— HOW TO — DEVELOP — A — PERSONNEL POLICY MANUAL

Sixth Edition

— HOW TO — DEVELOP — A — PERSONNEL POLICY MANUAL

Sixth Edition

Joseph W. R. Lawson II

AMACOM
American Management Association

New York • Atlanta • Boston • Chicago • Kansas City • San Francisco • Washington, D.C.
Brussels • Mexico City • Tokyo • Toronto

This book is available at a special
discount when ordered in bulk quantities.
For information, contact Special Sales Department,
AMACOM, a division of American Management Association,
1601 Broadway, New York, NY 10019.

This publication is designed to provide accurate and authoritative
information in regard to the subject matter covered. It is sold
with the understanding that the publisher is not engaged in
rendering legal, accounting, or other professional service. If
legal advice or other expert assistance is required, the services
of a competent professional person should be sought.

Library of Congress Cataloging-in-Publication Data

Lawson, Joseph W. R.
      How to develop a personnel policy manual / Joseph W.R. Lawson,
   II. — 6th ed.
      p.   cm.
      Includes index.
      ISBN 0-8144-7310-5
      1. Personnel management—Handbooks, manuals, etc.   I. Title.
   HF5549.17.L38   1998
   658.3—dc21   97-52038
                                                                             CIP

Printing number

10 9 8 7 6 5 4 3 2 1

Contents

Preface

This is the sixth edition of a book first published in 1967. This edition, like the first, was prepared for use by employee relations directors, human resources managers, industrial relations directors, and employers in every industry. Its purpose is to provide a practical approach to developing, drafting, and editing personnel policies and procedures for employees and supervisors.

In the five years since the fifth edition, far-ranging developments have brought about significant changes in the focus, development, interpretation, and application of personnel and human resources policy.

Of particular significance is the current high rate of judicial review of and interpretative changes to many existing personnel practices and policies. This greatly increased judicial review of "people-sensitive" human resources issues has resulted in much new material and a considerably different focus on these policies and practices. We caution our readers, in the light of this legal attentiveness, to keep abreast of the many new and changing policy determinations currently being made in our federal and state court systems.

In SESCO's first half-century of consulting with business and industry, we found that one of the greatest difficulties and challenges experienced by the employer and human resources manager is that of having to draft and finalize a particular personnel policy or procedure for the organization. The time element and the pressures of other important business matters have caused many firms, large and small, to procrastinate in this important phase of supervisor-employee communications, yet policies are certainly needed for successful employee relations.

This sixth edition has been revised to meet the continuing need of large and small employers for a simple, how-to-do-it approach to developing a personnel policy manual. Each section begins with a Policy Manual Checklist to give the user a concise and systemic approach to formulating and outlining policies covering all important phases of the employer-employee relationship. The person using this manual can simply place a check mark in the box beside each particular subject to be covered in the personnel policy manual. This checklist is the first step in tailoring personnel policies to fit the particular needs of each employer.

More important, the checklist is designed to stimulate thinking about various aspects of policy that should be formulated and covered in any manual. Recommendations on key aspects of personnel policy are included in several sections.

Sample policy statements are included in twelve sections. These examples enable the policy writer to review actual personnel policies that reflect and possess, in the author's judgment, these desirable characteristics:

1. Policies should provide an organization with flexibility and a high degree of permanency.
2. Policies should be harmonious with all other personnel policies.
3. Policies should be designed to meet the individual needs and differences of employees and supervisors.
4. Policies should be in compliance with all federal and state regulations.
5. Policies should be clear, concise, and avoid too much detail.
6. Policies should never be a liability to the interest of anyone involved in the employer-employee relationship, including owners and the public.
7. Policies should provide for effective communication among and understanding by all interested parties and users of the policy manual.
8. Policies should reflect careful study and analysis before being formulated and administered.

The sample policy statements are also of value because they provide ideas on current policy language. This helps in formulating concise terminology.

A final note: All policies, statements, and examples cited and used in this manual should be considered as guides and ideas to assist you in appropriately providing for your specific needs and requirements. The particulars of your organizational demands will largely dictate your specific courses of action.

We are deeply indebted and offer grateful appreciation to over 300 organizations that were asked to participate in this project. We are particularly grateful to those companies that provided us with their policy statements and manuals, employee handbooks, and personnel forms, and to those that gave us permission to use their company name and to quote their policy statements. However, because of the confidential nature of many policies, several companies have requested that their names not be mentioned in this publication. Therefore, no specific footnote or reference is made to the contributors of many of the various policy statements to be found in the various sections.

Joseph W. R. Lawson II
Chairman of the Board and Chief Executive Officer
SESCO Management Consultants

SECTION 1

How to Begin a Personnel Policy Manual

The following checklist can be used to help you determine the various policy items that should be incorporated in your policy manual. Sample policy statements covering many of the items in the checklist appear in this section. They can be used to guide your policy statements.

Policy Manual Checklist

Our Policy Manual Should Cover:

1. Purpose of the policy manual   Yes_____ No_____

2. Authority and distribution of policy manual   Yes_____ No_____

3. Supplements to the policy manual   Yes_____ No_____

4. Establishing new or revised policy   Yes_____ No_____

Purpose of a Personnel Policy Manual

The purpose of a personnel policy manual is to provide employers, human resources directors, industrial relations directors, and supervisors with a systematic approach to administering personnel policies and practices.

A policy manual should be designed as a fundamental communications tool for these members of management to clarify policies and practices and thus stop morale problems, complaints, and grievances before they arise.

Your policy manual should put an end to difficulties in understanding personnel policies and practices that have resulted from unwritten policy, inconsistent policy, and lack of proper communications. Above all, your personnel policy manual should be a working tool designed to help you and your organization in "affirmative action"—providing equal employment opportunities to everyone in your organization, regardless of race, sex, age, religion, national origin, physical or mental handicap, or veteran's status. It must show that you are in compliance with the Equal Employment Opportunity Act and with other state and federal laws.

How You Benefit From a Policy Manual

Preparing a policy manual provides many tangible and intangible benefits for an organization. Not the least of these benefits is the peace of mind that takes the place of the headaches and indecision that usually result when management must continuously meet to discuss and reach decisions concerning policies or practices.

Another major benefit is that a written policy manual provides everyone in management with a clear explanation of all existing personnel policies and practices. This in itself is an invaluable asset to communications. In many respects, the manual literally speaks for itself.

A third benefit is that a written manual can be used in conducting training courses for new supervisors and refreshing current supervisors' understanding of the organization's policies. Too many organizations, small and large, union and nonunion, spend endless hours and a great deal of money trying to decide what to teach supervisors. Their goal is to make the company or organization more efficient and to promote better employee morale, and they have made every effort to achieve this goal. However, many have found, to their dismay, that the programs that top management felt were best for everyone were poorly received.

Often management's hopes for improvement in personnel relations were doomed from the very conception of the idea. The employees were not to blame; the front and middle-line supervisors were not to blame. The responsibility can be laid at the doorstep of top management for failing to properly clarify and document personnel policy and practice, then train the supervisors and department heads to administer the policy.

A fourth benefit of a policy manual is that it is a written documentation of good faith in providing fair employment practices and equal employment opportunity for present employees and future job applicants. Title VII of the Civil Rights Act places great importance on such communication. Frankly, a manual should be the basis of good-faith efforts to prove nondiscrimination and to provide equal employment opportunity to everyone throughout all phases of human resources action. In communicating your equal employment opportunity policy, you may simply need to reaffirm your existing policy. However, you may find that your organization needs to make changes in order to establish fair employment practices that comply with new laws.

Needless to say, the development of a policy manual will not in itself guarantee compliance with Title VII. To comply effectively requires an active, good-faith effort. This implies, of course, communicating the contents of the manual to everyone who should know of this policy.

Since the enactment of Title VII and other federal and state nondiscrimination laws, many employers throughout the United States have found that one of the most likely areas of vulnerability under Fair Employment Practice Laws has been front and middle-line supervision. In interviewing supervisors, we find a great lack of understanding of company personnel policies and practices.

Without this understanding, supervisors cannot be expected to know how to protect your interest in what they do and say to job applicants and employees under their supervision.

We all know that management's greatest asset is a well-trained, qualified supervisor who is capable of administering policy in a fair and consistent manner. It is even more important today for supervisors to know how to interpret your policy effectively, clearly, and properly in order to avoid any possible unfair employment practice charge.

Whether we want to admit it or not, management has too often placed added responsibilities in the hands of supervisors while giving them no definite policy to guide them in their performance. Thus, your policy manual is highly important in helping them to clearly understand personnel policy and practices so that they can administer these policies fairly, firmly, and equally to all employees.

Who Should Use a Policy Manual

The individuals who use policy manuals differ from organization to organization. Generally speaking, the manual is designed for those individuals whose primary responsibility is to carry out and administer policies and practices. Thus, most employers provide policy manuals for the industrial relations director, the human resources director, the employment manager, department heads, and supervisors.

A realistic answer to the question of who should receive a policy manual depends largely on the nature of the contents. If the contents of the manual pertain to ways and means of communicating, getting the service performed or the product manufactured at the least cost in the smallest amount of time, with the goal of maintaining job satisfaction and high employee morale, then anyone responsible for these functions should have a copy of the manual.

There are certain dangers in limiting the distribution of the manual to only one level of management. For example, if you distribute the manual to only middle-line supervisors, they may feel that they are being singled out as a group that needs to be given rules to work under, while front-line supervisors have more freedom. In another case, if you limit the policy manual to production supervisors and exclude office supervisors, the office supervisors may feel that plant supervisors are given more authority and status.

We recommend that unless your organization has sound, specific reasons for limiting the distribution of the manual to certain ranks of supervision, you issue the same copy to all managerial employees, from the top corporate officer to the first level of supervision.

If an organization is so large that providing every supervisor with a manual would be impractical, it may be necessary to limit distribution to the middle and upper ranks of management. For example, if your organization has 4,000 supervisors, it could be both impractical and extremely expensive to distribute a large policy manual to all of them.

The Decision to Produce a Manual

If you are convinced that your organization is in need of a policy manual, or if it is obvious that your present manual is in need of revision, the first decision to be reached is a clear-cut go-ahead for the project. Topmost management is charged with making this decision.

The chief executive or the chief governing body of the company (board of directors, management committee) must:

1. Choose the person who will have the authority and responsibility for preparing the manual.
2. Outline the major sources of information for the manual.
3. Determine the ground rules covering what should and what should not go into the manual.
4. Put the final OK on the format and organization of the manual.

In most cases, policies already exist in some form. The production of a new manual will probably entail the revision of an old manual or the putting into writing of previously unwritten policies.

Some of the frequently expressed reasons for revision include the following:

1. Your organization has been unionized since your policy manual was written or last revised.
2. You have moved to an entirely different labor community.
3. You have not made the changes in your policies and practices required by the EEOC.
4. Your current written policies and practices have not been revised to conform to the latest minimum wage and overtime requirements of the Federal Wage-Hour Law.
5. Your present written policies or practices are in conflict with recent state or federal laws that might affect a particular classification of your employees.
6. Your organizational structure has grown substantially or your products and methods of manufacture or distribution have changed.

In summary, the most obvious reason for revision is that your manual is out of date.

Authority and Responsibility for Preparing the Manual

Once the decision to produce a manual has been made, it is up to top management to decide who is going to be in charge of producing it. It is highly recommended that one person have the responsibility, and that this person be a member of the management team.

Because the organizational structure differs so much among various types of companies and organizations, there is no one choice that is always right. The human resources department, for example, may seem the obvious choice. However, in many organizations this department has not yet been fully developed, and there may not be anyone of sufficient rank to handle the job. The office administrator may be capable of doing the job, but if this person's job mostly involves the purchasing of supplies and the maintenance of machines, he or she may not be the right choice either.

In every organization, there are several people who know current policy and perhaps formulate it on a day-to-day basis. One of these people should have enough background to take charge of the project. This person should be given the authority to set up a small committee of individuals who have working knowledge of the various departments and who can assist him or her in gathering the data necessary for a complete and comprehensive manual. Someone from human resources has background on employee relations; someone from accounting has access to wage and salary information; an industrial relations person knows all about the union. The committee should, in effect, do some of the legwork required to bring the necessary information to the committee chairperson.

This committee should be small enough to be functional. Its purpose is to reduce the effort that the chairperson-writer must put forth to produce a comprehensive manual. The committee's initial task is to gather data from specified departments. Individual members can make recommendations, and finally each member should carefully review the area of policy within his or her realm. It would be wise to set a time limit for each response.

The Role of the Supervisor

The committee should utilize the ideas and observations of supervisors to the fullest extent possible. The supervisors are on the firing line daily and are primarily responsible for administering company policies and practices. They know how past unwritten or written personnel policies have affected employee morale and productivity.

Supervisors should be interviewed for the purpose of learning what is going on now. They will be a great help in finding out where present policies, written or unwritten, are working and where they are not working. For example, the supervisors may be able to point out certain policies that have proved unworkable or are unnecessary, and should therefore be revised or abolished. They may also be able to recommend new policies that would be helpful in attaining greater efficiency and more job satisfaction for the employees. The supervisors will be the best informed source on areas of present policy and practices that are being administered inconsistently or unequally among their subordinates. Thus, the supervisors will prove of great benefit to the policy manual committee by helping them determine what the policy and practice should be concerning various subjects.

An indirect benefit of using supervisors as a source of information for the proposed policy manual or revision is that it gives them the opportunity to participate in the manual's development or revision. By participating, the supervisors are helping to "create" the new or revised manual. You will find that they will make a greater effort to support policies and practices, because they have helped create them.

For the supervisors to be effective in helping the policy manual committee, the committee itself must be systematic and practical in approaching the supervisors. Above all, committee members must be specific in their questioning. They should ask every supervisor to tell them what he or she thinks organization policy on a given subject is. If organization policy is silent or ambiguous on a particular subject, the supervisors should be asked how they actually handle problems that arise in that area. They should also be asked what changes in existing policies and practices need to be made.

For organizations developing a policy manual for the first time, members of the policy manual committee may find the following questionnaire extremely helpful in gathering information from supervisors. This set of questions can be applied to any given subject dealing with personnel policies:

1. Are you familiar with our policy on _____?
2. Do you think this policy is working in the best interests of both our organization and the employees?

3. Do you feel that this policy meets our present needs?
4. Do you feel that you know and understand this policy well enough to interpret and administer it correctly? Are you aware of any improper understanding or administration of this policy?
5. Do you feel that we need a new policy on the subject of _____?
6. What do you think the new policy should be?

This approach to interviewing supervisors has practical value. It can identify areas that have given rise to complaints, inconsistencies, grievances, and misunderstandings in the past, and it can assist in the development of new policies to prevent additional problems from arising in the future.

A questionnaire can also be of great value as an aid in reviewing overall personnel policies and procedures. We recommend that such a review be done at least once every year. Furthermore, supervisors can provide many good ideas on where present training programs need to be revised or improved for the benefit of new supervisors, new managers, and staff personnel.

Finally, the questionnaire approach, through in-depth interviewing of supervisors, can help keep present supervisors up to date on current policy and practice. Thus, it can prevent misunderstandings and incorrect or inconsistent interpretation and administration of your policies and practices from being passed down.

Sources of Information for the Manual

The written policies that already exist will form the main basis for the manual. All of these should be brought together with three things in mind:

1. *Comparison.* If the existing policies conflict or vary from area to area or department to department, they should be checked and unified. If written policy conflicts with present practice, the changes should be incorporated.

2. *Review.* Past and current policies should be examined in the light of new developments. Changes may be contemplated, and it is wise to make them a part of written policy now.

3. *Authenticity.* Practices currently in use, if not written in a policy manual, may be without basis. Perhaps managers or supervisors have inaugurated their own policies without submitting them formally to top management.

The existing policy manuals, employee handbooks, and even bulletin board notices will provide the bulk of the information needed to build the basic policy areas.

As an example, your vacation allowance policy is probably in writing, and is certainly well understood. A new employee usually is told exactly what the vacation allowance will be. On the other hand, holidays may be determined on a year-to-year or even on a month-to-month basis. Your files might yield a series of bulletin board announcements that will tell you what was done in past years.

If this area (holidays) is becoming a part of policy for the first time, it might be wise to collect as much information as possible about the present practices within your industry and area. Surveys are valuable guides. Industry organizations and management groups (Chamber of Commerce, Administrative Management Society) make frequent surveys in this area.

Wage and salary administration policies may not be as clear-cut within your organization as vacation allowances or holidays. If there is a definite policy (written or unwritten), you should make every effort to incorporate it into the policy manual. If top management is uneasy about dealing with this area of policy in writing, it would be of value to collect policy statements from other employers in similar industries to show top management what is being said.

Reviewing past policies, manuals, and guidebooks differs from comparing various current policy statements in the respect that many items will change. It is normally estimated that policies become out-of-date in about five years. This is not true of all policies, but it does apply in a good many areas—especially those involving benefits. The development of a new manual should obviously be a stimulus for reconsidering all present policies. Making changes at this point will eliminate the need for constant revision during the next period.

Authenticating known policies is a vital task. All department managers, supervisors, and even division heads should be requested to submit any information on policy that they have. This may require extensive research, but it should provide the greatest amount of information possible. Part of the job will be to trace the present policy to its source, if this is can be done. This can be revealing, and top management might wish to make sure that in the future, policy comes from only one source. It may also disclose excellent procedures in some areas that will work well for all areas of the organization.

What Should and Should Not Go Into a Policy Manual

A working policy manual must be a usable tool for supervision. The emphasis on clarity reflects the necessity for careful editing of the available material. Many rules, regulations, and procedures will be compiled during the initial search. This is one area where the working committee can be called upon to make decisions.

If the manual is to have general distribution, the bulk of the written material should deal with those policy areas that affect all human resources. If, for example, the rules governing leave of absence are the same for all departments or operations (plant and office), they can be stated in general terms, with or without procedures. However, if there are certain conditions that affect office help and not plant help, these may or may not be spelled out specifically in a single manual. They might be included in a departmental or operational manual designed specifically for the area involved.

The specific holidays a company grants would certainly be included in the policy manual by name—Independence Day, Washington's Birthday—but it wouldn't be practical to try to give the exact date. The manual is intended to be of value for at least three years, and perhaps as long as five years.

A big area for consideration in the development of a policy manual is the company's union status. In most cases the union agreement represents policy on seniority, holidays, remuneration, and job descriptions. If not all of the company is within union ranks, however, there will be separate policy for the nonunion personnel. For the sake of clarity, it is wisest to include both statements in the policy manual. The union agreement can stand as an appendix item and an entity, or the two areas can be ranked side by side within the sections designated. This is where management must make the final decisions.

Sources of Outside Help

With the help of this publication, you should be able to produce an effective working policy manual. However, under certain circumstances, it is not out of line to recommend the use of competent, professional outside assistance.

If the amount of time available is limited, there are specialists who will do the basic legwork and draft, compose, and edit a policy manual. There are also professional consultants who will act in an advisory capacity, providing suggestions and recommendations at various stages of the project.

One possibility might be the use of a management consultant to analyze and audit your entire organization before you write a policy manual. This is a valid approach if your company has never actually put its policy to writing before. Many areas of policy may not be presently covered in writing or practice. The suggested move here is to obtain guidance in formulating such policies or practices, which will then become a part of your organization.

Recommendations of consultants can be obtained by contacting various trade associations, Chambers of Commerce, or by corresponding with the Association of Management Consultants, New York City.

A final thought in this area is to have your corporate lawyer and/or industrial relations specialist check out all possible legal questions and affirm (if a union is involved) that union agreements are not violated.

If benefits such as a pension plan or annual bonuses are included in a policy statement, the statement had better be worded in a manner that protects all parties involved.

Format and Organization of the Manual

While the choice of format and organization is pretty much up to the individual in charge of preparing a policy manual, it is obvious that some type of outline should be developed and followed throughout.

A checklist for each major section of this guide has been developed for your convenience. These checklists are comprehensive, but you may still have to add items that are unique in your organization.

An immediate suggestion is to make copies of each checklist for committee members and key executives. These lists can be combined for an overall look at the requisites for a written policy. They can also serve as a springboard leading to a single checklist for your organization.

Early discussion can center on differences discovered in the outlining of policy areas. This is the best time to resolve these questions. When a master copy is finished, the writer-chairperson has a complete picture of what is needed. However, this does not dictate the order of the material.

After the various areas of policy that will be included in the manual have been determined, it is the job of the chairperson-writer and the committee to come up with the material (handbooks, previous policies, etc.) that will be the basis of the policy.

Once the research has been completed and the information is at hand, it is necessary to establish the organization or arrangement of the manual. The primary requirement here is that the material be organized in a logical manner. Several organizing techniques are used extensively. One of the simplest methods is to arrange the subjects in alphabetical order according to the name of the policy area. An example of this technique is as follows:

A   Absenteeism
         Absenteeism Report
B   Bonuses
         Bulletin Boards
C   Changes in Personnel Status
         Christmas Parties
         Company Benefits
D   Department Heads Manual
         Departmental Seniority
E   Employee Benefits
         Employee Discipline
         Employee Handbook
F   Fair Labor Standards Act
         Falsifying Records
         First Aid

This technique for organizing a policy manual is very simple. However, it has some disadvantages. For example, with such a system, locating a specific policy statement is often troublesome because it is not always evident what key word will have been chosen.

If your policy manual is to use a loose-leaf format, it is often impractical to number the pages consecutively. Thus, it is often desirable to use a different technique of arranging the material. For example, sections can be coded either alphabetically or numerically, or with a combination of the alphabet and numbers.

Alphabetical Code

With an alphabetical code, each main classification of policy statements is given a key letter. These major classifications are then broken down into smaller subdivisions, which are also given key letters. An example of such an arrangement is the following:

A　　　Employee Benefits
AA　　Paid Holidays
AB　　Number and Name of Holidays Observed
AC　　Arrangements for Christmas, Election Days, and Religious Holidays
AD　　Holidays Falling on Nonworking Days
B　　　Employee Relations
BA　　Position on Union Affiliation
BB　　Employee Relations Philosophy
BC　　Position of the Company on Equal Employment Opportunity
C　　　Hiring
CA　　Type of Job Applicants to Look For
CB　　Physical Examinations

The primary disadvantage of the alphabetical code technique is that there is often no logical connection between the code letters and the subject of the policy statement. If this system is used, it will be desirable to use an alphabetical code letter that is identical with the first letter of the subject of the policy statement. However, this is not always possible.

Numerical Code

The technique of arranging your policy manual by numerical code is very similar to arranging it by alphabetical code. With this technique, you use numbers instead of letters to identify the major classifications and subclassifications.

1. Employee Benefits
   1.1 Paid Holidays
   1.2 Number Observed
   1.3 Eligibility
   1.4 Holidays Falling on Nonworking Days
2. Safety Rules
   2.1 Equipment and Work Area
   2.2 Employee Responsibility
3. Termination of Employment
   3.1 How to Handle Resignations
   3.2 How to Handle Terminations for Cause
   3.3 Unemployment Compensation
   3.4 References

The numerical code technique can also be modified by organizing the major classifications of policy statements. Begin a major section with page 100, with the more detailed subject matter pertaining to the major classification on pages numbered consecutively from 100, i.e., 101, 102, 103. Once all the subject matter pertaining to the major classification has been coded by page number, the next major policy statement classification would begin on page 200.

Alphabetical and Numerical Combination

Under a combination of the two coding techniques, the major policy statement subjects are arranged alphabetically and the subdivisions or more detailed aspects of the major policy subjects are identified numerically. For example, an illustration of this combination technique is the following:

Section 1   Accidents on the Job
             1.1 Safety Rules
             1.2 Good Housekeeping
             1.3 Preventive Maintenance
Section 2   Bonuses
             2.1 Attendance Bonuses
             2.2 Discretionary Bonuses
             2.3 Production Bonuses

The technique used to organize and arrange the subject matter of your policy manual should be explained in your manual.

The Index or Table of Contents

It is desirable to have a table of contents and an index for a policy manual. Having both is particularly desirable if your company policy manual has a large number of pages.

The subjects listed in the table of contents vary according to the particular organization. Many factors account for this. The size and type of the organization involved, the purpose of the policy manual, and the types of human resources who are to receive and use the manual are all factors influencing the subjects listed in the table of contents. However, general subject headings such as the following may prove helpful:

1. Purpose of the Policy Manual
2. Supplements to the Policy Manual
3. How to Use the Policy Manual
4. Authority of the Policy Manual
5. Responsibilities of Supervisors and Department Heads
6. Employee Relations Policies
7. Hiring Policy
8. Job Training Policy
9. Hours of Work
10. Pay Policies and Procedures
11. Promotions, Transfers, and Layoffs
12. Employee Benefits
13. Attendance, Punctuality, and Absenteeism
14. Safety Rules Program
15. Security Rules
16. Rules of Conduct
17. Cost Control
18. Grievance and Complaint Procedure
19. Communications
20. Termination of Employment Policies
21. Labor Relations
22. Personnel Forms

The table of contents may consist of the short form as illustrated above, which is arranged by major subject headings in order of their appearance, or it may use a more detailed format giving major headings and subheadings for each key topic. The table of contents should, of course, be placed at the very beginning of the manual, where it can be located quickly.

It is recommended that the manual also be indexed alphabetically by page number. A general exception to this recommendation is whenever your policy manual is arranged in alphabetical order with tabs dividing the major subjects.

The index cannot, of course, be undertaken until the final draft of the manual has been written and approved.

In indexing the manual, you should read through the final draft. Have a package of 3- by 5-inch cards available as you read through the manual, and write the key subject and the page number(s) of each policy on a card. After you have finished writing down the subjects of all policy statements and practices, arrange the cards in alphabetical order. Then begin editing these cards. You may find that you have used different words to identify a particular subject on two different cards. Decide on the most logical word or words to identify the policy statement and discard the other word(s). If, for example, you have made references to "paid holidays" and "holidays," use the term that is more commonly used in your organization.

Once you have edited your cards, you are ready to combine all page references to the same key word in ascending order. Thus, your index should look something like the following:

A
Absence, 3, 20
Accidents, 64, 68
Applicants, 8, 10, 14, 25
Attendance, 30, 41, 50
Attendance Records, 40, 38
B
Bidding, 40, 42, 52
Buddy System, 19, 22, 37
C
Complaints, 20, 28
Cost Control, 28

Elements of a Policy and Procedure

A *policy* is a statement of your position. A *procedure* is the method by which a policy is implemented. Thus, your manual is a combination of theory and "how to." We have listed a few policies along with the kind of questions that should be answered in the procedure. In essence, you need to perform a type of brainstorming to answer the fundamental question: How do managers accomplish the objective when faced with the day-to-day situations?

Procedures should be drafted to answer the following types of questions:

◆ *Change of employee's address.* When should the employee notify you of a change of address? To whom should the notice be given? Why is it important that a current address be available?

◆ *Bulletin boards.* Where are they located? Who is entitled to post notices? What limitations are there on the subject matter of a notice? Who has jurisdiction over the bulletin board?

◆ *Absence.* What notice is required in case of absence? How should you be notified? Who should be notified? What about payment or nonpayment of wages in case of absence?

◆ *Continuous service.* What constitutes continuous service? Under what circumstances is continuous service broken? Termination? Layoff? Leave of absence? Quitting? Absence without reporting? What recognition is given for long-term service?

◆ *Time recording.* Time cards or time sheets? Location of time clocks? What is the penalty for punching someone else's time card? When is time recorded? Leaving premises? Meal break? Rest period?

◆ *Emergency work.* Is an employee required to work overtime when asked? What excuses from overtime are accepted? What action is taken when an employee refuses to accept overtime work without good cause?

◆ *Employee purchases.* Can an employee purchase items at a discount? What is the procedure? To whom is the privilege extended? What are the limitations on purchases? To whom is payment made?

◆ *Employment policy.* What are the qualifications required of applicants? Are employees classified as temporary, permanent, or seasonal—definition? Who is responsible for the decision as to what person is employed? Who is responsible for the "sign-in" paperwork?

◆ *Overtime*. What constitutes overtime? How is it authorized? Pay policy? Compensatory time off?

◆ *Payroll workweek*. What constitutes the payroll workweek? On what day are wages paid? What is the procedure when payday falls on a weekend or holiday? Night shifts—when they are paid and by whom?

◆ *Visitors*. Are visitors permitted? Under what conditions? Where do visitors report before going into the facility? Who is responsible for authorizing visitation?

◆ *Injuries*. What is the procedure in the event of injury? To what hospital or doctor is the employee taken? What compensation is provided? What follow-up procedure ascertains the progress of injured employees?

◆ *Holidays*. What holidays are recognized? For how many hours and at what rate is the employee paid? Does holiday pay include a shift differential, if any? Must the employee be working before and after the holiday to be eligible for holiday pay? Must the holiday fall in a regular workweek to be a paid holiday? Is a holiday considered as hours worked in the computation of overtime? What is the policy on holiday pay in case of leave of absence, excused absence, layoff?

Writing the Drafts of the Policy Manual

If you have followed the recommended steps in preparing and/or revising your policy manual, you should now be ready to begin writing the first draft. A good idea is to review the Checklist of Policy Statements at the beginning of each section. If you have checked off a policy area, you should have a policy statement prepared. The checklists provide you with a variety of policy areas that have been suggested by many companies.

Each section contains one or more policy statements that are in actual use or that have been adapted from an actual working policy manual. If one particular statement meets your needs, you can use or adapt it for your policy manual.

Use the margin of the pages in this guide to note statements that you wish to use, adding or deleting data or information to tailor each policy to your requirements. Keep a record of the page numbers of the policy statements that you are planning to use so that you can refer to each one quickly.

It is imperative at this point that you correlate the checklist and the policies that will be incorporated into your manual. There are several policy items on the checklist that do not appear in policy form in the section following. In most cases, the reason for this is that this particular policy should be entirely composed by the individual organization. Also keep in mind that these are actual policies, unchanged in wording, and were written to fit a specific company situation.

In this revised edition of this guide, you will find personnel policy statements covering many more areas than in previous editions. These policies are in a new "policy manual" format that makes it easier to visualize how they will look in manual form.

In drafting the first copy of your manual, you can use 8-1/2″ × 11″ sheets that will fit into a three-ring binder, or you can use index cards (3″ × 5″ cards) that can be kept in a file. If you wish to put the actual policy statements on cards, it is suggested that you use a larger size.

This guide can be adapted quickly to fit your basic need for a manual draft. Keeping the section guides, the checklists, and the policy statements you wish to use, you can develop your own manual. Add your policy statements within the sections. When all the topics have been covered, the manual can be alphabetized to fit your needs.

Keep Language Clear

At this point, it should be emphasized that a policy statement requires the utmost in clarity. Nothing can be more damaging to organization or morale than a policy that is not understood or that is not clear to the reader because it is ambiguous.

Writing expert Robert Gunning, in his book, *How to Take the Fog Out of Your Business Writing* (Chicago: Dartnel, 1994), offered excellent suggestions that should be considered before the first attempt is made:

- Break Up Long Sentences—If you want to keep your meaning clear, keep the length of the sentences used as short as possible. Express one idea at a time in a sentence.
- Prefer the Simple to the Complex—Many complex terms are unnecessary. When there is a simpler way of saying a thing, use it. Avoid complex sentences.
- Avoid Unneeded Words—Nothing weakens writing so much as extra words. Be critical of your own writing and make every word carry its weight.
- Put Action into Your Verbs—The heaviness of much business writing results from overworking the passive verbs. Prose can usually be kept impersonal and remain in the active voice.
- Use Terms Your Reader Can Picture—Abstract terms make writing dull and foggy. Choose short, concrete words that the reader can visualize.
- Tie In With Your Reader's Experience—The reader will not get your new idea unless you link it with some old idea he already has.
- Write the Way You Talk—As much as you can, use words and phrases that you would normally use in expressing the same thought orally.
- Write to Express, Not to Impress—Present your ideas simply and directly. The writer who makes the best impression is the one who can express complex ideas simply.

This final point reiterates the beginning statement—the policy statements must be absolutely clear. A policy manual is no place to display rhetorical ability in any other area.

Here are some other suggestions to keep in mind:

1. Keep your first draft flexible and open to additions and changes. Make your point as clear as possible, and find out if others agree that it is clear.
2. Tables and charts are always good when explaining a difficult area. Even breaking up a section into a table-like grouping can get the message across:
   Complete Shift Cycle
   12:00 (midnight) to 8:00 A.M.
   8:00 A.M. to 4:00 P.M.
   4:00 P.M. to 12:00 (midnight)
3. Be your own critic first. Don't be hesitant about rewriting something two or three times. Try to have the first draft as complete as it can be. This may eliminate extensive corrections at the review and cut down the number of times the manual will be subjected to review.
4. Make enough copies of your first draft to be sure that everyone who needs to review it will be able to do so. Keep track of these copies to avoid missing key corrections suggested by some member of the management team.

Get the First Draft Proofed and Reviewed

Once the policy statements have been selected, written to order, and checked for presentation, the first draft can be typed. This is the point at which the manual should be put into order, using the organization technique you have chosen. It is a good idea for you to retain the master copy and produce sufficient copies for distribution to key personnel who must help in the review.

Each of the copies should have the name of the individual who receives it written on the cover or first page. This will keep your record clear when it comes to checking any revisions. As well as making changes or suggestions, some of the executives will read the copy closely enough to catch possible typographical errors. These should be caught in proofreading, but experience shows that many such manuals do contain some errors.

After all the review copies have been returned, it probably will be up to the chairperson-writer to check each revision. The committee (at what is hopefully its final meeting) can resolve any differences or conflicts that might arise. This is the final chance to make revisions within the existing body of policy, and since the subject is a current one, some management ideas (changes for the future) might be included now.

Each committee member should OK his or her particular area of administration. For example, it is very important that personnel administration puts the final OK on the employment practices statement. It may also be wise to have the company lawyer look at this statement. It is important that financial officers OK the pension plan statement, again with legal concurrence.

Check with Supervisors

Since it is primarily the supervisors who will work with the policy manual, it is a good practice to have certain key members of this group read over the entire presentation. After they have studied the policies and policy statements, they might join with the committee for a brief question-and-answer session. Do they understand the policy? Do they know how to explain the policy to an employee? Do they feel that the policy, as it is written, will be understood by the employees?

If the supervisors have serious doubts about a policy statement, or if they are unable to interpret it, this is the time to change it. This doesn't mean that the supervisors have the final say, but policy is going to be hard to enforce if this group doesn't comprehend its meaning. Also, there will be a widespread problem of control if supervisors in one department interpret a policy in one way and supervisors in another department interpret it in another way. Besides avoiding confusion, this meeting will help to eventually cut time and money from the program.

Production of the Manual

When all corrections have been incorporated into a master copy, the next step is to have the manual printed or reproduced. Cost should be a factor here. It is up to management to set some ground rules. The size of the organization will probably determine the number of copies needed. (This also has had an effect on the actual page count of the manual. In general, the larger the company or organization, the larger the manual, but this is not a hard and fast rule.)

If you have been following the step-by-step procedures in this guide, you have already determined who will get a copy of the manual. The next step is to determine how many extra copies you will need (for replacement, etc.) and how long this particular manual will be in use. If you are producing a loose-leaf manual, you can make additions and changes on a periodic basis without too much difficulty. This means that the initial run can be a little larger than otherwise.

What Type of Manual?

The choice here is wide. If you have a printing facility, the person in charge will be your best source of information. If you have offset facilities, your shop can reduce an 81/2'' × 11'' typed page to half the size and produce a compact booklet. This may be harder to read, but it will fit conveniently in a desk drawer.

Remember, however, that if you decide on a printed and bound edition, there is really no opportunity to make a simple change without running the entire job through again.

It is recommended that the policy manual use a loose-leaf format. The pages can be printed, run on a mimeograph or duplicator, or, for that matter, photocopied and punched. The loose-leaf binder allows pages to be updated and changed with a minimum of difficulty. A new employee benefit can be quickly added to the policy manual by distributing new pages to the manual holders.

For a large manual (in pages), the three-ring binder is probably the best bet, but for smaller manuals, the Duo-tang binder (two holes) is adequate. Both of these allow for flexibility. Both can have either printed covers, or simple labels on the covers. Both plastic and paper covers are available from many sources (including the local stationery store), and the choice should be based on use and cost.

If the aim is to keep the manual for at least five years, a substantial cover is best. However, keep in mind that people dealing with policy matters are supposed to be fully aware of the policy, so reference to the manual will not be that frequent. It will spend a great deal of time in a desk drawer or in a file cabinet.

How to Keep Your Policy Manual Up-to-Date

As stated before, a policy manual can last for as long as five years, but it is recommended that you consider updating it at least every two years.

Many companies have found that revising a manual every time a single policy change is necessary is rather expensive and impractical. Instead, they keep management and supervisors informed of policy changes by issuing "Policy Bulletins" or other types of memoranda. Such bulletins can be retained in the front or rear of the manual, or, if it is a loose-leaf publication, inserted in place of the former statement.

One area where changes occur frequently is vacation and holiday benefits. If policy is explicit, then it is probably subject to biannual or even annual change.

Another technique for handling policy changes before revising the manual that some employers have found helpful is to set up a section in the manual entitled "New and Revised Policies and Practices." If this area gets extensive, however, maintaining a manual in usable condition becomes a chore. Secretaries, as well as managers, dislike filing pages in existing booklets or manuals. They are apt to drop them in anywhere, insisting that they will put them in the proper place at some time in the near future.

Getting Ready for Revision

The time will come when a policy manual will need revision. Most of the steps outlined in this section will have to be followed again, but the time required can be cut dramatically.

A policy file should be retained by the current writer of the manual. If someone else is given the assignment of revising the manual, this file will be valuable to this person. If the chairperson-writer is once again given the assignment, he or she will have most of the information at hand.

This does not mean that a committee will not be needed. If this is a true revision, each item of policy must be rechecked, and each must be approved again. At this point, suggestions for improvement of the manual—format, organization, presentation, etc.—can be sought.

This is also an excellent time for a critical evaluation of policy itself. Is the current policy up-to-date? Does the organization operate the same way it did five or two years ago? Have employees accepted the current policy, or has there been dissension?

The same type of evaluation should be conducted for the format of the manual. Has the manual held together? Has it been easy to use? Has it been criticized by members of the management team or by employees?

Making the Revision

Having had the experience of producing one manual, the writer-chairperson can proceed with confidence on the revision. Less time will probably be allocated, but it is wise to remind management that the job still must be thorough. A mistake in a revision is just as bad as a mistake in the original publication.

By repeating the steps in this section, the revised manual can be brought into being with a minimum of effort. Copies of the current policy statements can be made for the individuals concerned and directed to their attention. They can be asked to OK the current policy statement or make recommendations for revision.

Finally, when the new manual is released, be sure that old copies are collected and destroyed—except for record copies. This is the best way to prevent a serious problem, especially when the new and old manuals look pretty much the same.

On the following pages you will see actual company policy statements in actual ''policy manual'' format. You can use this form if you are devising your policy manual for the first time. It can be typeset to meet your needs.

The copy at the top of the form includes pertinent information necessary to control distribution—policy subject area, distribution, dates, approval, etc. The form can be punched for a binder so that pages can be added and removed when necessary.

The policy statement displayed in the book may be in different formats. The large majority of these policy statements were developed by a variety of actual companies, financial institutions, hospitals, and organizations to meet specific needs. They are presented for your adaptation or adoption.

On the following pages you will find sample policy statements related to the material in this section. Areas covered include:

Introduction to Policy Manual
Authority and Distribution of Manual
Policy Changes

PERSONNEL POLICIES AND PROCEDURES

DISTRIBUTION:		SUBJECT: INTRODUCTION TO POLICY MANUAL	
EFFECTIVE DATE:	PAGE 1 OF 1		FILE UNDER SECTION
REVISION DATE:	APPROVED BY:		

INTRODUCTION:

This manual contains statements of personnel policies and procedures to be followed by all managers and department heads. It is to serve as a permanent reference and working guide for supervisory and management human resources in the day-to-day administration of our personnel policies, procedures, and practices.

These written policies should increase understanding, eliminate the need for personal decisions on matters of companywide policy, and help to assure uniformity throughout our organization. It is the responsibility of each and every member of management to administer these policies in a consistent and impartial manner. If necessary for more complete understanding, employees should be permitted to read policies of interest in detail. It is essential that employees understand our policies if they are to be expected to obey them.

Procedures and practices in the field of human resources relations are subject to modification and further development in light of experience. Therefore, changes of intent, interpretation, and administration will occur periodically. All such changes will be recorded in the form of a policy or procedural statement and issued to holders of the manual routinely. Each store manager and member of management can assist in keeping our human resources program up-to-date by notifying the General Office whenever problems are encountered or improvements can be made in the administration of our personnel policies. It is your responsibility as a store manager or supervisor to be certain that the manual is kept current, that policies are understood by all employees, and that policies are interpreted and administered uniformly.

PERSONNEL POLICIES AND PROCEDURES

DISTRIBUTION:		SUBJECT: AUTHORITY AND DISTRIBUTION OF POLICY MANUAL	
EFFECTIVE DATE:	PAGE 1 OF 1	FILE UNDER SECTION	
REVISION DATE:	APPROVED BY:		

This Personnel Policy and Procedure Manual is being distributed to all store managers and department heads who have supervisory responsibilities of any magnitude.

This policy manual is issued to you as a means of providing you and your job with a very important human resources tool. It is designed to serve as a source of information you can look to with authority and completeness. If, for some reason, you leave your present supervisory position, please return this policy manual to the General Office.

You are receiving a copy of this policy manual because you are a part of our management team, and we believe you will find it useful in increasing your understanding of companywide personnel policies and practices, as well as procedures for operating your store. It will tell you how our human resources program should operate.

We believe that the policies and procedures of our human resources program presented in this policy manual will produce information essential to carry out our human resources program and to determine how well our program is meeting our company and employee needs.

SUPPLEMENTS TO THE POLICY MANUAL:

The personnel policies, procedures, and guidelines in this policy manual will remain in effect until changes are considered necessary as a result of internal growth, competitive forces, or general economic conditions pertaining to our particular industry. However, any such change to be made in any personnel policy or procedure will be made only after we give due consideration to the mutual advantages, benefits, and responsibilities of such changes for you as a manager or supervisor, and for other employees of our company. Should such changes be warranted and approved by the Policy Manual Committee, you will be notified immediately and given revised policy changes, which are to be placed where indicated in the policy manual.

If you have any question as to the interpretation or understanding of any revised policy or procedure, please discuss it in our store managers' meeting. It is most important that we continue to have full and complete understanding of all our personnel policies and procedures.

PERSONNEL POLICIES AND PROCEDURES

DISTRIBUTION:		SUBJECT: AUTHORITY AND DISTRIBUTION OF POLICY MANUAL	
EFFECTIVE DATE:	PAGE 1 OF 1	FILE UNDER SECTION	
REVISION DATE:	APPROVED BY:		

The attached manual is being assigned to all positions that entail supervisory responsibilities of any magnitude. Please notice that the manual is assigned to the position and not the incumbent of the position, and should remain with the position if the incumbent moves on.

We also ask your cooperation in keeping the manual up-to-date when page changes are sent to you in the future. With more than 100 copies in circulation, a great deal of confusion could arise if changes are not made. The manual can be a reliable and effective tool for good management if carefully maintained.

To avoid confusion, if you should have a copy of any previous manual in your possession, please return it to Human Resources.

PERSONNEL POLICIES AND PROCEDURES

DISTRIBUTION:		SUBJECT: POLICY CHANGES	
EFFECTIVE DATE:	PAGE 1 OF 1	FILE UNDER SECTION	
REVISION DATE:	APPROVED BY:		

POLICY:

Changes and revisions in established personnel policies will be promptly brought to all employees' attention. All policy changes must be approved by the Administrator and the Board of Trustees.

PURPOSE:

A. To make sure each employee is made aware of policy changes.

B. To maintain employee morale by keeping them informed.

PROCEDURE:

1. Suggestions for changes in existing policies are to be presented in writing through department heads to the Administrator.

2. The Human Resources Department will be responsible for complete dissemination of policy changes. This will be accomplished by:

A. Forwarding a copy of policy change memorandum to all department heads.

B. Department heads, in turn, will be responsible for ensuring that their departmental employees are informed of all policy changes.

PERSONNEL POLICIES AND PROCEDURES

DISTRIBUTION:		SUBJECT: ADMINISTRATIVE MANUAL	
EFFECTIVE DATE:	PAGE 1 OF 3	FILE UNDER SECTION	
REVISION DATE:	APPROVED BY:		

SCOPE:

This policy applies to all functional areas that are involved with the development and/or implementation of General Affairs policies, practices, or procedures.

PURPOSE:

The purpose of this policy is to describe the format that will be used throughout this manual. This policy will also detail the administrative procedures that will be utilized when developing, revising, approving, and implementing policies, practices, and procedures at (Name of Company).

POLICY:

A. Format

The Administrative Manual contains company policies and procedures. The manual itself is assembled in a "three-ring binder" format to facilitate addition or revision of policies.

B. Contents

The policies and procedures are grouped by subject and are designated by section numbers, which are outlined as follows:

Table of Contents

Section I	Introduction/Administration
Section II	Associate Relations
Section III	Employment
Section IV	Hours of Work
Section V	Attendance
Section VI	Wage/Salary Administration
Section VII	Benefits
Section VIII	Job Opportunity
Section IX	Work Rules/Discipline
Section X	Customer Relations
Section XI	Training
Section XII	Continuous Improvement
Section XIII	Terminations
Section XIV	Health/Medical
Section XV	Safety
Section XVI	Organization Chart

DISTRIBUTION:

Manuals will be distributed to all who have supervisory responsibility, and to all individuals in the specialist classification who have responsibility for development, implementation, interpretation, and communication of procedures.

PERSONNEL POLICIES AND PROCEDURES

DISTRIBUTION:		SUBJECT: ADMINISTRATIVE MANUAL	
EFFECTIVE DATE:	PAGE 2 OF 3	FILE UNDER SECTION	
REVISION DATE:	APPROVED BY:		

The information in the manuals will not be considered confidential; however, copies of policies or portions of the manual should not be distributed to associates without the approval of the General Affairs Department.

Every manual will be designated with a number; each person who receives a manual will be responsible for maintaining it. A listing of manual distribution by number/associate will be maintained by a member of the General Affairs Department.

FORMAT:

Each policy will be identified with a two-position numeric designation. The first position of the code will be a Roman numeral, and it will refer to the section of the manual in which the policy is located. The second number will be used to designate location within that section. Forms that support a policy will be included at the end of that location and will be numbered accordingly.

Each policy will have the same format and will have sections that detail the scope and the purpose of the policy, followed by the text.

POLICY DEVELOPMENT:

It is the responsibility of the General Manager to determine when a new policy should be developed, or when an existing policy should be revised. Input for this process can come from many different sources, including associates from any area of the company. Once the need for a policy is identified, an individual will be assigned to research and develop a new policy or revise an existing policy, depending upon the requirement. This research should include discussions with affected departments and coordinators and a review of area/industry practice, and may also involve the use of outside consultants, attorneys, etc.

When developing or revising policies, the factors to be considered will include:

- Applicable State and Federal Laws
- Impact on Safety, Quality, Production, Efficiency, etc.
- Competitive Cost Considerations
- Market Considerations
- EEO/Affirmative Action Impact
- Associate Relation Impact
- Industry Practice
- Area Practice

When the General Affairs Department has completed the policy formulation/revision process, the policy will be submitted to the vice president for review and comment.

Depending on the significance of the policy, a meeting involving representatives from areas affected by the policy may be conducted to review/discuss the final policy prior to submitting it for the approval process.

POLICY APPROVAL:

If the new policy is a revision of an existing policy, the document will be submitted for formal review and approval. If the new policy introduces significantly new ideas or methods, it should be introduced to all general managers at a Business-Review Meeting.

21

DISTRIBUTION:		SUBJECT: ADMINISTRATIVE MANUAL	
EFFECTIVE DATE:	PAGE 3 OF 3	FILE UNDER SECTION	
REVISION DATE:	APPROVED BY:		

Once a policy has been reviewed at a Business-Review Meeting, it will be prepared for approval signature of the president. The policy will be considered approved after it is signed by the president of the company.

POLICY IMPLEMENTATION:

Once a policy has received necessary approval, it will then be communicated and distributed for inclusion in the Administrative Manual.

Whenever a policy is implemented, a memo will be prepared by the General Affairs Department that communicates and explains the new policy. This memo will be posted on the company Controlled Communication Center and will be distributed to the supervisory staff along with a copy of the policy.

Any questions concerning application of any policy should be directed to the General Affairs Department.

HISTORICAL POLICY FILE:

It will be the responsibility of the General Affairs Department to maintain a historical file on each practice that details all changes that have been made to a policy since its initial implementation.

PERSONNEL POLICIES AND PROCEDURES

DISTRIBUTION:		SUBJECT: FOREWORD	
EFFECTIVE DATE:	PAGE 1 OF 1	FILE UNDER SECTION	
REVISION DATE:	APPROVED BY:		

This manual contains statements of personnel policies and procedures. It is designed to be a working guide for supervisory and human resources staff in the day-to-day administration of our company human resources program.

These written policies should increase understanding, eliminate the need for personal decisions on matters of companywide policy, and help to assure uniformity throughout the organization. It is the responsibility of each and every member of management to administer these policies in a consistent and impartial manner.

Procedures and practices in the field of human resources relations are subject to modification and further development in the light of experience. Each member of management can assist in keeping our human resources program up to date by notifying the Human Resources Department whenever problems are encountered or improvements can be made in the administration of our personnel policies.

PERSONNEL POLICIES AND PROCEDURES

DISTRIBUTION:		SUBJECT: PURPOSE OF POLICY MANUAL	
EFFECTIVE DATE:	PAGE 1 OF 1	FILE UNDER SECTION	
REVISION DATE:	APPROVED BY:		

Our Personnel Policy Manual is simply the company's personnel policies written into a usable guidebook for our managerial and supervisory staff. This manual not only outlines the company policy toward the various phases of our employee-employer relationship, but also indicates how policy is to be administered. Consequently, supervisors are able to use this manual as a guidebook when they need to apply company policy in a given situation.

Our experience has shown that written policies promote consistency, continuity, and understanding within our organization. When policies are put into writing, in the form of a manual, they add a visual effect to their overall import. Moreover, written policies help top management by obviating the need for time-consuming and expensive memos, bulletins, and announcements.

Written policies also aid our supervisors in consistently achieving fair and equitable interpretations of policy that requires human resources action on a regular, recurring basis. Moreover, our fellow employees feel a deeper understanding of their role in the organization when they realize that policies are written and thereby uniformly administered.

Basically, our Personnel Policy Manual is an important tool for supervision. We believe that supervisors work better when they know what is expected of them. They feel more secure, more confident, and more "at one" with the company when our policies are made clear for them.

We all tend to gravitate toward responsibility rather than away from it when we know there is written policy on which to rely. Furthermore, the ever-present tendency to pass the buck is reduced to a great extent.

Specifically speaking, this Personnel Policy Manual is designed to provide us with the following advantages:

◆ ◆ Understanding—Written company policy is one of the best antidotes in the human resources medicine chest for the troubles a company grapevine can cause. Even though everything is subject to interpretation, the odds overwhelmingly favor the written word as against the oral. It's incredible how a single fact can become so distorted by the word-of-mouth avenue.

   ◆ Line of Authority—Top management cannot make all the decisions that need to be made within our company. But so often they try, simply because they are afraid to release that authority to subordinates. Naturally, it follows that if top management felt that subordinates could make decisions like top management would, the reluctance would be relieved. Our Personnel Policy Manual achieves this desired relationship. It thus results in a solid delineation of authority.

   ◆ Consistency—The idea of consistent application of our company policies is coveted simply because it means that employees will be treated equally. It prevents, to a great extent, the seepage of prejudice and bias in the decisions of supervision. The achievement of this one human resources virtue is to take a colossal step in your maintenance of satisfactory employer-employee harmony.

   ◆ Planning—Many times we have found deficient policies that urgently needed changing. However, since all policy was orally transmitted, the need for change never seemed to achieve attention. Then, in preparing a policy manual, where all policy is together and coordinated, the need for change became quite apparent. Likewise, other existing policies that suddenly seemed out of place were deleted, changed, or amended. In short, we find that when developing our policy manual, we are more often than not made aware of incongruities in our present policies, which heretofore might have seemed quite sufficient.

We feel that no company is so small as to make a Personnel Policy Manual unnecessary. In short, no company is invulnerable to the fallacies of human nature.

PERSONNEL POLICIES AND PROCEDURES

DISTRIBUTION:		SUBJECT: PURPOSE OF POLICY MANUAL	
EFFECTIVE DATE:	PAGE 1 OF 1	FILE UNDER SECTION	
REVISION DATE:	APPROVED BY:		

POLICY:

Many of us are aware of the great need for leadership in government, churches, and schools, but, unfortunately, we have neglected some phases of industrial leadership. Much of our conscious time is spent at work. If we are to have daily satisfaction, it must come from our jobs as well as from our community and family activities. Therefore, it is our earnest hope that this manual will enable you to better understand your management duties and the responsibility of establishing leadership in the field of human relations. We know that if you understand the philosophy of management, you will furnish the present and future industrial leadership that is so sorely needed to continue the traditions that mean so much to each of us.

PERSONNEL POLICIES AND PROCEDURES

DISTRIBUTION:		SUBJECT: PURPOSE OF POLICY MANUAL	
EFFECTIVE DATE:	PAGE 1 OF 1	FILE UNDER SECTION	
REVISION DATE:	APPROVED BY:		

This Manual contains statements of personnel policies and procedures to be followed by all members of the management team of (Name of Hospital). It is designed to serve as a permanent reference and working guide for management and supervisory human resources in the administration of the hospital's personnel policies, procedures, and practices.

These written policies should increase understanding, eliminate the need for personal decisions on matters of hospitalwide policy, and help to ensure uniformity throughout the organization. It is the responsibility of each and every member of management to administer these policies in a consistent and impartial manner.

PERSONNEL POLICIES AND PROCEDURES

DISTRIBUTION:		SUBJECT: PURPOSE OF POLICY MANUAL	
EFFECTIVE DATE:	PAGE 1 OF 1	FILE UNDER SECTION	
REVISION DATE:	APPROVED BY:		

POLICY:

To All Who Supervise:

The management of our most valuable resource, the people who work for the company, is a constant and continuing challenge. As a supervisor your task is to achieve our common goal—the highest caliber of trust and investment service—through those who work with you and for you.

Set forth in this manual are standards of human conduct that are designed to help you achieve this common purpose. It is a tool designed specifically for your daily use.

It is the function of the Human Resources Division to codify and clarify the policies of management. In this revised and updated edition, human resources was assisted by many supervisors who made valuable suggestions for the implementation and clarification of these policies.

It is your responsibility to apply these policies in a consistent manner to assure the staff of our common purpose. In the meantime, human resources stands ready to assist at any time in interpretation.

PERSONNEL POLICIES AND PROCEDURES

DISTRIBUTION:		SUBJECT: AUTHORITY AND DISTRIBUTION OF POLICY MANUAL	
EFFECTIVE DATE:	PAGE 1 OF 1		FILE UNDER SECTION
REVISION DATE:	APPROVED BY:		

POLICY:

Every salaried supervisor of (Name of Company) is to receive a copy of this Policy Manual upon entering his or her supervisory position. This present Policy Manual is up-to-date and contains the complete and accurate policies of our company as of this date. It is to be carefully preserved in your desk at all times. We ask that this Policy Manual remain on the premises at all times in your department. Should you, for any reason, be transferred within our company, upgraded, or change your status for any other reason, please contact your immediate supervisor and return the Policy Manual to him/her. If he/she is not immediately available, please turn the Policy Manual over to our Director of Industrial Relations.

PERSONNEL POLICIES AND PROCEDURES

DISTRIBUTION:		SUBJECT: AUTHORITY AND DISTRIBUTION OF POLICY MANUAL	
EFFECTIVE DATE:	PAGE 1 OF 1		FILE UNDER SECTION
REVISION DATE:	APPROVED BY:		

Our Personnel Policy Manual is being made available to all supervisory human resources in our organization. Its purpose is to:

1. provide a basis for and objectives of our human resources program;

2. assign responsibility for carrying out the principles and practices of our human resources program;

3. provide recognized authority, consistent with applicable laws, on which action is to be taken and to minimize the possibility of unauthorized human resources action;

4. bring about understanding of our personnel policies and practices;

5. facilitate decisions and promote consistency of interpretation and application across organizational lines and over a period of time;

6. provide a record to guide future policy and serve as a framework for the revisions that appear to be desirable on the basis of experience.

PERSONNEL POLICIES AND PROCEDURES

DISTRIBUTION:		SUBJECT: SUPPLEMENTS TO POLICY MANUAL
EFFECTIVE DATE:	PAGE 1 OF 1	FILE UNDER SECTION
REVISION DATE:	APPROVED BY:	

From time to time, you will receive additional supplements to our Personnel Policy Manual. These new supplements will update and revise present policy and practice whenever deemed necessary. You will want to study the revised supplements carefully prior to placing them in your Policy Manual. Please be sure to remove old policy statements and procedures when recommended to do so in the memorandum attached to revised supplements. Should you have any questions concerning the intent or procedure to follow in the supplements to your Policy Manual, please see your immediate supervisor.

PERSONNEL POLICIES AND PROCEDURES

DISTRIBUTION:		SUBJECT: NEW OR REVISED POLICY	
EFFECTIVE DATE:	PAGE 1 OF 1		FILE UNDER SECTION
REVISION DATE:	APPROVED BY:		

Standard Policies and Procedures concerning the relationship between the company and its employees will be placed in writing and made available to all concerned.

When the need for a new or revised Standard Policy and Procedure is indicated, it will be referred to the Policy Board to consider the establishment of one. If it is decided by the Policy Board that such a policy or revision is desirable, the Board will outline or suggest the principal points that should be covered.

The Industrial Relations Department will prepare a preliminary draft of the policy and distribute this to the members of the Board.

The Policy Board will review the preliminary draft and provide the appropriate direction for preparation of a tentative draft.

The Industrial Relations Department may present the tentative draft of a new policy to Management Conferences for discussion and recommendations. Copies will be mailed to Conference members prior to the meeting.

The results of the Management Conferences or Managers meetings discussion and recommendations will be reported to the Policy Board.

The Policy Board will be responsible for the final draft of the proposed policy. A copy of the proposed policy in its final form will be sent to each member of the Policy Board for his/her signature of approval.

To assure coordination with Corporate policies, copies of the proposed policy will be sent to the Corporate Director of Industrial Relations before it is issued.

Standard Policies and Procedures become effective upon approval by the Division Manager.

The Industrial Relations Department will mail sufficient copies of the approved Standard Policy and Procedure to each Policy Board member for distribution and discussion to those supervisors having a copy of the Policy and Procedure Manual. Supervisors will be responsible for placing the new policy in the manual and destroying any superseded policy.

SECTION 2

Federal Regulations Affecting Personnel Policies and Procedures

This section is a guide to help you understand some of the more important federal regulations that affect the employer-employee relationship. It is not intended to be an exhaustive summary, it is a handy reference source for you. In addition, remember that in many jurisdictions there are also state and local laws that address the same issues as federal labor laws. Exhibits 2A-1 and 2A-2 provide a brief summary of laws that affect employees' rights with a column for you to indicate which laws apply to your employees.

Private Employers

Age Discrimination in Employment Act of 1967
29 USC Sections 621-634

Coverage: Employers with twenty or more employees who are engaged in an industry affecting commerce are prohibited from discriminating against individuals on the basis of age in hiring or discharge decisions or with respect to compensation, terms, conditions, or privileges of employment. The Age Discrimination in Employment Act (ADEA) protects employees who are at least forty years of age. There is no upper age limit. Employees of federal, state, and local governments are also protected.

Americans with Disabilities Act of 1990
42 USC 12101

This act prohibits discrimination in application, hiring, advancing, training, compensation, and other terms and conditions of employment against a qualified individual with a physical or mental disability. It also prohibits discrimination on the basis of disability in the enjoyment of goods, services, facilities, transportation, privileges, advantages, and accommodations provided by a place of business intended for nonresidential use and that affects commerce.

Bankruptcy Act
(As amended by the Bankruptcy Act Amendments of 1984)
11 USC Section 525

Coverage: Any private employer or the federal government may not terminate the employment of, or discriminate in terms and conditions of employment against, an individual who is or has been a debtor under the Bankruptcy Act.

32

Civil Rights Act of 1964
Title VI—Nondiscrimination in Federally Assisted Programs
42 USC Section 2000d

Coverage: Programs and activities that receive federal financial assistance are prohibited from excluding persons on the basis of race, color, or national origin.

Civil Rights Act of 1964
Title VII—Equal Employment Opportunity
42 USC Section 2000e et seq.

Coverage: Employers with fifteen or more employees are prohibited from discriminating against any individual with respect to compensation, terms, conditions, or privileges of employment because of that individual's race, color, religion, sex, or national origin.

Consolidated Omnibus Budget Reconciliation Act of 1986 (COBRA)
IRC Section 162(k)

All employers in the United States, excluding church groups and federal employers, with twenty or more employees must offer employees and their dependents the right to continue group health (and dental) plan coverage between eighteen and thirty-six months beyond the date it would otherwise end, depending upon the circumstances.

Consumer Credit Protection Act
15 USC Section 1673

Coverage: All employees are protected by this act. This act sets a national maximum on the amount of an employee's wages that can be withheld to satisfy a wage garnishment.

The amount withheld cannot exceed either (1) 25 percent of the employee's weekly disposable earnings or (2) the amount by which the employee's weekly disposable earnings exceed thirty times the current minimum wage set by the Department of Labor. Each state has its own statutes on garnishments; the federal standard is designed only to set the maximum that can be withheld. The federal act does not limit court-ordered wage deductions for the support of any person or wage deductions for state and federal tax debts. The act also prohibits an employer from discharging an employee whose wages are garnished for one indebtedness.

Employee Polygraph Protection Act of 1988

This act prohibits most private employers from using lie detector tests for applicants and employees.

Employee Retirement Income Security Act of 1974
29 USC Sections 1001–1461

Coverage: The Employee Retirement Income Security Act (ERISA) sets standards and requirements for the substantive provisions and administration of employee benefit plans and employee welfare benefit plans, including, for example, pension and profit-sharing plans. ERISA does not apply to plans maintained solely to comply with workers' compensation, unemployment compensation, or disability insurance laws; plans maintained outside the United States for nonresident aliens; and excess benefit plans.

Equal Pay Act of 1963
29 USC Section 206(d)

Coverage: The Equal Pay Act is an amendment to the Fair Labor Standards Act (FLSA), and covers the same employers. The requirements of the Equal Pay Act, however, are extended to apply to executive, administrative, and professional employees and outside salespeople, even though other FLSA requirements do not apply to these employees. The act prohibits an employer from discriminating on the basis of sex by paying persons of one sex less than the wage paid to persons of the opposite sex in the same establishment "for equal work on jobs the performance of which requires equal skill, effort, and responsibility and which are performed under similar working conditions." Excepted are wage differentials based on seniority, merit pay, and piecework, and a "differential based on any factor other than sex."

Fair Labor Standards Act of 1938
29 USC Sections 201–219

Coverage: The Fair Labor Standards Act (FLSA) covers most employers in the public and private sectors. The act requires, first, that employees be paid at least the minimum wage; second, in general, that they be paid time and one-half for hours worked in excess of forty in any given week; third, that persons employed in hazardous occupations be over eighteen years of age; and fourth, that minors employed in other occupations be above fourteen or sixteen years of age, depending on the type of work and employer.

Family and Medical Leave Act of 1993
29 USC Section 2601 et seq.

Coverage: This act covers employers with fifty or more employees within seventy-five miles in twenty or more workweeks within the current or preceding calendar year. The act provides for a total of up to twelve weeks unpaid, job-protected leave in any twelve-month period for the birth and to care for an employee's child; for the placement of a child with an employee for adoption or foster care; to care for an employee's spouse, parent, or child who has a serious health condition; and for an employee's own serious health condition that makes the employee unable to perform one or more essential functions of the employee's current position.

Federal Election Campaign Act of 1971
2 USC Sections 431–455

Coverage: The act limits the means that a corporate employer may use to solicit contributions from employees for the employer's political fund. The act also makes it unlawful for any corporation to make a contribution or expenditure in connection with any election in which citizens vote for presidential and vice presidential electors or a senator or representative in Congress. Contributions and expenditures in connection with any primary election or political convention or caucus held to select candidates for any such office are also prohibited. Note that, while this act applies only to elections for federal office, many states have similar statutes limiting the contributions of corporations in state and local elections. Corporations are permitted by the federal act to establish a separate segregated fund that may be utilized for political purposes.

Immigration Reform and Control Act
8 USC Section 1324(a) & (b) (1986)

Coverage: All employers, including state and local government employers, must verify that employees hired on or after November 7, 1986, are either U.S. citizens or authorized to work in the United States. There is no exception for employers with a small number of employees. As verification, new hires must produce specific documents proving their identity and employment eligibility and, further, both employee and employer must complete a government form, INS Form I-9, indicating that the new hire is eligible for employment. Form I-9 must be retained for three years from the date of hire or until one year after termination, whichever is later. Any employer who knowingly hires or continues to employ an unauthorized alien is subject to civil, and in some cases criminal, penalties.

In addition, the act makes it unlawful for employers with four or more employees to discriminate by hiring, recruiting, referring, or discharging employees on the basis of national origin, citizenship status, or intention to obtain citizenship, to the extent that such discrimination is not covered by Title VII of the Civil Rights Act of 1964. It also grants amnesty to aliens who were previously illegal, but who have resided continuously in the United States since January 1, 1982, have been physically present in the United States since the act was passed, and are otherwise admissible as immigrants. See Section 4 for policy statements related to the Immigration Reform and Control Act.

Internal Revenue Code
26 USC Sections 1–9602

Coverage: Covering all employers, the code defines the tax treatment of the full range of business expenditures and, therefore, has important implications for the benefits to be granted to employees.

Jurors' Protection Act
28 USC Sections 1363, 1875

Coverage: These statutes prohibit all employers from disciplining any regular employee for the employee's participation in jury service.

Labor-Management Reporting and Disclosure Act, 1957
29 USC Section 153

Coverage: The purpose of this act was the elimination of certain types of wrongdoing on the part of certain unions and their officers. A code of conduct was established for unions, union officers, employers, and consultants that guarantees union members certain inalienable rights within their union and imposes certain obligations on unions, union officers, employers, and consultants.

National Labor Relations Act of 1935
29 USC Sections 151–169

Coverage: The National Labor Relations Act (NLRA) applies to employees in all industries affecting commerce and to all employees except agricultural laborers, individuals employed in the domestic service of a family or person, individuals employed by their parent or spouse, independent contractors, and supervisors.

The NLRA gives employees the right to form, join, and assist labor organizations or to refrain from such activities and to bargain collectively with employers.

Norris-LaGuardia Act, 1932
29 USC Sections 101–110

The Norris-LaGuardia Act accords employees full freedom to organize and to negotiate the terms and conditions of their employment through representatives of their own choosing, and limits the jurisdiction and authority of the courts of the United States to issue restraining orders and injunctions.

Occupational Safety and Health Act of 1970
29 USC Sections 651-678

Coverage: Because this act applies to employers in businesses affecting commerce, most private employers are covered by it. Those that are excluded are generally subject to safety and health requirements established by other agencies. Employers are required to maintain a workplace that is free from recognized hazards likely to cause death or serious injury and to comply with the workplace safety and health standards promulgated by the Occupational Safety and Health Administration (OSHA). Employers are prohibited from discharging or in any other way discriminating against employees who exercise their rights under the act. This precludes an employer from discharging an employee who, acting under a reasonable apprehension, refuses in good faith to expose himself or herself to a hazardous workplace condition.

Older Workers Benefit Protection Act of 1990
29 USC 630 et seq.

The act prohibits employers from reducing benefits because of an employee's age and specifies rules for obtaining Age Discrimination in Employment Act waivers.

Portal to Portal Pay Act of 1947
29 USC Sections 251-262

Coverage: This act applies to all employers subject to the Fair Labor Standards Act (FLSA). The intent of the legislation was to abrogate certain judicial interpretations of the FLSA. The Supreme Court had held that the time employees spent in walking from the plant gates to their workbenches and in tasks that were preparatory to their day's work must be counted as hours worked in computing pay and overtime. To alter this holding, the act bans suits by employees to recover back pay for time spent on site before and after the completion of the employees' "principal activities" unless that time was considered compensable under a contract, custom, or practice in the plant.

Pregnancy Discrimination Act of 1978
42 USC Section 2000

The Pregnancy Discrimination Act prohibits disparate treatment of pregnant women for all employment-related purposes. This act prohibits termination of or refusal to hire or promote a woman solely because she is pregnant; bars mandatory leaves for pregnant women beginning at an arbitrarily set time in their pregnancy and not based on their individual inability to work; protects the reinstatement rights of women on leave for pregnancy-related reasons, including rights in regard to credit for previous service, accrued retirement benefits, and accumulated seniority; and prohibits employers from treating pregnancy disability and childbirth less favorably than they treat other causes of disability under fringe benefit plans.

Worker Adjustment and Retraining Notification Act (Plant Closing Law) 20 CFR-TT 639

Coverage: The plant closing law requires employers of 100 or more employees to give sixty days' notice before closing a facility or starting a layoff of 50 people or more. Part-time employees, who are described as those working fewer than twenty hours per week or who have been employed for fewer than six of the twelve months preceding the date on which the notices are required, are not counted when adding the number of employees under the law.

Federal Contractors

Executive Order No. 11246 of September 26, 1965 30 Fed. Reg. 12319

Coverage: By this order, every employer who holds a federal contract of $10,000 or more is prohibited from discriminating against employees or job applicants on the basis of race, color, religion, sex, or national origin. For contractors employing fifty or more employees and holding contracts exceeding $50,000, the order requires written affirmative action plans regarding the utilization of minority persons and females.

Service Contract Act 41 USC Sections 351–358

Coverage: Employees engaged in contracts executed by the United States or the District of Columbia are entitled to minimum wages by reasons of the Service Contract Act of 1965 if the principal purpose of the contract is to furnish services in the United States through the use of service employees. Both prime contractors and subcontractors are subject to the provisions of the statute.

Regardless of the contract amount, no employee performing work under such contract or subcontract may be paid less than the minimum wage schedules specified in the Fair Labor Standards Act.

Vietnam-Era Veterans' Readjustment Assistance Act of 1974 38 USC Sections 2011–2012

Coverage: Employers who have federal contracts of $10,000 or more are prohibited from discriminating against and are required to take affirmative action to employ and advance employment-qualified disabled veterans and Vietnam-era veterans. A written affirmative action plan is required of employers who hold contracts of $50,000 or more and who have fifty or more employees.

The Vocational Rehabilitation Act of 1973
29 USC Sections 701–796i, 793–794

Coverage: The mandate of this act is divided into two parts. The first part, commonly referred to as Section 503, covers private employers who are government contractors. The second part, Section 504, applies to programs and activities that receive federal financial assistance. For employers holding government contracts and subcontracts in excess of $1,000, Section 503 of the act prohibits discrimination against individuals with disabilities. If the employer's contract is $50,000 or greater and the employer has fifty or more employees, the employer is required to develop a written affirmative action program for the employment of individuals with disabilities. Section 504, on the other hand, only prohibits discrimination against individuals with disabilities and does not require an affirmative action plan.

The Uniformed Services Employment and Reemployment Act of 1994
38 USC Section 4301 et seq.

Coverage: The act replaces all veterans' rights laws enacted and amended since 1940 (except the Vietnam-Era Veterans' Readjustment Assistance Act) and codifies veterans' rights case law over the same period. The act eliminates the former distinction between active duty and reserve and national guard training duty, and adds uniformed services other than the military. All employers are covered, regardless of the number of employees. All employees are protected from discrimination on the basis of past, present, or future service in the uniformed services of the United States. The act guarantees reinstatement of employees who serve in the uniformed services, generally to the same or similar position with like status and pay, and with full credit for seniority and other rights and benefits determined by seniority that they had at the start of the leave plus full credit for the period of time spent in service (up to five years).

Exhibit 2A-1. Employees' Job Protection Laws and Rights (Understanding the Rules of Your Government Partners)

Government Act and Agency	Basis of Coverage	Type of Employee Protection	Applies to Us	Posters Required	Penalty for Noncompliance	Statute of Limitations
FAIR LABOR STANDARDS ACT (DOL)	At least two employees whose work affects goods for commerce. All employees of any business with $500,000 annual gross sales.	Minimum wage Overtime pay Recording of hours Child labor		Yes	• Injunctions • Back pay • Liquidated damages • Fines (up to $10,000) • Legal costs	2 years 3 years—willful violations 5 years—criminal violations
EQUAL PAY ACT (EEOC)	All employees of a single location	(Recordkeeping requirements.) No wage differential based on sex. Differences OK if based on merit, performance, seniority.		Yes (EEOC)	• Back pay, including wages theoretically lost • Liquidated damages	
IMMIGRATION REFORM AND CONTROL ACT (DOJ)	All employers	Employers must verify identity and employment eligibility of hirees.		Yes	• Injunctions • Civil penalties: Up to $1,000 per I-9 form Up to $2,000 per illegal alien • Criminal penalties	N/A
	Four or more employees	Prohibits discrimination on basis of national origin or citizenship status.			• Civil penalty—up to $2,000 per discriminatee • Remedial relief/back pay • Attorney's fees	180 days DOJ—120 days
FEDERAL AND STATE LAWS UNEMPLOYMENT COMPENSATION (State Agencies)	All employers	Compensation for temporary involuntary unemployment.		Yes	• Increased state tax based on claims	N/A

(continued)

39

EXHIBIT 2A-1. (*continued*)

Law	Coverage	Provisions	Required to sue?	Remedies	Filing deadline
STATE LAWS WORKERS' COMPENSATION (State Agencies)	All employers	Compensation for injured workers and occupational diseases. Some states don't allow termination.	Yes	• Reinstatement/back pay, medical costs, disability and death payments, rehabilitation costs, legal fees and costs • Fines up to $10,000 • Court actions	Individual state statutes
EMPLOYEE POLYGRAPH PROTECTION ACT (DOL)	Most private employers	Prohibits use of lie detector tests for applicants and employees	Yes		N/A
OSHA—OCCUPATIONAL SAFETY AND HEALTH ACT (State and Federal Agencies)	Any person engaged in a business affecting commerce	Prohibits workplace with unsafe and unhealthy conditions (Recordkeeping requirements.)	Yes	• Fines • Close facilities • Imprisonment	N/A
NATIONAL LABOR RELATIONS ACT (NMRB)	Two employees Interstate commerce $50,000/year nonretail $50,000/year retail Other thresholds	Nonrepresented employees Protected if engaged in: Concerted activity Union activity	No, except in violations	• Reinstatement • Back pay • Post notice • Recognize union	6 months
CIVIL RIGHTS ACT—Title VII (EEOC) (State and Federal Agencies)	15 or more employees working 20 or more calendar weeks	Prohibits discrimination on basis of race, color, religion, sex, or national origin.	Yes	• Reinstatement/hiring • Back pay/front pay • Can be class action • Legal fees and costs • Damages to $300,000 (no limit on race)	180 days* 300 days in deferral states
PREGNANCY DISCRIMINATION ACT (EEOC)	15 or more employees working 20 or more calendar weeks	Prohibits discrimination (Recordkeeping requirements.) Required to consider pregnancy as disability.	No	• Reinstatement/hiring • Back pay/front pay • Can be class action • Legal fees and costs • Damages to $300,000 (no limit on race)	180 days* 300 days in deferral states

Law (Agency)	Coverage	Provisions	Posting	Remedies	Filing Deadline
ADA—Americans with Disabilities Act (EEOC)	Title I, 15 employees	Prohibits discrimination against a qualified individual with a disability in application, hiring, advancing, training, compensating, discharging, and other terms and conditions.	Yes	• Injunctions • Reinstatement/hiring • Back pay/front pay • Attorney's fees and costs • Damages to $300,000	180 days* 300 days in deferral states
FMLA—Family and Medical Leave Act (DOL)	50 or more employees working 20 or more calendar weeks in current or previous year	12 weeks' leave must be granted for care of employee's child (birth, adoption, or foster); or own, spouse's, child's, or parent's serious health condition.	Yes	• Reinstatement • Back pay/damages for monetary loss • Liquidated damages • Attorney's fees and costs	2 years 3 years—willful violation
ADEA—Age Discrimination in Employment Act (EEOC)	20 or more employees	Prohibits discrimination on basis of age over 40	Yes	• Reinstatement • Back pay/benefits • Liquidated damages • Attorney's fees and costs	180 days* 300 days in deferral states EEOC—N/A†
COBRA—Consolidated Omnibus Budget Reconciliation Act (IRS, DOL)	20 or more employees during preceding calendar year	Allows for continuation of health-care protection for up to 36 months.	Notice to employee/spouse and dependent children	• Up to $200/day tax penalty • Up to $500,000 annual • Willful—unlimited • Past/future medical expenses • Compensatory/punitive damages • Attorney's fees and costs	Applicable state statutes

(continued)

EXHIBIT 2A-1. (*continued*)

ERISA—Employee Retirement Income Security Act (DOL)	Any employer engaged in business or in any industry or activity affecting commerce	Eligibility Funding Standards for managing Information disclosure	No	• Injunctions • Equitable, remedial relief, including removal from office • Up to $10,000 fine, jail	N/A
USERRA Uniformed Services Employment and Re-employment Rights Act (DOL)	All employers	Employment Re-employment Seniority Health insurance Pension benefits Nondiscrimination Reasonable accommodation Discharge	No	◆ Injunctions ◆ Reinstatement ◆ Lost wages, benefits ◆ Equitable relief ◆ Liquidated damages ◆ Attorney's fees ◆ Legal costs	None
WARN—Worker's Adjustment and Retraining Notification Act (DOL)	100 or more employees	Layoffs and closings	Written notice	◆ Back pay and benefits ◆ Civil penalty up to $30,000 ◆ Attorney's fees	Individual state statutes
State FEPSs—Fair Employment Practices Laws (State Agencies)	Often extend to smaller employers	Often more comprehensive and more restrictive	Yes	◆ Injunctive, equitable relief ◆ Some states—damages ◆ Often more than federal	Individual state statutes
State Courts	Violation of employment-at-will "Wrongful discharge"—defamation	Violation of public policy Bad-faith dealings Duration of agreement, either expressed or implied	No	◆ Equitable relief ◆ Unlimited financial recovery ◆ Some states—damages	Individual state statutes

Key: DOL = Department of Labor
DOJ = Department of Justice
IRS = Internal Revenue Service
EEOC = Equal Employment Opportunity Commission
NLRB = National Labor Relations Board
* Statute of limitations extends from 180 to 300 days in all states except AL, AR, MS. State law statute may be longer. Local FEP agency in AL, AR, MS could extend 180 to 300.
† The EEOC has the right to initiate action without a charge.
Source: © 1997 SESCO Management Consultants.

Exhibit 2A-2. Federal Contractor Employees' Job Protection Laws and Rights (Understanding the Rules of Federal Contractors' Government Partners)

Government Act and Agency	Basis of Coverage	Type of Employee Protection	Applies to Us	Posters Required	Penalty for Noncompliance	Statute of Limitations
Government Service Contracts Service Contract Act (DOL)	Federal government contracts exceeding $2,500	Minimum wages Overtime pay Fringe benefits Safety and health		Yes	◆ Withholding contract payments ◆ Contract cancellation ◆ Blacklisting ◆ Back pay	N/A
Public Works Contracts Davis-Bacon Act (DOL)	Federal government contracts exceeding $2,000	Minimum wages Overtime pay Fringe benefits Anti kickback		Yes	◆ Withholding contract payments ◆ Blacklisting	2 years 3 years (willful)
Drug-Free Workplace Act (DOL)	Federal government contracts exceeding $25,000	Drug-free America Program. Report drug convictions. Good-faith drug-free effort		Yes	◆ Debarment up to 5 years	N/A
Executive Order 11246 (DOL-OFCCP)	Federal government contracts exceeding $10,000	Prohibits discrimination by race, color, sex, religion, or national origin. Requires affirmative action.		Yes	◆ Judicial enforcement ◆ Contract cancellation and debarment ◆ Back pay ◆ Reinstatement	N/A
	Federal government contracts exceeding $50,000 and 50 employees	Requires written affirmative action program (AAP).				

(continued)

43

Exhibit 2A-2. (*continued*)

Rehabilitation Act Sections 503-504 (DOL-OFCCP)	Federal government contracts exceeding $10,000 Recipients of federal financial assistance	Requires affirmative action to employ and advance individuals with disabilities Requires written AAP	Federal government contracts exceeding $50,000 and 50 employees	Yes	• Judicial enforcement ♦ Withholding contract payments ♦ Contract cancellation and debarment ♦ Back pay/reinstatement	300 days
Vietnam Era Veteran's Readjustments Assistance Act (DOL-OFCCP)	Federal government contracts exceeding $10,000 Requires written AAP	Requires affirmative action to employ and advance disabled and Vietnam-era veterans	Contracts exceeding $50,000 and 50 employees	Yes	♦ Withholding contract payments ♦ Contract cancellation and debarment ♦ Back pay/reinstatement	180 days

44

SECTION 3

State and Local Employment Laws

All states and some counties and municipalities have enacted employment laws that affect personnel policies and practices, and therefore personnel policy manuals. This may mean that some policies must be modified, and others may be required or prohibited by applicable state and/or local laws and regulations.

Standard policies must be supplemented by policies needed to comply with statutory requirements applicable to employers doing business in the state(s) in which they have facilities and/or employees. Some state law provisions are preempted by, are identical to, or are automatically addressed by federal law reflected in policies addressed in this volume. Others may be unrelated to the requirements of federal law and are simply additional requirements that employers must address.

Where state and federal laws differ, the standard policy must be modified to reflect the most generous and/or protective provisions of the combined laws. In some instances (e.g., family, medical, pregnancy, maternity, paternity, parental, or adoption leave), employees not only may be entitled to the most generous or protective combination, but may enjoy state entitlement in addition to federal entitlement.

Clients with multistate operations must decide whether they want a separate policy manual for each state or one manual for all operations. In the latter case, policies must reflect the most generous and/or protective provisions of all of the state (and perhaps federal) laws that address the same issues. It is always permissible for an employer to grant rights or protections to employees who are not otherwise eligible for or entitled to such benefits.

It should be noted that some counties and municipalities have ordinances that affect private and/or public employers' personnel policies. Employers are well advised to contact such governing entities, since it would not be feasible to reflect all such laws in this volume.

State and local employment laws frequently affect the following employer policies and practices:

- EEO—additional protected categories
- Applicant/employee testing
- Jury duty/witness leave
- Family and medical leave
- Maternity/pregnancy disability leave
- Adoption leave
- School activity leave
- Time off to vote
- Military leave pay treatment
- Employee privacy
- Employee access to personnel records
- Smoking
- Deductions from (final) pay
- Termination pay—accrued benefits

45

State Law and the Family Medical Leave Act

Family, Medical, Pregnancy (Disability), Maternity, Parental, and Adoption Leave

Employers covered by both the federal Family Medical Leave Act (FMLA) and applicable state law must comply with the provisions of both. State leave policy should be separate from and follow FMLA policy. The FMLA is described in Section 2.

Employees are entitled to use the most advantageous combination of federal and state leave laws available to them. Therefore, employers must comply with any provisions of state or local law that provide family or medical leave rights that are greater than the rights established by the federal FMLA.

FMLA rights, protections, and procedures apply to concurrent leaves unless state law provides greater rights or protections, or provides for less restrictive procedures.

Leave taken under state law, whether or not concurrent, is not subject to any FMLA limitations (e.g., eligibility, twelve-month entitlement period, spousal) that are more restrictive than the state law.

When state leave is taken after FMLA leave entitlement expires, FMLA rights and protections no longer apply, and employee protection may be limited to that provided by the state provisions, unless the employer voluntarily grants FMLA rights and protections in such circumstances. If the employer does so, the state leave policy statement must be modified.

Leave taken under state law for a purpose not covered by the FMLA (to care for a seriously ill parent-in-law, for example) may not be charged against the employee's FMLA leave entitlement, and is subject only to state law provisions.

Where state law provides a shorter notice period than the FMLA for leave that is reasonably foreseeable, an employer must allow that shorter notice period unless the employee is requesting more leave than is required by the state law.

Where only one medical certification is required by state law, no additional certifications may be required by the employer unless the employee is requesting more leave than is required under state law.

Where state law does not contain an exemption from reinstatement for ''key'' employees, such employees may not be exempted from reinstatement under concurrent FMLA leave.

Where state law specifies a twelve-month entitlement calculation, employers must follow the method required by the state. Employers operating in multiple states with differing provisions for calculating the twelve-month period must follow the method required by each respective state. Absent a conflict with state law, employers must select a single, uniform policy covering the entire workforce.

Employers must comply with state leave law posting and/or notification requirements, if any.

SECTION 4

Employment, Induction, and Orientation

The following checklist can be used to help you determine the various policy items that should be incorporated in your policy manual. Sample policy statements covering many of the items in the checklist appear in this section. They can be used to guide your policy statements.

Policy Manual Checklist

Our Policy Manual Should Cover:

1. Equal employment opportunity   Yes_____ No_____

2. Affirmative action program   Yes_____ No_____

3. Employees with disabilities   Yes_____ No_____

4. Harassment guidelines   Yes_____ No_____

5. Introductory period/employment-at-will   Yes_____ No_____

6. Definition of employee status—full-time, part-time, temporary, nonexempt, exempt   Yes_____ No_____

7. Hiring former employees, friends, relatives, and the handicapped   Yes_____ No_____

8. Employee recruitment and selection   Yes_____ No_____

9. Employment of former employees   Yes_____ No_____

10. Employment of relatives   Yes_____ No_____

11. Employee referrals   Yes_____ No_____

12. Reception and evaluation of applicants (procedure)   Yes_____ No_____

13. Selection of employees (procedure)   Yes_____ No_____

14. Immigration Reform and Control Act   Yes_____ No_____

15. Pre-employment physical examination   Yes_____ No_____

16. Employment application retention requirements   Yes_____ No_____

17. Payment of fees for employment procurement   Yes_____ No_____

18. Induction and orientation procedure   Yes_____ No_____

The most valuable asset of an organization is its human resources—its employees. In light of the time, energy, and money you invest in each of your employees, you should realize that the employment process is the most important link in the formation of your human resources. Each of us has experienced numerous problems in our organization when the wrong person was selected for a job. Therefore, the selection process is of utmost importance.

The selection process must begin with a clear understanding of the answer to the question, "What characteristics are we looking for in the person who could best perform the duties of this position?" There should be agreement among all concerned—the interviewer, the department head, and the supervisor.

A Person's Specification is a written description of the mental and physical demands of the position. It is not the same as a job analysis or job description. However, if you have a formal job evaluation program, Person's Specifications can be prepared quickly and easily. For each characteristic, there should be a brief statement of what is required (or, in some cases, is not required).

These should not be considered absolute requirements that must be met. However, they will provide guidelines for the people doing the interviewing. Also, they may indicate the most effective recruiting source.

Typical characteristics that the Person's Specification should include and questions it should answer are:

1. Education:
   Academic level?
   Special knowledge?
   Specialized field, trade, or profession?

2. Experience:
   How long in related work?
   Other types of work and how long?

3. Knowledge:
   Speed of typing or shorthand?
   Technical terminology?
   Machine operation and type?

4. Physical demands:
   How much lifting?
   Walking?
   Aural acuity?
   Manual dexterity?

5. Integrity:
   Uses confidential information?
   Handles money or valuable property?

6. Contact with others:
   Deals with public?
   Must be persuasive?
   Poised?

7. Special requirements:
Shifts?
Overtime?
Weekend work?
Working conditions requiring extremes of heat or noise, or out-of-doors?

Once you have determined the qualifications of the person you want to fill a particular job, there is the problem of knowing where to find that person. There are many good sources of people. It is important that you keep all of them in mind so that you do not overlook any good possibility. Listed below are some recruiting sources.

1. *Sources within your organization.* It is a good policy to promote from within the organization wherever practical. All job openings, both regular and temporary, should be posted on appropriate bulletin boards to inform employees that positions exist so that they can apply for transfer or promotion to another job or department. This eliminates some of the uncertainties involved in hiring new people.

2. *Employee referrals.* Present employees should be encouraged to refer applicants for specific jobs. However, relatives and immediate family or persons living under the same roof as the employee who made the recommendation should not be employed in the same department as that employee.

3. *Advertising—newspaper and radio.* One of the most popular ways of finding job applicants is to advertise in the newspaper or on a local radio station. Every time you advertise, be sure that the statement, "We are an equal opportunity employer," is included in the advertisement. The enforcement agencies have developed guidelines for the equal employment regulations that outline the types of radio and newspaper advertising that may be considered discriminatory. These guidelines are frequently violated.

First, no advertisement should contain any indications of preference for one sex over the other. Second, no advertisement should express any preference for age that would discriminate against those persons over forty years old. Additionally, newspaper advertisements should not be listed under a male or female heading.

Terms That Cannot Be Used

Attention June grads
College dropout
College evening student
Counter boys
Fresh college graduate
Junior accountant
Junior position for high school grad
Junior secretary
Students 18 to 65
Maximum two to five years experience
Night student
Night watchman
Retired or pensioned
Student
Telephone girl
Young men or women ages 18 to 26
Youthful staff
Korean veteran

4. *Public and private employment agencies.* Private and state employment agencies also provide job applicants. Private agencies charge the applicant or employer for the service; state agencies do not. Also,

most trade schools, business schools, junior or community colleges, and high schools have counselors who refer students or graduates.

5. *Former employees.* Former employees who did a good job and had a good attitude may be available as temporary help. Except in emergencies or unusual circumstances, employees who have been terminated for cause should not be rehired.

6. *Striking workers in your community—to hire or not to hire.* A number of National Labor Relations Board decisions show that to refuse to hire strikers as such may be a violation, but if there are other reasons, the policy may not be a violation. The real reason for not hiring strikers is generally that the employer does not want to have to replace them when the strike is settled, and this real reason should be given, not a blanket refusal to hire strikers. Interviewers, supervisors, and others coming in contact with applicants should be informed of this.

Regardless of the recruiting methods used, there will be a wide variety of applicants, ranging from totally unqualified to very competent. Therefore, finding out as much as possible about each applicant before the interview and weeding out the obvious misfits will save you time and money. We recommend that this be accomplished by an application for employment, a report of medical history, and a background check.

You should develop your own checklist of realistic and practical characteristics to look for, and those to avoid, when selecting new people. Identify common traits of those present and former employees who have done well and of those who failed. Keep the list simple. Apply only those standards that are clearly helpful. Don't get hung up on nonessentials. Be sure your standards do not directly or indirectly screen out anyone because of race, creed, color, religion, handicap, sex, or age.

Many employers administer pre-employment tests, and many of these tests have proved to be very effective in screening potential employees. Although the Equal Employment Opportunity Commission has stated that it is perfectly all right to give employment tests and act upon the results, certain conditions must be met. These conditions make it difficult for most employers to use pre-employment tests, not because of discriminatory intent, but because of the difficult administrative procedures and guidelines that must be met before tests can be used.

Each employer is required to maintain evidence, based on the employer's own experience, that demonstrates that the tests accurately predict successful job performance. This evidence include statistical information that would permit an accurate judgment of the test's validity.

The EEOC will allow employers to use any generally accepted data-gathering technique they would like, but it recommends as a guide *Standards for Educational and Psychological Tests and Manuals*, published by the American Psychological Association, 1200 17th Street, NW, Washington, DC 20036.

A pre-employment interview should be conducted only if the information received on the employment application and the results of reference checks involving previous employers, personal references, the police, and credit sources indicate that the applicant is eligible for a position with your company.

The interview is a vital part of the hire/no hire process. It is an interchange of knowledge, information, personalities, concepts, and the ideas which are mutually beneficial to the parties concerned and from which decisions can be made. Thus, a successful interview requires planning and the use of learned techniques. It cannot be treated as a casual conversation.

Discrimination prohibited by federal law is most likely to occur at the point of hiring and particularly during the pre-employment interview because this stage of the hiring process has historically been based upon the interviewer's subjective opinions and evaluations. If your company is to avoid discrimination, the pre-employment interviewer, must not base the decision to hire or reject an applicant on subjective criteria. To do so would leave you with an inadequate defense if you were charged with an unlawful employment practice or with refusal or failure to hire based on race, color, religion, sex, age, national origin, or veteran's status. An interviewer's final evaluation and recommendation to hire or reject must be stated in objective terms to prove that you have not discriminated.

Whether the applicant is hired or rejected, the interviewer should write the exact reasons in terms of the minimum standards previously established and her or his evaluation of the applicant based upon the areas covered.

During any pre-employment interview, there are certain questions that you should ask and questions that you should not ask. EEOC guidelines on pre-employment inquiries state that you may ask any question that you wish; however, should you ask a discriminatory question (such as one concerning religion or national origin), the fact that you asked such a question will constitute permanent evidence of discrimination.

Some questions are blatantly discriminatory, and we recommend that you do not ask them at all. These relate to race, sex, religion, ethnic background, etc. Likewise you must avoid other questions that are not discriminatory in themselves but have the potential to be discriminatory.

Any question that even though it is asked equally of minorities and nonminorities, has the effect of screening out more minorities than nonminorities is looked upon as discriminatory by the EEOC. Therefore, if you ask a question such as, "Have you ever been convicted of a crime?" and use this question to screen out applicants, and this action results in a disproportionate screening out of minorities, then the question is discriminatory.

Accordingly, you must ask yourself two questions concerning any pre-employment inquiry:

1. Is it job-related?
2. Does it screen out a disproportionate number of minorities?

If the answer to either of these questions is yes, then you should give serious consideration to eliminating the question.

Remember that no one is perfect. Almost every prospect will reveal some "doubtful" area to the alert interviewer. A final decision depends on thorough consideration of both the pluses and minuses of the prospect.

Immediately after the job applicant leaves your office, try to relax and think about the impression that he or she made on you. Is the total feeling good or bad? Look back at the application form and review the notes you have made on answers to your question. What do they add up to? It is often very helpful to record your reactions on an interview form as soon as the individual leaves your office, while the interview is fresh in your mind. These notations will also serve as documentation of the reasons why you didn't hire a job applicant if you are ever charged with discrimination for any reason. If the applicant is not hired, this screening profile form should be retained along with the applicant's application form for a period of twenty-four months.

Americans with Disabilities Act

A general statement covering all employer obligations under the ADA is needed. This eliminates the necessity for interspersing statements concerning such obligations under pertinent topics throughout the policy manual, and it provides employees with disabilities with a single source of reassurance.

A general policy does not eliminate the need for other essential ADA policies. The purpose of a job accommodations policy is to enable employers to provide certain kinds of accommodation to employees who have disabilities that are not readily observable.

Under ADA, employers have an obligation to provide reasonable accommodation to employees with disabilities. Employers also have an obligation to maintain information pertaining to an employee's disability or health condition in strict confidence. ADA regulations specify who may have access to such information, and under what circumstances.

When an employer provides an accommodation for an employee with an obvious impairment (e.g., one who uses a wheelchair), coworkers will know, or may reasonably conclude, why the accommodation was made. However, if the only reason an employer would modify an individual employee's job would be to accommodate a disability, then making such a modification would automatically reveal to the entire workforce that the affected employee has a disability.

The three job modifications are ones that coworkers may be likely to question management about. The three circumstances are specified so that, when questioned, management can respond that the modification was made "in accordance with the company's Job Accommodation Policy" without revealing which one of the three apply.

Three Job Modifications

1. Modification of an individual employee's job duties by reassigning, reallocating, or redistributing nonessential, marginal functions
2. Modification of an individual's work schedule within the individual's normal shift
3. Modification of work flow and/or procedures affecting an individual employee's job tour

Three Circumstances

1. To accommodate the employment needs of an employee with a disability
2. To accommodate other extraordinary personal needs of an employee
3. To satisfy other needs of the business

This enables employers to fulfill both the reasonable accommodation and confidentiality obligations, safeguards affected employees' privacy, and minimizes potential disability harassment.

This policy is especially important where employees are represented by unions. Union representatives are not among those authorized by ADA to have access to employee medical information. Therefore, special administrative procedures are required to implement the policy.

Employers also have an obligation under ADA to make placements as outlined in an accommodation transfer policy. An accommodation transfer is the transfer of an employee to a lateral or downward vacancy (or soon-to-be vacancy) in order to accommodate a disability. Employers need not create a vacancy, but must consider any existing vacancy (that would not be a promotion) before filling it in any other way. Vacancies that are known to be imminent must also be considered. Case law has established that this ADA obligation takes precedence over conflicting collective bargaining agreement provisions.

Employees in need of accommodation need only be considered competitively for promotions, because ADA does not require preferential treatment.

Terminology may be modified or deleted where appropriate because of the employer's structure or other policies (e.g., no posting), but the basic procedure is mandatory.

Harassment

Harassment can take many forms, and it is not prudent for an employer to prohibit one form (e.g., sexual harassment) to the exclusion of other forms (harassment based on race, color, religion, national origin, age, or disability).

The Civil Rights Act of 1991 provides for compensatory and punitive damage awards for any unlawful harassment in the workplace. Although this act currently limits damage awards to from $50,000 to $300,000 (based upon number of employees) for each victim, damages for racial harassment are unlimited under federal law, and damages for any form of harassment may be unlimited under applicable state law.

A harassment policy statement should cover and describe the various forms of harassment, what employees should do if they feel they have been or are being harassed, and what the company will do when harassment is alleged to have occurred.

It may also be advisable to provide convenient, nonthreatening alternative avenues for employees to use to register their concerns. Home phone number(s) of appropriate management personnel and/or a phone number of a (noncompany) third party designated for this purpose should be provided.

On the following pages are examples of equal employment policies and policies dealing with the Americans with Disabilities Act, harassment, recruiting, and hiring. They appear in actual "policy manual" formats to offer some idea of what the various programs look like. Areas covered include:

Equal Opportunity Employment
Definition of an Employee
Affirmative Action Policies
Sexual Harassment Policy
Equal Employment Opportunity for Individuals with Disabilities
Job Accommodations
Accommodation Transfers
Disability Harassment
Introductory Period/Employment-at-Will
Employment Procedure
Employee Recruitment and Selection
Hiring Former Employees, Friends, and the Disabled
Employee Referrals
Screening and Checking References
Retention Requirements on Applications
Pre-employment Interviews
Fee Payment for Employment Procurement
New Employee Induction/Orientation
Employment Status
College Cooperative Program
Employment Classification
Employment/Recruitment Guidelines
Hiring Former Employees
Employment of Relatives

PERSONNEL POLICIES AND PROCEDURES

DISTRIBUTION:		SUBJECT: EQUAL OPPORTUNITY EMPLOYMENT	
EFFECTIVE DATE:	PAGE 1 OF 1		FILE UNDER SECTION
REVISION DATE:	APPROVED BY:		

POLICY STATEMENT:

(Organization's Name) employment policy shall provide for its employees the equality of opportunity regardless of race, color, sex, age, religion, national origin, citizenship status, physical or mental disability, or past, present, or future service in the uniformed services of the United States, and shall not show partiality or grant any special favors to any employee or group of employees in violation of applicable law.

PERSONNEL POLICIES AND PROCEDURES

DISTRIBUTION:		SUBJECT: EQUAL OPPORTUNITY EMPLOYMENT	
EFFECTIVE DATE:	PAGE 1 OF 1		FILE UNDER SECTION
REVISION DATE:	APPROVED BY:		

POLICY STATEMENT:

There shall be no discrimination on the part of either (Organization's Name) or the union on account of any employee's race, color, sex, age, religion, national origin, citizenship status, physical or mental disability, or past, present, or future service in the uniformed services of the United States.

PERSONNEL POLICIES AND PROCEDURES

DISTRIBUTION:		SUBJECT: EQUAL OPPORTUNITY EMPLOYMENT	
EFFECTIVE DATE:	PAGE 1 OF 1		FILE UNDER SECTION
REVISION DATE:	APPROVED BY:		

It is the policy of (Organization's Name) to grant equal employment opportunity to all qualified persons without regard to race, color, sex, age, religion, national origin, citizenship status, physical or mental disability, or past, present, or future service in the uniformed services of the United States. To deny one's contribution to our efforts because of such factors is an injustice, not only to the individual, but to the company and the nation as well. It is the intent and desire of the company that equal employment opportunity will be provided in employment, promotions, wages, benefits, and all other privileges, terms, and conditions of employment.

PERSONNEL POLICIES AND PROCEDURES

DISTRIBUTION:		SUBJECT: EQUAL OPPORTUNITY EMPLOYMENT	
EFFECTIVE DATE:	PAGE 1 OF 1	FILE UNDER SECTION	
REVISION DATE:	APPROVED BY:		

POLICY STATEMENT:

The progress of our organization requires that we utilize all available human resources to the fullest, regardless of race, color, sex, age, religion, national origin, citizenship status, physical or mental disability, or past, present, or future service in the uniformed services of the United States. To deny one's contribution to our efforts because of such factors is an injustice, not only to the individual, but to the company and the nation as well. The continuing pressure to find sufficiently qualified people makes it necessary that discriminatory practices, if they exist, be eliminated, and that individuals with talent be recognized and encouraged through equitable personnel policies. It is the policy of this organization to grant equal employment opportunity to all qualified persons regardless of race, color, sex, age, religion, national origin, citizenship status, physical or mental disability, or past, present, or future service in the uniformed services of the United States. This policy is based on the same philosophy as the Civil Rights Act of 1964, that discriminatory employment practices are unjust and economically wasteful.

In the past, it has been the practice of this company to show no discrimination to employees with respect to race, color, sex, age, religion, national origin, citizenship status, physical or mental disability, or past, present, or future service in the uniformed services of the United States. We feel it best to once again announce this practice as our policy.

PERSONNEL POLICIES AND PROCEDURES

DISTRIBUTION:		SUBJECT: EQUAL OPPORTUNITY EMPLOYMENT	
EFFECTIVE DATE:	PAGE 1 OF 2		FILE UNDER SECTION
REVISION DATE:	APPROVED BY:		

POLICY STATEMENT:

It is the policy of (Organization's Name) to provide equal employment opportunities without regard to race, color, sex, age, religion, national origin, citizenship status, physical or mental disability, or past, present, or future service in the uniformed services of the United States. This policy also includes disabled and Vietnam-era veterans. This policy relates to all phases of employment, including but not limited to recruitment, employment, placement, upgrading, demotion or transfer, layoff, recall, termination, rates of pay or other forms of compensation, selection for training, the use of all facilities, and participation in company-sponsored employee activities.

(Organization's Name) further recognizes that the effective application of a policy of merit employment involves more than just a policy statement and will, therefore, undertake a program of affirmative action to make known that equal employment opportunities are available on the basis of individual merit, and to strive for advancement on this basis.

GUIDELINES:

1. Dissemination of Policy—(Organization's Name) will take appropriate steps to ensure that all employees are advised of this policy of nondiscrimination and of its interest in actively and affirmatively providing equal employment opportunity, such as:

   A. Communication media, including bulletin boards, personal letters mailed to employees' homes, and in-house publications, will emphasize this subject.
   B. All management and any others in a position to implement this policy, including those engaged in recruiting, training, and other personnel activities, will be fully advised of the policy and of their responsibilities with respect to it.
   C. (Organization's Name) will establish a system of communication and feedback controls within all management and department levels to ensure application of the policy throughout the entire Organization.

2. Assignment of Responsibilities - The Director of Human Resources is responsible for the administration of (Organization's Name) Equal Employment Opportunity Program. This official will coordinate the efforts of all managers and advise and assist top management. They shall regularly report to the President of the Organization concerning the state of progress, with recommendations where appropriate.

3. Recruitment—(Organization's Name) will seek qualified female and minority-group applicants for all job categories and will make particular efforts to increase such female and minority-group representation in occupations at the higher levels of skill and responsibility.

   A. All schools, colleges, employment offices, and other recruiting sources used by (Organization's Name) will be advised in writing of this policy, and will be asked to refer qualified female and minority-group applicants.
   B. Recruiting programs at schools and colleges will include those attended by substantial numbers of female and minority-group members.
   C. Where appropriate, employment advertisements will be placed in newspapers which are widely read by, and devoted to the interest of, female or minority groups. In addition, (Organization's Name) will request appropriate female and minority-group agencies to assist in making known the Organization's policy and will advise such groups of available employment opportunities. It will also encourage similar employment referrals from present employees.

PERSONNEL POLICIES AND PROCEDURES

DISTRIBUTION:		SUBJECT: EQUAL OPPORTUNITY EMPLOYMENT
EFFECTIVE DATE:	PAGE 2 OF 2	FILE UNDER SECTION
REVISION DATE:	APPROVED BY:	

4. Placement and Promotions—(Organization's Name) will review job categories where few female and minority-group persons are presently employed, and seek to determine the cause for such situations. When necessary, remedial efforts may include such actions as the following:

   A. More vigorous recruitment of qualified female and minority-group candidates.
   B. Special discussions with appropriate management, supervisory or other personnel regarding Organization's policy and its desire to ensure utilization of qualified female and minority-group personnel at all job levels.
   C. Reevaluate qualifications of the lower echelon of female and minority-group employees to determine whether their skills and capabilities may be more fully utilized at higher job levels or would warrant their transfer to other types of jobs more readily leading to advancement.
   D. Monitoring of placement, promotion, and transfer activities, at all levels, to ensure that full consideration, as required by Organization policy, has been given to qualified female and minority-group employees.

5. Training—In-plant and on-the-job training programs, as well as all other training and educational programs to which (Organization's Name) gives support or sponsorship, will be regularly reviewed to ensure that qualified female and minority-group candidates, as well as all other employees, are provided the opportunity to participate.

   A. Appropriate steps will be taken to encourage female and minority-group employees to increase their skills and job potential through participation in available training and educational programs.
   B. (Organization's Name) will ensure that qualified female and minority group employees are included in Organization Management Development programs.
   C. (Organization's Name) will seek the inclusion of qualified female and minority-group members in any skilled training program which (Organization Name) may sponsor.

6. Layoffs, Terminations, and Downgrading—(Organization's Name) will ensure that layoffs, terminations, downgrading, and recalls from layoffs are made without regard to race, color, sex, age, religion, national origin, citizenship status, physical or mental disability, or past, present, or future service in the uniformed services of the United States.

7. Other Matters Affecting Employee Benefits and Status—(Organization's Name) will ensure that there is no disparity in the compensation received by female and minority-group employees and other employees for performing equivalent duties equally well, and that opportunities for performing overtime work or otherwise earning increased compensation are afforded without discrimination to all employees.

It is (Organization Name's) policy that any employee programs or activities which are sponsored or supported by the Organization will be equally available to all employees.

PERSONNEL POLICIES AND PROCEDURES

DISTRIBUTION:		SUBJECT: EQUAL OPPORTUNITY EMPLOYMENT
EFFECTIVE DATE:	PAGE 1 OF 1	FILE UNDER SECTION
REVISION DATE:	APPROVED BY:	

GENERAL:

It is the policy of (Name of Company) as a federal contractor, through a positive and continuing program, to provide equal opportunity in employment for all qualified persons; to prohibit discrimination in employment because of race, color, sex, age, religion, national origin, physical or mental disability, or status as a disabled or Vietnam-era veteran; and to take affirmative action to encourage the employment of such veterans.

SCOPE:

This is the policy for the Corporate plants and offices and its U.S. Divisions and Subsidiaries.

APPLICATION:

A. A positive program of equal employment opportunity will be established and maintained for all employees and applicants for employment.

B. Management and administrative personnel will plan and take affirmative action to achieve equal employment opportunity and thus improve the employment status of all such group members in employment, training, and promotional opportunities.

C. All advertising for employees shall include the statement, ''An Equal Opportunity Employer—M/F/D/V.''

D. The Company will cultivate communications channels with representatives of female, minority, disability, and veteran groups, and civic and community organizations.

E. All relations and decisions pertaining to employment, upgrading, demotion, transfer, recruiting, layoff, terminations, training, and rates of pay of employees will be executed without regard to race, color, religion, sex, national origin, physical or mental disability, or veterans' status.

PERSONNEL POLICIES AND PROCEDURES

DISTRIBUTION:		SUBJECT: EQUAL EMPLOYMENT OPPORTUNITY	
EFFECTIVE DATE:	PAGE 1 OF 1	FILE UNDER SECTION	
REVISION DATE:	APPROVED BY:		

PURPOSE:

The company will provide equal opportunities for all associates and applicants for employment without regard to sex, age, race, religion, national origin, citizenship status, physical or mental disability, or any service, past, present, or future, in the uniformed services of the United States.

Any illegal discrimination or harassment, regardless of its form, is unacceptable. The objective of the company is to provide a working environment that is free of discrimination for all associates.

POLICY:

It is the responsibility of all levels of management to ensure that equal opportunity and equal consideration be given to all applicants and associates in personnel actions, which include recruiting and hiring, selection for training, promotion, demotion, discipline, rates of pay or other compensation, transfer, layoff, recalls, and terminations.

The company's Equal Employment Opportunity Policy will be posted on a Controlled Communication Center at each location.

PERSONNEL POLICIES AND PROCEDURES

DISTRIBUTION:		SUBJECT: EQUAL EMPLOYMENT OPPORTUNITY FOR INDIVIDUALS WITH DISABILITIES (Federal Contractors)	
EFFECTIVE DATE:	PAGE 1 OF 1	FILE UNDER SECTION	
REVISION DATE:	APPROVED BY:		

POLICY STATEMENT:

The employment policies and statements of (Organization's Name) are to recruit and hire employees or applicants for employment without discrimination because of physical or mental disability in regard to any position for which the employee or applicant for employment is qualified, and to treat them equally in all employment practices such as the following:

Employment, upgrading, demotion or transfer, recruitment, advertising, layoff or termination, rate of pay or other forms of compensation, and selection for training.

PROCEDURE FOR COMPLIANCE:

As an indication of the company's affirmative action, it is further our policy to:

1. Post in conspicuous places, available to employees and applicants for employment, notices stating the company's obligation under the law to take affirmative action to employ and advance in employment qualified individuals with disabilities.

2. Include the "Affirmative Action for Individuals with Disabilities" clause in every subcontract or purchase of $10,000 or more.

RESPONSIBILITY:

The Director of Human Resources is responsible for the administration of this policy, and will coordinate the efforts of all managers and advise and assist top management.

PERSONNEL POLICIES AND PROCEDURES

DISTRIBUTION:		SUBJECT: DEFINITION OF AN EMPLOYEE	
EFFECTIVE DATE:	PAGE 1 OF 1	FILE UNDER SECTION	
REVISION DATE:	APPROVED BY:		

PURPOSE:

The purpose of this policy is to standardize terminology and ensure common understanding in our references to employees.

POLICY:

The terms below shall be interpreted as indicated:

A. Employees—All persons who receive wages or salaries from our company.

B. Regular Full-Time Employees—Those employees who work the customary number of hours weekly (at least thirty hours) and who maintain continuous regular employment status. Under special conditions (illness, etc.), a full-time employee may work less than thirty hours weekly for a specified short term (three months maximum) without losing full-time employee benefits. All regular full-time employees are eligible for all employee benefits, including the profit-sharing retirement plan, paid vacations, paid holidays, group insurance, discounts on purchases, paid sick leave, etc.

C. Regular Part-Time Employees—Those employees who work fewer than the customary number of full-time hours weekly (thirty hours), but in no event fewer than ten hours, and who maintain continuous regular employee status. Regular part-time employees will be eligible for the following employee benefit programs: Profit-sharing retirement plan (if they work at least twenty hours a week), group health and life insurance, employee discounts on purchases. Regular part-time employees are not eligible for paid vacations, paid holidays, or paid sick leave benefits.

D. Temporary Full-Time Employees—Those employees whose service is intended to be of limited duration, such as during summer months only, but who work the customary number of full-time hours. Temporary full-time employees are eligible for paid holidays, provided they meet the requirements as prescribed on Page XX of Employee Handbook.

E. Temporary Part-Time Employees—Those employees who work less than the customary number of full-time hours weekly and who do not maintain continuous regular employment status. Temporary part-time employees are not eligible for any employee benefits.

F. Nonexempt Employees—Employees who are not exempt from minimum wage, overtime, and time-card provisions of the Fair Labor Standards Act (Wage-Hour Law) as amended. These employees receive overtime premium pay for over forty hours per week.

G. Exempt Employees—Employees who are exempt from the minimum wage, time-card, and overtime provisions of the Fair Labor Standards Act (Wage-Hour Law) as amended. These executive, administrative, and supervisory employees do not receive overtime pay.

PERSONNEL POLICIES AND PROCEDURES

DISTRIBUTION:		SUBJECT: ASSOCIATE CLASSIFICATIONS	
EFFECTIVE DATE:	PAGE 1 OF 1	FILE UNDER SECTION	
REVISION DATE:	APPROVED BY:		

PURPOSE:

It is the purpose of this policy to use standardized terminology with reference to employment categories within the company.

POLICY:

A. The terms below shall be interpreted as indicated:

1. Associates—All persons who receive wages or salaries from the company
2. New Associates in Orientation/Evaluation Period—The first ninety (90) calendar days of employment are considered an associate's orientation/evaluation period. If his/her performance is satisfactory during this period, his/her status will be changed to a regular, full-time associate after ninety (90) calendar days.
3. Regular Associates—If an associate successfully completes his/her new associate orientation/evaluation period, he/she is called a regular associate. A regular, full-time associate works at least a scheduled workweek of thirty (30) hours.
4. Nonexempt Associates—Nonexempt, full-time associates are paid on a salary basis. Whenever they work authorized hours in excess of forty (40) hours in a workweek, they are entitled to overtime premium pay.
5. Exempt Associates—Associates who are exempt from the minimum wage, timecard, and overtime provisions of the Fair Labor Standards Act (Wage-Hour Law) as amended. These executive, administrative, and supervisory associates do not receive overtime pay.
6. Regular Part-Time Associates—Those associates who work fewer than the customary number of full-time hours [(30) hours], but in no event fewer than ten (10) hours, and who maintain continuous regular associate status.
7. Temporary Full-Time Associates—Those associates whose work service is intended to be of limited duration, such as during summer months only, but who work the customary number of full-time hours.
8. Temporary Part-Time Associates—Those who work less than the customary number of full-time hours weekly and who do not maintain continuous regular employment status.

B. Job Duration:

Since all associates are hired for an unspecified duration, these job classifications do not guarantee employment for any specific length of time. Employment is at the mutual consent of the associate and the company. Either an associate or the company can terminate the employment relationship at will, at any time, with or without cause or advance notice.

PERSONNEL POLICIES AND PROCEDURES

DISTRIBUTION:		SUBJECT: AFFIRMATIVE ACTION PLAN	
EFFECTIVE DATE:	PAGE 1 OF 3	FILE UNDER SECTION	
REVISION DATE:	APPROVED BY:		

PURPOSE OF POLICY:

To provide guidelines for Equal Employment Opportunity by means of Affirmative Action Program.

BACKGROUND OF POLICY STATEMENT:

It has been the established personnel policy of our company to effectively utilize our available human resources by selecting the best qualified person for the job to be performed. We have always given appropriate attention to such factors as educational background, previous experience, proven skills, desirable character traits, and potential for growth and development. The personnel we have hired and promoted in the past and those to be hired and promoted in the future have been and will continue to be selected from all applicants on the basis of qualifications which we feel are essential in order that an employee may perform well. These include such factors as ability, availability, capability, aptitude, experience, education, health, and a willingness to work and serve.

Moreover, since the objective of this personnel policy is to use all qualified available manpower to the fullest, we feel we must administer this policy in such a manner as not to discriminate against any person, employee, or job applicant for employment because of race, color, sex, age, religion, national origin, citizenship status, physical or mental disability, or past, present, or future service in the uniformed services of the United States.

AFFIRMATIVE ACTION POLICY:

It is our policy to offer equal employment opportunity to all persons without regard to race, color, sex, national origin, religion, physical or mental disability, or disabled or Vietnam-Era veterans' status. No applicant is to be discriminated against or given preference because of these factors. This policy is intended to apply to recruiting, hiring, promotions, upgrading, layoffs, compensation, benefits, termination, and all other privileges, terms, and conditions of employment.

Since it is recognized that effective utilization of qualified, available human resources at our locations requires more than a statement of policy, we believe it is timely to make known and follow up a program of affirmative action. This program will communicate the important guidelines and procedures that will be followed in providing equal employment and advancement opportunities at (Name of Company) on the basis of individual qualifications and job performance.

AFFIRMATIVE ACTION PROGRAM:

1. Recruitment: We will consider all qualified female and minority, disabled and veteran applicants for vacancies in all job classifications in conjunction with our established policy of advancement and promotion from within on the basis of individual qualifications, potential, and job performance.
   A. Public and private employment offices used by given locations will be advised in writing of our equal employment policy and will be urged to refer qualified female, minority, disabled, and veteran applicants to us as the need arises. (See sample letter attached.)
   B. When advertising in newspapers and on radio, we will use the term "Equal Opportunity Employer—M/F/D/V" in all such employment advertisements.
   C. When recruiting is necessary at schools and colleges, we will include those attended by women and minority members.

2. Job Placement and Promotions: We will provide promotional and upgrading opportunities to all qualified female and

PERSONNEL POLICIES AND PROCEDURES

minority employees, employees with known disabilities, and employees who are disabled or Vietnam-era veterans by the following action:

A. Communicate policy of promotion from within of qualified individuals to such employees during performance reviews.
B. Brief supervisors at all levels of management that our company intends to ensure utilization of such qualified employees at all job levels.
C. Review objectively all qualifications of all candidates for promotions from within.

3. Training and Development
   A. All training and educational programs conducted on the job will be reviewed periodically to be certain that all personnel are given equal opportunity to participate in these programs.
   B. All company-supported or company-sponsored training seminars for supervision will be available for female, minority-group, disabled, and veteran supervisors, and they will be encouraged to participate.

4. Compensation and Employee Benefits: We will pay all personnel fairly according to their job classification. Company-supported benefit programs for employees will be made equally available to all employees without discrimination.

5. Layoffs and Terminations: Whenever necessary to reduce our workforce, layoff or recall to work will be made without regard to race, color, sex, age, religion, national origin, citizenship status, physical or mental disability, or past, present, or future service in the uniformed services of the United States. When it becomes necessary to terminate any employees, such termination will be without discrimination due to race, color, religion, sex, age, national origin, physical or mental handicap, or veterans' status.

6. Communication of EEO Policies: Our company will take appropriate steps to ensure that all employees know of our sincere desire to support and take affirmative action toward providing equal employment opportunity such as the following:
   A. Bulletin boards showing official EEOC poster and company EEO policy
   B. Employee Handbook
   C. Policy Manual
   D. Affirmative Action Program
   E. Employee Newsletter
   F. Supervisory-employee meetings
   G. Supervisory staff meetings

7. Affirmative Action Program Coordinator: There will be appointed within our company an Equal Employment Policy Coordinator. This person will be given appropriate authority and responsibility to administer and coordinate this program. This official will coordinate the efforts of all managerial and supervisory personnel. This coordinator will advise and assist top management of our corporation and will make periodic reports of progress under this Affirmative Action Program to the Corporate President and Executive Committee, with recommendations whenever appropriate.

PERSONNEL POLICIES AND PROCEDURES

DISTRIBUTION:		SUBJECT: AFFIRMATIVE ACTION PLAN	
EFFECTIVE DATE:	PAGE 3 OF 3	FILE UNDER SECTION	
REVISION DATE:	APPROVED BY:		

(Suggested letter to state employment offices and private sources of employees that have been used in the past—including trade and business schools, nearby colleges.)

Dear Sir/Madam:

This letter is to advise you that (Name of Company) maintains a firm policy of granting equal employment opportunities to all qualified persons without regard to race color, sex, national origin, religion, physical or mental diability, or disabled or Vietnam-Era veteran's status. We deem it opportune to reannounce our policy specifically to you at this time and further inform you that we will consider all qualified applicants that you may refer to us for openings on which we may have requested assistance.

Should we have openings in our company and need your assistance, we will advise you and request that you refer qualified applicants to us as the need arises.

Should you have any questions, please contact me by telephone or by letter.

Sincerely yours,

(Name of Company)

_____

(Title)

PERSONNEL POLICIES AND PROCEDURES

DISTRIBUTION:		SUBJECT: EQUAL EMPLOYMENT OPPORTUNITY FOR INDIVIDUALS WITH DISABILITIES	
EFFECTIVE DATE:	PAGE 1 OF 1	FILE UNDER SECTION	
REVISION DATE:	APPROVED BY:		

POLICY STATEMENT:

The employment policy of (Company Name) is to treat all applicants and employees without discrimination because of physical or mental disability in regard to any position for which the applicant or employee is qualified, and to treat them equally in all employment practices such as the following:

Advertising; employment; rate of pay or other forms of compensation; benefits; training, upgrade, transfer or demotion, layoff, or termination; and all other terms, conditions, and privileges of employment.

PROCEDURE:

The company will post in conspicuous places, available to employees and applicants for employment, notices stating the company's obligation under the law to employ and advance in employment qualified persons with disabilities.

The company will make reasonable accommodation to the known physical or mental limitations of a qualified applicant or employee with a disability, to enable them to perform essential job duties, unless such accommodation would impose an undue hardship on the operation of the business.

The company will remove architectural and structural barriers to an employee's workplace accessibility and usability where such removal is needed and is readily achievable.

The company will maintain all company information regarding the medical condition or history of applicants, employees, and employees' dependents on separate forms and in separate locked medical files, and treat such information as a confidential medical record, to be utilized only as permitted by law.

Employees in need of accommodation for workplace accessibility or usability, to perform essential job duties, or to participate in company-sponsored programs and activities; who need alternative accessible formats for company communications; or who may need emergency treatment or emergency evacuation assistance should make such needs known to their immediate supervisors.

Further, any employee who feels that this policy is not being adequately fulfilled should make such feelings known to his/her immediate supervisor.

Employee accommodation requests and related information will be treated as confidential by the company to the maximum extent feasible.

PERSONNEL POLICIES AND PROCEDURES

DISTRIBUTION:		SUBJECT: JOB ACCOMMODATIONS	
EFFECTIVE DATE:	PAGE 1 OF 1	FILE UNDER SECTION	
REVISION DATE:	APPROVED BY:		

POLICY STATEMENT:

The company may make certain modifications to an individual employee's job under appropriate circumstances.

PROCEDURE:

The following modifications will be considered by the company:

1. Modification of an individual employee's job duties by reassigning, reallocating, or redistributing nonessential, marginal functions.

2. Modification of an individual's work schedule within the individual's normal shift.

3. Modification of work flow and/or procedures affecting an individual employee's job tour.

The company may take such actions under the following circumstances:

1. To accommodate the needs of an employee with a disability.

2. To accommodate other extraordinary personal needs of an employee.

3. To satisfy other needs of the business.

Any employee who has a need for such accommodation should make the need known to his/her immediate supervisor. After appropriate discussion and consideration, a decision will be made by the company and the affected employee will be informed. If the request for an accommodation is denied, the employee will have an opportunity to appeal.

Employee accommodation requests and related information will be treated as confidential by the company. Any and all documentation pertaining to actions taken by the company under this policy will be maintained in a separate, confidential file and will not be available or otherwise made known to persons not specifically authorized by the company.

PERSONNEL POLICIES AND PROCEDURES

DISTRIBUTION:		SUBJECT: ACCOMMODATION TRANSFERS	
EFFECTIVE DATE:	PAGE 1 OF 1	FILE UNDER SECTION	
REVISION DATE:	APPROVED BY:		

POLICY STATEMENT:

If an employee can no longer perform, with or without accommodation, his/her current position because of a disability, the company will, as a reasonable accommodation, attempt to make transfer placements as outlined below.

PROCEDURE:

The employee will be placed on a lateral basis in an existing (or soon to be) vacancy for which he/she is qualified and can perform the essential job duties, with or without accommodation.

If no such vacancy exists, or the employee declines such placement, the employee will be placed in an existing (or soon to be) vacancy on successively lower levels for which he/she is qualified and can perform the essential job duties, with or without accommodation.

If no such vacancies exist, or the employee declines such placement, the employee will be terminated.

Employees in need of an accommodation transfer will be given first consideration (before posting) for such vacancies on a lateral or downgrade basis.

Employees in need of an accommodation transfer will be considered on a promotion basis along with other internal candidates without priority or preference.

PERSONNEL POLICIES AND PROCEDURES

DISTRIBUTION:		SUBJECT: DISABILITY HARASSMENT	
EFFECTIVE DATE:	PAGE 1 OF 1	FILE UNDER SECTION	
REVISION DATE:	APPROVED BY:		

POLICY STATEMENT:

The Company is committed to maintaining a safe and healthy work environment for all employees and one that is free from illegal harassment of any kind. Consistent with this commitment, the company will treat employees with life-threatening diseases and other disabilities with compassion and understanding and will provide support and reasonable accommodation to the fullest extent possible. The company will also treat employees with communicable diseases in a like manner, consistent with reasonable precaution that relies on the most current medical knowledge.

It is the policy of the Company to allow and assist all such employees to continue to work as long as they are medically able to perform their work satisfactorily and do not pose a direct threat to their own health or safety, or to the health or safety of others in the workplace. Coworkers are expected to cooperate with this policy.

Accordingly, coworkers who refuse to work with, refuse to cooperate with, harass or otherwise intimidate, demean, or isolate such employees will be subject to discipline.

Employees who have concerns related to this policy are encouraged to contact their immediate superior or designated Human Resources Representative to discuss their concerns and to obtain additional information as appropriate.

PERSONNEL POLICIES AND PROCEDURES

DISTRIBUTION:		SUBJECT: HARASSMENT	
EFFECTIVE DATE:	PAGE 1 OF 2	FILE UNDER SECTION	
REVISION DATE:	APPROVED BY:		

PURPOSE:

The purpose of this policy is to define the company's position with regard to any form of illegal harassment in the workplace.

POLICY:

A. Company's Position on Harassment

The Company is committed to maintaining a work environment that is free from discrimination where associates at all levels of the company are able to devote their full attention and best efforts to the job. Harassment, either intentional or unintentional, has no place in the work environment. Accordingly, the company does not authorize and will not tolerate any form of harassment of or by any associate (i.e., supervisory or nonsupervisory) or nonassociate based on race, sex, religion, color, national origin, age, disability, or other factor protected by law. The term "harassment" for all purposes includes, but is not limited to, offensive language, jokes, or other verbal, graphic, or physical conduct relating to an associate's race, sex, religion, color, national origin, age, disability, or other factor protected by law which would make the reasonable person experiencing such harassment uncomfortable in the work environment or which could interfere with the person's job performance. This policy will be posted and distributed to all associates.

1. Sexual Harassment:

No associate, leader, coordinator, or other person, whether employed by the company or not, shall threaten or suggest that another associate's refusal to submit to sexual harassment will adversely affect that person's employment, work status, evaluation, wages, advancement, assigned duties, shifts, or any other terms or conditions of employment. Similarly, no associate, regardless of job title, shall promise, imply, or grant any preferential treatment in return for another associate's acceptance of conduct which is sexually harassing.

Sexual harassment may be overt or subtle. Some behavior which is appropriate in a social setting may not be appropriate in the workplace. Sexual harassment does not refer to behavior or occasional compliments of a socially acceptable nature. It refers to behavior that is personally offensive. Some examples of conduct that may constitute sexual harassment include:

(a) making unwelcome sexual flirtations, advances, requests for sexual favors, or other verbal, visual, or physical conduct of a sexual nature a condition of employment; or

(b) creating an intimidating, hostile, or offensive working environment by such conduct as:

    (1) sexual innuendo or sexually suggestive comments, including but not limited to sexually oriented "kidding," "teasing," or "practical jokes"; jokes about gender-specific traits; foul or obscene language or gestures;

    (2) subtle or direct pressure or requests for sexual activities;

    (3) unnecessary touching of an individual, such as pinching, patting, or brushing up against another body;

    (4) graphic verbal comments about an individual's body or appearance;

    (5) sexually degrading words used to describe an individual;

    (6) the reading or display in the workplace of sexually suggestive or revealing words, objects, or pictures;

    (7) sexually explicit or offensive jokes;

    (8) physical assault; or

    (9) other explicit or implied conduct of a sexual nature which relates to or affects an individual's employment.

PERSONNEL POLICIES AND PROCEDURES

DISTRIBUTION:		SUBJECT: HARASSMENT	
EFFECTIVE DATE:	PAGE 1 OF 2	FILE UNDER SECTION	
REVISION DATE:	APPROVED BY:		

2. Other Harassment:

All associates are entitled to work in an atmosphere free of harassment of any kind. Associates may occasionally make statements or display or use words, objects, or pictures that others could interpret as being insulting, derogatory, or slurs towards persons based upon their race, color, national origin, religion, sex, age, or disability. Such conduct may make a reasonable person uncomfortable in the work environment or could interfere with an associate's ability to perform his/her job. Comments or actions of this type, even if intended as a joking matter among friends, are always inappropriate in the workplace and will not be tolerated. No leader, coordinator, or any other member of management should participate in such behavior and must take immediate action, including discipline up to and including discharge, if necessary, to stop others who are known or suspected of being involved in such conduct.

B. How to Report Instances of Harassment:

The company cannot resolve matters that are not brought to its attention. Any associate, regardless of position, who has a complaint of or who witnesses harassment at work by anyone, including leaders, coordinators, associates, or even nonassociates, has a responsibility to immediately bring the matter to the company's attention. Associates may bring their complaint of or observation of harassment to their leader, coordinator, manager, or plant Human Resources representative. If the associate is uncomfortable discussing the matter with these individuals, or if the complaint or observation of harassment involves someone in the associate's direct line of supervision, the associate is urged to go to another company manager, or the associate should contact the senior vice president of the General Affairs Department. Associates who do not feel comfortable discussing their concern or problem with any of the individuals listed above should contact our Corporate Training Department at (502) 782-7397, extension 240.

C. How the Company Will Investigate Complaints:

The company will thoroughly and promptly investigate all claims of harassment. The company will meet with the complaining associate to discuss the results of the investigation and, where appropriate, review the proposed resolution of the matter. If an investigation confirms that harassment has occurred, the company will take action, including such discipline, up to and including immediate termination of employment, as is appropriate. Claims of assault or the threat of assault, if proven, will result in discharge.

PERSONNEL POLICIES AND PROCEDURES

DISTRIBUTION:		SUBJECT: HARASSMENT	
EFFECTIVE DATE:	PAGE 1 OF 1	FILE UNDER SECTION	
REVISION DATE:	APPROVED BY:		

POLICY STATEMENT:

We expect every person at (Company name) to be treated with fairness, respect, and dignity. Accordingly, any form of harassment based on an individual's race, color, sex, religion, national origin, age, or disability is a violation of this policy and will be treated as a disciplinary matter.

For these purposes, the term harassment includes slurs and any other offensive remarks, jokes, graphic material, or other offensive verbal, written, or physical conduct.

Unwelcome sexual advances, requests for sexual favors, and any other unwelcome, unbecoming verbal or physical conduct will not be tolerated and is not a condition of employment. Neither submission to nor rejection of such conduct will be used as a basis for employment decisions.

The company is committed to maintaining a safe and healthy work environment and takes all appropriate health and safety precautions consistent with current medical knowledge. Accordingly, employees may not refuse to work with or cooperate with, withhold services from, or otherwise harass, intimidate, demean, or isolate a coworker because of a known or suspected disability or disease, or because of a coworker's association with a person with a disability or disease.

PROCEDURE:

Employees who have questions about what constitutes harassing behavior should ask their supervisor.

Employees who believe they have been subjected to unwelcome sexual advances or conduct should inform the perpetrator (preferably at the time of the unwelcome advance) of the specific behavior that is unwelcome and request the perpetrator to stop.

The company will take all steps necessary to prevent any form of harassment from occurring. All supervisors and managers are informed of this policy and have been instructed as to what constitutes proper and improper behavior. We are prepared to promptly take steps necessary to enforce this policy.

Violation of this policy by any employee will subject that employee to disciplinary action, possibly including dismissal. If you feel that you have been a victim of harassment by a coworker, member of management, vendor, visitor, or customer of this organization, or if you become aware of such behavior around you, please contact your supervisor, the Human Resources Manager, or any member of management with whom you feel comfortable discussing your concern.

The company will promptly investigate all complaints and will endeavor to handle these matters expeditiously, confidentially, and in a professional manner so as to protect the offended individual and other individuals providing relevant information. When the situation is fully understood by management, prompt and appropriate action will be taken. There will be no retaliation against anyone for stepping forward with a concern regarding any type of harassment.

PERSONNEL POLICIES AND PROCEDURES

DISTRIBUTION:		SUBJECT: INTRODUCTORY PERIOD/EMPLOYMENT-AT-WILL	
EFFECTIVE DATE:	PAGE 1 OF 1	FILE UNDER SECTION	
REVISION DATE:	APPROVED BY:		

POLICY STATEMENT:

We welcome new employees to our company and want them to enjoy their work, receive good job satisfaction, and share in the rewards of a job well done. Our management team is pledged to help them in every way.

During the early stages of their career, they will find their supervisors and coworkers alike working more closely with them than at any other time of their employment. Their years of experience will give a welcomed "lift" and "head start" with orientation and job training.

Throughout their career, we will always be interested and involved with them and their employment here. Should an employee ever wish to leave our employ or should we desire to sever the employment relationship, we both are free to separate at will. If this is ever necessary, we encourage advance counseling on our part and a notice of separation on the employee's part, giving us both time to prepare and hopefully prevent any misunderstandings or unfortunate separations.

As an employee's position and length of service makes him or her eligible, the employee's supervisor and/or our Coordinator of Human Resources will introduce and explain various benefit programs we offer our employees and their families.

PROCEDURE:

It has been erroneously felt that once employees get by the "probationary period," they are relatively home-free, since they have made it through "probation." The fact is that we must carefully counsel, train, scrutinize, and evaluate employees' performance continually, not just during the "probationary period." Thus, employees—if they are truly accountable in employment—are truly accountable continuously and not just during the first ninety or so days of their employment. Therefore, at (Organization's Name), we have no formal "probationary period" for our employees, and we will base our employment relationships on the concept of employment-at-will, as stated in the policy above.

PERSONNEL POLICIES AND PROCEDURES

DISTRIBUTION:		SUBJECT: ORIENTATION EVALUATION	
EFFECTIVE DATE:	PAGE 1 OF 2	FILE UNDER SECTION	
REVISION DATE:	APPROVED BY:		

PURPOSE:

The purpose of this policy is to evaluate new associates to determine suitability for regular, full-time employment.

POLICY:

A. All new associates will serve a ninety- (90-) calendar-day orientation and evaluation period. The purpose of this period of evaluation is to accommodate an individual's normal learning curve and to determine if the new associate is capable of meeting the performance requirements of the job. This period will also provide the associate with the opportunity to evaluate the company and determine if he/she wishes to continue employment with the company.

B. If at the end of the ninety- (90-) calendar-day orientation period it is determined that the new associate can satisfactorily meet the performance requirements of his/her job, the individual will become a regular associate.

C. (Name of Company) would like for all of its new hires to successfully complete their ninety- (90-) day orientation/evaluation period. If an associate develops a performance problem during this initial period, the associate's leader and coordinator will work with the individual to help him/her correct the performance problem.

If it is determined that the individual is not meeting the performance requirements established by the company, his/her employment with the company will be terminated. This termination will be effective at the point an individual demonstrates that he/she is not likely to complete the evaluation period. It will not be the policy of this company to provide associates an automatic ninety (90) days of employment regardless of their performance.

D. The time worked during a person's ninety- (90-) day orientation/evaluation period will count towards the associate's length of service for the purpose of determining eligibility for company benefit programs. A new associate's length of service will not be considered in any other programs, such as job/shift transfer, vacation scheduling, etc., until the associate has successfully completed his/her ninety- (90-) day orientation/evaluation period and has become a regular associate.

E. While an associate is serving his/her ninety- (90-) day orientation/evaluation period, the company may assign the individual to different shifts/areas without regard to his/her length of service in order to meet production requirements.

F. During a person's ninety- (90-) day orientation/evaluation period, he/she will be covered by legally required benefits such as overtime, worker's compensation, social security, etc. Eligibility periods for other company benefits will vary and will be communicated to associates at their time of hire.

PROCEDURES:

A. All new associates will undergo initial training and orientation. At the end of their training, they will be assigned to an area and work group.

B. The coordinator will assign each new associate to a specific job after consulting with the trainer as to the new associate's strengths and weaknesses.

PERSONNEL POLICIES AND PROCEDURES

DISTRIBUTION:		SUBJECT: ORIENTATION EVALUATION	
EFFECTIVE DATE:	PAGE 2 OF 2	FILE UNDER SECTION	
REVISION DATE:	APPROVED BY:		

C. Leaders will train new associates and monitor progress. This monitoring should include documentation of when the new associate is doing well and when the new associate is not doing as well as expected.

It is the leader's responsibility to inform the new associate when he/she fails to meet expectations.

D. At the end of each thirty (30) calendar days of employment the coordinator will review the new associate's performance. This evaluation should be done at the end of the thirty- (30-) day cycle. Associates not meeting expectations should be informed as to what improvements must be made before the next appraisal if they are to be allowed to continue employment.

If the associate's performance is far below an acceptable level or the coordinator doubts significant improvement is possible, then the coordinator should consult the Human Resources Section and a decision should be made to either terminate employment or develop an aggressive action plan to achieve the necessary performance improvement.

E. New hires are expected to follow all company rules and policies as outlined in:
1. The Employee Handbook
2. Notices on the Controlled Communication Centers
3. Orientation training

PERSONNEL POLICIES AND PROCEDURES

DISTRIBUTION:		SUBJECT: EMPLOYMENT PROCEDURE	
EFFECTIVE DATE:	PAGE 1 OF 1	FILE UNDER SECTION	
REVISION DATE:	APPROVED BY:		

PURPOSE:

System-wide controls are required to maintain an orderly method to place new employees on the payroll and accurate employee personnel files.

NONBARGAINING—EXEMPT AND NONEXEMPT EMPLOYEES:

1. Application: Our standard application form with inserts must be completed (in duplicate or copied) thoroughly in accordance with the personnel policy and procedure on applications. A copy of this application is to be sent to Human Resources to be placed in the employee's personnel folder.

2. Telephone Reference Check: The telephone reference check is part of the application form. It is included with the application to let candidates know what questions will be asked about them. The questions are designed to reveal any misrepresentation and general character of the applicant. This form must be completed prior to the decision to hire.

   The individual making the telephone reference check must note the individual spoken to and the date and sign the reference check. A copy of this telephone reference check is to be sent to Human Resources to be placed in the employee's personnel folder.

3. Insurance Enrollment Card: An enrollment card must be completed on all regular full-time employees. This card should be completed in accordance with the personnel policy and procedure on insurance and is to be sent to Human Resources with the other employment papers.

4. Physical Examination: All employees must have a physical prior to the final decision to hire. Normally this is done via a conditional offer to employ contingent upon the results of the physical. The results of the physical will be filed in a separate confidential medical file. The Company will bear the expense. The approved bills are to be sent to Accounts Payable.

5. Federal Withholding W-4 Form: All employees will complete the W-4 Form. This form can be received from the local Post Office or Internal Revenue Service. This form is to accompany the employment papers to Human Resources.

6. Federal Immigration I-9 Form: All employees will complete the I-9 Form. This form can be received from the local Immigration Office or Human Resources. This form is to accompany other employment papers to Human Resources.

PERSONNEL POLICIES AND PROCEDURES

DISTRIBUTION:		SUBJECT: EMPLOYEE RECRUITMENT AND SELECTION	
EFFECTIVE DATE:	PAGE 1 OF 3	FILE UNDER SECTION	
REVISION DATE:	APPROVED BY:		

POLICY STATEMENT:

The policy and procedures for employee recruitment and selection at (Organization's Name) are established to facilitate the company's commitment to equal opportunity employment, hiring the best-suited applicants for available positions, making the best use of their abilities and providing job satisfaction, and ensuring that appropriate communications, records, and human resources controls are maintained.

The employment functions are centralized in the Human Resources Department in (Organization's Name), and all recruitment and selection procedures at the company headquarters and nearby locations will be initiated by the Coordinator of Human Resources. Appropriate communications between distant satellite locations and the Human Resources Department should be maintained as specified in this policy.

PROCEDURE:

A. Employee Requisition

To initiate the recruitment process at company headquarters and nearby facilities, the hiring manager must submit to Human Resources an Employee Requisition, identifying the position to be filled, the reason it was vacated or why it is to be added, by whom it was vacated, etc., along with pertinent information for the recruitment process, such as hours to be worked, minimum qualifications, etc. This requisition must be signed by the interviewing manager and his superior at the Vice President level.

Managers at distant satellite locations may initiate recruitment procedures themselves for replacement positions, but must complete the requisition process above for newly created positions and for new or replacement management positions.

Upon receipt of the Employee Requisition, the Coordinator of Human Resources will notify the manager who submitted the Employee Requisition of authorization to recruit for newly created positions and coordinate plans for recruitment.

B. Applicant Resources

All managers should attempt to fill positions in-house before recruiting someone from outside the company. The Coordinator of Human Resources will maintain a record of employees who have identified their interest in moving into another position or location, and will attempt to match in-house candidates with position availability. Managers should encourage their employees to notify the Human Resources Department of their career goals and interests. While managers in outlying areas may not be able to practically and expediently consider in-house candidates for all job openings, they should determine from Human Resources if there are in-house candidates for managerial positions prior to seeking outside candidates.

Additional resources that should be considered when attempting to fill a position include: applications on file, trade school/college/university placement offices, high school guidance counselors, temporary employment agencies, employee referrals, newspaper/trade publication advertisements.

The Coordinator of Human Resources must either place or approve (by phone) all employment advertisements to ensure language consistent with (Organization's Name)'s commitment to Equal Opportunity Employment.

C. Employment Applications

Form—The company utilizes a standard Application for Employment form for all potential employment candidates,

DISTRIBUTION:		SUBJECT: EMPLOYEE RECRUITMENT AND SELECTION	
EFFECTIVE DATE:	PAGE 2 OF 3	FILE UNDER SECTION	
REVISION DATE:	APPROVED BY:		

which must be completed and signed by an applicant prior to being considered for employment. Candidates who submit résumés should be required to complete an application form at the time of their interview. A supply of these application forms will be made available to satellite store managers through the Human Resources Department.

Receipt—Individuals interested in completing an application for employment at (Organization's Name) may do so at any time during business hours at the company headquarters and at distant satellite offices. Applicants should be made aware that their application will remain on active file for three months, and if we desire to interview them should a suitable opening occur, we will contact them. Applicants should be treated professionally, courteously, and with respect, as we would a customer.

Review—Applications should be carefully reviewed prior to the applicant's leaving to ensure that the application has been thoroughly completed and signed. Personnel receiving and reviewing applications should take care to avoid writing notes of any kind on applications or résumés.

Retention—Each month application files should be purged by the Coordinator of Human Resources at the company headquarters and by managers at distant satellite stores to ensure that applications remain on ''active'' file for three months and are placed in ''inactive'' file for an additional twelve months. This will ensure the company's compliance with federal regulations covering the application process and our ability to maintain a defensible posture should an EEOC charge be filed against our company relative to our hiring practices.

Copies of applications and résumés of managerial candidates received by distant satellite store management should be forwarded to the Coordinator of Human Resources for filing.

D. Pre-employment Interviews

If in-house candidates are to be considered for available positions, the Coordinator of Human Resources will arrange interviews to be conducted by the hiring manager with suitable candidates.

Pre-employment interviews for outside candidates will be arranged and conducted by the Coordinator of Human Resources for the company headquarters and nearby satellite stores, following a review of applications with the hiring manager. Managers of distant satellite stores will conduct their own interviews.

All managerial employees who conduct pre-employment interviews should study and practice the recommendations for interview procedures and fair employment practices that follow in this section.

E. Reference Checks

All employment at (Organization's Name) is subject to the receipt of acceptable references unless extenuating circumstances occur, in which case the President must approve a hiring decision.

Reference checks of former employers and/or teachers will be conducted by the Coordinator of Human Resources or, in distant satellite offices, by the hiring manager. Managers should use the enclosed reference check form, a supply of which can be obtained through the Human Resources Department, and should follow the enclosed guidelines for conducting reference checks.

If an applicant is rejected on the basis of reference information, it is important that the source of this information be protected so as to avoid a lawsuit on the basis of derogatory, slanderous information. You are not obligated to and should not reveal to the applicant the source or content of the reference check information. It is confidential and for our use in the hiring decision only.

PERSONNEL POLICIES AND PROCEDURES

DISTRIBUTION:		SUBJECT: EMPLOYEE RECRUITMENT AND SELECTION	
EFFECTIVE DATE:	PAGE 3 OF 3	FILE UNDER SECTION	
REVISION DATE:	APPROVED BY:		

NOTE: All requests from other companies for reference information on the company's current or previous employees must be referred to the Coordinator of Human Resources. No one else, except the President or his designee, may release any employment information.

F. Physical Examinations

An employee may be required to undergo a physical examination prior to or during employment. The company reserves the right to designate the physician to conduct the examination, and the examination will be at the company's expense.

G. Accepting/Rejecting Applicants

Before a hiring decision can be made, the candidate must be interviewed by the manager of the division in which he/she will be working, and by the Division's Market Manager or Supervisor if possible. Manager-level employees and higher will be interviewed by the President, in addition to the Supervisor or Market Manager.

The Supervisor or Manager to whom the candidate will be reporting should extend the offer of employment once appropriate approvals from higher levels, as necessary, have been obtained. Managers at company headquarters and nearby satellite offices should review plans to offer employment with the Coordinator of Human Resources prior to the offer's being extended.

In-house job candidates who are not selected for a position should be notified by the Coordinator of Human Resources. Rejected outside candidates should be notified, by letter, that someone else was chosen for the position; this is to be accomplished by the Coordinator of Human Resources at the company headquarters and by the interviewing manager at distant satellite operations. A sample rejection letter is provided and should be used as a guide for proper wording of such a letter.

Rejected applications should be filed according to the schedule established in this manual.

Dear Ms. Jones:

Thank you for the interest you expressed in (Company Name) by applying for the Purchasing Clerk position. We appreciate the opportunity to exchange information in our interview, and we hope you left with a positive impression of (Company Name).

After careful consideration, the Purchasing Clerk position has been filled by another applicant. We believe we have made the best choice in view of our current needs; however, we would like to retain your application in our file and contact you should a future opening suitable to your background and experience occur.

Again, we appreciate your interest in (Company Name), and we wish you success as you pursue satisfying employment.

Sincerely,

PERSONNEL POLICIES AND PROCEDURES

DISTRIBUTION:		SUBJECT: EMPLOYEE REFERRAL AWARD PROGRAM
EFFECTIVE DATE:	PAGE 1 OF 2	FILE UNDER SECTION
REVISION DATE:	APPROVED BY:	

A. Objective

This policy is established to define the procedure and establish the qualifications required for the employee referral award program.

B. Purpose

1. To provide eligible employees with an incentive to refer qualified candidates to be hired for exempt, regular, full-time positions as designated and announced by the organization/location employment manager.

2. To establish a uniform procedure that will standardize:
   a. Location/organization approval procedure
   b. Referral award amount and method of payment
   c. Eligibility criteria

3. To supersede all existing organization/location employee referral programs within the company.

C. Organization/Location Approval

Activation of this program for/at any organization/location requires prior approval of the Vice President, Human Resources. Organizations requesting approval should submit a written request, which must include:

1. Major activity or specific project(s) that require and could benefit from activation of this program.

2. Specific positions or critical skill areas to be eligible for award consideration.

3. Specific time period for which the program is to be in effect for/at the organization/location, e.g., "effective April 1, 19___ through September 30, 19___."

4. Planned method of communication to employees, e.g., payroll stuffers, home mail-outs, posters, etc.

Any requests for extension beyond the initially requested/approved time period require the same approval as the initial request to activate the program.

D. Eligibility

All employees of (Company Name) except:
1. Supervisory/management employees
2. Human Resources Department employees

E. Criteria

1. The referring employee's name and employee number must appear on the bottom of the front page of the application for employment, in the "employment source" section. Also, the application must bear the employing organization's stamp, which clearly shows the date it was received.

2. In the event of a former company employee being referred for rehire, only those former employees who will have a rehire date exceeding 365 days since date of termination will be eligible under this program.

3. Awards will not be issued for candidates hired as a result of search firm, agency placement, direct write-ins, response to advertising, college/technical school recruitment, walk-ins, company layoff lists, job/career fair recruitment, transfers within the corporation, or other recruitment sources.

4. Awards will be issued:
   a. Only after a written offer of regular, full-time employment is made and accepted, and the newly hired employee has completed thirty-one days of active employment.

DISTRIBUTION:		SUBJECT: EMPLOYEE REFERRAL AWARD PROGRAM	
EFFECTIVE DATE:	PAGE 2 OF 2		FILE UNDER SECTION
REVISION DATE:	APPROVED BY:		

    b. Only if the referred candidate's application is received within the specified time period as announced by the organization/location employment manager if/when the program is activated at/for a specified organization/location.

F. AWARDS

Eligible employees who refer candidates who are employed under this program will be awarded an amount that yields $500 after taxes. The actual cost of this tax gross-up will depend upon the referring employee's tax bracket. The award will be paid by direct deposit at all locations where the direct deposit program is available.

G. Administration

This program is administered by the organization/location employment manager. His/her specific responsibilities are to:

1. Obtain approval for activation of this program for/at his/her organization/location as specified in Section C of this procedure.
2. Implement the communication of the program to employees (Ref. Section C.4).
3. Make all decisions regarding eligibility of both referring employees and referred candidates.
4. Process appropriate referral award documentation, specifically:
   a. Front page of the application for employment which identifies the newly hired employee and the referring employee
   b. Request for Payment Form Exhibit A
5. Ensure that the award is paid as expediently as possible after the newly hired employee has been employed for thirty-one days.

PERSONNEL POLICIES AND PROCEDURES

DISTRIBUTION:		SUBJECT: SCREENING AND CHECKING REFERENCES	
EFFECTIVE DATE:	PAGE 1 OF 2	FILE UNDER SECTION	
REVISION DATE:	APPROVED BY:		

PURPOSE OF PROCEDURE:

It is the purpose of this policy to fill job vacancies as they occur with the most qualified job applicants available and to build up a reserve of qualified personnel who can be promoted to higher positions within our organization.

PROCEDURE:

It is our policy to hire job applicants only after they have been carefully screened and interviewed by the store manager, warehouse manager, or a department head that has been delegated such authority and responsibility.

The following sources of pre-employment references will be used in our company:

1. Previous employers. (Contact at least two most recent employers as shown on the employment application.)

2. Call local police department or county sheriff's office to see if job applicant has been convicted of a job-related crime.

3. Personal character references. Often these are not satisfactory. But you may wish to contact a character reference even though most are not willing to say anything that would keep a person from getting a job. Try to get them to give you the names of the applicant's friends and personal acquaintances. Please check with these people, too. These "secondary" personal references often give more valuable information about the applicant than the personal reference the applicant put on the application form.

4. Former school teachers. In the case of high school students or students who have quit after high school or quit during school, it is desirable to talk with the school principal or the homeroom teacher. If the job applicant gave a teacher or the school trouble, it's possible he or she will give our supervisors more of the same. Most teachers are happy to get their feelings off their chest. If the applicant was a good student and had a good attitude, most teachers will tell you this.

A word of caution in the treatment of job applicants and their references:

It is most important that we maintain good public relations throughout the screening and interviewing process with job applicants and their references. Many job applicants, whether they are hired or not, will form definite opinions of our organization. They may spread good will for us, or their attitude may be unfavorable and detrimental in their communities. Therefore, it is our policy to follow these guidelines consistently in the treatment of all job applicants:

1. All job applicants will be looked upon as potential customers and will be treated with the same consideration as we would show our customers.

2. We will not use "No Help Wanted" signs in any store at any time.

PERSONNEL POLICIES AND PROCEDURES

DISTRIBUTION:		SUBJECT: SCREENING AND CHECKING REFERENCES	
EFFECTIVE DATE:	PAGE 2 OF 2	FILE UNDER SECTION	
REVISION DATE:	APPROVED BY:		

3. We will avoid all practices that create ill will. We will not give applicants false hope. If there is no chance of employing an applicant, we will tell that person so. We should not make vague promises about a job in the future or tell the applicant to keep checking back with us. Unless there is a bona fide job vacancy to be filled, or unless you anticipate a vacancy in the immediate future, we will not give out an employment application to anyone who comes into a store or warehouse asking for a job.

PERSONNEL POLICIES AND PROCEDURES

DISTRIBUTION:		SUBJECT: RETENTION REQUIREMENT ON ALL EMPLOYMENT APPLICATIONS	
EFFECTIVE DATE:	PAGE 1 OF 1	FILE UNDER SECTION	
REVISION DATE:	APPROVED BY:		

POLICY STATEMENT:

All employment applicants that are received from job applicants will be considered "active" for a period of thirty calendar days from the date of the application form. Once employment applications become over thirty days old, they are considered "inactive" and will be filed separately and retained for a period of one year.

PROCEDURE:

1. Set up two employment application retention file folders. Label one file "Applicants for Employment—Less than thirty days old—Active." Label the second file "Applications for Employment—Over thirty days old—Inactive".

2. When a job applicant completes an employment application for a vacancy, it is to be placed in the "Active" application retention file and remain there until thirty days from the date on the application. Applications for employment in the "Active" retention file will be considered first for qualified Employees. Once an application becomes more than thirty days old, it will be placed in the "Inactive" retention file. Applicants in that group will not be considered for hire unless you are not able to find qualified personnel among the "Active" applications.

3. Once applications in the "Inactive" file become twelve months old from the date on the application form itself, they may be destroyed.

4. Once a job applicant is hired, the employment application form that had been completed should be placed in the "Employee Personnel File" folder and retained as part of our permanent personnel record system. In addition to the application, all reference forms, résumés, and any other pre-employment forms or records used will be placed in the employee's personnel file folder.

5. Results of physical examinations, reasonable accommodation information, and all other health-related information must be maintained in a separate confidential medical file.

PURPOSE OF THIS PROCEDURE:

The purpose of this recordkeeping procedure is to comply with various Federal Wage-Hour and EEO recordkeeping requirements. The "Active" and "Inactive" application retention files are simply designed as a means to treat all applicants fairly and consistently without illegal discrimination of any kind.

PERSONNEL POLICIES AND PROCEDURES

DISTRIBUTION:		SUBJECT: PRE-EMPLOYMENT INTERVIEWS OF JOB APPLICANTS	
EFFECTIVE DATE:	PAGE 1 OF 4	FILE UNDER SECTION	
REVISION DATE:	APPROVED BY:		

POLICY STATEMENT:

A pre-employment interview will be conducted with job applicants if the information received on the employment application, along with the reference checks from previous employers, personal references, and other sources, indicates that the applicant is still eligible for a position with our organization.

PROCEDURE:

1. Set up a time for the pre-employment interview that is mutually convenient for both you and the job applicant. Try to hold the interview in an office or room where there will be complete privacy from interruptions by telephone calls and from other employees.

2. Make every effort to put the applicant at ease. Use a friendly and courteous introduction. Call the applicant by his or her last name. Show an interest in the applicant, but do not talk about yourself. Get the applicant to talk, as your objective is to learn as much as possible about his or her background. Start with a question or request such as the following:

   "Tell me about yourself."
   "Tell me about your last job."
   "Why are your interested in working for our company?"

   After the preliminaries, move on to the actual interview. You will want to describe the particular job needed to be filled very clearly, including the work schedule, rate of pay, working conditions, type of work, etc.

3. Ask questions and listen carefully to the applicant's answers.

   Ask questions about experience, job record, wages, immediate supervisors. Even brief answers to these questions by the applicant will tell you very basic important attitudes the person possesses.

4. Find out about each job the applicant held in the past. Find out first what his or her duties were and then determine the kind of people he or she worked with in each situation.

5. Job applicants who feel that they have always worked for poor supervisors and unfair managers will probably find you to be the same. A job applicant who has found interesting people he or she worked with in previous jobs will probably find them in your location, too. This interview is the best way to find out real attitudes toward immediate supervision, fellow workers, and the whole idea of cooperation.

6. Length of interview: Your pre-employment interview can be as short as fifteen minutes but should not go much beyond an hour for most jobs. The length of the pre-employment interview will depend upon the type of job you are trying to fill. Remember that if you expect to keep an applicant as a long-term employee, you will want to interview him or her as carefully as you can.

DISTRIBUTION:		SUBJECT: PRE-EMPLOYMENT INTERVIEWS OF JOB APPLICANTS
EFFECTIVE DATE:	PAGE 2 OF 4	FILE UNDER SECTION
REVISION DATE:	APPROVED BY:	

7. In sizing up prospective employees, it is necessary to consider the "whole person" and not just past experiences. Job applicants bring us their health, their ambitions, their attitudes, their worries, and the influence of their families. All these things and others will affect their potential with our company.

8. **What An Interviewer Must Not Ask or Require on an Application Before Hiring** (Many of these questions may be asked, however, after hire if required for fringe benefits programs.)

    ◆ Do not ask the applicant's age.
    ◆ Do not ask the applicant's date of birth.
    ◆ Do not ask the applicant what church he/she attends or the name of his/her priest, rabbi, or minister.
    ◆ Do not ask the applicant what his/her father's surname is.
    ◆ Do not ask the female applicant what her maiden name was.
    ◆ Do not ask the applicant whether he/she is married, divorced, separated, widowed, or single (but you may ask Mr., Mrs., Miss, or Ms.).
    ◆ Do not ask the applicant who resides with him/her.
    ◆ Do not ask the applicant how many children he/she has.
    ◆ Do not ask the ages of any children of the applicant.
    ◆ Do not ask who will care for the children while the applicant is working.
    ◆ Do not ask the applicant where a spouse or parent resides or works (although you may ask whether relatives of the applicant are or have been employed by the company).
    ◆ Do not ask the applicant if he/she owns or rents his/her place of residence.
    ◆ Do not ask the applicant whether he/she was ever arrested.
    ◆ Do not ask the applicant about present or past health conditions or disabilities.
    ◆ Do not ask the applicant about previous health-care claims or worker's compensation claims.
    ◆ Do not ask the applicant about previous attendance record.

    You Can Ask Questions About the Applicant's Past Job and Check His/Her Suitability for the Present Position:
    The interviewer should do little talking here. The applicant should encouraged to talk. Try to avoid asking questions that can be answered with "yes" or "no."

A. Job Experience

    ◆ Your last job was with XYZ company. What did you do exactly?
    ◆ How did you like your work?
    ◆ Tell me something about your working relationship with your supervisor.
    ◆ You know we will have to talk to your former employers to check your references. You do not have objections, do you?
    ◆ In your application you are not too clear about why you left your last job. How about telling me some of the reasons.
    ◆ How did you find the working atmosphere in your last place of employment?
    ◆ In what accomplishments on your last job did you take the most pride?
    ◆ Did your former boss encourage suggestions or ideas for improvements? Tell me about any suggestions that you made on your own.
    ◆ Discuss your relationship with your associates.
    ◆ For what kind of company do you think you can do your best work?
    ◆ Did you ever become involved in emergency situations and work long hours under pressure? Tell me about such an experience.

PERSONNEL POLICIES AND PROCEDURES

DISTRIBUTION:		SUBJECT: PRE-EMPLOYMENT INTERVIEWS OF JOB APPLICANTS	
EFFECTIVE DATE:	PAGE 3 OF 4	FILE UNDER SECTION	
REVISION DATE:	APPROVED BY:		

B. Suitability for Available Position

- I have explained the duties of our job. How do you think your qualifications/experience fits you for it?
- Do you think you would have difficulty in performing any of the job duties?
- Can you tell me about your satisfaction or lack of satisfaction with the rate of advancement at your former company?
- Suppose you take this job. What are your immediate goals?
- What do you think are your strong points?
- Tell me what you consider your greatest abilities and how they will help you in this job.
- Do you have any weak spots in your work habits? What are you doing to overcome them?
- Have you taken any courses or home study programs relating to your field of work? Tell me about them?

9. **Danger Cues in Pre-employment Interviews:** There are several danger cues in interviews. Please remember that no one is perfect. Almost every prospect will reveal some "doubtful area" to the alert interviewer. A final decision depends on thorough consideration of both "pluses" and "minuses" of the prospect. A danger cue in itself is not a conclusion; it is simply a signal to the interviewer that digging further may be in order. Following are possible danger cues:

A. Danger cues in actions: Sudden nervousness, blushing, stammering, fidgeting, or clamming up may indicate that you are about uncover unfavorable facts. A sudden change of pace in talking or in the rate of reply to questions is a potential cue. An attempt to change the subject or to laugh it off merits digging in by the interviewer.

B. Danger cues in what is said: Gap in the record—was he or she loafing? In jail? Pursuing another job listlessly? Frequent changes in jobs, schools, or places of residence—was he or she in trouble (marital or alcohol)? Discrepancies in the records: Are there discrepancies between the application blank and interview—clear them up.

C. Reluctance to furnish references: Was the person in trouble? Do you have his or her real reason for leaving the last job? Is the person a troublemaker? Beware of a person with a record of trouble—trouble begets trouble. Be cautious if the person received a "dirty deal" from the last boss, or thinks the last boss was a stinker.

D. Be cautious of dependent characters—if they have a habit of depending on someone else to make their decisions, or if they can get by without working, someone will take care of them.

E. What to do with danger cues: Do not show surprise, approval, or disapproval. Keep them talking. Use questions and requests such as: Why do you say that? Why do you know that? What makes you think that? Give me some concrete examples. Tell me why you feel this way. I don't quite get your point; please explain further. In short—dig in.

Look for "danger" cues in your pre-employment interviews. If you find in interviewing a certain individual that he or she is totally undesirable for the job, then you need not go all the way through the interview. Your time is valuable and should not be wasted on an applicant that you know is undesirable. An interview can be concluded at any point. Dismiss poor risk applicants quickly. Don't hesitate to tell them the answer is "no." Do not leave anyone hopeful of a job offer that he/she will never get. A delayed "no" often invites further waste of time with useless phone calls, correspondence, or both. We must always keep good public relations in mind by saying "no." A short explanation such as the following will help you:

"You have some good qualifications, but we honestly feel that our job is not the kind in which you are apt to do your best. But thank you for applying for a position with our organization. We appreciate your time and your interest."

PERSONNEL POLICIES AND PROCEDURES

DISTRIBUTION:		SUBJECT: PRE-EMPLOYMENT INTERVIEWS OF JOB APPLICANTS
EFFECTIVE DATE:	PAGE 4 OF 4	FILE UNDER SECTION
REVISION DATE:	APPROVED BY:	

10. **Put your evaluation of applicant during interview on "Applicant Screening Profile" Form 7:** Immediately after the job applicant leaves your office, try to relax and think about the impression he or she has made on you. If you have reacted at all, he or she has certainly left you with a definite feeling. Is the total feeling good or bad? Look back on the application form and review the notes you have made of the answers to your questions. What do they add up to? It is often very helpful to record your reactions on an interview form just as soon as the individual leaves your office and while the interview is fresh in your mind.

    If the job applicant is hired: Put the application form and other reference check forms and information in an "Employee Personnel File" folder. A confidential personnel file folder should be on file for every employee hired.

    The "personnel file" folder also serves as a "hiring checklist" along with sections containing the permanent record of the employee's pay increases, job assignments, recommendations, reprimands, testing, training courses, vacations, annual earnings, and a record of any company handbooks and rules issued to the employee. This file folder also contains a record of the reason for separation from employment.

    Be sure to put any information pertaining to the hired person's health, disabilities, and reasonable accommodation in a separate, confidential medical file. This includes results of any physical examination or tests.

11. **If the job applicant is not hired:** Put any information pertaining to the rejected applicant's health, disabilities, and reasonable accommodations in a separate, confidential medical file. This includes the results of any physical examinations or tests.

    Put all other information in a rejected applicant file. This will serve as documentation on the reasons why you failed or refused to hire a job applicant if and when we are ever charged with discrimination for any reason by any applicant. If the applicant is not hired following your interview, then you must retain the applicant's job application form and all other information for a period of twelve months.

PERSONNEL POLICIES AND PROCEDURES

DISTRIBUTION:		SUBJECT: FEE PAYMENT FOR EMPLOYMENT PROCUREMENT	
EFFECTIVE DATE:	PAGE 1 OF 1	FILE UNDER SECTION	
REVISION DATE:	APPROVED BY:		

POLICY STATEMENT:

Employment agency fees for procurement of (Organization's Name) Sales Trainees and Salespersons will be borne by the Company.

GUIDELINES:

Use of Agencies

1. Personnel responsible for the recruiting of Sales Trainees and Salespersons (e.g., Manpower Development Manager, Regional Manager, District Manager, Human Resources Manager) will minimize the use of employment agencies. Agencies should be used as a last resort and *only* after all other sources of recruiting have been exhausted.

2. Agencies must guarantee the new employee for ninety days. That is, should an agency-procured employee leave the company's employ within three months from the date of employment, the agency must agree to furnish a suitable, fully qualified replacement.

LIMITATION OF FEES

Agency fees will not be paid in excess of 15 percent of the candidate's yearly base salary unless approved in advance by the Director of Human Resources.

Method of Payment

1. Invoices will be approved by the Regional Manager concerned and forwarded to the Human Resources Department for payment. (This expense is charged to Employment Procurement Account.)

2. In no event may costs be charged to the Employment Procurement Account without prior knowledge and approval of the Director of Human Resources. These include costs incurred in employment advertisements, interview expenses, employment agency fees, etc.

PERSONNEL POLICIES AND PROCEDURES

DISTRIBUTION:		SUBJECT: EMPLOYMENT STATUS	
EFFECTIVE DATE:	PAGE 1 OF 1	FILE UNDER SECTION	
REVISION DATE:	APPROVED BY:		

POLICY STATEMENT:

A. Part-time

Anyone employed less than thirty-five hours a week is considered part-time. A part-time employee is eligible for fringe benefits depending upon the regularity of employment and the number of scheduled hours.

B. Temporary

Anyone employed for a specific period (such as summer) or for a specific purpose (to replace a sick employee) is considered temporary. A temporary employee is not eligible for fringe benefits.

C. Outside Employment

Holding a second job elsewhere is subject to critical appraisal only if it conflicts with the full performance of the employee and interests of the Company.

PERSONNEL POLICIES AND PROCEDURES

DISTRIBUTION:		SUBJECT: COLLEGE COOPERATIVE PROGRAM	
EFFECTIVE DATE:	PAGE 1 OF 1	FILE UNDER SECTION	
REVISION DATE:	APPROVED BY:		

The Company from time to time employs college students who work less than the normal 37-1/2-hour week during the academic year, while attending college on a full-time basis. Work programs and benefits for college co-ops are modified as follows:

A. Working Hours

    (1) Normal Academic Year—25 hours weekly.

    (2) Summer and Midyear Vacation Periods—37-1/2 hours weekly.

    (3) Specific starting and quitting times will be determined by the department head directly involved.

B. Salary

    (1) One standard rate for all clerical work performed by college co-ops is determined by market conditions.

    (2) Hours in excess of 25 per week will be reimbursed at the rate of $_____ an hour.

    (3) Hours in excess of 37-1/2 (when performing a full workweek schedule) shall be at 1-1/2 times the employee's current base pay.

C. Leaves of Absence

Leaves of absence will not be granted for the sole purpose of study.

D. Benefits

College co-ops are eligible for all fringe benefits except tuition refund, provided they are employed on a regular part-time basis for a workweek of no less than 30 hours.

PERSONNEL POLICIES AND PROCEDURES

DISTRIBUTION:		SUBJECT: EMPLOYMENT CLASSIFICATION	
EFFECTIVE DATE:	PAGE 1 OF 1	FILE UNDER SECTION	
REVISION DATE:	APPROVED BY:		

POLICY STATEMENT:

A. Part-time

A part-time employee is one who consistently works less than thirty hours per week and is paid on an hourly or daily salary basis. He or she is not eligible for any employee benefits except the following: free parking and workers' compensation insurance.

B. Regular

A regular employee is one who has successfully completed his or her orientation period and who consistently works thirty or more hours per week as assigned by the department head. This employee is eligible for all of the employee benefits given by the hospital, such as group insurance, holidays, vacation, sick leave, leaves of absence, and other benefits.

C. Temporary

A fully qualified person who offers his or her services on a relief basis when needed by the hospital or for short-term employment, such as summer employment, is considered a temporary employee. This employee is not eligible for any employee benefits except the following: free parking and workers' compensation insurance.

PERSONNEL POLICIES AND PROCEDURES

DISTRIBUTION:		SUBJECT: NEW EMPLOYEE INDUCTION/ORIENTATION
EFFECTIVE DATE:	PAGE 1 OF 1	FILE UNDER SECTION
REVISION DATE:	APPROVED BY:	

POLICY STATEMENT:

New employees at (Organization's Name) will be required to complete new hire paperwork on their first day of employment to ensure proper and timely payroll and benefits processing. Additionally, a well-planned orientation to our company and to the employee's specific job will be provided by appropriate management personnel to assist new employees in feeling welcome and comfortable in their new work environment and in becoming fully productive in their position as quickly as possible.

PROCEDURE:

A. New Employee Paperwork—New employees should report to the Human Resources Department or in distant satellite operations to the Manager at the beginning of their first day of employment. At that time, they should complete the necessary paperwork to result in an "employment package" which will be used to initiate their paycheck and appropriate employee benefits and to set up their personnel file. Satellite managers should forward this package, retaining a copy for their files, to the Coordinator of Human Resources, who will forward the necessary information to the Payroll Department.

The following information should be included in the employment package, with proper authorizations:

- Completed Employment Application, résumé if obtained, and reference check documentation.
- W-4 Form signed, designating actual hire date.
- Work Permit, if necessary.*
- Insurance enrollment card for qualifying employees.
- Retirement Enrollment Application or Revocation on qualifying employees.
- Agreement for opening a charge account.
- Waiver of Incentive Payment Agreement.
- Form I-9.
- Completed Employment Checklist.

*Each state has regulations applicable to the employment of miners as it relates to hours of work, duties allowed to be performed, etc. Managers should consult the Coordinator of Human Resources to ensure the company's compliance with Child Labor regulations.

B. Employment Agreement—Certain employees may be required to enter into an employment agreement with the company that would restrict competition with the company in the event of termination. A sample employment agreement is included in this section. However, managers must consult with the President in determining who should be required to enter into such an agreement and in determining specific terms of the agreement.

C. New Employee Orientation—To ensure that all new employees will receive needed information and that the orientation process will proceed in an orderly sequence, the supervisor or manager to whom a new employee reports must complete a New Employee Induction/Orientation Checklist within the first two weeks of hire of a new employee. This completed checklist will be placed in the employee's personnel file.

Additionally, managers should review and adopt the enclosed recommendations for providing job training to new employees.

PERSONNEL POLICIES AND PROCEDURES

DISTRIBUTION:		SUBJECT: EMPLOYMENT/RECRUITMENT GUIDELINES
EFFECTIVE DATE:	PAGE 1 OF 2	FILE UNDER SECTION
REVISION DATE:	APPROVED BY:	

POLICY STATEMENT:

(Organization's Name) believes that all persons are entitled to equal employment opportunity and will adhere to all aspects of Personnel Policies regarding such matters and, in addition, follow the company's affirmative action plan regarding minorities, females, Vietnam-era veterans, handicapped, and those who are over the age of forty.

PURPOSE:

The purpose of these guidelines is to reaffirm (Organization's Name)'s position relating to employment.

DEFINITION OF TERMS:

Regular Employees—Full-time employment in an established, budgeted position. Will participate in all benefits programs.

Part-time Employees—Employment in an established, budgeted position requiring less than thirty hours per week. Will not participate in benefits programs.

Temporary Employees—Employment in a position established (not budgeted) for a specific period of time but not to exceed 1,000 hours. Will not participate in benefits programs.

As a condition of employment, all employees are informed and agree by their signature that employment and compensation can be terminated, with or without cause, and without notice, at any time, at the option of either the Company or the employee, and further, that no representative or agent of (Company Name) with the exception of the President has authority to enter into any agreement for any specified period of time, or to make any agreement contrary to the foregoing.

PROMOTION FROM WITHIN:

Vacancies are filled by promotions from within the company whenever possible. Open positions will be posted for three working days on all bulletin boards and interested employees may apply, by receiving an application form from the Human Resources Department. Employees with the greatest seniority will be given first consideration should more than one candidate be equally qualified.

Temporary or part-time employees who apply for a "regular" employee position and are accepted will be given seniority credit for all time worked, provided there is no break in employment. If a fully qualified candidate is not already available on the staff, a new employee will be secured from the outside.

RECRUITMENT:

New employees will be selected on the basis of qualifications criteria pertaining to the vacant position. Such criteria are specified in the position description. Other factors to be considered are previous work history, dependability, character, and aptitude.

PERSONNEL POLICIES AND PROCEDURES

DISTRIBUTION:		SUBJECT: EMPLOYMENT/RECRUITMENT GUIDELINES	
EFFECTIVE DATE:	PAGE 2 OF 2		FILE UNDER SECTION
REVISION DATE:	APPROVED BY:		

FORMER EMPLOYEES:

Employees who left the company voluntarily or through no fault of their own and who make application for reemployment will be given consideration. It is our policy not to reemploy those who are discharged for cause. A reemployed person waives all rights accruing from prior service.

RELATIVES:

The employment of relatives will be permitted, but not in the same department. In the event employees in the same department marry, the more junior employee from a seniority viewpoint will be transferred to another department in an equal position with no loss of pay or benefits, if such a position is available.

PHYSICAL EXAMINATION:

After a conditional job offer, it is necessary that the applicant submit to a physical examination to ensure that the individual is physically capable of performing the essential job duties. Employment is contingent upon the results of the examination.

EMPLOYEE REFERRALS:

Referrals from employees are encouraged; however, all such referrals will be given the same consideration as any other applicants.

OVERTIME:

Employees are expected to work overtime as requested. Supervisors will make every effort to notify those concerned as early in the workweek as possible to avoid any undue hardships.

APPLICATIONS:

Employment applications will be kept on file for a period of twelve months from the date received in the Human Resources Department.

PERSONNEL POLICIES AND PROCEDURES

DISTRIBUTION:		SUBJECT: HIRING FORMER EMPLOYEES, FRIENDS, AND DISABLED
EFFECTIVE DATE:	PAGE 1 OF 1	FILE UNDER SECTION
REVISION DATE:	APPROVED BY:	

POLICY:

Vacancies are filled by promotion from within the Company whenever possible. If a suitable candidate is not already available on the payroll, a new employee is secured in accordance with the following policies:

1. Recruitment
   A. Preference is given to applicants who are recommended by employees and friends of our company, provided they meet all job requirements, and provided this is consistent with equal employment policies.
   B. No employee is to solicit applicants from among employees of another company.

2. Selection
   Employees are selected on the basis of past performance, education, salary compatibility, experience, interviews, and validated tests, when administered. Qualifications for the job at hand as well as for future advancement are given prime consideration.

3. Age
   Applicants under eighteen years of age will not be considered. Age is not a factor in employment except for those openings in which bona fide occupational qualifications are paramount.

4. Education
   Applicants without a high school diploma or equivalent business experience can be considered for only a relatively small number of positions.

5. Former Employees
   Employees who left our company voluntarily or through no fault of their own and who make application for reemployment will be given consideration. It is our policy not to reemploy those who are discharged. A reemployed person must waive all rights accruing from prior service.

6. Nondiscrimination
   There will be no discrimination in employment because of race, color, religion, sex, age, national origin, citizenship status, physical or mental disability, or past, present, or future service in the uniformed services of the United States.

7. Physical or Mental Disability
   Individuals with known physical or mental disabilities will be considered for employment on the basis of their capability to perform a particular job with or without accommodation. Disabilities that do not prevent such performance shall not disqualify them if they do not constitute a direct threat to the health or safety of others in the workplace.

   The company will make reasonable accommodation to enable applicants and employees with disabilities to perform essential job functions unless to do so would be an undue hardship.

PERSONNEL POLICIES AND PROCEDURES

DISTRIBUTION:		SUBJECT: HIRING FORMER EMPLOYEES	
EFFECTIVE DATE:	PAGE 1 OF 1	FILE UNDER SECTION	
REVISION DATE:	APPROVED BY:		

POLICY STATEMENT:

(Organization's Name) will give employment consideration when staff openings occur to former employees who have performed satisfactorily, who have terminated their employment under favorable circumstances, and who desire to return to work. Each application will be considered on its own merits after a review of the applicant's record, the type of job available, and other relevant factors.

PROCEDURE:

Before pursuing the recruitment and selection process with a former employee, the hiring official must contact the President or the Coordinator of Human Resources for a review of the job opening and the former employee's record. The President will provide final authorization for reemployment after a review of the circumstances.

Should a former employee be rehired, normally the person will be reinstated with his or her original hire date for the purpose of determining seniority and benefits eligibility, provided that the employee is rehired within six months of the termination date. However, the President reserves the right to alter this practice as he or she sees fit in light of the circumstances surrounding the reemployment.

PERSONNEL POLICIES AND PROCEDURES

DISTRIBUTION:		SUBJECT: EMPLOYMENT OF RELATIVES	
EFFECTIVE DATE:	PAGE 1 OF 1	FILE UNDER SECTION	
REVISION DATE:	APPROVED BY:		

POLICY STATEMENT:

It is the goal of (Organization's Name) to avoid creating or perpetuating circumstances in which the possibility of favoritism, conflicts of interest, or impairment of efficient operations may occur. Therefore, while relatives of employees may be hired, relatives may not work in a direct reporting relationship.

For purposes of this policy, relatives are defined as: father, mother, son, daughter, brother, sister, wife, husband, grandparent, nephew, or individual who has acquired such a relationship through marriage or who makes his or her home with an employee, and is in any way related to that employee.

PROCEDURE:

Managers should exercise caution in hiring decisions to ensure that a new employee is not placed in a direct reporting relationship with a relative, as defined by this policy.

Should two employees in a reporting relationship become relatives, as defined in this policy, during their employment at (Organization's Name), the choice will be theirs as to which employee accepts a transfer into an available position, suitable to his or her skill and experience. If, between the two employees, a decision cannot be made, the employee with the least seniority must transfer into the next available position suitable to his or her skill and experience.

The existing employment of relatives in a direct reporting relationship will be ''grandfathered'' into this policy so that employees can remain in their current position. However, all related employees who are hired or employees who become relatives after the effective date of this policy must abide by this policy.

Managers should contact the Coordinator of Human Resources for assistance in facilitating a transfer.

PERSONNEL POLICIES AND PROCEDURES

DISTRIBUTION:		SUBJECT: EMPLOYMENT OF RELATIVES	
EFFECTIVE DATE:	PAGE 1 OF 1	FILE UNDER SECTION	
REVISION DATE:	APPROVED BY:		

PURPOSE:

The purpose of this policy is to establish guidelines with respect to the employment and placement of relatives of associates.

POLICY:

A. It is the policy of (Name of Company) to hire the best qualified individual for each job opening. Although relatives of active associates will not be given preference, they will be allowed to participate in our pre-employment selection process like any other applicant, and if they satisfactorily meet our employment standards, they will be considered for employment.

B. The following guidelines will apply to the employment of relatives of (Name of Company) associates:
1. No associate will be permitted to directly or indirectly supervise the work of anyone in his or her immediate family. "Indirectly supervise" is defined as supervising a relative from a second level of supervision.
2. Third-level supervision will be allowed if the other guidelines of this policy can be followed.
3. Personnel movement or associate transfers will not be allowed when this movement or transfer results in a supervisory/subordinate relationship or a second level of supervision between associates in the immediate family, or when the possibility exists that this type of relationship is likely to result from the personnel move or transfer.
4. Relationships within the organization will not be permitted where an associate handles cash transactions involving a relative, or where his/her relative is responsible for control over those items.
5. No organizational relationship involving relatives will be allowed to exist, regardless of their positions, if it creates a disruption, violates confidentiality rules, or has a negative impact on the work and business at (Name of Company).

PROCEDURE:

A. Leaders are considered the first level of supervision and they will not be allowed to supervise any relative covered under this policy.

B. It is the responsibility of the associate in the supervisory role to notify the Human Resources Section of any violation or potential violation of this practice. Failure to notify the company of a violation of this policy on the part of the associate in the supervisory position will result in discipline to that associate.
1. A person will not be considered for a promotion if it would result in a violation of this policy. The company will not take responsibility of initiating transfers to allow a promotion. It is entirely up to the associates to consider the family implications of transfers and promotions and make appropriate decisions.
2. If a violation of this policy occurs as a result of a reassignment due to downsizing of a department, layoffs, etc., the Human Resources Section should be notified immediately.
   a) Every reasonable attempt will be made to find another location for the associate who was reassigned without violating seniority rules.
   b) If no reasonable alternatives are available, this policy may be waived until a reasonable solution can be found. Approval by the Vice President of General Affairs is required for a temporary waiver of this policy.

101

PERSONNEL POLICIES AND PROCEDURES

DISTRIBUTION:		SUBJECT: COMPANY'S POSITION ON UNIONISM	
EFFECTIVE DATE:	PAGE 1 OF 1	FILE UNDER SECTION	
REVISION DATE:	APPROVED BY:		

PURPOSE:

(Name of Company) believes that any problem can best be settled through the various communication programs at our company and not through the use of a third party.

POLICY:

Whenever appropriate, the company will express its feelings concerning unions and share information the company considers important. The following statement is to be included in the Associate Handbook and communicated to associates during their orientation training:

(Name of Company) is a union-free company. Our coworkers have chosen to keep it that way! Their experience has shown that it is completely unnecessary for anyone to have to pay union dues or to have a union contract to enjoy our company's excellent benefits and programs.

The excellent working conditions and benefits that are enjoyed by the coworkers were achieved through the strong working relationship among all levels of company associates. They are made possible by a continuing relationship based upon an attitude of teamwork and pulling together—not from one of pulling apart caused by union dissension and union troubles. Your company is dedicated to keeping it that way.

The competitive advantage that the company has with its customers is made possible because our customers can depend upon us. They do not have to worry about possible strikes or other work stoppages. Our customers require dependability and need a source for their wiring harnesses and components that will always be reliable and not subject to interruption of services.

You do not need a union at (Name of Company) in order to get attention to problems or concerns you may have that affect you or your work. Your company has well-communicated procedures that enable you to discuss any complaint or problem you may have. We also provide opportunities that enable you to appeal any decision that you do not feel is correct. In addition, you may use steps to go around any levels of management that you feel might prevent you from getting a fair hearing of your problems. You are guaranteed those rights by the company. You do not need to pay money to a group of outsiders to talk for you.

Federal law guarantees you the right to oppose any unionizing attempts, and it guarantees you protection from any union threats or harassment. You are not required to yield to pressures from anyone to sign union membership cards or union authorization cards of any kind. Union organizers sometimes use your fellow associates to try to get their membership cards signed. Please do not let anyone talk you into signing a card or document unless you are ready to turn over your future to outsiders and strangers who want to tax your paychecks and want you to pay them for empty promises. We encourage you not to risk turning over your future welfare and the welfare of this company to any outside interests.

The company is interested in you. Its personnel policies and associate benefit programs were voluntarily created and provided to our coworkers because of a desire to meet the needs of associates and their families—not as a result of any union threats, union promises, union boycotts, or union strikes.

Please help to keep your company union-free. It is the best way for us to succeed and to compete in a volatile, changing marketplace.

PERSONNEL POLICIES AND PROCEDURES

DISTRIBUTION:		SUBJECT: POST-EMPLOYMENT-OFFER MEDICAL EXAMINATIONS	
EFFECTIVE DATE:	PAGE 1 OF 1		FILE UNDER SECTION
REVISION DATE:	APPROVED BY:		

PURPOSE:

To ensure that applicants brought into the workforce are free of medical and health conditions that would prohibit them from performing the essential functions of the job for which they have applied.

POLICY:

All applicants to whom an offer of employment has been extended will be required to have a company-paid physical examination before starting work.

This medical examination will be performed either at the plant by a Company physician or at a designated physician's office.

Employment will be contingent upon successful completion and acceptable results of this medical examination.

If the medical examination reveals work restrictions or direct threats to the applicant or to others, efforts will be made to provide accommodations in accordance with the Americans with Disabilities Act.

All information involving medical examinations shall be treated as confidential medical information. All such information will be accessible only to those Company officials and designated medical or professional persons with a valid need to know the results. No information collected under this policy or any related procedure will be provided to any other party without the expressed, written consent of the applicant pursuant to administrative or legal procedure or process. Any associate who willfully discloses such information in violation of Company policy will be subject to disciplinary action, up to and including discharge.

PERSONNEL POLICIES AND PROCEDURES

DISTRIBUTION:		SUBJECT: IMMIGRATION REFORM AND CONTROL ACT	
EFFECTIVE DATE:	PAGE 1 OF 3	FILE UNDER SECTION	
REVISION DATE:	APPROVED BY:		

POLICY STATEMENT:

It is the policy of the company to fully comply with the regulations of the Immigration Reform and Control Act of 1986 (as amended) enforced by the Immigration and Naturalization Service. Our company will hire only American citizens and aliens who are authorized to work in the United States.

REQUIREMENTS:

The law requires our company to do five things:
1. Have new employees fill out Section 1 of the I-9 form before they start to work.
2. Check documents establishing employees' identity and eligibility to work.
3. Fully complete Section 2 of Form I-9.
4. Retain the form for at least three years. (If the company employs the person for more than three years, the company must retain the form until one year after the person leaves our employment.)
5. Present the form for inspection to an INS or Department of Labor officer upon request. (At least three days advance notice will be given.)

PROCEDURE:

After they have accepted a job offer, have new hires complete section 1 of the I-9 form before they start to work. The company must fully complete section 2 of the I-9 within three business days of the date of hire. (If an employee is hired for less than three days, the company must complete Form I-9 before the end of the employee's first working day.)

Examine the appropriate document and check the corresponding document. Fill in document number and expiration date.

Read, fill in appropriate information, and sign the certification section.

The employee will need to provide a document or documents that establish identity and employment eligibility. Some documents establish both identity and employment eligibility. These documents appear in LIST A of the bottom half of the form. Other documents establish identity alone (LIST B) or employment eligibility alone (LIST C). The following is a complete list of acceptable documents:

LIST A:

Documents That Establish Identity and Employment Eligibility
- United States Passport (unexpired or expired).
- Certificate of United States Citizenship (INS Form N-560 or N-561).
- Certificate of Naturalization (INS Form N-560 or N-570).
- Unexpired foreign passport that:
  —Contains an unexpired stamp that reads "Processed for I-551. Temporary Evidence of Lawful Admission for permanent residence. Valid until _____. Employment authorized"; or

DISTRIBUTION:		SUBJECT: IMMIGRATION REFORM AND CONTROL ACT
EFFECTIVE DATE:	PAGE 2 OF 3	FILE UNDER SECTION
REVISION DATE:	APPROVED BY:	

—Has attached thereto a Form I-94 bearing the same name as the passport and contains an employment authorization stamp, so long as the period of endorsement has not yet expired and the proposed employment is not in conflict with any restrictions or limitations identified on the Form I-94.

- Alien Registration Receipt Card (INS Form I-151) or Resident Alien Card (INS Form I-551), provided that it contains a photograph of the bearer.
- Temporary Resident Card (INS Form I-688).
- Unexpired Employment Authorization Card (INS Form I-688A).
- Unexpired reentry permit (INS Form I-327).
- Unexpired Refugee Travel Document (INS Form I-571)
- Unexpired Employment Authorization Document issued by the INS that contains a photograph (INS Form I-688 B)

LIST B:

Documents that Establish Identity
- For individuals eighteen years of age or older:

- Driver's license or identification card issued by a state or outlying possession of the United States, provided it contains a photograph. If the driver's license or identification card does not contain a photograph, identifying information should be included, such as name, date of birth, sex, height, color of eyes, and address.
- School identification card with a photograph.
- Voter registration card.
- United States Military card or draft record.
- Identification card issued by federal, state, or local government agencies, provided it contains a photograph or information such as name, date of birth, sex, height, eye color, and address.
- Military dependent's identification card.
- Native American tribal documents.
- United States Coast Guard Merchant Mariner Card.
- Driver's license issued by a Canadian government authority.
- For individuals under age eighteen who are unable to produce one of the documents listed above:
- School record or report card
- Clinic, doctor, or hospital record
- Daycare or nursery school record

LIST C:

Documents that Establish Employment Eligibility
- U.S. Social Security Number card, other than one that has printed on its face "not valid for employment purposes." Note: This must be a card issued by the Social Security Administration; a facsimile (such as a metal or plastic reproduction that people can buy) is not acceptable.
- An original or certified copy of a birth certificate issued by a state, country, or municipal authority bearing an official seal.
- Unexpired INS employment authorization.
- Certification of Birth issued by the Department of State (Form FS-545).
- Certification of Birth Abroad issued by the Department of State (Form FS-545 or Form DS-1350).

PERSONNEL POLICIES AND PROCEDURES

DISTRIBUTION:		SUBJECT: IMMIGRATION REFORM AND CONTROL ACT	
EFFECTIVE DATE:	PAGE 3 OF 3		FILE UNDER SECTION
REVISION DATE:	APPROVED BY:		

- United States Citizen Identification Card (INS Form I-197).
- Native American tribal document.
- Identification Card for use of Resident Citizen in the United States (INS Form I-179).

The new immigration law also prohibits discrimination by employers with four or more employees. Our company will not discriminate against any individual (other than an unauthorized alien) in hiring, discharging, or recruiting or referring for a fee because of that individual's national origin or, in the case of a citizen or intending citizen, because of his or her citizenship status.

SECTION 5

Attendance and Absenteeism

The following checklist can be used to help you determine the various policy items that should be incorporated in your policy manual. Sample policy statements covering many of the items in the checklist appear in this section. They can be used to guide your policy statements.

Policy Manual Checklist

Our Policy Manual Should Cover:

1. Defining absenteeism:	Yes_____	No_____
A. Authorized	Yes_____	No_____
B. Unauthorized	Yes_____	No_____
2. Punctuality	Yes_____	No_____
3. Time away from work	Yes_____	No_____
4. Policy on excessive absenteeism	Yes_____	No_____
5. Policy on attendance control	Yes_____	No_____
6. Policy on return to work after illness/injury	Yes_____	No_____
7. Leaves of absence	Yes_____	No_____
8. Paid sick leave	Yes_____	No_____
9. Family and medical leave	Yes_____	No_____
10. Disability leave	Yes_____	No_____
A. Exempt employees	Yes_____	No_____
11. Personal leave of absence	Yes_____	No_____
12. Uniformed services leave	Yes_____	No_____
13. Jury duty	Yes_____	No_____
15. Hours of work	Yes_____	No_____

Absenteeism is not unique to one specific industry or one geographic locale. It is a major problem for every public- and private-sector organization, and the economic costs are between $20 and $25 billion a year.

More specifically, any form of absenteeism, excused or unexcused, results in disruption of work schedules, breakdown in work accomplishments, added supervisory workload, and increased payroll costs.

It has been said that an organization gets the attendance it expects, or the absenteeism it accepts. Employees generally regard work attendance and absence the same way the organization's management does.

Too many organizations, unfortunately, take little or no action on an employee's absenteeism until the situation becomes extreme. This is often a case of too little, too late. Trying to correct out-of-control absenteeism at this stage is often futile. Additionally, if action is taken only in extreme cases, other employees will see this as a sign that less severe absenteeism doesn't matter.

An important aspect of each organization is the organization's attendance culture. The idea that organizations have cultures is not new. In recent years there has been an increased focus on the culture of organizations as managers and researchers try to find ways to better understand and tap the human resources within organizations. For the manager or human resources practitioner faced with absentee problems, a direct, practical understanding of the concept of attendance culture can be useful.

This culture in an organization consists of the values, beliefs, and norms about attendance and absenteeism in that organization. It is manifested in the attitudes and behaviors of managers, supervisors, and employees regarding attendance. If the prevailing organization culture values good attendance—management sets expectations, recognizes good attendance, pays attention to all absences, and deals with related problems directly—then the attendance level of most employees will be good. If, on the other hand, the prevailing attendance culture is one in which no standards for attendance exist—good attendance is not recognized, absences go unnoticed, and action is taken only in the most extreme cases—then employee attendance is generally less than satisfactory.

The key to reducing absenteeism, therefore, is the management of all types of attendance behavior. Attendance behavior is defined as the degree to which an employee attends or is absent from regularly scheduled work. It includes both the frequency or the number of incidences of absence and the duration or length of absence, and it also takes into consideration patterns of and reasons for absence.

To effectively manage attendance and reduce overall absenteeism, a supervisor must use preventive as well as corrective measures. The focus should be on the entire spectrum of attendance behaviors:

- *Excellent attendance.* This behavior describes perfect or near-perfect attendance at work, with only rare and legitimate absences.
- *Good attendance.* Similar to ''excellent attendance''; with this behavior there are slightly higher frequencies of absence, particularly one-day absences.
- *Problem attendance.* These employees have a greater frequency of absence and are generally unreliable.
- *Chronic absenteeism.* Chronic absenteeism is extensive and recurring. The reason may be ongoing ill health, a series of unrelated extended absences, or a long-running history of frequent short-duration absences for a variety of reasons.

Attendance behavior covers these four different types of attendance, and people in each group will respond differently to the actions taken by an organization and its supervision to deal with attendance. Listed below are several actions that an organization must take to properly deal with absenteeism.

Awareness

Managers and supervisors must be aware of the exact levels of absenteeism for their work units, including each employee's specific attendance patterns and the nature of each absence. This information dictates the required action in each case. Without it, the wrong techniques may be applied, with disastrous results.

Expectations

Employees must know what is expected of them. Company standards and policies regarding work attendance and absences should be officially communicated to employees and reiterated to those whose attendance starts to slip.

Example

Managers and supervisors set the standard for employee attendance by example. Whether it is good or poor, the supervisor's attendance is seen by employees as the accepted standard.

Recognition

Everyone appreciates recognition for good performance; attendance is no different. Employees with consistently excellent or good attendance should be recognized, as should those who improve poor attendance. Many forms of recognition can be used—tangible rewards, intangible rewards, formal presentations, letters of recognition—but the most powerful form is usually genuine praise from the immediate supervisor. Let employees know that their attendance matters to the company and the entire work team.

Recognition also includes ''recognizing'' every absence of every employee, regardless of the employee's attendance record. Whenever an employee returns to work from an absence of any duration, the supervisor should greet the employee, indicating that the employee was missed while he or she was absent and that the supervisor is glad to see him or her back at work.

When an employee is absent for an extended period, supervisors should call (or visit) the absent employee periodically to express concern about the employee's (or the employee's family member's) progress, to determine whether there are any significant changes in the employee's circumstances, and to reconfirm the employee's expected return to work date.

Supervisors may protest that they are ''too busy,'' but an important part of any supervisor's job is to control costs. While such practices have obvious employee relations value, industrial experience has also demonstrated that such practices help to reduce both the incidence of absenteeism and the associated costs across the spectrum of employees.

Additional Attention

Some employees need more supervisory attention than others, whether for reasons of job performance, work habits, or attendance. While it is important to talk with each employee after each absence, it is equally important to have more specific discussions when an employee's attendance is not up to expectations and to point out the potential consequences.

Direct Action

Some types of attendance behavior, especially chronic absenteeism, require direct action from the supervisor. Direct action, which begins with documented interviews, helps to improve the attendance of some employees (or, in the extreme, causes them to leave the organization). More important, it will be seen by other employees as a sign that the organization is serious about reducing absenteeism.

The keys to success in managing any aspect of organizational life—safety, quality, cost control, productivity, attendance—are consistency and persistence. The comprehensive and continuing use of these techniques and skills at all levels in an organization produces immediate and long-lasting improvements in employee attendance.

Accurate information about attendance is essential. Although computerized approaches to collection and feedback of absence data are immensely valuable, a simple manual calendar tracking system may also be used. This system consists of a twelve-month calendar with a note-keeping space on the opposite side for each employee. This provides up-to-date, continuous attendance records for each employee.

A policy on attendance at work is the critical building block for attendance management. It should reflect what the organization expects in the way of attendance; the procedures regarding the use of various leave provisions, notification of absence procedures, return to work procedures, and required documentation for an absence; and what action should be taken in case of unacceptable levels of absenteeism.

On the following pages of this section are sample policy statements on many of the subjects listed on the checklist that you can use to describe your policies. Your written or unwritten present policy should be included in this section of the manual.

As indicated by the length of the Policy Manual Checklist, there are many areas where policy should be clearly stated. In some cases, you will not require policy on all of the checklist subjects.

This is also an area governed by state laws, so it is necessary to comply with these regulations. The policy statements and exhibits on the following pages cover the majority of policy areas in detail. Areas covered include:

Attendance and Punctuality
Excessive Absenteeism
Attendance Control
Authorized Absences
Return to Work After Illness or Injury
Leave of Absence
Paid Sick Leave
Disability Leave—Exempt Employees
Personal Leave of Absence
Uniformed Services Leave
Jury Duty
Hours of Work

PERSONNEL POLICIES AND PROCEDURES

DISTRIBUTION:		SUBJECT: ABSENCES	
EFFECTIVE DATE:	PAGE 1 OF 1	FILE UNDER SECTION	
REVISION DATE:	APPROVED BY:		

POLICY STATEMENT:

Our policies are designed to return an absentee to active service at the earliest moment commensurate with good health, safety, and reasonable personal considerations. Absences are classified as normal, excessive, or prolonged.

Excessive absence is defined as:

A. Ten days or more in one calendar year, spread over two or more separate absences.

B. Five or more different absences in one calendar year.

Prolonged absence is defined as continuous absence in excess of twenty working days.

The department head is responsible for determining the true cause of all absences and for making appropriate arrangements for the employee's return to work in cases of normal and excessive absences. Human Resources is responsible for arrangements for prolonged absences, since such absences usually involve medical, salary, tax, and insurance problems.

Absences are also classified according to reason: sickness, family or medical, death in family, marriage, pregnancy, jury duty, uniformed service, personal leave of absence, preretirement, and temporary. Policies and procedures governing these types of absence are dealt with separately in sections which follow.

PERSONNEL POLICIES AND PROCEDURES

DISTRIBUTION:		SUBJECT: ATTENDANCE AND PUNCTUALITY	
EFFECTIVE DATE:	PAGE 1 OF 2	FILE UNDER SECTION	
REVISION DATE:	APPROVED BY:		

POLICY STATEMENT:

Excessive absenteeism and tardiness adversely affects productivity, disrupts normal operating effectiveness, and overburdens other employees who must cover for the employee who is absent. Excessive absenteeism and tardiness will be grounds for disciplinary action, up to and including termination.

PROCEDURE:

A. Attendance—Occasionally, it may be necessary for an employee to be absent from work as a result of illness or injury, or for personal reasons. In such cases, employees are expected to give their supervisor as much advance notice as possible before the beginning of their scheduled starting time. This advance notification is necessary in order that proper arrangements can be made to handle their work during their absence. If the absence cannot be predicted in advance, they should notify their supervisor within the first half-hour of their starting time on the first day of absence. If they must leave work, their supervisor should be notified as far in advance as possible.

Absences are classified into two categories, Authorized and Unauthorized, as follows:

Authorized Absences—Excused absences are a result of factors beyond an employee's control, such as holidays, vacation days, work compensatory time, leaves of absence, and sick time. Should an employee need to be absent for more than three consecutive work days as a result of illness, he/she must provide the supervisor with a physician's statement indicating inability to work.

Unauthorized Absences—Unexcused absences occur upon failure to report to work as expected. Any unauthorized absence of any duration will be considered an occurrence. Employees receive a disciplinary warning for each occurrence. Two or more occurrences of unauthorized absence within a ninety-day period will result in disciplinary measures up to and including dismissal. Three or more occurrences of unauthorized absence within a twelve-month period will result in dismissal. Two consecutive days in which an employee fails to report to work as expected and without notice will be considered a voluntary quit on the part of the employee.

B. Punctuality—Being on time is most important to the efficient operation of our company. Tardiness disrupts productivity and makes it difficult for our company to function effectively and to meet our customers' needs. It is your responsibility to be at your work station at your scheduled starting time and to return from lunch periods no later than the allotted time.

Occasionally unavoidable circumstances may cause you to be late, and you are requested to notify your supervisor if you should find yourself in this situation. Two or more occurrences of tardiness within a thirty-day period will result in disciplinary action up to and including dismissal; if two such incidents occur in a thirty-day period, they will be considered as one occurrence of unexcused absence.

C. Reporting Time Away from Work—Whenever an employee is off work for a period of more than one hour, an "Off Work Report" must be completed and turned in to the Supervisor. It is the Supervisor's responsibility to see that this report is turned in complete and on a timely basis and signed by the Supervisor. In the event an employee is not capable of submitting this report, the Supervisor is to prepare the report.

If for some reason, such as an illness or emergency that comes up quickly, an employee is unable to come to work, he/she is to notify the Supervisor of the situation as soon as possible prior to the scheduled time to work. Under this situation, the Supervisor should initiate the "Off Work Report" and have the employee sign it upon return to work.

Normally time off is either without pay or charged against vacation pay. If for some reason a Manager feels that the time off should be with pay and charged to regular pay, this will require approval from the employee's Manager or

PERSONNEL POLICIES AND PROCEDURES

DISTRIBUTION:		SUBJECT: ATTENDANCE AND PUNCTUALITY	
EFFECTIVE DATE:	PAGE 2 OF 2	FILE UNDER SECTION	
REVISION DATE:	APPROVED BY:		

Officer. The Manager should denote the reasons the employee is requesting that this time off be with pay and should also indicate what is going to be required of the employee to make up the lost productivity while off work.

A separate ''Off Work Report'' should be completed for each payroll period.

The Company wishes to stress to all Management Personnel the importance of completing this form. Our Payroll records designate whether an employee is being paid for vacation or regular pay. They also keep track of any time off in an employee's file to assist us in evaluating the employee's performance and productivity. No employee or Supervisor has the authority to waive using the ''Off Work Report.''

A copy of this report is included in this manual for further reference.

PERSONNEL POLICIES AND PROCEDURES

DISTRIBUTION:		SUBJECT: ATTENDANCE AND ABSENTEEISM	
EFFECTIVE DATE:	PAGE 1 OF 2		FILE UNDER SECTION
REVISION DATE:	APPROVED BY:		

PURPOSE:

The purpose of this policy is to define a reasonable and acceptable level of absenteeism while providing fairness and consistency in disciplining associates whose level of absenteeism exceeds the maximum acceptable level.

POLICY:

The ability of the company to operate efficiently and meet its schedules depends upon regular attendance. All associates who are to be absent or tardy are expected to report the absence to the local facility switchboard attendant or their coordinator before the shift begins. If a prolonged absence is anticipated, the Human Resources Section or the coordinator should be contacted about a leave of absence.

Absence is defined as being absent from work on any scheduled workday. Each absence will be counted as one occurrence. The first two (2) workdays of consecutive absence due to a medical condition, illness, or injury of the associate or the associate's dependent child under eighteen (18) years of age living at home will be recorded as one (1) occurrence.

Additional consecutive days of absence, after the first two (2) workdays, due to the same illness or injury of the associate or the associate's dependent child under eighteen (18) years of age living at home, up to a maximum of seven (7) calendar days, will be recorded as the same single occurrence if a medical excuse for those days is provided within two (2) days of the associate's return to work.

In cases where a doctor schedules return visits for the same medical problem of the associate or the associate's dependent child, those visits occurring within ninety (90) days of the original visit will not be counted against the associate's attendance record provided written notice of the medical visit is given to the immediate supervisor prior to the scheduled visit.

Such notice should include the date and time of the return visit and should be signed by the doctor or the appropriate member of the doctor's staff. If advance notice is not possible due to the nature of the illness, then notice should be given to the immediate supervisor as soon as possible and an acceptable medical excuse provided within two days of return to work. The excuse must state that the visit was related to a prior medical condition, illness, or injury of the associate or his/her dependent child. The immediate supervisor must approve this visit prior to the return visit and may require that the date or time of the return visit be changed to limit interference with scheduled working time. Otherwise, return visits shall be considered separate occurrences.

If an associate has not requested an official leave of absence by the end of his/her shift on the seventh consecutive calendar day beginning with the first day of any period of absence, the associate will be subject to termination.

Tardiness—Tardiness is defined as reporting to work or returning from meal break after the scheduled starting time, but no later than thirty (30) minutes after the scheduled starting time. One occasion of tardiness will be charged as one-fourth of an occurrence.

Partial Day Absence—Associates who report to work later than thirty (30) minutes after the scheduled starting time or leave before the end of the shift (with management's permission) will be charged with one-half of an occurrence.

Reporting Absence—Associates who are absent a full day and do not call the designated office personnel before their scheduled starting time will be charged with one (1) additional occurrence for that occasion unless the associate calls as soon as possible and, within twenty-four (24) hours of returning to work, the associate provides documentation to show that he/she was medically incapacitated and that it was not possible to notify the company.

Approved Absences—The following absences will not count as an occurrence:
* Approved periods of bereavement leave

PERSONNEL POLICIES AND PROCEDURES

DISTRIBUTION:		SUBJECT: ATTENDANCE AND ABSENTEEISM	
EFFECTIVE DATE:	PAGE 2 OF 2	FILE UNDER SECTION	
REVISION DATE:	APPROVED BY:		

- Jury duty (must provide document in advance from clerk of court)
- Subpoenaed to appear in court (must provide documentation in advance from clerk of court)
- Approved medical treatment due to company-related workers' compensation injury
- Approved vacation and/or holiday time
- Properly reported floating holiday
- Approved leaves of absence*
- Approved military leave

Disciplinary Action–Absence records will be maintained for twelve- (12-) month periods beginning January 1 and ending December 31 of each year.

Corrective discipline will normally be administered according to the following:

Four (4) occurrences:	Verbal warning
Six (6) occurrences:	Written warning
Eight (8) occurrences:	Shall normally result in termination after review by General Affairs

Circumstances sometimes result in a verbal or written warning not being administered in accordance with this schedule, but any person who accumulates eight (8) occurrences shall be subject to termination.

Any associate who fails to contact the company prior to the start of his/her scheduled shift on the third (3rd) consecutive workday absent shall be deemed to have abandoned the job, and his/her employment will be terminated.

Regardless of any other provision of this policy, any associate who receives a combination of four (4) verbal and written warnings for absenteeism during any rolling twelve- (12-) month period shall normally be terminated after review by General Affairs.

*NOTE: Under certain conditions, consecutive day absences of more than three (3) days and/or the need for intermittent or partial day absences may make an associate eligible for a leave of absence under the provisions of the Family and Medical Leave Act of 1993 (the ''FMLA''). The specific conditions for such leaves are summarized in the FMLA policy. If an associate qualifies for a leave mandated by the FMLA, no absence occurrence will be charged against the associate for the time away from work on an approved leave of absence.

PERSONNEL POLICIES AND PROCEDURES

DISTRIBUTION:		SUBJECT: EXCESSIVE ABSENTEEISM	
EFFECTIVE DATE:	PAGE 1 OF 2	FILE UNDER SECTION	
REVISION DATE:	APPROVED BY:		

COVERAGE: All Personnel

Definition of Terms

- *Casual Absences:* Those absences that are of short duration. This includes personal business, illness, etc. As an example, the pattern is usually absences of one to two days that occur frequently. Absences that are never considered "casual" are bereavement and job injury.
- *Medical Absences:* Those absences of longer duration that usually require hospitalization. This would include, for example, time off for surgery. In most cases the absence is for a long duration but is a rare occurrence. Except for a medical absence, the employee concerned will usually have a proven record of dependability, i.e., rarely absent.
- *Occasion:* An absence that is two hours or more.

Corrective Action Guidelines for Excessive Casual Absence

1. Seven occasions of casual absence during the calendar year—Employee will be verbally counseled and told that absences are approaching an excessive level. This is simply a reminder of the policy and a request for corrective action.

2. Should an employee experience twelve (12) occurrences of casual absence during the calendar year (an average of one per month), the employee will be informed by the supervisor through the use of a written correction that his/her casual absences are excessive. The supervisor will also counsel the employee as to suggested methods for corrective action, and explain that the written correction becomes a part of the employee's personnel file, normally for a period of six months. Since attendance and punctuality are a necessary component of efficient production, the supervisor should further explain that excessive absence has an adverse effect on other employees who must be called upon to perform the absent employee's work. The supervisor should emphasize that the correction is not a form of punishment but is simply a method to alleviate an undesirable situation. In order to ensure corrective action on the part of the employee, pay raises may not be considered while the correction is on file. Dependability is one of the most important employee responsibilities; therefore, all employees concerned will be treated equally under the terms of the policy.

3. An employee who will not or cannot correct a chronic excessive absence program will be replaced by someone more dependable. Mitigating or aggravating circumstances, length of service, etc., will be discussed before any disciplinary action is taken.

Personal Business Absences

Supervisors have the authority to approve such absences; however, absences of this type should be very rare and the employee questioned to determine if the particular problem cannot be solved after working hours. The supervisor should remember that (s)he has an obligation to treat all employees equitably.

Unauthorized Absences

(As determined by supervisor after consulting with the Human Resources Department.) Any employee who fails to notify his/her supervisor when (s)he cannot report to work will receive an unauthorized absence. Each such incident will be evaluated on its merit to determine if the employee could have notified the supervisor. For example, an employee who is hospitalized as the result of an emergency may not be able to notify the supervisor; thus the absence would be authorized.

PERSONNEL POLICIES AND PROCEDURES

DISTRIBUTION:		SUBJECT: EXCESSIVE ABSENTEEISM	
EFFECTIVE DATE:	PAGE 2 OF 2	FILE UNDER SECTION	
REVISION DATE:	APPROVED BY:		

Corrective Action for Unauthorized Absence

- One day unauthorized absence—WRITTEN CORRECTION.
- Two days unauthorized absence (not necessarily consecutive) within a twelve-month period—DISCHARGE.

General

1. The immediate supervisor has the authority to ask for a physician's statement for any employee absent for personal illness. This normally is not done unless the employee has an excessive absence record.

2. It is important that all concerned bear in mind that even one day's absence can be excessive if it adversely affects other employees or the performance of the workgroup. It would, therefore, be improper to believe that any absences up to seven occasions are acceptable.

Less than 1/2 to 1 percent of (Company's Name) employees fall into the "Excessive Casual Absence" category, and it is unfair for the majority of our people to suffer as the result of "chronic offenders."

PERSONNEL POLICIES AND PROCEDURES

DISTRIBUTION:		SUBJECT: ATTENDANCE CONTROL	
EFFECTIVE DATE:	PAGE 1 OF 2	FILE UNDER SECTION	
REVISION DATE:	APPROVED BY:		

DEPARTMENT HEAD AND SUPERVISOR'S RESPONSIBILITY:

Department heads and supervisors are responsible for the proper and efficient use of employees assigned to them. They are accountable for prudent management of the investment and expense these employees represent.

When employees are absent, their share of the work must be performed by others. In most instances, absent employees are paid for time not worked. Lost time must be controlled. Therefore, the department head or supervisor must:

1. Know thoroughly the content of the organization's Attendance and Sick Leave policies.

2. Make certain that all employees reporting to them are aware of their obligations under these policies.

3. Maintain day-by-day the attendance records of employees under their supervision.

4. Speak to an employee upon his/her return to work after an absence; make appropriate notes on the employee's attendance record of all discussions with him/her concerning attendance.

5. Review frequently the attendance records of employees reporting to him/her.

6. Commend the employee whose attendance is good, encouraging him/her to maintain a good record.

7. Counsel with and, as required, warn the employee whose attendance is unsatisfactory.

8. Dismiss the employee whose attendance continues to be unsatisfactory.

ATTENDANCE CONTROL ADMINISTRATION:

1. Attendance Records

   Keep them. It is a fact of life that memory weakens with passage of time—more with some individuals, less with others, but to some extent with all. A written record remains constant. For this reason it is absolutely essential to maintain good records of all lost time, including tardiness, with complete related information.

   An Employee Attendance Record for each individual reporting to him/her is to be kept by every supervisor in a readily accessible place. These records must be kept up to date daily and reviewed regularly.

   Act on them. Attendance records are not an end in themselves but a means to an end. They are necessary tools for correction of unsatisfactory attendance. Therefore, attendance records must be utilized.

2. Reviewing Attendance Records

   Each employee's record stands alone. An employee's record of attendance is an individual record—a record each makes. What constitutes unsatisfactory attendance, therefore, must be determined on a case-by-case basis. For example, if an employee is absent only one day during a year, but this one day's absence was avoidable, this employee's attendance record was less than satisfactory, On the other hand, if an employee is absent for several weeks because of a single incapacitating illness or injury, then such an absence, by itself, does not create an unsatisfactory attendance

DISTRIBUTION:		SUBJECT: ATTENDANCE CONTROL	
EFFECTIVE DATE:	PAGE 2 OF 2	FILE UNDER SECTION	
REVISION DATE:	APPROVED BY:		

record. For eligible employees, such absences will qualify for leave under the Family and Medical Leave Act and, as such, cannot be counted against an employee's attendance record.

Detect poor attendance habits. It is essential to detect, at an early date, the beginning of poor attendance habits and to determine the underlying reasons for an individual's absences and/or tardiness. With knowledge of the reasons, the supervisor may be able to aid and rehabilitate the employee whose attendance habits are not satisfactory. The employee may have a problem that is purely administrative and can be solved by the supervisor. It may be determined that the problem can be solved only by appropriate warning and, if such action proves ineffective, by dismissal.

Consider these factors (among others) when reviewing attendance records:

* Frequency of absence
* Patterns of absence
* When absences were reported, and any unreported
* Causes of absence
* Tardiness record

Unsatisfactory attendance: Short-term and frequent absences, including tardiness, constitute an unsatisfactory record because they involve both dependability and attitude. One who is chronically unable to be present at work, whatever the reasons, simply cannot fulfill the role for which he/she was hired.

3. Disciplinary Action for Unsatisfactory Attendance

Should an employee fail to correct an unsatisfactory attendance record in spite of counseling, disciplinary action must be taken.

PERSONNEL POLICIES AND PROCEDURES

DISTRIBUTION:		SUBJECT: TIME AND ATTENDANCE ADMINISTRATION	
EFFECTIVE DATE:	PAGE 1 OF 2	FILE UNDER SECTION	
REVISION DATE:	APPROVED BY:		

PURPOSE:

The purpose of this policy is to define procedures and responsibilities for the administration of the company time and attendance procedures.

POLICY:

The immediate supervisor/coordinator is responsible for explaining to associates the company's position regarding attendance procedures and practices as well as maintaining accurate records of each associate's absences.
The supervisor's responsibilities are:

1. Checking the clock-in sheet daily and communicating the reasons for any early clock-in to the timekeeper. Associates should be instructed not to clock in earlier than twenty (20) minutes before the start of their shift unless authorized by their supervisor for overtime purposes. Associates who repeatedly clock in early after being coached will receive disciplinary action in accordance with the corrective action policy.

2. Any overtime worked by an associate should be approved in advance by his/her supervisor/coordinator.

3. Absences, tardies, and leave earlies should be noted on the associate's attendance sheet and an absentee report filled out and turned in to the timekeeper before the end of the shift.

4. It is the supervisor/coordinator's responsibility to verify if the associate has available the paid time off requested for either a floating holiday or vacation days.

PROCEDURES FOR COMPLETION OF ABSENTEE REPORT:

1. NAME: Complete, correct name (no nicknames) must be used.

2. DATE: The date shown must be the actual date of the absence. It should be listed as abbreviated weekday name, month, day, year.

3. ASSOCIATE NUMBER: Supervisor/coordinator must ensure that the correct associate number is entered on the absentee report.

4. REPORTED ABSENCE: Any absence reported to a company representative prior to the beginning of the associate's shift.

5. UNREPORTED ABSENCE: Any absence not reported to a company representative prior to the beginning of the associate's shift.

PERSONNEL POLICIES AND PROCEDURES

DISTRIBUTION:		SUBJECT: TIME AND ATTENDANCE ADMINISTRATION
EFFECTIVE DATE:	PAGE 2 OF 2	FILE UNDER SECTION
REVISION DATE:	APPROVED BY:	

PAID ABSENCES:

Absences for which an associate is paid under one of the company benefits. Hours of a paid absence are reported as hours worked for the purpose of overtime calculations or in determining holiday pay eligibility with the exception of paid time off on Saturday. These absences do not count as days missed under the Attendance Policy and Perfect Attendance Policy.

1. VACATION TIME: The associate must schedule vacation time by requesting the vacation no later than the end of his/her shift on the last day worked prior to the requested vacation day, and the request must be approved by his/her immediate supervisor. Whole or half vacation days may be taken on an unscheduled call-in basis on up to three (3) occasions in a calendar year.

    Whole or half vacation days taken on an unscheduled, call-in basis must be reported to the plant prior to the beginning of the shift, except in cases of emergencies approved by the general manager or his/her designee. In such emergency cases an associate may report his/her whole or half vacation day up to one and one-half (1-1/2) hours after the beginning of the shift.

2. JURY DUTY: An associate who is called to jury duty must contact his/her coordinator and/or Human Resources representative to discuss work requirements under this policy.

3. BEREAVEMENT: Time off for a death of an immediate family member is defined under the Bereavement Policy.

4. FLOATING HOLIDAY: An associate may take a floating holiday on either a scheduled or an unscheduled call-in basis. Floating holidays taken on a call-in basis must be reported to the plant prior to the beginning of the associate's scheduled shift.

UNPAID EXCUSED:

Absences that do not count against an associate's attendance record.

1. BEREAVEMENT: Bereavement day to attend the funeral of designated relatives who are not members of the associate's immediate family, but covered under the Bereavement Policy.

2. VOLUNTARY ABSENCE: Time distinguished by the company in which an associate may either accept work that the company provides or request time off without pay or penalty.

3. SUBPOENA: A required appearance in court for reasons other than jury duty. Documentation must be provided by the associate.

4. LEAVE OF ABSENCE: Any approved leave of absence, regardless of the length, will not count against an associate's attendance record and should be handled through the leave of absence forms.

ASSOCIATE ATTENDANCE RECORD:

Each supervisor/coordinator will keep an attendance record of his/her associates, upon which are to be listed any absences, tardies, leave of absences, etc.

When an associate is transferred to another area, his/her attendance record should be transferred to his/her assigned coordinator.

PERSONNEL POLICIES AND PROCEDURES

DISTRIBUTION:		SUBJECT: AUTHORIZED ABSENCES	
EFFECTIVE DATE:	PAGE 1 OF 1	FILE UNDER SECTION	
REVISION DATE:	APPROVED BY:		

A. APPLICABLE

This procedure applies to all regular, full-time employees of (Company Name) and is established to recognize the need of employees to be excused from work for periods of time and to mitigate any hardship by granting pay for such absences in specific circumstances.

B. POLICY

It is the policy of (Company Name) that:

1. Emergency absences, with pay, of up to five days per year are authorized for such reasons as a brief bona fide minor illness, bereavement in the immediate family, or other compelling reasons.

   This time is authorized only after assurance of the validity and bona fide purpose of the absence and is to be administered as an automatic entitlement of time off.

2. Leaves of absence indicated below are granted with pay where the conditions noted apply:

   A. Disability—Entitlement to short-term disability benefits requires thirty-one days of continuous service with the company. Benefits commence on the third day of disability. Benefits include any benefits payable under statutory laws, except in those states that require payment directly to the disabled employee. Combined benefits payable under short-term disability, statutory laws, workers' compensation, Social Security, or any similar laws will not exceed 100 percent of pay while employee is actively at work.

   Disability benefits beyond twenty-six weeks may be payable if the employee is enrolled and eligible for long-term disability benefits. Long-term disability benefits are reduced when combined with statutory benefits, workers' compensation, Social Security, or any similar laws, not to exceed 66-2/3 percent of pay while actively at work.

   B. Uniformed Service—Any employee absence for any service in the Uniformed Services of the United States of up to thirty days, including absence to take physical examinations for such service.

   C. Jury Duty—Eligible employees receive regular base rate of pay during the time served on jury duty. The employee retains all compensation received from the governmental agency.

3. Leaves of absence without pay may be authorized for the following purposes:

   A. Family and Medical—Up to twelve weeks in any twelve-month period (eligible employee).

   B. Extended Illness—Maximum: one year (less any disability leave, emergency absence, and vacation time for which paid).

   C. Military Service Longer than Thirty Days (voluntary or involuntary—any employee)—Maximum: Five years plus any involuntary extension.

   D. Approved Personal Leave—Maximum: One year.

   Peace Corps Service is considered under the same terms and conditions as a personal leave of absence. The maximum of one year for a personal leave may be extended to two years for Peace Corps duty.

4. Employees returning from extended leave (such as personal leaves of absence) are tendered such job opportunities as their qualifications and experience may warrant, consistent with position vacancies existing at that time. Where the law provides otherwise, as in the case of employees returning from uniformed service leave, the specific re-employment requirements are observed.

5. Employees returning from a family or medical leave will be reinstated to the same or an equivalent job. Employees returning from a medical leave in excess of three consecutive calendar days must provide a medical certificate of fitness to resume normal work activities, including any limitations or restrictions.

PERSONNEL POLICIES AND PROCEDURES

DISTRIBUTION:		SUBJECT: RETURN TO WORK AFTER ILLNESS OR INJURY	
EFFECTIVE DATE:	PAGE 1 OF 1	FILE UNDER SECTION	
REVISION DATE:	APPROVED BY:		

POLICY STATEMENT:

Employees who are off the job due to illness or injury for more than three workdays will be required to secure return-to-work permission from the Health and Safety Administrator.

GUIDELINES:

1. In no event may the supervisors concerned allow an employee who has been absent due to illness or injury of more than three consecutive calendar days to report to work without a medical certification.

2. If any illness or injury requires the services of an attending physician or practitioner, the employee must present to the company medical certification of fitness for duty from the physician that (s)he is able to return to work and specify any restrictions or direct threats.

3. No employee may return to work unless (s)he has been certified as being able to return to work and perform safely in his/her normal job. This means that employees who have restrictions placed upon them by the attending physician or practitioner that are related to specific duties will be allowed to return to work only after consideration of appropriate accommodation of the restriction(s).

4. When an employee has been certified by a physician or practitioner as "totally and permanently disabled" and begins receiving long-term disability benefits through workers' compensation, long-term disability, or Social Security insurance, the employee may be terminated at that time from active employment. Hospitalization, major medical, and life insurance coverage will remain in effect as outlined in these policies.

5. Employees who apply for sick pay, weekly indemnity, or other health-care benefits will be required to complete the appropriate forms. Payment of such benefits will begin only when the employee concerned provides this important documentation.

6. In case of occupational disability, employees *will not* be eligible for sick pay or weekly indemnity benefits. They will, however, receive workers' compensation benefits as outlined in the appropriate state laws.

PERSONNEL POLICIES AND PROCEDURES

DISTRIBUTION:		SUBJECT: WORK INTERRUPTIONS	
EFFECTIVE DATE:	PAGE 1 OF 1	FILE UNDER SECTION	
REVISION DATE:	APPROVED BY:		

POLICY STATEMENT:

A. Lunch Hour

The lunch period is forty-five minutes. On paydays the period is extended to one hour to permit the cashing of salary checks.

Variations from the policy are subject to the following instructions.

1. Shorter lunch hour

   a. The department head may not arrange for a lunch period shorter than forty-five minutes.
   b. Employees may not forgo the lunch period in order to shorten the workday.

2. Longer lunch hour

   The department head may, at his or her discretion, arrange for a longer period on occasion, but not as a regular matter.

B. Supper Period

1. Overtime workers

   A supper period of not less than twenty minutes to be taken between 5 and 7 P.M. must be granted to all employees whose work period commences before 12 noon and continues after 7 P.M.

2. Second-shift workers

   A meal period of not less than forty-five minutes to be taken midway in the shift must be granted to all employees beginning work between 1 P.M. and 6 A.M.

C. Other Work Interruptions

There is an official coffee break of no more than fifteen minutes' duration once a day. There are no other official breaks.

Employees may not leave the building during normal working hours without consent except for business purposes.

PERSONNEL POLICIES AND PROCEDURES

DISTRIBUTION:		SUBJECT: PERSONAL LEAVE OF ABSENCE	
EFFECTIVE DATE:	PAGE 1 OF 2	FILE UNDER SECTION	
REVISION DATE:	APPROVED BY:		

PURPOSE:

The purpose of this policy is to define the procedure under which an associate may receive an approved leave of absence for personal reasons.

POLICY:

The company realizes that there may be times when urgent personal situations may result in associates needing to have time away from work. For this reason, a Personal Leave may be granted for a minimum period of seven (7) consecutive calendar days and a maximum of thirty-six (36) weeks within a rolling twelve- (12-) month period, looking back in time from the date the request for Personal Leave is submitted.

PROCEDURE:

A. To be eligible for a Personal Leave, an associate must have been employed for ninety (90) days prior to the date the requested leave of absence is to begin. If an associate wishes to take an emergency Personal Leave of Absence, he/she should submit a Leave of Absence Request form to his/her supervisor/coordinator. If the need for Personal Leave is foreseeable, the associate will be required to complete a "Leave of Absence Request" form at least thirty (30) days prior to the date the requested Personal Leave is to begin. If the need for Personal Leave is not foreseeable, the associate must notify his/her supervisor/coordinator as soon as practicable under the circumstances.

B. Personal Leaves will not be granted for vacation purposes or to attend to routine personal business that could be handled during normal, nonworking hours. Personal Leaves will not be granted for reasons related to a second job or for additional sources of income. Instead, Personal Leaves are intended to allow associates with urgent personal situations that are not covered by other leave of absence policies to take time off to deal with those situations.

C. Each Personal Leave request will be carefully evaluated by the affected supervisor and Human Resources Department representative. If a Personal Leave is approved, the associate will be required to use any accrued, unused vacation during the approved Personal Leave, unless the leave is for the associate's own health condition. Associates on approved Personal Leave will not receive pay for time lost or holiday pay, other than earned, unused vacation days or shutdown pay.

D. Associates will not lose seniority or other benefits that were accumulated before the Personal Leave began. Associates will not, however, be entitled to discretionary raises, promotions, or other benefits that become available during the period of leave, and no additional paid leave will accrue during a leave of absence. Additional benefits will not be earned by an associate until he/she returns to work on a regular basis.

E. Associates on approved leave of absence will have the right to return to their regular job provided they return within ninety (90) days of the date on which the leave began. Associates who fail to return from an approved leave within ninety (90) days of the date on which the leave began will have the right to return to their regular work group provided they return within one hundred eighty (180) days of the date on which the leave began.

125

DISTRIBUTION:		SUBJECT: PERSONAL LEAVE OF ABSENCE
EFFECTIVE DATE:	PAGE 2 OF 2	FILE UNDER SECTION
REVISION DATE:	APPROVED BY:	

F. If the associate's most recent job or a comparable job for which he/she is qualified is not available at the time the leave of absence ends, the associate will be given the opportunity to accept other open jobs for which he/she is qualified and eligible. The maximum leave period is forty-eight (48) weeks [twelve (12) weeks of FMLA, plus thirty-six (36) weeks of Personal Leave].

G. If an associate fails to return to work at the beginning of his/her regular shift on the agreed-upon date of return, or if he/she fails to notify the company at the beginning of his/her regular shift of his/her inability to return to work as scheduled so that a determination can be made as to the availability of additional leave, his/her employment will terminate effective at the beginning of the shift on the first scheduled workday that is missed by the associate following the expiration of the leave.

H. An associate who is granted a leave of absence may continue his/her insurance coverage, but must arrange with the Human Resources Department to pay all required premiums.

PERSONNEL POLICIES AND PROCEDURES

DISTRIBUTION:		SUBJECT: PERSONAL LEAVE OF ABSENCE	
EFFECTIVE DATE:	PAGE 1 OF 2	FILE UNDER SECTION	
REVISION DATE:	APPROVED BY:		

A. INTRODUCTION

(Company Name) employees may be granted personal leave without pay for periods not to exceed one year. Peace Corps service is considered under the same terms and conditions as a personal leave, with the exception that the maximum may be extended to two years for such duty.

B. CONDITIONS

1. Compelling Personal Reasons—Conditions under which personal leave may be granted include such compelling personal reasons as bereavement, pursuits connected with the employee's present or future work, or similar personal reasons.

2. Time Limitations—When granted immediately following a disability leave, the combined total leave period cannot exceed one year.

3. Payment for unused vacation when the employee is granted a personal leave is made as a lump sum immediately at the time the employee is placed on a personal leave. The vacation lump-sum payment does not extend the one-year limit in combining a disability leave and an approved personal leave without pay. However, personal leave may not normally be used for the purpose of extending a vacation.

4. Status of an employee is not changed to a return to work status to accommodate the vacation payment when going from a paid medical leave to an unpaid personal leave.

C. INITIATING PERSONAL LEAVE

1. Employees request a personal leave in writing through their supervisors, stating the reason for the leave and the period of time to be covered. The request should be made at least one month in advance whenever possible.

2. Supervisors initiate a personal leave using the proper forms, to be effective on the employee's last day of work. If the employee has not exhausted all vacation time, the leave should begin on the date the vacation is exhausted. The forms should then be forwarded to the next level of supervision for approval, after which they are to be sent to the Human Resources Manager.

3. The Human Resources Manager must provide the employee with written advice outlining the notification process stated in paragraph F.1.

D. REINSTATEMENT FROM PERSONAL LEAVE

1. Position Availability—The granting of a personal leave implies that employees returning from leaves of short duration (60 days or less) will be returned to their former positions. Employees on longer leaves will be considered for their former positions or like available positions for which they are qualified. Employees not returned to active employment are laid off provided they comply with paragraph F.1 of this procedure.

2. Vacation Reinstatement—Employees who return to the active payroll by the expiration date of an approved leave will have the accrued vacation standing to their credit at the beginning of the leave reinstated.

3. Instrument—The instrument executing a reinstatement from personal leave is the employee status and change notice. It is prepared by the cognizant supervisor, subject to approval by the Human Resources Department concerned.

PERSONNEL POLICIES AND PROCEDURES

DISTRIBUTION:		SUBJECT: PERSONAL LEAVE OF ABSENCE
EFFECTIVE DATE:	PAGE 2 OF 2	FILE UNDER SECTION
REVISION DATE:	APPROVED BY:	

E. TERMINATION FROM PERSONAL LEAVE

1. Other Employment—Employees accepting gainful employment or entering into personal business ventures while on an approved personal leave are deemed to have "quit without notice" and are terminated as of the starting day of the leave.

2. Failure to Return—Employees who do not return to active employment at the expiration of an approved leave are terminated as of the last date of the approved leave and will be paid for any vacation that had accrued to their credit at the time the leave began.

3. Instrument—Terminations from personal leave are executed by the department supervisor on the standard employee status and change notice in accordance with notice given by the Human Resources Department. Effective the date of termination, all employment rights, nonvested benefits, and insurance coverage in effect are forfeited, with the exception of life insurance, which, if still in effect, continues for thirty-one days following the date of termination.

F. LAYOFF FROM PERSONAL LEAVE

1. If the company is not able to offer the employee his or her former position or a like available position upon return from a leave of sixty days or less, the employee is laid off.

   Employees on personal leave of more than sixty days' duration are subject to the following: The employee must contact his/her Human Resources Department in writing thirty days prior to the end of a leave stating the date (s)he intends to return to work. If, after receiving the notice required, the company is not able to offer the employee his/her former position or a like available position, the employee is laid off. Failure to comply with this notification process will result in termination not classified as layoff.

2. In cases of layoff, the employee will be paid for any vacation that had been accrued to his/her credit at the time the leave began.

3. Instrument—A layoff from personal leave is executed by the department supervisor on an employee status and change notice in accordance with notice given by the cognizant Human Resources Department. Effective the date of layoff, all employment rights, nonvested benefits, and any insurance coverage in effect are forfeited, with the exception of life insurance, which, if still in effect, continues for thirty-one days following the date of layoff.

PERSONNEL POLICIES AND PROCEDURES

DISTRIBUTION:		SUBJECT: SICK LEAVE	
EFFECTIVE DATE:	PAGE 1 OF 1	FILE UNDER SECTION	
REVISION DATE:	APPROVED BY:		

PURPOSE:

To establish the company's policy and to define the conditions under which paid sick leave is authorized.

POLICY:

The company realizes that inability to work because of illness or injury may cause serious economic hardship. For this reason, we provide a paid-sick-leave plan for all full-time employees. The following schedule details payments that will be made to full-time employees.

1. All full-time employees who have worked at least six months will be eligible for wage continuation during periods of illness.

2. After six months of employment, each employee will be credited with six (6) days' sick-leave credit. For each month of employment thereafter, the employee will receive one-half (1/2) day's sick leave credit for each month of continued employment.

3. Sick leave will be paid only for those days regularly scheduled for work. Upon written request, vacation may be substituted for sick leave after twelve months regular service.

4. Sick-leave payments will be made by separate check upon return to work, or once each month in case of extended illnesses.

5. Employees receiving workers' compensation benefits are not entitled to sick-leave payments also.

6. It is the responsibility of the employee's supervisor, in conjunction with the store manager, to determine that absence from work is due to actual illness or injury. If a serious health condition absence exceeds three (3) consecutive calendar days, the employee must provide medical certification within fifteen (15) calendar days to support the absence and give it to the store manager or department head. Failure to comply may result in delay or denial of leave.

PERSONNEL POLICIES AND PROCEDURES

DISTRIBUTION:		SUBJECT: DISABILITY LEAVE (SALARIED EXEMPT PERSONNEL)	
EFFECTIVE DATE:	PAGE 1 OF 1	FILE UNDER SECTION	
REVISION DATE:	APPROVED BY:		

POLICY STATEMENT:

It is the policy of (Company Name) to provide financial aid to all regular, full-time, salaried (exempt) employees who are unable to work due to personal illness or injury.

ELIGIBILITY:

All regular, salaried (exempt), full-time employees are eligible for paid-sick-leave benefits from the first day of employment, except those employees who are absent from work due to illnesses or injuries which are job-related. In this event, such employees are eligible for Workers' Compensation benefits only. Compensation will differ by state according to benefits outlined in the particular state's laws.

GUIDELINES:

1. No reduction in pay will be made for absence, due to non-job-related illness or accident, not to exceed two months.

2. Any exempt employee required to be absent from work, due to non-job-related sickness or accident, beyond two months will be compensated at 65 percent of base pay for a period not to exceed an additional four months.

3. At the termination of the above four-month period, salary continuation will cease, at which time the employee may apply for Long-Term Disability benefits.

4. In no event may a salaried (exempt) employee exceed the above specified allowance in any twelve-month period. In addition, once the full amount of sick pay has been exhausted during the twelve-month period, no additional sick pay is provided until said employee has returned to work and been on the active payroll for a period of one year. Deviation from this stipulation must be approved in advance by the Management Committee.

PERSONNEL POLICIES AND PROCEDURES

DISTRIBUTION:		SUBJECT: UNIFORMED SERVICES LEAVE OF ABSENCE	
EFFECTIVE DATE:	PAGE 1 OF 3	FILE UNDER SECTION	
REVISION DATE:	APPROVED BY:		

PURPOSE:

The purpose of this policy is to describe the company's position with respect to associates who request a leave of absence in order to satisfy a military obligation.

POLICY:

It is the policy of the company to support and accommodate associates who volunteer or who are called to serve military obligations (voluntary or involuntary) in the Armed Services of the United States, or any of the reserve components of these services.

PROCEDURE:

A. ACTIVE MILITARY SERVICE:

1. Associates who are called or volunteer to serve on active status in any of the military services components will be provided a Uniformed Services Leave of Absence (USLA) from work to cover the time missed as a result of the military service.

2. Leaves of absence in these cases will be limited to a maximum of five (5) years unless extended in accordance with federal law.

3. Associates who enlist or who are called to active military service should complete a "Request for Uniformed Services Leave of Absence" in advance and attach a copy of their written orders to report to duty.

4. Associates who are called or who volunteer to serve on active military status will not receive company pay or company-paid benefits during the time they are on active duty.

5. Associates who are discharged from the service following active military service must apply for re-employment within ninety (90) days of the date of their discharge, unless such period is extended by law or mutual agreement between the company and the associate.

    Associates in these situations will be re-employed in the same job classification they held prior to their active military service and will be given the same length of service, benefits and pay level that they would have been entitled to had they not served in the military. Information on their qualified plan status can be found in the Summary Plan Description for these benefits.

    In certain situations it may not be possible because of current production requirements to place associates returning from active military service in the same job that they held previously. They will, however, be returned to the same job classification and will be assigned to the area/shift where current openings exist.

6. All associates who have been on a USLA for at least seven (7) consecutive calendar days will be required to submit to a drug and alcohol screening as a condition for returning to work.

B. EXTENDED MILITARY TRAINING:

1. Associates may request a USLA to cover extended periods of military training [more than thirty (30) days] in the Uniformed Services of the United States.

2. To request a USLA for extended military training leave, associates must complete a "Request for Uniform Services Leave of Absence" form and attach a copy of the written orders.

PERSONNEL POLICIES AND PROCEDURES

DISTRIBUTION:		SUBJECT: UNIFORMED SERVICES LEAVE OF ABSENCE
EFFECTIVE DATE:	PAGE 2 OF 3	FILE UNDER SECTION
REVISION DATE:	APPROVED BY:	

3. While associates are on USLA, they will not receive any compensation from the company beyond that referred to in Section C-3, and benefits will remain in effect for up to thirty (30) calendar days.

4. After completion of their training, associates must notify the company and must return to work at the beginning of the next regularly scheduled working period unless the leave period is extended by mutual agreement.

5. Associates returning from USLA will be returned to the same job classification that they held prior to their leave and will be given length of service, pay level, and other rights and benefits that they would have been entitled to had they not been on USLA.

    In certain situations, it may not be possible because of current production requirements to place associates returning from an extended leave in the same job that they held previously. They will, however, be returned to the same job classification and will be assigned to the area/shift where current openings exist.

6. All associates who have been on a USLA for at least seven (7) consecutive calendar days will be required to submit to a drug and alcohol screening as a condition for returning to work.

C. SHORT-TERM MILITARY TRAINING: SUMMER CAMP/WEEKEND TRAINING:

1. Associates who are members of the Uniformed Services of the United States and who are called to perform short-term military training will be granted a USLA to cover the time that is missed from work (including reasonable travel time).

2. To receive approval for the leave outlined in Section C-1, associates must complete a "Request for Uniformed Services Leave of Absence" form and submit it to their coordinator/supervisor for review/approval. A copy of the associate's military orders, which details the dates to be served, must be included with this request.

3. Regular associates who are serving on short-term military training will receive payment from the company equal to the difference between their regular base rate of pay (including premiums, if applicable) and the amount of military pay they actually receive (excluding meals, lodging, and travel) for each regularly scheduled workday in a regular workweek up to a maximum of ten (10) regular workdays in a calendar year.

    The pay will not exceed eight (8) hours per day and will be limited to a maximum of ten (10) regular workdays in a calendar year.

4. Associates who participate in short-term military training must report for work at the beginning of the next regularly scheduled workday after completion of training.

5. In order to receive company-paid benefits for short-term military training, the associate must submit a copy of his/her military pay record to the company.

6. Associates may elect to take vacation to cover their time spent on short-term military duty. In these cases they will receive full vacation benefits and will experience no reduction in vacation pay due to any military pay received.

7. During USLA for short-term military training, associate benefits and length of service will remain in effect and the associate will be provided the opportunity to return to the same position he/she held prior to the leave.

8. All associates who have been on a USLA for at least seven (7) consecutive calendar days will be required to submit to a drug and alcohol screening as a condition for returning to work.

9. Absence due to USLA for short-term military training will not affect the associate's attendance record.

PERSONNEL POLICIES AND PROCEDURES

DISTRIBUTION:		SUBJECT: UNIFORMED SERVICES LEAVE OF ABSENCE	
EFFECTIVE DATE:	PAGE 3 OF 3	FILE UNDER SECTION	
REVISION DATE:	APPROVED BY:		

D. PUBLIC EMERGENCY:

1. If an associate is called to serve in the Uniformed Services of the United States because of a public emergency, he/she will be granted a USLA to cover the amount of time lost from work.

    In these situations associates should complete a "Request for Uniformed Services Leave of Absence" form and attach a copy of their written orders.

2. In case of a public emergency, associates will receive the difference in compensation as outlined for up to thirty (30) calendar days in each calendar year.

3. Associates serving in cases of a public emergency will be covered by company benefit plans (subject to normal exclusions contained in those plans) for up to six (6) months of such active duty.

4. If a period of active service for public emergency extends beyond six (6) months, it will be considered active military service as described and associates will be afforded rights as detailed in that section.

5. All associates who have been on a USLA for at least seven (7) consecutive calendar days will be required to submit to a drug and alcohol screening as a condition for returning to work.

PERSONNEL POLICIES AND PROCEDURES

DISTRIBUTION:		SUBJECT: JURY DUTY	
EFFECTIVE DATE:	PAGE 1 OF 1	FILE UNDER SECTION	
REVISION DATE:	APPROVED BY:		

A. APPLICABLE

Jury duty leave will be granted to nonbargaining employees called for such duty. (Company Name) will continue the employment of employees called for the duration of the jury duty assignment. The company expects employees to meet their assigned responsibilities to the best of their ability during such periods.

B. DEFINITION

Jury duty is defined as the duty requested by any legally constituted court or governmental unit, whether of a municipal, county, district, state, or federal nature. Jury duty is further defined as including not only active participation as a juror but also where an employee is summoned for examination as a possible jury member or where an employee is called as a witness in a worker's compensation action involving another employee and the company.

C. PROCEDURE

1. Summons to Jury Duty—A call to jury duty is recognized by the company only through submission, by the employee, of an authentic summons issued by the court of the governmental unit involved.

2. Time Record—Employees receiving a call to jury duty will immediately report this information to their supervisors and show the summons. Absence for jury duty will be recorded as such on an employee's regular attendance report forms.

PERSONNEL POLICIES AND PROCEDURES

DISTRIBUTION:		SUBJECT: JURY DUTY	
EFFECTIVE DATE:	PAGE 1 OF 1		FILE UNDER SECTION
REVISION DATE:	APPROVED BY:		

PURPOSE:

The purpose of this policy is to define the company's position with respect to associates who are called to serve on jury duty or who are subpoenaed to appear in court.

POLICY:

The company supports associates who fulfill their duty as citizens to their communities. If they are summoned for jury duty or are subpoenaed to appear in court, they will be excused from work for the period of time served. Service includes required reporting for jury duty when summoned, whether or not they are selected.

PROCEDURE:

A. An associate who is called to serve on jury duty should notify his/her supervisor or coordinator. He/she will issue a "Jury Duty Pass" for each day the associate serves on the jury.

   The jury duty summons or court subpoena must be presented to document the necessity of the absence.

B. The associate's supervisor/coordinator will arrange for him/her to receive regular straight-time pay for scheduled lost work time due to jury duty as outlined below:

   1. If the associate is able to work at least one (1) hour prior to reporting for jury duty, or if the associate can return to work at least one (1) hour after being excused from jury duty, he/she is expected to do so.

   2. Travel time for associates who live outside the county in which the plant is located will be determined by plant management and communicated to associates by posting on the Controlled Communication Center.

   3. Second- and third-shift associates will be exempt from overtime at the end of the shift on the day before jury duty, but will be expected to work all regularly scheduled hours.

   4. Associates using the time schedule below may work longer than the hours listed, but will be paid only a maximum of eight (8) hours unless the associate worked outside the normal work hours of his/her shift and is otherwise qualified for the overtime.

   5. Regardless of overtime eligibility, the associate will be compensated at his/her overtime rate for any time outside of his/her normal work hours in conjunction with the time schedule.

   6. It is the responsibility of the associate to discuss jury duty requirements with his/her coordinator/supervisor and/or Human Resources representative.

   7. Second- and third-shift associates will be expected to work a reduced schedule based on time at jury duty.

C. If an associate is subpoenaed, he/she will not receive regular pay for time lost; however, it will not affect his/her attendance record.

D. Absences due to appearances in court outside the immediate geographical region that require an absence of several full days will be dealt with on a case-by-case basis by the Human Resources Section.

PERSONNEL POLICIES AND PROCEDURES

DISTRIBUTION:		SUBJECT: EMERGENCY ABSENCE	
EFFECTIVE DATE:	PAGE 1 OF 1	FILE UNDER SECTION	
REVISION DATE:	APPROVED BY:		

A. APPLICABLE

Emergency absence is an absence of short duration granted for minor illness, bereavement in the immediate family, or other compelling personal reasons. Emergency absence should be used when a (Company Name) employee determines that he or she cannot come to or remain at work because of hazardous weather conditions. Emergency absence normally should not be used for absences that exceed five (5) consecutive workdays when such absence is for bereavement in the immediate family or other compelling personal reasons. Emergency absence, if available, must be used for absences due to minor illness up to two consecutive workdays for each period of disability.

B. ALLOWANCES

Employees with one or more years of continuous employment with the company will be granted an allowance of six (6) days per year of emergency absence with pay, credited to the employee on the anniversary hire date.

1. Newly hired nonexempt employees shall accrue emergency absence allowance at the rate of one day per month worked to a maximum of six (6) days allowance during the first year of employment.

2. Newly hired exempt employees will be eligible for the full six (6) days annual allowance effective as of their hire date.

3. Exempt employees are eligible for full salary if absent only part of a week even though emergency absence allowance may have been exhausted. Salary for any full week not worked when emergency absence allowance has been exhausted may be considered at the discretion of the supervisor. Scheduled company-designated holidays are considered as workdays for this purpose. Approval of an exempt employee's pay when emergency absence has been exhausted is at the discretion of the supervisor, by coding the timecard ''to pay'' or ''not to pay.''

4. When ''with pay'' allowance has been exhausted, emergency absence without pay shall be granted to the degree that it is warranted, and with the provision that habitual or excessive absenteeism will not be condoned or encouraged.

5. Emergency absence allowance unused during any year shall not be carried over into the next year. An employee who is on excused absence as of the anniversary hire date shall not be eligible for the next year's emergency absence allowance until the employee returns to work.

6. Upon return from an unpaid leave of absence, the employee's emergency absence balance is reinstated if the employee's anniversary hire date did not occur during the leave period. The full six (6) days are reinstated if the employee's anniversary date did occur within the leave period.

C. GENERAL

1. Employees who begin emergency absence for sickness that continues through an excess of two consecutive workdays will be paid from the short-term disability plan.

2. Payments for emergency absence will be reduced by the amount of legislated compensation excluding state statutory disability benefits that may be paid to the employee. State statutory disability benefits are included in emergency absence pay not to exceed 100 percent of pay while actively at work.

3. Even though the company provides six (6) days per year of emergency absence, these days are to be used only for the absences cited in the introduction. These days are not intended as additional vacation days or to be used for noncompany scheduled local, legal, religious, or ethnic holidays.

4. Approved nonemergency absences should be charged to unused vacation, personal floater holiday, or unpaid absence.

DISTRIBUTION:		SUBJECT: FAMILY AND MEDICAL LEAVE OF ABSENCE	
EFFECTIVE DATE:	PAGE 1 OF 4	FILE UNDER SECTION	
REVISION DATE:	APPROVED BY:		

PURPOSE:

The purpose of this policy is to define the company's position with respect to associates who need to miss work due to personal or family medical situations.

POLICY:

(Name of Company) is covered by the federal Family and Medical Leave Act (the "FMLA") and will comply with the requirements of the Act. Under the provisions of the FMLA, eligible associates are entitled to take a leave for the following reasons:

A. Parental Leave:

1. Birth of a child or in order to care for a child [must be taken within twelve (12) months of the birth];
2. The adoption or foster care of a child [must be taken within twelve (12) months of the adoption or placement in foster care].

B. Medical Leave

1. The need to care for an associate's spouse, son,* daughter,* or parent who has a serious health condition; or
2. The associate's own serious health condition.

*Children must be either under the age of eighteen (18), or age eighteen (18) or older and "incapable of self-care" because of a mental or physical disability.

Although leave may be taken for any of the above-listed reasons, an associate is entitled to a total of twelve (12) weeks of FMLA-covered leave within a rolling twelve- (12-) month period, measured backward from the date of the most recent request for a covered leave of absence. This means that each time an associate requests a leave under the provisions of this policy, the available time for a leave of absence will be the balance of the total twelve (12) weeks that has not been used during the twelve (12) month period immediately preceding the commencement of leave.

ELIGIBILITY:

To be eligible for leave, an associate must have been employed by (Name of Company) for at least twelve (12) months and have worked for at least 1,250 hours during the twelve- (12-) month period immediately preceding the commencement of leave.

NOTICE REQUIREMENTS:

Anyone requesting a leave of absence under this policy should see his/her Human Resources representative and complete the proper leave request form.

PERSONNEL POLICIES AND PROCEDURES

DISTRIBUTION:		SUBJECT: FAMILY AND MEDICAL LEAVE OF ABSENCE	
EFFECTIVE DATE:	PAGE 2 OF 4	FILE UNDER SECTION	
REVISION DATE:	APPROVED BY:		

Where the need for leave is foreseeable, the request must be submitted at least thirty (30) days prior to the desired beginning of the leave of absence. Failure to give at least thirty (30) days notice of foreseeable need for a leave of absence may delay the start of such leave until thirty (30) days after the date the notice is received by the company.

If the need for a leave is not foreseeable, the associate must provide at least verbal notification to his/her supervisor/coordinator within three (3) days of learning of the need for leave. In such an event, the associate must submit a written request for leave to his/her Human Resources Section as soon as practicable after giving verbal notice.

CERTIFICATION OF THE NEED FOR LEAVE:

In addition to providing notice of the need for leave, any associate who needs to have an FMLA-covered Medical Leave of Absence must present certification of the need for a leave of absence. This certification must be provided within fifteen (15) days of the request unless it is not practicable under the circumstances. The Human Resources Department has forms available for an associate to have completed by his/her health-care provider. Failure to provide certification may result in the associate's leave being delayed, denied, or revoked.

NOTE: (Name of Company) reserves the right to a second or third medical certification at company expense. (Name of Company) further reserves the right to require recertification of the continuance of a serious health condition at thirty-(30-) day intervals. Recertification may also be required if:

♦ An associate requests an extension of leave;
♦ Circumstances described by the original certification have changed significantly;
♦ (Name of Company) receives information that casts doubt upon the continuing validity of the certification; or
♦ An associate is unable to return to work because of the continuation, recurrence, or onset of a serious health condition.

INTERMITTENT LEAVE:

Generally, FMLA leave must be taken in a single block. Under certain circumstances, however, FMLA leave may be taken on an intermittent or reduced work schedule basis.

A Parental Leave of Absence may be taken intermittently or on a reduced work schedule basis if the associate and the company can agree on the schedule requested by the associate.

A Medical Leave of Absence may be taken intermittently or on a reduced work schedule basis if the requesting associate produces the required certification that there is a medical need for a leave of absence and that the medical need is best accommodated through an intermittent leave or reduced work schedule.

NOTE: (Name of Company) reserves the right to require a second or third medical opinion in appropriate cases where authorized to do so by the FMLA.

If medical leave is requested on an intermittent or reduced work schedule basis, the company may, at the discretion of management, transfer the associate temporarily to an available alternative position for which the associate is qualified and which better accommodates recurring periods of leave than does the associate's regular position. Any such transfer will be to a job that offers pay and benefits that are equivalent to those available in the associate's regular job.

PERSONNEL POLICIES AND PROCEDURES

DISTRIBUTION:		SUBJECT: FAMILY AND MEDICAL LEAVE OF ABSENCE	
EFFECTIVE DATE:	PAGE 3 OF 4	FILE UNDER SECTION	
REVISION DATE:	APPROVED BY:		

FMLA LEAVE IS UNPAID LEAVE FOR HOURLY ASSOCIATES:

Associates on approved FMLA leave of absence will be required to use any earned, unused vacation days during the approved leave of absence unless the leave is for the associate's own serious health condition.

Hourly associates on approved FMLA leave of absence will not receive pay for lost time other than earned, unused vacation or shutdown pay.

RETURN TO WORK:

An associate returning from a leave taken because of his/her own health condition must provide certification from his/her health-care provider that he/she is able to return to work. An associate on approved leave of absence will have the right to return to his/her regular job provided he/she returns within ninety (90) days of the date on which the leave began. An associate who fails to return from an approved leave within ninety (90) days of the date on which the leave began will have the right to return to his/her regular workgroup provided he/she returns within one hundred eighty (180) days of the date on which the leave began.

Associates will not lose any seniority or other benefits that were accumulated before FMLA leave was taken. Associates may not, however, be entitled to discretionary raises, promotions, or other benefits that become available during the period of leave.

If an associate does not return to work when his/her leave of absence expires or notifies the company of his/her inability to return in order to determine whether additional leave is available, (Name of Company) will terminate his/her employment effective at the beginning of the associate's shift on the first scheduled workday that is missed following the expiration of the FMLA leave of absence.

EXEMPTION FOR CERTAIN ASSOCIATES:

Salaried associates in the highest-paid ten percent (10%) of the company workforce are not guaranteed job restoration if returning such associates to work would cause substantial and grievous economic injury to the company. However, these associates will still be entitled to continuation of health benefits throughout the leave period. (Name of Company) will notify associates in writing at the time leave is requested or at such time as the company determines that the associate qualifies for this exemption. If the leave has already begun, the associate will be given the option of deciding whether or not to return to work after receiving the notice. An associate who will not be restored will be considered to be on leave for the duration of his/her leave.

SPOUSE AGGREGATION:

In the case where both an associate and his/her spouse are employed by (Name of Company), the aggregate number of weeks to which both associates are entitled because of the birth or placement of a child or to care for a parent with a serious health condition will be limited to twelve (12) workweeks during any twelve- (12-) month period. This limitation does not apply in instances where leave is taken because of an associate's own serious health condition or to care for a spouse or child with a serious health condition.

PERSONNEL POLICIES AND PROCEDURES

DISTRIBUTION:		SUBJECT: FAMILY AND MEDICAL LEAVE OF ABSENCE
EFFECTIVE DATE:	PAGE 4 OF 4	FILE UNDER SECTION
REVISION DATE:	APPROVED BY:	

HEALTH INSURANCE:

An associate away from work due to FMLA leave may continue medical insurance coverage while on leave by timely payment of his/her portion of the monthly insurance premium on the same day such payment would be required if payment were made by payroll deduction. Where the need for family leave of absence is foreseeable, the associate will be asked to sign an agreement before the leave of absence begins that:

* Discloses the amount that the associate must remit on a timely basis to retain the coverage; and
* Indicates that the associate understands his/her insurance premium payment obligations.

If the FMLA leave is not foreseeable, this agreement must be signed as soon as possible after the leave begins.

An associate's failure to pay premiums within thirty (30) days of the due date for such premiums will result in the loss of his/her insurance coverage.

If an associate does not return to work at the end of an approved FMLA leave, he/she may be required to repay the company for the insurance premiums it paid.

SECTION 6

Wage and Salary Administration

The following checklist can be used to help you determine the various policy items that should be incorporated in your policy manual. Sample policy statements covering many of the items in the checklist appear in this section. They can be used to guide your policy statements.

Policy Manual Checklist

Our Policy Manual Should Cover:

1. Basic wage and salary policies   Yes_____ No_____

2. How wages and salaries are determined   Yes_____ No_____
   - A. Job evaluation plan   Yes_____ No_____
   - B. Merit or performance rating plans   Yes_____ No_____
   - C. Rate range by classifications   Yes_____ No_____
   - D. Length of service raises   Yes_____ No_____
   - E. Incentive wage policies   Yes_____ No_____

3. Wage and salary differentials   Yes_____ No_____
   - A. Shift differentials   Yes_____ No_____
   - B. Differentials for learners and apprentices   Yes_____ No_____
   - C. Call-in pay   Yes_____ No_____

4. Overtime pay policies   Yes_____ No_____
   - A. Employees subject to overtime pay   Yes_____ No_____
   - B. Supervisor overtime   Yes_____ No_____

Whether your business has 10 employees or 10,000, you still face the same problem: How do you pay your employees an amount that is fair and proper in a way that your employees will understand and accept, and at the same time pay them an amount you can afford?

For the smaller employer, the obvious and quick answer to these questions is often to simply pay an employee a rate that ''seems'' proper at the time. You may look at what you ''usually'' pay for this job, see what the employee has been making at his or her previous employer, determine that rate seems ''all right,'' and then pay the employee on that basis.

But the nagging question still remains: How do you know that the rate of pay you have decided upon is the right one for your organization, for this job, and for this employee? How does this rate of pay compare to those of other employees who do the same or similar work? How does it compare to rates paid by other similar establishments in your industry and in your area? These questions can be answered only through the development of an effective wage and salary administration program.

You should always be aware that payroll costs are usually the largest single controllable cost of any employer. Administration of this cost through a formalized plan and system is essential in maintaining above-average profitability along with high productivity and good employee relations.

A wage and salary administration program does not have to be complex to be effective and successful. It does, however, need to be thorough and complete, and it needs to relate to other jobs within your organization, area, and industry.

Every position in an organization has a ''right price.'' The right price is a blend of what the market is paying for that particular skill and the organization's ability to pay. It is essential that you identify the right price for each position in the organization, help employees attain that price within a specified period of time, and do everything within your power to keep that ''price'' competitive.

Determining Salary Levels

Factor 1: Your Ability to Pay

The amount of money you pay in wages directly affects your gross profit margin. If you pay too little, your wage rates may not be competitive enough to attract qualified employees. If you pay too much, your financial security is threatened. Thus, obtaining an optimum price is important. To obtain ''your ability to pay,'' consider the following steps:

Step 1. Determine how much of your total sales dollars are to be allocated to payroll. Determine this budgetary amount by obtaining information from industry standards or past practices.

Step 2. Establish your staffing requirements. Write a job description for each job and determine how many individuals and annual hours are required for each.

Factor 2: Marketplace Price

Go to the marketplace and determine the going rate for every position in your company. This market data should include the hire rate, the average going rate, and the maximum rate for each position. You can get this information by:

1. Conducting an area wage survey.
2. Purchasing or obtaining local and regional wage survey data from:
   - State and national associations
   - Chamber of Commerce
   - State Employment Commission
   - U.S. Department of Labor

Combining Factors 1 and 2

Armed with these two basic factors, you are now ready to assemble the system. You should apply the market price to each position, then modify this going rate by your ability to pay. The results will look something like Exhibit 6-1. The schedule for hourly personnel in the exhibit shows the *labor grade* assigned to each hourly position. Normally, the grades progress from the lowest paying to the highest paying positions. The *position* is the company's official title for each hourly job in the organization. The *hire rate* is the entry level or beginning rate for the position. The progression dates that follow show the wages the employ will receive after meeting certain length of service requirements.

The schedule for salaried personnel show the *labor grade* assigned to each salaried position. The *position* is the company's official title for each salaried job in the organization. The progression columns show the minimum or entry level pay for the position and progresses to the middle and maximum ranges for each position.

Exhibit 6-1. Wage progression schedules.
Sample 1
Standard Flying Service
Progression Schedule for Hourly Personnel

Effective Date: _____

Labor Grade	Position	Hire Rate	3 Mos.	6 Mos.	1 Year	24 Mos.
1	Receptionist	4.75	4.95	5.20	5.40	5.60
2	Custodian Line Personnel	5.00	5.20	5.40	5.80	6.25
3	Secretary	5.75	6.00	6.25	6.50	7.00
4	Mechanic	6.50	6.75	7.00	7.50	8.00

Sample 2
Standard Flying Service
Progression Schedule for Salaried Personnel

Effective Date: _____

Labor Grade	Position	Min.	Mid.	Max.
1	Line Supervisor Flight Instructor	16,125	20,000	23,875
2	Parts Supervisor	20,750	25,000	29,150
3	Chief Pilot	25,075	30,000	34,620

Most organizations cannot be the highest payer in town. Fortunately, this is OK, as employees are primarily concerned about fairness and that their wages are relatively competitive with the market. Top wages are not motivators in themselves. Essentially, employees are normally very satisfied with their compensation when they feel the employer knows what it is doing with regard to compensation practices.

As the theories of Maslow and Herzberg show, not all employees are motivated by money. In fact, by a substantial margin, most employees are not. Sustained long-term motivation comes from within—from feelings of personal self-worth, competency, and contribution. This in turn is supported by the external factors of recognition and admiration from others.

One of the most important questions in the mind of every employee is, "How am I doing?" Accordingly, it is important for every organization to establish a performance appraisal system. This will:

1. Establish a means to evaluate employee performance in a fair and consistent manner.
2. Establish a basis for wage increases and other personnel action.
3. Determine whether an employee is performing up to established standards.
4. Provide documentation for personnel actions such as promotion and discharge.
5. Let an employee know how he or she is getting along.

There are two other points to remember:

1. Without a formalized wage program, it is likely that an employee will know more about wages in the labor market than the employer does.
2. A wage program should describe and communicate an organization's pay practices as candidly and openly as vacation, holiday, or other personnel programs.

Exhibit 6-2 graphically illustrates the key elements of wage administration.

Exhibit 6-2. Key elements of wage administration.

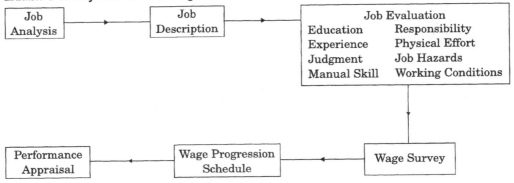

The Involvement of Federal Agencies in Wage and Salary Administration

Federal regulations have an important impact on wage and salary administration. Without going into too much detail on this subject (because it is lengthy and complicated), there are a number of federal agencies that have regulations governing how you pay your employees. The three principal ones are the Wage-Hour Division of the Department of Labor, the National Labor Relations Board, and the Equal Employment Opportunity Commission.

The Wage-Hour Division enforces the Fair Labor Standards Act (the "Wage and Hour Law") and deals primarily with timecards, minimum wages, and overtime compensation. This definition is simplified, but its importance should not be discounted, since this agency imposes millions of dollars in back pay on unsuspecting employers each year.

By developing a wage administration program, you automatically eliminate a number of technical and complicated areas of vulnerability that could lead the Wage-Hour Division to calculate back pay for your employees in terms of overtime compensation and minimum wages.

The National Labor Relations Board (NLRB) is a complex and intriguing agency. The NLRB enforces the National Labor Relations Act mainly in the area of protected concerted activity by employees. For example, it is against NLRB regulations to prohibit discussions of wages, hours, and working conditions among employees. If you formulate a rule that prohibits wage discussions and discipline employees for breaking that rule, then you (as an employer) can be taken before the NLRB and be forced to retract the discipline that you have imposed. Personnel policies that you formulate should take into account the employees' rights concerning concerted activity involving wages, hours, and the conditions of employment.

The Equal Employment Opportunity Commission (EEOC) is a solid triple threat. Not only does this agency enforce Title VII of the Civil Rights Act, but it also enforces age, race, and sex discrimination regulations and the equal pay for equal work regulations. Although the EEOC has not been highly efficient, it has been highly visible and is strongly supported by the federal courts.

Should you have difficulty with the EEOC, it probably will not be because you intentionally did something improper, it will be because of the difficult and complex regulations that this agency has developed and the technical manner in which they are enforced.

As an example, if you have two employees of different sexes who are performing the same or a similar job, then you must pay them at the same rate, unless you can show that any difference is based on something other than sex. If a discrimination charge is brought before the EEOC, the burden of proof is squarely on the shoulders of the employer. If the employer cannot prove that its compensation procedures are correct, the EEOC will automatically assume that they are incorrect and may find the employer guilty of sex discrimination. (No doubt you have read of the multimillion-dollar back wage settlements for wages theoretically lost by employees.)

A sound wage and salary administration program will go a long way toward eliminating potential discrimination areas from the standpoint of the EEOC.

In Summary—Ensuring Your Peace of Mind

The last major advantage of a wage and salary program is one that is dear to the heart of every manager who is concerned with efficiency: ease of administration. The pure and simple fact is that a salary administration program will make the day-to-day management of your organization's pay rates and salaries much easier. No longer will you have to grope for proper pay rates or agonize over the size of an employee's pay raise. These questions will have already been worked out in policy decisions in your wage and salary program. The time that you spend administering your wages and salaries could be cut in half or more.

If you have not developed a formal wage and salary administration program at your organization, the odds are very good that you have pay rates that are "out of line." The longer you wait to develop such a program, the more difficult it will become to bring these rates back in line and implement your new program.

Further, you simply will not be able to attract and retain good, qualified employees without fair and competitive rates of pay, and the only way that you will know for sure that your rates of pay are proper is through the development of a formal wage and salary administration program. Otherwise, it's simply a hit-and-miss affair.

Fair Labor Standards Act

Salary Basis

An employee is considered to be paid "on a salary basis" if under his or her employment agreement he or she regularly receives each pay period, on a weekly or less frequent basis, a predetermined amount constituting all or part of his or her compensation, which amount is not subject to reduction because of variations in the quality or quantity of the work performed.

Subject to the exceptions provided below, salaried employees must receive their full salary for any week in which they perform any work, without regard to the number of days or hours worked. As a general rule, salaried employees need not be paid for any workweek in which they perform no work.

Impermissible deductions from exempt salaried employees' salaries would subject the affected employees to loss of exempt status. Impermissible deductions from exempt or nonexempt employees' salaries would subject the affected employees to treatment as hourly employees for wage-hour law purposes, and therefore for all other purposes.

If DOL finds a policy or pattern of impermissible docking of salaried employees' pay, it may determine that the affected employee(s), *and all those in similar positions*, have become hourly workers, entitled to back pay for all overtime hours worked.

Deductions for the following *will not* defeat the salary basis requirement:

1. Absence from work for a day or more (days) for any personal reasons, whether discretionary, mandatory (e.g., legal), or otherwise unavoidable.

2. Absence from work for a day or more (days) for sickness or disability (including industrial accidents) before an employee has qualified under and after he or she has exhausted leave allowance under the employer's plan, policy, or practice that provides compensation for loss of salary occasioned by both sickness and disability.

3. Absence for day(s) for which an employee receives compensation for leave under:

    a. The employer's sickness or disability plan, policy, or practice

    b. A private sickness and disability insurance plan

    c. A state sickness and disability insurance law

    d. A state workers' compensation law (*provided* that the employer also has a plan, policy, or practice providing compensation for sickness and disability not relating to industrial accidents)

4. Periods of absence during an illness when an employee receives no pay, or when the leave pay pursuant to a disability insurance plan is less than the employee's predetermined salary. (When an insurance plan is bona fide, compliance with its terms is compliance with the salary basis of payment even though a waiting period in excess of one or more days is required before the employee becomes eligible for inclusion in the plan, or there is a waiting period for each illness before benefits are paid.)

5. Substitution of or reduction of accrued paid leave for time an employee is absent from work, provided the employee receives in total payment an amount equal to his or her guaranteed salary.

6. Deductions for any period of unpaid FMLA leave.

7. Deductions for board, lodging, and other facilities, provided the remaining portion of the salary is paid free and clear and meets the applicable minimum salary test.

8. Penalties imposed for infractions of safety rules of major significance, i.e., those relating to the prevention of serious danger to the plant or to other employees (e.g., rules prohibiting smoking in explosive plants, oil refineries, and coal mines).

9. Deductions or penalties imposed on employees for infractions of security regulations required by a government agency.

10. Absences of a day or more (days) when the time is spent in collective bargaining activities and that time *is not* counted as hours worked under FLSA.

11. Proportionate deduction for time not worked during the initial or terminal week of employment (including the start and end of uniformed services leaves of longer than thirty days).

Deductions for the following *will* defeat the salary basis requirement (reminder: Salaried employees need not be paid for any workweek in which they perform no work):

1. Absence from work of less than a day for any reason (except FMLA).

2. Absence from work for a day or more (days) for sickness or disability (including industrial accidents) if the employer does not have a plan, policy, or practice that provides compensation for loss of salary occasioned by both sickness and disability.

3. Absences of a day or more (days) when the time is spent in collective bargaining activities and that time *is* counted as hours worked under FLSA.

Note: An employer may require the substitution of accrued paid leave or reduce accrued paid leave for absences under the above three circumstances without defeating the salary basis requirement.

4. Absence for day(s) for which an employee receives compensation for leave under a state workers' compensation law if the employer does not also have a plan, policy, or practice providing compensation for sickness and disability not relating to industrial accidents. The employer may offset any amounts received by an employee as compensation benefits during a particular week against the salary due for that particular week.

5. Deductions for absences occasioned by the employer or by the operating requirements of the business (e.g., business closed or a shutdown because of snow, inventory, machinery repair, et al.). If the employee is ready, willing, and able to work, deductions may not be made for time when work is not available.

6. Deductions for absences caused by jury duty, attendance as a witness, or temporary (less than thirty-one days) uniformed service leave, or absence for uniformed service fitness examination. The employer may offset any amounts received by an employee as jury or witness fees or uniformed service pay for a particular week against the salary due for that particular week.

7. Deductions or penalties imposed (e.g., suspension without pay) for infractions of the employer's personnel policies or for infractions of the employer's work, conduct, or safety rules (unless of major safety significance).

8. Deductions for cash register shortages.

9. Deductions for reasons not stated in Reg. 541.118(a) or otherwise specified by the Wage-Hour Division.

Adjusting Grievances (§ 785.42)

Time spent in adjusting grievances between an employer and employees during the time the employees are required to be on the premises is hours worked, but if a bona fide union is involved, the counting of such time will, as a matter of enforcement policy, be left to the process of collective bargaining or to the custom or practice under the collective bargaining agreement.

Holidays

Many employers have a policy of not paying holiday pay unless an employee works the day before and the day after the holiday.

This policy is not applicable to salaried employees (exempt or nonexempt). If an employer's business operations (with respect to affected employees) are closed for a holiday and affected employees are ready, willing, and able to work, withholding holiday pay from a salaried employee would defeat (violate) the FLSA salary basis requirement.

Withholding holiday pay from *any* employee because he or she is on jury duty during one (or both) of those surrounding days has been found to be intimidation and coercion in violation of the federal juror protection law.

Sick Leave

An employer that does not have a policy that provides compensation for loss of salary occasioned by both sickness and disability should be advised that salaried employees (exempt and nonexempt) must receive their full salary for any week in which they perform any work.

The employer may not deduct for absences from work of a day or longer for sickness or disability (including industrial accidents). An employer may reduce any accrued paid time off (personal days, vacation) for such absences. The employer's paid personal days policy and/or vacation policy should reflect this.

The employer must pay a salaried employee his or her full salary for any week during which the employee is absent and receives compensation under a state workers' compensation law for one or more days. The employer may offset any amounts received by an employee as workers' compensation benefits during a particular week against the salary due for that particular week. The employer's workers' compensation policy statement should reflect this.

Paid Time Off: Sick Leave, Personal Days, Vacation

If an employer's policy or practice is to substitute or reduce accrued paid leave for time that salaried employees are absent from work during any week in which they perform any work, the employer's respective paid time off policies and the employer's absence/attendance policy statements should reflect that fact.

Jury Duty Leave

We recommend at least differential pay for all employees accepting this important civic duty.

Salaried employees (exempt and nonexempt) must receive full salary for any week in which they perform any work, without regard to the number of days or hours worked. During any such week, deductions may not be made for absences caused by jury duty or attendance as a witness. Jury or witness fees may be used to offset the salary due.

Many employers have a policy of not paying holiday pay unless an employee works the day before and the day after the holiday. Withholding holiday pay from an employee because he or she is on jury duty during one (or both) of those surrounding days has been found to be intimidation and coercion in violation of the federal juror protection law.

Tardiness (Early Quit and Partial Day Time Off)

An employer policy or practice of docking salaried exempt or nonexempt employees' pay for tardiness, leaving early, or other absences of less than one day for any reason (except FMLA) will defeat the FLSA salary basis requirement.

If an employer's particular plan, policy, or practice provides for the accrual of paid vacation, personal time, family time, or sick time, the employer may require a reduction in such unused accruals proportionate to the amount of time less than a day that a salaried employee absents himself or herself (for any purpose), if the employee receives in payment an amount equal to his or her guaranteed salary. Leave banks do not constitute salary, and such reductions would not therefore be a deduction from an employee's salary. (Such reductions are not possible before an employee has qualified for such accruals or if all such accruals have been exhausted.)

Employers covered by the Family and Medical Leave Act may make deductions from a salaried employee's salary for any hours taken as intermittent or reduced FMLA leave within a workweek, provided that the employee is eligible for FMLA leave, the absence qualifies as an FMLA leave, and there are not unused accrued paid permissible substitutions available.

Absences

Salaried employees (exempt and nonexempt) must receive full salary for any week in which they perform any work. Accordingly, salaried employees may not be suspended without pay for less than a full workweek for excessive absence.

Progressive Discipline

Salaried employees (exempt and nonexempt) must receive full salary for any week in which they perform any work. Accordingly, salaried employees may not be suspended without pay for less than a full workweek for infractions of the employer's personnel policies or for infractions of the employer's work, conduct, or safety rules (except those of major safety significance).

Time Off to Vote

Salaried employees (exempt and nonexempt) must receive full salary for any week in which they perform any work. Accordingly, deductions may not be made from a salaried employee's pay for any time off to vote, if granted.

The section of the manual covering wages and salaries should be carefully thought out and as detailed as possible. The extensive Policy Manual Checklist covers most of the conditions that require policy. Many will be included in every manual; some will not.

On the following pages of this section there are sample policy statements on many of the subjects listed on the checklist that you can use to describe your policies. In other cases, your written or unwritten present policy should be included in this section of the manual. Areas covered include:

Corporate Salary Administration
Management and Supervisor Compensation
Job Rates Determination
Exempt Salary Review
Shift Premium
Overtime
Guide Service
Payment for Time Spent at Company-Sponsored Affairs
Call-In Pay
Employees Medically Classified for Light Work Only
Credit for Prior Experience

PERSONNEL POLICIES AND PROCEDURES

DISTRIBUTION:		SUBJECT: MANAGEMENT AND SUPERVISOR COMPENSATION	
EFFECTIVE DATE:	PAGE 1 OF 1	FILE UNDER SECTION	
REVISION DATE:	APPROVED BY:		

POLICY:

The company recognizes management and supervisory personnel as an integrated and highly important segment of management, regardless of the level or nature of the individual occupation. The company recognizes that promotion into or upward through the supervisory organization causes an increased demand on the abilities and time of the individual and requires a greater degree of contribution, in terms of participation and interest in the job and in the company. Since recognition of the contribution and position of each supervisor is a basic responsibility of top management, it is both necessary and desirable to enunciate the company policy as it concerns the compensation of supervisory personnel.

PERSONNEL POLICIES AND PROCEDURES

DISTRIBUTION:		SUBJECT: MANAGEMENT AND SUPERVISOR COMPENSATION	
EFFECTIVE DATE:	PAGE 1 OF 4	FILE UNDER SECTION	
REVISION DATE:	APPROVED BY:		

POLICY:

The company will maintain a salary administration program which (1) will provide for payment of salaries comparable to or better than those paid for similar positions and services in the surrounding area, in the industry, and nationwide, and (2) will provide for recognition of and reward for differences in individual ability and performance.

FOUNDATION OF SALARY ADMINISTRATION PROGRAM:

The foundation of our company salary administration program is described under the following:

1. Position Evaluation
2. Salary Schedule

1. Position Evaluation

   a. What it is—Position Evaluation is a systematic procedure for analyzing, measuring, and classifying positions in terms of four common elements or factors found in every position. These factors are:

      (1) Knowledge and Skills
      (2) Difficulty and Complexity
      (3) Responsibility for Supervision
      (4) Responsibility for Profits

   b. How the plan works—The extent to which a factor exists in one position may be different from the extent to which that same factor exists in another position. For example, position A may require a greater amount of Knowledge and Skill than position B. It is possible, therefore, to rank one position relative to other positions in terms of its Knowledge and Skill requirement. Likewise, a position can be ranked in terms of Difficulty and Complexity, Responsibility for Supervision, and Responsibility for Profits. The result is a ranking for each of the four factors listed in 1. a. above. These final rankings are added together to give a total point value for the position. The position is then placed in a salary grade according to its total point value.

   c. How the plan is maintained—Each department manager is responsible for maintaining equitable and properly evaluated position relationships in his or her department. Newly created positions or major changes in the functions and responsibilities of a position should be reported to the Industrial Relations Department in order to initiate an evaluation study to establish the new position or to reclassify an existing position. The Industrial Relations Department is responsible for auditing the classifications of all salaried positions once each year.

   d. Approval of ratings—All evaluation ratings must be approved by the Executive Vice President before the position is placed in a salary grade.

2. Salary Schedule

   a. How the schedule is established—The salary is based upon information obtained from area, industry, and national surveys performed by the federal government, individual companies, private compensation services, and the trade associations. The schedule is prepared and issued by the Industrial Relations Department after being approved by the Executive Vice President.

   b. How the schedule is maintained—The Industrial Relations Department is responsible for auditing the salary schedule once each year. It compares area, industry, and national salary information with the company schedule.

PERSONNEL POLICIES AND PROCEDURES

DISTRIBUTION:		SUBJECT: MANAGEMENT AND SUPERVISOR COMPENSATION	
EFFECTIVE DATE:	PAGE 2 OF 4	FILE UNDER SECTION	
REVISION DATE:	APPROVED BY:		

A revised schedule is prepared and issued, whenever appropriate, in order to maintain ranges comparable to or better than prevailing area, industry, and national salaries.

SALARY ADMINISTRATION:

The administration of the salary program is described under the following:

1. Determination of Salary—New Employee
2. Salary Adjustments
3. Coordination of Program

1. Determination of Salary—New Employee

    A new employee will receive the minimum salary for the position classification to which he or she is assigned. Exceptions to this are as follows:

    a. A person who has directly related experience that is immediately usable may be employed at a salary within the first quartile of the range.

    b. A person who is not fully qualified may be employed at a salary below the range minimum for the position. This exception applies only in cases where an employee has sufficient potential to meet minimum position requirements within a six- to twelve-month period and can be raised to the minimum within that time.

2. Salary Adjustments

    Adjustments in an individual's salary are based upon the individual's record of performance in the position as follows:

    a. Review Schedule

        (1) New Employee—At least once during the first year of employment. In most instances this will be after the first six months of employment.

        (2) Employee Remaining in the Same Position—At least once each twelve months. (An anniversary year begins on the date of the last review.)

        (3) Employee Transferred to Another Assignment or Promoted to a Higher Grade—Not sooner than six months after the transfer or promotion took place. The length of the orientation period assigned to a transferred or promoted employee is dependent upon such factors as the individual's prior experience, training, and rate of progress in the new position.

    b. Tickler System

        Review dates for each employee are established by the employee's supervisor. The dates are based upon the nature of each employee's position and the employee's rate of progress in the position. The Industrial Relations Department will maintain a tickler system and will send each supervisor, one month in advance, a memo reminding him or her that a review is due the following month.

    c. Performance Analysis and Appraisal Procedure

        Each supervisor will conduct a performance analysis to evaluate each employee in terms of the actual requirements of his or her position.

PERSONNEL POLICIES AND PROCEDURES

DISTRIBUTION:		SUBJECT: MANAGEMENT AND SUPERVISOR COMPENSATION	
EFFECTIVE DATE:	PAGE 3 OF 4		FILE UNDER SECTION
REVISION DATE:	APPROVED BY:		

d. Necessity for Granting Increases

The foregoing is not intended to indicate that salary adjustments must always be given upon completion of each individual's performance appraisal. The mere fact that an employee has continued to be employed by the company is not justification for a salary adjustment. Performance is the key factor—not length of service. Consequently, salary adjustments must be based upon a thorough review of an employee's performance and noted improvement in performance or continued excellent performance.

e. Determination of Salary Adjustments

Each supervisor is responsible for submitting recommended salary adjustments to his or her supervisor for approval. Such recommendations must be made in accordance with the following general guides.

(1) Normal Adjustment Amounts

Salary adjustments within the salary range for a position will normally be in amounts varying from 5 to 10 percent of an employee's salary in any twelve-month period (5 to 15 percent in cases of promotion—see f. below).

(2) Determination of the Specific Amounts

(a) Performance vs. Position Requirements
How well does the employee's performance meet the requirements of the position?

(b) Performance vs. Performance of Others
How does the employee's performance compare with the performance of others in the same work group and salary grade?

(c) Salary History
What has been the employee's rate of progress—frequency and amount of past salary adjustments?

(d) Position in the Salary Range
Where does an employee's salary fit in the range? What effect does performance have on this determination? The following are basic guides:

Salary Below Range Minimum
For persons not fully qualified to perform at the minimum acceptable level, or trainees.

Salary Between Minimum and First Quartile
Person considered to have the potential to become fully qualified for position with further effort and experience; normal starting range. FAIR performance.

Salary Between First Quartile and Midpoint
Person is progressively acquiring experience needed to meet essential requirements of position. SATISFACTORY performance.

Salary Between Midpoint and Third Quartile
Person fully meets position requirements and consistently achieves performance above the satisfactory level in several major areas. VERY GOOD performance.

Salary Between Third Quartile and Maximum
Person's performance has exceeded the satisfactory level in most areas over an extended period. OUTSTANDING performance.

(3) Special 20 percent Guide—First-Line Supervision
The salary of a first-line supervisor whose overall performance is classified as "Satisfactory" or better will be at a level no less than 20 percent above the annual straight-time rate of pay of the highest hourly employee

153

DISTRIBUTION:		SUBJECT: MANAGEMENT AND SUPERVISOR COMPENSATION	
EFFECTIVE DATE:	PAGE 4 OF 4	FILE UNDER SECTION	
REVISION DATE:	APPROVED BY:		

he or she directly supervises. This calculation will be made at the time of each performance appraisal, and will be one of the factors used in the final determination of a supervisor's salary.

(4) Schedule and Range Limitations

Only salary rates appearing on the currently authorized salary schedule may be used. Salary adjustments will not be granted that will raise an employee's salary above the salary range for the position.

(5) Minimum Adjustments

Salary adjustments should be granted to reward noted improvement in an employee's performance or continued "Outstanding" or "Very Good" performance. In cases where the degree of improvement in an employee's performance has not been significant enough to warrant at least a 5 percent salary adjustment, and in cases where an employee's overall performance has not been at a level high enough to warrant at least a 5 percent salary adjustment, no salary adjustment should be granted.

An exception to this 5 percent minimum restriction is the case where an employee's performance warrants a salary adjustment but where his or her present salary is less than 5 percent from the maximum salary for the grade. In such cases, an adjustment of less than 5 percent may be granted.

(6) Effective Dates

Salary adjustments will become effective at the beginning of the first pay period following the date of final approval. (See Procedure No. 2 for details.) No retroactive salary adjustments will be granted.

f. Promotions

In accordance with the principle that employees will be rewarded in proportion to their contribution to the company, promotional salary adjustments normally will be granted upon the assumption of positions involving greater duties and responsibilities. A promotional salary adjustment must be based upon a bona fide change in duties that raises the person to a higher salary grade. The following general guides will apply in these cases:

Present Salary Lower Than New Minimum (less than 15 percent lower)—Raise person's salary to new minimum.

Present Salary Substantially Lower Than New Minimum (more than 15 percent lower)—Raise person's salary a portion of the way toward the new minimum. Schedule a performance analysis and appraisal within six months. Then consider increasing the salary to the minimum, based upon the results of the performance appraisal.

Present Salary At or Above Minimum—Leave salary at present level or increase, based upon prior performance, training, and history of salary adjustments.

g. Frequency of Salary Adjustments

Recommendations for salary adjustments must be substantiated by completed performance analysis and appraisal forms. Consequently, frequency of salary adjustments is determined by the frequency of performance reviews.

3. Coordination of Program

The Industrial Relations Department is responsible for coordinating all salary adjustments in order to maintain uniform and consistent administration of salaries for positions in all salary grades. Supervisors preparing salary adjustment recommendations should work closely with the Industrial Relations Department in order to keep their recommendations in line with general departmental and company trends. In order to assist the Industrial Relations Department in maintaining uniform and consistent administration, when not procedurally involved with a recommendation, the Executive Vice President and/or Vice President—Operations will review each completed performance analysis and appraisal.

PERSONNEL POLICIES AND PROCEDURES

DISTRIBUTION:		SUBJECT: JOB RATES DETERMINATION	
EFFECTIVE DATE:	PAGE 1 OF 2	FILE UNDER SECTION	
REVISION DATE:	APPROVED BY:		

POLICY:

The base rate for each hourly rate job and the salary range for each job that is nonexempt from payment of overtime shall be established by job evaluation according to the duties and requirements of the job.

Hourly Rate Jobs: Each hourly rate job will be analyzed by the Wage and Salary Section. Specifications that explain the duties and requirements of the job will be written by the job analyst and approved by the head of the department involved. The job specifications will include information pertaining to the following:

Job Duties
Physical Requirements
Working Conditions
Mental Requirements
Skill Requirements
Responsibilities

A Job Evaluation Committee will meet to set up the necessary evaluation data to be used in determining an equitable rate for the job.

The Committee will be made up of an hourly rate employee from the department involved, an hourly rate employee from another department, the job analyst, the supervisor of the department in which the job is performed, and a member of management from another department. The member of management will be selected by the supervisor of the department in which the job is performed.

Selection of the hourly rate employee representatives will be as follows:

The hourly rate representative for the department involved will be selected by employees from the job or jobs involved.

The hourly rate employee from another department will be chosen by the hourly rate representative of the job to be studied in conjunction with the job analyst from a list of hourly rate employees in other departments, preference being given to employees who have previously served on this committee. The list will be drawn up by the job analyst.

The General Hourly Evaluation Committee will meet to review the job's evaluation, as set up by the Job Evaluation Committee, and to recommend a rate for the job. The General Hourly Evaluation Committee will consist of members of the higher managerial level, as appointed by the Division Manager. In all cases, the area manager of the department involved will serve on this committee.

All rates recommended by the General Hourly Evaluation Committee must be approved by the Division Manager before becoming effective.

The department manager of the job involved will be notified in writing by the Wage and Salary Section as to the final outcome of the evaluation and is responsible for the prompt relaying of this information to the supervisor of the employees concerned.

Temporary Hourly Rates: When a new job is established, the Wage and Salary Section will be notified immediately by letter from the department manager involved, requesting that a temporary rate be set.

A preliminary study of the job will be made and presented to the General Hourly Evaluation Committee along with a suggested temporary rate.

Upon approval, the rate established by the committee will be entered in the rate book designated as "temporary." This rate will be paid only until the job is formally evaluated.

All temporary jobs will be reviewed every three months by the Wage and Salary Section with the department manager to determine the status of the temporary job.

When the duties of the job are stabilized, the manager concerned will request, in writing to the Wage and Salary Section, that the job be evaluated.

PERSONNEL POLICIES AND PROCEDURES

DISTRIBUTION:		SUBJECT: JOB RATES DETERMINATION	
EFFECTIVE DATE:	PAGE 2 OF 2	FILE UNDER SECTION	
REVISION DATE:	APPROVED BY:		

Nonexempt Salary Jobs: The salary range of each salary job that is nonexempt from payment of overtime shall be established according to the duties and requirements of the job.

Each job will be analyzed by the Wage and Salary Section. Specifications that explain the duties and requirements of the job will be written by the job analyst and approved by the head of the department involved. The job specifications will include information pertaining to the following:

Job Duties
Mental Requirements
Skill Requirements
Physical Requirements
Responsibilities
Supervision

The First Salary Evaluation Committee will evaluate the job in relation to other jobs and recommend a salary range for the job. The committee will be made up of two nonexempt employees (one from the department involved and one from another department), the job analyst, the supervisor of the department in which the job is performed, and a member of management from another department. The member of management will be selected by the supervisor of the department in which the job is performed.

The General Salary Evaluation Committee will meet to review the job evaluation and salary range as set up by the Salary Evaluation Committee, and to recommend a salary range for the job. The General Salary Evaluation Committee will consist of members of the higher managerial capacity, as appointed by the Division Manager. In all cases the area manager of the department involved will serve on this committee.

The department manager of each job involved will receive a written notification of the job's approved salary range, and will be responsible for prompt notification to the supervisor and employees concerned.

General: Approved evaluated salary ranges and hourly rates will remain in effect until either the duties and requirements of the job undergo a sufficient change to merit reevaluation, or a general increase or decrease is effected.

A job will be reevaluated when sufficient changes occur in the job's duties and requirements, if all of the following procedures are complied with:

A written request for the reevaluation will be submitted by the department head involved to the Wage and Salary Section.

A job analyst will contact the supervisor and an employee on the job involved, and will conduct a thorough analysis of the situation.

A report of the situation will be presented to the General Evaluation Committee by the Wage and Salary Section.

The General Evaluation Committee may approve or deny a reevaluation, using the new job specifications.

The Wage and Salary Section will notify the department manager, in writing, as to the decision of the General Evaluation Committee.

General increases will apply to evaluated rates only.

Special rates, temporary rates, and preevaluated rates will be given individual attention.

General decreases will apply to all rates.

PERSONNEL POLICIES AND PROCEDURES

DISTRIBUTION:		SUBJECT: EXEMPT SALARY REVIEW	
EFFECTIVE DATE:	PAGE 1 OF 1	FILE UNDER SECTION	
REVISION DATE:	APPROVED BY:		

POLICY:

The salary and each performance of each exempt employee shall be reviewed at regular intervals, as set forth in this policy. Adjustments in salary will be based on individual merit, proper differential with those supervised, and equitable relationship with all other exempt salaries in the division.

Each month a comparison of four-week and year-to-date total earnings of exempt and the top group of nonexempt and hourly rate employees in each department will be prepared by the Wage and Salary Section for the manager concerned. The Division Manager will receive a composite report covering all departments. Apparent gross inequities will be called to the attention of both the manager concerned and the Division Manager.

Annual reviews will be made on an individual basis. Beginning anniversary on the job will determine the time of annual review. The annual review will be based on starting date of the job or date of last increase, whichever is later.

In the event an individual starts on a new job without a salary adjustment, his or her salary will be reviewed within six months.

Salary increases should not be more frequent than once each year unless circumstances merit the consideration.

One month prior to the applicable review date the manager will receive a notice from the Wage and Salary Section concerning those under their supervision who are eligible for consideration.

A composite listing of all who are eligible, and pertinent information concerning each, will be furnished the Division Manager.

Based on the annual performance review, the manager will, through the Wage and Salary Section, make the appropriate recommendation (increase, decrease, or no change) to the Division Manager.

The Division Manager will review all recommendations and give a decision in each case. This decision, with the supporting reasons, will be forwarded to the Wage and Salary Section and the appropriate manager for necessary action.

Each manager will be responsible for seeing that each of his or her exempt employees has been informed of the salary adjustment or nonadjustment, and the reason this decision was reached. This must be completed before the review date.

An exempt salary employee who has not been talked to concerning a review, or is dissatisfied with the results of the review, may request and receive an interview with the next higher supervisor. This procedure may be followed through to the Division Manager, if necessary.

The intent of this policy is to ensure periodic exempt reviews so that they may be kept up to date, fair, and equitable, and is not to be construed as a guarantee of, or automatic, salary increase.

PERSONNEL POLICIES AND PROCEDURES

DISTRIBUTION:		SUBJECT: SHIFT PREMIUM	
EFFECTIVE DATE:	PAGE 1 OF 1	FILE UNDER SECTION	
REVISION DATE:	APPROVED BY:		

POLICY:

An employee who is assigned to work in the second and third shifts will be paid shift premium to compensate for the inconvenience of such working hours.

The amount of shift premium paid will be 7 cents for the second shift, and 12 cents for the third shift.

The hours of each shift will be as follows:

Shift No. 1 (Day Shift) — 7 A.M. to 3 P.M.
Shift No. 2 (Afternoon Shift) — 3 P.M. to 11 P.M.
Shift No. 3 (Night Shift) — 11 P.M. to 7 A.M.

The regular scheduled shifts of 8 A.M. to 4 P.M., 4 P.M. to 12 midnight, and 12 midnight to 8 A.M., as worked in some departments, will be considered to be first, second, and third shifts, respectively, for the purpose of shift premium payment for these departments.

The day work schedule of 8 A.M. to 5 P.M. or 8 A.M. to 4 P.M. will be considered as first shift for all day workers.

All hourly rate and nonexempt salary employees will be paid the shift premium of the shift in which their work occurs.

Overtime will be paid on shift premium.

An employee who is required to work prior to the regular shift or into the next shift will receive the shift premium for the hours worked in that shift. An employee who works the third shift and continues working into the first shift will receive third-shift premium for those first-shift hours.

Application of payment for special nonstandard shift schedules may differ from this by mutual agreement between the employees involved and the department manager.

Shift differential has been included in the salary of exempt supervisors who regularly work shift work, but will not be paid on an occasional basis to those who normally work day work.

PERSONNEL POLICIES AND PROCEDURES

DISTRIBUTION:		SUBJECT: OVERTIME	
EFFECTIVE DATE:	PAGE 1 OF 1		FILE UNDER SECTION
REVISION DATE:	APPROVED BY:		

POLICY:

The Company embraces the general policy that regularly scheduled overtime work within a department will be distributed as equally as possible among employees within that department who are capable of performing the work to be done. The company further believes that casual overtime should go to the employee who regularly does the job on which the overtime work occurs.

Casual overtime means overtime of an irregular nature, not expected to continue for more than a day or two. Casual overtime occurs at infrequent intervals and is of such a nature that it cannot be accurately predicted for any given period of time. An example of casual overtime is overtime authorized to meet emergencies caused by machine breakdown or by unexpected absenteeism in a department. Casual overtime includes daily or Saturday work provided the above conditions are met.

Regularly scheduled overtime means overtime that occurs at regular intervals and that can be accurately predicted for a given period of time. For instance, if because of production needs you announced to your department that a certain number of people would be required to work thirteen hours' overtime each week for the next six weeks, this would be classed as regularly scheduled overtime.

The following rules will be used as guides in interpreting and applying the company's Overtime Distribution Policy:

A. Employees assigned overtime work must be capable of performing the work to be done.

B. Casual overtime on a particular job will be assigned to the employee who has been working on that job during the course of the regular shift.

C. Saturday overtime of a casual nature will be assigned to the employee who does this work during the course of the regular week.

D. There will be no partiality shown to any employee in the distribution of overtime.

E. For regularly scheduled overtime, supervisors will maintain an overtime roster and will record the amount of overtime worked by each individual employed. As far as possible, the differential between the highest and lowest person on this roster will not exceed twenty hours (forty hours in Maintenance and Tool Room). This roster, as closely as is possible, will be leveled out annually.

F. In Maintenance Department and Tool Room, rotation will be within classifications. Employees in Maintenance or Tool Room who are normally assigned to a particular repair or Tool Room job will normally be assigned casual overtime on that job.

G. Employees will be expected to work overtime when assigned by their supervisor. In any event, if an employee does not work assigned overtime through his or her own choice, he or she will be charged that amount of overtime on the overtime roster.

PERSONNEL POLICIES AND PROCEDURES

DISTRIBUTION:		SUBJECT: GUIDE SERVICE	
EFFECTIVE DATE:	PAGE 1 OF 1	FILE UNDER SECTION	
REVISION DATE:	APPROVED BY:		

POLICY STATEMENT:

The Company will pay hourly rate and nonexempt salary employees who volunteer to serve as guides to conduct visitors through the mill.

A roster of employees who have volunteered to serve as guides during the hours when they are not working will be maintained by the Industrial and Community Relations Department.

In unusual circumstances supervisors may be requested to release employees from the job to serve as guides.

Substitute supervisors will be solicited and encouraged to volunteer to serve as guides.

Employees serving as guides on company-scheduled tours will be required to bring their time cards both in and out for timekeeping purposes.

An employee who serves as a guide at a time other than regular working hours will be paid for a minimum of 2½ hours or the actual hours served, whichever is greater.

When guide service continues beyond the regular working hours, the employee will be paid for the hours actually worked in guide service.

When an employee serves as a guide during the regular working hours, he/she will be paid regular pay, except incentive bonus.

PERSONNEL POLICIES AND PROCEDURES

DISTRIBUTION:		SUBJECT: PAYMENT FOR TIME SPENT AT COMPANY-SPONSORED AFFAIRS	
EFFECTIVE DATE:	PAGE 1 OF 1	FILE UNDER SECTION	
REVISION DATE:	APPROVED BY:		

POLICY STATEMENT:

The Company will encourage and assist employees to take an active part in civic and approved company-sponsored affairs, but expects such participation to be secondary to job duties.

The intent of this policy is to provide a plan whereby employees may participate in approved civic and approved company-sponsored affairs:

With the least interruption to production.

With the least disruption of work schedules.

At a minimum of expense to the company.

Company-sponsored affairs will include:

Meetings of standing committees of the company, as approved by the Vice President and Division Manager.

Special recreational activities as approved by the Vice President and Division Manager.

Special company affairs for which wage payment has been approved by the Vice President and Division Manager.

Approved civic affairs will include:

Meetings of general community interest in which the company desires representation by delegates, as approved by the Human Resource Administration Manager.

The employee will be paid for attendance at the functions listed above according to the following conditions, and his or her time deviated to the proper Human Resources Administration burden charge.

A written request for an employee to be away from the job will be made to the supervisor by an authorized representative of the organization or activity with the approval of the Human Resources Manager.

The written request must be in the hands of the supervisor at least 48 hours prior to the requested day of absence.

The written request will be required for both rearrangement of schedule and/or receipt of payment for time off.

Payments will not be made to an employee for attendance or participation in the above-mentioned functions during scheduled time off from his or her job.

PERSONNEL POLICIES AND PROCEDURES

DISTRIBUTION:		SUBJECT: CALL-IN PAY	
EFFECTIVE DATE:	PAGE 1 OF 1	FILE UNDER SECTION	
REVISION DATE:	APPROVED BY:		

POLICY STATEMENT:

Any time an employee reports for work, he or she shall be assured of receiving at least four hours' pay.

An employee scheduled to work or called in to work shall receive a minimum of four hours' work or its equivalent in total money earned between the time the employee reports for work and the time he or she goes home.

An employee called in with less than eight hours' notice for all work other than absence relief will be provided with a minimum of four hours' work during the off shift period, or receive a minimum of four hours' pay for the ''off shift'' work.

PERSONNEL POLICIES AND PROCEDURES

DISTRIBUTION:		SUBJECT: CALL-IN PAY	
EFFECTIVE DATE:	PAGE 1 OF 1	FILE UNDER SECTION	
REVISION DATE:	APPROVED BY:		

POLICY STATEMENT:

Due to certain emergency situations that may arise, it may be necessary to call an employee back to duty after he/she has left the premises or prior to his/her regular starting time. It is the policy of (Company Name) to reimburse such employees for their inconvenience in accordance with the provisions herein.

ELIGIBILITY:

This policy is applicable only to hourly and salaried (nonexempt) employees.

GUIDELINES:

1. Should an employee be called in four hours or more prior to the beginning of the normal shift, the employee will be paid at the rate of time and one-half the regular hourly rate (provided the employee will qualify for overtime during that workweek), but in no event shall the employee be paid less than four hours at the regular straight-time rate.

2. Should an employee be called in less than four hours before the beginning of the shift, the employee will be paid at the rate of time and one-half the regular hourly rate (provided the employee will qualify for overtime during that workweek), but in no event shall the employee be paid less than two hours at the regular straight-time rate.

3. Emergencies that require an employee to work past the normal end of the shift will be considered as scheduled overtime and not subject to call-in provisions.

PERSONNEL POLICIES AND PROCEDURES

DISTRIBUTION:		SUBJECT: EMPLOYEES MEDICALLY CLASSIFIED FOR LIGHT WORK ONLY	
EFFECTIVE DATE:	PAGE 1 OF 1		FILE UNDER SECTION
REVISION DATE:	APPROVED BY:		

POLICY STATEMENT:

Every effort will be made to find suitable work for employees who become physically unable to perform their regular job because of nonoccupational illness or a nonoccupational injury. If a reduction in rate of pay would result and the employees have one year continuous service, their pay shall be "stepped down" to give them time to make the proper adjustment in their personal finances.

An employee who is temporarily classified by the Medical Department for "light work only" will be provided light work when and if it is available.

Employees will receive the base rate of their previous job classification during their temporary assignment to light work.

Employees who are permanently classified by the Medical Department for "light work only" will be assigned to a light work pool for a predetermined maximum period of time.

The Employment Section and the employee's supervisor will determine a suitable length of time the employee will be retained in the light work pool pending regular assignment, and the employee shall be advised as to the length of this period.

If no permanent assignment has become available during this predetermined period, the employee's case shall be reviewed and a decision will be made as to whether the period will be extended or the employee will be laid off.

If an employee refuses a permanent assignment that is suitable to his or her physical condition as determined by the Medical Department, his or her employment shall be terminated.

While the employee is in the light work pool, the Employment Section shall make every effort to find suitable work to which the employee may be permanently assigned.

PERSONNEL POLICIES AND PROCEDURES

DISTRIBUTION:		SUBJECT: CREDIT FOR PRIOR EXPERIENCE	
EFFECTIVE DATE:	PAGE 1 OF 1	FILE UNDER SECTION	
REVISION DATE:	APPROVED BY:		

POLICY:

Although a minimum or base hiring rate has been established for each position in the hospital, provisions have been made to hire an employee with previous experience at a higher adjusted rate. Employees with verifiable and acceptable prior experience may qualify and be considered according to the following years of prior experience:

- Two to five years' prior experience—2.5 percent above base hourly rate of pay.
- More than five years' prior experience—5 percent above base hourly rate of pay.

EXPERIENCE REQUIREMENTS:

1. The experience must have been full-time, continuous experience (part-time experience is disallowed).

2. The experience must have been directly related to the position for which application for employment is made.

3. There must not be a break of two years or more in the experience; if so, then that period of prior experience is disallowed.

4. For Nursing Service applicants, only hospital experience—not nursing home or extended-care facility experience—is allowed.

PERSONNEL POLICIES AND PROCEDURES

DISTRIBUTION:		SUBJECT: GENERAL PAY POLICY	
EFFECTIVE DATE:	PAGE 1 OF 1	FILE UNDER SECTION	
REVISION DATE:	APPROVED BY:		

POLICY STATEMENT:

It is the policy of (Company Name) to pay wages and salaries that are consistent with job performance and that are comparable to rates being paid for similar work in the community. The company recognizes the importance of equitable pay differentials for varied types of work and provides incentives for maximum contribution to the company, self-improvement, and advancement.

It is the policy of (Company Name) to regularly review and evaluate the performance of each employee. Performance reviews are conducted by the immediate supervisor and discussed with the employee at established intervals. A performance review does not guarantee a wage increase. However, each employee's performance and rate of pay will be reviewed at least annually to ensure that it is equitable in comparison with similar jobs in the area labor market and to ensure that satisfactory and/or exceptional performance is recognized through additional compensation.

The company will adjust wages and salaries based on job performance, business growth, general economic conditions of the company, and comparable wages in this area.

PROCEDURE:

A. Paychecks—The pay period for all employees is Monday through Sunday, with checks being processed the following week and normally being distributed the second Monday after the end of the pay period. Paychecks will be mailed to each division, and each manager is responsible for giving each employee his/her paycheck on Monday. Should the employee be absent on payday, the paycheck should be mailed by the manager the next day unless the employee telephones and requests that the paycheck be held until he/she returns to work. Employees may authorize someone else to pick up their paycheck; however, managers should request to see identification before releasing the paycheck. Bonus, incentive, and spiff payments are paid approximately thirty days after the completion of the bonus period. Certain employees are eligible for incentive programs. Each manager will be provided a copy of the current year's incentive programs applicable to his/her area of responsibility.

B. Once employees receive their payroll checks (or expense checks), they become the employees' responsibility. Should an employee lose one of these checks, costs associated with duplicating the check or stopping payment will be the responsibility of the employee.

Should an employee find the original check, it should be returned to the Payroll Department at the home office.

C. Payroll Deductions—The company is required to deduct certain federal and state taxes from each paycheck. Additionally, we will make deductions from an employee's paycheck as authorized by the employee for benefits such as retirement, insurance, etc. Employees should complete the necessary paperwork identifying those deductions they authorize at the beginning of their employment. Should an employee wish to make any changes in his/her deductions, the appropriate form can be obtained through the employee's supervisor or through the Human Resources Department.

D. Garnishment—Any actions on the part of employees that may result in involving the company in legal proceedings started by employees' creditors is viewed as a serious matter. If unusual or emergency situations develop that create a financial burden on an employee, it is imperative that provisions be made so that neither actions for collection nor garnishment of wages will occur.

If a creditor obtains a garnishment on an employee's earnings, we are required by law to deduct the necessary payment.

PERSONNEL POLICIES AND PROCEDURES

DISTRIBUTION:		SUBJECT: PAYDAY POLICY	
EFFECTIVE DATE:	PAGE 1 OF 2	FILE UNDER SECTION	
REVISION DATE:	APPROVED BY:		

PURPOSE:

The purpose of this policy is to describe the company's pay cycles and pay practices that support the company's operational requirements.

POLICY:

A. PAY PERIOD:

1. Hourly:
   The pay period begins on Monday and ends on the following Sunday. Payment is made for the time worked the previous week.

2. Salary:

   a. Nonexempt
   Office/clerical associates who are paid on a salaried basis are classified as salaried nonexempt. These associates are paid on a biweekly basis but are compensated for overtime work [all hours worked over forty (40) in a workweek]. Salaried nonexempt associates are paid on a current basis except for overtime pay.

   b. Exempt
   Supervisory, management, professional, and some technical associates who are classified as salaried exempt are paid on a biweekly basis, but do not receive compensation for overtime worked other than that provided in the policy on compensatory time. These associates are paid on a current basis.

B. PAYROLL CHECK DISTRIBUTION:

1. Payroll checks will be distributed on the following schedule and will cover hours worked during the prior week:

   a. First-shift associates—Friday morning
   b. Second-shift associates— Thursday evening
   c. Third-shift associates—Friday morning
   d. Weekend-shift associates—Friday morning

2. It will not be our regular policy to release payroll checks in advance except in the following situations:

   a. The associate has scheduled a vacation, floating holiday, or comp day for Friday.
   b. The associate is on an approved leave of absence.
   c. In case of emergencies, which will require the approval of the general manager.
   d. In no case will a check be released before 3:00 P.M. Thursday.

3. If a holiday falls on a payday, every attempt will be made to distribute checks on the last workday prior to the holiday.

4. If an associate does not report for work on the regular payday, the following procedures will be followed:

   a. The associate's check will be held until he/she returns to work.
   b. Request for someone else to pick up the associate's check must be made in writing, and that individual will be required to show proper identification in order to receive the associate's check.
   c. Checks not claimed will be mailed to the associate's home.

PERSONNEL POLICIES AND PROCEDURES

DISTRIBUTION:		SUBJECT: PAYDAY POLICY	
EFFECTIVE DATE:	PAGE 2 OF 2	FILE UNDER SECTION	
REVISION DATE:	APPROVED BY:		

LOST/DESTROYED PAYCHECKS:

Lost, stolen, or destroyed checks should be reported to the associate's immediate supervisor as soon as possible. In these cases, the company will issue a duplicate check; however, the associate may be responsible for any stop payment charges that are assessed by the bank. If a check is found after a stop payment request has been made to the bank, the associate is responsible for notifying the company and returning the check as soon as possible.

DIRECT DEPOSIT:

The company provides associates with the optional benefit of direct deposit of payroll, whereby as associate may elect to have his/her payroll funds deposited electronically into his/her account(s) at a bank or other financial institution. Funds are available in the associate's account at the beginning of the business day on payday, and the associate receives a receipt to document his/her pay, deductions, and deposit.

PERSONNEL POLICIES AND PROCEDURES

DISTRIBUTION:		SUBJECT: HOURS OF WORK	
EFFECTIVE DATE:	PAGE 1 OF 1	FILE UNDER SECTION	
REVISION DATE:	APPROVED BY:		

POLICY STATEMENT:

(Company Name) will maintain work hours for its employees in accordance with federal and state regulations, production needs, and the maintenance of an efficient and effective schedule of work.

The Fair Labor Standards Act requires employers to maintain an accurate record of hours worked and to pay one and one-half times the regular hourly rate of pay to every nonexempt employee who works overtime. Overtime will be defined as all hours worked over forty in a workweek. The Fair Labor Standards Act permits exemption of certain professional, administrative, and executive positions and certain sales positions, as defined in the statutes, from compliance with the act. For assistance in determining specific positions that are exempt under these definitions, managers must contact the Coordinator of Human Resources.

PROCEDURE:

A. Workweek—The official workweek for all employees at (Company Name) begins at 12:01 A.M. on Monday and ends at 12:00 midnight the following Sunday.

B. Meal Periods—Each employee's meal period will be established by his/her supervisor. Each employee must be provided the opportunity to take a full thirty minutes of uninterrupted time for his/her meal period, and this thirty minutes of uninterrupted time should be reflected on the time record.

C. Break Periods—Each employee's break will be scheduled by the employee's manager, in keeping with work schedules and customer demands. Break times are paid for by the company.

D. Training Time—Any meetings, lectures, and training programs that an employee is required to attend will be considered compensable time.

E. Recording of Hours Worked—Unless otherwise exempt, all employees are required to record when they start each workday, when they leave for and return from lunch, and when they leave work each evening. All hourly employees are required to punch a time clock for the recording of hours. Managers are responsible for ensuring that the following procedures are followed when employees are using a time clock:

- Each timecard should have the name and the employee number entered on the front and on the back of the timecard. Employees should sign their timecards at the end of each week to authorize that the hours shown on the timecard are the true and accurate hours actually worked.
- Employees are not to punch in prior to five minutes before their scheduled working time or punch out later than five minutes past their scheduled quitting time unless authorized. Employees are required to punch out when they leave company premises other than on company business. Under no circumstances is an employee to punch another employee's timecard; this is grounds for disciplinary action.
- Employees are required to have their supervisor correct and initial any changes made on their timecards.
- Managers should review all timecards prior to submitting them to payroll to ensure that they are completed thoroughly and accurately.

PERSONNEL POLICIES AND PROCEDURES

DISTRIBUTION:		SUBJECT: HOURS OF WORK	
EFFECTIVE DATE:	PAGE 1 OF 1		FILE UNDER SECTION
REVISION DATE:	APPROVED BY:		

PURPOSE:

The purpose of this policy is to define a regular work schedule for hourly associates.

POLICY:

A. Posting Requirement
    The official work schedules will be posted on the Controlled Communication Centers at each facility. An associate's work schedule will depend on the job and the shift to which he/she is assigned. Changing conditions in operations may require changes in work schedules. Such changes will be announced as far in advance as practicable.

B. Regular Workshifts
    In the regular eight and one-half- (8-½) hour workday, associates will have a one-half- (½) hour unpaid lunch period along with two rest breaks. Normal work schedules will allow associates a ten- (10) minute break in the first half of the shift and a ten- (10) minute break in the second half of the shift.

C. Irregular Workshifts
    The company may create alternative workshifts as necessary. Legal requirements and consistency of work operations will be considered before alternative workshifts are scheduled.

D. Workshifts cannot be altered without approval of the Human Resources Section.

PROCEDURE:

Hourly associates are required to clock in and clock out each workday using an identification (ID) badge with their name, photo, and payroll number on it. Associates will not be charged for badges that must be replaced due to normal wear, but associates will be charged $3.00 for replacement of badges lost or damaged due to negligence.

An associate should not clock in more than twenty (20) minutes before their scheduled starting time or clock out more than twenty (20) minutes after their scheduled quitting time unless requested to do so by his/her supervisor.

If an associate forgets to clock in or out or feels that an error has been made, he/she should notify his/her supervisor. It is the supervisor's responsibility to see that the correction is made.

DISCIPLINE:

Clocking in or out for another associate or having another associate clock in or out for you is prohibited. This is an intolerable work rule violation, and will be grounds for termination for both associates.

PERSONNEL POLICIES AND PROCEDURES

DISTRIBUTION:		SUBJECT: SALARY ADMINISTRATION, NONEXEMPT AND EXEMPT EMPLOYEES
EFFECTIVE DATE:	PAGE 1 OF 3	FILE UNDER SECTION
REVISION DATE:	APPROVED BY:	

A. PURPOSE

It is the desire of the management to establish a salary policy that will:

1. Improve morale by clearly outlining promotional opportunities and by providing visible job and salary growth.

2. Maintain equitable salaries among individuals.

3. Provide controls that will eliminate excessive salary payments.

4. Provide positive incentives toward outstanding performance and negative incentives toward mediocrity.

5. Keep pace with the current inflationary job market and enable us to retain present and attract new employees.

6. Provide strong financial motivation for employees at all levels, thereby improving the Company's profitability.

B. DEFINITIONS

1. Merit increases are given to reward:

   a. Improved performance.

   b. Increased responsibility without a change in job classification.

2. Promotional increases are given in recognition of promotion from one job classification to a higher classification.

3. General increases are not given to exempt or nonexempt personnel.

C. TIMING OF INCREASES

1. Merit increases given are subject to the following guidelines:

   a. Exempt employees:

      (1) Exempt employees who exhibit good to superior performance and are in the following position classifications—trainee, transferred six months or less previously, promoted nine months or less previously—may receive an increase between six and nine months after assuming the position. The length of time that should elapse before an increase is given is determined by the standard of the employee's performance. For instance, an employee having a good performance level should not receive an increase in less than nine months, but an employee with superior performance could receive an increase in six months.

      (2) Exempt employees who demonstrate good to superior performance and are in an established position classification may receive an increase between nine and eighteen months from the last increase. The length of time that should elapse before an increase is given is determined by the standard of the employee's performance. For instance, if an employee had a good level of performance, he/she would be eligible for an increase at approximately fifteen to eighteen months, but an employee having superior performance would be eligible for an increase at between nine and twelve months.

   b. Nonexempt, nonbargaining employees:

      (1) Nonexempt, nonbargaining employees who demonstrate good to superior performance and are in the following position classifications—trainee, transferred six months or less previously, promoted nine months or less previously—may receive an increase between three and nine months after assuming the position. The length of time that should elapse before an increase is given is determined by the standard of the employee's performance.

DISTRIBUTION:		SUBJECT: SALARY ADMINISTRATION, NONEXEMPT AND EXEMPT EMPLOYEES	
EFFECTIVE DATE:	PAGE 2 OF 3	FILE UNDER SECTION	
REVISION DATE:	APPROVED BY:		

(2) Nonexempt, nonbargaining employees who demonstrate good to superior performance and are in an established position classification may receive an increase between nine and fifteen months from the last increase. The length of time that should elapse before an increase is given is determined by the employee's performance.

(3) The review of an employee's salary for increase is to ensure that all employees are given consideration and are not forgotten. However, a review is not synonymous with an increase. Therefore, the employee should not necessarily receive an increase every six, nine, or eighteen months, as the case may be.

2. Increases for employees of multiemployee departments or terminals will be submitted with different effective dates. Any increase for two or more employees in the same department, to be effective on the same date, will require the approval of the Director of Human Resources.

D. PROMOTIONAL INCREASES

Normally each employee would receive a promotional increase effective on the date that the employee assumes the responsibilities of the new position. In certain circumstances, it may be desirable to delay the promotional increase until the employee has successfully completed a trial period, not to exceed three months in the new position.

E. DETERMINING INCREASE AMOUNTS

1. Merit Increases: The following factors should be considered in determining the amounts of increases that an employee will receive:

a. Performance since last merit increase.
b. Potential for further advancement.
c. Assumption of increased responsibility in the job.

2. A reasonable standard for merit increase, stated as a percentage of base salary, based upon performance is:

a. Unsatisfactory—0 percent
b. Good—5 to 7.5 percent
c. Very good—7.5 to 10 percent
d. Superior—10 to 12.5 percent
e. Outstanding—12.5 percent plus

Increases should not be given in amounts that are less than 5 percent of the employee's base salary.

3. Promotional increases: The following factors should determine the amount of a promotional increase:

a. Degree of increased responsibility.
b. Performance since last merit or promotional increase.
c. Length of time since last increase.

No guidelines may be set for the amount of a promotional increase; however, the amount of this increase should be somewhat greater (2 to 4 percent) than the merit increase that the employee would have received.

F. SALARY INCREASE APPROVAL PROCEDURE

1. Salary increase requests are to be submitted to the Human Resources Department fourteen (14) days or more in advance of the requested date.

PERSONNEL POLICIES AND PROCEDURES

DISTRIBUTION:		SUBJECT: SALARY ADMINISTRATION, NONEXEMPT AND EXEMPT EMPLOYEES	
EFFECTIVE DATE:	PAGE 3 OF 3	FILE UNDER SECTION	
REVISION DATE:	APPROVED BY:		

2. The requested increase date is the effective date of the increase, which is normally the first day of the payroll period.

3. The request is to be submitted on a Personnel Action Form and completed as indicated. The following information must be completed:

   a. Employee's name (last, first, and middle initial).
   b. Employee's six-digit employee number.
   c. Terminal code.
   d. Employee's department accounting code number.
   e. Employee's date of hire.
   f. Employee's pay classification (exempt, nonexempt, bargaining unit).
   g. Employee's job title.
   h. Employee's department and location.
   i. Employee's previous increase—amount.
   j. Employee's present rate of pay—amount, effective date, and percentage.
   k. Employee's proposed rate of pay—amount, effective date, and percentage.

4. Each level of supervision should retain one copy of the Personnel Action Form as it is given to them for approval. Once each level of supervision has signed the form, they should separate their copy and send the remainder to the next level. Unless each level of supervision is notified that an increase has been disapproved, they may assume that the increase was granted on the date as indicated.

5. Should the request reach the Human Resources Department less than fourteen (14) days before the proposed effective date, the effective date will be changed accordingly.

6. All retroactive pay adjustments must be approved by the Director of Human Resources.

7. Employees are not to be advised of a pending increase until the effective date of the increase.

PERSONNEL POLICIES AND PROCEDURES

DISTRIBUTION:		SUBJECT: CORPORATE SALARY ADMINISTRATION	
EFFECTIVE DATE:	PAGE 1 OF 2		FILE UNDER SECTION
REVISION DATE:	APPROVED BY:		

It is the intent of the Company to establish throughout the organization a sound salary policy in order to:

A. Develop a better understanding of the principles of salary administration and of the Company's salary program on the part of all those responsible for its application.

B. Develop and maintain sound, practical guides to effective salary administration at each location. Such guides are developed in conjunction with Division Heads and local management, and designed to meet specific needs of the location.

C. Permit optimum delegation of authority and responsibility to appropriate management for the administration of salaries within the framework of the salary policy.

D. Facilitate work with each Division, Department, and Plant Manager to properly translate the results of performance reviews into meaningful salary administration for each salaried employee.

E. Maintain salary levels and a salary program consistent with those of the general industry through the medium of periodic reviews and surveys.

F. Provide incentives, through the proper administration of salaries and other forms of compensation, for each individual to put forth his or her best efforts on the job. This means that each individual's progress on a job is reviewed regularly, recognizing the individual's achievements and suggesting areas of possible improvement.

G. Determine a uniform structure of job relationships that will adequately compensate the individual for work performed and provide opportunities for advancement, promotion, and transfer.

H. Keep the individual informed of compensation matters affecting him or her and bring about the realization by each individual that he or she is being treated consistently and equitably with respect to salary.

POLICY:

It is the policy of the Company to pay each salaried employee for the value of his or her contribution through assigned work to the success of the company. In doing so, it will maintain competitive salary relationships with other companies in order to retain its own qualified personnel and attract competent applicants.

AUTHORITY:

The Salary Committee has been empowered by the Executive Committee of the company to develop the salary structure for the organization. The Salary Committee, in turn, delegates the overall responsibility for developing, implementing, and administering the salary program to the Industrial Relations Division, while retaining the final authority in the following areas:

PERSONNEL POLICIES AND PROCEDURES

DISTRIBUTION:		SUBJECT: CORPORATE SALARY ADMINISTRATION	
EFFECTIVE DATE:	PAGE 2 OF 2	FILE UNDER SECTION	
REVISION DATE:	APPROVED BY:		

A. Approval of new or revised salary classifications and corresponding salaries.

B. Approval of salary increases, except as delegated to other levels of management as indicated in the Salary Manual.

C. Recommending to the Executive Committee of the company adjustments in the salary structure based on determinations made by the Industrial Relations Division.

D. Development and implementation of additional methods of compensation.

DESCRIPTIVE SALARY INFORMATION:

The plan conforms to the wage and hour provisions of the Walsh-Healey Public Contracts Act and the Fair Labor Standards Act in that jobs classified as "Executive, Administrative, Professional, and Outside Salesmen" are described as exempt. All other salaried jobs not falling in these classifications are described as nonexempt.

The company uses the guideline* method in evaluating jobs. This method utilizes primarily American Management Association surveys for prevailing rates and ranges in exempt functions, and local surveys for comparable information on nonexempt functions.

The corporate salary program is needed to eliminate undue pressure on the company's payroll costs. Generally, pressure on payroll costs results when (1) higher individual pay rates are granted as seniority is acquired, (2) the traditional approach is practiced—i.e., that progress in individual pay rates should be continuous, (3) responsible executives are reluctant to reduce rates when a function has less market value than it did formerly, and (4) increases to salaried employees are granted as a result of an increase to the hourly employees.

This program will assist in accurately forecasting salary costs for budgetary purposes.

*The guideline method deals in results rather than approaches and provides a valid, simple, flexible, and economical evaluation plan for management jobs. The guideline method bases evaluation on comparison with standard job descriptions and ranks functions in competitive salary ranges for the exempt group. Each range is made up of a minimum, a midpoint, and a maximum salary level. The midpoint of the range represents the average salary paid by other employers as determined from survey data. This method eliminates the time-consuming element found in a "point" or "factor" evaluation plan. New jobs can be evaluated or reevaluation of existing jobs accomplished without tying up line management for unreasonable periods of time. Record-keeping and paperwork requirements are minimal.

PERSONNEL POLICIES AND PROCEDURES

DISTRIBUTION:		SUBJECT: SALARY ADMINISTRATION	
EFFECTIVE DATE:	PAGE 1 OF 5	FILE UNDER SECTION	
REVISION DATE:	APPROVED BY:		

A. SCOPE

This procedure applies to the planning and administration of all salary actions to the active, non-bargaining-unit employees who are administered by U.S. salary range structures. This policy is not intended to create a contract of employment with any employee but should be used as a guide in administering the salary program.

B. INTENT

Individual employee performance is to be used as the basis for achieving (Company Name) "pay for performance" goals in its salary administration program. The company's objective is to administer salary actions that will ultimately move an individual's salary to a position that falls between the minimum and maximum of the salary quintile range that is most consistent with the employee's job performance level, as assessed through the performance appraisal program.

C. POLICY

It is the policy of (Company Name) that:

1. Salaries paid to employees compare favorably with those paid in the general market for workers with the same or similar skills, training, and ability. Salaries are paid within established salary ranges that provide the flexibility to motivate and reward employees in relation to their contributions.

D. GENERAL GUIDELINES

The following guidelines apply to the applicable employee groups and may be changed by the senior vice president—human resources, or designee, due to unique requirements arising from economic conditions, government regulations, etc.:

1. Salary Levels for New Employees (Exempt and Nonexempt)

   Hiring rate will normally fall between the minimum and midpoint of the range in which a position is classified. Offers above the midpoint should be made only for reasons of unusual market demand.

2. Promotional Increases (Exempt and Nonexempt)

   A. Bona fide promotions may occur at any time and are usually unplanned salary actions. Promotional increases to a salary in the lower half of the range of the new position should normally be fully adequate. Promotional increases that result in a salary that is in excess of the salary range midpoint should be considered only in exceptional situations. (In these situations, some supporting documentation must be retained in the individual's location or department personnel file.)

   B. Salary actions must bring the employee's salary at least to the minimum of the new salary range.

3. Individual Salary Increases (Exempt and Nonexempt)

   An individual employee's movement toward a position within the salary range quintile will be based upon achieved level of performance, current position in the salary range, and the overall application of the company's salary spending budget guidelines, which reflect competitive conditions and economic factors. The frequency and amount of individual increases are directed at achieving proper salary positioning within the salary range and will vary, with review consideration being given at least once during the company's salary planning period, typically each fiscal year. However, employees on a properly documented performance improvement program should have their salary increase delayed until performance improvement goals are met.

   Proper salary positioning within a given range results from the translation of an employee's performance rating, as assessed by management, into one of five range segments, which have been defined to reward specific levels of performance. See "Definitions" for performance ratings and associated range segments.

PERSONNEL POLICIES AND PROCEDURES

DISTRIBUTION:		SUBJECT: SALARY ADMINISTRATION	
EFFECTIVE DATE:	PAGE 2 OF 5	FILE UNDER SECTION	
REVISION DATE:	APPROVED BY:		

4. Salary Budget Spending Guidelines (Exempt and Nonexempt)

   These guidelines, usually expressed in average percentage budget increase amounts and average increase frequencies, are developed for and applied to the overall planning of salary increases as part of the company's fiscal budget plan. They are not meant as achievable targets among small groups of employees, or for individual salary determination. Because increases are based on individual situations as described in this procedure, there is no company intent to establish an average increase for "satisfactory" or any other level of performance.

5. Salary Range Minimums (Exempt and Nonexempt)

   All employees must be paid at least the minimum rate of the salary range for their job classification. However, when new salary ranges are adopted, some employees' salaries will fall below the new range minimums. Employees with salaries below the range minimum may be considered for an increase nine (9) months from the date of the last salary increase, unless they are on a current performance improvement program, in which case increases will be delayed until improvement goals are met. The amount of the increase is to be determined on an individual basis, but the salary action must bring the employee to at least the range minimum.

6. Individual Salary Increase Eligibility Schedule (Nonexempt Employees)

   Normally, the first increase eligibility date is at the completion of six (6) months of employment. The second eligibility date is six (6) months from the date of the first increase, and subsequent eligibility dates occur at intervals of at least one year (usually one planning period) from the date of last increase.

7. Salary Range Maximums (Exempt and Nonexempt)

   Salary actions should not result in salaries that exceed established range maximums (red circle rates).

   If a job change, with resultant reduction in grade, causes a salary to exceed the range maximum, consideration of an appropriate reduction in salary should be given. Generally, if the change is performance-related, a reduction should be made. If the red circle rate results for any other reason, management, at its discretion, may or may not implement a reduction.

8. Employees Currently on or Returning from Leave of Absence (Exempt and Nonexempt)

   Salary actions for employees currently on an approved disability leave with pay may be processed as long as the action (1) was previously planned and (2) is to be effective on or prior to the last day of the month following the month in which the disability leave is effective. Otherwise, salary actions will not be processed while employees are on leaves of absence. Any other previously approved increases may become effective on the first pay date of the month following the employees' return to work.

   Employees returning from leaves of absence of sixty (60) consecutive calendar days should be reinstated with an extension of their review cycle equivalent to the length of their leave, i.e., the amount of time absent should be added to their normal review cycle timeframe. However, once an employee returning from a medical or military leave has completed nine (9) months' active service [or six (6) months for nonexempt new hires] since the date of the last increase, he/she may be considered for a salary increase, regardless of the length of the leave, depending on performance, position in range, and market conditions.

E. SALARY PLANNING

   As an aid to management in planning and equitably distributing salary dollars, an automated salary planning system is utilized throughout the company. This system is designed as a management tool and is not intended to infringe on management's prerogative to assess performance and review and approve planned actions.

   The system provides for the building and verification of an employee planning base and the review and modification of system-generated salary action recommendations for each employee. (Line management may modify the recommended actions where a properly documented need for adjustments to selected employees in the same budget group

DISTRIBUTION:		SUBJECT: SALARY ADMINISTRATION	
EFFECTIVE DATE:	PAGE 3 OF 5	FILE UNDER SECTION	
REVISION DATE:	APPROVED BY:		

exists. Such adjustments may be shared appropriately among other employees in the budgeting group.) The system also provides a prescribed approval process to ensure management's concurrence with individual salary actions and total costs at the beginning of the planning period.

As salary actions become due for implementation, the approved plan provides a framework for effecting planned actions and for identifying actions that are exceptions to plan. The processing of these actions is done through established electronic and/or document-based systems.

F. APPROVAL REQUIREMENTS

The following authorizations are required to institute plans generated from the company's salary planning system:

A. Line or staff executive reporting to the president and chief operating officer and, at minimum, two lower levels of direct reporting management are required to authorize by signature the summary of salary plan costs for their respective organization.

In addition, each of the three management levels is required to sign a list of individual salary actions, which includes, for their respective organization:

- Resulting salaries that exceed delegated approval levels.
- The need for the second level of line management approval.
- Individual actions in excess of 16 percent.
- Individual merit actions that are less than six months in frequency for new hire nonexempt employees, and less than nine months in frequency for all other employees.
- Actions that result in salaries that are below the minimum or exceed the maximum of the salary ranges.

B. President and Chief Executive Officer authorizes by signature the list of individual salary actions, which includes:

- Resulting salaries that exceed delegated approval levels; and
- The need for the second level of line management approval.

2. Salary Action Approvals

The following authorizations are required to effect salary actions as specified:

A. Salary Actions within an Approved Salary Plan

Salary actions that are processed against an approved salary plan require the following approvals:

Originating line management may approve actions that:

- Comply exactly with plan, or
- Vary from plan increase percentage by no more than minus 2 percent of base salary, or
- Are postponed beyond the planned effective date.

B. Changes to the Approved Salary Plan

The level of line management with the proper approval authority must approve a change that:

Exceeds the approved plan increase percentage, and/or

Reduces the planned percentage by more than minus 2 percent of base salary, and/or

- Is less than the planned increase frequency (unless action is a result of a bona fide promotion), or
- Exceeds the delegated approval authority of the first level of management above the manager initiating the change, provided that the action does not exceed 16 percent of the base salary, or is below the minimum or above the maximum of the salary range, or is less than six months in frequency for all other employees (unless action is a result of a bona fide promotion). The line or staff executive reporting to the president and chief operating officer must approve these actions. This approval may be delegated to the next level.

PERSONNEL POLICIES AND PROCEDURES

DISTRIBUTION:		SUBJECT: SALARY ADMINISTRATION	
EFFECTIVE DATE:	PAGE 4 OF 5	FILE UNDER SECTION	
REVISION DATE:	APPROVED BY:		

C. Unplanned Salary Actions

The following approvals are required for all unplanned salary actions:

- Resultant salaries require specific management approval.
- At least two levels of line management approval are required.
- The line or staff executive reporting to the president and chief operating officer must approve salary actions: In excess of 16 percent; below the minimum or above the maximum of the salary range; and less than six months in frequency for new hire nonexempt employees and less than nine months for all other employees (unless action is a result of a bona fide promotion). This approval may be delegated to the next level.

D. General Increase Programs

General increase programs require the approvals of the affected line executive reporting to the president and chief operating officer and the staff vice president for corporate compensation or their designees.

3. Cognizant human resources management is accountable for assuring that required approvals and supporting documentation are obtained and properly retained for audit purposes before salary plans or salary actions are implemented.

G. SALARY INCREASE PROCESSING

There is to be no retroactive processing of salary increases.

Increases for weekly payroll employees must be received in the payroll department by the end of the next to the last working day of the month preceding the effective date of the increase.

Increases for monthly payroll employees must be received by the seventh of the month in which the increase is to be effective.

Any exception to these dates must be approved by the executive reporting to the president and chief operating officer. This approval may be delegated to the next level.

H. DEFINITIONS

The following performance levels apply to specific segments of the salary range:

"O" Outstanding—This level is associated with the top quintile of the range: The employee consistently performs all assignments at a level significantly above the position requirements and rarely achieved by others. Performance is characterized by exceptional contribution and extraordinary accomplishment.

"A" Above Satisfactory—The fourth quintile is a level in which an employee's performance continually exceeds the position requirements. The employee maintains a high level of achievement on a sustained basis.

"S" Satisfactory—The middle, third quintile is represented by this level where performance meets all position requirements. The employee generally fulfills all key assignments satisfactorily.

"I" Improvement Required—Relates to the second quintile of the range and applies when the employee's performance of position requirements is at a less than fully satisfactory level. The employee may require more than normal assistance, guidance, or supervision. Improvement is required.

"M" Marginal—Relates to the bottom, first quintile of the range and applies when the employee's performance does not meet the minimum acceptable position requirements and demands close supervision and frequent review of work. Performance at this level is not acceptable and demands immediate improvement.

Salary actions are identified by the following:

PERSONNEL POLICIES AND PROCEDURES

DISTRIBUTION:		SUBJECT: SALARY ADMINISTRATION	
EFFECTIVE DATE:	PAGE 5 OF 5	FILE UNDER SECTION	
REVISION DATE:	APPROVED BY:		

Type of Action	*Definition*
Merit Increase	Salary action granted to an employee within present job classification that takes into consideration job performance, position within salary range, budget, and competitive market conditions.
Promotional Increase	Salary action associated with a promotion to a higher grade where the duties, responsibilities, and accountabilities of an employee have substantially increased from the previous position. Growth reclassifications within the same established functional hierarchies are excluded.
Merit/Grade Advancement Increase	Salary action associated with an advancement to a higher grade, up to and including the fourth level, within the same established functional hierarchy. These actions usually occur at the normal merit salary increase review time.
Adjustment	Salary action, granted on a selected or limited basis, to correct a specific salary rate problem—i.e., compression caused by accelerating hiring rates, unfavorable salary market position, etc. Adjustments are normally granted simultaneously to a group of employees but may be granted to an individual employee to correct a severe salary inequity that demands immediate attention. This type of salary action will not interrupt an employee's merit review cycle.
Reduction	Salary action resulting in a reduction of salary or hourly rate for any reason.
Rate Progression	Salary action granted to an individual employee or to bring an individual employee to the appropriate incremental rate of an approved step progression program. This is not to be used for general increases or for a promotion to a significantly different classification at a higher grade level.
General Increase	Market adjustment given simultaneously to all employees on an approved step progression program when their rate structure is revised. Includes individual rate progression increase when given at the same time as general increase.
Merit Increase Accelerated Frequency	Merit increase granted under guidelines that call for increase frequency that is no more than one-half of the normal merit frequency. This applies to such employees as nonexempt new hires, trainees, etc.

All of the above actions, with the exception of ''Adjustments,'' will recycle the employee onto a new merit review cycle.

I. AUDIT

The corporate compensation programs activity, or designee human resources departments, are accountable for conducting periodic audits of compliance with the requirements of this procedure.

PERSONNEL POLICIES AND PROCEDURES

DISTRIBUTION:		SUBJECT: STATEMENT ON JOB EVALUATION
EFFECTIVE DATE:	PAGE 1 OF 1	FILE UNDER SECTION
REVISION DATE:	APPROVED BY:	

No business can overlook the importance of providing people with fair salaries, proper job training, and the opportunity for advancement relative to ability, performance, and experience.

The purpose of job evaluation is to ensure fair and equitable salaries according to job responsibilities and to be sure each person understands clearly what is expected in his/her particular job. To ensure this, every position has been evaluated. Jobs are scored for their degree of difficulty, with the following factors taken into consideration: education required, special training, responsibility, physical or mental effort, manual dexterity, and working environment.

Each position is given a specific salary range with an established minimum and maximum. The range is ample enough to allow generous incentives for improved performance, job proficiency, and exceptional individual effort. To keep up to date, we review our job evaluation program at least once a year.

Employee performance on the job is continually checked. Supervisors make periodic reports on employees' progress that become a permanent part of their personnel files. These files are referred to for salary reviews and when opportunities for promotion exist. They are also used as background material should supervisors feel the need to discuss improvement in an individual's work.

The quality of an employee's work, ability to get along with coworkers, job performance, willingness to cooperate, ability to lead, attendance and promptness records, appearance, and personal initiative are all measured for salary review or in a case where a promotion is to be made.

PERSONNEL POLICIES AND PROCEDURES

DISTRIBUTION:		SUBJECT: EXEMPT SALARY TEST FOR "EXECUTIVE" WAGE-HOUR CLASSIFICATION
EFFECTIVE DATE:	PAGE 1 OF 2	FILE UNDER SECTION
REVISION DATE:	APPROVED BY:	

THE "EXECUTIVE" SALARY CLASSIFICATION TESTS
WHITE-COLLAR EXEMPTION:

There are six federal wage-hour accounting tests that must be met before an individual can qualify for a guaranteed straight salary, thus being free from minimum wage, overtime compensation, and the recording of hours. The tests are as follows:

The employee:

1. Must have as a primary duty the management of an establishment, department, or subdivision of the organization.

2. Must regularly direct the work of at least two full-time employees.

3. Must have the authority to hire or fire, or else have the authority to effectively recommend personnel changes with reference to hiring, firing, or other personnel actions, with reference to employees under his/her supervision. These recommendations must be given particular weight by the immediate supervisor.

4. Must regularly exercise discretion and independent judgment, rather than simply a skill or skills on a regular, recurring basis.

5. Must spend less than 20 percent of the total hours of work in a workweek in "nonexempt" work (40 percent in retail and health-care facilities). This is similar to the type of work performed by employees under supervision, such as manual production work or routine clerical duties unrelated to the primary supervisory responsibilities.

6. Present minimum salary test for a person trying to qualify in the "Executive" white-collar classification is $155 a week guaranteed. However, if an employee is paid $250 a week guaranteed, he/she would be eligible for the "Executive" salary classification provided the first two accounting tests outlined above are met. (Use current minimum.)

THE "EXECUTIVE" TESTS AMPLIFIED

Management duties must involve having charge of and managing a recognized unit that has a continuing function. Those who usually qualify as managers are: department heads, office managers, foremen, and superintendents, among others.

Supervision must involve customary and regular supervision of two other full-time employees (or the equivalent), and they must be in the department managed by the executive. Supervision needn't be constant but must be more than occasional. If an employee supervises four part-time employees, two working mornings and two working in the afternoons, that is equivalent to two full-time employees.

Hiring or firing includes direct action by the executive employee or recommendations to those to whom hiring and firing functions are delegated. Recommendations as to promotions, pay increases, and the like must also be given weight. Exercise of discretion must be performed customarily and regularly. It needn't be exercised constantly, but only more frequently than occasionally. Nonexecutive duties are those that are not directly and closely related to executive work, usually those that are performed by subordinates. Thus, production work done during subordinates' ab-

DISTRIBUTION:		SUBJECT: EXEMPT SALARY TEST FOR "EXECUTIVE" WAGE-HOUR CLASSIFICATION	
EFFECTIVE DATE:	PAGE 2 OF 2		FILE UNDER SECTION
REVISION DATE:	APPROVED BY:		

sences for lunch periods is part of the 20 percent tolerance that was mentioned above (40 percent in retail and health-care facilities).

Three types of employees are not governed by the 20 percent or 40 percent test for the Executive salary classification: (1) those in sole charge of an establishment having a fixed location and separated from other company property, (2) those who own a 20 percent interest in the organization, and (3) those who are paid $250 a week and who meet the first two tests (management and supervision), as outlined above. (Use current minimum.)

PERSONNEL POLICIES AND PROCEDURES

DISTRIBUTION:		SUBJECT: EXEMPT SALARY TEST FOR "ADMINISTRATIVE" OR COMBINATION "EXECUTIVE/ADMINISTRATIVE" SALARY CLASSIFICATION
EFFECTIVE DATE:	PAGE 1 OF 1	FILE UNDER SECTION
REVISION DATE:	APPROVED BY:	

THE "ADMINISTRATIVE" SALARY CLASSIFICATION TESTS
WHITE-COLLAR EXEMPTION:

There are five federal wage-hour accounting tests that apply to personnel qualifying for the "Administrative" white-collar salary classification. There are generally three types or classifications usually eligible for the administrative white-collar classification exemption from the minimum wage and overtime requirements: (1) an assistant to a top-level executive, (2) a staff employee, and (3) those persons who do special assignments under only general supervision. An administrator establishes or carries out policies and is principally distinguished from the "Executive" in that he/she does not directly supervise the work of others in the department or subdivision.

To qualify as an "Administrative" salary employee and be free from the recording of hours of work on a daily basis, minimum wage, and overtime compensation after forty hours in a workweek, an employee must meet the following tests:

The employee:

1. Must, as the primary duty, do office or nonmanual work directly related to management policy and/or decisions affecting customers of the business.

2. Must regularly exercise independent discretion and judgment on significant matters.

3. Must assist an owner, an executive, or another administrative employee or do specialized work under general supervision.

4. Must spend less than 20 percent of his/her total hours worked in the workweek in performing nonadministrative, nonexempt work (40 percent in retail and health-care facilities).

5. The present minimum guaranteed salary or fee test for an administrative employee is no less than $155 a week. (Use current minimum.)

"Administrative" personnel who are paid a current minimum, guaranteed, or the equivalent for periods longer than a week, are eligible for the "administrative" salary classification, if they meet the first two accounting tests outlined above.

However, even at the minimum guarantee or the equivalent, such administrative personnel cannot spend more than 50 percent of their total time in their workweek in nonadministrative duties such as manual office clerical work, operating bookkeeping or accounting machines, and other general-type clerical work.

PERSONNEL POLICIES AND PROCEDURES

DISTRIBUTION:		SUBJECT: EXEMPT SALARY TEST FOR "PROFESSIONAL" WAGE-HOUR CLASSIFICATION	
EFFECTIVE DATE:	PAGE 1 OF 1	FILE UNDER SECTION	
REVISION DATE:	APPROVED BY:		

THE "PROFESSIONAL" SALARY CLASSIFICATION TESTS
WHITE-COLLAR EXEMPTION:

There are five (5) federal wage-hour accounting tests that must be met before an individual can qualify for a guaranteed straight salary, thus being free from minimum wage, overtime compensation, and the recording of hours. The tests are as follows:

1. The primary duty of the professional is to perform work requiring knowledge of an advanced type in a field of science or learning customarily acquired by a prolonged course of specialized intellectual instruction and study, as distinguished from a general academic education and from an apprenticeship and from training in the performance of routine mental, manual, or physical processes. This requirement is generally met by such professions as law, medicine, accountancy, engineering, architecture, etc., and the best evidence thereof is the appropriate academic degree.

2. This work requires the consistent exercise of discretion and judgment in its performance.

3. This work is predominately intellectual and varied in character (as opposed to routine mental, manual, mechanical, or physical work) and is of such character that the output produced or the results accomplished cannot be standardized on a time basis.

4. The individual must spend less than 20 percent of the total hours of work in a workweek in nonexempt work. (Routine work is exempt if it is directly and closely related to the performance of the professional duties, and it is also "an essential part of and necessarily incident to" the professional work.)

5. The present minimum fee or salary test for a professional employee is at least $170 per week. (Use current minimum.) However, if the individual is paid at least $250 per week, eligibility for the "Professional" salary classification is made provided the first two accounting tests outlined above are met.

PERSONNEL POLICIES AND PROCEDURES

DISTRIBUTION:		SUBJECT: EXEMPT SALARY TEST FOR "OUTSIDE SALESPERSON" OR "COMBINATION EXECUTIVE/OUTSIDE SALESPERSON"
EFFECTIVE DATE:	PAGE 1 OF 1	FILE UNDER SECTION
REVISION DATE:	APPROVED BY:	

THE "OUTSIDE SALESPERSON" SALARY CLASSIFICATION TESTS
WHITE-COLLAR EXEMPTION:

The Wage-Hour Division defines the classification of "Outside Salesperson" as any employee primarily hired in the capacity of an outside sales representative who performs the following job duties and responsibilities on a regular, recurring basis:

1. Employed for the purpose of and customarily away from the place or places of business in making sales or obtaining orders or contracts for services, or for the use of facilities for which a consideration is paid by the customer.

2. Hours of work in performing duties other than those described above do not exceed 20 percent of the hours worked in a workweek by nonsales and nonsupervisory employees. However, work performed by a salesperson that is incidental to or in conjunction with his/her own outside sales or solicitations, including incidental bookkeeping, collections, and deliveries, would not be looked upon as nonsales duties by the Wage-Hour Division.

It is general enforcement policy of the Wage-Hour Division that so-called "house salespeople who are engaged primarily in taking orders by telephone on a daily basis are not eligible for the "Outside Salesperson" salary classification free from the minimum wage and overtime requirements. Of course, there is no minimum salary required for personnel meeting the "Outside Salesperson" accounting tests.

PERSONNEL POLICIES AND PROCEDURES

DISTRIBUTION:		SUBJECT: REPORT PAY	
EFFECTIVE DATE:	PAGE 1 OF 1	FILE UNDER SECTION	
REVISION DATE:	APPROVED BY:		

PURPOSE:

The purpose of this policy is to ensure that associates who report for work are provided either a minimum of four (4) hours' work or four (4) hours' pay if work is not available for reasons within the control of the company.

POLICY:

Unless attempts have been made by telephone or through the designated public media to notify associates that work is not available, if they report at their regular starting time, associates will receive either four (4) hours of work or four (4) hours of pay. Every effort should be made to provide four (4) hours of work. Under this policy, associates may be assigned to any job on which work is available.

This provision for a minimum of four (4) hours' work or pay does not apply if the lack of work is due to weather, utility failures, or other causes beyond the control of the company.

Associates will be advised by a notice posted on the Controlled Communications Center at each location of radio and television stations on which announcements regarding the operation of the plant will be made.

PERSONNEL POLICIES AND PROCEDURES

DISTRIBUTION:		SUBJECT: OVERTIME—HOURLY AND SALARIED (NONEXEMPT) PAYROLLS
EFFECTIVE DATE:	PAGE 1 OF 3	FILE UNDER SECTION
REVISION DATE:	APPROVED BY:	

POLICY STATEMENT:

For all workers except our security officers, it is the policy of (Company Name) that work shall be completed, insofar as possible, with one shift only. When overtime work must be scheduled, equal opportunity for participation will be given within the department concerned as equally as possible among the employees who are capable of performing the work to be done.

DEFINITION OF TERMS:

1. Casual Overtime:

   Means overtime of an irregular nature, not expected to continue for more than a day or so. Casual overtime occurs at infrequent intervals and is of such a nature that it cannot be accurately predicted for any given period of time. An example of casual overtime is overtime authorized to meet an emergency caused by machine breakdown or unexpected absenteeism or production demand in the department. Casual overtime includes daily or Saturday work provided the above conditions are met.

2. Regularly Scheduled Overtime:

   Means overtime that occurs at regular intervals and that is usually accurately predicted for any given period of time. For instance, if because of production need a department head announces to his/her department that a certain number of people would be required to work ten hours overtime each week for the next six weeks, this would be classed as regularly scheduled overtime.

GENERAL:

1. Employees assigned overtime work must be judged by the company as capable of performing the work to be done.

2. Opportunity for casual overtime on a particular job will normally be given to the employee who has been working on that job during the regular shift.

3. Opportunity for Saturday overtime of a casual nature will normally be given to the employee who does this work during the regular week.

4. There will be no partiality shown to any employee in the distribution of overtime.

5. For regularly scheduled overtime, the Management Committee Member concerned will approve a memo of justification and indicate the approximate date the overtime will cease. A copy of the justification memo will be kept in the human resources department reflected on the appropriate payroll ledger cards.

PERSONNEL POLICIES AND PROCEDURES

DISTRIBUTION:		SUBJECT: OVERTIME—HOURLY AND SALARIED (NONEXEMPT) PAYROLLS
EFFECTIVE DATE:	PAGE 2 OF 3	FILE UNDER SECTION
REVISION DATE:	APPROVED BY:	

6. For casual overtime, the Management Committee Member concerned must approve an Overtime Authorization Request Form listing employees selected for overtime.

7. As a condition of employment, an employee is expected to work overtime and on any shift when assigned by his/her immediate supervisor. In the event an employee has a justifiable excuse and is unable to work overtime, he/she should notify his/her immediate supervisor so that an alternate may be selected.

OVERTIME REQUESTS—APPROVALS:

1. All overtime requests must be approved by the appropriate Management Committee Member or in his/her absence by a Manager specifically authorized to make the decision.

2. In the event of an "emergency" the Director of Human Resources may approve overtime requests for any department.

METHOD OF PAYMENT:

1. Overtime will be paid to hourly and salaried (nonexempt) payroll employees for those hours worked over and above forty hours in a workweek at the rate of 1 1/2 times regular base rate.

   a. For the purpose of this policy, paid holidays and paid vacations will be treated as time worked.

   b. No other absence will be counted as time worked.

   c. Sunday will be considered as a regular workday.

2. Those hourly and salaried (nonexempt) payroll employees who work on government contracts will be paid at a rate not less than one and one-half times the base rate for all overtime hours worked in any workweek in excess of eight in a day or forty in a week, whichever is the greater number.

3. The normal workweek for hourly payroll personnel begins at 7:30 A.M. on Monday and ends at 4:00 P.M. on Friday. The normal workweek for salaried (nonexempt) payroll personnel begins at 8:00 A.M. on Monday and ends at 4:30 P.M. on Friday. The calendar workweek begins at 4:00 P.M. (hourly payroll) or 4:30 P.M. [salaried (nonexempt) payroll] each Friday.

MISCELLANEOUS:

1. No employee will be asked or required to take time off from his/her regular work schedule due to his/her having worked overtime.

PERSONNEL POLICIES AND PROCEDURES

DISTRIBUTION:		SUBJECT: OVERTIME—HOURLY AND SALARIED (NONEXEMPT) PAYROLLS
EFFECTIVE DATE:	PAGE 3 OF 3	FILE UNDER SECTION
REVISION DATE:	APPROVED BY:	

2. Any hourly or salaried (nonexempt) employee found on the premises at other than normal work hours without an approved ''overtime authorization request'' will be asked to ''clock out'' but will, of course, be paid for the full time worked.

3. Violations of this policy will be brought to the attention of the Management Committee Member concerned for appropriate corrective action.

PERSONNEL POLICIES AND PROCEDURES

DISTRIBUTION:		SUBJECT: SUPERVISOR OVERTIME AND SHIFT BONUS	
EFFECTIVE DATE:	PAGE 1 OF 2		FILE UNDER SECTION
REVISION DATE:	APPROVED BY:		

POLICY STATEMENT:

It is the policy of the company to pay an overtime allowance to Exempt Supervisors, Salary Grade 1B and below, when required to supervise nonexempt employees during approved scheduled overtime.

DEFINITION OF TERMS:

1. Scheduled Overtime:

   Planned work hours extended beyond the normal forty-hour workweek specifically designated to accomplish some agreed-upon task.

2. Emergency Overtime:

   Extra work hours beyond normal schedule that occur because of some unforeseen condition—e.g., breakdown of equipment that will be needed the following work period. The unexpected condition would require supervision of nonexempt employees and should be no more than three hours in duration.

3. Casual Overtime:

   Hours spent beyond the normal work schedule to accomplish administrative duties, briefings, training, meetings, or the like.

4. Allowance Approvals:

   Extra work hours eligible to be compensated with an overtime allowance. Approval must be made by the appropriate Management Committee Member or designate.

5. Overtime Allowance Rate:

   One times the supervisor's regular hourly base rate (annual rate divided by 2080) multiplied by the number of hours worked.

GUIDELINES:

1. For supervisors to be paid the overtime allowance, the overtime must be (a) approved and (b) categorized as either scheduled or emergency, and (c) they must work the hours accounted for.

2. Casual overtime is not eligible for compensation of an overtime allowance.

3. All compensable overtime (scheduled or emergency) must be requested and approved prior to working any overtime.

4. Total hours worked in one week must exceed forty hours before overtime allowances can be paid.

PERSONNEL POLICIES AND PROCEDURES

DISTRIBUTION:		SUBJECT: SUPERVISOR OVERTIME AND SHIFT BONUS	
EFFECTIVE DATE:	PAGE 2 OF 2	FILE UNDER SECTION	
REVISION DATE:	APPROVED BY:		

5. The Vice President of Human Resources has initial and final approval of any position's eligibility designation for supervisory overtime allowance.

6. Supervisors paid overtime allowance cannot have compensatory time off for working overtime.

7. Supervisors assigned to the designated second or third shift would receive a shift premium bonus of 50 cents per hour. For supervisors assigned to the second or third shift, calculations of overtime allowances would include the shift premium.

REPORTING OF OVERTIME AND SHIFT PREMIUM:

Weekly the respective department manager is responsible for submitting, for those exempt supervisors under his or her charge, an Overtime Report to the Human Resources Department for processing. The Supervisory Overtime Report will include the name of the supervisor, number of hours, date, and shift worked. (No report is necessary for first shift and when no overtime was worked.) All reports submitted must be signed.

RESPONSIBILITIES:

1. The Human Resources Manager will cosign and forward the report to payroll.

2. The Payroll Department calculates and adds shift premiums and overtime allowances to the appropriate Supervisory Employee's pay.

GENERAL:

1. Overtime and shift premium worked during the payroll input cutoff week will be paid the following payroll period.

PERSONNEL POLICIES AND PROCEDURES

DISTRIBUTION:		SUBJECT: SHIFT DIFFERENTIAL	
EFFECTIVE DATE:	PAGE 1 OF 1	FILE UNDER SECTION	
REVISION DATE:	APPROVED BY:		

POLICY STATEMENT:

Each hourly or salaried (nonexempt) payroll employee who is assigned to work on the second shift or third shift will be paid a shift premium to compensate for the inconvenience of such working hours.

ELIGIBILITY:

Employees who are assigned to work on a job such that two-thirds of their hours fall on the second or third shift will be eligible for shift differential; however, shift differential will not be paid to regular day-shift employees working overtime on the second or third shifts.

PREMIUM:

The amount of shift premium paid will be 35 cents for the second shift and 50 cents for the third shift.

SHIFT HOURS:

Shift No. 1—Day Shift	7:30 A.M. to 4:00 P.M.
	8:00 A.M. to 4:30 P.M.
Shift No. 2—Afternoon Shift	4:00 P.M. to 12:30 A.M.
	4:30 P.M. to 1:00 A.M.
Shift No. 3—Night Shift	11:00 P.M. to 7:30 A.M.
	11:30 P.M. to 8:00 A.M.

There may be variances from the above schedule for second- and third-shift operations as required by production needs. Hours scheduled for the first shift, however, will not be changed without prior approval of the Vice President—Human Resources.

SALARIED (EXEMPT) PAYROLL EMPLOYEES:

Shift differential will be included in the salary of salaried (exempt) payroll personnel who regularly work shift work but will not be paid on an occasional basis to those who normally work day shift.

PERSONNEL POLICIES AND PROCEDURES

DISTRIBUTION:		SUBJECT: CALLBACK PAY	
EFFECTIVE DATE:	PAGE 1 OF 1	FILE UNDER SECTION	
REVISION DATE:	APPROVED BY:		

PURPOSE:

The purpose of this policy is to ensure that associates who are called back to work outside their regular shift are provided either the opportunity to work four (4) hours or four (4) hours' pay.

POLICY:

A. Callback:

If an associate is called back to work outside his/her regular shift period, the associate will be compensated under the provisions of this policy.

Should an associate be called back to work after completion of a regular shift, he/she will be provided either four (4) hours' work or four (4) hours' pay, including premiums for work performed.

If an associate is called back to work during his/her scheduled paid time off, he/she will receive his/her pay for the scheduled time off in addition to the ''callback'' pay.

B. Pay Rates:

Rate of pay for hours worked for callback or report situations is subject to the provisions of the overtime policy and always includes any shift, leader, or other differentials that the associate normally receives.

If an associate is called back to work, every effort should be made to provide at least four (4) hours' work. If there are at least four (4) hours' work available and the associate exercises an option to work less than four (4) hours, the associate will be paid only for actual hours worked. Overtime premium is not paid for time not worked.

PERSONNEL POLICIES AND PROCEDURES

DISTRIBUTION:		SUBJECT: OVERTIME HOURS	
EFFECTIVE DATE:	PAGE 1 OF 2		FILE UNDER SECTION
REVISION DATE:	APPROVED BY:		

PURPOSE:

The purpose of this policy is to define guidelines for payment of overtime compensation to all hourly associates.

POLICY:

A. Overtime Hours

    1. Overtime hours are all hours worked in a workweek exceeding forty (40) hours and will be paid at one and one-half (1-½) times the associate's hourly rate of pay. Vacation, bereavement, or jury duty time worked during the regular workweek is considered the same as hours worked for overtime calculations unless specified differently in this manual. Pay for accrued or earned benefits is not considered hours worked. Overtime premium is not paid for time not worked.

    2. Except for regularly scheduled Sunday work that is part of a regular work schedule, any work performed on Sunday will be considered overtime and will be paid at double the associate's straight-time rate of pay.

PROCEDURE:

Special effort is made to schedule and finish production and maintenance work within a normal work schedule. However, on occasion, due to customer demands, it is necessary to schedule work past the normal scheduled workshift and workweek. Should that need arise, it is expected that every associate will cooperate to work the assigned overtime. Associates will be notified of daily or weekly overtime assignments by their leader, coordinator, or supervisor at the earliest opportunity. There may be occasions when overtime work occurs because of production requirements that give little time for notification.

A. Scheduling of Overtime:

    1. Immediate supervisors are responsible for notification of overtime hours scheduled.

    2. When overtime is scheduled, the immediate supervisor must announce if the overtime is mandatory or voluntary. If the overtime is voluntary and an associate volunteers, the overtime then becomes mandatory for that associate, and if the associate fails to work all or part of that overtime, he/she will be penalized in accordance with the attendance policy.

B. Notification of Overtime:

    1. Daily overtime before or after the regular shift: Unless assigned to a job where overtime work is routinely expected, an associate will be notified by his/her immediate supervisor before mid-shift for overtime after the regular shift and before quitting time if the overtime is to be worked before the next scheduled shift.

    2. If daily mandatory overtime is scheduled and an associate notifies his/her supervisor or coordinator one (1) day in advance of a scheduled appointment (doctor's appointment, etc.), that one (1) occurrence will not count against his/her attendance record. Only two (2) such occurrences are allowed per month. If the daily overtime is announced on the same day that it is to be worked, the associate must notify her/his supervisor of the appointment as soon as reasonably possible.

PERSONNEL POLICIES AND PROCEDURES

DISTRIBUTION:		SUBJECT: OVERTIME HOURS	
EFFECTIVE DATE:	PAGE 2 OF 2	FILE UNDER SECTION	
REVISION DATE:	APPROVED BY:		

3. If Saturday overtime is scheduled, all affected associates will be notified of mandatory overtime by mid-shift Thursday preceding the Saturday work.

4. Sunday overtime is considered voluntary, except in extreme emergencies determined by the company president.

5. Failure to work scheduled mandatory overtime will count against an associate's attendance record. Scheduled mandatory overtime missed before or after the normal workshift will constitute one-half day of absence. Scheduled mandatory overtime missed on Saturday will count as one (1) day of absence. Paid time off taken on Saturdays will not be considered as time worked and will be paid at the straight-time rate.

6. If an associate takes a whole vacation day or floating holiday on Friday, he/she will be excused from mandatory overtime scheduled on Saturday. However, if an associate takes a half vacation day on Friday, he/she will not be excused from mandatory overtime scheduled on Saturday.

7. Weekend shift associates who are to be scheduled for mandatory overtime during the week will be notified by their supervisor by mid-shift of their last regularly scheduled workday before the scheduled overtime.

PERSONNEL POLICIES AND PROCEDURES

DISTRIBUTION:		SUBJECT: OVERTIME COMPENSATION	
EFFECTIVE DATE:	PAGE 1 OF 1	FILE UNDER SECTION	
REVISION DATE:	APPROVED BY:		

PURPOSE:

The purpose of this policy is to define guidelines for calculations of overtime compensation to all hourly associates.

POLICY:

Associates who work more than forty (40) hours during their workweek will be paid an hourly rate of pay equal to one and one-half (1-½) times their hourly rate, plus shift and other premiums, for all hours actually worked beyond forty (40).

Except for regularly scheduled Sunday work, any work performed on Sunday will be paid at double the associate's straight-time hourly rate of pay, plus shift and other premiums.

Time for which an associate is paid for a floating holiday, vacation days, jury duty, or bereavement will be counted as hours worked for the purpose of overtime calculations except when the paid time off is taken on Saturday. Overtime premium is not paid for time not worked.

PERSONNEL POLICIES AND PROCEDURES

DISTRIBUTION:		SUBJECT: EXEMPT OVERTIME COMPENSATION	
EFFECTIVE DATE:	PAGE 1 OF 1	FILE UNDER SECTION	
REVISION DATE:	APPROVED BY:		

PURPOSE:

To compensate eligible exempt associates who are required to work full shifts [minimum of eight (8) hours] on weekends or holidays.

POLICY:

Associates who are eligible to earn Comp Days are those in the following job titles:

Coordinator	Senior Engineer
Supervisor	Production Planner
Specialist	Material Planner
Plant Nurse	Programmer
Cost Accountant	Senior Programmer
Staff Accountant	Senior MRO Buyer
Engineer	

PROCEDURE:

Comp Days may be earned by eligible associates who work a minimum of eight (8) hours on a weekend day or holiday, provided the day worked is not part of the associate's normal work schedule.

Weekend shift associates may earn Comp Days by working full shifts [minimum of eight (8) hours] on any day that is not part of their normal work schedule.

Comp Days may be earned only for those days on which there is a requirement for the associate to work and which are approved in advance by the associate's immediate supervisor.

Documentation for Comp Days earned must be completed by the Comp Day Records Keeper at each location and approved by his/her general manager.

Requests for Comp Day payment must be forwarded to salaried payroll and must be received no later than Monday prior to a Friday pay date. Comp Day payment will be included on associates' regular paycheck.

Associates may elect to receive pay for Comp Days earned or to take compensatory time off from work. Comp Days will be paid at eight (8) times the associate's hourly rate. Hourly rate is calculated by dividing annual salary by 2080 hours.

Compensatory time off must be scheduled and approved in advance other than in cases of emergency.

Compensatory time taken must be documented on an Absentee Report in the same manner as any other absence.

Comp Days earned must be taken off or paid for in the calendar year in which they are earned except in the case of Comp Days earned in the month of December. Those days may be carried over through January of the following year.

Exempt associates who are absent from work during the week for reasons other than vacation, holiday, bereavement, jury duty, or comp time taken will not earn a Comp Day for that weekend or a holiday worked during that week.

PERSONNEL POLICIES AND PROCEDURES

DISTRIBUTION:		SUBJECT: SALARY CONTINUATION	
EFFECTIVE DATE:	PAGE 1 OF 1	FILE UNDER SECTION	
REVISION DATE:	APPROVED BY:		

SCOPE:

All Exempt and Salaried Nonexempt Associates Who Have Completed Their Ninety- (90-) Day Evaluation/Orientation Period

PURPOSE:

The purpose of this policy is to compensate salaried associates on an approved Personal Medical Leave of Absence.

POLICY:

1. Exempt and nonexempt salaried associates on an approved Personal Medical Leave of Absence will be paid full salary for a maximum of sixty (60) calendar days.
2. Approval of salary continuation will be contingent upon the associate's providing appropriate documentation in a timely manner as set forth in the company's Leave of Absence Policy. In addition, the associate may be required to undergo a company-paid medical examination to support his/her claim for benefits under this policy.
3. During the maximum period of sixty (60) continuous calendar days in which an associate may receive salary continuation, all regular payroll deductions will continue.
4. If an associate has not returned to work after the sixty (60) continuous calendar days have lapsed, he/she must contact a Human Resources representative to make arrangements to pay his/her portion of group and/or optional insurance.
5. The company provides long-term disability insurance for all salaried associates. Salaried associates must be continuously disabled for ninety (90) days before application can be made for long-term disability benefits.
6. Information concerning claims applications and procedures is contained in the Long-Term Disability Insurance Summary Plan Description, which can be obtained from a Human Resources representative.
7. An explanation of the Salary Continuation Policy should be provided to the associate by a Human Resources representative at the time the request is made.

Section 7

Management Development and Training

The following checklist can be used to help you determine the various policy items that should be incorporated in your policy manual. Sample policy statements covering many of the items in the checklist appear in this section. They can be used to guide your policy statements.

Policy Manual Checklist

Our Policy Manual Should Cover:

1. Company Mission Statement	Yes _____	No _____
2. Company Training Philosophy Statement	Yes _____	No _____
3. Orientation and Training	Yes _____	No _____
4. Meeting/Seminar Attendance	Yes _____	No _____
5. Supervisor's Responsibilities to Subordinates	Yes _____	No _____
6. Supervisor's Responsibility to Cost Control	Yes _____	No _____
7. Performance Appraisals	Yes _____	No _____
(a) Hourly and Nonexempt Employees	Yes _____	No _____
(b) Exempt Employees	Yes _____	No _____
(c) Levels of Performance	Yes _____	No _____
(d) Specific Review Factors	Yes _____	No _____
(e) When to Conduct	Yes _____	No _____
8. Promotion from Within	Yes _____	No _____
9. Job Posting	Yes _____	No _____
10. Training and Educational Assistance	Yes _____	No _____
11. Tuition Reimbursement	Yes _____	No _____
12. Quality Statement and Policy	Yes _____	No _____
13. Forms for Administration of Training Programs	Yes _____	No _____
14. Forms for Management of Performance Appraisals	Yes _____	No _____

The Importance of Human Resources

As we near the end of the twentieth century and stand on the threshold of the twenty-first century, human resources have become the most important assets of our organizations. As we move from the Industrial Age into the Information Age, human resources will become even more the driving force in the workplace. Because human resources are so important, it is imperative that today's organization focus on preserving and developing these resources.

In the years ahead, we will be experiencing the following trends:

1. The workforce will be aging. There will be more persons past forty in the workforce than under it. As this "graying" of the workforce takes place, we will have to learn to utilize the skills of these older workers and adapt our policies and procedures to the particular needs of the older adult. This will present new challenges to the employer.

2. There will be more women in the workforce. There will be more and more women at the executive level of organizations and more women doing traditional "male" jobs. They will demand greater flexibility in the workplace.

3. The younger workers that come into the workforce will be a new breed. They will be better educated and will know their rights and demand them. They will want work that is challenging and not routine. They will not be committed to one job for a lifetime.

4. There will be the need for training and retraining. As we move further into the Information Age, more and more jobs will become obsolete. To preserve and develop our human resources, we will have to provide continued training and retraining throughout the worker's life. It will no longer be possible to train a worker for one job and keep him or her in that job for a lifetime.

5. There will be a shortage of potential employees available. There will be a smaller and smaller pool to draw from. There will be fewer qualified persons to take the available jobs.

These trends present some unique challenges to the organization in the latter part of this century and the first part of the next century. These challenges are:

1. To make every effort to develop and preserve the resources we have.
2. To plan for the training and retraining of the resources that we have. There will be the need for lifelong learning plans.
3. To adapt our organization to the older worker and his or her particular needs.
4. To provide for the career development of the younger worker.
5. To meet the challenge of the woman in the workplace.

Organizations must meet these challenges with effective policies and procedures in the years ahead.

Recommendations for Providing Initial Job Training

The following recommendations will improve employee orientation and initial training:

1. Introduce your new employee to a work climate that will encourage a desire to learn the job and to develop abilities and skills as rapidly as possible. Let the person know that you can be depended upon for the training and backup he or she needs to become a fully trained member of your staff.

2. Establish progressively more difficult standards of performance that the new employee can accept as fair and challenging. Develop methods of measuring performance so that both you and the employee can measure progress.

3. Allow some freedom in performance. Give the employee the opportunity to show you what he or she can accomplish on the job. Don't be so critical of the employee that each workday becomes a frustrating experience that leads to exhaustion without a sense of achievement.

4. Develop a routine of checking with the employee as often as necessary based upon the performance levels that are expected and the possible cost of improper performance.

5. Develop an employee on-the-job training program that includes the special coaching that is required to meet your standards of performance. Follow the three basic steps in employee on-the-job training:

a. The first time, have the employee observe the tasks to be performed.

b. The second time, have the employee assist in performing the tasks.

c. The third time, have the employee perform the task under very close observation.

Repeat these three steps several times if necessary to ensure that the employee can perform the duties to your standards and can perform them safely.

If you cannot spend the time with the trainee, assign a senior employee as an instructor. Have the senior employee report to you regularly on the trainee's progress.

6. Don't put yourself and your company in a bind if the employee is not making satisfactory progress. Immediate counseling is a must. If the performance continues to be unsatisfactory, don't keep the trainee on the payroll; it's not fair to either you or the employee.

No matter how carefully pre-employment screening is conducted, selection mistakes do happen. If the employee can't measure up to your requirements, termination is the best resolution to the mistake. Be sure to properly document all errors and signs of incompetence to assure conformity with the many state and federal regulations. Do not put off this unpleasant, but necessary, task.

On the following pages you will find policies covering:

Mission Statements
Orientation and Training
Professional Development
Supervisor's Responsibility to Subordinates
Supervisor's Responsibility to Cost Control
Performance Appraisals
Promotion from Within
Job Posting
Training and Educational Assistance
Tuition Reimbursement
Quality

PERSONNEL POLICIES AND PROCEDURES

DISTRIBUTION:		SUBJECT: MISSION STATEMENT	
EFFECTIVE DATE:	PAGE 1 OF 1		FILE UNDER SECTION
REVISION DATE:	APPROVED BY:		

The mission of (Company Name) is to be the leader in providing funeral services in the state of (Name of State) that will fully meet the needs of families at the time of the death of a family member, friend, or other significant person in their lives. This will be achieved by providing a full range of services at prices affordable to all, a full range of support services, innovative merchandising, excellent facilities, expansion by purchase and consolidation, and a staff of professionals. This will result in an excellent reputation and a reasonable profit.

PERSONNEL POLICIES AND PROCEDURES

DISTRIBUTION:		SUBJECT: MISSION STATEMENT	
EFFECTIVE DATE:	PAGE 1 OF 1	FILE UNDER SECTION	
REVISION DATE:	APPROVED BY:		

The mission of (Company Name) is to provide the customer with the finest automobile available, backed by excellent customer service that brings complete satisfaction. It will have a staff of professionals who are well trained and always perform at the highest levels. We will strive to be the largest Mercedes dealer in our state. We will be the best dealership in our city. We will be a good citizen of the community through meaningful involvement. This will result in a reasonable profit for the owner and employees.

PERSONNEL POLICIES AND PROCEDURES

DISTRIBUTION:		SUBJECT: TRAINING PHILOSOPHY	
EFFECTIVE DATE:	PAGE 1 OF 1	FILE UNDER SECTION	
REVISION DATE:	APPROVED BY:		

STATEMENT:

(Company Name) is committed to providing all of the training necessary to do the job effectively for all employees. This includes orientation for new employees, training for present employees, and retraining for employees whose jobs become obsolete. The management of (Company Name) is committed to developing the Human Resources of the company to the fullest.

PERSONNEL POLICIES AND PROCEDURES

DISTRIBUTION:		SUBJECT: ORIENTATION AND TRAINING	
EFFECTIVE DATE:	PAGE 1 OF 1	FILE UNDER SECTION	
REVISION DATE:	APPROVED BY:		

POLICY:

It is the policy of the company to conduct orientation and training programs when it feels such programs will help employees.

PROCEDURES

A. An orientation program will be conducted for all newly hired employees. The primary purpose of this program is to familiarize employees with company rules and policies. Additional subjects and the scheduling of the programs will be determined by the Human Resources Department.

B. Employees may be required to participate in and satisfactorily complete continuing education and training programs when such instruction is considered necessary for satisfactory job performance.

C. It will be the general responsibility of supervisors to perform on-the-job training as necessary to teach knowledge of new methods, equipment, techniques, and duties beyond what is normally expected of the employee. Nonsupervisory employees may be designated as on-the-job trainers. Such training will be conducted during normal working hours unless otherwise approved by supervision.

D. Employees will be made aware of safety and health matters as necessary and as required by federal and state law.

E. Special training programs may be developed and conducted when considered necessary by the company. For example: Supervisory and management development, quality improvement, cost reduction, government regulations, etc.

F. When employees are required to obtain licensing or recertification of a license, the company may consider the possibility of sponsoring and conducting the programs. The company will apply for approval by the licensing authority and will comply with all requirements established by such authority. The company, at its discretion, may cancel the program or modify its direction and withdraw it from certification.

G. Self-instructional programs and materials may be made available for employees' use.

H. Company-sponsored or company-conducted orientation and training programs, in-house or in-plant, may be evaluated as to the quality of the instruction, the content, and the results. In such cases:
   1. Evaluation forms may be prepared and distributed by the Human Resources Department for each program.
   2. Supervisors of employees participating in such programs may be requested to evaluate the effectiveness of the programs.
   3. Participants in such programs may be required to take tests to determine the extent to which they have learned the knowledge and skills being taught.

I. Certificates of completion may be awarded to employees who successfully complete such programs.

J. Records will be maintained by the Human Resources Department of all training programs completed by each employee.

PERSONNEL POLICIES AND PROCEDURES

DISTRIBUTION:		SUBJECT: ORIENTATION AND TRAINING	
EFFECTIVE DATE:	PAGE 1 OF 1	FILE UNDER SECTION	
REVISION DATE:	APPROVED BY:		

PURPOSE:

The purpose of this policy is to provide associates with an appropriate orientation to the company, facility, and job to which they have been hired. Such orientation is to welcome new associates to the company, and to provide employing sections with associates who are acclimated and ready to perform the duties of their new position.

POLICY:

1. The General Affairs Department is responsible for the development of orientation and initial training programs for associates at all levels. Changes to these programs must be approved by the manager of training and organizational development, the manager of associate relations, or the vice president of General Affairs.

2. Facility Human Resources Sections are responsible for scheduling all new hires for the orientation program appropriate for their position. Individuals changing positions within the company may also require orientation to the new position. It is the responsibility of the Human Resources professional approving the status change and the immediate supervisor to arrange for the appropriate orientation as needed.

3. Supervisors are responsible for making new associates available for the appropriate company orientation. Supervisors are also responsible for orientation to the work group and instruction on the specific job. This must include, but is not limited to, introduction to coworkers, location of facilities such as time clocks, cafeterias, restrooms, etc., and specific duties and expectations of the job.

PERSONNEL POLICIES AND PROCEDURES

DISTRIBUTION:		SUBJECT: PROFESSIONAL DEVELOPMENT THROUGH MEETING/SEMINAR ATTENDANCE
EFFECTIVE DATE:	PAGE 1 OF 1	FILE UNDER SECTION
REVISION DATE:	APPROVED BY:	

POLICY STATEMENT:

(Company Name) encourages the professional development of employees through attendance and participation in approved meetings, seminars, etc., that are directly related to the Company's operations, activities, and objectives and that will place employees in a position to improve their job performance.

GUIDELINES:

This policy covers meetings, seminars, etc., that are conducted or sponsored by colleges and universities and organizations such as the American Management Association, American Chemical Society, Pharmaceutical Manufacturers Association, and Packaging Institute.

PROCEDURE:

A. An employee shall prepare a Meeting/Seminar Attendance Application Form, which may be obtained from the Human Resources Department, and forward it to his/her immediate supervisor for approval.

B. If the immediate supervisor recommends approval of the application, he/she shall sign in the appropriate section and forward for the following required approvals:

   (1) Department Manager/Regional Sales Manager

   (2) Appropriate Management Committee Member

C. A copy of the approved application must be forwarded to the Director of Human Resources for inclusion in the appropriate history folder. The immediate supervisor will, in turn, notify the employee concerned.

MISCELLANEOUS:

1. This policy provides for payment in full by the Company of registration fees; expenses for hotel/motel accommodations, meals, and travel; and other expenses incurred (payable under standards of Expense Reporting system) by employees attending approved meetings, seminars, or other Company-related activities.

2. All expenses incurred for professional development through meeting/seminar attendance will be charged to the expense center concerned.

PERSONNEL POLICIES AND PROCEDURES

DISTRIBUTION:		SUBJECT: SUPERVISOR'S RESPONSIBILITY TO SUBORDINATES	
EFFECTIVE DATE:	PAGE 1 OF 2	FILE UNDER SECTION	
REVISION DATE:	APPROVED BY:		

POLICY STATEMENT:

We all know that good, sound leadership is important in our company—in fact, it is an absolute necessity. Effective, sound leadership requires that you deal with your subordinates in a way that encourages them to get the job done in the safest, least expensive, and most effective way and still achieve the quantity and quality of service we desire. To do this, you must be ever mindful of the importance of trying to meet the individual, personal needs of your subordinates on a daily basis.

We must realize, as supervisors, that subordinates will follow us if we prove to them that we understand their needs and will try to help them meet their needs better than anyone else. Therefore, every supervisor in our company must recognize his or her obligations to subordinates, as well as his or her responsibilities to them, in order to gain respect, cooperation, and team effort from these subordinates. To achieve this goal, you, as a supervisor, must meet the following responsibilities to the employees under your supervision:

1. It is the policy of this organization that each employee is to have the opportunity to earn a fair day's pay for a fair day's work, and that each employee will have the opportunity to grow and be advanced to better jobs according to his or her effort and ability and according to opportunity within the organization.

2. Supervisors are to evaluate each subordinate and each job so that every employee can be given job duties according to his or her qualifications and present ability. Supervisors should always make every effort to place their subordinates in congenial work groups whenever possible.

3. Every supervisor is responsible for giving the best possible training on the job to every employee. To accomplish this goal, the supervisor must be skilled in the techniques of job instruction. The supervisor must also be able to supervise job instruction given by an assistant.

4. Supervisors are to be sure that each employee is trained to do the job as efficiently and as satisfactorily as possible. Each employee is to be provided with suitable tools, equipment, and materials at all times.

5. The supervisor is to take the necessary steps to be sure that each employee thoroughly understands the job duties, responsibilities, and authority. The employee must know how to perform these duties and have the incentive to constantly improve performance.

6. It is the supervisor's responsibility to properly indoctrinate all employees concerning present and future company rules and personnel policies that affect them. The supervisor must know these rules and policies well enough to interpret them clearly and simply to the employees so that they will understand them.

7. Every supervisor is responsible for letting each worker know how he or she stands on the job. Supervisors are to be liberal in giving praise and credit where due. The supervisor is to be sure that each employee's skill and ability are being used to the fullest at all times.

8. Supervisors are to know how to correct the employee's work performance and personal conduct without giving personal offense to the employee. The supervisor is to know when to be friendly and easygoing and when to be fair and firm. Above all, the supervisor is to be consistent in all disciplinary action with employees at all times.

PERSONNEL POLICIES AND PROCEDURES

DISTRIBUTION:		SUBJECT: SUPERVISOR'S RESPONSIBILITY TO SUBORDINATES
EFFECTIVE DATE:	PAGE 2 OF 2	FILE UNDER SECTION
REVISION DATE:	APPROVED BY:	

9. Supervisors are to be alert to potential sources of friction within their departments at all times.

10. Supervisors are to be responsible to the employees in seeing that their working areas are kept as clean and safe as possible at all times under present facilities.

11. Supervisors are to provide the fullest possible protection for the employees' personal safety and welfare. Supervisors are to be responsible for eliminating and correcting all potential hazards, and making full use of all present and future safety equipment, first-aid techniques, and the fundamentals of good safety practices.

12. Every supervisor is responsible for seeing that each employee has a clear and correct understanding of how the method of payment is computed on the payroll.

13. Supervisors are responsible for communicating the correct feelings and attitudes of employees to top management. In the same manner, supervisors are primarily responsible for conveying to the employees the plans, intentions, and expressions of top management to the extent necessary to build continued team spirit and high employee morale and job satisfaction.

PERSONNEL POLICIES AND PROCEDURES

DISTRIBUTION:		SUBJECT: SUPERVISOR'S RESPONSIBILITY TO COST CONTROL
EFFECTIVE DATE:	PAGE 1 OF 1	FILE UNDER SECTION
REVISION DATE:	APPROVED BY:	

POLICY STATEMENT:

Our company cannot continue to progress and expand unless we continue to watch our costs and keep operating expenses to a minimum. As a supervisor, you can assist in this effort by ensuring your compliance with your assigned budget/expense authorization, and by creating in your employees a genuine interest in cost reduction. The following guidelines are recommended to gain cooperation of your employees in this important area:

1. Create in each of your employees a feeling of being important and of being "in" on things. Try to make the employee feel that he or she is a part of your department and of the organization rather than thinking, "I just work here."

2. Make every effort to show your newer employees, as you introduce them to their jobs during the orientation process, how company costs are directly related to long-range job security and direct income. Show the new employee how our customer, the real boss, won't buy from us unless our costs are competitive, our quality is superior, and our service is excellent.

3. Make every effort to look out for wasted utilities such as light, heat, water, etc., and other costly services when they are not in use or being needed.

4. Constantly search for ways to eliminate wasted materials in your department. By all means, set an example daily for your employees to follow.

5. When possible, explain to your employees the reasons for our large expenditures for new equipment, supplies, and materials so that they will understand the reason for spending by the company. It all results in our continuing efforts to make our company the best possible place to work for everyone so that we can have excellent, safe, and pleasant working conditions and make everyone's work easier.

PERSONNEL POLICIES AND PROCEDURES

DISTRIBUTION:		SUBJECT: PERFORMANCE APPRAISALS	
EFFECTIVE DATE:	PAGE 1 OF 1	FILE UNDER SECTION	
REVISION DATE:	APPROVED BY:		

POLICY STATEMENT:

While the performance of each employee is under constant review, overall performance and pay level shall be appraised in detail not less often than once during each twelve-month period. Such review will determine the performance pay increase to be given, if any, and the interval of time between increases. Change in the pay of an individual will primarily reflect competence in the performance of all assigned duties and sustained accomplishment of the company's objectives set for the position.

PROCEDURE:

Performance will be judged by those in management having direct and supervisory responsibility for the job. Market managers must have input regarding salary for new hires, promotions, and any other salary increases, following any applicable pay scales that may be in existence at the time. Any increase over 10 percent must be approved by the Coordinator of Human Resources and the President.

Prior to the review of a wage increase with an employee, the employee's supervisor must complete the Employee Rate Recommendation form and submit it through the proper channels for authorization and implementation. Additionally, prior to the supervisor/manager's meeting with the employee, a Pre-Evaluation Information form must be completed by the evaluator conducting the performance appraisal with the employee.

The Employee Evaluation Form is to be completed by the evaluator during the performance appraisal meeting, in the presence of the employee.

The Employee Evaluation Form should be signed by both the evaluator and the employee. The employee's signature does not indicate agreement with the appraisal; it does, however, indicate that the employee has had the information reviewed with him/her. Should an employee refuse to sign an evaluation form, the evaluator should call in another supervisor to witness this refusal to sign. The Employee Evaluation Form should be filed in the employee's personnel file, ensuring that appropriate signatures have been obtained and payroll has been notified of the salary increase. Also at each review, the employee should complete the Employee Update Form and give it to the evaluator, who will ensure that it is placed in the employee's personnel file.

Should an employee's performance not warrant a salary increase, the manager may wish to place the employee on a thirty-day probation with the expected behavior and performance during this time clearly outlined and documented. Should the employee improve behavior or performance according to standards, the salary increase can be given following the probationary period. If the employee does not improve, additional disciplinary steps should be taken in conjunction with our progressive disciplinary procedure.

Supervisors and managers are encouraged to follow the enclosed guidelines for performance appraisal.

PERSONNEL POLICIES AND PROCEDURES

DISTRIBUTION:		SUBJECT: PERFORMANCE EVALUATION	
EFFECTIVE DATE:	PAGE 1 OF 1	FILE UNDER SECTION	
REVISION DATE:	APPROVED BY:		

PURPOSE:

The purpose of this policy is to define the company's evaluation procedure for hourly and salaried associates. The purposes for the evaluation are as follows:

1. To evaluate associate performance and measure actual performance against the requirements of the job;

2. To provide two-way discussion about job performance and understanding of job requirements;

3. To create awareness of potential and to motivate the associate to improve performance;

4. To establish goals and timetables for improvement and provide feedback on progress toward achievement of goals;

5. To deal candidly and fairly with marginal or unsatisfactory performance and to establish time frames for elevation of performance to a satisfactory level.

POLICY:

A. SALARIED ASSOCIATES

All salaried exempt and salaried nonexempt associates will have annual performance appraisals and reviews normally given during the first quarter of each year.

The level of performance on this appraisal as indicated in the evaluation will be one of the factors considered in determining the amount of increase in salary.

B. LEADER/ENGINEERING ASSISTANTS HOURLY ASSOCIATES

1. Newly promoted leaders will serve a ninety- (90-) day probationary period, during which appraisals will be given at thirty (30), sixty (60), and ninety (90) days. These appraisals will point out areas of strengths and weaknesses and will be used to determine whether an associate will be retained in the leader classification.

2. A leader class associate will have a performance evaluation as a condition of and prior to his/her fifteen- (15-) month increase. Any leader whose performance is below standard at the time of the appraisal will have his/her increase delayed until satisfactory performance is attained. Leaders and immediate supervisors will develop an action plan, and if significant improvement has not been attained within three (3) months, disciplinary action will be taken.

C. HOURLY NEW-HIRES

Hourly new-hires will undergo an orientation/evaluation period for ninety (90) calendar days. Evaluations will be given to these associates at thirty (30), sixty (60), and ninety (90) days.

At the end of each thirty (30) calendar days of employment, the coordinator will review the new associate's performance. Associates not meeting expectations should be informed as to what improvements must be made before the next appraisal if they are to be allowed to continue employment.

If the associate's performance is far below an acceptable level or the coordinator doubts that significant improvement is possible, then the coordinator should consult the Human Resources Section and a decision should be made to either terminate employment or develop an aggressive action plan to achieve the necessary performance improvements.

Although the purpose of these appraisals is to provide feedback to the associate that will allow him/her to improve performance, unsatisfactory effort or poor performance may result in termination of employment at any point in the orientation/evaluation period.

PERSONNEL POLICIES AND PROCEDURES

DISTRIBUTION:		SUBJECT: PERFORMANCE APPRAISALS	
EFFECTIVE DATE:	PAGE 1 OF 3	FILE UNDER SECTION	
REVISION DATE:	APPROVED BY:		

A. PURPOSE

Each terminal manager, division manager, or department supervisor should prepare a periodic performance appraisal for each employee under his/her direction to:

1. Assist the terminal manager, division manager, or department supervisor in determining the employee's potential for further advancement and development.

2. Advise employees of their strengths and weaknesses and what is expected of them in their position.

3. Build and strengthen the supervisor-subordinate relationship.

B. LEVELS OF PERFORMANCE

The following guidelines are levels of performance for each specific factor:

1. Unsatisfactory: Performance meets minimum acceptable standards in most instances, but is unsatisfactory in some cases; improvement is necessary. Assignments are occasionally submitted late and/or are incomplete. Detailed direction and frequent progress checks are usually required. The employee is normally in a learning phase or of questionable ability to meet job requirements.

2. Good: Performance of most duties is adequate; meets most standards in an acceptable manner. Some improvement may be necessary. Occasionally may fail to complete assignments on time and/or comprehensively. Requires direction and review of major parts of assignments. May hesitate to undertake work outside his/her defined area of responsibility. Understands most duties and overall objectives of the job. The employee is beyond the learning phase and is making measurable contributions within limited areas.

3. Very Good: Performs all duties and responsibilities in a comprehensive manner. Little need for improvement to be considered fully adequate for the job. Infrequently may not complete specific assignments on schedule. Generally works independently. Requires infrequent progress reviews. Handles assignments in a professional manner and seeks out work in a related area. Makes contributions to the overall effectiveness of the department or terminal.

4. Outstanding: Performs all duties and responsibilities in a thoroughly comprehensive manner. Some duties are carried out in a superior manner. Efficiently uses time, personnel, and funds in carrying out assignments. Considered highly knowledgeable by superiors, peers, and subordinates. Sought out for advice and assistance; consistently makes significant contributions to the overall effectiveness of the department or terminal.

5. Superior: All duties and responsibilities are conducted in a thoughtful and judicious manner with little or no need for direction, resulting in outstanding contributions on a continuing basis. Typically accurate, timely, decisive, and comprehensive in carrying out assignments and/or making recommendations. Recognized as an expert in his/her profession and frequently sought out for advice, counsel, and direction. Aggressively seeks to expand scope of activity and assumes additional responsibility.

C. FACTORS TO BE APPRAISED

1. Specific Review Factors:

   a. Ability to get along with others

   b. Acceptance of responsibility

   c. Attendance and promptness

   d. Attitude

   e. Ingenuity

   f. Initiative

DISTRIBUTION:		SUBJECT: PERFORMANCE APPRAISALS	
EFFECTIVE DATE:	PAGE 2 OF 3	FILE UNDER SECTION	
REVISION DATE:	APPROVED BY:		

    g. Job knowledge

    h. Judgment

    i. Promptness in completing assignments

    j. Quality of work

    k. Quantity of work

2. Overall Appraisal of Performance: The supervisor is to indicate the general overall performance of the employee.

3. Overall Performance: The supervisor is to indicate additional comments to explain any fluctuation in the employee's overall performance. The reviewing supervisor is to indicate any difference of opinion or additional comments regarding the employee being reviewed.

4. General Review of Current Performance and Potential for Advancement:

    a. Employee Strong Points: Every employee has strong points that qualify him/her for his/her current position (e.g., intelligence, good attitude, enthusiasm, excellent job knowledge, etc.).

    b. Employee Weak Points: Every employee has weak points that may keep him/her from growing within his/her job or from being promoted (e.g., lacks job knowledge, doesn't delegate, fears responsibility, is afraid to discipline employees, is constantly late for work, has excessive absenteeism, can't follow instructions, etc.).

    c. Recommendation for Improvement: The supervisor is to set mutual goals for the employee to reach before the next performance appraisal. The recommendations should specifically state methods to correct weaknesses or prepare the employee for a future promotion.

    d. Employee Potential for Increased Responsibility: The supervisor should indicate where an employee could be ready for further responsibility. Can the employee handle larger workloads? Can the employee handle duties in some supervisory position? Does he/she possess skills that would make him/her promotable? Does he/she show eagerness for more responsibility?

5. Future Consideration: The supervisor is to indicate whether or not more time on the present job is needed to correct weaknesses or improve performance. Some employees are ready for promotion when a higher-level position is available. The supervisor should indicate what type of position the employee is ready to assume and, after reasonable probation, can handle.

6. Acquired Skills Not Being Utilized on Present Job: The supervisor should indicate any skills that the employee is not using on his/her present job (e.g., typing, shorthand, computer keypunching, leadership ability, accounting, etc.).

7. Employee Reaction to Review: The supervisor, after the employee has left, should indicate what the employee's reaction was to the appraisal. Indications should be whether the employee accepted constructive criticism, had a favorable or negative response, etc.

8. Employee Comments: The supervisor is to write what the employee thought of the appraisal (e.g., Was it objective? Did he/she agree with what was said? Where does he/she disagree with what was said? etc.).

D. PITFALLS IN MAKING PERFORMANCE APPRAISALS

1. "Halo": This is a tendency to appraise an employee in general as rather good or inferior and to color judgments about the specific qualities of this employee by this general feeling.

2. The tendency to rate all employees in a group as superior, outstanding, very good, good, or unsatisfactory.

3. The supervisor should remember that even the best employees have weaknesses that can be remedied, and even the poorest employees have some strong points.

PERSONNEL POLICIES AND PROCEDURES

DISTRIBUTION:		SUBJECT: PERFORMANCE APPRAISALS	
EFFECTIVE DATE:	PAGE 3 OF 3	FILE UNDER SECTION	
REVISION DATE:	APPROVED BY:		

4. No department has a monopoly on superior or unsatisfactory personnel. Generally, some employees in each department will warrant a superior rating, some outstanding, some very good, some good, some unsatisfactory. The following table represents a normal distribution of all appraised employees in a department:

Superior—10 percent
Outstanding—20 percent
Very Good—40 percent
Good—20 percent
Unsatisfactory—10 percent

E. WHEN TO CONDUCT PERFORMANCE APPRAISALS

1. Exempt Employees

   a. An exempt employee shall receive a performance appraisal after the completion of six months of service.

   b. An exempt employee shall receive a performance appraisal during his or her anniversary month of employment.

2. Nonexempt Supervisors

   a. Nonexempt supervisors shall receive a performance appraisal after the completion of the first six and twelve months of service after the date transferred to supervision.

   b. Nonexempt supervisors shall receive a performance appraisal during their anniversary month of employment.

3. Nonexempt, nonbargaining employees shall receive a performance appraisal during their anniversary month of employment.

F. GENERAL

1. Nonexempt supervisors and nonexempt, nonbargaining employees shall not be eligible for a monetary increase during their anniversary month of employment. This month is to be used to appraise employees at a time when they know that no increase will be given and to encourage dialogue between the supervisor and employees concerning their performance in their position.

2. The central Human Resources Department will maintain the employment dates of all employees specified in Paragraphs 1, 2, and 3 above, and in accordance with such paragraphs, shall notify responsible supervisors that a performance appraisal is required on one of their employees.

3. The supervisor shall prepare two copies of the performance appraisal, completing all areas marked with an ''X.'' Employees should be appraised according to what is expected of them in their position.

4. The immediate supervisor shall discuss the performance appraisal, in detail, with the employee concerned. Upon completion of such discussion, the supervisor will sign and date the form. The supervisor will then complete the sections ''Employee's Reaction to Review'' and ''Employee Comments.''

5. The appraisal form is forwarded to the next higher level of supervision for review of the employee's performance and the immediate supervisor's appraisal. The executive will note any differences or additional comments that he or she may have under the section ''Overall Performance'' and sign the form.

6. After the performance appraisal has been completed in accordance with the preceding four steps, the original appraisal and the copy will be forwarded to the central Human Resources Department for further processing and filing. The second copy will be returned for filing at the location or in the department. The completed appraisal is to be forwarded to the Human Resources Department within fourteen calendar days after the anniversary month of the employee's appraisal.

PERSONNEL POLICIES AND PROCEDURES

DISTRIBUTION:		SUBJECT: PROMOTION FROM WITHIN	
EFFECTIVE DATE:	PAGE 1 OF 1	FILE UNDER SECTION	
REVISION DATE:	APPROVED BY:		

It is Company policy to aid, encourage, and train employees so that they may rise to the highest position possible. Promotion from within is a preferred policy. The Company is continuously seeking employees who have the ability, training, and experience to fill better positions. There is always a great deal of opportunity for capable and ambitious persons.

In all selections for promotions, the person chosen will be the one who is best suited for the job, taking the following into consideration: job knowledge, ability, attitude, loyalty, and personality.

PERSONNEL POLICIES AND PROCEDURES

DISTRIBUTION:		SUBJECT: JOB POSTING	
EFFECTIVE DATE:	PAGE 1 OF 3	FILE UNDER SECTION	
REVISION DATE:	APPROVED BY:		

RATIONALE:

It is in the interest of every company to avail itself of the established and latent talents of its employees. Two basic reasons are:

1. The company's cost of training and loss of skill continuity is reduced, and

2. Employee loyalty may be further enhanced by the advantages that promotions bring.

One other compelling reason exists aside from human factors: Denied opportunity is often a major issue in drives for union organization. If a company does not have opportunity, that's one thing. If it has opportunity, but does not make it available to existing employees on a qualified basis, that is quite another issue.

BIDDING PROCEDURE:

1. When a vacancy occurs, the department in which it occurs must submit a requisition to the Employee Relations Manager.

2. The Employee Relations Department will generate a notice of position vacancy (job posting) to be posted at regularly appointed locations readily accessible for viewing throughout the company.

   A. Postings shall be confined to positions Labor Grade 2 and above. Labor Grade 1, being the lowest position, should have no promotional appeal, and therefore will not be posted, nor will part-time or short-term temporary vacancies be posted.

   B. Lead person positions shall not be posted, inasmuch as such positions are appointive based upon demonstrated maximum job knowledge, knowledge of overall departmental/shop operation, and self-application.

   C. Job postings shall remain in full view for employees to consider for a period of seventy-two (72) consecutive working hours (exclusive of any Saturdays, Sundays, or holidays).

   D. Basic information contained in each job posting shall include:

      (1) Date and time of posting

      (2) Date and time of removal

      (3) Identification of the job vacancy:

         (a) Title

         (b) Labor grade

         (c) Rate range

         (d) Department and shift

         (e) Permanent or temporary

         (f) Any special mandatory skill requirements for consideration or unusual conditions the successful candidate must accept; for example, split or rotating shifts

   E. Employees shall be given information on how to bid, how selection is to be made, what will be done if there are no bidders or successful bidders, etc.:

PERSONNEL POLICIES AND PROCEDURES

DISTRIBUTION:		SUBJECT: JOB POSTING	
EFFECTIVE DATE:	PAGE 2 OF 3	FILE UNDER SECTION	
REVISION DATE:	APPROVED BY:		

    (1) Where to go to get bid forms and whom to seek for help in filling them out.

    (2) When to apply.

    (3) Selection is primarily based on minimum requirements of: regular employee, prior experience (if any), attendance record, supervisory interview, and length of service. There must be a substantive, clear-cut reason why the senior employee is not the successful bidder.

    (4) No department is required to accept employees with marginal work records, whatever the reason.

    (5) Vacancies having no bidders or no qualified bidders shall be released for external hire.

F. At the close of the posting period, the Employee Relations Department shall review the bid forms of each bidder, taking careful note to examine:

    (1) Adherence to preset qualifications specified (if any).

    (2) Whether the bidder is a qualified bidder (i.e., length of service and full-time employee).

    (3) The work history of each, including attendance (and tardiness) record.

G. The acquiring Foreman shall be contacted and the candidates reviewed in detail with him or her. At the same time, the Foreman in each department containing a prospective candidate shall be advised.

H. The Foreman shall personally interview each prospective candidate to examine with each the demands of the job, performance, expectations, the employee's expectations, and the employee's experience to weigh the suitability of the candidate for the job.

I. The Foreman, with the guidance of the Employee Relations Manager, shall select the successful candidate and notify the candidate of the job award.

J. All unsuccessful candidates for the job shall be immediately notified by a memo. A copy shall be placed in the Personnel file jacket.

K. In cases where there are two or more equally qualified bidders, the award will be made to the employee who possesses the greatest length of continuous service.

ELIGIBLE BIDDERS

1. Any regular, full-time hourly employee who has completed ninety (90) days of service is available to bid while the announcement is posted for bidding.

2. Interested nonexempt personnel may bid and be awarded a job in the hourly ranks provided there were no other bidders and they are the most senior employee with prior satisfactory performance on the exact job being bid upon.

TRIAL PERIOD:

1. The trial period on a newly awarded job shall be thirty (30) days.

2. A bidder who is unable to perform the new job satisfactorily within the above period shall be returned to his or her former position at the same seniority and pay level without prejudice.

PERSONNEL POLICIES AND PROCEDURES

DISTRIBUTION:		SUBJECT: JOB POSTING	
EFFECTIVE DATE:	PAGE 2 OF 3	FILE UNDER SECTION	
REVISION DATE:	APPROVED BY:		

2. A bidder who apparently is able to perform the job satisfactorily, but who desires to opt out of the new position within the thirty- (30-) day trial period, may return to his or her former job only if it has not been filled. Otherwise, consideration must be given to other current vacancies.

LIMITATIONS:

Successful job bidders shall be limited to one successful award every six months to avoid uncontrolled job-hopping.

PERSONNEL POLICIES AND PROCEDURES

DISTRIBUTION:		SUBJECT: TRAINING AND EDUCATIONAL ASSISTANCE	
EFFECTIVE DATE:	PAGE 1 OF 1	FILE UNDER SECTION	
REVISION DATE:	APPROVED BY:		

POLICY STATEMENT:

It is a joint obligation of management and the employees to ensure that employees are knowledgeable about their job and its requirements. Management should ensure that training is available to all employees periodically in various fashions, such as on-the-job training, a library of videocassettes, training meetings, and personal consultation. In addition to this in-house training, many of the company's suppliers provide additional training, either for a fee or on a no-charge basis.

PROCEDURE:

As a general rule, managers will determine what training employees are required to have and what training courses they should attend. In the event that an employee has identified some training available to him/her that he/she would like to have and feels would be beneficial to the performance of his/her job, the employee should contact his/her supervisor to discuss the feasibility of company participation in the expense of the training.

Managers are authorized to send employees to special training programs if the cost is within the division's budget and the manager's established spending authority. Otherwise, the manager must receive authorization from the President to incur the cost of employee training.

Managers should document any special training an employee receives and should ensure that this documentation is placed in the employee's personnel file. This information will prove valuable in determining an employee's capability and suitability for positions of advancement.

Normally, training occurs on the job and the company absorbs all expenses associated with the training. If an hourly employee is required to attend a training session, the employee will be compensated for the time involved in the training. All expenses associated with a preapproved training program that the company requires an employee to attend will be covered by the operating division in which the employee is assigned.

An employee who incurs any expenses associated with training must complete an expense report attaching the appropriate receipts and submit it to his/her immediate manager for authorization. The manager will forward it through proper channels to secure reimbursement for the employee. All claims for reimbursement must be filed within thirty days. The amounts for reimbursement such as vehicle mileage, meals, etc., should comply with the standard company policies.

PERSONNEL POLICIES AND PROCEDURES

DISTRIBUTION:		SUBJECT: TUITION REIMBURSEMENT	
EFFECTIVE DATE:	PAGE 1 OF 2	FILE UNDER SECTION	
REVISION DATE:	APPROVED BY:		

POLICY:

It is the policy of the Company to reimburse full-time employees for tuition fees for college credit courses that have received advance approval from Management.

Funds for this purpose are separate from those set aside for the ''Training Program.''

ELIGIBILITY FOR REIMBURSEMENT:

To be eligible for reimbursement, the employee must have been employed by the Company or an affiliated company for one year and must receive a passing grade in the course. Any approved course(s) taken during the first year of employment will be reimbursed retroactively after the employee's first anniversary date.

APPROVAL OF COURSES:

For each course for which reimbursement will be sought, a ''Tuition Approval/Refund Request'' form should be filled out by the employee and approved by signature by the employee's Department Head and by the Manager of Administration. This should be done prior to payment of the tuition fee. The Administration Department will keep the original and give the copies of the request form to the Department Head and to the employee:

To qualify as reimbursable, the course must:

1. Be directly related to the employee's present job or enhance the employee's worth to the Company.

2. Be a requirement for an undergraduate or graduate degree.

Any degree-granting program should be reviewed by the employee's Department Head and by the Manager of Administration before the employee registers for courses. The course of study must be job-related. Each course will be considered for approval on an individual basis.

Any course beginning prior to employment is not eligible for reimbursement.

REIMBURSEMENT PROCEDURE:

Reimbursement for tuition fees can be made upon presentation to the Administration Department of an invoice from the school and proof of payment. An employee who has not completed one year of employment with the Company or an affiliated company will be reimbursed after his/her first anniversary date upon presentation of the above documents, provided the course(s) was approved in advance by his/her Department Head and by the Manager of Administration using the ''Tuition Approval/Refund Request'' form.

Reimbursement will be for tuition only, not for registration fees, other miscellaneous fees, books, transportation, etc.

PERSONNEL POLICIES AND PROCEDURES

DISTRIBUTION:		SUBJECT:
		TUITION REIMBURSEMENT
EFFECTIVE DATE:	PAGE 2 OF 2	FILE UNDER SECTION
REVISION DATE:	APPROVED BY:	

FINAL GRADE:

Upon completion of the course, a copy of the final grade transcript should be presented to the Administration Department. If the employee fails to complete the course(s) or receives a nonpassing grade, the Company will require repayment of the tuition fees for those courses.

CORRESPONDENCE COURSES:

This policy is limited to bona fide classroom lecture courses taken after working hours. Correspondence courses are discouraged because experience has shown that they are not always effective due to the high degree of commitment required on the part of the student. However, if examinations are successfully completed, retroactive payment may be considered.

SPECIAL PROGRAMS:

Special "concentrated study" programs such as the Executive Development Programs at Harvard University and at London Business School must be approved by the Executive Vice President in charge of Administration. These courses require completion of a special application form.

PERSONNEL POLICIES AND PROCEDURES

DISTRIBUTION:		SUBJECT: EDUCATIONAL ASSISTANCE	
EFFECTIVE DATE:	PAGE 1 OF 2	FILE UNDER SECTION	
REVISION DATE:	APPROVED BY:		

PURPOSE:

It is the intent of this policy to describe the guidelines whereby associates may receive educational assistance. The company recognizes that the educational development of our associates is important to the company's success. For this reason, this policy is established to provide an opportunity for all associates to obtain additional education or training in order to increase their competence in their present jobs and to prepare for possible advancement in the future. It is also intended to ensure the company of a reasonable return on our investment in the development of our associates.

ELIGIBILITY:

This practice applies to all regular, full-time associates provided their plan of study does not interfere with their work schedule. In addition, the eligible associate must have completed six (6) months of continuous service before starting the course. The maximum course load must be limited to not more than six (6) credit hours or two (2) courses (whichever is greater) in any single semester. Summer and bi-term classes are discouraged due to their demands on the associates' time. Approval of summer and bi-term classes will be limited to one (1) course at a time.

Associates already entitled to educational aid extended by a governmental agency, private agencies, foundations, scholarships, or other such programs should use those funds first. They may be excluded from this program if such funding covers all reimbursable expenses. However, where such programs do not fully cover the cost of tuition and books, the company will reimburse for any difference if the associate meets all other requirements.

Courses eligible for reimbursement must be offered by an accredited university, college, or business, trade, or technical school. The course must relate to a degree program or plan of study approved by the associate's immediate supervisor and the Human Resources manager for that facility. Degree programs or plans of study must be business-related, in that completion of the same would qualify the associate for some position to which he or she could aspire within the company.

LIMITS TO ELIGIBILITY:

To apply for participation in the Educational Assistance Program, an associate must complete an initial letter of intent and obtain approval from local management and the General Affairs Department prior to registration for classes. Additionally, an Educational Assistance Form must be completed prior to each course period.

The company maintains the right to set limits on the number of associates in any particular study area based upon projected job openings. Also, those associates seeking second or advanced degrees, or those receiving information through satellite or computer-aided delivery (on-line or off-line), may be required to meet additional qualifications. Responsibility for determining limits and additional qualifications will rest with the plant or section manager, the manager of training, and the General Affairs or Human Resources Section.

REIMBURSEMENT:

Only those courses that have been preapproved by local management and the General Affairs Section are eligible for reimbursement. The associate is responsible for actual admission and enrollment fees. After successful completion of a preapproved course the associate must submit receipts for actual expenses and proof of grade to the Human Resources Section in his or her plant or office. Successful completion is defined as a grade of "C" or above and/or receipt of a certificate of completion in vocational or technical courses. Reimbursable expenses are restricted to registration, tuition, laboratory fees, and books; no other fees or costs will be covered.

PERSONNEL POLICIES AND PROCEDURES

DISTRIBUTION:		SUBJECT: EDUCATIONAL ASSISTANCE	
EFFECTIVE DATE:	PAGE 2 OF 2	FILE UNDER SECTION	
REVISION DATE:	APPROVED BY:		

LIMITS TO REIMBURSEMENT:

Reimbursement shall be made only to the individual associate. Any financial obligation pertaining to a reimbursable course must be settled by that associate. The company will not make payment directly to any third party, lending institution, or educational institution. Reimbursements are subject to all applicable local, state, and federal taxes. In cases of second or advanced degrees or distance delivery programs, reimbursement will be fifty (50) percent of covered expenses as listed above.

PERSONNEL POLICIES AND PROCEDURES

DISTRIBUTION:		SUBJECT: QUALITY	
EFFECTIVE DATE:	PAGE 1 OF 1	FILE UNDER SECTION	
REVISION DATE:	APPROVED BY:		

POLICY STATEMENT:

Our company is committed to delivering defect-free competitive products and services on time to our customers. We shall strive for excellence in all endeavors. We shall set goals to achieve total customer satisfaction and to deliver error-free products on time, with service second to none.

PROCEDURE:

A. It is the policy of our company that the function of quality management shall exist in each manufacturing and service operation to the degree necessary to ensure that:

    1. The acceptance and performance standards of our products and services are met.

    2. The cost of quality goals for each operation are achieved.

B. The company General Manager is responsible for establishing the proper degree of quality function in each operation. The General Manager shall take affirmative steps to ensure that the employees understand that the quality policy of the company is to perform exactly like the requirement or cause the requirement to be officially changed to what we and our customer really need.

C. To ensure its effectiveness, the quality function must be exercised in an objective and unbiased manner. As such, the head of the quality function in each unit shall report directly to the General Manager.

D. The responsibilities of the quality function include:

    1. Product/service acceptance at all levels.

    2. Supplier quality.

    3. Quality engineering

    4. Data analysis and status reporting.

    5. Corrective action.

    6. Planning.

    7. Qualification approval of products, processes, and procedures.

    8. Audit.

    9. Quality education.

    10. Quality improvement.

    11. Consumer affairs.

    12. Product safety.

E. The company shall produce cost of quality reports in accordance with the comptroller's procedure and will create regular quality status reports for presentation to all management personnel.

PERSONNEL POLICIES AND PROCEDURES

DISTRIBUTION:		SUBJECT: CUSTOMER SERVICE	
EFFECTIVE DATE:	PAGE 1 OF 1	FILE UNDER SECTION	
REVISION DATE:	APPROVED BY:		

OBJECTIVES OF THE CUSTOMER SERVICE PROGRAM:

* To ensure that the customer's point of view regarding company policies, practices, and procedures is systematically incorporated in the company's decision-making process in the same way that the financial considerations are today.

* To provide a central clearing point for information on customer concerns, available from a number of internal and external sources.

* To ensure that appropriate persons are in regular contact with consumer leaders in the areas the company serves and that communications with our customers are open and helpful.

(Company Name) welcomes the consumer movement and supports its goal to reaffirm consumer rights in the marketplace. We view consumerism not as a contest between company and customer, but as a constructive social movement that will benefit both parties by creating new channels of communication. Through this open and responsible interchange of ideas, our customers' needs can be more accurately defined and incorporated into the making of our policies and procedures.

We have long recognized that our license to serve depends entirely on public trust—a trust built on a long history of service but always dependent on the last customer contact. By its very nature our business is consumer-oriented. We also recognize that consumer trust depends on our service. Our employees take pride in their spirit of service—a long tradition of faithful performance of everyday duty to provide the best communication service in the world. And as we grow larger, we must strive harder to personally uphold and renew this tradition in every community we serve.

Our concern for continuing our tradition of service and renewing the public trust is more than a matter of prudent public relations, it is a reflection of deep management conviction. For we recognize that just as we have grown and changed as a company, so have the expectations, concerns, and interests of our customers. And if we are to be responsive, we must develop an environment in which our company and customers can communicate, reason, and compromise with understanding and confidence.

We, therefore, declare the following standards to be an integral part of our management philosophy and actual practice:

* We view the consumer movement as a constructive force in our society and strive to develop and maintain an effective working relationship with its representatives.

* We reaffirm the provision of reasonably priced high-quality products and services as our main objective.

* We promise to continue to safeguard the long-standing right of our customers to privacy of their communications with us.

* We rededicate ourselves to the promise that our treatment of our customers shall be totally open and completely fair.

* We pledge to continually review our existing practices and policies to ensure that they are responsive to the current needs and desires of our customers and the communities we serve.

* We commit ourselves to actively seeking customer attitudes and opinions and to using these interests as we shape future practice and policy.

Finally, we recognize that although we aim at perfection, we do not claim to have achieved it. Whenever actual practice falls short of these standards, we will strive to bring our performance up to the high levels that we have set for ourselves and that our customers have every right to expect and receive from us.

SECTION 8

Employee Benefits Administration

The following checklist can be used to help you determine the various policy items that should be incorporated in your policy manual. Sample policy statements covering many of the items in the checklist appear in this section. They can be used to guide your policy statements.

Policy Manual Checklist

Our Policy Manual Should Cover:

Paid Vacations

1. Length of vacations   Yes_____ No_____

2. Eligibility and amount of vacation pay   Yes_____ No_____

3. Scheduling vacation time   Yes_____ No_____

4. Illness during vacation   Yes_____ No_____

5. Extending, accumulating, or splitting vacation   Yes_____ No_____

6. Uniformed service duty during vacation   Yes_____ No_____

7. Effect of layoffs and absences   Yes_____ No_____

8. Effect of discharge and resignation   Yes_____ No_____

9. Part-time and temporary employees   Yes_____ No_____

Paid Holidays

1. Number and name of paid and unpaid holidays   Yes_____ No_____

2. Arrangements for Christmas and religious holidays   Yes_____ No_____

3. Holidays falling on nonworking days   Yes_____ No_____

4. Arrangements for long holiday weekends   Yes_____ No_____

5. Eligibility requirements for paid holidays   Yes_____ No_____

6. Amount of holiday pay and computation procedure   Yes____ No____

7. Pay for worked holidays   Yes____ No____

8. "Floating" holidays   Yes____ No____

Group Health Insurance

1. Health Plan specifics   Yes____ No____
   - A. Type and amount of benefits provided   Yes____ No____
   - B. Kind of plan—self-funded, indemnity, HMO, etc.   Yes____ No____
   - C. Eligibility requirements for employees/dependents   Yes____ No____
   - D. Contributory or noncontributory plan—percentage contributions   Yes____ No____
   - E. Coverage—individual or family   Yes____ No____
   - F. Maximum out-of-pocket, lifetime, etc.   Yes____ No____
   - G. Deductibles   Yes____ No____
   - H. Limitations and exclusions   Yes____ No____

2. Continuation provisions   Yes____ No____
   - A. Extended coverage   Yes____ No____
   - B. COBRA administration   Yes____ No____
   - C. Conversion privileges   Yes____ No____

Group Life Insurance

1. Defining group life insurance   Yes____ No____

2. Eligibility requirements   Yes____ No____
   - A. Employee   Yes____ No____
   - B. Dependents   Yes____ No____

3. Amount of coverage   Yes____ No____

4. Contributory or noncontributory plan   Yes____ No____

5. Conversion privileges after termination for any reason   Yes____ No____

6. Accidental death or dismemberment insurance rider   Yes____ No____

7. Continuation of life insurance after employee's retirement   Yes____ No____

Group Accident and Sickness Insurance (Salary Continuance)

1. Employees eligible for coverage   Yes____ No____
   - A. Nonexempt   Yes____ No____
   - B. Exempt   Yes____ No____

2. Type and amount of benefits provided   Yes____ No____

3. Contributory or noncontributory plan   Yes____ No____

4. Proof of disability   Yes_____ No_____

5. Re-employment obligations for employee   Yes_____ No_____

6. Insurance continuation during excused absences   Yes_____ No_____

Profit-Sharing Plans

1. Current profit-sharing plans   Yes_____ No_____
   A. Cash plans   Yes_____ No_____
      (1) Defining net profits for purposes of the cash plan   Yes_____ No_____
      (2) Defining the distribution formula   Yes_____ No_____
      (3) Frequency of distributing profit-sharing earnings   Yes_____ No_____
   B. Wage dividend plans   Yes_____ No_____
      (1) Defining net profits for purposes of wage dividend plan   Yes_____ No_____
      (2) Defining the distribution formula   Yes_____ No_____
      (3) Frequency of distributing profit-sharing earnings   Yes_____ No_____
   C. Production-sharing or cost-saving plans   Yes_____ No_____

2. Deferred profit-sharing plans   Yes_____ No_____
   A. Defining "profit" in plan   Yes_____ No_____
   B. Eligibility requirements   Yes_____ No_____
   C. Percentage of profits that will be distributed   Yes_____ No_____
   D. Description of distribution formula   Yes_____ No_____
   E. How and when benefits will be distributed to employees   Yes_____ No_____
   F. Contributory or noncontributory plan   Yes_____ No_____
   G. Description of how plan will be administered   Yes_____ No_____

Retirement Plan

1. Type of funding arrangement   Yes_____ No_____
   A. Group annuities   Yes_____ No_____
   B. Individual policy   Yes_____ No_____
   C. Group life retirement plan   Yes_____ No_____
   D. Uninsured or self-administered plan   Yes_____ No_____
   E. Deposit administration plan   Yes_____ No_____
   F. Self-administered and insured combination plan   Yes_____ No_____

2. Contributory or noncontributory plan   Yes_____ No_____

3. Employee eligibility requirements   Yes_____ No_____

4. Retirement age requirements   Yes_____ No_____

5. Amount of retirement benefits   Yes_____ No_____

6. Description of retirement benefit formulas   Yes_____ No_____

7. Vesting rights of employees   Yes_____ No_____

8. Death and disability benefits   Yes_____ No_____

Bonuses

1. Discretionary year-end and Christmas bonuses   Yes_____ No_____

2. Nondiscretionary production-incentive bonus plans   Yes_____ No_____
   A. Method of paying overtime compensation on production and
      incentive-type bonuses   Yes_____ No_____

Other Benefit Plans

1. Severance pay plan   Yes_____ No_____

2. Unemployment insurance   Yes_____ No_____

3. Workers' compensation   Yes_____ No_____

4. Social Security benefits and payments   Yes_____ No_____

5. Physical examinations   Yes_____ No_____

Employee Services, Recognition, and Privileges

1. Length of service awards   Yes_____ No_____

2. Employee discounts   Yes_____ No_____

3. Employee loans and advances   Yes_____ No_____

4. Credit union   Yes_____ No_____

5. Employee food services   Yes_____ No_____

6. Employee counseling   Yes_____ No_____

7. Financial aid for commuting employees   Yes_____ No_____

8. Medical services on the premises   Yes_____ No_____

9. Safety shoes   Yes_____ No_____

10. Recreation programs   Yes_____ No_____

11. Employee charge accounts   Yes_____ No_____

12. Employee uniforms   Yes_____ No_____

13. Charitable contributions   Yes_____ No_____

Employee benefits is an interesting field because it is a field of constant change. This is both self-imposed as managers redesign programs to get the most out of them and environmentally imposed (as a result of shifting economic, demographic, regulatory, and legislative conditions).

Employee benefits will remain a central area for any organization that employs people. Employee benefit programs are found at every level of government, with employers of every size. They can be mandatory or voluntary, tax-favored or non-tax-favored.

You should realize that the future is now with regard to employee benefits. Employee benefit programs are far-reaching and can represent a true economic safety net. With that in mind, more and more comprehensive economic security planning is being done with individual employees and the growth of financial planning can be expected to move us further along this path.

Flexible benefit programs with an emphasis on setting clear objectives are moving us in the direction of this comprehensive approach. The creation of benefit planning staffs in the largest corporations is further evidence of this. The 1990s saw both government and the private sector focus on the "effectiveness and efficiency" of benefit programs and expenditures. That focus will remain with us for decades to come.

How, then, can a company prepare for the future? Listed below are several points that your company should consider in developing its employee benefit plan for the future.

1. Determine why your company offers the benefit program that it does. For example, what is the rationale for the way your fringe benefits as a whole are set up? Here are some reasons that you may examine for offering the benefits that you do:

A. What other companies in the area or industry are offering. Naturally you want to remain competitive, and fringe benefits are often a deciding factor in an employee's choice of job. You can unofficially survey other companies in your area, or you can obtain the results of a professionally conducted survey by an outside consultant. Either way, you should stay informed on what competitive firms are offering in the way of insurance programs so that your employees don't end up getting short-changed.

B. Top management's stand on benefits. How far is your company's management team willing to go to provide financial security for its employees? How much influence does it think benefit programs have on the company's ability to maintain a competitive edge in the labor market? Without top management's support, there is little likelihood that you will be able to bring about improvements in fringe benefit offerings or develop a more progressive policy statement.

C. Employees' wishes. Surveys now indicate a trend toward letting employees choose, from among a number of available options, the types of insurance coverage or benefit programs they want. These are called "flexible" benefit plans or "cafeteria" plans. They are designed to reflect the different needs of various employee groups. An employee survey is an excellent means of determining the needs of your employees and the extent to which your benefit plans are currently meeting those needs. Thousands of employees who have participated in hundreds of employee opinion surveys have been asked if their present benefits meet the needs of their family. Surprisingly, 63 percent of those who participated responded by saying yes.

D. Your company's employee profile. It is very important that you take a close look at your employee profile and compare it to your current benefit programs. You may discover that some significant changes have taken place over the last ten years or so. Demographic trends have a nice side to them. You may not be able to control them, but at least you know what to expect in the next few years: fewer new, young entrants to the workforce; more women in the workforce; more single-parent families; more two-income families; more older workers; more retirees; more older retirees; and more geographic movement. Many employers have multiple benefit plans, such as holidays and vacations, disability leaves, short-term and long-term disability plans, comprehensive health plans, dental plans, employee assistance programs, group life insurance plans, accidental death plans, business travel-accident plans, dependent life, retirement plans, profit-sharing plans, severance pay plans, bonuses, unemployment insurance, and workers' compensation. You should make sure that your plans do not duplicate one another and that none are overlooked in your review.

2. Your company must come to realize the value of the employees' "other paycheck." Every employee receives two paychecks. The wage or salary check creates the standard of living for employees and their families. The second, a "hidden" or "invisible" paycheck, is the benefits they receive that protect their standard of living. Thus, your employees' total compensation—and your total cost of labor—is the sum of these two checks.

The second paycheck is really money that you, as a company, have paid for the security and leisure of your employees and their families. It is true that some of these payments are called taxes (Social Security, unemployment compensation, workers' compensation, and state statutory disability), but they are, in fact, insurance premiums that you have paid on your employees' behalf. This insurance provides income protection for your employees when, through no fault of their own, they are unable to work or after they have retired.

Again, thousands of employees who have participated in hundreds of employee opinion surveys have been asked these questions:

"Do you know what all of your benefits are?"—78 percent said yes.
"Do you know the value of your employee benefits in dollars?"—38 percent said no.
"Do you understand your benefits?"—67.9 percent said yes.

It is the challenge and responsibility of a cost-conscious employer to set the record straight. One way to do so is to use an inexpensive itemized statement of the invisible or hidden paycheck to show your employees and their families the size of the payments that you make on their behalf. Such a statement is shown in Exhibit 8-1. This statement lists the benefits and either the average cost for employee or the total cost to you.

Economic factors are important in employee benefits planning. It is never easy to predict what the economy will do with total accuracy, and even when a bit of insight is possible, we have a tendency to ignore the implications. Furthermore, the arrival of reality is sometimes forestalled through regulations and subsidies. The current debate over trade legislation is an example of our unwillingness to accept the arrival of a true world economy. Yet, it is that world economy that will determine how much companies can afford to spend on employee benefit programs.

A second economic factor of major importance is the federal budget deficit. Cutbacks in social programs and the restructuring of tax incentives for employee benefits have both been results, and this pressure can be expected to continue in the future. The government is increasingly asking whether the social value of a given employee benefit is worth the current cost in forgone federal tax revenues.

A third economic factor relates to the company structure of our nation. We are becoming more and more reliant on small employers for jobs. The current surge of early retirement and workforce reduction programs in large businesses will only speed this transition. This change will make sponsors look more closely at the types of programs they want in the future. The government will see reductions in coverage and will question the voluntary tax incentive approach now in the law. The question of mandatory private programs will reemerge as the structure of the economy continues to shift.

A fourth economic factor is the level of inflation in general, and in health care in particular. The accelerating cost of benefits in the 1970s created the movement toward redesign and cost containment. If inflation were to come back, it would intensify the need for cost control and also bring demands for postretirement benefit increases.

A fifth economic factor is the level of taxation owners and employees are subjected to. This changes periodically as a result of congressional action, and it will have a significant impact on the need for specific employee benefit plans in the future.

Employer costs will continue to be a major consideration. Efforts toward cost sharing with both active workers and retirees will be undertaken. Workers will demand greater flexibility and more value at younger ages. Workers will also demand better communication about employee benefits as the tax benefits wither. You will increasingly be challenged to minimize the cost of benefits and at the same time to achieve maximum efficiency. "Offering less while having workers think they are getting more"—that is the phrase that sums up the marketing of flexible benefit programs. The emphasis on health-care cost containment that has been at the center of the spread of flexible benefits has helped to increase competition in the health-care market. The health-care inflation rate has slowed, but it still shows a problematic tendency to stay higher than general inflation.

3. Determine provisions for updating fringe benefits for the future. What does your company intend to do to help employees keep pace with increasing health-care costs? For example, if certain types of coverage are linked to length of service, you may want to emphasize the fact that the company encourages and rewards employees who stay with the firm by increasing the provisions for their financial security. Listed below are six areas that you may want to consider in updating your benefit plans for the future:

Exhibit 8-1. A way to tell your benefit story—the big picture.

The Benefits	Who Pays?	Who's Eligible?	(Employer's Name) Paid in 19___	Paid in 19___
PROTECTION FOR YOU AND YOUR FAMILY Life Insurance Benefits	_____	_____	$_____	$_____
Hospitalization	_____	_____	$_____	$_____
Dental Insurance	_____	_____	$_____	$_____
Workers' Compensation	_____	_____	$_____	$_____
Disability Leave	_____	_____	$_____	$_____
Unemployment Insurance	_____	_____	$_____	$_____
FINANCIAL PLANNING FOR YOUR FUTURE Pension Plan	_____	_____	$_____	$_____
Social Security	_____	_____	$_____	$_____
RECOGNITION FOR PERFORMANCE Merit Increase	_____	_____	$_____	$_____
Employee Service Awards	_____	_____	$_____	$_____
PERSONAL SATISFACTION THROUGH PLANNED RECREATION AND EDUCATION Educational Assistance	_____	_____	$_____	$_____
In-house Education	_____	_____	$_____	$_____
Employee Publications	_____	_____	$_____	$_____
Social Activities	_____	_____	$_____	$_____
Vacation	_____	_____	$_____	$_____
Holidays				
LITTLE THINGS THAT REALLY COUNT Discount on Meals	_____	_____	$_____	$_____
Free Parking	_____	_____	$_____	$_____
Coffee Breaks	_____	_____	$_____	$_____
Bereavement Leave	_____	_____	$_____	$_____
Christmas Gifts	_____	_____	$_____	$_____
Jury Pay	_____	_____	$_____	$_____

A. Carrier. What insurance company is providing the best coverage (most cost-effective coverage) for the particular plans?

B. Eligibility. How long must the employee be on the payroll before he or she qualifies for coverage?

C. Coverage. This includes deductible amounts, the percentage of costs covered above and beyond the deductible, and maximum benefits (in terms of either dollar amounts or number of days).

D. Employee costs. Does the company pay the full premium, or must the employee contribute a certain amount?

E. Continuation of healthcare coverage after the separation of the employee. It is common to cover employees for a certain number of days after they have left the company. With the implementation of COBRA, this continuation is now mandatory for employers with twenty or more employees. The major question here is how long your company will continue insurance before COBRA is implemented.

F. Additional coverage available. In some cases, coverage greater than your present benefit may be available at no increase in cost.

The importance of the employee benefit function and employee benefit programs will increase in the years ahead as demographic and economic change, combined with regulatory and legislative change, makes benefits an increasingly important part of both human resources and financial aspects of the corporation.

On the following pages you will find policies covering:

Paid Vacations (Exempt and Nonexempt)
Company-Paid Holidays
"Floating Birthday" Holidays
Salary Continuance Plan (Exempt and Nonexempt)
Benefits Continuance during Excused Absences
Health Insurance
COBRA Administration
Retirement Savings Plan [401(k)]
Insurance Plans (Comprehensive)
Severance Pay
Unemployment Insurance
Workers' Compensation
Social Security Benefits and Payments
Physical Exams
Employee Uniforms
Employee Discounts
Employee Charge Accounts
Service Recognition Awards
Safety Shoes
Athletic and Recreational Programs
Charitable Contributions

PERSONNEL POLICIES AND PROCEDURES

DISTRIBUTION:		SUBJECT: PAID VACATIONS	
EFFECTIVE DATE:	PAGE 1 OF 3	FILE UNDER SECTION	
REVISION DATE:	APPROVED BY:		

POLICY STATEMENT:

The company provides vacations with pay for all eligible employees for the purposes of rest and relaxation.

A. Eligibility

(1) All regular employees are eligible to receive vacations with pay. Temporary and part-time employees are not eligible.

(2) Employees become eligible for vacations as of April 1 each year, in accordance with:

    a. the length of their continuous service (measured from Company Service Date to April 1 of any year).

    b. the number of weeks worked during the prior twelve months in the period from April 1 through March 31.

B. Length of Vacation

(1) *Length of Continuous Service* *(as of April 1 each year)*	*Weeks Worked* *(April 1–March 31)*	*Days of Vacation*
1 year to 5 years	40 weeks or more	10 days
6 years to 19 years	40 weeks or more	15 days
20 years or more	40 weeks or more	20 days
Less than 1 year	40 weeks or more	10 days
	36–39 weeks	9 days
	32–35 weeks	8 days
	28–31 weeks	7 days
	24–27 weeks	6 days
	20–23 weeks	5 days
	16–19 weeks	4 days
	12–15 weeks	3 days
	8–11 weeks	2 days
	4–7 weeks	1 day

(2) An employee who has one year or more of continuous service, but who has worked less than 40 weeks during the prior period from April 1 through March 31, is eligible for a prorated vacation based upon the number of weeks actually worked. (For example, an employee with four years of continuous service who has worked 30 weeks in the period April 1 through March 31 is eligible for 30/40 × 10 days = 7.5 days of vacation.)

(3) Definitions

    a. Continuous Service—uninterrupted employment while classified as a regular employee.

    b. Weeks Worked—calendar weeks during which time an employee was on the job performing his or her assigned duties and responsibilities. (Partial weeks worked count as full weeks.)

C. Vacation Periods

(1) An employee who is eligible for up to two weeks' vacation will take it during the company's vacation shutdown period or during the summer months of June, July, and August in accordance with the following general guides:

    a. Plant production employees—will take their vacations during the shutdown period.

DISTRIBUTION:		SUBJECT: PAID VACATIONS	
EFFECTIVE DATE:	PAGE 2 OF 3	FILE UNDER SECTION	
REVISION DATE:	APPROVED BY:		

Exception: Employees required to remain during the plant shutdown period for plant maintenance, housekeeping, or special production operations will take their vacations at such other times as can be conveniently arranged with their supervisors.

    b. Office clerical employees—will take their vacations during the months of June, July, and August.

        Exception: Employees may take their vacations in months other than the three above for special reasons—such as marriage, scheduling of a vacation trip with a spouse, accompanying parents on a vacation, etc.—with the approval of their supervisor and the manager of the department.

        The vacations of office clerical employees should be scheduled in such a way as to not hamper the normal operating efficiency of the department. Work cycles, special project completion dates, and the capabilities of employees to perform each other's regular assignments must be taken into consideration when scheduling vacations. A basic rule of thumb to follow is:

        Department of 1–6 employees—no more than one person should be on vacation at any one time.

        Department of 7–12 employees—no more than two persons should be on vacation at any one time.

        Department of 13–18 employees—no more than three persons should be on vacation at any one time.

        Department of 19–24 employees—no more than four persons should be on vacation at any one time.

    c. All salaried employees—will take their vacations at such times as can be conveniently arranged with their supervisors. The following points should be considered in scheduling vacations for salaried employees:

        i. Vacations should be scheduled in such a way as to not hamper the normal operating efficiency of the department.

        ii. Manufacturing salaried employees involved in direct supervision of plant production employees or involved in functions directly related to manufacturing operations (production planning, scheduling, inventory control, etc.) should take their vacations during the plant shutdown period.

        iii. Marketing or staff salaried employees in departments where the level of activity drops off during the shutdown period should take their vacations at that time.

  (2) An employee who has additional days of vacation will take it at such times as can be conveniently arranged with his or her supervisor in accordance with company and departmental operating schedules and needs.

  (3) An employee who is eligible for less than two weeks' vacation and who is in a department where operations cease during a plant shutdown period may take the time off without pay or work during all or a portion of the shutdown period, at the discretion of the company.

D. Use of Vacation Time

Vacations resulting from service in the prior twelve months (April 1–March 31), must be taken within the present vacation year. Vacation days not used within a vacation year will be forfeited. No payments will be made for forfeited vacation days. (An employee may not be given additional pay in lieu of vacation days not taken.)

PERSONNEL POLICIES AND PROCEDURES

DISTRIBUTION:		SUBJECT: PAID VACATIONS	
EFFECTIVE DATE:	PAGE 3 OF 3	FILE UNDER SECTION	
REVISION DATE:	APPROVED BY:		

E. Notification

The company will notify all employees of the dates for the two-week vacation shutdown period at least five months prior to the period.

F. Holiday Within Vacation Period

In the event that a holiday observed by the company falls within a vacation period, the additional day of vacation will be allowed at another time.

G. Effect on Overtime

Vacation days count as time worked for purposes of overtime calculations.

H. Termination of Employment

Persons terminating employment with the company will receive any vacation allowance resulting from continuous employment during the prior twelve months (April 1–March 31), and not yet taken. An employee who has not completed a vacation eligibility year at the time of his or her termination of employment (leaves prior to April 1, the beginning of a new vacation year) is not eligible to receive a prorated vacation.

I. Uniformed Service

(1) Entering Service—An employee entering a uniformed service will be eligible for any vacation allowance resulting from continuous employment during the prior twelve months (April 1–March 31) and not yet taken as well as a prorated vacation based upon the number of weeks actually worked from April 1 to date of entering into service.

(2) Returning from Service—An employee returning from service will receive a prorated vacation based upon the number of weeks actually worked between the date of his or her return and the following March 31.

PERSONNEL POLICIES AND PROCEDURES

DISTRIBUTION:		SUBJECT: PAID VACATIONS	
EFFECTIVE DATE:	PAGE 1 OF 1	FILE UNDER SECTION	
REVISION DATE:	APPROVED BY:		

POLICY STATEMENT:

The company grants annual paid vacations and is convinced that both the employees and the company benefit thereby. Vacations are given as a reward for the completion of a year's work, and to prepare the employee for better service in the coming year. Under certain circumstances a vacation is considered an earned right and will be granted in the form of money rather than time off. These policies are further clarified as follows:

A. Splits

Eligible officers and employees are required to take no less than two consecutive weeks of vacation. (For exceptions, see Procedure under Department Head.) Those entitled to more than two weeks of vacation may take the remaining time by weeks or by days. For purposes of calculating split vacations, a week of vacation is equivalent to five business days, and a month of vacation is equivalent to twenty-two days.

B. Extensions

A vacation may be extended by reason of certain events occurring during the authorized period:
(1) Legal holiday
(2) Temporary recall to work

A vacation is not automatically extended by reason of these events:
(1) Illness
(2) Death in family

In such cases the department head has the right to reschedule the vacation at a future date, if the circumstances warrant.

C. Holdovers

A vacation may be postponed to a subsequent year only for the convenience of the company and not of the individual.

D. Cancellations

Additional pay will not be given in lieu of a vacation that is not taken.

PERSONNEL POLICIES AND PROCEDURES

DISTRIBUTION:		SUBJECT: VACATIONS	
EFFECTIVE DATE:	PAGE 1 OF 2	FILE UNDER SECTION	
REVISION DATE:	APPROVED BY:		

PURPOSE:

The purpose of this policy is to define vacation benefits for associates and to describe the administrative procedures associated with the vacation process.

POLICY:

Paid vacation is one of the ways we recognize length of service with the company and allows paid time off work.

ELIGIBILITY:

A. Regular, full-time associates earn a paid vacation based on length of continuous service as follows:

1 year	5 days
3 years	10 days
8 years	15 days
15 years	20 days

B. Regular, full-time associates are eligible to earn a paid vacation based on the following requirements:

1. Completion of the required number of years of continuous employment.

2. In order to qualify for paid vacation an associate must have worked at least 1,250 hours in the twelve- (12-) month period preceding the anniversary date. Time off for which the associate receives pay from the company, excluding leaves of absence, will count as hours worked for purposes of vacation eligibility.

PROCEDURES:

A. The associate will have one year from the day on which he/she earns vacation to take his/her vacation.

B. Whole- or half-day vacation may be taken on an unscheduled call-in basis on up to three (3) occasions per calendar year. The associate must report this vacation by calling the plant prior to the beginning of the scheduled shift, except in cases approved by the general manager or his/her designee. In such emergency cases, an associate may report his/her whole or half vacation day up to one and one-half (1-½) hours after the beginning of the shift.

C. Vacation time must be scheduled as follows:

1. Up to six (6) vacation days may be taken in increments of half days.

2. Four (4) additional vacation days may be taken in whole-day increments.

3. All other earned vacation must be taken in a block of five (5) consecutive days at a time.

D. Vacation periods should be scheduled as far in advance as possible. Vacation periods should be scheduled and approved by the associate's supervisor at least two (2) weeks prior to the date requested. Preference in selection of

PERSONNEL POLICIES AND PROCEDURES

DISTRIBUTION:		SUBJECT: VACATIONS	
EFFECTIVE DATE:	PAGE 2 OF 2		FILE UNDER SECTION
REVISION DATE:	APPROVED BY:		

dates will be granted based on length of service. Local management will determine the method of advance scheduling of vacation, taking into consideration the production requirements of that facility.

E. Each supervisor will maintain a vacation schedule for his/her group and a record of the vacation time taken by each associate.

F. A written authorization should be submitted in all instances where the associate is granted a vacation day(s).

G. Vacation time other than that taken on an unscheduled call-in basis must be scheduled no later than the end of the workshift on the last workday prior to the vacation time.

H. Scheduled vacation must be canceled no later than the end of the workshift on the last workday prior to the scheduled vacation time.

I. Vacation days cannot be borrowed from future years.

J. Associates on leave of absence or layoff on their anniversary date will be eligible to receive earned vacation pay provided they have worked the minimum 1,250 hours in the preceding twelve- (12-) month period.

GUIDELINES FOR COMPUTING AMOUNT OF VACATION PAY:

A. Vacation pay is the associate's regular rate of pay (including leader and shift premium, if applicable) for eight (8) hours per day of vacation.

B. Associates not using all their vacation entitlement will be paid automatically for any unused portion at the end of their anniversary year.

C. Hourly associates will receive vacation pay for whole payroll weeks of vacation on the last regular payday prior to the start of vacation, where vacation has been scheduled two (2) weeks prior to that date and a written request for payment has been submitted by the associate.

D. Vacation time counts as time worked for purposes of overtime calculations except for vacation taken on Saturday.

TERMINATION:

A. Associates with less than one (1) year of continuous service will not be entitled to vacation.

B. Associates with more than one (1) year of continuous service will be paid any earned unused vacation for the previous year plus any prorated vacation for the current year provided the associate has met the minimum hours requirement.

C. Vacation will be prorated based on completed years of service.

PERSONNEL POLICIES AND PROCEDURES

DISTRIBUTION:		SUBJECT: PAID VACATIONS	
EFFECTIVE DATE:	PAGE 1 OF 2	FILE UNDER SECTION	
REVISION DATE:	APPROVED BY:		

PURPOSE:

To recognize each employee's length of service and performance and to show our appreciation to him/her by providing time off with pay.

PROCEDURE:

Eligibility Requirements

1. Eligibility for vacation pay is determined by the number of full months the employee has worked prior to December 31 of any calendar year.

2. An earned vacation must be taken in the year it comes due and cannot be carried forward from one year to the next.

3. Vacation pay will not be given to anyone unless time off is actually taken except with permission of the General Office.

4. For each full month of employment prior to the employee's first December 31, he/she will earn one-half day of vacation that will be taken in the following calendar year. Example: If an employee began work on February 5, by next January 1 he/she would be entitled to five (5) days paid vacation. [March through December is ten (10) months times one-half day equals five (5) paid days of vacation.]

   After one full calendar year has been completed by an employee, he/she will earn one (1) full day vacation for each month of employment. Example: In the above illustration, on the second January anniversary of his/her employment, employee would have two (2) weeks paid vacation due him/her, which he/she may schedule at any time during the calendar year.

5. After fifteen (15) full calendar years of service, employees will be eligible to earn one and one-half days of paid vacation for each month of active employment, which will entitle them to a maximum of three (3) weeks paid vacation each calendar year.

Amount of Vacation Pay

A. Hourly Employees—vacation pay will be forty (40) hours at the regular straight-time hourly rate for each week of eligible vacation.

B. Commission Sales Employees—vacation pay for sales personnel paid on a salary plus commission basis will be their regular weekly base salary.

C. Fluctuating Workweek Salary-Paid Employees—vacation pay for employees paid by the fluctuating workweek salary plan will be their weekly guaranteed base salary (overtime premium not included).

DISTRIBUTION:		SUBJECT: PAID VACATIONS	
EFFECTIVE DATE:	PAGE 2 OF 2	FILE UNDER SECTION	
REVISION DATE:	APPROVED BY:		

D. Exempt Salaried Personnel—vacation pay for exempt salaried personnel will be their regular guaranteed weekly salary.

Ineligibility for Vacation Pay

1. Any employee who voluntarily quits without giving at least two weeks' notice forfeits all vacation pay eligibility rights. Only employees who voluntarily leave with at least two weeks' notice after being employed at least twelve (12) continuous months will be paid for any unused vacation.

2. Employees discharged or dismissed for cause shall not be eligible for any unused paid vacation.

Vacation Scheduling

A. Vacations for eligible employees should be scheduled by the store manager or department head in such a way that we can best serve our customers by maintaining sufficient help to meet their needs. Advise employees to give you at least thirty (30) days notice in advance of the desired time off.

Should there be a conflict in scheduling vacation time off between employees in the same department, the employee with the greatest length of service will be given first choice of vacation time.

B. If a paid holiday falls during an employee's scheduled vacation period, he or she will be given an additional day off with pay or an extra day's pay, at the discretion of the store manager.

C. Except in unusual circumstances, employees who are eligible for at least one week of vacation should take it all at one time. However, when it is not practical for an employee to take as much as one week of vacation at one time, it will be permissible for that employee to take vacation time two days or more at a time, but not for periods of less than two (2) days. If an employee is entitled to only three (3) days' vacation, he or she would have to take it all at one time. However, if an employee were entitled to a full week, he or she could take three (3) days at one time and later take the remaining two (2) days. FMLA-eligible employees may substitute paid vacation for unpaid FMLA leave in any necessary increment.

PERSONNEL POLICIES AND PROCEDURES

DISTRIBUTION:		SUBJECT: EXEMPT AND NONEXEMPT VACATIONS	
EFFECTIVE DATE:	PAGE 1 OF 3	FILE UNDER SECTION	
REVISION DATE:	APPROVED BY:		

PURPOSE:

The company grants vacation with pay in accordance with two convictions:

1. That its employees will benefit mentally and physically from a period of rest and relaxation during the year.

2. That its employees are entitled to vacation based upon length of continuous service.

VACATION PERIOD:

Employees may take their vacation at any time during the twelve months following their anniversary date of hire. Employees are encouraged to schedule their vacation prior to June 1 of each year. However, each employee must take his or her vacation by the end of each anniversary year, since no vacation credit will be accumulated from one anniversary year to another and no payment will be made in lieu of vacation.

VACATION ELIGIBILITY

Nonexempt Employees

1. Regular, full-time, nonexempt employees are granted vacation credit in accordance with the following years of continuous service:
   A. Regular, full-time, nonexempt employees who have completed twelve months of continuous service shall be eligible, after their anniversary date, for one week's vacation.
   B. Regular, full-time, nonexempt employees who have completed twenty-four months of continuous service shall be eligible, after their anniversary date, for two weeks' vacation.
   C. Regular, full-time, nonexempt employees who have completed 120 months of continuous service shall be eligible, after their anniversary date, for three weeks' vacation.
   D. Regular, full-time, nonexempt employees who have completed 180 months of continuous service shall be eligible, after their anniversary date, for four weeks' vacation.

2. Regular, part-time, nonexempt employees who have completed the eligibility requirements above shall be eligible, on a prorated basis, for vacation credit (based on the normal hours worked in a forty-hour week).

3. Temporary, part-time, nonexempt employees shall not be eligible for vacation credit or vacation payment.

4. Holidays during nonexempt employees' vacation period: If a holiday occurs during an employee's vacation period, the employee will be allowed to take an additional day off, with pay, at a time different from the vacation period.

PERSONNEL POLICIES AND PROCEDURES

DISTRIBUTION:		SUBJECT: EXEMPT AND NONEXEMPT VACATIONS	
EFFECTIVE DATE:	PAGE 2 OF 3	FILE UNDER SECTION	
REVISION DATE:	APPROVED BY:		

VACATION ELIGIBILITY:

Exempt Employees

1. Regular, full-time exempt employees are granted vacation credit in accordance with the following years of continuous service:

    A. Regular, full-time, exempt employees who have completed 12 months of continuous service shall be eligible, after their anniversary date, for two weeks' vacation.

    B. Regular, full-time, exempt employees who have completed 120 months of continuous service shall be eligible, after their anniversary date, for three weeks' vacation.

    C. Regular, full-time, exempt employees who have completed 180 months of continuous service shall be eligible, after their anniversary date, for four weeks' vacation.

2. Holidays during exempt employees' vacation period: If a holiday occurs during an exempt employees' vacation period, he or she forfeits the holiday and shall not receive holiday pay or additional time off.

3. Exception to eligibility: The Executive Committee, at its discretion, may alter vacation eligibility on an exception basis.

4. Regular part-time and temporary part-time exempt employees shall not be eligible for vacation credit or vacation payment.

GENERAL:

1. Splitting vacation credit

    A. Regular, full-time exempt and nonexempt employees who are eligible for two weeks' vacation credit shall be eligible to take one week's vacation at any time and split the remaining vacation credit into one-day increments, but at no time shall they split their vacation credit into partial days except as substitution for unpaid FMLA leave.

    B. Regular, full-time exempt and nonexempt employees who are eligible for two weeks' or more vacation credit shall be eligible to take two weeks' vacation at any time and split the remaining credit into one-day increments, but at no time shall they split their vacation credit into partial days.

    C. Regular, full-time exempt and nonexempt employees who are eligible for more than two weeks' vacation shall not use their vacation credit for more than two weeks at any one time. Exceptions to this policy shall be made at the discretion of the Executive Committee.

2. Continuous Service: Continuous service shall be deemed to have been broken if the employee has terminated his or her employment voluntarily or for cause or has taken a leave of absence in excess of twelve continuous months. Exceptions to this policy shall be made at the discretion of the Executive Committee.

PERSONNEL POLICIES AND PROCEDURES

DISTRIBUTION:		SUBJECT: EXEMPT AND NONEXEMPT VACATIONS	
EFFECTIVE DATE:	PAGE 3 OF 3	FILE UNDER SECTION	
REVISION DATE:	APPROVED BY:		

3. Recordkeeping: Department heads shall keep, annually, in the employee's personnel file, when an employee has used his or her vacation credit, a record of the dates.

4. Termination of Employment:

   A. Regular, full-time employees who have voluntarily terminated their employment shall receive, in their final paycheck, payment of any unused vacation credit provided two weeks' notice has been given and served prior to termination.

   B. Regular, full-time employees who terminated their employment because of death or retirement shall receive, in their final paycheck, payment for any unused vacation credit.

PERSONNEL POLICIES AND PROCEDURES

DISTRIBUTION:		SUBJECT: HOLIDAYS	
EFFECTIVE DATE:	PAGE 1 OF 1	FILE UNDER SECTION	
REVISION DATE:	APPROVED BY:		

POLICY STATEMENT:

The company recognizes certain days during the year as paid holidays for its employees. The specific holidays observed at each location are contained in the Company Directory.

Due to the nature of our business, it may be necessary for some of our employees to work on a holiday. If this occurs, those nonexempt employees required to work will be paid overtime in accordance with the prevailing practice at the specific location involved.

PERSONNEL POLICIES AND PROCEDURES

DISTRIBUTION:		SUBJECT: HOLIDAYS	
EFFECTIVE DATE:	PAGE 1 OF 1	FILE UNDER SECTION	
REVISION DATE:	APPROVED BY:		

POLICY STATEMENT:

The following days will be observed as paid holidays for company employees:

New Year's Day
Memorial Day
Independence Day (July 4)
Labor Day
Thanksgiving Day
Christmas Day

If one of these holidays falls on a Sunday, it will usually be observed on the following Monday. If a holiday falls on Saturday, we will either pay eligible employees for the holiday or select another regular workday as substitute holiday.

Eligibility

Hourly-rated factory employees will be eligible for eight hours' pay at their straight-time rate if they lose work because of a holiday, provided that they meet the following requirements:

A. The employee must work within the payroll period during which the holiday occurs.

B. The employee must work a full shift the day before the holiday and a full shift immediately following the holiday. There will be no exceptions to this rule for any reason.

C. The employee must have completed his/her introductory period.

D. Temporary employees will not receive holiday pay.

Miscellaneous

A. If a holiday is postponed, or observed at a time other than the date the holiday actually falls on, the employee must meet his/her eligibility requirements at the time the holiday is observed.

B. A paid holiday will be counted as eight hours worked by the employee in the computation of overtime pay, provided that the employee meets all the eligibility requirements.

PERSONNEL POLICIES AND PROCEDURES

DISTRIBUTION:		SUBJECT: COMPANY-PAID HOLIDAYS	
EFFECTIVE DATE:	PAGE 1 OF 2	FILE UNDER SECTION	
REVISION DATE:	APPROVED BY:		

POLICY STATEMENT:

(Company Name) recognizes certain days of religious and historic importance as holidays and pays employees for time off on these days in accordance with its special eligibility rules.

HOLIDAYS OBSERVED:

The following days will be observed as paid holidays for company employees:

New Year's Day	Thanksgiving Day
Washington's Birthday	Friday after Thanksgiving
Good Friday	Day before Christmas
Memorial Day	Christmas Day
Independence Day	Floating Holiday
Labor Day	Employee's Birthday
Presidential Election Day	

Whenever any of the holidays falls on a Saturday or Sunday, the preceding Friday or the following Monday, whichever is closer, will be recognized as a paid holiday.

ELIGIBILITY REQUIREMENTS:

1. All regular, full-time active employees are eligible to receive holiday pay. Persons classified as temporary are not eligible.

2. Hourly employees are required to work their regular scheduled hours preceding and their regular scheduled hours following a holiday in order to receive holiday pay.

   A day of vacation or any other excused and paid day off (paid for in accordance with standard payroll policies) is considered as a day worked for purposes of holiday eligibility.

3. In the event it is necessary for an hourly employee to be absent the day before or the day after a holiday, the immediate supervisor, through the Department Head, Management Committee Member, and Director of Human Resources, must submit in writing beforehand his/her recommendation concerning pay. If approved by all concerned, holiday pay will be granted.

4. Should a holiday occur during an employee's vacation period, an additional day of vacation will be allowed.

5. In the case of monthly salaried personnel, when it becomes necessary to schedule work on a recognized holiday, the person concerned should receive an alternative day off in lieu of taking the holiday.

6. The Director of Human Resources will be the final authority concerned in the interpretation of this policy regarding eligibility for holiday pay.

DISTRIBUTION:		SUBJECT: COMPANY-PAID HOLIDAYS	
EFFECTIVE DATE:	PAGE 2 OF 2	FILE UNDER SECTION	
REVISION DATE:	APPROVED BY:		

7. If an employee terminates employment for any reason, he/she will not be eligible for holiday pay for any holidays that occur beyond the date of termination.

HOLIDAY PAY COUNTING TOWARD OVERTIME:

Holiday pay will be considered as the equivalent hours worked in computing overtime for the week in which the holiday falls, except when an employee may have worked on a holiday.

WORK ON A HOLIDAY:

A regular, full-time, active employee who works on a holiday will receive, in addition to holiday pay, compensation at the rate of one and one-half of regular base pay for the actual hours worked.

PERSONNEL POLICIES AND PROCEDURES

DISTRIBUTION:		SUBJECT: HOLIDAYS	
EFFECTIVE DATE:	PAGE 1 OF 2	FILE UNDER SECTION	
REVISION DATE:	APPROVED BY:		

PURPOSE:

The purpose of this policy is to set forth the procedures related to the administration of the company's paid Holiday Program.

POLICY:

A. The company recognizes certain days as holidays and pays eligible associates for time off on these days as follows:

   HOLIDAYS OBSERVED:
   - New Year's Day
   - Good Friday
   - Memorial Day
   - Independence Day
   - Labor Day
   - Thanksgiving Day
   - Friday following Thanksgiving Day
   - Christmas Eve
   - Christmas Day
   - Floating Holiday

B. Holiday Pay:

   An associate will be paid eight (8) hours pay at his/her regular rate of pay, including shift or leader premium.

C. Observance of Holidays:

   1. Monday through Friday

      If a holiday occurs on a regular workday (Monday through Friday), it is observed on that day.

   2. Saturdays and Sundays

      If a holiday occurs on a Saturday or Sunday, normally it will be observed either on the Friday preceding it or on the following Monday.

D. Working on a Holiday

   1. Regular Workshift

      Hourly and salaried nonexempt associates who are required to work on a holiday will be paid eight hours holiday pay (as outlined above) and one and one-half (1-1/2) times their regular rate for all hours worked on that day.

   2. Irregular Workshift

      Associates who work irregular workshifts will have the day that they are to be off work in observance of the holiday communicated to them as far in advance as practical.

PERSONNEL POLICIES AND PROCEDURES

DISTRIBUTION:		SUBJECT: HOLIDAYS	
EFFECTIVE DATE:	PAGE 2 OF 2	FILE UNDER SECTION	
REVISION DATE:	APPROVED BY:		

3. Weekend Shift

Associates who work a weekend shift will not be eligible for holiday pay.

E. Eligibility Requirements:

Full-time permanent associates are entitled to receive holiday pay if they work all scheduled hours on the last workday before and the first workday after the holiday.

Paid time off work on the last workday before the holiday or the first workday after the holiday will be considered an absence "excused in accordance with the Attendance Policy" and will therefore be considered to be the same as time worked in determining eligibility for holiday pay.

Associates on leave of absence when a holiday occurs are not eligible to receive holiday pay.

PERSONNEL POLICIES AND PROCEDURES

DISTRIBUTION:		SUBJECT: HOLIDAY—BIRTHDAY	
EFFECTIVE DATE:	PAGE 1 OF 1	FILE UNDER SECTION	
REVISION DATE:	APPROVED BY:		

POLICY STATEMENT:

In addition to those certain holidays that (Company Name) recognizes as being of historic importance, the company grants time off with pay for each employee's birthday. Employees receive this paid day off in accordance with the following eligibility requirements.

ELIGIBILITY REQUIREMENTS:

1. All regular, full-time, active employees are eligible to receive a paid day off on their birth date. Persons classified as temporary are not eligible.

2. This day is not considered a "floating" day off, i.e., employees must take the actual day off coinciding with their birth date. If the actual day is not taken, the paid day off is lost.

3. Employees are required to work their regularly scheduled hours preceding and their regularly scheduled hours following their birthday in order to receive pay for time off. A day of vacation or any other excused paid day off (paid for in accordance with standard payroll policies) is considered as a day worked for purposes of birthday pay eligibility.

4. In the event it is necessary for an employee to be absent the day before or the day after a birthday, the immediate supervisor, through the Department Head, Management Committee Member, and Director of Human Resources, must submit in writing beforehand his/her recommendation concerning birthday pay. If approved by all concerned, birthday pay will be granted.

GUIDELINES:

1. Should a birthday occur during an employee's vacation period, an additional day of vacation will be allowed.

2. Should a birthday fall on a Saturday or Sunday, the preceding Friday or the following Monday, at the discretion of the employee, will be recognized as a paid day off.

3. It is the responsibility of all employees to mark their individual time record cards when off due to a birthday. The initials "BD" will be written on the card, rather than "B," which is the coding for bereavement.

BIRTHDAY PAY COUNTING TOWARD OVERTIME:

Birthday pay will be considered as the equivalent hours worked in calculating overtime for the week in which the birthday falls.

WORK ON A BIRTHDAY:

A regular, full-time, hourly or salaried (nonexempt) employee who, due to emergency, works on his/her birthday at the request of the immediate supervisor will receive, in addition to birthday pay, compensation at the rate of 1-1/2 times regular base pay for the actual hours worked. Authorization must be obtained in advance from the appropriate Management Committee Member concerned, and an Overtime Authorization Request Form must be completed.

PERSONNEL POLICIES AND PROCEDURES

DISTRIBUTION:		SUBJECT: GROUP LIFE INSURANCE	
EFFECTIVE DATE:	PAGE 1 OF 1	FILE UNDER SECTION	
REVISION DATE:	APPROVED BY:		

POLICY STATEMENT:

The company has established a Group Life Insurance Plan to provide basic protection for every permanent employee at no cost, and to provide additional coverage for which employees may subscribe at reduced rates.

In addition, the company pays to the dependent heir or heirs of a deceased active employee:

A. Current salary due.

B. Gift equal to one week's salary for each year of service.

PERSONNEL POLICIES AND PROCEDURES

DISTRIBUTION:		SUBJECT: HEALTH INSURANCE	
EFFECTIVE DATE:	PAGE 1 OF 1	FILE UNDER SECTION	
REVISION DATE:	APPROVED BY:		

POLICY STATEMENT:

(Company Name) Group Health Care Plan is designed to cover most of the medical expenses employees will incur. With a lifetime maximum of one million dollars coverage, employees can be assured of financial security for their medical care needs. The company also provides dental and vision care insurance plans. Regular, full-time employees who have completed ninety days of continuous employment are eligible to participate in (Company Name) group health insurance, dental, and vision care plans.

PROCEDURE:

Supervisors and managers should become familiar with the health insurance plans provided by the company to its employees, free of charge, by reading the following information, as well as the Group Health Plan booklets. Employees' questions that cannot be answered by a supervisor should be referred to the Coordinator of Human Resources.

Employers are required by law to notify employees of their rights under COBRA (Consolidated Omnibus Reconciliation Act of 1985), which deals with group health insurance continuance upon termination of employment or reduction in hours of work that results in a loss of coverage. Supervisors and managers must ensure timely notification of an employee's termination or reduction in hours to the Coordinator of Human Resources Department so that this notice will be sent out.

It is important as well as beneficial for employees to understand (Company Name) Group Health Care Plans, in order to use them effectively. Employees will gain a basic understanding of how the plans work if they review the booklets provided upon enrollment. Additional knowledge about the programs will be gained as the benefits are used. Each time employees seek medical, dental, or vision care, they should review the contents outlined in the Plan booklet to determine if the Plan pays for the care and, if so, how it pays and what they can expect to receive.

The ''Benefits Summary'' chart on the inside back cover of the booklets provides a brief review of the benefits available and their payment schedule. The ''Description of Benefits'' section provides greater detail about the benefits. The ''Exclusions'' section outlines coverage not taken care of by the Plans.

For employees who are eligible for this Plan, there is no deduction from their paycheck. At the time of employment, employees are asked to complete a group enrollment card for this Plan, which will be retained in the Payroll Office until the completion of ninety days of employment. At that time, the employee's enrollment card will be forwarded to the Company's Group Health Care Plan Administrator for processing.

If an employee is originally hired as a part-time employee and is subsequently converted to full time, he/she will become eligible for enrollment in the Company's Group Health Care Plan on the first day of the month following or coincident with the completion of ninety days of continuous, full-time employment. If an employee's employment status changes from full-time to part-time, he/she will no longer be eligible for the Plan, but will be eligible for continuation coverage under COBRA.

The cost of the continuation coverage will be approximately equal to the ''applicable premium'' that is provided to other employees and/or beneficiaries under the group benefit plan whose coverage continues to be maintained by the employer. The individual will be required to pay this premium on a monthly schedule.

GROUP CONVERSION INSURANCE/INDIVIDUAL INSURANCE POLICY PROVISION:

In addition to the ''Continuation of Coverage/Self-Pay Provision'' outlined above, covered employees and dependents may elect to purchase a group conversion insurance policy. This may be done at the time when an employee or family members are no longer eligible under the group benefit plan or following the maximum COBRA continuation period.

This policy will be similar to but not necessarily a duplication of the group benefit plan. Employees will be eligible for this personal medical program without providing evidence of insurability. Employees will need to make written application for this privilege within thirty-one days after they or a family member become ineligible for further coverage.

255

PERSONNEL POLICIES AND PROCEDURES

DISTRIBUTION:		SUBJECT: GROUP INSURANCE PLANS	
EFFECTIVE DATE:	PAGE 1 OF 2	FILE UNDER SECTION	
REVISION DATE:	APPROVED BY:		

All full-time employees are entitled to coverage under the company's Group Insurance Plans.

MEDICAL AND HOSPITAL INSURANCE:

Basic hospital expenses incurred by you or members of your family are covered by (name of insurance carrier). This plan pays 100 percent for the first 21 days and 50 percent for the next 180 days for semiprivate hospital accommodations and most general hospital services. The high expenses that can result from serious illness or injury are covered by major medical insurance, which pays for doctors' bills, drugs, nursing costs, and most other medical expenses. You and each of your dependents can receive up to $250,000 in benefits in your lifetime. Coverage under major medical insurance begins after you have paid $100 toward the cost of your treatment, or a dependent's, each year (but subject to a maximum yearly family deductible of $200). The insurance pays for 80 percent of expenses above the deductible up to $2,000 and 100 percent of expenses over $2,000 in a calendar year. You are covered on your date of employment for hospital and major medical insurance. Your children may be covered dependents until they are age 19, or until age 24 if they are full-time students.

DENTAL INSURANCE:

From your first day of employment, you will be covered for dental insurance at the following coinsurance amounts: 100 percent for routine oral examinations; 80 percent for basic restorative; 50 percent for major restorative and orthodontia. The deductible for routine oral examinations and for basic and major restorative is combined with the major medical program. There is a separate $100 deductible per calendar year for orthodontia.

LIFE INSURANCE:

From the day you are employed, your life is insured under our group life insurance plan for an amount equal to two times your annual compensation taken to the next higher $100, if not already an exact multiple thereof, to a maximum of $300,000. You may name anyone as your beneficiary for this insurance and may change your beneficiary at any time. Payments may be arranged as a cash settlement, a monthly income, or as a combination of the two. If you should leave the company, you may convert your coverage (for your own account) to an individual policy with no medical examination required.

ACCIDENT INSURANCE:

If you should lose your life through an accident, your beneficiary will receive an additional amount equivalent to your life insurance. If you should become disabled by the loss of limbs or eyesight through an accident, you will receive a substantial settlement. This insurance begins on your first day of employment.

SALARY CONTINUANCE PLAN:

You are covered by a salary continuance plan that guarantees you 60 percent of salary, including government compensation, if you should have an accident or illness that prevents you from working. The plan itself will pay 60 per-

PERSONNEL POLICIES AND PROCEDURES

DISTRIBUTION:		SUBJECT: GROUP INSURANCE PLANS	
EFFECTIVE DATE:	PAGE 2 OF 2	FILE UNDER SECTION	
REVISION DATE:	APPROVED BY:		

cent of your monthly salary up to a maximum of $2,500. Payments begin 180 days after your disability occurs and can continue until you reach 70 or are able to return to work. Coverage begins on your date of employment.

SURVIVOR INCOME BENEFITS:

In addition to your life insurance, we provide your dependents with a partial continuation of your salary in the event of your death. Your spouse gets 30 percent of your salary payable until remarriage, death, or age 62; each child gets 10 percent up to a maximum of 20 percent for all your children, payable until marriage, death, or age 19 (not to exceed a maximum of $1,500 per month). Coverage begins after you have been with the company for a year. You need to submit evidence of your insurability only if your widowed spouse's and surviving children's total benefit exceeds $1,000 a month.

RETIREMENT PLAN:

The company provides a noncontributory deferred compensation plan (pension) which is designed to provide income for all covered employees beyond the working years. To be eligible, an employee must have completed one year of service and must be 21 years of age. However, once in the plan, the employee will be credited for all service with the company.

Compensation base is the average of the highest consecutive five years' income during the last ten years of service. Benefits are computed as 1¾ percent of compensation base multiplied by the number of years of service (maximum forty) less 1¼ percent of the employee's primary Social Security benefit multiplied by the number of years of service (maximum forty).

Benefits are fully vested after five years of service, which means that after five years in the plan, the benefits accrued to the employee's account are irrevocably assigned to the employee even if he/she leaves the company, and may be claimed by him/her at retirement age. Normal retirement age is 65, although earlier retirement is possible in certain circumstances. For more detailed information concerning the plan, see the Retirement Plan booklet.

If you should have any questions regarding any of the insurance coverages, please contact Human Resources.

PERSONNEL POLICIES AND PROCEDURES

DISTRIBUTION:		SUBJECT: INSURANCE PROGRAMS	
EFFECTIVE DATE:	PAGE 1 OF 2	FILE UNDER SECTION	
REVISION DATE:	APPROVED BY:		

PURPOSE:

To provide associates with a comprehensive insurance program.

POLICY:

The company provides the following insurance programs:
- Group Medical
- Group Dental
- Group Life with Accidental Death and Dismemberment
- Optional Insurances

Associates become eligible to participate in these insurance programs on the ninety-first (91st) day of continuous employment.

A. Group Medical Insurance

All associates and eligible dependents are provided the opportunity to participate in the group medical plan. The company pays a significant portion of the group insurance premium, with the remaining portion being deducted from associate paychecks.

Subject to a $200 individual and $600 family deductible per year, the plan will pay a percentage of reasonable and customary charges for medical services.

The company has chosen to affiliate with the Center Care Preferred Provider Organization (PPO), which offers the following features:

An extensive network of physicians and hospitals including most of those in our geographical area

- Discounted fees from network physicians and hospitals
- Lower co-pay for in-network services
- Free annual health fairs

The Summary Plan Description of the group medical plan details services and percentage of expenses covered.

Options for continued health insurance coverage under the COBRA Act are available for up to eighteen (18) months in the event of an associate's resignation, reduction of hours, layoff, or termination (except where termination results from gross misconduct), and for up to thirty-six (36) months for an associate's spouse and/or dependent children in the event of the associate's death, divorce, or separation, coverage under Medicare, or a covered child who ceases to be a dependent as defined in the plan.

B. Group Dental Insurance

All associates and eligible dependents are provided the opportunity to participate in the group dental plan. The company pays the entire group dental premium.

The group dental plan pays eighty (80) percent of reasonable and customary charges for covered diagnostic and preventive services and fifty (50) percent of reasonable and customary charges for other covered major dental services.

The maximum annual benefit payable under the group dental plan is $1,000 per person.

The Summary Plan Description of the group dental plan details services and percentage of expenses covered.

Options for continued dental insurance coverage under the COBRA Act are available for up to eighteen (18) months

PERSONNEL POLICIES AND PROCEDURES

DISTRIBUTION:		SUBJECT: INSURANCE PROGRAMS	
EFFECTIVE DATE:	PAGE 2 OF 2	FILE UNDER SECTION	
REVISION DATE:	APPROVED BY:		

in the event of an associate's resignation, reduction of hours, layoff, or termination (except where termination results from gross misconduct), and for up to thirty-six (36) months for an associate's spouse and/or dependent children in the event of the associate's death, divorce, or separation, coverage under Medicare, or a covered child who ceases to be a dependent as defined in the plan.

C. Group Life Insurance with Accidental Death and Dismemberment

All regular, full-time associates are eligible to participate in the group life insurance plan. The company pays the entire group life insurance premium.

All eligible associates are covered by a life insurance benefit equal to twice their annual base salary. Additional coverage for the same amount is provided in the event of accidental death or dismemberment.

The Summary Plan Description of the group life insurance plan details coverage.

In the event of termination, an associate's life insurance benefit will terminate on the same day as his or her employment terminates.

D. Prescription Drug Program

The company has made available to all associates and eligible dependents a Prescription Drug Program through Caremark, Inc., which consists of the following elements:

1. Prescription Drug Card

Covered associates and dependents are issued drug cards to be used at network pharmacies to obtain short-term prescriptions [up to a thirty- (30-) day supply].

Associates and dependents pay only ten (10) percent of discounted network price for generic or twenty (20) percent of the discounted network price for brand-name medication per prescription.

2. Mail Order Program

Prescriptions for medications that are taken on a long-term basis may be filled through the mail service for up to a ninety- (90-) day supply. The associate or dependent pays only eight (8) dollars for generic or fifteen (15) dollars for brand-name medication per prescription.

E. Optional Insurances

All associates are provided the opportunity to select any of the following optional insurance plans:

Supplemental Life Insurance

Cancer Insurance

Intensive Care Insurance

Short-Term Disability Insurance (hourly associates only)

Associates who select either the supplemental life insurance, cancer insurance, or intensive care insurance may cover themselves as well as any eligible dependents and will be required to pay one hundred (100) percent of applicable premiums. A representative of the appropriate insurance carrier will explain covered services, premiums, and percentage of expenses covered.

Hourly associates who select the short-term disability insurance may cover only themselves and will be required to pay fifty (50) percent of the premium, with the company paying the remaining fifty (50) percent. This plan provides up to twenty-six (26) weeks of disability insurance. The Summary Plan Description of the short-term disability insurance details the administration of this benefit.

PERSONNEL POLICIES AND PROCEDURES

DISTRIBUTION:		SUBJECT: SALARY CONTINUANCE PLAN— EXEMPT
EFFECTIVE DATE:	PAGE 1 OF 1	FILE UNDER SECTION
REVISION DATE:	APPROVED BY:	

GENERAL:

Eligible exempt salaried employees are protected by a salary continuance program when they are absent due to sickness or accident. This is a self-insured program provided by the company.

SCOPE:

This is the policy for all regular, full-time exempt salaried employees.

ELIGIBILITY:

This Plan applies to all regular, full-time exempt salaried employees on the active payroll. The coverage becomes effective the first day of work in the next month following the date of employment.

SCHEDULE OF BENEFITS:

A. The company will continue to pay the percentage of basic salary shown below for an exempt salaried employee who is absent from work as a result of sickness or accident.

    1. Less than one year of company service—75 percent of basic monthly salary.

    2. One year and over—100 percent of basic monthly salary.

    The above benefits will be paid for a maximum period of twenty-six weeks.

B. If an exempt salaried employee is disabled from work after he/she has received twenty-six weeks of absence pay, he/she may be eligible for long-term disability benefits.

PERSONNEL POLICIES AND PROCEDURES

DISTRIBUTION:		SUBJECT: INSURED WEEKLY INCOME PLAN— NONEXEMPT SALARIED EMPLOYEES
EFFECTIVE DATE:	PAGE 1 OF 2	FILE UNDER SECTION
REVISION DATE:	APPROVED BY:	

GENERAL:

All nonexempt salaried employees who are eligible are provided with an Insured Weekly Income Plan for protection of earnings during an extended absence due to accident (nonoccupational) or illness. The cost of this protection is paid for entirely by the company.

SCOPE:

This is the policy for all regular, full-time nonexempt salaried exempt employees.

ELIGIBILITY:

The Insured Weekly Income Plan applies to all regular, full-time nonexempt salaried employees on the active payroll. The coverage becomes effective after the first day of work in the next month following the date of employment.

SCHEDULE OF BENEFITS:

After the Twelve-Day Sick Pay Plan has been exhausted, or if the employee is not eligible for the Twelve-Day Sick Pay Plan, the Insured Weekly Income Plan will go into effect per the insurance contract.

For eligible nonexempt salaried employees, the weekly payment is 70 percent of the basic salary up to a maximum of $70 per week, including a make-up difference between the Workers' Compensation benefit and the nonoccupational benefit.

The Insured Weekly Income Plan is a "1-8-26" Plan with benefits beginning on the date following the last day of benefits paid under the Twelve-Day Sick Pay Plan or the date specified below, whichever is the latter, with the following provisions.

A. Benefits begin the first day if the absence is the result of an accident, either occupational or nonoccupational. Occupational in this definition means, "(Name of Company) Occupational." If an employee is injured while working for another employer (including being engaged in business for profit for his/her own account), this benefit is not payable.

B. Benefits begin the eighth day of sickness unless hospitalized prior to the eighth day. In this event, benefits become payable from the first day of hospitalization.

C. Benefits become payable, if the employee is otherwise eligible, after the benefits from the Twelve-Day Sick Pay Plan have been exhausted and will continue up to a maximum of twenty-six (26) weeks per period of absence.

D. In the event benefits are being paid for an absence resulting from a nonoccupational accident, the benefits are coordinated with the Twelve-Day Sick Pay Plan.

DISTRIBUTION:		SUBJECT: INSURED WEEKLY INCOME PLAN— NONEXEMPT SALARIED EMPLOYEES
EFFECTIVE DATE:	PAGE 2 OF 2	FILE UNDER SECTION
REVISION DATE:	APPROVED BY:	

In administering such claims, the company will report these claims for payment after allowing for these twelve (12) days of paid sick leave.

For Example: An employee who is injured or hospitalized the first day of illness and has not used any of his/her twelve (12) days of sick leave would not collect the Insured Weekly Income Plan benefits until his/her absence had gone beyond the twelve (12) days of paid sick leave time. The Insured Weekly Income Plan would then begin paying after the twelfth scheduled working day and continue up to a maximum of twenty-six (26) weeks.

E. If a nonexempt salaried employee is unable to return to work after exhausting his/her Insured Weekly Income Plan benefits, he/she may be eligible for long-term disability benefits.

PERSONNEL POLICIES AND PROCEDURES

DISTRIBUTION:		SUBJECT: CONTINUATION OF BENEFITS DURING EXCUSED ABSENCE
EFFECTIVE DATE:	PAGE 1 OF 3	FILE UNDER SECTION
REVISION DATE:	APPROVED BY:	

APPLICABLE:

Employee benefits coverage continues during the period in which a nonbargaining employee is on leave of absence with pay. Payments for which the employee is responsible as a participant in a contributory plan will be deducted from income continuation payments made during a leave of absence.

During a leave of absence without pay, employee benefits will be continued or interrupted in accordance with the following:

GROUP INSURANCE BENEFITS:

1. Disability Leave

    A. During approved short-term disability leave with pay:

    (1) Group medical benefits, dental plan benefits, and use of the flexible spending account for enrolled employees and their eligible dependents remain in effect.

    (2) Company-paid life insurance remains in effect at no cost; optional life, dependent life, and AD & D may be continued providing contributions are maintained.

    (3) Employee contributions through payroll deductions remain in effect for all contributory benefits, except for any that the employee elects to cancel.

    B. During disability leave without pay:

    (1) Group medical, dental, and vision care coverage and benefits for enrolled employees and their eligible dependents continue on the same basis as before the leave. The employee may qualify for disability benefits from the company's long-term disability plan or Social Security disability benefits, regardless of age or length of service. Dependent coverage contributions are required.

    Use of the flexible spending account designated for health or dependent care expenses continues through the end of the current calendar year.

    Cash or 401(k) designations are distributed at the end of the current calendar year or the date of medical layoff, whichever date occurs first. Contributions to these plans during an unpaid period of leave cannot be made because contributions on other than a salary deferral basis are prohibited, but contributions will be resumed immediately upon return to work.

    (2) Company-paid life insurance continues at no cost to the employee, subject to approval by the insurance company. If the insurance company does not approve the continuation, life insurance continues for thirty-one (31) days following the date of medical layoff. Optional life may be continued with required contributions providing the company-paid life insurance is approved by the insurance company. Dependent life and AD & D coverages are discontinued.

    C. During anticipatory disability leave:

    (1) Group medical, dental, and vision care insurance, company-paid life insurance, optional life insurance, dependent life insurance, and AD & D in effect will be continued if the employee makes the appropriate contributions.

DISTRIBUTION:		SUBJECT: CONTINUATION OF BENEFITS DURING EXCUSED ABSENCE	
EFFECTIVE DATE:	PAGE 2 OF 3	FILE UNDER SECTION	
REVISION DATE:	APPROVED BY:		

2. Uniformed Service Leave—Participation in medical, dental, and disability benefit plans is discontinued on the last day worked prior to a uniformed service leave of absence without pay of longer than thirty (30) days. Life insurance remains in effect for thirty-one (31) days from commencement of such leave.

3. Approved Personal Leave without Pay—Participation in medical, dental, and company-paid life insurance plans is continued for a maximum of three months. Employees who are members of contributory plans may continue coverage in those plans for a period not to exceed three months provided they make the appropriate contributions for such period prior to the start of the leave.

   Life insurance coverage ceases thirty-one (31) days after the end of the period for which a contribution has been made.

   Participation in short-term disability and long-term disability benefit plans is discontinued on the last day worked prior to the personal leave of absence without pay, except for statutory requirements.

LENGTH OF SERVICE:

1. Accrual is continued through the duration of any approved leave of absence. The maximum limit of such accrual is one year, with the exception of personal leave for Peace Corps duty, which is two years, and uniformed service leave, which is five years.

2. Length of service—For employees on uniformed service, leave is continued in excess of five years only when service is prolonged involuntarily by reasons of national emergency. A voluntary extension of military service by an employee automatically severs length of service accrual as well as entitlement to reinstatement if such an extension causes the uniformed leave to exceed five years.

EMERGENCY ABSENCE AND VACATION:

Benefits accrue to employees on paid uniformed service leave, approved family or medical leave of absence with pay, and jury duty. Time granted for other types of leave is not considered as time worked when computing these benefit entitlements. Upon an employee's return from a leave of absence, the employee's emergency absence balance is reinstated if the employee's anniversary date did not occur during the leave period. The full ten (10) days is reinstated if the employee's anniversary date did occur within the leave period.

HOLIDAYS:

Holiday pay is received by employees when a paid holiday falls during a paid leave of absence. Employees on leave of absence without pay do not receive holiday pay.

DISTRIBUTION:		SUBJECT: CONTINUATION OF BENEFITS DURING EXCUSED ABSENCE	
EFFECTIVE DATE:	PAGE 3 OF 3		FILE UNDER SECTION
REVISION DATE:	APPROVED BY:		

RETIREMENT PROGRAM:

The first twelve (12) months of any authorized leave of absence, as determined by the company, is counted as service for all purposes of the program. If an employee leaves the service of the company to enter the uniformed services of the United States, the period of the absence is counted as service, provided the employee returns to the service of the company within the period as provided by law for the protection of re-employment rights after discharge or release from active duty in the uniformed services of the United States.

PERSONNEL POLICIES AND PROCEDURES

DISTRIBUTION:		SUBJECT: DISABILITY BENEFITS	
EFFECTIVE DATE:	PAGE 1 OF 1	FILE UNDER SECTION	
REVISION DATE:	APPROVED BY:		

The company provides for continuation of salary to employees who are disabled through sickness or injury. The amount of salary and duration of payments shall be no less than the minimum required under state law.

PERSONNEL POLICIES AND PROCEDURES

DISTRIBUTION:		SUBJECT: DISABILITY INSURANCE	
EFFECTIVE DATE:	PAGE 1 OF 1	FILE UNDER SECTION	
REVISION DATE:	APPROVED BY:		

POLICY STATEMENT:

The salaries of personnel will be continued in whole or in part during absences resulting from disabling personal illness or injury.

Salary continuation is intended to preserve the normal employment relationship during brief periods of disability based on the assumption that the employee will return to work when the disability ceases.

The duration of coverage is determined by the employee's length of service, at the time he/she becomes disabled, as follows:

Years of Service	Plan I Full Pay (Weeks)	Plan II Half Pay (Weeks)
0	6	20
1	7	19
2	8	18
3	9	17
4	10	16
5	11	15
6	12	14
7	13	13
8	14	12
9	15	11
10	16	10
11	18	8
12	20	6
13	22	4
14	24	2
15+	26	—

PERSONNEL POLICIES AND PROCEDURES

DISTRIBUTION:		SUBJECT: TRAVEL ACCIDENT INSURANCE	
EFFECTIVE DATE:	PAGE 1 OF 1	FILE UNDER SECTION	
REVISION DATE:	APPROVED BY:		

POLICY STATEMENT:

You are protected, whenever you are required to travel on company business, by a Group Travel Accident Insurance Plan. This plan, underwritten by (name of insurance company), provides coverage against loss of life or loss resulting from bodily injury sustained solely through accidental means. This insurance is provided at no cost to you.

PERSONNEL POLICIES AND PROCEDURES

DISTRIBUTION:		SUBJECT: TRAVEL ACCIDENT INSURANCE	
EFFECTIVE DATE:	PAGE 1 OF 1	FILE UNDER SECTION	
REVISION DATE:	APPROVED BY:		

POLICY STATEMENT:

Employees who leave the company premises for business purposes are exposed to greater risks and hazards, and are therefore protected by Travel Accident Insurance, as a supplement to Workers' Compensation Insurance. Death or dismemberment claims arising out of an accident involving an employee engaged in company business will be honored as follows:

Classification	Death Claim	Dismemberment Claim
Officer	$ 50,000–150,000	$7,500 maximum
Nonofficer	$ 25,000	$1,250 maximum

PERSONNEL POLICIES AND PROCEDURES

DISTRIBUTION:		SUBJECT: 401(k) PROFIT- SHARING/RETIREMENT PLAN	
EFFECTIVE DATE:	PAGE 1 OF 1	FILE UNDER SECTION	
REVISION DATE:	APPROVED BY:		

PURPOSE:

The purpose of this plan is to provide associates with a means of saving money on a pretax basis and building financial resources for retirement.

POLICY:

All associates who have completed a minimum of six (6) months of employment are eligible to participate in the plan as outlined in the Summary Plan Description.

There are two parts to the 401(k) Profit-Sharing/Retirement Plan:

- Associate Contributions
- Profit Sharing

A. Associate Contributions

Eligible associates may choose to have the company withhold a fixed percentage, not to exceed ten (10) percent, of their gross annual earnings through payroll deductions and contribute that amount to the 401(k) plan as a pretax savings contribution.

The company will match an amount equal to fifty (50) percent of the associate's contribution up to a maximum of four (4) percent of the associate's annual gross income.

Associates may invest their savings in any of several different investment options. An election of contribution percentage and fund allocation will be made by associates prior to their eligibility date.

There is a toll-free phone number through which associates may obtain account information and elect changes in fund allocation between funds set up on the daily valuation system. Contribution percentage may be changed only during the months of June and December.

B. Profit-Sharing Plan

The company may elect to contribute a discretionary percentage to each associate's account.

Associates may invest their profit sharing in any of several different investment options. Changes in fund allocation may be made through use of the toll-free phone number.

PERSONNEL POLICIES AND PROCEDURES

DISTRIBUTION:		SUBJECT: RETIREMENT SAVINGS PLAN [401(k)]	
EFFECTIVE DATE:	PAGE 1 OF 1		FILE UNDER SECTION
REVISION DATE:	APPROVED BY:		

POLICY STATEMENT:

(Company Name) and Subsidiaries Retirement Savings Plan is a Defined-Contribution Pension and Profit-Sharing Plan established under section 401(k) of the Internal Revenue Code. This type of plan results in the lowering of federal and state income taxes to the employees who elect to participate. When employees elect to defer a portion of their gross wage, their W-2 (tax statement) at the end of the year shows the gross wage net of what the employees have elected to defer, thus lowering the income subject to income tax.

PROCEDURE:

Supervisors and managers should be familiar with the Retirement Savings plan [401(k)] and should encourage employees' participation in the plan. Specific questions may be referred to the Coordinator of Human Resources for clarification.

Presently, all employees who are 21 years of age and are scheduled to work a minimum of 1,000 hours per year are eligible to enroll upon completion of one full year of continuous service. They may elect to have deducted from their gross pay any percentage from 2-½ percent to 12-½ percent. The Company matches the first 2-½ percent of the employee's gross pay. To encourage participation and as federal law allows, the employee contribution will be deducted from the employee's paycheck before taxes, thereby reducing the amount of income subject to federal income taxes. This will provide an additional benefit to the employee due to tax savings.

The funds that the employees and employer contribute are forwarded monthly to (name of insurance company) and are administered by (name of administrator). Employee contributions are invested in guaranteed accounts earning competitive rates of interest. Employer contributions are invested in a high-quality equity portfolio. After an employee has participated in the fund for three years and if the employee is less than 50 years of age, the Company purchases a $10,000 whole life insurance policy. Funds remaining after payment of the premium are still invested in the equity accounts.

If an employee terminates employment before becoming fully vested, the employee will be entitled to a cash payment equal to the value of his/her contribution and interest, plus a share of the value of the employer's account determined as follows:

VESTING:

Years of Service	Percent of Employer's Contribution Entitled To
0–2 Years	0
3 Years	20
4 Years	40
5 Years	60
6 Years	80
7 Years	100

The employee is always 100 percent vested in the value of his/her contributions plus interest. Employees who have reached the age of 55 may, at their own option, choose early retirement and are considered fully vested.

Employees who have reached the age of 62 may, at their option, retire and be entitled to Social Security benefits in addition to the Company pension program.

271

PERSONNEL POLICIES AND PROCEDURES

DISTRIBUTION:		SUBJECT: RETIREMENT	
EFFECTIVE DATE:	PAGE 1 OF 1	FILE UNDER SECTION	
REVISION DATE:	APPROVED BY:		

POLICY STATEMENT:

In accordance with common industrial practice and in the belief that individuals earn and merit retirement status after completing a normal work-life cycle, it is the intent of the company to provide a retirement plan for employees.

PERSONNEL POLICIES AND PROCEDURES

DISTRIBUTION:		SUBJECT: RETIREMENT	
EFFECTIVE DATE:	PAGE 1 OF 1	FILE UNDER SECTION	
REVISION DATE:	APPROVED BY:		

POLICY STATEMENT:

Subject: Retirement Observances

It is the company's wish that the retirement of an employee be made an occasion for special recognition of the employee. It is the further wish that the company take the leadership in the planning for any retirement observance that takes place. To implement this, the following policy is being established:

A. The company will plan a retirement observance for each retiring employee.

B. The observance will be normally in the form of a dinner or similar gathering for the retiree, his or her spouse, and fellow employees.

C. The company will cover the costs of the dinner for the honored retiree, his or her spouse, and the fellow employees. The employees may bring guests (their wives, etc.), but they will then personally pay for such additional dinners.

D. The company's participation in any gift for the retiring employee will be nominal, with the gift, if there is to be one, coming primarily from the fellow employees.

E. Each Department, District, or Plant will be expected to plan and execute its own observances. However, the Human Resources Department is available for consultation and should be advised when such observances are scheduled.

F. Special invitations should be issued by the Department, District, or Plant to any of those outside the group whom it is the wish to have attend.

PERSONNEL POLICIES AND PROCEDURES

DISTRIBUTION:		SUBJECT: DEATH OF ACTIVE OR RETIRED EMPLOYEE
EFFECTIVE DATE:	PAGE 1 OF 4	FILE UNDER SECTION
REVISION DATE:	APPROVED BY:	

POLICY STATEMENT:

Realizing that the death of an employee brings certain hardships to the employee's family, the company has provided this policy to accomplish as quickly as possible those actions it believes are necessary at the time of death.

It is the policy of our company to provide assistance in meeting the difficulties encountered when death occurs to an employee.

NOTIFICATION:

When an employee dies, it is the responsibility of the location Human Resources Manager to obtain as much of the following information as possible and relay it immediately to the industrial relations division:

A. Name of deceased employee.

B. Date of death.

C. Cause of death.

D. Last day worked.

E. Name and address of widow or next of kin.

The location Human Resources Manager should immediately prepare and send:

A. A preliminary personnel change authorization form P-51 to the payroll department. A final notice may be prepared if all necessary information is available.

B. A notification of death form to the President's office.

SETTLEMENT OF ACCOUNTS:

The following payments are to be made to the next of kin where allowed by law:

A. Wage, salary, or pension through the date of death.

B. Vacation earned but not taken through the date of death.

C. Any other amounts due the deceased employee.

DISTRIBUTION:		SUBJECT: DEATH OF ACTIVE OR RETIRED EMPLOYEE	
EFFECTIVE DATE:	PAGE 2 OF 4		FILE UNDER SECTION
REVISION DATE:	APPROVED BY:		

When there is an administration of the employee's estate, a short form of the court order certifying the appointment and qualification of the executor or administrator of the estate must be obtained in duplicate.

In such cases, the payments listed above are to be made to the executor or administrator as required by law.

Items of indebtedness to the company are to be deducted from any monies due to the employee. If the amount of indebtedness exceeds the money due, an arrangement for repayment of the balance should be made by the location Human Resources Manager.

All payments are to be made by the payroll department handling the wages of the deceased upon receipt of the final personnel change authorization form P-51, and are to be sent, together with a withholding tax statement form W-2, to the location Human Resources Manager for delivery to the payee.

If the deceased employee has full-time use of a company automobile, it is to be offered to the surviving spouse at the wholesale price listed in the Official Used Car Guide issued by the National Automobile Dealers Association for the month in which the sale is made. The wholesale price determination is to be made by the corporate purchasing department.

GIFT:

A gift equivalent to four weeks' pay or pension is to be made to the surviving spouse by the headquarters payroll department upon receipt of a check request from the location Human Resources Manager. If the employee was employed at an hourly rate, the gift shall equal 160 hours' straight-time pay.

If the deceased is not survived by a spouse but is survived by other dependents who are resident in their household, payment will be made to one of the following in the order named:

A. Oldest child

B. Father

C. Mother

D. Brother

E. Sister

If the recipient is a minor, payment will be made to the legal guardian. Reasonable proof of the survivor's dependency and residency status will be required. The gift check is to be sent to the location Human Resources Manager for delivery.

GROUP INSURANCE:

Accident-Sickness Insurance: Unfiled claims are to be processed by the location Human Resources department.

PERSONNEL POLICIES AND PROCEDURES

DISTRIBUTION:		SUBJECT: DEATH OF ACTIVE OR RETIRED EMPLOYEE	
EFFECTIVE DATE:	PAGE 3 OF 4	FILE UNDER SECTION	
REVISION DATE:	APPROVED BY:		

HOSPITAL-SURGICAL-MEDICAL INSURANCE:

A. Outstanding claims are to be processed by the location Human Resources department immediately.

B. Dependent hospital-surgical-medical insurance, if in force, will be continued for thirteen weeks after the employee's death. COBRA notification is to be provided the surviving spouse and/or dependents within fourteen days.

LIFE INSURANCE:

The location Human Resources Manager should send to the industrial relations division:

A. The employee's group insurance certificates.

B. The mode of settlement selected by beneficiary.

C. Two copies of the completed proof of death form for basic group life insurance carried by (name of insurance carrier).

D. An official certificate of death for each additional life insurance policy involved, such as supplemental or travel accident. Special claim forms will be supplied by the industrial relations division.

WORKER'S COMPENSATION:

If death occurred at work or was related to an occupational accident, the Worker's Compensation carrier is to be notified immediately and the necessary form filed thereafter.

CONDOLENCE:

The established practice of sending a letter of condolence from the President's office is to be continued. A floral remembrance is to be sent by the location in which the deceased was employed. The amount of expenditure should not exceed $40. If another form of remembrance is suggested instead of flowers, an amount equal to the cost of a floral remembrance is to be donated by the location.

SOCIAL SECURITY:

The location Human Resources Manager should advise the survivor to notify the nearest Social Security office of the employee's death and to file a claim for benefits.

PERSONNEL POLICIES AND PROCEDURES

DISTRIBUTION:		SUBJECT: DEATH OF ACTIVE OR RETIRED EMPLOYEE	
EFFECTIVE DATE:	PAGE 4 OF 4	FILE UNDER SECTION	
REVISION DATE:	APPROVED BY:		

LETTER OF SETTLEMENT:

A letter to the next of kin is to be written and delivered by the location Human Resources Manager or district sales manager. It should include explanations of the following items:

- Unpaid wages and other amounts due deceased employee
- Withholding tax statement
- Status of debts to company
- Company's gift
- Settlement of group insurance claims
- Continued hospitalization coverage
- COBRA notification letter
- Social Security procedure to be followed by next of kin

PERSONNEL POLICIES AND PROCEDURES

DISTRIBUTION:		SUBJECT: UNEMPLOYMENT INSURANCE	
EFFECTIVE DATE:	PAGE 1 OF 1	FILE UNDER SECTION	
REVISION DATE:	APPROVED BY:		

POLICY STATEMENT:

(Company Name) pays the entire cost of unemployment insurance. Its purpose is to provide temporary income for workers and their families when they have been laid off from their job through no fault of their own. If an employee becomes unemployed for this reason, he/she may be eligible for unemployment compensation for a limited period of time.

If an employee becomes unemployed due to his/her own resignation, dismissal, or any other nonqualifying reason, the company will take the position with the state authorities governing the unemployment insurance that the employee is not entitled to unemployment compensation, and the company will object to any claims and will appeal any claims.

PROCEDURE:

Whenever an employee terminates, whether voluntarily or involuntarily, the manager must complete a Separation of Employment form that provides the reason for termination, along with any appropriate documentation such as counseling records, etc. This information will be maintained in the terminated employee's file and will be used by the Coordinator of Human Resources for defense in unemployment claims should an employee file for unemployment inappropriately.

Managers may be required to appear at unemployment hearings from time to time. Any such efforst should be coordinated through the Coordinator of Human Resources.

PERSONNEL POLICIES AND PROCEDURES

DISTRIBUTION:		SUBJECT: WORKERS' COMPENSATION	
EFFECTIVE DATE:	PAGE 1 OF 1	FILE UNDER SECTION	
REVISION DATE:	APPROVED BY:		

POLICY STATEMENT:

Employees are provided Workers' Compensation coverage from the day they begin work. The company pays the entire cost of this coverage. Employees are covered by Workers' Compensation if they are incapacitated by injury or illness arising out of their employment.

Employees begin collecting Workers' Compensation after they are off work three (3) working days. Other benefits may include medical expenses, compensation for total or partial permanent disability, and death benefits.

PROCEDURE:

Employees must report all accidents to their supervisor, regardless of how minor. If a work-related injury requires medical attention by a physician or any other medical facility that produces a bill, a claim must be made out that same day by the employee's supervisor. If the injury causes the person to be away from work beyond three days, this injury must be reported to the state Workers' Compensation Division. The store manager and/or the employee's supervisor is responsible for submitting a copy of the original claim to the state office. Additionally, a copy of this claim must be forwarded to the Coordinator of Human Resources, who will forward it to the insurance company.

Employees are not authorized to go to a physician without first advising their supervisor or manager. Employees will not be eligible for regular compensation or vacation or holiday pay in addition to any Workers' Compensation received.

Workers' Compensation absences that also qualify as Family and Medical Leaves will be charged concurrently against the employee's annual twelve-week FMLA entitlement. In those circumstances, all FMLA rights and protections apply, but Workers' Compensation procedures apply.

PERSONNEL POLICIES AND PROCEDURES

DISTRIBUTION:		SUBJECT: SOCIAL SECURITY BENEFITS AND PAYMENTS	
EFFECTIVE DATE:	PAGE 1 OF 1	FILE UNDER SECTION	
REVISION DATE:	APPROVED BY:		

POLICY STATEMENT:

Federal Social Security provides a variety of benefits, including retirement income, death benefits, disability benefits, and monthly income payments for certain dependent survivors of covered employees.

PROCEDURE:

A percentage of an employee's gross earnings is deducted as his/her contribution for Social Security protection, and the company contributes an amount established by law. Normally, an employee will be eligible to receive a monthly income from Social Security when he/she retires or in the event of a total or permanent disability.

Employees should contact the Payroll Department at the home office should they have questions regarding Social Security payments or benefits.

PERSONNEL POLICIES AND PROCEDURES

DISTRIBUTION:		SUBJECT: MOVING EXPENSES	
EFFECTIVE DATE:	PAGE 1 OF 1		FILE UNDER SECTION
REVISION DATE:	APPROVED BY:		

POLICY STATEMENT:

Employees who are transferred from one location in the company to another, either at the request of the company or as the result of bidding on a posted position, will have expenses incurred in the moving of household furnishings paid by the company, subject to the following conditions:

A. The company must be notified as far ahead as possible as to the preferred date or dates for the move.

B. Arrangements for the move must be made by the company or by authorization of the company.

    (1) Where possible, at least two reputable bonded transfer companies are to be contacted for a complete quotation. (Name of Company) Form No. 000, "Bid on Moving Company Employees," is to be completed in every case. These forms are available through the Human Resources Department.

    (2) Completed Form No. 000 should be passed along to the Human Resources Department, together with any recommendations that might appear in order.

    (3) The Human Resources Department will consult with the Purchasing Department and determine who should do the moving. The Human Resources Department will then initiate the necessary requisition and authorization for the move.

C. The employees to be moved must assume the responsibility for any expenses incurred on the following.

    (1) Packing expenses over and above those regarded as normal or necessary if the transfer company is to assume responsibility for goods. The employee is expected to contribute his/her share to the expense of a move by having all household goods possible packed in necessary cartons, etc., and in readiness for the move. (Reasonable wardrobe service will be paid for by the company.)

    (2) Any transit insurance requested over and above the normal protection afforded by the bonded transfer company.

PERSONNEL POLICIES AND PROCEDURES

DISTRIBUTION:		SUBJECT: MATCHING GIFTS TO COLLEGES	
EFFECTIVE DATE:	PAGE 1 OF 1	FILE UNDER SECTION	
REVISION DATE:	APPROVED BY:		

POLICY STATEMENT:

The company aids outstanding institutions of higher education through the United States Trust Company Foundation. It also encourages all members of the staff to support colleges and universities that they have attended, through a Matching Gifts Program.

Any member of the staff who makes a contribution may apply for a matching gift under the following terms:

A. What colleges are eligible?

   Any college or university granting a two- or four-year degree, including junior and community colleges, private or tax-supported, situated in the United States or its possessions.

B. Who is eligible?

   Anyone who has attended the institution to which he/she is making the contribution for at least one semester and has served the Trust Company for at least three months on a permanent, full-time basis.

C. What gifts qualify?

   Personal gifts, either in cash or securities having a quoted market value, which qualify for exemption under the federal income tax laws. Gifts may be for restricted or unrestricted purposes, for alumni or capital campaigns and for endowments or scholarships, and may be made to more than one college or university.

   The maximum contribution by the Trust Company Foundation in matching an individual's gift (or gifts) may not in any one calendar year exceed $500. The minimum matching contribution will be $5. Gifts of securities should be reported at the fair market value on the effective date of the donation. The foundation's matching gifts will always be for unrestricted purposes.

PERSONNEL POLICIES AND PROCEDURES

DISTRIBUTION:		SUBJECT: COMPANY-SPONSORED MEMBERSHIPS	
EFFECTIVE DATE:	PAGE 1 OF 1	FILE UNDER SECTION	
REVISION DATE:	APPROVED BY:		

POLICY STATEMENT:

The company recognizes that employee memberships in business, technical, professional, and civic organization can be of benefit to the company, and it will support such memberships consistent with sound and prudent fiscal policies as may be determined from time to time.

The responsibility for the judicious use of company funds in sponsoring employee memberships shall be assigned to each department manager, subject to initial approval and periodic review by the Division Manager.

The following criteria shall be used in evaluating such memberships:

* Who will benefit by such membership?

* Will the individual be more effective on his or her job as a result of such membership?

* Is there a direct relationship between the function of the organization and the job duties of the individual being considered for membership?

* Will there be a desirable community impact as a result of such membership?

* If a membership renewal is under consideration, has the individual demonstrated personal interest by reasonable participation during the past year?

* Is the expenditure in keeping with the current fiscal policy?

* Except in unusual circumstances, company-sponsored memberships will be available only to exempt salaried individuals.

* Expenses connected with maintaining company-sponsored memberships.

PERSONNEL POLICIES AND PROCEDURES

DISTRIBUTION:		SUBJECT: PHYSICAL EXAMINATION	
EFFECTIVE DATE:	PAGE 1 OF 1	FILE UNDER SECTION	
REVISION DATE:	APPROVED BY:		

POLICY STATEMENT:

In an effort to assure continuity of management, and believing that more efficient management will result from employees in good health, the company has instituted this physical examination program to assist its management personnel in maintaining their physical well-being.

The company recommends and will pay all expenses in connection with a periodic comprehensive physical examination for certain of its management personnel. Participation in this program is on a voluntary basis, but all eligible employees are encouraged to participate.

PERSONNEL POLICIES AND PROCEDURES

DISTRIBUTION:		SUBJECT: PERIODIC PHYSICAL EXAMINATIONS—EXEMPT EMPLOYEES	
EFFECTIVE DATE:	PAGE 1 OF 1		FILE UNDER SECTION
REVISION DATE:	APPROVED BY:		

GENERAL:

In the interest of employees' health and continued ability to serve, the company offers all exempt employees a yearly physical examination at company expense. Participation is strictly voluntary.

It is the responsibility of the Employee Relations Department to assist in arranging for these examinations.

DEFINITIONS:

Exempt employees so classified for Payroll purposes shall fall into this category.

RESULTS OF EXAMINATION:

The results of the examination are communicated solely to the employee. The employee may discuss the results with the examining physician and seek advice regarding an appropriate course of action, as needed. The company receives no report from the examining physician other than that the examination was completed.

ADDITIONAL DIAGNOSTIC WORK:

If, in the process of examination, it is determined by the physician that additional diagnostic information is desirable or necessary, the company will pay the additional cost if the employee's company-paid health insurance program does not provide the necessary coverage for the added diagnostic work, and the employee requests payment.

WORK RESTRICTIONS:

If the examining physician determines that an employee needs work restrictions that would affect the employee's ability to perform his/her job, the employee may consider asking for a reasonable accommodation.

PERSONNEL POLICIES AND PROCEDURES

DISTRIBUTION:		SUBJECT: RECREATIONAL PROGRAMS	
EFFECTIVE DATE:	PAGE 1 OF 1	FILE UNDER SECTION	
REVISION DATE:	APPROVED BY:		

POLICY STATEMENT:

The company encourages a sports and activities program for employees to stimulate better working relationships among employees and to promote teamwork.

Participation in recreation activities will be limited to employees. If, however, the majority of employee participants in a recreation group approve, spouses of husbands or wives, or immediate families, may participate provided that the participation of the spouse or family is done with the understanding that the employee will be solely responsible for all expenses that they incur.

PERSONNEL POLICIES AND PROCEDURES

DISTRIBUTION:		SUBJECT: RECREATIONAL PROGRAMS
EFFECTIVE DATE:	PAGE 1 OF 1	FILE UNDER SECTION
REVISION DATE:	APPROVED BY:	

POLICY:

It is the policy of (Company Name) to encourage employees to participate in athletic and recreational programs.

PROCEDURE:

A. Intercompany competition in various athletic events will be sponsored by the company with the following guidelines:
   1. Participation on company teams will be voluntary.
   2. The company will provide proper uniforms and equipment necessary for the teams to participate.
   3. Practice and competition will be held during nonworking hours and will not be considered time worked.
   4. Expenses for travel, etc., will be considered by the company on a per event basis.
   5. The program will be under the direction of the Employee Relations Manager, who may issue other communications as necessary.

B. Interdepartmental competition in a variety of athletic events will be sponsored by the company with the following guidelines:
   1. Teams will be organized and directed by the employees in each department in which there is sufficient interest to compete in an organized program. Participation will be voluntary.
   2. The company will provide equipment necessary for participation.
   3. Any cost of using proper facilities for practice and competition will be paid by the company with approval of the Employee Relations Manager.
   4. Prizes for the winners of each program will be provided by the company.
   5. Practice and competition will be held during nonworking hours and will not be considered time worked.
   6. The Employee Relations Manager will be responsible for coordination of all athletic competition and for the costs involved.

C. Exercise programs may be organized by the Employee Relations Manager and employees invited to attend. These will be scheduled during meal periods and after regular working hours. Facilities both within and outside the company's premises may be utilized. All costs of instructors and facilities will be paid by the company.

D. The Employee Relations Manager, along with the Safety Manager, will arrange for adequate insurance coverage for the company in the event of injuries resulting from these athletic and recreational programs.

E. Any employee participating on company teams in intercompany competition may be required to furnish proof of his/her physical capabilities for participating as deemed necessary by the Employee Relations Manager.

F. Any employee with a disability who requires accommodation in order to participate in any company athletic or recreational program should make the need known to the Employee Relations Manager. All employee accommodation requests and related information will be treated as confidential by the company to the maximum feasible extent.

PERSONNEL POLICIES AND PROCEDURES

DISTRIBUTION:		SUBJECT: RECREATIONAL ACTIVITIES	
EFFECTIVE DATE:	PAGE 1 OF 1	FILE UNDER SECTION	
REVISION DATE:	APPROVED BY:		

PURPOSE:

The purpose of this policy is to define the company's position on sponsoring, approving, funding, and establishing guidelines for associates' participation in company-sponsored activities during nonwork hours.

It is the objective of the company to encourage participation and provide recreational activities for the greatest possible percentage of associates.

POLICY:

It is the policy of the company to approve of associates' participating in company-sponsored recreational activities during nonwork time provided the activity meets certain guidelines.

PROCEDURE:

A. Except in cases approved in advance by management, the activity should not interfere with work operations.

B. When activities are planned, the leader (captain, coach, etc.) must obtain the approval of the Human Resources representative and/or plant manager in advance.

C. Funding requests for approved recreational activities must be submitted in advance to the Human Resources Section for processing.

D. In case of associate activities approved by the company, associates will be notified in advance what portion of expenses, if any, will be paid by the company.

E. Following is a list of the types of recreational activities that the company will consider for sponsorship, funding, or partial funding.
   - Softball
   - Basketball
   - Volleyball
   - Golf
   - Hunting/Fishing
   - Bowling
   - Walking/Running Events
   - Plant Picnic
   - Exercise Room
   - Health-Related Activities

   Other activities will be considered if requested.

PERSONNEL POLICIES AND PROCEDURES

DISTRIBUTION:		SUBJECT: ATHLETIC AND RECREATIONAL PROGRAMS	
EFFECTIVE DATE:	PAGE 1 OF 2	FILE UNDER SECTION	
REVISION DATE:	APPROVED BY:		

POLICY:

The company wishes to encourage employees to promote their wellness through various athletic and recreational programs while minimizing the company's risk and exposure. The company feels that such events and activities promote morale and "team" spirit, which contribute to improved workplace productivity.

PROCEDURES:

1. All company-sponsored athletic and recreational activities will be coordinated, approved, and administered by the Director—Human Resources or his/her designee.

2. From time to time, the company may form an advisory committee consisting of employees from several various departments to assist the Human Resources Department in the coordination of events, determining employee interest in and support for various programs, advising on the extent of company support for various programs, and helping in the promotion of such events. The committee will be chaired by the Director—Human Resources or his/her designee. In no case shall the committee consist of more than ten (10) employees who are appointed by the Director—Human Resources or his/her designee. All attempts shall be made to properly represent the majority of the employees in the facility, including employees with disabilities. Where possible, meetings shall be held so as to minimize lost work time. Time spent in committee meetings is considered as work time, and employees will be so compensated.

3. The Director—Human Resources is charged with the responsibility of formulating and including in the Human Resources budget expenses for such athletic and recreational programs. Items eligible include, but are not limited to:

   - Uniforms
   - Awards
   - Facility rental
   - Equipment
   - Out-of-town transportation costs
   - Entry fees
   - Miscellaneous supplies
   - Reasonable accommodation

4. Participation in company-sponsored athletic and recreational activities by employees is strictly voluntary and is open to all employees and company retirees. Activities should typically take place outside of normal working time. In certain cases, where approved, participation may include employee families and guests.

5. Employees participating in athletic events may be required to provide certification from their attending physician as to their ability to participate safely in such events and/or information on any restrictions that they may have. Employees are required to notify the Human Resources Department of any known limitation or need for accommodation as soon as it becomes known. All attempts shall be made to make reasonable accommodations to enable employees with disabilities to fully participate in these activities. The Director—Human Resources, in conjunction with the

DISTRIBUTION:		SUBJECT: ATHLETIC AND RECREATIONAL PROGRAMS	
EFFECTIVE DATE:	PAGE 2 OF 2	FILE UNDER SECTION	
REVISION DATE:	APPROVED BY:		

company's Medical Department, has the final determination as to whether employees may or may not participate in these activities based upon available medical evidence at the time.

6. Employees participating in athletic events may be required to sign waiver of liability forms by the company and other outside sponsoring organizations. Participation in such events may be limited to those employees who sign the requested waivers.

7. In conjunction with the company's Medical Department, the Human Resources Department may offer company-sponsored wellness programs that encourage regular exercise, proper diet, and a healthy lifestyle. Such programs may be presented during working hours and may utilize outside organizations and personnel, as approved.

PERSONNEL POLICIES AND PROCEDURES

DISTRIBUTION:		SUBJECT: LENGTH OF SERVICE RECOGNITION	
EFFECTIVE DATE:	PAGE 1 OF 1	FILE UNDER SECTION	
REVISION DATE:	APPROVED BY:		

POLICY STATEMENT:

Company policy is to give official recognition to employee service on a quinquennial basis through the presentation of appropriate service emblems and special service anniversary ceremonies.

PERSONNEL POLICIES AND PROCEDURES

DISTRIBUTION:		SUBJECT: LENGTH OF SERVICE RECOGNITION	
EFFECTIVE DATE:	PAGE 1 OF 1	FILE UNDER SECTION	
REVISION DATE:	APPROVED BY:		

POLICY STATEMENT:

The company recognizes long and faithful service and the value of the skill, knowledge, and judgment gained through years of experience. Each employee is honored on specified milestones in his/her career.

Recognition Points

Year of Service	*Increased Vacation*	*Recognition*
5th	From 2 to 3 weeks	
20th	From 3 to 4 weeks	
25th	Extra week	Gold watch, scroll, roses, ceremony, membership in Twenty-five-Year Club
30th	Extra week	Congratulations by senior officers
35th	Extra week	$500
40th	Extra week	Congratulations by senior officers
45th	Extra week	$500
At retirement		Guest of honor at special luncheon, letter of appreciation from President

PERSONNEL POLICIES AND PROCEDURES

DISTRIBUTION:		SUBJECT: SERVICE RECOGNITION AWARDS	
EFFECTIVE DATE:	PAGE 1 OF 1	FILE UNDER SECTION	
REVISION DATE:	APPROVED BY:		

POLICY STATEMENT:

(Company Name) is appreciative of the loyalty and faithful service of its employees. Each regular employee will be honored on specified milestones in his/her career. Therefore, it is the policy of our company to recognize length of service by giving service awards to those employees who have demonstrated their loyalty to the company.

PROCEDURE:

A. Length of Service Awards—The company will present awards in the forms of certificates, plaques, and/or pins to employees who complete the following prescribed number of years of continuous service.

   3 Years
   5 Years
   10 Years
   15 Years
   20 Years
   25 Years

   Additionally, special events such as employee awards dinners, receptions, etc., will be held to honor employees who have completed the prescribed number of years of continuous service.

B. Employee-of-the-Month Awards—The Employee-of-the-Month Program is a program that selects one employee each month for recognition of outstanding performance through nomination by other employees. Nomination forms are mailed out in employee paychecks along with an announcement of that month's Employee of the Month. The committee meets the first Monday after the tenth of the month. Each of the six members of the committee votes for one employee he/she thinks deserves to be elected. The selection is submitted to the President for final approval.

   All (Company Name) employees—full- or part-time—are eligible to be nominated and selected as Employee of the Month. A finder's fee is presented to the person who nominated the selected Employee of the Month. The Employee of the Month will receive a plaque with his/her name engraved on it, and a plate is also posted on the master plaque in the Main Office. He/she also receives a gift from the Company for the recognition.

PERSONNEL POLICIES AND PROCEDURES

DISTRIBUTION:		SUBJECT: SERVICE RECOGNITION AWARDS	
EFFECTIVE DATE:	PAGE 1 OF 1	FILE UNDER SECTION	
REVISION DATE:	APPROVED BY:		

PURPOSE:

The purpose of this policy is to give associates recognition for service with the company by presenting service awards upon the completion of certain service anniversaries.

POLICY:

It is the policy of (Name of Company) to recognize service of regular full-time associates by presenting them with appropriate awards recognizing service during their career with the company. A Service Award is presented upon the attainment of five- (5-), ten- (10-), fifteen- (15-), and twenty- (20-) year periods of service with the company.

PROCEDURE:

1. A designated associated of the Human Resources Section at each location will order service plaques and gifts for eligible associates at least two (2) months prior to the beginning of the quarter.

2. Associates on leave of absence will not receive a service award until after returning to active employment.

3. The local plant manager and corporate representatives will make the Service Award presentation on or as near as possible to the associate's service date.

PERSONNEL POLICIES AND PROCEDURES

DISTRIBUTION:		SUBJECT: GUIDELINES FOR SHUTDOWN	
EFFECTIVE DATE:	PAGE 1 OF 1	FILE UNDER SECTION	
REVISION DATE:	APPROVED BY:		

PURPOSE:

The purpose of this policy is to define shutdown benefits for eligible associates and describe the procedures associated with the Shutdown Policy.

POLICY:

The company will normally schedule a summer shutdown period during which most associates will not be scheduled to work. This shutdown period will normally consist of one (1) paid holiday and four (4) paid shutdown days for all associates who meet the eligibility requirements for payment for these days.

To qualify for paid shutdown days, an associate must have successfully completed his/her ninety- (90-) day orientation/evaluation period and be either actively at work or on an approved Leave of Absence.

All associates scheduled to work during shutdown will be scheduled to work all four (4) workdays during the week.

Associates who are required to work during shutdown will be allowed to schedule and take time off work to make up for shutdown time worked under the following conditions:

1. Time off must be scheduled in advance with the associate's supervisor.

2. The period available for associates to schedule the time off will be between the payroll period following shutdown and the last payroll period in September.

3. Time off to make up for shutdown time worked must be taken in a single block of time that falls within a single payroll week.

4. Time off to make up for shutdown time worked may not be carried over beyond the period designated.

5. Time off to make up for shutdown time worked will be without pay, since the associate will have already been paid shutdown pay as well as pay for time worked during shutdown.

PERSONNEL POLICIES AND PROCEDURES

DISTRIBUTION:		SUBJECT: CAFETERIA BENEFITS PROGRAM	
EFFECTIVE DATE:	PAGE 1 OF 4	FILE UNDER SECTION	
REVISION DATE:	APPROVED BY:		

PURPOSE:

The (Company Name) flexible benefit program was designed to meet a series of objectives encompassing company and employee considerations:

- To provide a uniform benefit structure for all employees
- To control company and employee costs
- To respond to changing business needs and demographic characteristics of the workforce
- To reflect a total compensation approach
- To rank in the "second quartile" when compared to a selected group of competitors
- To be used positively by employees relative to their costs

POLICY:

(Company Name) has established a flexible benefit plan for employees in which employees can elect benefits in the form of health, life, and long-term disability insurance premiums; dependent care; and salary deferral. The program will be funded partly through participant salary reduction and partly with company contributions. Each benefit option is assigned a monthly dollar "price tag" and can be purchased by participants in varying combinations.

Each participant, in selecting which benefits to "purchase," uses the building-block approach to tailor his or her benefits package. During an election period, participants elect benefits and agree to salary reduction under the terms of the plan. Participation is mandatory for all (Company Name) employees.

COVERAGE:

The flexible benefit plan of (Company Name) covers all company employees who work an average of thirty-five hours per week.

PROCEDURES:

Flexible benefit programs (also termed cafeteria plans) are governed by Section 125 of the Internal Revenue Code, which allows employees to choose between two or more taxable and/or nontaxable benefits while incurring tax liability only to the extent that taxable benefits are received. A flexible benefit program must meet several formal requirements. The program must be set forth in a written plan document, may only include employees as plan participants, and must offer two or more benefit options. In addition, flexible benefit programs must comply with a number of discrimination rules.

The (Company Name) cafeteria benefit program is established as an umbrella program that encompasses several component plans (i.e., one plan for each benefit option). This allows monies to be contributed to the umbrella account and to be paid out under the terms of the component plan, as elected by each participant. The employee has the option of receiving cash instead of the various plan participations.

If the employees choose the benefits, the insurance premiums paid and company contributions paid in their behalf are excluded from their income and are therefore not subject to federal or state income tax or to Social Security or Medicare tax. If employees choose cash instead, it is included as income and is fully taxable.

PERSONNEL POLICIES AND PROCEDURES

DISTRIBUTION:		SUBJECT: CAFETERIA BENEFITS PROGRAM	
EFFECTIVE DATE:	PAGE 2 OF 4	FILE UNDER SECTION	
REVISION DATE:	APPROVED BY:		

Benefit Options

The (Company Name) cafeteria benefits program offers the following options:

- Health insurance premiums
- Long-term disability insurance premiums
- Accident insurance premiums
- Life insurance premiums
- Dependent care assistance
- Contributions to retirement plan
- Contributions to medical reimbursement account
- Elective vacation days
- Salary deferral
- Cash

These benefits base tax liability as detailed below:

1. Health insurance premiums are excluded from employee gross income.

2. Company-provided long-term disability insurance premiums are excluded from employee gross income. However, if an employee becomes disabled, disability payments under the plan that are attributable to company contributions or that were pretax are includable in the employee's gross income.

3. Company-paid premiums for the first $50,000 of group term life insurance coverage are excluded from employee gross income. Premiums for coverage in excess of $50,000 are a taxable benefit to the employee. The amount of the taxable benefit is determined under the Table 1 Computed Income Schedule.

4. Company-provided dependent care is excluded from employee gross income to the extent that the benefit does not exceed the lesser of the employee's earned income or his or her spouse's earned income. In general, dependent care benefits are taxable to employees with nonworking spouses. (A special rule applies to students' spouses and spouses who lack capacity.)

5. Salary-deferral amounts deposited in the company's 401(k) plan are excluded from gross income and thus not subject to current taxation. However, these amounts are taxable when distributed at retirement, termination, or hardship.

6. Cash is a taxable benefit.

DISCRIMINATION RULES:

The cafeteria benefit plan of (Company Name) must meet certain discrimination tests under Section 125 of the Internal Revenue Code. If the plan is found to be discriminatory under these rules, the majority of participants will not be affected. However, "highly compensated" participants will be taxed on the entire sum available to them through the program, whether the employee elects taxable or nontaxable benefits. The major rules regarding cafeteria benefits are as follows:

DISTRIBUTION:		SUBJECT: CAFETERIA BENEFITS PROGRAM	
EFFECTIVE DATE:	PAGE 3 OF 4	FILE UNDER SECTION	
REVISION DATE:	APPROVED BY:		

1. A cafeteria plan may not discriminate in favor of "highly compensated individuals" regarding eligibility to participate.

2. The company's cafeteria plan may not discriminate in favor of "highly compensated individuals" regarding contributions and benefits.

3. The company's cafeteria plan's health insurance benefits must meet both a percentage test and an excess test. Contributions for each participant must equal:

   ♦ 100 percent of the cost of health coverage for the majority of similarly situated, highly compensated participants; or

   ♦ 75 percent of the cost of the most expensive health coverage elected by any similarly situated participant.

   In addition, the "excess" contributions or benefits provided by the plan must bear a uniform relationship to the employee's compensation.

   Each benefit option offered under the cafeteria benefits plan may be required to meet certain nondiscrimination tests as required by the Internal Revenue Code. These tests and requirements are defined in the different plan documents and policies.

PLAN CONTRIBUTIONS:

On an annual basis, the company will determine the amount that will be contributed per employee to the cafeteria benefits program, in monthly installments. In addition, in an annual enrollment period, each company employee will complete an enrollment form electing both the benefit options and the amount of annual salary reduction, which will be accomplished through regular (monthly or biweekly) payroll deduction.

The enrollment period will be conducted for all employees each fall preceding the new plan year. Changes in the annual enrollment election during the year will be allowed only for the following changes in family status:

♦ Marriage, divorce, or legal separation

♦ Birth or adoption of a child

♦ Death of a spouse or other dependent

♦ If the spouse loses or gains his/her job and benefits

♦ Employee's dependent becomes employed or eligibility for benefits

♦ An unmarried, dependent child gains or loses dependent eligibility

Should a change in family status occur, the employee has thirty days from the date of the change in status to enroll and/or make changes in the election.

The company will determine on an annual basis the premium costs for each benefit option, which may depend upon the amount of coverage, the amount of any deductible, and whether benefits are covered. Dependent care assistance benefits are preset amounts from which the employee may choose. The "cost" of salary deferral and cash equals the amount any participant elects to defer or continue receiving in cash as regular pay. The total dollar amount in each employee's account dictates the amounts of benefits each employee may elect. Any difference between the total contributions for a participant and the cost of his or her benefits package as elected during the annual enrollment period is deemed a cash benefit and is included in the participant's regular paycheck throughout the year.

PERSONNEL POLICIES AND PROCEDURES

DISTRIBUTION:		SUBJECT: CAFETERIA BENEFITS PROGRAM	
EFFECTIVE DATE:	PAGE 4 OF 4	FILE UNDER SECTION	
REVISION DATE:	APPROVED BY:		

RESPONSIBILITIES:

The corporate Human Resources Department is charged with the responsibility of assuring compliance with the Department of Labor requirements as well as coordinating the annual enrollment and determining the company's projected costs for each year. The corporate Tax Department is charged with the responsibility of assuring compliance with the Internal Revenue Code and any applicable IRS rules, including the filing of Form 5500 and any other necessary reports.

With the company President's approval, either the corporate Human Resources Department and/or the corporate Tax Department may utilize and delegate certain responsibilities to outside consultants or organizations.

PERSONNEL POLICIES AND PROCEDURES

DISTRIBUTION:		SUBJECT: SEVERANCE PAY	
EFFECTIVE DATE:	PAGE 1 OF 1	FILE UNDER SECTION	
REVISION DATE:	APPROVED BY:		

POLICY STATEMENT

The purpose of this policy is to provide an equitable measure of compensation for eligible employees whose employment has been terminated by the company, and to encourage management to take prompt action whenever an employee lacks the ability to perform the duties of his/her position satisfactorily. Special consideration has been given to those employees with long service, since they may experience difficulty in obtaining suitable new employment.

It is the company's intent to provide regular employment to all employees; however, conditions may arise that necessitate the dismissal of an employee or a decrease in working force. When a termination of employment other than discharge for cause has been initiated by the company, management believes that some payment should be made to the employee that will assist him/her in making an adjustment until other employment is found. In all other cases of termination, management believes no payment should be made.

DEFINITION OF TERMS

A. Temporary Employees—All employees who have been hired for limited tenure of employment are considered temporary employees.

B. Regular Full-Time Employees—All employees other than temporary employees.

C. Release—A permanent separation initiated by the company due to lack of work or the employee's inability to satisfactorily perform the duties of his/her position.

D. Discharge—A permanent separation for cause initiated by the company.

E. Resignation—A voluntary, permanent separation initiated by the employee.

F. Salary—The basic pay rate, not including overtime, bonuses, or other premium pay.

TERMINATION PAY

A. Regular full-time employees are entitled to severance pay in accordance with the following schedule:

Reason for Termination	*Amount of Severance Pay*
Release:	
◆ Under one year of service	None
◆ Over one year of service	One week's salary for each year of service completed (minimum of two weeks)
Discharge	None
Resignation	None
Retirement and Death	Benefits payable at retirement or death of an employee are covered in separate policies on these subjects.

B. Temporary employees are not entitled to severance pay.

C. Severance pay for those eligible shall be paid at the regular time the paycheck is due, until the entire severance pay allowance is paid out.

D. Acceptance of this allowance by the employee will terminate his/her status as an employee. If he/she is subsequently re-employed, he/she shall be considered as a new employee.

E. In unusual situations or cases involving key management personnel, severance pay in excess of this schedule may be approved by the Management Committee.

PERSONNEL POLICIES AND PROCEDURES

DISTRIBUTION:		SUBJECT: EMPLOYEE UNIFORMS	
EFFECTIVE DATE:	PAGE 1 OF 1	FILE UNDER SECTION	
REVISION DATE:	APPROVED BY:		

POLICY STATEMENT:

Company policy requires that employees in certain positions and job classifications wear an approved uniform while working. In those positions and classifications where uniforms are required, the cost of the uniform will be a Company expense and will be charged against payroll for the Division to which the employee is assigned. This will include normal cleaning and normal replacement costs.

PROCEDURE:

Uniforms are to be worn when working only and when commuting to and from work where necessary. They are not to be worn as personal clothing. Cost for uniforms lost, damaged, or destroyed will be charged to the employee.

The quantity, style, type, and color of the uniforms will be requested by the Market Manager or Supervisor responsible for the Division on a provided authorization form for Company-paid uniforms. This request will require the approval of the President of the Company. It will be the Market Manager's or Supervisor's responsibility to review the authorization with the Store Managers or Division Managers under their responsibility to be sure that they understand what is authorized and that they are in compliance.

Uniforms should not be ordered for temporary employees or for new employees until their three months of continuous service have been completed and the Manager feels confident that the employee will be continuing with the Company.

Head wear is considered a part of an employee's uniform. Employees who choose to wear head wear are required to wear appropriate or authorized head wear only. Appropriate or authorized head wear is that which is provided by the Company bearing the Company's name or logo or the name or logo of one of its major suppliers or head wear bearing no identification.

Head wear bearing identification or advertising products not distributed by the Company is prohibited while working on behalf of the Company. This requirement applies whether an employee is on the Company Uniform Program or not.

Managers are expected to use conservative measures to keep uniform costs reasonable while maintaining good employee image.

All employees terminating their employment with the Company will be held accountable for all uniforms assigned to them. They are required to turn in their uniforms to their Supervisor immediately upon termination of employment.

PERSONNEL POLICIES AND PROCEDURES

DISTRIBUTION:		SUBJECT: DISCOUNTS ON EMPLOYEE PURCHASES	
EFFECTIVE DATE:	PAGE 1 OF 1	FILE UNDER SECTION	
REVISION DATE:	APPROVED BY:		

POLICY:

After completing six months of continuous service, employees are entitled to the benefit of purchasing regular stock merchandise on a reduced-cost basis as follows:

PROCEDURE:

1. Purchases for cash at time of purchase
    A. More than thirty days but less than six months continuous service:
        (1) Furniture—selling price less 25 percent.
        (2) Appliances, televisions, and stereos—selling price less 10 percent.
    B. Continuous service of six months and over:
        (1) Sold at cost, payable at time of purchase.
        (2) Services required on appliances, televisions, and stereos will be charged to the employees at our regular service charge cost, even though the set may still be in warranty.

2. Purchase on credit after six months of service
    A. Employees will buy at selling price plus normal carrying charges and a 10 percent down payment, with the following adjustment to selling price:
        (1) Furniture—less 20 percent.
        (2) Appliances, televisions, and stereos—less 10 percent.

3. No commissions will be paid to salespeople for employee purchases. The store manager will sell all items to employees.

4. It is understood that all purchases at discount prices by employees must be for their immediate personal use only. Employees will not be eligible to buy company merchandise for friends or neighbors.

PERSONNEL POLICIES AND PROCEDURES

DISTRIBUTION:		SUBJECT: EMPLOYEE CHARGE ACCOUNTS	
EFFECTIVE DATE:	PAGE 1 OF 1	FILE UNDER SECTION	
REVISION DATE:	APPROVED BY:		

POLICY STATEMENT:

(Company Name) utilizes credit cards at most of its retail operations and encourages employees to sign up for these credit card programs and to use them whenever possible.

PROCEDURE:

The company will consider extending credit to an employee on an open account basis under the following conditions:

1. The employee must complete a credit application.

2. The employee will be required to sign a collateralization agreement to protect the company in the event the employee's account runs over thirty days past due or the employee terminates his/her employment with the company.

The company reserves the right to deny any employee this open account privilege.

Employees should submit their credit application to their respective managers, who will forward it for processing.

PERSONNEL POLICIES AND PROCEDURES

DISTRIBUTION:		SUBJECT: SAFETY SHOES	
EFFECTIVE DATE:	PAGE 1 OF 1	FILE UNDER SECTION	
REVISION DATE:	APPROVED BY:		

POLICY:

Safety shoes have been proven to be an excellent protective device for preventing foot injuries. In view of this, (Company Name) personnel are encouraged to wear safety shoes at all times while on the premises.

GUIDELINES:

1. In order to provide "extra" incentive to wear safety shoes in hazardous areas of the organization, (Company Name) will grant an $18.00 rebate toward the purchase of safety shoes to any employee who is regularly exposed to or works in an area where foot injuries are most likely to occur. Normal freight charges for safety shoes ordered through the company will be paid by the company.

2. The rebate will cover a calendar-year period with a maximum of two $18.00 allowances per year ($36.00 maximum per employee per calendar year).

3. Safety shoes may be purchased from any source; however, for the convenience of employees, catalogues will be available in the Maintenance Department.

4. (Company Name) will assume no responsibility for quality, fit, lost orders, etc., concerning safety shoes.

5. If, while performing his/her normal job, an employee prevents a foot injury as a result of wearing safety shoes, damaged shoes will be replaced by the company.

RESPONSIBILITY:

(Company Name) Safety Committee shall have primary responsibility for the administration of the Safety Shoe Program.

PERSONNEL POLICIES AND PROCEDURES

DISTRIBUTION:		SUBJECT: CHARITABLE CONTRIBUTIONS	
EFFECTIVE DATE:	PAGE 1 OF 2	FILE UNDER SECTION	
REVISION DATE:	APPROVED BY:		

GENERAL:

It is the policy of (Name of Company) to make monetary contributions to established, recognized, and eligible agencies or institutions engaged in providing and improving education, welfare, and civic enterprises in communities that they serve nationally or locally. This standard operating procedure outlines the approved method for requesting and processing such contributions.

SCOPE:

This is the policy for the corporate departments and all Divisions and Subsidiaries of the Company.

APPLICATION:

A. As soon as possible after May 1, a listing should be forwarded to the Employee Relations Department. This listing will contain the following information:
   1. All anticipated contributions for the fiscal year, showing the agency involved and the amount that is to be contributed.
   2. A list of the contributions for the previous fiscal year, indicating the name of the agency and the amount contributed.

B. Each anticipated contribution in an amount greater than $100.00 must also be submitted on a "Contributions Request" form for individual consideration and approval.

COMMITTEE ON CHARITABLE CONTRIBUTIONS:

This committee, consisting of appointed members, is responsible for the review, consideration, and approval or rejection of contribution requests included in projected budgetary listings or for other interim and exceptional contribution requests as submitted.

PROCEDURE:

A. As a portion of annual budget preparation, each specified location will include an itemized listing of anticipated, annual contributions. In addition, the previous fiscal year's contribution list, along with an appropriate explanatory statement of any projected revisions, shall be prepared and will accompany this itemized listing.

B. Should individual contributions be requested for amounts greater than $100.00, even though itemized in the listing, a separate form shall be prepared and submitted.

C. The annual listing with the accompanying data is forwarded to the Director—Employee Relations by no later than June 1 of each current year for analysis and presentation to the Committee on Charitable Contributions. The contribution year is from July 1 to June 30.

PERSONNEL POLICIES AND PROCEDURES

D. The Committee on Charitable Contributions will convene for the purposes of considering requests, and either approval or rejection will result.

E. The Director—Employee Relations informs the requester of accepted or rejected requests for processing accordingly.

RELATED INFORMATION:

A. Locations Making Contributions from Local Company Funds

    For acceptable contributions donated from locations making payment from local Company funds, a ''Contribution Account'' shall be established and accountability reports of such payments provided.

B. Unacceptable Solicitation

    Solicitations for contributions received from political, fraternal, and labor organizations or from organizations that are recipients of United Fund monies are not acceptable for consideration. When exceptions exist because of unusual circumstances, such requests should be forwarded to the Director—Employee Relations for additional analysis and consideration.

C. Miscellaneous Contributions

    Contributions categorized in budgetary listings and approved as ''miscellaneous'' shall be distributed at the discretion of the qualified requester.

D. Donations for Advertisement

    Donations made for newspaper, radio, television, and other such communication media for local enterprises, such as school yearbooks, Junior Achievement, civic programs, etc., shall not be considered in budgetary listings. Such donation requests shall be forwarded to the Advertising and Public Relations Department.

E. Interim Requests

    Requests arising during the fiscal year, other than incidental disbursements, shall be submitted on the ''Contributions Request'' form to the Director—Employee Relations for review and consideration prior to making the disbursement.

PERSONNEL POLICIES AND PROCEDURES

DISTRIBUTION:		SUBJECT: BEREAVEMENT GUIDELINES	
EFFECTIVE DATE:	PAGE 1 OF 1	FILE UNDER SECTION	
REVISION DATE:	APPROVED BY:		

PURPOSE:

The purpose of this policy is to provide compensation for associates who must be off work during a period of bereavement as defined in this policy.

POLICY:

Associates will be paid their regular straight-time wages for eight (8) hours per day up to three (3) workdays lost due to the death of any member of their immediate family as defined in this policy. The bereavement period will begin no earlier than the day of death and will extend through the day following the funeral.

Bereavement pay will not be allowed for holidays or for time outside the normal work schedule.

Bereavement pay will be paid for work time lost on mandatory overtime days scheduled for weekends. Overtime premium will not be paid for work time lost under the bereavement policy.

The immediate family is defined as full or step-members as follows:

Wife/husband
Half-brother/sister
Mother/father (and in-law)
Grandchildren
Daughter/son (and in-law)
Grandparent
Sister/brother (and in-law)
Great-grandparent

If a relative dies who is not a member of an associate's "immediate family" as defined in this policy, the associate may be excused without pay for one (1) scheduled workday to attend the funeral. Documentation of attendance at the funeral may be required. Relatives covered include the full or step: aunt, uncle, first cousin, nephew, or niece. A spouse's grandparent, brother-in-law, or sister-in-law is also included.

Documentation of the death and/or relationship may be required.

PROCEDURES:

Associates should inform their supervisor/coordinator or Human Resources representative as soon as possible following the death in order to ensure that the absence is properly recorded and bereavement pay is approved.

An associate's supervisor/coordinator and Human Resources representative may grant additional time off without pay in conjunction with the bereavement period.

PERSONNEL POLICIES AND PROCEDURES

DISTRIBUTION:		SUBJECT: COMPANY NEWSLETTER	
EFFECTIVE DATE:	PAGE 1 OF 1	FILE UNDER SECTION	
REVISION DATE:	APPROVED BY:		

PURPOSE:

The purpose of the newsletter is to inform and communicate with associates and their families about matters of concern and interest affecting the company and its associates. The newsletter will recognize associates and groups of associates for significant work-related accomplishments and should contribute to the improvement of associate morale. In addition, the company wants to use the newsletter to help promote a sense of unity among associates at the various locations of the company.

POLICY:

It is the policy of the company to keep the communication systems open. In order to achieve this goal, the Company will publish a newsletter and distribute it to associates. Its purpose will be to inform associates of news. It will also contain occasional articles on non-work-related activities of company associates as well as information from our parent companies and other matters of interest.

SECTION 9

Seniority, Promotions, Transfers, and Layoffs

The following checklist can be used to help determine the various policy items that should be incorporated in your policy manual. Sample policy statements covering many of the items in the checklist appear in this section. They can be used to guide your policy statement.

Policy Manual Checklist

Our Policy Manual Should Cover

Seniority

1. Defining types or units of seniority	Yes____	No____
2. Exceptions to seniority	Yes____	No____
3. How seniority can be lost	Yes____	No____
4. Accumulation of seniority	Yes____	No____
5. How seniority works	Yes____	No____
A. Layoffs	Yes____	No____
B. Recall	Yes____	No____
C. Promotions and demotions	Yes____	No____
D. Transfers	Yes____	No____
E. Overtime work distribution	Yes____	No____
F. Vacation scheduling	Yes____	No____
6. Seniority lists	Yes____	No____
7. Seniority by classification	Yes____	No____
A. Stewards—union officials	Yes____	No____
B. Supervision	Yes____	No____
C. Employees on strike	Yes____	No____
D. Uniformed service veterans	Yes____	No____
8. Job bidding procedure	Yes____	No____

Promotions

9. Defining types of promotions	Yes____	No____
10. Performance reviews	Yes____	No____

11. Ability, skill, and length of service   Yes_____ No_____

12. How promotion affects seniority   Yes_____ No_____

13. How promotion affects pay   Yes_____ No_____

Transfers

14. Definitions of transfer   Yes_____ No_____

15. Procedure for an employee wanting a transfer Yes_____ No_____

16. Procedure for an employer initiating employee transferral Yes_____ No_____

17. Transfers within department   Yes_____ No_____

18. Transfers outside department   Yes_____ No_____

19. Transfers outside bargaining unit   Yes_____ No_____

20. Transfers and bumping procedure   Yes_____ No_____

21. How transfers affect seniority   Yes_____ No_____

22. How transfers affect pay   Yes_____ No_____

Layoffs

23. Definitions—temporary and permanent layoffs   Yes_____ No_____

24. Reasons for layoffs   Yes_____ No_____

25. Advance notice of layoffs   Yes_____ No_____

26. How seniority will be affected by short or prolonged layoffs Yes_____ No_____

27. Effect of layoff on employee benefits   Yes_____ No_____

28. Layoff procedure   Yes_____ No_____

29. Bumping procedure during layoff   Yes_____ No_____

30. Recall procedure   Yes_____ No_____

31. Income Assistance Plan   Yes_____ No_____

Employee Values—Do They Make a Difference?

One of a manager's most difficult jobs is motivating his or her employees. Without properly motivated employees, an organization will be inefficient and unproductive, and will suffer the loss of quality personnel. One of the most neglected and unappreciated areas in understanding our motivational scheme is employee values.

Values are becoming more and more important in the workplace as we move into the twenty-first century. They are becoming a basis for employee motivation, pay, and job satisfaction. Today's employees are seeking to find an organization that has values congruent with their own. This is particularly true for the Generation X person.

Dr. Morris Massey, a professor at the University of Colorado, has done pioneering work in the area of values in the workplace. In his book, *The People Puzzle* (Weston, Va.: Reston, 1979), he indicates that we are motivated either by values or needs in the workplace. Thus, it's very important for today's employer to understand the value system out of which the person is operating. Massey says, "Your values system determines how you relate to your family, what products you buy, how you vote, and how you perform your job. It dictates your leisure time activities, what information you absorb, and your religious convictions."

Work values are powerful shapers and motivators of employee behavior. Today's manager cannot afford to not know the workers' values. We must know what turns them on. According to Massey, there are five groups of workers characterized by their value systems in the workplace today. They are:

1. Traditionalists
2. In-betweeners
3. Challengers
4. Synthesizers
5. Fantasizers

The traditionalist group is made up of those who are in the senior age group in the workforce. Their primary focus is to preserve and promote very traditional, fixed values. These people are very loyal to the organization of which they are part and will give a fair day's work for a fair day's pay. They value the job and what it stands for very highly.

The in-betweener group is made up of employees in their forties and fifties, or the Boomer group. They are seeking the meaning of life and are optimists. Work for them is a means to an end. They expect to get the money they need to do what they want in life, and they expect to have all the good things in life: the car, the house, the boat, and personal fulfillment.

The third group is the challengers. This is the same age group as the in-betweeners, but their focus is pessimistic. They also want to find the meaning of life and have the good life, but they doubt that they will ever achieve it. They tend to focus on disenchantment. Their motivation for work is to get the money they need to find meaning in life.

The fourth group is the synthesizers. This group wants to be in harmony with everybody and the organization of which they are a part. They do whatever they need to do to support the company. They are very loyal and willing to do whatever the company needs to be done. Their focus is on supporting the organization of which they are a part.

The fifth group is the fantasizers, this is the younger generation, or Generation X. This group wants immediate gratification, and work is the means to get it. They are not loyal to one company and will go from place to place depending on what values they encounter. They are group-oriented and value relationships highly.

Do you know the values of the people in your workplace? If you do not, you may be running into motivation problems. Your employees may not have the commitment you think they should have, and you have a collision of values. To alleviate this, you may want to see what the values of the organization are and how the people can fit into those values. You may want to compare the individual's values to those of the organization.

On the following pages, you will find policy statements covering:

Service Record
Recognition of Seniority
Anniversary Date
Policy on Promotions
Transfers and Promotions
Employee Requested Transfers

Layoffs and Recall
Layoffs (Union)
Layoff and Recall Procedure
Hourly Employees
Salaried Employees
Force Reductions
Income Assistance Plan

PERSONNEL POLICIES AND PROCEDURES

DISTRIBUTION:		SUBJECT: SERVICE RECORD	
EFFECTIVE DATE:	PAGE 1 OF 1	FILE UNDER SECTION	
REVISION DATE:	APPROVED BY:		

GENERAL:

Each employee's length of service is based on his/her most recent hiring date with the company.

DETERMINATION OF SERVICE:

A. Length of service will not be broken and time lost will be added to the length of service record in the following instances:
   1. In the event that an employee is transferred to another department or location.
   2. Sick leave up to 730 consecutive days or less.
   3. Time lost due to accidents that occur on the job.
   4. In the event that an employee is laid off and recalled to work within 730 consecutive days.
   5. Leave of absence of thirty (30) calendar days or less.
   6. In the uniformed service of the United States (if an employee has satisfactorily met legal requirements).

B. Length of service will not be broken but time lost will not be added to length of service record when a leave of absence granted by the company is in excess of thirty (30) calendar days.

C. Length of service will be broken by:
   1. Resignation.
   2. Discharge.
   3. Layoff for a consecutive period of longer than three (3) years.
   4. Failure to report back to work within three (3) working days after being requested by the company to do so.
   5. Absence for a period of two (2) consecutive scheduled working days without permission or without notice to the company.

D. In the event that an employee resigns and is rehired at a later date, he/she should be informed that his/her service date must correspond with his/her rehire date and that all previous service has been lost.

DISTRIBUTION:		SUBJECT: SENIORITY	
EFFECTIVE DATE:	PAGE 1 OF 1	FILE UNDER SECTION	
REVISION DATE:	APPROVED BY:		

POLICY:

Seniority is the amount of continuous employment with the hospital and/or within a job classification. Employees accumulate seniority by continuing at their work without unauthorized interruptions or termination. Employee seniority is important to the hospital, as it assures the availability of an experienced and stable workforce. Seniority is important for employees, as it enables them to continue their self-improvement and advancement to qualify for higher wages and promotion opportunities. Certain employee benefits are based on an employee's length of continuous employment. Seniority is also taken into consideration when scheduling holidays and vacations.

In considering employees for wage increases, promotions, and transfers, selection will be based on performance and the ability to do the job. Where candidates have equal ability and performance, additional consideration will be given to the candidate with the greatest seniority.

PURPOSE:

The purpose of this policy is to ensure a fair, impartial, and uniform procedure for the calculation of seniority.

PROCEDURE FOR THE CALCULATION OF SENIORITY:

For the first ninety continuous days of employment, the employee has no seniority status. At the end of this period, his/her seniority will date back to the date of hire. Seniority is not accumulated for temporary employees. The accumulation of seniority will be interrupted when the employee is granted a leave of absence or is temporarily laid off. No seniority will be accumulated during a leave of absence; however, the employee on an approved leave of absence will receive credit for all seniority accumulated prior to the leave of absence.

PERSONNEL POLICIES AND PROCEDURES

DISTRIBUTION:		SUBJECT: SENIORITY	
EFFECTIVE DATE:	PAGE 1 OF 2	FILE UNDER SECTION	
REVISION DATE:	APPROVED BY:		

POLICY STATEMENT:

Seniority refers to time that the employee has worked for the company. It gives the employee certain preferences or ranking when decisions must be made in regard to promotions, reduction in forces, and determination of eligibility for various benefits.

DETERMINATION OF SENIORITY

Seniority is determined by a specific date. In most cases, this date is the date of original hire with the company; however, if seniority was broken through resignation, discharge, or extended layoff, then the seniority date becomes the last date the employee was hired, following the break in seniority.

LOSS OF SENIORITY:

There are several ways an employee can lose seniority. The following things will result in loss of seniority:

A. Resigning: An employee absent for two (2) consecutive workdays without notice will be regarded as a voluntary resignation and lose all seniority. If an employee must be absent, he/she must be sure to notify the plant nurse or the Human Resources office as quickly as possible and never later than the third day of the absence or he/she will lose his/her seniority.

B. Discharge: Reasons for this could include violation of rules, unsatisfactory work performance, or improper conduct.

C. Layoff of More than One Year: Employees with more than one year of service at time of layoff may retain seniority for another year if they notify the Human Resources office during the twelveth month of layoff that they wish to be retained on the recall list for another year.

D. Failure to Report for Work within Two Days After Employee Receives a Certified Mail Notice of Recall: Such notices will be sent to the last address that employee has given to the Human Resources office. In all cases, employee must report not more than five (5) days after such notice has been mailed. If for any reason employee cannot report for work immediately when he/she receives notice of recall, he/she should get in touch with the Human Resources office as quickly as possible to see what arrangements can be made.

E. Overstaying a Leave of Absence
   Division Seniority
   The work of the plants is divided into three divisions, each doing a certain type of work quite different from that of each of the other divisions. These divisions are the Cabinet plant, the Electronics plant, and the Maintenance and Occupancy division. The divisions are divided into occupational groups, with each group doing similar work.

   When employees are hired, they are assigned to one of the three divisions, and in most cases, they will remain in that division throughout their employment with the company. Their seniority will accumulate in the division, and they will have no seniority in other divisions, just as employees in other divisions will not develop seniority in their division. Within their division, they will usually be assigned to a job in Grade 1, which is the starting grade. When openings develop in higher-rated jobs within their division, they will have the opportunity to bid for such jobs in accordance with the promotion procedure, which will be explained later. Once they start up the ladder of promotions with a particular occupational group, they will normally continue to progress in this group as they develop greater skills and longer seniority in the particular occupational group where they are working.

When reductions in force are necessary, employees are reduced in grade according to assigned seniority in reverse order to the manner in which they were promoted in the occupational group. However, employees reduced to Grade (1) will be permitted to use their seniority throughout the division rather than just in the occupational group, with the employees in Grade (1) having the least seniority being laid off first. When employees are recalled to a division, they are considered in reverse order of layoff, with the people on layoff holding the greatest seniority being recalled first to the Grade (1) jobs.

EXCEPTIONS TO SENIORITY

A. If senior employees are not qualified to perform the available work.

B. Temporary layoff. There will be times when shortages of materials or other problems will develop in spite of every effort on the part of the company to avoid them. Under these conditions, it is sometimes necessary to have short interruptions of work in some parts of the plant. To avoid the difficulties that would be created if it were necessary to apply the regular seniority provisions for these short periods of time, temporary layoffs may be made without regard to seniority for such periods, but they will not exceed five consecutive working days. These temporary layoffs will affect only those employees whose jobs may have been shut down.

If there is any temporary work available when these temporary layoffs are required, the employees to fill the temporary jobs will be selected by seniority from among those whose jobs have shut down if they are qualified to perform the temporary work.

C. The starting of a new line or the resumption of work after shutdown. Employees recalled to such work may be recalled within a three-day period without consideration of the seniority of employees within the group. Likewise, when a line is being shut down, employees may be laid off from their line as their operations are completed over a three-day period without consideration of their seniority as compared to others in the group involved.

D. The company reserves the right to hire or retain employees without regard to seniority because their special training, ability, or experience is needed for the continuing operation of the plant. There shall never be more than thirty employees in each division included within this group.

PERSONNEL POLICIES AND PROCEDURES

DISTRIBUTION:		SUBJECT: SENIORITY	
EFFECTIVE DATE:	PAGE 1 OF 1		FILE UNDER SECTION
REVISION DATE:	APPROVED BY:		

POLICY STATEMENT:

(Name of Company) embraces the general policy of providing the maximum employment security, consistent with sound business principles, to those employees with the greatest amount of employment service within appropriate seniority units. Further, the company recognizes employees' length of employment service as one of the major factors applicable to the accumulation of employee benefits, such as vacations, holidays, job opportunity, insurance, etc.

PERSONNEL POLICIES AND PROCEDURES

DISTRIBUTION:		SUBJECT: SENIORITY	
EFFECTIVE DATE:	PAGE 1 OF 1	FILE UNDER SECTION	
REVISION DATE:	APPROVED BY:		

PURPOSE:

The purpose of this policy is to recognize the length of service of associates for the purpose of earning certain employment privileges and benefits pertaining to promotions, transfers, reductions in force, layoffs, and recalls.

POLICY:

An associate's length of service (seniority) is recognized by the company for regular, full-time associates within a plant or company facility. The term "seniority" means an associate's continuous, uninterrupted period of regular, full-time employment beginning with his/her last date of hire. For associates having the same date of hire, seniority rights are determined by the last four digits of the associate's Social Security number, with the associate with the lowest number having the highest seniority.

After an associate successfully completes his/her ninety (90) calendar day orientation/evaluation period, he/she will become a regular associate with ninety (90) days of seniority.

An associate's seniority will continue during an approved leave of absence. However, an associate's seniority will be broken for the following reasons:

- If an associate voluntarily quits or resigns
- If employment is terminated for any reason
- If an associate fails to perform any work for a period of forty-eight (48) weeks (for an associate who is eligible for FMLA) or thirty-six (36) weeks (for an associate who is not eligible for FMLA) or for a period equal to the associate's total length of service, whichever is less
- When an associate retires or becomes permanently totally disabled

318

PERSONNEL POLICIES AND PROCEDURES

DISTRIBUTION:		SUBJECT: LENGTH OF SERVICE; RECOGNITION OF SENIORITY	
EFFECTIVE DATE:	PAGE 1 OF 1	FILE UNDER SECTION	
REVISION DATE:	APPROVED BY:		

POLICY:

To recognize an employee's length of service as a benefit that entitles him/her to certain privileges and considerations. We recognize the principle of seniority between regular, full-time employees by job classification within a department.

PROCEDURE:

1. Accumulation of Seniority—New employees must complete 180 calendar days of service before becoming eligible for seniority privileges. After completion of 180 calendar days of service, seniority privileges will become effective, and the new employee will receive seniority credit for the first 180 days. Seniority will mean continuous employment at our stores, beginning with the date on which the employee began to work after last being hired, plus any time spent in uniformed services.

2. How Seniority Can Be Lost or Broken

   A. If employee voluntarily quits or resigns

   B. If employee is discharged or dismissed

   C. If employee retires

   D. If employee fails to report to work and is absent without notification or acceptable excuse for a period of two (2) consecutive scheduled workdays.

   E. If employee is laid off for a period of more than six (6) consecutive months.

   F. If employee overstays his/her vacation without an excuse acceptable to management.

   G. If employee is on an authorized sick leave of absence longer than twelve (12) consecutive months unless an extension has been granted by the company.

   H. If employee gives a false reason for leave of absence or accepts unauthorized employment elsewhere during a leave of absence.

   I. If employee falsifies information on any pre-employment or post-employment personnel forms.

PERSONNEL POLICIES AND PROCEDURES

DISTRIBUTION:		SUBJECT: SENIORITY	
EFFECTIVE DATE:	PAGE 1 OF 1	FILE UNDER SECTION	
REVISION DATE:	APPROVED BY:		

JOB SENIORITY:

Job seniority is the amount of time employed in a full-time status in a job classification of the seniority group. Job seniority is accrued by an employee simultaneously on his/her current job and on all lower jobs in the line of progression.

DEPARTMENT SENIORITY:

Department seniority is the amount of time employed in a full-time (plus retroactive temporary, where applicable) status in the department seniority group.

CLASSIFICATION SENIORITY:

When there are more employees in a job classification than the number required, the employee with the least department seniority in that job classification will move to the next lower job classification to which department seniority entitles him/her, displacing the employee with the least department seniority in that lower job classification. Similarly, this displaced employee moves down under the same procedure and so on until the excess employee with the least departmental seniority is displaced to the Transfer Pool.

An employee moving down must take the job assignment that is vacated by the employee displaced by seniority. He or she cannot displace any other employee for a job assignment with that classification.

When a rearrangement of machines or processes or circumstances results in a vacancy of a specific job assignment, but no excess employees in the job classification, the job assignment will be open for bid only to those already classified in that job classification. The resulting vacancies in job assignments will be similarly posted and filled until an unassigned employee fills the remaining vacancy.

PERSONNEL POLICIES AND PROCEDURES

DISTRIBUTION:		SUBJECT: ANNIVERSARY DATE	
EFFECTIVE DATE:	PAGE 1 OF 1	FILE UNDER SECTION	
REVISION DATE:	APPROVED BY:		

POLICY:

All employees establish an anniversary date on the date of their employment or re-employment. This date will be the basis from which the service date will be computed as explained below.

SERVICE DATE:

This date will be identical to the anniversary date when the employee was first employed. It will be moved forward by an equal amount of time each period that the employee is absent from work without pay in excess of ten (10) working days except for U.S. uniformed service. It is the service date that is used in determining an employee's eligibility for wage increases and fringe benefits that are related to length of service. Service awards are given annually in the following categories: 3 years, 6 years, 10 years, 15 years, 20 years, and 25 years.

RAISE DATE:

A special record is maintained in the Human Resources Department of the date(s) an employee receives an increase in wages. It is this date that is used for consideration of further programmed merit wage increases. Wage increases based on merit are determined by the hospital's performance evaluation program, and one such evaluation must precede each merit wage increase.

PERSONNEL POLICIES AND PROCEDURES

DISTRIBUTION:		SUBJECT: TERMINATION OF SENIORITY	
EFFECTIVE DATE:	PAGE 1 OF 1	FILE UNDER SECTION	
REVISION DATE:	APPROVED BY:		

Employees will cease to have seniority of any type, and their names will be removed from the Seniority Roster(s), in the event that:

A. They are discharged, quit, or terminated.

B. They take unauthorized employment with another company during a Leave of Absence or give false reason(s) for obtaining a Leave of Absence.

C. They fail to report for work immediately following a Leave of Absence. (If they fail to report for work because of personal illness, they must make arrangements with the Human Resources Department for a Medical Leave, which may or may not be granted at management's discretion.)

D. They are laid off and are not recalled to work within the one-year period immediately following the date of layoff.

E. They fail to report their intentions within two days of receipt of notice to report from layoff, or fail to report for work within five working days of receipt of such notice. (If they fail to report for work because of personal illness, they must make arrangements with the Human Resources Department for a Medical Leave, which may or may not be granted at management's discretion.)

F. They are absent from work for two consecutive days without good cause.

G. They are absent from work for two consecutive days without notifying the Human Resources Office directly or through their supervisor of the reason for absence not later than 5:00 P.M. of the second day absent (second- and third-shift employees must make notification not later than 9:00 A.M. of the morning following the second day absent).

PERSONNEL POLICIES AND PROCEDURES

DISTRIBUTION:		SUBJECT: PROMOTIONS	
EFFECTIVE DATE:	PAGE 1 OF 1		FILE UNDER SECTION
REVISION DATE:	APPROVED BY:		

POLICY:

It is our policy to fill job vacancies and higher-rated jobs by the promotion of qualified employees within our company whenever possible.

PROCEDURE:

1. In the selection of an employee to fill an upgraded job, the following qualifications will be carefully considered:
   A. Attitude, skill, ability, and past performance
   B. Efficiency
   C. Physical and mental qualifications
   D. Disciplinary record
   E. Attendance record
   F. Length of service

2. Should any store not have available, qualified employees for promotions, or should the company not have a qualified person available in another store for transfer or promotion, then the store manager should seek qualified employees from outside.

3. Where the above qualification factors are considered relatively equal among two or more employees considered for an upgraded or promoted job, length of service will be the determining factor.

PERSONNEL POLICIES AND PROCEDURES

DISTRIBUTION:		SUBJECT: TRANSFERS AND PROMOTIONS	
EFFECTIVE DATE:	PAGE 1 OF 1	FILE UNDER SECTION	
REVISION DATE:	APPROVED BY:		

POLICY:

It is the policy of the hospital to transfer and promote from within the hospital whenever possible. Employees are urged to obtain the necessary skills, training, education, and professional registration in order to be eligible candidates for transfer or promotion.

Employees who request a transfer within a department or to another department will be given preference over applicants from the outside if they are equally or better qualified. However, it is the responsibility of the Human Resources Department to fill job openings with the best qualified people available.

All job vacancies except executive positions will be posted for a reasonable period of time in the Human Resources Department and on the official employee bulletin boards located at each timeclock to allow employees the opportunity to apply for the identified job(s). Outside applications will be accepted at the same time positions are posted within, but employees will be given priority consideration.

ELIGIBILITY REQUIREMENTS:

Only employees who have completed ninety days' service will be eligible for transfer or promotion. Employees must be dependable and be doing satisfactory work in their present department. There is no limit to the number of jobs employees can apply for. All applicants must meet the requirements defined in the job description before a transfer will be considered.

PROCEDURE:

The employee desiring a transfer must submit a written request to the Human Resources Department. The Human Resources Department, in turn, will interview the employee to determine qualification, reasons for request for transfer, and the requirements of the department concerned.

An interview will be arranged between the department head with the job opening and each qualified employee applying for that job. If the employee is selected for the new job, he or she will not be transferred for two weeks or until a replacement is found.

The successful bidder or promoted employee will have a trial period of ninety days. If unable to perform the required work, he or she will be given the first opportunity for a job in his or her former capacity when an opening occurs, be given the chance to apply for another opening for which he or she is qualified, or be terminated if no position is available. If after ninety days an employee is able to perform all elements of the job, the transfer will be official and seniority will be credited. All employees will be paid the rate of the new job when they are transferred or promoted. All accrued benefits will transfer with the employee to the new position.

PERSONNEL POLICIES AND PROCEDURES

DISTRIBUTION:		SUBJECT: CAREER OPPORTUNITIES	
EFFECTIVE DATE:	PAGE 1 OF 1	FILE UNDER SECTION	
REVISION DATE:	APPROVED BY:		

PURPOSE:

This policy provides for the posting of notices of open exempt salaried positions in the classification of superintendent and below whenever such openings occur in any of the company locations.

Along with the job title, location, and shift of the open position, the following information will be included on the posting:

Basic Position Duties
Position Requirements
Special Skills or Experience Desired

POLICY:

1. Whenever an opening occurs in an exempt salaried position at the level of superintendent or below, the Human Resources Section at the facility where the opening exists will prepare a "Career Opportunity" notice. All relevant information regarding the position and qualification requirements will be completed.

2. Copies of the "Career Opportunity" notice for posting will be sent by fax to the Human Resources Sections at all other locations.

3. "Career Opportunity" notices will be posted for one week, and the beginning and expiration dates will be indicated on the notice.

4. Associates will be informed on each "Career Opportunity" notice that if they meet the minimum requirements of the job from the standpoint of education, experience, and qualifications and wish to be considered for the vacancy, they should submit an updated résumé to the Human Resources Section at their location no later than the expiration date shown on the notice. The Human Resources Section of the plant of the associate who submits the résumé will be responsible for submitting the résumé to the Human Resources Section of the facility where the opening exists.

5. Internal candidates who apply for a vacant position and who meet the stated requirements for the position should receive consideration for the vacancy, with appropriate credit given for company service and employment record.

   No single factor or qualification for a position will be considered a determining factor, and there is no requirement that an internal candidate be awarded a position over an outside candidate.

PERSONNEL POLICIES AND PROCEDURES

DISTRIBUTION:		SUBJECT: JOB POSTING PROCEDURE	
EFFECTIVE DATE:	PAGE 1 OF 2	FILE UNDER SECTION	
REVISION DATE:	APPROVED BY:		

PURPOSE:

The purpose of this policy is to provide a system by which job openings are filled by seniority among eligible associates who apply for the position.

POLICY:

Each plant will display a list from which regular full-time jobs will be posted when job openings occur. This list will be updated as needed. All regular full-time associates may apply for posted positions through the Job Posting Procedure.

PROCEDURE:

Job openings will be posted on a designated Controlled Communication Center at each plant for two (2) consecutive workdays. During this time any eligible associate who desires to apply for a posted job opening must sign up at the designated location.

Positions will be filled by the most senior eligible associate who bids. If an associate rejects a position, the opening will be awarded to the next most senior eligible associate. In some instances a test will be administered to determine whether applicants meet the minimum qualifications of the job. In these cases, the job will be awarded to the most senior qualified applicant.

For vacancies for which testing is required, if additional openings in the same position occur within ninety (90) days of the initial posting, those additional openings will be filled from the pool of qualified applicants remaining from the original posting. Additional applicants will not be accepted or tested within the ninety- (90-) day period unless the pool of tested and qualified applicants has been exhausted.

ELIGIBILITY:

1. Associate must be a regular full-time associate who has completed at least six (6) months of service.

2. Associate must not be under a written warning for any reason.

3. If the associate is under medical restrictions, the associate must be able to perform the essential functions of the job posted.

The following provisions will apply to this procedure:

1. If an associate rejects a posted position that he/she has applied for and been offered, he/she will not be eligible to bid for another posted position for a six- (6-) month period.

2. If an associate accepts a posted position, he/she will have a six- (6-) month commitment to that area before being eligible to apply for any other posted position. A six- (6-) month restriction will also apply to moves within a

PERSONNEL POLICIES AND PROCEDURES

DISTRIBUTION:		SUBJECT: JOB POSTING PROCEDURE	
EFFECTIVE DATE:	PAGE 2 OF 2	FILE UNDER SECTION	
REVISION DATE:	APPROVED BY:		

designated job group. These restrictions will not apply to an individual bidding on a job that would be a promotion or an individual who has been displaced through job elimination or formation change.

3. Associates who are awarded a posted leader class position, including production leaders, engineering assistants, setup operators, maintenance leaders, and quality assurance leaders, will have a twelve- (12-) month commitment to that area before being eligible to apply for any other open hourly position.

4. Posted jobs for which no one bids will be filled by new hires.

The company will ensure that every effort will be made to transfer the associate who has been selected to his/her new position as soon as practicable.

PERSONNEL POLICIES AND PROCEDURES

DISTRIBUTION:		SUBJECT: WAIVER OF PROMOTION	
EFFECTIVE DATE:	PAGE 1 OF 1	FILE UNDER SECTION	
REVISION DATE:	APPROVED BY:		

POLICY STATEMENT:

An employee may relinquish his/her rights to a promotion or job progression by signing a waiver.

Any hourly rated employee who declines a promotion or progression must sign a written waiver stating that he/she has knowingly and willingly declined the next highest job within his/her progression group.

Upon signing the waiver, the employee relinquishes any rights to promotion or progression until six months after his/her written request to be released from waiver is received by his/her supervisor.

He/she will be bypassed by employees below him/her on the seniority list so long as he/she remains on the waiver.

He/she relinquishes any rights to temporary promotion or progression brought about by vacations, sick relief, etc.

He/she will not lose his/her seniority status, which is considered for layoffs, vacations, etc., and will maintain his/her relative seniority status in the classification that he/she was on when going on waiver.

PERSONNEL POLICIES AND PROCEDURES

DISTRIBUTION:		SUBJECT: TRANSFERS	
EFFECTIVE DATE:	PAGE 1 OF 1	FILE UNDER SECTION	
REVISION DATE:	APPROVED BY:		

POLICY STATEMENT:

To provide equitable consideration and opportunity for qualified employees to fill hourly rate job vacancies within the Division, transfers and job assignments between departments will be made according to the prescribed methods and procedures that follow. Only where unusually special qualifications are required for a job and employees are not available within the Division may other methods be used for filling the vacancy.

TRANSFER TO LOWER-RATE JOB:

Any employee who has over one year of continuous service with the company and who is displaced at company request for any reason other than incompetence, disciplinary actions, or physical inability to do the job, will have his/her pay "stepped down" gradually to give him/her time to make the proper adjustment in personal finances.

PERSONNEL POLICIES AND PROCEDURES

DISTRIBUTION:		SUBJECT: EMPLOYEE REQUESTED TRANSFERS	
EFFECTIVE DATE:	PAGE 1 OF 2	FILE UNDER SECTION	
REVISION DATE:	APPROVED BY:		

SCOPE:

Subject to the review of the cognizant Human Resources Department following approval of the line operating management concerned, any (Company Name) employee may request transfer to another type of work, organization, shift, or geographical location in order to make better use of his/her capabilities; to take advantage of career growth or promotional opportunity; or to solve personal problems.

PROCEDURE:

1. Transfer applications are submitted to the employee's Human Resources Department in memorandum form, approved by the employee's immediate supervisor. They specify the employee's job title, number, location, and organization. They are valid for ninety (90) days and may be reviewed for an additional ninety (90) if necessary to provide thorough replacement exposure.

2. An application for transfer is reviewed based on the following criteria:
   A. Job performance
   B. Attendance
   C. The employee's qualifications for the job under consideration
   D. Reasonable length of service with the company

3. Transfer applications are continuously compared by the Human Resources Department against open requisitions and existing manpower plans to ensure that transfer applicants receive adequate consideration.

   All reasonable consideration is given to accommodating employee transfer requests, including those involving lateral transfer, when they are not to the material disadvantage of the company. In weighing transfer requests, the most effective utilization of employee capabilities is the controlling factor in management decisions.

4. All qualified employees are given equal consideration for transfer without regard to age, sex, race, color, religion, or national origin. Selection is subject only to job requirements.

5. Disability accommodation transfers will be given first consideration.

6. Consistent with the above, the employee is released by operating management for transfer consideration unless:
   A. It can be clearly shown that an adequate replacement cannot be obtained.
   B. The employee's reason for requesting a transfer cannot be satisfied within the present organization.
   C. The action is inconsistent with the staffing plans.

7. An employee selected for transfer is normally released to the new assignment within ten (10) workdays from the date of acceptance. Longer retention is a matter of agreement between the losing and gaining organizations.

PERSONNEL POLICIES AND PROCEDURES

DISTRIBUTION:		SUBJECT: EMPLOYEE REQUESTED TRANSFERS	
EFFECTIVE DATE:	PAGE 2 OF 2	FILE UNDER SECTION	
REVISION DATE:	APPROVED BY:		

8. When transfer applicants in the local labor market area possess qualifications at least comparable to those of new-hire candidates, the transfer applicants are given precedence. Similarly, qualified transfer applicants from outside the local market area take precedence over nonlocal recruits unless it can be clearly shown that a significant improvement in capability is represented by the recruit.

9. Employees whose applications for transfer are not accepted are so advised by the cognizant Human Resources Department. In addition, they are counseled as to why their applications were not accepted, and how and when they might expect further consideration for similar transfer opportunity.

PERSONNEL POLICIES AND PROCEDURES

DISTRIBUTION:		SUBJECT: ACCOMMODATION TRANSFERS	
EFFECTIVE DATE:	PAGE 1 OF 1	FILE UNDER SECTION	
REVISION DATE:	APPROVED BY:		

An employee who can no longer perform, with or without accommodation, his/her current position because of a disability will be placed on a lateral basis in an existing (or soon to be) vacancy for which he/she is qualified and can perform the essential job duties, with or without accommodation.

If no such vacancy exists, or the employee declines such placement, the employee will be placed in an existing (or soon to be) vacancy on successively lower levels for which he/she is qualified and can perform the essential job duties, with or without accommodation.

If no such vacancies exist, or the employee declines such placement, the employee will be terminated.

Employees in need of an accommodation transfer will be given first consideration (before posting) for such vacancies on a lateral or downgrade basis.

Employees in need of an accommodation transfer will be considered on a promotion basis along with other internal candidates without priority or preference.

PERSONNEL POLICIES AND PROCEDURES

DISTRIBUTION:		SUBJECT: LAYOFFS	
EFFECTIVE DATE:	PAGE 1 OF 1	FILE UNDER SECTION	
REVISION DATE:	APPROVED BY:		

POLICY STATEMENT:

A layoff is the discontinuance of employment for any period of time when no work is available. If it is possible to determine the approximate time and conditions under which the employee will return to work, he/she will be so advised.

A layoff for less than one calendar week will be made according to the equipment or shift involved, and every effort will be made to equalize the lost time.

Should it become necessary to lay off a regular employee for one week or more due to lack of work, layoff will be made according to mill seniority, provided those employees who are eligible for reassignment to avoid layoff are qualified to do the available work or can be trained to do it in a reasonable period of time.

Except for layoffs of less than one week, all employees must be laid off by transferring to the Transfer Pool. (Example: The employee with the lowest mill seniority who is to be laid off is assigned to the Machine Room. Supervision of the Machine Room will transfer him/her to the Transfer Pool; layoff from the company will be made from there.)

NOTICE OF LAYOFF:

Except for emergencies, such as equipment breakdown and acts of God, an employee who is to be laid off for more than one week due to lack of work will be given two weeks' notice.

Advance notice will not be given for disciplinary layoff or discharge.

RECALL:

Recall from layoff of all qualified employees will be made before employment of others for one year from date of layoff. Recall will be made in reverse order of layoff. Employees will be recalled as full-time employees.

Recalled employees who have been laid off for more than thirty days will be given a physical examination by the company's physician or by a physician designated by the company before returning to work.

PERSONNEL POLICIES AND PROCEDURES

DISTRIBUTION:		SUBJECT: LAYOFFS (UNION)	
EFFECTIVE DATE:	PAGE 1 OF 1	FILE UNDER SECTION	
REVISION DATE:	APPROVED BY:		

PURPOSE:

On those occasions when there is a need to decrease the number employed, it is essential that the terms of the appropriate union contract be followed explicitly. As detailed below, there are few instances when an employee's seniority date is not the determining factor. And, whenever such an instance seems appropriate, the supervisor should notify the Industrial Relations Manager before proceeding to keep a person with less seniority and lay off a more senior person.

PROCEDURE:

In any decrease of the working force, temporary employees are the first to be dismissed.

◆ Temporary Layoffs

As regards temporary layoffs [those scheduled to last thirty (30) days or less], seniority shall be the factor determining which employees shall be retained, providing the employees have clearly demonstrated their ability to perform all phases of the job to be performed.

◆ Permanent Layoffs

Whenever it becomes necessary to decrease the working force permanently, the following factors shall be weighed in arriving at the selection of those employees to be retained:

(1) Demonstrated skill and efficiency in performing the particular work available and

(2) Seniority

Where demonstrated skill and efficiency in performing the particular work available are relatively equal between two or more employees, seniority shall be the determining factor.

The company shall be the judge of an employee's skill and efficiency. The union reserves the right to institute grievance procedures if it disagrees with any such decision of the company, and if the dispute is not settled by such procedure, the same may be submitted to arbitration.

Whenever the workforce within a department is to be reduced on a permanent basis, the employee(s) within that department having the least seniority shall be notified by the departmental foreperson twenty-four (24) hours in advance of the last hour the employee is scheduled to work.

PERSONNEL POLICIES AND PROCEDURES

DISTRIBUTION:		SUBJECT: LAYOFF AND RECALL PROCEDURE (Hourly and Weekly Salaried Employees)
EFFECTIVE DATE:	PAGE 1 OF 1	FILE UNDER SECTION
REVISION DATE:	APPROVED BY:	

POLICY:

The purpose of this policy is to establish a layoff and recall procedure that will provide a systematic method to accomplish a reduction/recall in the workforce while providing the company with a means to retain the necessary skills and abilities to comply with customer requirements.

ELIGIBILITY:

All full-time hourly and weekly salaried employees.

PROCEDURES FOR LAYOFF:

Employees will be laid off in order of seniority by classification within an occupation, within their department.

Affected employees in the higher classifications within the occupation will be allowed to displace junior employees in a lower classification in the same occupation or take the layoff. Where applicable, there will be a corresponding adjustment in pay rate.

PROCEDURES FOR RECALL:

When the workload increases, the senior employee(s) on layoff will be recalled to the classification within the occupation from which they are on layoff.

LENGTH OF RECALL PRIVILEGES:

Employees with more than ninety (90) days but less than seven (7) years of continuous service at the time of layoff will have recall privileges for one (1) year from the date of their layoff.

Employees with more than seven (7) years of continuous service at the time of layoff will have recall privileges for two (2) years from the date of their layoff.

PERSONNEL POLICIES AND PROCEDURES

DISTRIBUTION:		SUBJECT: LAYOFF AND RECALL PROCEDURE (Hourly)
EFFECTIVE DATE:	PAGE 1 OF 3	FILE UNDER SECTION
REVISION DATE:	APPROVED BY:	

COVERAGE:

Hourly Employees

ASSUMPTIONS

1. The ability of the plant to operate effectively is the primary objective.

2. The ability of a displaced employee to perform the job classification to which he/she has been bumped is essential to the achievement of the stated primary objective.

3. Every consideration for length of service (seniority) will be extended as long as the primary objective is achieved.

4. After thirty (30) days of assignment in a department, an employee's job and department seniority shall always equal his/her plant seniority, provided the employee has developed the ability to perform the job satisfactorily.

5. Discrimination plays no part in the layoff logic.

RATIONALE:

Periods of reduced business activity demand reduction of staffing levels to maintain a financially acceptable position. Implementation of staff reduction activities is to be based on a uniform and logical procedural system. This system shall provide the utmost equity and job protection for senior employees in descending order.

PROCEDURE:

1. The Plant Manager shall provide the Employee Relations Manager with a list of job classifications, by department, which are to be reduced.

2. The Employee Relations Manager shall prepare a list ranking employees by seniority within each job classification, by department.

3. The list prepared in item 2 shall be used to identify the person(s) with the least seniority within each job classification that will be affected by the company's layoff plans. The list will also be used to identify those individuals whose jobs are vulnerable to the "bumping" sequence.

4. The "bumping" sequence to be utilized by the affected person(s) is as follows:
    A. A person affected is eligible to "bump" the least senior person in his/her job grade, providing that person possesses less plant seniority.

DISTRIBUTION:		SUBJECT: LAYOFF AND RECALL PROCEDURE (Hourly)	
EFFECTIVE DATE:	PAGE 2 OF 3	FILE UNDER SECTION	
REVISION DATE:	APPROVED BY:		

B. If there is no person with less plant seniority within the job grade of the affected person, then the affected person is eligible to examine the least senior person in each successive lower job grade until a person is found whose plant seniority is less than that of the affected person.

C. Each person who is bumped from his/her job classification may likewise examine each lower grade for the least senior person in that grade with less plant seniority than himself/herself and replace the lower-grade employee. This process may be repeated until the person with the least plant seniority shall be forced out of the plant on layoff.

D. Where several persons may become displaced in each successively lower job grade, the choice of job selections available within each lower job grade shall be made in descending order of seniority.

E. Where a displaced person is not qualified to perform the job that is available to him/her in the bumping sequence, he/she may examine the least senior incumbent in each successively lower job grade until he/she finds someone with less plant seniority whose job he/she can perform satisfactorily.

F. Where a person is unqualified or unwilling to accept the terms of layoff to a lower job grade, he/she has the option of either accepting a layoff without reassignment or resigning.

G. A person shall not be permitted to skip an available job in the layoff procedure to get a job he/she is unqualified to perform the available job.

All of the foregoing is based upon ability to do the job.

OTHER LIMITS:

1. The company will enter into reasonable training programs to maintain seniority order. New or recalled skills necessary to perform the layoff assignment must be acquired at standard levels inside of four weeks.

2. Voluntary switching among employees will not be permitted in the interest of expediency and to reduce controversy.

RECALL PROCEDURE:

1. As the build-up in each job classification occurs, the employees displaced or laid off out of these job classifications will be recalled to them in reverse order of the layoff (highest seniority to lowest). Returning to a job classification higher than the one an employee left is not permitted.

Exception: Part-time employees have no recall rights, having been terminated. They may be rehired at the discretion of the company, after all the full-time employees available for recall from layoff are placed.

If employees laid off out of a job classification do not possess a particular skill required in the build-up process, full-time employees laid off out of the plant who possess the essential skill may be recalled as needed out of the normal recall order. If the skill does not exist in acceptable form within the active or inactive workforce, hiring from outside will occur.

2. Recall notification will be accomplished by dispatch of telegram to the employee's last known address. It is highly recommended that verification of delivery or nondelivery be demanded for our file, to defend the company in the event of complaint.

DISTRIBUTION:		SUBJECT: LAYOFF AND RECALL PROCEDURE (Hourly)
EFFECTIVE DATE:	PAGE 3 OF 3	FILE UNDER SECTION
REVISION DATE:	APPROVED BY:	

3. Recall rights shall be maintained for a length of time equal to the individual employee's service up to a maximum of twelve (12) months. When the recall rights are exhausted, the employee shall be terminated, subject to rehire at the discretion of the company.

4. Recall rights shall also terminate if, upon dispatch of recall notification, no response in the form of report-in or written notice of acceptable reason for not reporting in is forthcoming within three (3) working days of dispatch of a recall notice.

MAINTAINING SENIORITY:

Employees recalled within six (6) months of layoff shall maintain accumulated seniority including time on layoff. Employees recalled within six (6) to twelve (12) months shall cease accumulation of seniority beyond one (1) month.

SHORT-TERM LAYOFFS:

Production curtailments involving ten (10) working days or less and small numbers of people may be more effectively handled by asking for volunteers to go on layoff. If this cannot be effectively arranged, the regular layoff procedure should be followed regardless of time involved.

PERSONNEL POLICIES AND PROCEDURES

DISTRIBUTION:		SUBJECT: FORCE REDUCTIONS	
EFFECTIVE DATE:	PAGE 1 OF 1	FILE UNDER SECTION	
REVISION DATE:	APPROVED BY:		

OBJECTIVE:

This policy is established to provide objective criteria to be applied when a workforce outside of a bargaining unit must be reduced because of decreased workload, decrease in volume of business, discontinued functions, or halt in operations of activities.

POLICY:

It is the policy of (Company Name) that reductions in the workforce are processed in the following manner:

1. Nonexempt Employees: Seniority is the primary factor in determining reduction in force order among individuals qualified to perform the remaining work, except where a reasonable business need requires the retention of less senior employees who possess required unique skills.

2. Exempt Employees: Selections are based upon employees' qualifications to perform the remaining work and their job performance. Length of service is considered in those cases where the individuals otherwise possess equivalent qualifications.

3. For a period of one year following termination, employees who have one or more years of service at the time of a force reduction are eligible for consideration for re-employment to the same job classification, salary grade, and geographic location from which they left.

PERSONNEL POLICIES AND PROCEDURES

DISTRIBUTION:		SUBJECT: INCOME ASSISTANCE PLAN	
EFFECTIVE DATE:	PAGE 1 OF 3	FILE UNDER SECTION	
REVISION DATE:	APPROVED BY:		

OBJECTIVE:

To provide an income assistance allowance to eligible U.S. (Company Name) employees. This allowance is intended to facilitate economic adjustment resulting from termination of employment through layoff and ensuing loss of income.

GENERAL:

Specifically excluded from the income assistance are employees who resign, die, are transferred between business entities, are totally disabled, are discharged, or are terminated due to inability to perform the job satisfactorily or terminated at the end of a personal leave of absence in excess of sixty days. Income assistance is not paid when termination of employment results from the sale of a company facility or function to a successor company, and the terminated employee accepts employment with the successor company.

Employees who retire are excluded from receiving income assistance unless they are being laid off and are eligible for income assistance.

DEFINITIONS:

1. Eligible Employee—Any active, full-time United States employee other than employees who are specifically excluded. Generally, it does not include those employees whose benefits are negotiated by a collective bargaining agent except where such negotiated agreement specifically provides for participation in this plan.

2. Base Plan—The employee's base weekly pay immediately preceding termination of employment. Overtime, commissions, bonuses, and premiums are excluded from this calculation. The base salary of employees paid on a monthly basis is determined by multiplying the monthly salary by 18 and then dividing the resulting product by 69.

3. Continuous Service—All unbroken service with (Company Name) or its wholly owned subsidiaries, or in the case of broken service, the amount of total service credited to the employee's retirement date as defined under the company's retirement plan.

PROCEDURE:

Income Assistance Allowance—Eligible employees are provided income assistance based on length of continuous service as defined in C, Definitions. Maximum income assistance is determined by multiplying the employee's weekly base pay by the appropriate number of weeks contained in the following schedules:

340

PERSONNEL POLICIES AND PROCEDURES

Full Years of Service	Weeks of Payment
Less than 1 year	1 week
1 year to 3 years	2 weeks
4 years to 6 years	4 weeks
7 years to 9 years	6 weeks
10 years to 12 years	8 weeks
13 years to 15 years	10 weeks
16 years to 18 years	12 weeks
19 years to 21 years	14 weeks
22 years to 24 years	18 weeks
25 years to 27 years	18 weeks
28 years to 30 years	22 weeks
31 years and over	26 weeks Maximum

NOTE: The total number of weeks indicated in the foregoing schedules will not be reduced by the number of weeks pay in lieu of notice granted to the employees.

EMPLOYMENT OFFER:

A terminated employee who has been offered other employment by the company or any other business group within the same geographic area at a base pay of at least 85 percent of current base pay and who declines such employment will be considered to have resigned and will be ineligible for consideration of an income assistance allowance.

PAYMENT:

The income assistance plan is effective on the day following the expiration of the period represented by any pay in lieu of notice. Payments to eligible employees will be made in a lump sum (maximum six weeks) for length of service less than ten years. For employees eligible for more than six weeks' income assistance, commencing with the seventh week, payments will be made weekly and continue until the laid-off employee:

1. Is paid the maximum number of weeks according to length of service; or

2. Is reinstated before the maximum number of weeks have been paid; or

3. Is employed full-time by another employer before the maximum number of weeks have been paid; or

4. Dies during the payment period. In this event, the remaining payments are paid in a lump sum to the employee's beneficiary as designated under the retirement program.

PERSONNEL POLICIES AND PROCEDURES

DISTRIBUTION:		SUBJECT: INCOME ASSISTANCE PLAN	
EFFECTIVE DATE:	PAGE 3 OF 3	FILE UNDER SECTION	
REVISION DATE:	APPROVED BY:		

SPECIAL CONDITIONS:

An employee who has been paid a lump sum and is then reinstated prior to the expiration of the period represented by the lump-sum payment shall be required to return to the company that portion that covers the period following reinstatement. Repayment may be made either in a lump sum or by payroll deduction.

A reinstated employee to whom an income assistance allowance has once been paid by any (Company Name) business group and who is again laid off within one year of recall will be considered only for an income assistance allowance based upon total length of continuous service less the number of weeks of income assistance previously paid. An employee laid off in excess of one year from previous recall will be entitled to the full income assistance allowance based on total length of continuous service.

No holiday pay, including the unused personal floater, will be paid at the time of layoff or during the layoff period.

RESPONSIBILITY:

1. This income assistance plan is managed and controlled by the executive committee of the company as the named fiduciary pursuant to the requirements of the Employee Retirement Income Security Act of 1974 (ERISA), and may be modified or amended by them at any time.

2. Exceptions to this policy are to be submitted in writing and approved in advance by the executive committee.

3. The plan administrator for the purpose of ERISA is (Company Name).

Section 10

Conduct, Discipline, and Termination

The following checklist can be used to help you determine the various policy items that should be incorporated in your policy manual. Sample policy statements covering many of the items in the checklist appear in this section. They can be used to guide your policy statements.

Policy Manual Checklist

Safety Plant Rules

1. Must rules be submitted to the union before they can become effective?   Yes_____ No_____
   A. For notification purposes only   Yes_____ No_____
   B. For union approval   Yes_____ No_____

2. Can rules be added, revised, or withdrawn at any time?   Yes_____ No_____
   A. At management's discretion and judgment   Yes_____ No_____
   B. If organized, after notifying the union   Yes_____ No_____
   C. If organized, by joint agreement with the union   Yes_____ No_____

3. How rules are to be publicized   Yes_____ No_____
   A. Employee handbook   Yes_____ No_____
   B. Bulletins and bulletin boards   Yes_____ No_____
   C. Labor agreements   Yes_____ No_____
   D. Employee publications   Yes_____ No_____
   E. Special rule book   Yes_____ No_____
   F. Individual meetings with immediate supervisor   Yes_____ No_____

4. Type of penalty given employees for rule violations   Yes_____ No_____
   A. Penalty to be at the discretion of supervisor and immediate superior   Yes_____ No_____
   B. If organized, penalty to be determined by mutual consent of management and employee or union representatives   Yes_____ No_____
   C. Penalty determined by a disciplinary committee composed of management and employee or union representatives   Yes_____ No_____
   D. Penalty determined by specific guidelines in writing according to seriousness of violation   Yes_____ No_____

5. Type of disciplinary action   Yes_____ No_____
   A. Oral reprimand—warning   Yes_____ No_____

343

B. Written reprimand—warning   Yes_____ No_____
C. Disciplinary layoff   Yes_____ No_____
D. Loss of special privileges   Yes_____ No_____
E. Demotion   Yes_____ No_____
F. Fine   Yes_____ No_____
G. Loss of seniority   Yes_____ No_____
H. Discharge   Yes_____ No_____

6. If organized, shall the union have the right to appeal any disciplinary action taken by management?   Yes_____ No_____

7. If not organized, does the employee have the right to appeal any disciplinary action taken through a nonunion grievance procedure?   Yes_____ No_____

8. Shall disciplinary policy provide that after a period of time previous written reprimands or other disciplinary action on file will become void, giving the employee a clean slate for the future?   Yes_____ No_____

9. Procedure for supervisors to follow in administering discipline verbally and in writing.   Yes_____ No_____

Discharge Policy and Procedure

1. Description of misconduct that warrants the discharge of employees immediately, without prior warning   Yes_____ No_____

2. Policy providing that employee is to be suspended before a discharge is made final and effective   Yes_____ No_____

3. Policy stating that management has the right to determine what is cause for immediate discharge   Yes_____ No_____

4. Policy and procedure to be followed in issuing written warnings in less severe types of disciplinary action before discharge   Yes_____ No_____

5. Requirements on documenting discharge without notice   Yes_____ No_____
   A. To be given to employee   Yes_____ No_____
   B. To be given to union   Yes_____ No_____
   C. To be given to Human Resources office for employee's personnel file   Yes_____ No_____

6. Policy on when termination of employment notice is to be given   Yes_____ No_____
   A. Minimum period prior to discharge   Yes_____ No_____
   B. At time of discharge   Yes_____ No_____
   C. Within a specified period of time following discharge   Yes_____ No_____

7. Type of form of termination notice
   A. Oral   Yes_____ No_____
   B. Written   Yes_____ No_____

8. Contents of termination notice   Yes_____ No_____

9. Policy providing that all discharges are subject to final approval and authorization of supervisor's immediate superior   Yes_____ No_____

10. Policy on providing discharged employees with dismissal or severance pay   Yes_____ No_____
   A. Eligibility requirements for dismissal or severance pay, including reason for discharge   Yes_____ No_____
   B. Amount of severance or dismissal pay—minimum and maximum   Yes_____ No_____
   C. Policy statement providing inclusion or exclusion of monies due employee from contributions to benefit plans in determining maximum amount of severance pay   Yes_____ No_____
   D. Policy on making all necessary tax deductions from severance pay   Yes_____ No_____
   E. Policy on giving severance pay based upon giving or not giving advance notice of termination   Yes_____ No_____

11. Policy on performing exit interviews   Yes_____ No_____

12. Policy on discharges being subject to grievance procedure   Yes_____ No_____

13. Policy on reinstating employees if the employer is found to be in error through grievance procedure   Yes_____ No_____

14. Policy on reinstated employee being eligible for back pay for time lost   Yes_____ No_____

15. Policy of COBRA extension of benefits administration   Yes_____ No_____

Resignation Policy and Procedure

1. Policy statement requiring or not requiring employee notice of intent to resign   Yes_____ No_____
   A. Verbal or written notification and time limit   Yes_____ No_____

2. Policy on a penalty provided for failure to notify the employer of intent to resign   Yes_____ No_____
   A. No recommendation   Yes_____ No_____
   B. Loss of severance or dismissal pay   Yes_____ No_____

3. Policy on issuing letters of reference for terminated employees   Yes_____ No_____

4. Policy on providing employees who quit or resign with termination form describing reason for termination   Yes_____ No_____
   A. Retaining copy of termination of employment form in personnel file   Yes_____ No_____
   B. Giving copy of termination of employment form to employee   Yes_____ No_____

Progressive Discipline—A Tool or a Weapon?

If any one word has been linked with human resources administration over the past two decades, it has been *documentation*. Employers besieged by governmental intervention found that a successful defense against a charge of discrimination was a heavy paper trail showing that efforts had been made to communicate the need for corrective action in an objective way, and that the employee was sufficiently warned before discipline was applied.

We formalized the process and called it progressive discipline (see Exhibit 10-1). As an employee's job behavior becomes more intolerable or increasing levels of discipline are provided, usually beginning with verbal correction followed by written correction, with suspension or termination looming on the horizon.

The process is well intended and usually effective. However, too often this discipline process loses sight of the real reason for the exercise—to change undesirable behavior. We mistakenly believe that a "written notice" will automatically correct every employee's erring ways. Then we compound the problem by writing up the employee so early in the process that we create the atmosphere of a police officer writing tickets.

As a supervisor, you must keep a strong focus on the fact that progressive discipline and documentation is an important, necessary, and accepted management tool. However, it is secondary to your primary role: leadership. Before you use discipline to correct undesirable behavior, you must first have exercised a host of other leadership tools, including orientation, training, counseling, coaching, evaluation, listening, caring, support, and feedback.

These primary tools foster dialogue with employees. Discussions should be private, forthright, sincere, and, in the humanitarian sense, loving. Private supervisory written notes of the discussion(s) are in order, but only as triggers to help further counseling sessions. Such private confirmation of verbal corrections is rarely used as defensive documentation per se. It is in the atmosphere of, "How may I help you to improve your

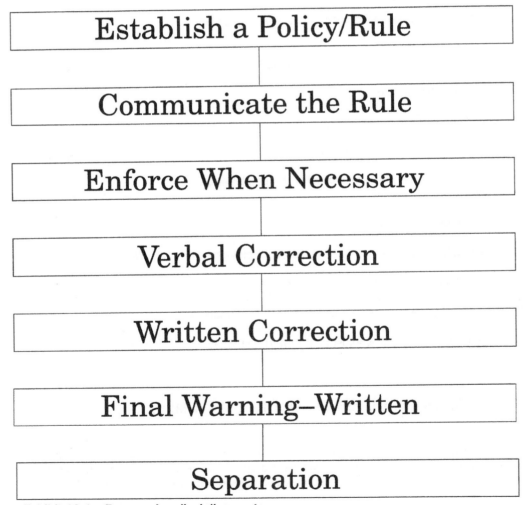

Exhibit 10-1. Progressive discipline system.

job performance? I am interested and concerned in your success,'' that true behavior improvement has a better chance of taking place. This is not the time to write up an employee formally and obtain a confirming signature.

You must also remember that as a supervisor, you are part of the solution, for it is your problem also. Either you made a wrong hiring decision, or you didn't properly apply the helping skills in your leadership responsibilities. In any case, you are suffering the consequences of the problem, so it is now your problem as well.

Only when repeated counseling is disregarded and the behavior has (after ample discussion) gone unchecked should a written correction be made. Ultimately, one or two written corrections on a given topic, following earlier discussions, are enough; then the situation must be brought to a head. (This scenario doesn't cover those occasional job behaviors that are so serious that written correction, suspension, and/or termination may occur immediately after the inappropriate act or behavior. But this type of behavior is relatively infrequent in comparison to day-to-day overall troublesome behavioral actions.)

In the final written stage, you want to confront the employee and say, ''Jim, do you realize that if this (specific) behavior continues, it will be grounds for separation?'' This conversation is a critical, pivotal point in the discipline process, for in effect, the supervisor has relinquished responsibility for and ownership of the corrective action. Continued employment now lies squarely on the employee's shoulders.

Prior to every termination, you must ask yourself the question, ''If I fire Jim tomorrow, will it be a surprise to him?'' If the answer is yes, progressive discipline has not been properly applied, and the process should be repeated from the very beginning.

It is important that you do not allow the process of progressive discipline to lead to an arm's-length, adversarial relationship with employees to like that found in many bureaucracies and union workplaces.

In actuality, your employees are replacing you, since they are doing the job on your behalf—the job that you once did. In turn, you will be rated on their performance and delivery. Their success is, in effect, your success. Remember once again that, for the most part, you truly are in the ''people business.'' Progressive discipline, to be truly effective, should encompass more than written warnings, for they by themselves very rarely bring about improved job performance.

Who Is Challenging Your Right to Hire and Fire?

As a member of management, you are a legal agent for your organization. What you say and do can commit the organization just as easily as if it were said by the chief executive officer. This ''agent status'' is a very important consideration, for there are several major employment regulations that could override your discharge decision. Failure to recognize these guidelines could be both awkward and costly!

When you discharge someone, you must evaluate the impact of these regulations and have proper documentation that provides convincing evidence that your action has not violated the person's employment rights.

Immediately following a discharge, charges of discrimination are very likely. Unless you can provide adequate proof of the reasons for the discharge, the Wage-Hour Division, National Labor Relations Board, Equal Employment Opportunity Commission, or another labor-related agency might quickly find merit in a charge of discrimination, and require you to reinstate the employee with back pay.

Other agencies, like the State Unemployment Department, will award the employee weekly compensation benefits for a stated period of time, usually thirteen to twenty-six weeks, if the separation was not the fault of the employee. This protection is paid for by the employer through a premium charge of a percentage of payroll. Usually, the higher the rate of separations, the higher the employer premium. Thus, it is most important that all separations, whenever possible, document the inappropriate actions or poor performance of the employee, and confirm that the supervisor made repeated attempts to help the employee correct such actions.

Guidelines for Administration of Discipline and Discharge Procedures

As you begin to formulate your disciplinary policies and procedures, you should be aware of the importance not only of communicating these both orally and in writing to your hourly, nonexempt employees, but also ensuring that managers and supervisors have a clear understanding of them. This includes not only a knowledge of what the rules mean and how to determine if the employee has violated them, but of the importance of consistency and documentation when discipline is administered as a result of a rule's violation. Without consistency and documentation, company policies and procedures are of little effect in either remedying problem behaviors of salvageable employees or preventing costly unemployment claims and other employment-related litigation. These terms can best be understood as follows:

1. *Consistency*: Administering disciplinary action equally to all employees without regard to sex, age, race, religion, national origin, citizenship status, disability, veteran status, or any other legally protected status. Consistency also means administering disciplinary action without singling out more productive or cooperative employees for exceptional treatment and avoiding the supervisor's inherent bias to allow the best employees to commit minor or infrequent disciplinary infractions with impunity.

2. *Documentation*: Ensuring that each disciplinary action is accompanied by a written report indicating the date of the infraction, the nature of the infraction, the particular rule or policy violated, any and all previous disciplinary actions within a relevant period (usually one year), and the consequence of any future infraction within a relevant period (usually one year). Giving the employee an opportunity to ''wipe the slate clean'' by a year of service without any repeated violations of company policy or procedure provides a positive incentive to discourage these offenses. However, if no documentation or insufficient documentation exists, you will have the burden of proving—particularly for purposes of an unemployment compensation appeal hearing—that the employee knew of the rule or policy and had been made aware not only of his or her violation, but of the consequences of the final violation which resulted in the discharge.

On the following pages are sample policies covering conduct, corrective discipline, performance, and termination. Included in this grouping are:

Guide for Disciplinary Action
Work Rules
Employee Misconduct
Disciplinary Procedures
Responsibilities, Rules, and Discipline
Resignation
How to Avoid Firing Mistakes—Use Termination Checklist
Termination of Employment

PERSONNEL POLICIES AND PROCEDURES

DISTRIBUTION:		SUBJECT: DISCIPLINE	
EFFECTIVE DATE:	PAGE 1 OF 1		FILE UNDER SECTION
REVISION DATE:	APPROVED BY:		

POLICY STATEMENT:

The company at all times wants to be fair and uniform in its handling of personnel. Employee releases have consistently been troublesome, not usually because there was insufficient reason for the release, but because adequate written records were not made of an employee's misconduct or of the warnings and second chances given.

It is the company's wish, therefore, that a uniform policy be followed by its supervisors. This will mean:

* First, that an employee will have had sufficient notice that a continuance of improper actions will bring about discharge and,
* Second, that a report in writing is made of all warnings given and disciplinary measures taken.

The following, therefore, is to be viewed as the guiding policy insofar as taking disciplinary action for infractions of company rules and misconduct is concerned:

A. At first offense, if not in itself serious enough to warrant suspension or discharge, give warning and advise that another offense will result in suspension for two weeks without pay as a disciplinary measure.

B. At second offense, if not in itself serious enough to warrant discharge, give two weeks' suspension without pay and warn that another offense will result in discharge.

C. At third offense, discharge, and point out to employee that he or she brought about the action and left the supervisor with no alternative.

D. Make a written report of each offense and disciplinary measures taken, with the report routed through regular channels to the Human Resources Department. Use Report of Employee Failure Form No. 292 for the report or give the information in a letter.

Insofar as employees' conduct off the job is concerned, the following indicates the minimum that is required of employees in the way of proper conduct:

A. They must conduct themselves in such a manner that their actions do not reflect on either the company or their fellow employees.

B. They must conduct themselves in such a manner that their actions do not affect their ability to assume the full responsibility of their job at the regular starting time for the day.

The company realizes that the above is made necessary because of the misconduct and offenses of only a small number of employees. It does not in any way want the great majority of the employees who are performing loyally and efficiently and who actually make the company a respected organization to feel that the above is any reflection on them.

PERSONNEL POLICIES AND PROCEDURES

DISTRIBUTION:		SUBJECT: DISCIPLINE	
EFFECTIVE DATE:	PAGE 1 OF 1	FILE UNDER SECTION	
REVISION DATE:	APPROVED BY:		

POLICY STATEMENT:

Management recognizes its continuing responsibility to develop and administer the necessary company regulations and disciplinary measures in a fair and consistent manner, and the obligations of all employees to conform with those company rules and regulations applicable to their assignment.

The company's management seeks to establish and maintain appropriate administrative procedures, company rules, and regulations that will provide the most efficient and effective operation and to provide for proper disciplinary action whenever an employee (or employees) fails to observe such company rules and regulations.

PERSONNEL POLICIES AND PROCEDURES

DISTRIBUTION:		SUBJECT: DISCIPLINARY PROCEDURES	
EFFECTIVE DATE:	PAGE 1 OF 1	FILE UNDER SECTION	
REVISION DATE:	APPROVED BY:		

POLICY STATEMENT:

Whenever an employee commits an offense warranting disciplinary action, his/her supervisor may begin disciplinary action with any of the steps listed below, depending on the seriousness of the offense committed:

A. For minor offenses, the employee should be given a verbal warning. If this does not correct the situation within a reasonable length of time, the supervisor should then use the second step of this procedure.

B. Written warning. The employee may be given a written warning, a description of which appears as an attachment to this policy.

C. If a second offense occurs within a period of one year from the date of the first written warning, the employee may be suspended from work without pay for a period of time up to five days, the length of the suspension depending on the seriousness of the offense.

D. If a third similar offense occurs within a period of one year from the date of the first written warning, the employee may be suspended without pay, pending discharge.

It should be emphasized again that supervisors are not required to go through all four steps in this disciplinary procedure. Discipline may begin at any step in the procedure depending on the seriousness of the offense committed. Any discipline administered by a supervisor should be commensurate with the offense committed. In addition, the supervisor may repeat any of the first three steps of this procedure when he/she feels it is necessary, so long as the discipline is commensurate with the offense committed. If there is any doubt on the part of the supervisor as to what step to begin with, he/she should consult with the Plant Manager and/or the Director of Industrial Relations.

PERSONNEL POLICIES AND PROCEDURES

DISTRIBUTION:		SUBJECT: DISCIPLINARY PROCEDURES	
EFFECTIVE DATE:	PAGE 1 OF 2	FILE UNDER SECTION	
REVISION DATE:	APPROVED BY:		

POLICY STATEMENT:

The role of supervisor or manager is to counsel an employee effectively in order to obtain the best possible job performance and job behavior. To the extent that either of these is not consistent with desired work standards, it is a supervisory responsibility to counsel with each employee to achieve this acceptable performance.

To be effective, disciplinary action should emphasize correcting the problem rather than punishing the offender. It should maintain the employee's dignity and self-respect. It should provide for increasingly serious steps if the problem is not resolved. And, it should result in a change in the employee's behavior and performance.

In keeping with the company's commitment to nondiscriminatory practices, consistency and proper documentation are required of all supervisors and managers in the disciplinary process.

Verbal Correction—The first step in the progressive disciplinary procedure is for the supervisor to meet with the employee to discuss the behavioral or performance problem. The supervisor must explain to the employee the reason for the rule that has been violated, explain to the employee the specific changes that are required, offer assistance as necessary, and express confidence that the employee will correct the problem and that no further action will be needed. The supervisor makes a note of the conversation on a Verbal Correction Report and retains the report in his/her file unless additional counseling is needed. In this case, the supervisor should forward a copy of the Verbal Correction Report to the employee's personnel file, along with a copy of a written Correction Notice.

Written Correction—If the problem continues, the supervisor must again approach the employee. The supervisor must tell the employee what is suspected and ask the employee to confirm that he or she knows what changes must be made. The supervisor must prepare a written summary telling the inappropriate behavior or performance and the corrective action desired. The employee must sign this written notice, signifying that this conversation took place, and the manager should provide the employee with a copy of the written notice, as well as ensuring that a copy is placed in the employee's personnel file.

If the unacceptable job performance or behavior continues, there should be further progressive discipline. With each application of discipline, a record in writing must be made. The number of corrective steps will depend upon the severity of the questionable actions of the employee and the degree of improvement shown.

Decision-Making Leave—With the next level of management approval and input, the supervisor may choose to suspend the employee who refuses to make the necessary changes. The employee is told to stay home for a day (with or without pay at management's discretion), and to take time to make a final decision as to whether he or she can meet your organization's standards. The employee is told that the company wants to keep him or her as a productive member of the workforce, but that the decision is up to the employee—and future violations will result in termination. The employee is told to report back to the supervisor after the decision-making leave day to let the supervisor know his or her decision. Conversations and decisions surrounding the suspension of an employee should be documented in memo form, signed by the employee and supervisor, and placed in the employee's personnel file.

Termination—If discharge becomes necessary, it will mean in most cases that the counseling efforts have failed. Accordingly, when the discharge decision is ultimately communicated to the employee, it should not be a surprise because the discussion prior to the discharge should have warned him or her of the pending consequences. Each discharge should be fully documented. The exact reasons for separation should be noted in writing, and the document must be signed by the employee and the supervisor, as well as the next level of management. This document should then be filed in the employee's permanent personnel file. The Separation of Employment form should be used to document all terminations and should be placed in the personnel file. A copy must go to the president, and another to the Human Resources Department.

Prior to terminating an employee, the employee's supervisor/manager must consult the Coordinator of Human Resources for details regarding the distribution of the employee's final paycheck. In Iowa, an employer is required to pay wages

352

PERSONNEL POLICIES AND PROCEDURES

DISTRIBUTION:		SUBJECT: DISCIPLINARY PROCEDURES	
EFFECTIVE DATE:	PAGE 2 OF 2	FILE UNDER SECTION	
REVISION DATE:	APPROVED BY:		

due to a terminated employee no later than the next regularly scheduled payday. In Minnesota, wages due an employee who voluntarily terminates are due and payable within five days thereafter; an employee who is discharged must be paid within twenty-four hours after the employee demands payment. In Wisconsin, an employee (except commissioned salespeople) who voluntarily terminates must be paid in full within fifteen days of termination; an employee who is discharged must be paid in full within three days. Supervisors must retrieve from the employee all company property, keys, manuals, equipment, etc., before the employee leaves the premises.

In the event that an employee terminates his or her employment with the company, the manager in charge must do the following:

1. Contact the Coordinator of Human Resources and/or the Payroll Department at the home office the same day you are aware of the resignation and/or termination; supply them with the employee's name, termination date, number of hours worked in that pay period if requested, etc.

2. Follow up the call by sending a completed Personnel Action Notice, a Separation of Employment form, and, if conducted, an Exit Interview Form. A completed Exit Interview Form is not required in the case of a dismissal.

Supervisory and management personnel are encouraged to review and follow the recommendations regarding conducting a disciplinary interview. While the above-mentioned progressive disciplinary procedure is preferred and recommended, discipline may begin at any step in the procedure depending on the seriousness and nature of the offense committed. Discipline administered by supervisors should be commensurate with the offense. The seriousness of some offenses, however, may warrant immediate suspension and/or termination. However, a termination decision cannot be made without the input of a market manager–level manager or above.

PERSONNEL POLICIES AND PROCEDURES

DISTRIBUTION:		SUBJECT: HOW TO CONDUCT A DISCIPLINARY INTERVIEW	
EFFECTIVE DATE:	PAGE 1 OF 2	FILE UNDER SECTION	
REVISION DATE:	APPROVED BY:		

If an employee knows he/she has made a mistake and has learned by it, your words may only increase his/her embarrassment and serve no purpose. However, where a rule has been broken or misconduct has taken place, correction or discipline is in order. The following steps are recommended to correct an employee properly:

1. Don't talk about the problem standing up. Sitting down reduces the chances of either person's getting angry.

2. Sit opposite the employee, but not behind the desk. This softens the atmosphere of confrontation.

3. Don't start with an accusation—win the confidence of the employee by describing the problem as one that both have to work at solving.

4. Don't start with chitchat. Your aim is to gather information by encouraging the employee to talk.

5. Don't deliver a sermon or make any wild promises. Try to influence by developing an emotional bond through honest discussion.

6. Avoid prejudging the problem from your point of view alone. Consider enlisting the help of an impartial third person to keep the situation from becoming too emotionally charged.

7. Never criticize, correct, or reprimand an employee in the presence of others. Discipline and correction is a private matter. You should find a quiet place where you can sit down and discuss the problem or mistake calmly, coolly, and objectively.

8. Never try to correct or reprimand an employee when tensions are high. Always do so when matters have calmed down.

9. Listen. Listen quietly to your employee's point of view of what happened. He/she may see the situation more clearly than you do. Even if he/she has a distorted view, let him/her talk. You need to understand the employee's point of view if you hope to work with that person intelligently.

10. Share the blame if necessary. Accept your part of the responsibility for the mistake. Perhaps you didn't give your employee adequate training or preparation. Or maybe you didn't forewarn the employee that this type of problem or situation might arise. Your becoming a "center" with him/her helps ease the load and assures him/her that he/she is not alone.

11. Discuss the problem rather than the employee. Be concerned with correcting the mistake because it is a mistake. Don't focus on the person or his/her personality. To all of us, our person and personality are usually sacred ground.

12. Deal with "why" as well as "how." Many supervisors tell employees what they are doing wrong, but not why they should do something another way. Explain your recommendations fully. Make certain that you and the employee are shooting at the same target with the same kind of gun.

PERSONNEL POLICIES AND PROCEDURES

DISTRIBUTION:		SUBJECT: HOW TO CONDUCT A DISCIPLINARY INTERVIEW	
EFFECTIVE DATE:	PAGE 2 OF 2	FILE UNDER SECTION	
REVISION DATE:	APPROVED BY:		

13. Find a better way. A correction or disciplinary interview is not a success unless there is agreement on a better way. No one likes to be told flatly that he/she is doing something wrong. The person will dislike it even more if he/she is left up in the air with no solution to the problem. Through free give-and-take, try to settle on an approach that you both agree will be better.

14. Finish your correcting and disciplinary interview on a high note. End on a note of optimism and confidence. Don't let your employee feel you have less confidence in him/her because the problem arose.

PERSONNEL POLICIES AND PROCEDURES

DISTRIBUTION:		SUBJECT: GUIDE FOR DISCIPLINARY ACTION
EFFECTIVE DATE:	PAGE 1 OF 3	FILE UNDER SECTION
REVISION DATE:	APPROVED BY:	

POLICY STATEMENT:

Rules and regulations are essential to the efficient operation of any company. They are the cornerstone of any successful operation. This guide for disciplinary action has been established for the common good of all of us at (Company Name). The following rules are fundamental in character. They are designed for the convenience and protection of all of us, and they provide for a more efficient and successful operation.

It is the policy of (Company Name) to be patient, sympathetic, and fair in the administration of discipline. It is the sincere desire of management to help all employees so that we may go forward together in a successful future. However, willful and inexcusable breaches of these rules will be dealt with firmly under policies that apply uniformly to all departments and all individuals.

Penalties consisting of written corrections must be approved by the Director of Human Resources.

Penalties involving suspension or dismissal require approval of the Director of Human Resources, the appropriate Management Committee Member, and the President. In all circumstances with respect to fixing penalties, prior consultation with the Director of Human Resources is required.

Committing any violation of a company rule or regulation will be sufficient grounds for disciplinary action, ranging from verbal correction to immediate dismissal depending on the seriousness in the judgment of management.

RULES AND REGULATIONS

Offense	Range of Disciplinary Action
1. Misrepresentation or omission of facts in obtaining employment.	Dismissal
2. Punching or altering the time card of another employee or allowing someone else to punch, alter, or falsify your time card or time sheet; altering or falsifying a time card or record in any way.	Dismissal
3. Making or permitting a false or untrue company record, e.g., relating to production or quality control records, or other company records relating to materials or work.	Suspension to dismissal
4. Defacing, damaging, or destroying property of the company or of another employee.	Verbal correction to dismissal
5. Interfering with, obstructing, or otherwise hindering the production of the work performance of another employee.	Verbal correction to dismissal
6. Causing a disturbance by running, yelling, playing practical jokes, horseplay, throwing things, or in other ways.	Verbal correction to dismissal
7. Originating or spreading false statements concerning employees or the company.	Verbal correction to dismissal
8. Revealing, disclosing, or making available any confidential or private company information to any person who is not authorized or entitled to receive it, and who does not need to know it; or acting in a reckless, irresponsible, negligent, or wanton way that might lead to or make possible the unauthorized disclosure of classified information.	Written correction to dismissal

PERSONNEL POLICIES AND PROCEDURES

DISTRIBUTION:		SUBJECT: GUIDE FOR DISCIPLINARY ACTION	
EFFECTIVE DATE:	PAGE 2 OF 3	FILE UNDER SECTION	
REVISION DATE:	APPROVED BY:		

Offense — Range of Disciplinary Action

9. Assisting any person to gain unauthorized entrance to or exit from any portion of the company's premises. — Suspension to dismissal

10. Participating in any way in bookmaking or in organized gambling or in any card, dice, or other game of chance for money or other consideration. — Dismissal

11. Fighting or causing bodily injury to another; all other forms of disorderly conduct. — Dismissal

12. Immoral or indecent conduct. — Dismissal

13. Leaving work area without permission, wasting time, loitering, or sleeping during work hours. — Verbal correction to dismissal

14. Careless or inefficient performance of duties, including failure to maintain standards of workmanship or productivity. — Verbal correction to dismissal

15. Refusal to accept or follow orders or directions from proper authority or any other form of insubordination. — Dismissal

16. Reporting to work or working under the influence of intoxicants or illegal drugs; or without appropriate management approval bringing in, possessing, or using of intoxicants or illegal drugs. — Dismissal

17. Selling, soliciting, canvassing, or distributing during work hours on company property without prior approval of the Director of Human Resources. — Dismissal

18. Failure to comply with plantwide or individual departmental safety rules or health rules, instructions, or practices. — Verbal correction to dismissal

19. Operating or using any piece of equipment or property without being authorized to do so. — Written correction to dismissal

20. Excessive tardiness or absence; failure to report for work without a satisfactory reason. — Verbal correction to dismissal

21. Theft, pilferage, or unauthorized removal of property of the company or of others. — Dismissal

22. Smoking in areas where smoking is prohibited. — Verbal correction to dismissal

23. Bringing in, possessing, or using weapons or explosives on company premises without appropriate management approval. — Verbal correction to dismissal

24. Harassment in any form. — Verbal correction to dismissal

25. Intimidating, threatening, or verbally or physically abusing another person. — Verbal correction to dismissal

26. Criminal, dishonest, or notoriously unethical conduct. — Dismissal

27. Failure to work full days (8:30 A.M. to 5:00 P.M.) — Dismissal

28. Interacting with a customer in such a manner as to reflect adversely on the company. — Dismissal

DISTRIBUTION:		SUBJECT: GUIDE FOR DISCIPLINARY ACTION	
EFFECTIVE DATE:	PAGE 3 OF 3	FILE UNDER SECTION	
REVISION DATE:	APPROVED BY:		

Offense

Range of Disciplinary Action

29. Giving a false reason for a leave of absence or accepting employment elsewhere during an authorized leave of absence.

Dismissal

Types of Disciplinary Action*

◆ Simple correction with information and reason for it
◆ Verbal correction
◆ Written correction
◆ Suspension (with or without pay)
◆ Dismissal

* This list is not restrictive or all-inclusive but includes the most frequently used penalties, stated from top to bottom, in the order of their severity.

PERSONNEL POLICIES AND PROCEDURES

DISTRIBUTION:		SUBJECT: WORK RULES AND CORRECTIVE DISCIPLINE	
EFFECTIVE DATE:	PAGE 1 OF 4		FILE UNDER SECTION
REVISION DATE:	APPROVED BY:		

PURPOSE:

The purpose of this policy is to inform associates what the company expects of them in the area of performance/behavior. This policy also describes the types of behavior that are unacceptable and the corrective action that will be taken to address unacceptable associate behavior.

POLICY:

If an individual fails to respond favorably to corrective action or if the associate's actions are so serious that the company feels they are intolerable, then the associate may be discharged in accordance with the corrective discipline policy.

WORK RULES:

There are three levels of violations of work rules (General, Major, and Intolerable). Listed below are examples of violations from each level. This is not a complete list of offenses or activities and practices that may subject an associate to discipline or corrective action. Other activities that adversely affect the welfare of other associates or the company will be dealt with by the company according to management's judgment of the seriousness of the activity.

A. General Violations:

— Do not constitute a significant threat to the operation of the business;

— Do not pose a significant threat to the safety and well-being of the individual or other associates.

Examples of General Violations

1. Failure to wear safety equipment in designated areas
2. Running in the plant
3. Horseplay
4. Failure to report injury on shift it occurs
5. Smoking in restricted areas
6. Poor housekeeping or littering on company property
7. Using profane or abusive language
8. Leaving assigned work areas without permission
9. Failure to perform reasonable quantity of acceptable quality of work
10. Unauthorized posting of materials or tampering with bulletin boards
11. Sleeping while on duty—unintentional
12. Stopping work or making preparations to leave work before the specified quitting time at breaks, lunch, or the end of the shift
13. Failure to be at the job site ready to start work at the beginning of the shift or at the end of lunch and break periods

PERSONNEL POLICIES AND PROCEDURES

14. Failure to comply with the instructions of a security officer

15. Loafing and/or wasting time during work hours

16. Unauthorized use of company telephones

17. Unauthorized presence on plant production floor more than twenty (20) minutes prior to or after assigned shifts

18. Violations of solicitation or distribution rules

19. Excessive breaks

20. Improper parking or improper operation of any vehicle on company property

21. Repeated or intentional failure to clock in or out

22. Repetitive wage attachments from multiple sources

23. Repeated violation of company dress code

24. Putting unauthorized markings or drawings on parts, labels, or boxes

B. Major Violations:

Acts of dishonesty or acts that seriously threaten the operation of the business or the safety and well-being of any associate.

Examples of Major Violations

1. Operating machines without required guards

2. Horseplay with potential for serious injury

3. Violation of safety rules where risk of injury to self or others is significant

4. Failure to report for medical attention as instructed

5. Habitual carelessness and/or recklessness

6. Threatening or intimidating fellow associates at any time

7. Unauthorized use of company time, materials, tools, or equipment for personal projects

8. Unauthorized or unlicensed operation of company equipment

9. Taking company property or the personal property of another from the plant without permission (pilferage)

10. Abusive language to supervisor or member of management

11. Unauthorized alteration of company machinery or equipment

12. Intentional abuse of any structures or equipment on company property

13. Testing at a level between .04 percent and .07 percent on a company-administered alcohol test

14. Disruptive and/or inappropriate behavior

C. Intolerable Violations:

Actions of such serious nature that they may result in termination on the first offense. Examples of Intolerable Violations

1. Sleeping while on duty—intentional

2. Punching another associate's time card or permitting another associate to punch your time card

DISTRIBUTION:		SUBJECT: WORK RULES AND CORRECTIVE DISCIPLINE	
EFFECTIVE DATE:	PAGE 3 OF 4		FILE UNDER SECTION
REVISION DATE:	APPROVED BY:		

3. Theft

4. Falsification of an application or any company records

5. Unauthorized disclosure of confidential information

6. Physical altercations

7. Serious violation of harassment or other policies

8. Sabotage, intentionally interfering with operations or quality, or intentionally allowing defective materials to pass

9. Defacing company property

10. Deliberately damaging company property or property of another associate or property of vendors performing work on company property

11. Leaving facility without authorization or job abandonment

12. Directing threatening language to a member of management, including supervisors and leaders

13. Refusal or failure to cooperate with the investigation of any work-related matter conducted by the company, including the failure or refusal to submit to or sign a release concerning a drug or alcohol test

14. Reporting to work or being on company property under the influence, or the unauthorized use, consumption, possession, distribution, sale, or offering for sale of alcohol, drugs, or any controlled substances at any time

15. Possession of guns, knives, weapons (or objects generally accepted as weapons), explosives, including fireworks or other incendiary material on company property at any time

16. Performing unauthorized work for personal gain while on an approved leave of absence

17. Participating in activities that would aggravate a work-related injury or condition that has caused an associate to be disabled or restricted from performing the regular duties of his or her job.

18. Insubordination

19. Indecent or immoral behavior on company property

20. Testing positive on a company-administered drug test

21. Testing at a level of .08 percent or higher on a company-administered alcohol test

22. Conviction of a felony

23. Conviction of a drug-related criminal offense

CORRECTIVE ACTION PROGRAM:

Every supervisor/coordinator will be expected to use the Corrective Action Program. A Human Resources representative will be involved in all stages of each problem.

The company uses a six-step progressive discipline policy. For each general violation of work rules, the associate moves up one step in the system. For each major violation of a work rule, the associate will progress two steps in the system. A notice of counseling is issued at the first step. A written warning is issued at the second and/or third step. At the fourth and/or the fifth step, the associate will be issued a written warning and suspended three (3) days without pay. Any associate who reaches the sixth and final step, or who commits an ''intolerable'' work rule violation, is subject to discharge.

PERSONNEL POLICIES AND PROCEDURES

DISTRIBUTION:		SUBJECT: WORK RULES AND CORRECTIVE DISCIPLINE	
EFFECTIVE DATE:	PAGE 4 OF 4	FILE UNDER SECTION	
REVISION DATE:	APPROVED BY:		

PROGRESSIVE DISCIPLINE CORRECTIVE STEPS:

Step 1:	A notice of counseling (verbal counseling by the supervisor)
Step 2/3:	A written warning acknowledged by the associate, supervisor, and Human Resources representative
Step 4/5:	Written warning and three-day suspension
Step 6:	Discharge

A. Notice of Counseling:

(General violation of a work rule)—Supervisor/coordinator will discuss the problem with the associate. The problem will be stated on paper and acknowledged by the associate, supervisor, and Human Resources representative. The notice of counseling will be placed in the associate's personnel file and remain active for the next twelve calendar months.

B. Written Warning:

Any general violation after the notice of counseling, or any major violation of a work rule will result in a written warning. The problem will be stated on paper and acknowledged by the associate, supervisor, and Human Resources representative. The warning will be placed in the associate's personnel file and remain active for the next twelve calendar months.

C. Written Warning/Three-Day Suspension

Any general violation after the third step, or any major violation after the second step will result in a written warning with three-day suspension. The problem will be stated on paper and acknowledged by the associate, supervisor, and Human Resources representative. The warning will be placed in the associate's personnel file and remain active for the next twelve calendar months. The associate is then placed on an unpaid three-day suspension. The associate is to return through the Human Resources Section. If an associate is on the fourth step and commits a general violation, the associate will receive additional corrective action.

D. Subject to Discharge:

If the associate is on the fourth step and commits a major violation or is on the fifth step and commits any violation, he/she is subject to discharge. Any intolerable violation may result in discharge. A Human Resources representative is required to be present during these discussions.

Corporate General Affairs will review all cases in which discharge has been recommended.

PERSONNEL POLICIES AND PROCEDURES

DISTRIBUTION:		SUBJECT: WORK RULES	
EFFECTIVE DATE:	PAGE 1 OF 2	FILE UNDER SECTION	
REVISION DATE:	APPROVED BY:		

POLICY STATEMENT:

(Company Name) wants to provide a good work environment for all employees. In turn, it is reasonable to expect a good productive effort and the recognition of responsibility of the part of employees. Each of us has the responsibility to our fellow workers to conduct ourselves according to certain rules of good behavior, conduct, and performance. In any business, some rules are needed to help everyone work together by letting them know what they can and cannot do. (Company Name) expects its employees to follow our company rules; for this reason, a sample of work rules are listed, and employees are expected to read, understand, and follow these rules in their day-to-day work.

PROCEDURE:

Failure to follow company work rules must result in disciplinary action, from verbal correction to termination, depending upon the nature of the offense. Measures should follow the progressive disciplinary policy when practical. We will recognize a twelve-month "washout" period: If an employee does not violate company work rules within a twelve-month period, the company will "wipe the slate clean" and the employee will have a clean record.

While the following list is not all-inclusive, some of the violations that can result in disciplinary action from verbal correction to discharge are:

1. Misrepresentation or omission of facts in seeking employment.

2. Falsification of time records, clocking of another employee's time, or having another employee clock your time.

3. Making or permitting a false record relating to any material or work.

4. Defacing, damaging, or destroying property of the company or of another employee.

5. Possession or consumption on company premises or reporting to work under the influence of alcohol or illegal drugs.

6. Theft, pilferage, or unauthorized removal of property of the company, customers, or others.

7. Bringing in, possessing, or using weapons or explosives on company property without prior management approval.

8. Assisting any person to gain unauthorized entrance to any portion of company premises.

9. Failure to follow required safety procedures or careless or negligent use or operation of company tools, equipment, or vehicles.

10. Excessive absence or tardiness.

11. Fighting or causing bodily injury to another employee or other forms of disorderly conduct.

12. Refusal to accept or follow orders or directions from proper authority or any other form of insubordination.

13. Use of company facilities after normal working hours without authorization.

PERSONNEL POLICIES AND PROCEDURES

DISTRIBUTION:		SUBJECT: WORK RULES	
EFFECTIVE DATE:	PAGE 2 OF 2	FILE UNDER SECTION	
REVISION DATE:	APPROVED BY:		

14. Interfering with, obstruction of, or otherwise hindering the production or work performance of another employee.

15. Engaging in horseplay, running, scuffling, or throwing objects on company premises.

16. Originating or spreading false statements concerning employees or the company.

17. Immoral or indecent conduct on company premises.

18. Leaving work area without permission, wasting time, loitering, or sleeping during working hours.

19. Using any piece of equipment or property without being authorized to do so.

20. Failure to meet quality or quantity requirements.

21. Inefficiency or lack of application on the job.

22. Threatening, intimidating, or abusive language or conduct to any supervisor or employee.

23. Contributing to unsanitary conditions.

24. Violations of company policy on fair treatment, equal opportunity, and nondiscrimination.

25. Harassment in any form.

PERSONNEL POLICIES AND PROCEDURES

DISTRIBUTION:		SUBJECT: EMPLOYEE MISCONDUCT	
EFFECTIVE DATE:	PAGE 1 OF 2	FILE UNDER SECTION	
REVISION DATE:	APPROVED BY:		

PURPOSE:

To give all employees guidance as to those actions that are considered as misconduct.

GENERAL:

The following is a noninclusive list of misconduct that may lead to immediate adverse personnel action (e.g., discipline, suspension, discharge) or placement on a release action.

1. Theft.

2. Intentional destruction or unauthorized use of company property.

3. Language or actions that are inappropriate to the workplace or that create a racially or sexually harassing environment.

4. Intentional falsification of company records, such as time records, employment applications, medical records, expense reports, etc.

5. Threatening, assaulting, or abusing any employee, customer, supplier, or company visitor.

6. Failure to follow company policies or procedures.

7. Unauthorized use or possession of firearms or explosives on company premises during working hours.

8. Intoxication or excessive use of alcohol during working time or on company premises.

9. Use, sale, possession, or functioning under the influence of unlawful drugs, or other controlled substances on company premises or during working time.

10. Excessive absences or lateness as determined by the business needs of the operating unit.

11. Failure to adhere to the scheduled or approved work hours.

12. Sleeping during work time, neglecting duties, or disrupting the performance of other employees.

13. Gambling on company premises or during working time.

14. Insubordination, including refusal to follow work direction.

15. Violations of company safety regulations or the gross or intentional endangerment of the safety of self or coworkers.

16. Violations of company security regulations, including acts of espionage or other subversive activities.

17. Solicitations not related to the performance of the employee's job during working time. Such solicitations are not permitted. Exceptions are company-sponsored drives such as United Way, blood drive, etc.

DISTRIBUTION:		SUBJECT: EMPLOYEE MISCONDUCT	
EFFECTIVE DATE:	PAGE 2 OF 2	FILE UNDER SECTION	
REVISION DATE:	APPROVED BY:		

18. Distributing literature, pamphlets, photographs, or other printed matter other than work-related information necessary to proper job performance.

19. Failure to deal ethically and honestly with other employees, suppliers, or company visitors.

20. Failure to protect company technology, product information, manufacturing process, and business and planning data.

21. Engaging in outside business activities that conflict with company interests or interfere with proper performance of job duties.

22. Giving or receiving compensation, gifts, or other benefits contrary to the company's policy on business ethics.

PERSONNEL POLICIES AND PROCEDURES

DISTRIBUTION:		SUBJECT: DISCHARGES	
EFFECTIVE DATE:	PAGE 1 OF 2	FILE UNDER SECTION	
REVISION DATE:	APPROVED BY:		

POLICY STATEMENT:

It is our policy to make every effort to avoid unwarranted discharges. However, it is necessary to enforce our company rules fairly and consistently. Violations of company rules as set forth shall result in one or more of the following disciplinary actions according to the frequency, seriousness, and circumstances of the offense.

A. Verbal Warning

   (1) The foreman will review the facts of the case in private with the employee involved.

   (2) The employee will be told what action will be taken if another violation occurs.

   (3) The foreman should keep a record of the verbal warning given by having a copy placed in the employee's personnel file.

B. Written Warning

   (1) The foreman will review the facts of the case with the employee involved in the presence of the general supervisor or department manager and, if deemed advisable, a representative from the Industrial Relations Department.

   (2) The employee will be told what action will be considered if another violation occurs.

   (3) A record of the meeting, stating the facts that were reviewed with the employee and the action taken or to be taken, will be prepared by the general supervisor. The general supervisor will then review the warning memo with the employee, give a copy to the employee, and send copies to the Personnel Records Section and the Industrial Relations Department Manager.

      a. If no other violations of any regulations are committed for a period of two years, the warning letter will be removed from the employee's folder upon his/her request and the recommendation of the employee's immediate supervisor and the Industrial Relations Manager.

   (4) If employees disagree with the record or want to appeal the decision, they may do so through the Grievance Procedure as provided in Standard Policy and Procedure M-4.

C. Disciplinary Layoff (Suspension from work without pay)

   (1) When immediate action is necessary, or when the facts are not all available, the foreman may have an employee register his or her time card and leave the plant until a final decision is reached.

   (2) After all the facts are accumulated, the case will be reviewed by the foreman, the department manager, and a representative from the Industrial Relations Department as quickly as possible.

   (3) The employee will be called in for a meeting with the foreman, department manager, and an Industrial Relations representative, at which time he or she will be given a chance to state his or her side of the case.

      a. If an employee wishes, he or she may bring one fellow employee of choice to this meeting.

   (4) After the meeting, the foreman, department manager, and Industrial Relations representative will reach a decision and advise the employee immediately.

      a. The decision may be that the time between the incident and the meeting was sufficient layoff, or additional days of layoff may be imposed as a penalty.

      b. Should the investigation absolve the employee of blame for the suspension, the foreman, department manager, and Industrial Relations representative may decide to pay the employee for the time lost in this layoff.

   (5) A written record shall be made by the Industrial Relations Department representative of all the facts and the decision reached.

PERSONNEL POLICIES AND PROCEDURES

DISTRIBUTION:		SUBJECT: DISCHARGES	
EFFECTIVE DATE:	PAGE 2 OF 2	FILE UNDER SECTION	
REVISION DATE:	APPROVED BY:		

D. Discharge

    (1) If, as a result of the meeting prescribed in paragraph C.3, a discharge is indicated, the employee shall be separated from the company.

        a. A written record shall be made by the Industrial Relations Department representative of all the facts and the decision reached.

    (2) The discharge of an employee for repeated minor violations must be preceded by former verbal or written warnings.

    (3) In the event of a discharge, the Division Manager will be advised of the action.

PERSONNEL POLICIES AND PROCEDURES

DISTRIBUTION:		SUBJECT: DISCHARGES	
EFFECTIVE DATE:	PAGE 1 OF 2	FILE UNDER SECTION	
REVISION DATE:	APPROVED BY:		

POLICY STATEMENT:

In an effort to head off unwarranted discharges, yet to enforce rules fairly and consistently, all supervisory personnel should review the following procedure before terminating any employee.

PROCEDURE:

Human Resources

1. Prepares Separation Worksheet.

2. Secures a current performance review.

3. Prepares all copies of the Separation from Staff form.

4. Routes one copy of the Separation from Staff form, as indicated, for ultimate return.

5. Distributes copies of the Separation from Staff form to General Accounting and Auditing for processing and retention.

6. Obtains from Payroll Section checks for net salary due, separation allowance, overtime, supper money, and savings bond refunds where applicable.

7. Arranges and conducts an exit interview at a time mutually convenient for the employee's supervisor and the Human Resources officer. Uses Exit Interview checklist.

8. Secures acknowledgment of precise reason for dismissal or resignation.

9. Explains reference policies.

10. Discusses unemployment and/or workers' compensation laws where applicable.

11. Discusses effects of termination on life, disability, and hospitalization insurance.

12. COBRA eligibility letter to employee's home address (unless gross misconduct).

13. Reviews Separation Worksheet to ensure full completion.

14. Enters the termination date in the Personnel Tickler file.

15. Deletes employee's name from Personnel Roster and reduces actual staff totals of affected units by one.

16. Enters date of separation and summary of reasons for separation on progress record in Personnel folder.

17. Enters in Personnel Journal employee's name, summary of reasons for separation, and termination date and reduces the cumulative staff total to reflect change.

369

PERSONNEL POLICIES AND PROCEDURES

DISTRIBUTION:		SUBJECT: DISCHARGES	
EFFECTIVE DATE:	PAGE 2 OF 2	FILE UNDER SECTION	
REVISION DATE:	APPROVED BY:		

18. Cancels (type of insurance), notifies (name of insurance carrier) on date of termination, and initials Separation Worksheet in appropriate space.

19. Marks "resigned" or "terminated" across the face of insurance cards together with effective date and inserts in Personnel folder.

20. Transfers personnel records:
    a. Folders
        i. To inactive file for three years, then
        ii. To Records Retention Center indefinitely. (A Former Employee Card is substituted.)
    b. Statistical Cards
        i. To separation file, coded for separation reason.
    c. Time sheet or cards
        i. File for three years.

PERSONNEL POLICIES AND PROCEDURES

DISTRIBUTION:		SUBJECT: QUITS—DISCHARGES	
EFFECTIVE DATE:	PAGE 1 OF 1	FILE UNDER SECTION	
REVISION DATE:	APPROVED BY:		

POLICY STATEMENT:

Employees who quit, are discharged, or fail to respond to a recall will be regarded as permanently separated from employment with the company, with no seniority, recall, or other rights. Should such separated employees be rehired, they will be re-employed as new employees.

SEPARATION:

Separation policies are designed to achieve fairness and equity for all who leave our employ. These include adequate warning, full and mutual understanding, proper severance pay, and reasonable opportunity to establish another connection.

Separations are either voluntary or involuntary. "Mutual agreement" separations must be classified as either voluntary or involuntary so that they may be processed in accordance with the separation policies and procedures that follow.

Voluntary separations are initiated at the request of the employee. Involuntary separations are for:

A. Discipline (unsatisfactory services, etc.)

B. Poor health (poor attendance record)

A separation allowance may be granted in accordance with the following schedule.

Reason	*No. of weeks salary for each year of service*
Voluntary	None
Involuntary	
—Discipline	
—Unsatisfactory services	1
—Dishonesty	None
—Health	1
—Military	
6 months' duty	1 only
18 months or more	4 only
—Death	1 (payable to spouse)

Any separation allowance granted to a full-time employee (as distinct from temporary, or part-time) who leaves involuntarily shall not be less than two weeks' salary, or two weeks' continued employment in lieu of separation allowance. Exception: six months' military service.

A vacation allowance shall be granted to all full-time employees who leave for any cause whatsoever. In the case of retirement with a pension, the employee should be urged to take a vacation prior to retirement, because no allowance is granted.

PERSONNEL POLICIES AND PROCEDURES

DISTRIBUTION:		SUBJECT: HOW TO AVOID FIRING MISTAKES	
EFFECTIVE DATE:	PAGE 1 OF 1	FILE UNDER SECTION	
REVISION DATE:	APPROVED BY:		

When an employee continues to disregard rules and disciplinary action, where an offense is repeated, or when misconduct is serious enough for discharge on the first offense, decisive action must be taken.

To help guide you through this area, we suggest you stop and review very carefully the following checklist before any employee is ever terminated. Chronic rule violators who continue to menace efficient operations must be dealt with—sometimes severely. On the other hand, every employee represents an investment in time and money. Your employees are your company's most valuable assets. Ask yourself these questions before you fire an employee:

1. Has the company policy or rule been properly communicated to the employee?

2. Have I been objective and treated this employee the same as another would be treated for the same offense?

3. Have I accumulated all of the facts accurately?

4. If it is a repeated offense, has the employee been properly reprimanded in the past, and have written corrections been issued?

5. Is the employee guilty by his or her own actions or by association with another employee?

6. Am I taking action against the employee because he or she has "challenged my authority"?

7. Does the punishment fit the offense?

8. Was the employee's guilt supported by direct objective evidence, as opposed to just suspicion?

9. Has a top management official reviewed the facts and approved the discharge?

10. Is the employee involved in "protected concerted activity," complaining about a job-related problem involving wages, hours, or conditions of employment?

Remember, this recommended checklist is not very helpful after a discharge. If there is any question about facts or reasons for discharge, suspend the employee instead of firing, while you investigate the facts supporting both sides.

When a discharge is found to be justified, proper documentation of the specific reasons for "separation of employment" is most important. As we know, charges for discrimination are very likely to occur immediately following a discharge. Unless you can provide adequate proof for the reasons behind the discharge, the NLRB, EEOC, or Wage-Hour Division might quickly find merit in a charge of discrimination and recommend that you reinstate the employee with back pay.

PERSONNEL POLICIES AND PROCEDURES

DISTRIBUTION:		SUBJECT: TERMINATION OF EMPLOYMENT	
EFFECTIVE DATE:	PAGE 1 OF 6	FILE UNDER SECTION	
REVISION DATE:	APPROVED BY:		

A. APPLICABLE

This procedure is intended to be a guideline for management in addressing voluntary and involuntary termination of employment for all (Company Name) employees not covered by a collective bargaining agreement.

All employment is on an "at will" basis. Nothing contained herein shall be construed to constitute a contract of employment, either expressed or implied, nor shall anything contained herein be construed to modify the employment-at-will relationship that exists between (Company Name) and its employees.

B. DEFINITIONS

1. Involuntary terminations are those initiated by the company and include:

   a. Layoff resulting from force reduction.

   b. Separation due to failure to return from approved leave of absence.

   c. Separation due to exhaustion of approved leave of absence entitlement.

   d. Release for inability to perform duties or to meet prescribed standards on the job, after reasonable efforts have been made to assist the employee in meeting the standards expected by (Company Name).

   e. Discharge for conduct not in the best interest of the company.

2. Voluntary and other terminations are those not initiated by the company and include:

   a. Resignation.

   b. Retirement.

   c. Death.

   d. Unexcused absences that are unreported for a period of two or more consecutive scheduled workdays without sufficient justification.

C. PROCEDURE—INVOLUNTARY TERMINATIONS

1. The following requirements apply to all involuntary terminations:

   a. Termination of all employees aged 40 or more or any employee with a known disability must have prior approval of the staff vice president of industrial relations and the cognizant divisional human resources director who reports to a member of the staff of either the president/COO or chairperson/CEO as appropriate.

   b. Termination of employees at ten years of service or exceeding either the salary or the service levels shown below must be reviewed and approved by the divisional human resources director and the staff vice president of industrial relations as well as having prior approval as indicated:

Annual Salary	Years of Service	Prior Approval
$40,000	15	Cognizant divisional human resources director and the line executive reporting to a member of the staff of either the president/COO or chairperson/CEO as appropriate.
$60,000	20	Cognizant divisional human resources director and the member of the staff of either the president/COO or chairperson/CEO as appropriate.
$80,000	25	Senior vice president of human resources and the member of the staff of either the president/COO or chairperson/CEO as appropriate.

PERSONNEL POLICIES AND PROCEDURES

DISTRIBUTION:		SUBJECT: TERMINATION OF EMPLOYMENT	
EFFECTIVE DATE:	PAGE 2 OF 6	FILE UNDER SECTION	
REVISION DATE:	APPROVED BY:		

2. Layoff

    a. Layoffs are initiated when one or more jobs are eliminated because of various situations such as declining volume of business, reduced profitability, or discontinued functions, operations, or activities.

    b. The cognizant human resources manager or a designee at each location is responsible for processing layoffs. The human resources department normally requires two weeks' advance notice to provide for appropriate processing.

    c. Decisions regarding layoff of any salaried employee must be reviewed and approved by two levels of line management and the cognizant human resources director before implementation. Any proposed layoff of a protected class employee, with the exception of nonexempt production and maintenance employees, must also be reviewed with the industrial relations department prior to implementation. All employees to be laid off must be personally notified by their immediate line manager of the layoff action. An exit interview will be conducted by the human resources department, or by line management in the absence of an on-site human resources department.

    d. It is the responsibility of each manager to be affected by a layoff to determine the business objectives and the staffing needs of the affected organization.

        (1) A determination should be made to identify those job functions that have the least impact on the organization's ability to meet its business objectives.

        (2) Then an evaluation should be conducted to determine job requirements necessary to perform the remaining work.

        (3) An analysis of all individuals in the department should be done to determine which have the qualifications to perform the remaining work and their job performance.

            (a) Except where a reasonable business need requires retention of less senior individuals possessing unique qualifications, seniority will be the primary factor in determining the layoff order among nonexempt individuals qualified to perform the remaining work, provided that they do not have a current history of poor performance. Individuals not qualified to perform the remaining work and individuals with a current history of poor performance may be released regardless of their seniority order, provided that appropriate documentation exists.

            (b) Among exempt personnel, layoff selections will be based upon qualifications to perform the remaining work and job performance. Length of service will be considered in those cases where the individuals selected for layoff otherwise possess equivalent qualifications. Individuals lacking the qualifications to perform the remaining work will be laid off first. Individuals qualified to do the remaining work but with an ongoing record of poor performance will be laid off next. Additional layoff selections, if necessary, will be based upon the qualifications, job performance, and length of service of the remaining employees.

    e. Placement service may be provided by the cognizant human resources manager. This may include: (1) assistance in the preparation and duplication of resumes; (2) guidance regarding the use of professional placement agencies; (3) information on other job search techniques and interviewing skills; and (4) assistance in registering for unemployment compensation.

    f. Notification of impending layoff may be made to the state employment services, to professional placement agencies, and to other employers in the vicinity. Sufficient detail will be provided to these contacts so that placement may be expedited.

    g. Employees terminated under this section are eligible for two weeks' notice or pay in lieu of notice; the effective date of termination is the last day of the approved notice period. They are also eligible for the provisions of the income assistance policy and for payment for unused vacation earned in the prior fiscal year as well as for prorated vacation accrued in the current fiscal year.

PERSONNEL POLICIES AND PROCEDURES

DISTRIBUTION:		SUBJECT: TERMINATION OF EMPLOYMENT	
EFFECTIVE DATE:	PAGE 3 OF 6	FILE UNDER SECTION	
REVISION DATE:	APPROVED BY:		

h. Employees laid off under this section, with the exception of those laid off for documented poor performance, will be actively considered for re-employment if they had one year of service prior to layoff. As openings occur, for a period of one year from the time the employee was laid off, in the same job classification, salary grade, and geographic location from which an employee was laid off, individuals qualified for the specific openings in their job classification will be contacted regarding their interest in interviewing for them.

i. Employees interested in being considered for employment in other job classifications, grades, or geographic locations within the company must file a new application form with the appropriate human resources department indicating such interest.

j. A written statement notifying the employee of the facts in paragraphs (h) and (i) must be provided at the time of his/her layoff.

3. Release

Employees who fail to adequately perform their job duties or to meet prescribed standards on the job after formal corrective efforts have been made to assist them in improving their performance by meeting the standards prescribed by the company are released. Inadequate performance includes, but is not limited to, (a) excessive tardiness, (b) excessive absenteeism, (c) lack of application to the job, (d) lack of qualifications for the job, and (e) adverse conduct toward the company, one's supervisor, fellow employees, work assignments, and/or established policies and procedures.

a. When a performance problem has developed, and informal counseling efforts to assist the employee have failed, the following corrective personnel action should be taken by the appropriate line manager to initiate an employee release action plan.

(1) Contact the human resources manager/or designee and establish a plan of action. The human resources manager and the line manager shall ensure that adverse evaluation of the employee is justified and that the recommended corrective actions are realistic and, if completed, will lead to adequate performance.

(2) The employee's supervisor will meet with the employee and provide the employee with written documentation specifically indicating the deficiencies, the actions required for performance improvement, and the time limitations for required improvement.

(3) Individual action plans should allow time for specific improvements to take place and should provide for supervisory counseling/feedback on progress, or lack of such, at established intervals. Written documentation must be provided to both the employee and the human resources manager, summarizing each counseling session. The employee should acknowledge receipt of this documentation.

(4) Salary increases for an employee on a release action plan are to be delayed until the performance goals are met.

(5) In the event that the unsatisfactory performance continues and termination appears to be in order, the entire matter will be reviewed by the human resources manager and the appropriate next-level line manager and additional approvals. If all are satisfied that the employee has been given sufficient guidance and time to improve, release will be approved.

(6) The approval process set out in this procedure should be started by the appropriate line manager working with his/her human resources representative, on a schedule that will coincide with the timing set out in the performance improvement.

(7) A released employee is eligible for payment of unused vacation earned in the prior fiscal year and two weeks' notice or pay in lieu of notice. He/she is not eligible for rehire without first checking with the employee's human resources department.

PERSONNEL POLICIES AND PROCEDURES

DISTRIBUTION:		SUBJECT: TERMINATION OF EMPLOYMENT	
EFFECTIVE DATE:	PAGE 4 OF 6	FILE UNDER SECTION	
REVISION DATE:	APPROVED BY:		

4. Discipline/Discharge

Employees who are believed to have been guilty of misconduct are liable for immediate adverse personnel actions. These actions may range from written reprimand, delayed salary action, or reduction in grade and/or salary to discharge for serious misconduct. The term misconduct is defined as those incidents that are the result of acts of intentional wrongdoing, failure to act, or negligent acts that are clearly contrary to the safe and efficient business purpose of the operation. Also included are those incidents that are clearly contrary to company policy or procedure, or federal, state, or local laws or regulations.

a. Compliance with policies and procedures is the responsibility of each employee.

b. Adverse personnel actions for infractions of a serious nature not involving immediate discharge will be reviewed and approved by the immediate supervisor, the next-level line manager, and the appropriate human resources manager prior to imposition. The affected employee will be given the opportunity to state his/her position prior to a final determination by the reviewing managers.

c. In order to discharge an employee, the interested supervisor, the human resources manager, and the appropriate line manager must each be given an opportunity to state his or her position. The content of this meeting must be documented in a written report, which is placed in the personnel file.

d. When it is necessary to take immediate action on a discharge and not all of the aforementioned individuals are readily available, the supervisor shall suspend the employee without pay and instruct the employee to leave the premises. The actions outlined above shall be taken within ten working days.

e. Suspension without pay is appropriate when the situation is serious in nature, when it is clear that allowing the employee to remain on company premises would result in severe disruption of business, or when the situation is sensitive or potentially explosive. Suspension is also appropriate when more time is needed to investigate the situation.

f. An employee who refuses to leave the company premises should be advised by the manager/supervisor that: (1) the employee is temporarily suspended, (2) the employee is trespassing on company property, and (3) security and local police authorities will be contacted, if necessary.

 (1) If the employee still refuses to leave company premises, the manager/supervisor should contact the human resources department and the security authorities to arrange for notification of local police authorities. The manager/supervisor should then document the details of the employee's misconduct and the action items taken.

g. If, after the actions outlined above are taken, it is determined that a suspension is unsubstantiated, the employee shall be reinstated without any loss of pay or notation in his or her record. When discharge is in order, the employee is terminated immediately, or, in the case of suspension, as of the date of suspension.

h. Discharged employees are eligible for payment of unused vacation earned in the prior fiscal year. They are not eligible for income assistance, notice of termination, pay in lieu of notice, or prorated vacation. A discharged employee is not eligible for rehire.

D. PROCEDURE—VOLUNTARY TERMINATIONS

1. Resignations

a. The company requests at least two weeks' notice of intended resignation. Notice in excess of thirty days must be approved by the human resources manager. The effective date of termination is the last day of the approved notice period.

b. Employees who fail to report to work for a period of two consecutive scheduled workdays will be considered

PERSONNEL POLICIES AND PROCEDURES

DISTRIBUTION:		SUBJECT: TERMINATION OF EMPLOYMENT	
EFFECTIVE DATE:	PAGE 5 OF 6	FILE UNDER SECTION	
REVISION DATE:	APPROVED BY:		

as voluntarily terminating their employment unless such absence is excused by their immediate supervisor. Unusual circumstances preventing the employee from obtaining permission or presenting proper notice should be considered by the supervisor requested to reconsider the employee's resignation status.

   c. Employees who accept other unauthorized full-time employment while on an approved leave of absence, or who are presumed to have abandoned their positions without notice, are terminated and are considered to have resigned. Prior to the termination of employees who are presumed to have resigned, a registered letter, return receipt requested, or a telegram shall be sent to their last known address informing them of the company's intent to terminate their employment unless acceptable explanation can be given within twenty-four hours, justifying their continued absence from work.

   d. An employee who resigns is eligible for payment of unused vacation entitlement earned in the prior fiscal year, and for vacation accrued during the current fiscal year.

   e. Employees who fail to return from an approved leave of absence, in accordance with the applicable excused absence procedure, are considered to have resigned.

   f. Employees who fail to provide medical documentation necessary to support a medical leave are considered to have resigned.

2. Retirement between ages 55 and 70 and retirement at age 70 or older—Employees are eligible to retire after reaching age 55 if they have at least ten years of credited service, or after attaining age 60 (if hired prior to 1/1/79) or after attaining age 65 (if hired on or after 1/1/79) regardless of length of service.

The effective date of termination is the last day of actual work. Any remaining unused and accrued vacation balance will be paid to the employee in a lump sum.

The effective date of retirement (unless a deferred settlement is elected) will be the first of the next month following the month in which the employee last worked.

Income assistance and pay in lieu of notice are not applicable at retirement, unless the employee is laid off and eligible.

3. Death—If an employee dies, payment is made to the estate in accordance with statutory requirements for unused vacation earned in the prior fiscal year as well as for prorated vacation accrued in the current fiscal year and salary due at the time of death. Salary for the remainder of the pay period during which death occurred is paid to a surviving spouse only.

E. INFORMATION PROCESSING

In all cases of employee termination, specific information must be supplied to the Human Resources Department. The individual's final time card(s) must be forwarded as soon as possible to the Human Resources Department.

F. TERMINATION CHECKOUT

The cognizant supervisor will assure that the terminating employee has been properly checked out prior to departure. The purpose of the checkout is to make certain that credit cards and other company property have been returned, accounts have been settled, and all termination documents have been executed. The cognizant Human Resources Manager provides guidance with respect to these items. A termination checklist is used at plant locations for this purpose. The list is reviewed by the Human Resources Department at the time of exit interview.

G. EXIT INTERVIEW

An exit interview is conducted by the Human Resources Department for all terminating salaried employees, unless unusual circumstances preclude doing so. During the interview, a confidential information and invention agreement

PERSONNEL POLICIES AND PROCEDURES

DISTRIBUTION:		SUBJECT: TERMINATION OF EMPLOYMENT	
EFFECTIVE DATE:	PAGE 6 OF 6	FILE UNDER SECTION	
REVISION DATE:	APPROVED BY:		

is presented to the employee for signature and placed in the employee's personnel file. If the employee refuses to sign the form, a copy of the form is sent to the employee's home, requesting that it be completed and returned. A notation of the action taken is added to the personnel file.

H. REINSTATEMENT

Laid-off employees and terminated employees who return to the active payroll within two years and employees returning from an approved leave of absence within the time limits and other conditions relating to the approved leave may have their service reinstated.

PERSONNEL POLICIES AND PROCEDURES

DISTRIBUTION:		SUBJECT: RESIGNATIONS	
EFFECTIVE DATE:	PAGE 1 OF 1	FILE UNDER SECTION	
REVISION DATE:	APPROVED BY:		

POLICY STATEMENT:

Resignation is a voluntary decision by an employee to terminate his/her employment with the company.

PROCEDURE:

Should an employee resign employment with the company, he/she should give a minimum notice of two weeks—ten working days—preferably in writing. This advance notification allows supervisors time to adjust work schedules and secure a replacement. The degree of advance notice given in a resignation is noted in an employee's personnel file. Should an employee fail to give advance notice as outlined above, he/she will forfeit any unused, accrued vacation days and will not be paid for them.

On the employee's last day, an Exit Interview will be conducted by the Coordinator of Human Resources, or by the employee's manager in distant satellite locations, using the form included in this section. The completed form, signed by the employee and the one conducting the interview, should be placed in the employee's personnel file. At the Exit Interview, company property in the possession of the employee should be retrieved, and information regarding the final paycheck should be discussed.

Managers should proceed with the following upon an employee's resignation:

1. Contact the Coordinator of Human Resources and/or the Payroll Department at the home office the same day they become aware of the resignation and/or termination; supply them with the employee's name, termination date, number of hours worked in that pay period if requested, etc.

2. Follow up the call by sending a completed Personnel Action Notice, a Separation of Employment form, and, if conducted, an Exit Interview form. A completed Exit Interview form is not required in the case of a dismissal.

PERSONNEL POLICIES AND PROCEDURES

DISTRIBUTION:		SUBJECT: EXIT INTERVIEWS	
EFFECTIVE DATE:	PAGE 1 OF 1	FILE UNDER SECTION	
REVISION DATE:	APPROVED BY:		

PURPOSE:

The purpose of this policy is to obtain feedback from terminating associates concerning working conditions, policies, supervision, and other matters related to their employment with the company.

The company will use information obtained from exit interviews to identify problem areas and consider changes for their improvement.

POLICY:

Except where circumstances make it impractical, an exit interview will be conducted with each terminated associate prior to the release of the final paycheck.

This interview will normally be conducted by a member of the Human Resources Section.

In addition to the information concerning the associate's opinion of the company, other matters to be covered include the return of company property and confirmation of mailing address.

Insofar as possible, comments made by associates during exit interviews will be kept confidential.

One copy of the exit interview should be retained in the associate's personnel file and the second copy should be kept in a file containing all completed exit interviews to be maintained by a member of the Human Resources Section.

Periodic reviews of exit interview forms should be conducted and summarized in order to identify recurring problems or complaints.

The plant Human Resources manager should prepare a semiannual report for the general manager of the facility and the Corporate Associates Relations Section that summarizes the results of the review of the exit interview forms.

PERSONNEL POLICIES AND PROCEDURES

DISTRIBUTION:		SUBJECT: DRESS CODE	
EFFECTIVE DATE:	PAGE 1 OF 1	FILE UNDER SECTION	
REVISION DATE:	APPROVED BY:		

PURPOSE:

(Name of Company) believes that a proper dress code is essential in a business where:

A. Certain types of clothing can be safety hazards to the person wearing them.

B. Certain types of clothing are unprofessional in our office or plant areas.

C. Developing customer respect and confidence is necessary for long-term growth and prosperity.

POLICY:

A. Associates may wear: company shirts, smocks, T-shirts, sweatshirts, hooded sweat jackets, company jackets, long pants, rubber-soled shoes. No softball, picnic, etc., shirts will be permitted.

B. Coupons are provided upon hire date, completion of orientation/evaluation period, and anniversary date to purchase company-authorized clothing. A list of authorized clothing is available on the company store order form.

C. To adjust for personal comfort, noncompany sweatshirts or long-sleeved shirts may be worn under a company shirt, smock, or jacket.

D. Long pants must be worn on the factory floor. Shorts, leggings, spandex-type clothing, or holes in pants will not be permitted.

E. Rubber-soled, nonscuffing shoes are required on the factory floor. No open-toed shoes or sandals are allowed.

PERSONNEL POLICIES AND PROCEDURES

DISTRIBUTION:		SUBJECT: PERSONAL APPEARANCE	
EFFECTIVE DATE:	PAGE 1 OF 1	FILE UNDER SECTION	
REVISION DATE:	APPROVED BY:		

POLICY STATEMENT:

Employees engaged in work that puts them in a position where they meet the public are expected to present a neat appearance to the customers. This means good personal grooming habits and the proper attire for their position with the Company.

PROCEDURE:

— Men must be cleanly shaven, with the following exception: A neatly trimmed mustache or beard is permitted.

— Hair must be clean and groomed.

— Blue jeans are not appropriate attire for an office setting.

— Tennis shoes or similar lightweight shoes should not be worn in manufacturing and service facilities and in areas where there is a potential risk that equipment or products may fall and drop on the feet.

— Women must wear dress slacks, skirts and blouses, suits, or a dress when working in the office; men must wear dress slacks, shirt, and tie when working in the office.

Those employees engaged in working around machinery with moving parts must have the cuffs of their shirts buttoned if wearing long-sleeve shirts and also have their shirts tucked in.

Care must be given not to be wearing anything that could be caught in moving machinery.

Managers and supervisors should monitor their employees' appearance to ensure appropriate, safe dress.

PERSONNEL POLICIES AND PROCEDURES

DISTRIBUTION:		SUBJECT: GARNISHMENTS	
EFFECTIVE DATE:	PAGE 1 OF 1	FILE UNDER SECTION	
REVISION DATE:	APPROVED BY:		

POLICY STATEMENT:

An excessive number of garnishments on the wages of an employee will result in disciplinary action.

A court-ordered legal claim against the wages of a company employee by a creditor for nonpayment of a debt and served by the constituted legal authority is called a garnishment, and it must be recognized and executed by the company.

When a garnishment is received by the company, the Employment Section will:

* Determine whether or not the employee has had previous garnishments of wages.

* Advise the employee that a garnishment has been served on the company.

* Notify the employee's supervisor or department manager.

If the garnishment is the first one received by an employee:

* The employee will be called into the Human Resources Administration Department, Employment Section, with the supervisor's or department manager's consent, and advised of the consequences of further garnishments by the Employment Supervisor and the company's legal advisor.

* Every reasonable effort to counsel the employee through referral to an agency will be made by Human Resources Administration in order to assist the employee in working out his or her financial difficulties.

If the garnishment is the second one received by an employee:

* A meeting will be arranged between the employee, his or her supervisor or department manager, the Employment Section supervisor, the Human Resources Administration manager, and the company's legal advisor.

* Depending on the circumstances, the employee will be given assistance, if possible, and a written warning that further garnishments of wages will result in disciplinary action.

Any exception to this provision must be recommended by the Human Resources Administration Department and approved by the Vice President and Division Manager.

PERSONNEL POLICIES AND PROCEDURES

DISTRIBUTION:		SUBJECT: COMPANY POSITION ON EMPLOYEES WORKING FOR OTHERS	
EFFECTIVE DATE:	PAGE 1 OF 2		FILE UNDER SECTION
REVISION DATE:	APPROVED BY:		

POLICY STATEMENT:

The company discourages employees from engaging in practices wherein they are:

A. Working for hire outside of the company, whether in their trade or not.

B. Working in their trade for another utility or municipality as an accommodation, whether as custom work on an overtime basis or not.

C. Working for themselves because of the financial return involved in a pursuit demanding much of their off-duty time and effort.

The company likewise discourages any tendency on the part of management or supervisory personnel to approve or otherwise condone such practices as are indicated above. The employees of the company should have brought to their attention that the company has a very real basis for concern whenever any one of the above situations is permitted to exist.

A. The company loses:
   (1) When employees put time and effort into jobs outside of the company and tire themselves to the extent that they cannot produce as efficiently and as safely as they could were their normal efforts made in behalf of the company.
   (2) If an employee should be hurt, the company then loses the services of an experienced person who must either be replaced or lost to the company indefinitely.
   (3) If an employee should be injured, the company stands a real loss by reason of the administrative detail and investigation that would be brought about by the accident.

B. Employees lose:
   (1) If they cannot perform up to par and jeopardize their advancement opportunities with the company.
   (2) By jeopardizing the protection they have through workers' compensation should they get hurt while working outside the company. They also make it possible for the company to very legitimately question any injury that they report while on their regular jobs, if the injury does not occur because of a specific accident or is not witnessed by fellow workers.
   (3) If they jeopardize the protection they have through the group health and accident insurance that normally covers the employees in all of their activities outside of the company. If an employee works for an employer other than the company, he/she must look to that employer for any protection that is to be his/hers while working for the other employer.

C. The employees' families lose:
   (1) If employees are hurt without adequate protection, the families could lose materially in the form of lost income.

PERSONNEL POLICIES AND PROCEDURES

DISTRIBUTION:		SUBJECT: COMPANY POSITION ON EMPLOYEES WORKING FOR OTHERS	
EFFECTIVE DATE:	PAGE 2 OF 2	FILE UNDER SECTION	
REVISION DATE:	APPROVED BY:		

(2) If an employee should be killed, which possibility does exist when an employee works for another without due regard for the safety aspects of the job, the family is deprived of a loved one and all that such means in the way of heartbreak and loss of income and security.

The employees of the company should also have brought to their attention that the company's concern as indicated above is based on more than just a possibility of some unfortunate occurrence. Injury, permanent disability, and death have all been the result of employees' working in their trade and outside their trade for hire for others than the Company.

SECTION 11

Complaint and Grievance Procedures

The following checklist can be used to help you determine the various policy items that should be incorporated in your policy manual. Sample policy statements covering many of the items in the checklist appear in this section. They can be used to guide your policy statements. Our Policy Manual Should Cover

Policy Manual Checklist

Our Policy Manual Should Cover

1. Defining the term *grievance*   Yes_____ No_____
   A. What is a grievance?   Yes_____ No_____
   B. What is not a grievance?   Yes_____ No_____

2. Steps to be followed in the grievance procedure   Yes_____ No_____
   A. Number of steps or levels in the procedure   Yes_____ No_____
   B. Defining the parties involved at each step of the procedure   Yes_____ No_____

3. If unionized, can an individual employee take a grievance to
   arbitration?   Yes_____ No_____

4. Will policy permit the union the right to participate in case it does
   not support?   Yes_____ No_____

5. Defining time intervals for each step of the procedure in which a
   decision is to be made and between each step of the procedure   Yes_____ No_____

6. Policy stating that a grievance will be considered settled if it is not
   taken to the next higher step within established time limits   Yes_____ No_____

7. Policy requiring grievances to be written out   Yes_____ No_____
   A. Recommended form and number of copies   Yes_____ No_____
   B. Type of information to be included in written grievance   Yes_____ No_____

8. If organized, policy statement defining union representatives who
   have the right to investigate and assist in the settlement of
   employee grievances at various steps of the procedure   Yes_____ No_____

9. Policy setting forth the establishment of a joint committee for settling
   grievances that cannot be settled at the first or second step of the
   procedure   Yes_____ No_____

386

A. Representation of members on committee   Yes_____ No_____
B. Method of making a decision as to settlement   Yes_____ No_____
C. Requirements for frequency and notification of committee
    meetings to discuss grievances   Yes_____ No_____

10. Policy statement on establishing grievance sessions during workday
    or after working hours   Yes_____ No_____

11. Policy statement on how employees are to be paid for time spent in
    processing grievances   Yes_____ No_____
    A. Employer to make payment and on what computation procedure   Yes_____ No_____
    B. Union to make payment and on what computation procedure   Yes_____ No_____

12. Payment for time spent in processing grievances to apply under
    which situations?   Yes_____ No_____
    A. Grievance sessions during working hours   Yes_____ No_____
    B. Grievance sessions after working hours   Yes_____ No_____
    C. Grievance sessions at specific steps of the grievance procedure Yes_____ No_____
    D. Grievance session called only by the management   Yes_____ No_____

13. If organized, policy statement designed to prevent union
    representatives from abusing time spent on employee grievances   Yes_____ No_____
    A. Excessive time spent on processing grievances   Yes_____ No_____
    B. Interfering with the work of other employees and production
        activity   Yes_____ No_____
    C. Limitation on the number of employee union representatives
        eligible to participate on any one grievance   Yes_____ No_____

14. Policy statement requiring employee union representatives to obtain
    prior approval from supervisor before leaving their work station or
    department   Yes_____ No_____

15. Policy statement requiring employee union representatives to obtain
    prior approval of supervisor in charge of department where
    representatives wish to investigate the grievance   Yes_____ No_____

16. If arbitration is final step of grievance procedure, policy statement to
    define how many arbitrators involved at final steps   Yes_____ No_____
    A. Individual arbitrator or panel or arbitrators   Yes_____ No_____

17. Policy statement defining how arbitrators are to be selected   Yes_____ No_____

18. Policy statement describing arbitrator's decision as final and binding
    on both parties   Yes_____ No_____

19. Policy on who shall pay arbitrator's fee   Yes_____ No_____

20. Policy to encourage constructive suggestions and reward those
    suggestions that are accepted   Yes_____ No_____

Discontented employees are easy marks for union organizers. An unsatisfactory method of handling employee complaints and grievances is second only to pay inequities as the thing most likely to convince employees that a union is the solution to their problems.

A formal grievance procedure is an effective way for an employer to keep workers content in their jobs.

A formal method for hearing and resolving employee complaints offers protection against union incursions. Only the employer who fails to recognize the signs of unionization believes that such a procedure is unnecessary or a waste of time. Few employers are so imbued with tact and regard for workers' reactions that they can deal with employees' grievances without the benefit of a formalized grievance procedure.

Furthermore, the grievance procedure provides a safety valve. Good employee relations are based on employees' belief that their employer gives them a fair deal—not only in terms of pay, hours, and benefits, but also through reasonable work rules, consistent discipline, unbiased supervision, and appropriate treatment on the job. As a wise executive, you strive to establish policies and practices that emphasize the employer's fairness. But the managers and supervisors who administer policy to the rank and file can't always be perfectly impartial. Errors in judgment, misunderstandings, and other human shortcomings are bound to enter the picture sometimes. The result is real or imagined injustices from your employees' point of view.

And remember, it doesn't matter whether an employee actually suffers an injustice or only thinks he or she has. Goodwill is damaged either way unless the employee has a chance to air the complaint and seek relief from higher management. A formal grievance procedure guarantees your employees a fair shake by providing a channel for appeal that goes all the way to the top.

The goal of a grievance procedure is not to eliminate grievances, but to provide for a prompt, friendly, and mutually satisfactory settlement of differences between management and employees. If your grievance system meets these criteria, you can be sure that it will repay your investment of effort many times over.

Elaborate Procedure Not Needed

It is not necessary to create an elaborate grievance- or complaint-handling procedure. But the procedure should be in writing and should be communicated as a benefit to supervisors and employees. Use your handbook or bulletin boards to explain what it is, why it is beneficial, and how it works.

The number of steps in the formal grievance procedure is important. A good system provides for orderly appeal up through successive levels of management.

Step 1 involves informal discussion of the problem between the employee and his or her supervisor. If agreement is not reached, the grievance is reduced to writing and progresses to the next step.

The number of succeeding steps will depend on your organizational structure. Typically, there are two or three steps, with the president, owner, or senior administrative person making the final decision.

Be sure to set a time limit within which a grievance must be filed and target dates for action at each step. Otherwise, long-forgotten complaints may be revived to plague you or there may be undue delays in reaching a mutually satisfactory conclusion to the grievance.

The key to the effective adjustment of employee problems lies in the attitude of the supervisors as it reflects the attitude and philosophy of the employer. If a supervisor is willing to listen to an employee's complaint and take action when it is legitimate, grievances will not be too much of a problem.

Guidelines for Supervisors

1. An employee has the right to talk to his or her supervisor about a problem, real or imagined, and the supervisor is responsible for listening with interest and attention.
2. When an employee has a justified complaint, the supervisor should take immediate remedial action. If such action cannot be taken, an acceptable explanation should be given.
3. A supervisor should never promise action and not follow through. An employee who is left in a state of uncertainty is likely to be one whose grievance will grow and fester.

All grievance machinery, even the most elaborate, is based upon these simple maxims. They are a practical application of the Golden Rule.

No nonunion grievance procedure will work unless it has the wholehearted backing of top management. It must be clearly understood that the successful resolution of employee complaints is an integral part of each manager's job duties.

Train the Managers

The following points should be included when training managers to settle employee complaints and grievances effectively and to promote more harmonious employee-employer relationships:

1. To an employee, a grievance, whether real or imaginary, is a grievance and requires fair, open-minded, patient, and considerate treatment.
2. The employee's immediate supervisor is the first person to whom a grievance should be taken.
3. The grievance procedure allows an employee to appeal or take a grievance to a higher supervisory level if it is ignored, neglected, or unfairly handled, or if the request is refused by the immediate supervisor.
4. Every employee should know that he or she has the right to grieve and that your personnel procedures assure this right.
5. When employees have complaints or grievances, the supervisor should listen sincerely, get the employee's explanation or view of the facts, withhold immediate judgment or snap decisions, discuss the grievance in private, and take prompt action on the problem.
6. In dealing with an employee complaint or grievance, the supervisor should discuss, not argue; be friendly, not antagonistic or defensive; and avoid any implication or threat of retaliation because the employee has voiced a complaint or grievance.
7. Whether the grievance is justified or not, the employee should receive a timely decision and an explanation of the basis for the decision.
8. If someone is at fault or has made a mistake, it should be frankly admitted and action taken to make amends.
9. Don't pass the buck in accepting a grievance, in acting on a grievance, in explaining the decision, or in saying no when justified by proper review. If you lack the authority to handle the grievance, get the answer from someone who does have the authority.
10. Give a fair hearing; judge the employee's story objectively. If a past action of yours has been unintentionally unfair, admit it, and set the situation straight. You will gain the respect of the employees by doing so.

Maintain a file of grievances and complaints and document all final answers and solutions made in settlements. Review this file periodically and take action to remove or correct all possible areas that could jeopardize overall job satisfaction and high morale. Exhibit 11-1 shows very basic complaint procedure as it would be communicated to employees, and Exhibit 11-2 gives the complaint procedure as it would appear in the policy manual.

Committee Meetings

Many employers are finding that an Employees Committee helps them stay in touch with their employees' opinions and at the same time satisfies the employees' urge to have a voice in those company affairs that affect them. Other employers fear that an Employees Committee is a risky undertaking, not only because of its questionable legality but also because committee activity can suggest the idea of employee organization or provide a natural vehicle through which a union can infiltrate a facility.

There are obvious advantages in having an Employees Committee representing all employee classifications at your company. The main advantage is that you have established an excellent way to communicate with employees through their selected or chosen representatives. When problems in such areas as customer relationships, employee complaints or grievances, how the company can better meet the needs of the employees, or safety need to be dealt with they can be brainstormed and discussed with such a Committee.

An Employees Committee is an excellent sounding board for employee complaints and problems that need to be aired before they become so serious that the entire workforce is frustrated and does not know where to go or what they can do about their problem other than stage a walkout. Often these frustrations are vented by means of signing a union card.

Exhibit 11-1. Sample complaint procedure.

(A Policy Guideline)

OUR COMPLAINT PROCEDURE—IF YOU HAVE A PROBLEM

Your complaints or problems are of concern to us. It will always be our policy to let an employee tell his or her side of the story and to give full consideration to the problem or complaint. If you follow these steps, no one will criticize or penalize you in any way. Remember, the only way we can help you answer your questions or solve your problem is for you to tell us about them.

1. If you have a complaint to make or if you feel that any action by your employer or supervisor is unjust, go to your immediate supervisor about it. That person knows more about you and your job than any member of management, and is in the best position to handle your complaint properly and quickly. Be sure to talk with your supervisor within two (2) consecutive workdays. If the problem or complaint you have is with your supervisor, you may omit Step 1 and go directly to Step 2.

2. If you have not received a satisfactory answer or settlement from your immediate supervisor, you will be allowed five (5) days to refer your problem in writing to your department manager. You may obtain assistance from the Personnel Office in preparing the written presentation of your problem, and you may then present your problem to the department manager, who will give you an answer within five (5) days of your presentation.

3. If you are not satisfied with the recommendation provided by your department manager, you will have an additional five (5) days to request an appointment for a personal interview with the _____ , who will discuss the problem with you and review all aspects of it thoroughly. The _____ will respond within five (5) days of the personal interview. Any decision rendered by the _____ must be regarded as final and binding.

Please remember that the only purpose of our complaint procedure is to give us an opportunity to clear up any problems or complaints of any kind. In order for this complaint procedure to work, you must want it to work and use it. It is for your benefit. When things go wrong, we would like to have a chance to correct them if we can.

Needless to say, many employers have set up and encouraged Employees Committees to help reduce the need for an outside labor union to represent employees. Of course, a bona fide independent union can be recognized by an employer provided it operates as an independent union within the guidelines and enforcement policy of the National Labor Relations Board, and not as one dominated by an employer that eventually becomes no more than a "company union." Company unions are not permitted under the present enforcement policy of the NLRB.

[Under Section 8(a)(2) of the National Labor Relations Act, it is an unfair labor practice for an employer "to dominate or interfere with the formation or administration of any labor organization or contribute financial or other support to it." The prohibition protects from employer influence only those employee groups that are, in fact, labor organizations, which is defined to mean "any organization of any kind, or any agency or employee representation committee or plan, in which employees participate and which exists for the purpose, in whole or in part, of dealing with employers concerning grievances, labor disputes, wages, and rates of pay." When it is determined that a committee is a labor organization, the next element is usually easy to find, i.e., that the committee is employer-dominated or employer-supported.]

The following are suggested guidelines for establishing an Employees Committee:

1. Meetings of the committee should be held off the premises outside of working hours, if at all possible. Perhaps a dinner meeting once a month would be in order.
2. Do not pay for time spent at these meetings.
3. Employees should select their own representatives.
4. It would be desirable to exclude from the Employees Committee any department head or supervisor in management.

Exhibit 11-2. Policy manual description of complaint procedure

Policy Statement

The policy of the grievance setup is explained to supervisors in the following statement, which they, in turn, relay to employees.

It is our purpose to provide an effective and acceptable means for employees to bring problems and complaints concerning their well-being at work to the attention of management. Therefore, a formal grievance procedure has been established for the benefit and use of employees.

A grievance is defined as "any condition of employment that the employee thinks or feels is unjust or inequitable." Under the plan, hourly employees and nonexempt salaried employees may submit grievances in the following sequence:

Step One

1. To assure prompt attention, grievances should be submitted within five days of the event prompting the grievance.
2. Grievances are presented orally to the employee's immediate supervisor.
3. The employee submits the grievance personally, but may elect a fellow employee to appear with him/her.
4. The supervisor should make every effort to resolve the grievance at the initial step. The grievance shall be written out, whether resolved or not, so that there can be a permanent record, and signed by the supervisor and employee.

Step Two

1. If the grievance cannot be settled by the employee's immediate supervisor, the supervisor should, within two working days, indicate steps taken to resolve the problem.
2. The written grievance is then submitted directly to the department head, manager of employee relations, or someone in a comparable position.

Resolving the Grievance

1. The department head or manager of employee relations, or a designee, attempts to resolve the question and respond within three working days.
2. When the grievance cannot be resolved by the department head or manager of employee relations, the grievance is referred to the division director having administrative responsibility over the employee and supervisor or to the chief executive.

The aggrieved worker who presents or processes a grievance during scheduled working hours is paid for such time. Employees who feel they have been unjustly discharged can file a grievance within two working days after discharge, asking that the matter be reconsidered. See enclosure (Exhibit 11-3) for a sample grievance form.

Ferreting Out Grievances

Recognizing that employees may be too timid at first to register grievances, management follows up the supervisor's explanation of the plan by having the company manager review the procedure with employee groups of from twenty to thirty, stressing the company's sincere desire to have them make full use of the plan. The details of the plan are also well publicized on the bulletin board.

Exhibit 11-3 is a suggested outline of how an Employees Committee could be established.

Complaint and Grievance Procedure

Policy and procedure come very close together in this area, since the policy usually relies on the grievance procedure to develop its strength.

On the following pages, you will find policies covering:

Grievance Procedures
Suggestions and Complaints
Suggestion Program

Exhibit 11-3. Establishment of an employees committee.

SUBJECT: EMPLOYEE RELATIONS COMMITTEE

PURPOSE:

At the request of employees, it is the purpose of this committee to promote closer relationships between the employees and management and to give the employees a method of discussing with management how to continue to better serve the needs of customers and how to better meet the needs of all personnel of the company; keeping informed through effective two-way communications in these important areas; and continually improving the overall operations of the company.

COMPOSITION OF EMPLOYEE RELATIONS COMMITTEE:

1. The committee will be composed of one representative for approximately every fifty employees.
2. Employees who occupy positions in management or who are department heads will not be eligible to serve on the committee.
3. One employee representative will be elected from each of the following departments and shifts:
   (a) Department
   (b) Department
   (c) Department
   (d) First shift
   (e) Second shift

PROCEDURE FOR SELECTING COMMITTEE OF EMPLOYEES:

1. All employees eligible to serve on the committee will be eligible to vote in the selection of committee members.
2. Each employee eligible to vote may cast a vote for one employee within his/her job or shift as defined above.
3. Selection of committee members will be conducted between the hours of _____ and _____ on _____ day.
4. For the first year, _____ will serve as election officer. His/her duty will be to supervise the conduct of the voting. He/she will be supplied with a list of eligible voters in each category, with ample blanks to allow each eligible voter to cast his or her vote for the employee to represent him/her in the respective job classification or department.
5. The election official will determine the winner for each job classification as the employee in each classification having the greatest number of ballots cast. A majority of votes will be decisive. The officials will then declare and certify the selected committee members. In the event of a tie in any category, a special runoff election for that category will be held on the following Monday between the hours described above, and under the rules described above.
6. Each selected committee member will hold office for six months, which term shall terminate on December 31 or June 30 of each year, as the case may be. An elected representative may not be reelected for two successive terms. Prior to the expiration of the six months' term of office, the committee will hold an election so that new elected representatives will be able to take office at the expiration of the preceding term.

DUTIES AND FUNCTIONS OF THE SELECTED COMMITTEE:

1. Each member of the committee will represent the employees in his or her respective classification and department.
2. The committee of employees will meet at least once each month with a representative of management. The committee shall meet on the first _____ of each month at _____ P.M. unless such day is a legal holiday, in which case the committee will meet on the following Friday. The chairman of the committee may also request a meeting with management as circumstances may require at any time.
3. Meetings of the Employees' Committee and the company president will serve as a method for discussing companywide problems, including but not limited to employee problems, customer problems, and problems of management. The primary purpose of the meeting is to bring to management matters relating to the administration of employee benefit programs, sharing information on present and future personnel policies, employee problems, and safety, and to promote better understanding, communication, and good will between management and employees.
4. The committee, at its first meeting, will elect a chairperson from among its members, who will serve for a six months term. The chairperson may stand for reelection. The chairperson will be elected by a majority vote of the representatives in attendance at the meeting. The chairperson will preside at all meetings of the committee and serve as chief spokesperson for the committee.
5. Grievances: Grievances that arise between an employee and a supervisor will be resolved by the following procedure:

Exhibit 11-3. *(continued)*

First Step: An employee shall inform the supervisor of his/her department of the grievance as soon as practicable on the working day on which the event giving rise to the grievance occurs, and both the employee and the supervisor shall make every effort to resolve the problem that day.

Second Step: If the matter is not resolved to the satisfaction of either the employee or the supervisor on the day the grievance arises, the matter shall be referred to the group representative of such department, and he/she, together with the employee, the departmental supervisor, and the warehouse manager, shall attempt to resolve the matter. These persons shall meet no later than on the working day following the day on which the event giving rise to the grievance occurs.

Third Step: If the matter is not resolved by the above procedure to the satisfaction of either the employee or the supervisor, the matter shall then be referred to the Chairman of the Employee Relations Committee, who may request a meeting with the Chief Executive Officer of the company or his/her designated representative. At the requested meeting, which shall occur within five working days following the day on which the event giving rise to the grievance occurs, the employee and the supervisor shall present the grievance, which shall be resolved at this meeting, and the grievance procedure will be exhausted.

6. Conduct of Employee Relations Committee and Management: It is to be noted that all parties to the grievance procedure are encouraged to approach each situation with an open mind and to give each and every problem that may arise fair consideration. Every effort should be made by all parties involved in the dispute to make a settlement of the matter without becoming involved in lengthy debates, discussions, or meetings that would disrupt the operation of the company.

Grievance Format

On the following pages are suggested formats for the procedure outlined above, covering all the steps.

Employee

Step One
5 Days

Name of Employee _____   Date _____

Clock No. _____   Department _____

Complaint of Employee

Signature of Supervisor _____

Signature of Employee _____

Supervisor

Step Two
2 Days

Name of Employee _____   Date _____

Clock No. _____   Department _____

Problem and Steps Taken for Correction

Signature of Supervisor _____

Superintendent or Manager

Step Three
3 Days

Name of Employee _____   Date _____

Clock No. _____   Department _____

Recommendations of Manager or Superintendent

Signature of Manager or Superintendent _____

Findings of General Manager

Signature of General Manager _____

PERSONNEL POLICIES AND PROCEDURES

DISTRIBUTION:		SUBJECT: COMPLAINT AND GRIEVANCE PROCEDURE	
EFFECTIVE DATE:	PAGE 1 OF 2	FILE UNDER SECTION	
REVISION DATE:	APPROVED BY:		

POLICY STATEMENT:

When an employee thinks or feels that any condition affecting him/her is unjust, inequitable, or a hindrance to effective operation, or creates a problem, the employee should use the following procedure for the solution of such problem(s) without fear of recrimination. The same procedure may be followed by a group of employees.

Step 1

The employee should bring the situation to the attention of his/her shift foreman or immediate supervisor, explaining the nature of the problem and his/her suggested solution, if any. If it is a group problem, one or more of the group should talk to the foreman or immediate supervisor about the problem.

- The supervisor may give the employee or group his/her reply immediately or may postpone the answer to study the situation and/or obtain more information, but in any case, an answer must be given to the employee or group within three weekdays (Monday through Friday).

- If the reply the supervisor gives the employee does not clear up the situation, the employee may talk to the supervisor's superior or the Industrial Relations Manager.

If the answer the employee or group was given by the supervisor, the superior, or the Industrial Relations Manager did not clear up the situation for the employee(s), the employee(s) may follow the written procedure outlined in Step 2 below.

Step 2

The employee, or group, should write out the grievance on a Grievance Report form, copies of which are available throughout the plant.

The employee, or group, should give or mail one copy of the Grievance Report to the department manager, and one copy to the Industrial Relations Manager, and should keep the third copy.

When the Industrial Relations Manager receives a Grievance Report, he/she will:

- Advise the employee's department manager immediately and determine if Step 1 has been followed.

    If the provisions of Step 1 have not been fully complied with, the Industrial Relations manager will meet with the employee(s) and explain the basic necessity for following the Step 1 procedure. The Industrial Relations Manager will return the Grievance Report to the employee(s) for Step 1 procedure. The Industrial Relations Manager will also advise the department manager of the conversation, the action taken, and any comments relative to the situation.

Talk with the employee(s) to get any clarification of the problem.

Talk with the department manager and the supervisor to get any further clarification of the problem.

Schedule a meeting (within four weekdays, Monday through Friday) of the employee, the employee's immediate supervisor, the department manager or his designated representative, and the Industrial Relations Manager. If a group is involved, one or more representatives may be asked to attend the meeting.

- If the employee so desires, he/she may have a fellow employee attend the meeting with him/her to speak for him/her or on his/her behalf.

- If the department manager so desires, he/she may have one other member of departmental supervision also attend the meeting. He/she will act as chairperson of the meeting, record all proceedings of the meeting and the decision reached, and provide all concerned with copies of the record of the meeting.

DISTRIBUTION:		SUBJECT: COMPLAINT AND GRIEVANCE PROCEDURE	
EFFECTIVE DATE:	PAGE 2 OF 2	FILE UNDER SECTION	
REVISION DATE:	APPROVED BY:		

Step 3

If the meeting did not clear up the situation for the employee(s), the employee(s) may appeal the decision reached to the Division Manager.

  ◆ A request to appeal may be made verbally or in writing to the Industrial Relations Manager.

When the Industrial Relations Manager receives an appeal, he/she will:

  ◆ Advise all those who attended the meeting that an appeal has been made.
  ◆ Provide the Division Manager with a full record of the problem and proceedings to date; and
  ◆ Arrange for a meeting (within seven weekdays) of the employee or representatives, with copies to all who attended the original meeting.

The Division Manager shall render his judgment on the appeal in writing to the employee or representatives, with copies to all who attended the original meeting.

PERSONNEL POLICIES AND PROCEDURES

DISTRIBUTION:		SUBJECT: GRIEVANCE PROCEDURE	
EFFECTIVE DATE:	PAGE 1 OF 1	FILE UNDER SECTION	
REVISION DATE:	APPROVED BY:		

POLICY STATEMENT:

It is the policy of this company that all employees have the right to voice their complaints.

We recognize the meaningful value and importance of full discussion in resolving misunderstandings and preserving good relations between management and our employees. Accordingly, we believe that the following procedure will ensure that complaints receive full consideration.

Should a condition exist that an employee feels is unsatisfactory, it is important that he or she brings it to the attention of the appropriate person in the proper manner.

PROCEDURE:

Step 1: An employee with a complaint will initially approach his or her supervisor. The supervisor knows more about the employee and his/her job than any other member of management and is in the best position to resolve the problem satisfactorily. It is the supervisor's responsibility to ensure that any complaint brought before him/her receives prompt attention.

It is of the utmost importance that in all instances the supervisor notify the employee of the action to be taken to correct the situation. If the supervisor believes no action is warranted or possible, the employee should receive an explanation as to the reasoning behind such decision. The supervisor shall reply to the employee within three (3) working days.

Step 2: In the event that the employee feels that the problem remains unresolved, following discussions with the supervisor, the employee may submit the complaint in writing for reconsideration. A written complaint is to be submitted to the Branch Manager. Upon reviewing the complaint, the Branch Manager will render a decision in writing within three (3) days after receipt of the written complaint.

In certain cases, the Branch Manager and the supervisor may wish to meet personally with the employee to provide a fuller explanation of the action taken.

Normally, complaints will be resolved at this step of the grievance procedure.

Step 3: An employee who feels that his/her complaint has not received adequate attention in Step 2 may direct the complaint to the corporate Employee Relations Manager.

Such complaints are to be made in writing, on the complaint form, Step 3, within three (3) days of receiving the answer provided in Step 2. The corporate Employee Relations Manager will review the complaint with the Branch Manager and arrange a meeting with the employee within three (3) days of receiving the complaint. At this step the company President may be consulted for a final decision in the matter.

The "Open Door" policy, providing for a review by Human Resources management, is a safeguard against any possible inequitable treatment. All employees may therefore be assured that every effort will be made to resolve problems to their satisfaction. Under no circumstances will an employee be penalized for presenting his/her complaint to his/her supervisor or to members of management.

PERSONNEL POLICIES AND PROCEDURES

DISTRIBUTION:		SUBJECT: GRIEVANCE PROCEDURE	
EFFECTIVE DATE:	PAGE 1 OF 2	FILE UNDER SECTION	
REVISION DATE:	APPROVED BY:		

POLICY:

It is the sincere intent of the hospital to be fair and reasonable with all employees at all times. However, in the relationship of employee to employee or employee to employer, problems may develop. Generally, satisfactory solutions to any problems employees may encounter are not found by discussing these problems with fellow employees or other members of the staff. A problem or complaint cannot be handled fairly if employees do not let the proper people know of its existence.

If any employee has a question about interpretation or application of hospital policy, is in disagreement with a fellow worker or supervisor, or feels that he/she has been treated unfairly or that some problem has not been resolved to his/her satisfaction, he/she may use the following three-step procedure for solution of such problems without fear of recrimination. Failure to comply with any of the time limits listed below shall constitute a waiver of the grievance.

PURPOSE:

The purpose of the Grievance Procedure is to ensure fair and equitable treatment for all employees, eliminate dissatisfaction, and resolve problems so that constructive work-producing relationships can be maintained for the benefit of all.

PROCEDURE:

Step 1—The Immediate Supervisor

The employee will bring the situation to the attention of his/her immediate supervisor within ten (10) working days of the occurrence of the problem creating the grievance, explaining the nature of the problem, and the suggested solution if he/she has one.

After being confronted verbally with the grievance, the supervisor will investigate, and provide a solution or an explanation to the employee within five (5) working days.

In the event that the supervisor fails to respond to the grievance within five (5) working days, the employee will proceed to Step 2.

Step 2—The Department Head

If the answer or settlement the supervisor gives the employee does not clear the situation, the employee will be allowed five (5) working days to refer his/her problem in writing to the department head. The employee should obtain a Grievance Report from the Human Resources Department, where he/she may also obtain assistance in preparing the written presentation of his/her problem.

The department head will provide an answer to the employee within five (5) working days of his/her written presentation of the grievance.

In the event that the department head fails to respond to the grievance within five (5) working days, the employee will proceed to Step 3.

Step 3—The Administrator

If the employee is dissatisfied with the solution provided by the department head, he/she will have an additional five (5) working days to appeal his/her grievance to the Administrator.

When the Administrator receives the Grievance Report, he/she will determine if Steps 1 and 2 were followed. If Steps 1 and 2 have been followed, he/she will:

PERSONNEL POLICIES AND PROCEDURES

DISTRIBUTION:		SUBJECT: GRIEVANCE PROCEDURE	
EFFECTIVE DATE:	PAGE 2 OF 2	FILE UNDER SECTION	
REVISION DATE:	APPROVED BY:		

A. Talk with the employee to get further clarification of the problem.

B. Talk with the supervisor and department head to get further clarification of the problem.

C. If necessary, schedule a meeting between the employee, the department head, and administration. Both the employee and the department head may have additional representatives at this meeting. The Administrator will record all proceedings of the meeting and will provide all concerned with copies of the minutes of the meeting.

After careful consideration of all facts, but within five (5) working days, the Administrator will render a final decision in writing to the employee or his/her representative. Because the full responsibility for the operation of the hospital rests with the Administrator, any decision rendered in a problem situation by the Administrator must be regarded as final and binding.

PERSONNEL POLICIES AND PROCEDURES

DISTRIBUTION:		SUBJECT: PROBLEM-SOLVING PROCEDURE	
EFFECTIVE DATE:	PAGE 1 OF 2	FILE UNDER SECTION	
REVISION DATE:	APPROVED BY:		

PURPOSE:

The purpose of this policy is to provide associates with a procedure that will allow them to bring concerns and problems to the attention of management. If any associate is not satisfied with the answer he/she are given, he/she can use the following problem-solving procedure until his/her complaint has been satisfactorily addressed or he/she has exhausted this procedure.

POLICY:

It is the policy of this company that all associates have the right to voice their complaints.

We recognize the value and importance of full discussion in resolving misunderstandings and preserving good relations between management and associates. Accordingly, we believe that the following procedure will ensure that complaints receive full consideration.

Should a situation or work condition exist that an associate feels is unsatisfactory, he or she should bring it to the attention of the appropriate person in the proper manner.

PROCEDURE:

Each facility will have posted in a prominent location the company's Five-Step Problem-Solving Procedure. Instruction and training will be provided to all associates with supervisory responsibility to familiarize them with the procedure and enable them to answer questions regarding its use.

DO YOU HAVE A PROBLEM?

Please Start with Your Immediate Supervisor

It is anticipated that most problems you encounter can be solved by you and your leader. If there is something bothering you concerning your job, please discuss it with your leader.

If you and your leader are unable to solve the problem, you can bring your problem out in the open by discussing it with your coordinator/supervisor. Your coordinator/supervisor will courteously discuss the matter with you and attempt to solve your problem. In many cases, a satisfactory answer to your problem can be quickly reached, and there will be no need to go further.

Human Resources Specialist

If your leader or coordinator/supervisor is unable to solve your problem, please see your Human Resources specialist. That person's job is to investigate and help to resolve problems by listening and gathering the necessary information to make an informed decision. At this step, the Human Resources specialist will help you put your concern in writing.

General Manager or Assistant

Your plant manager and assistants are interested in the welfare and problems of every associate. Either one will listen, evaluate, and look for an appropriate solution to the problem. At this step, you should arrange for a specific meeting with your plant manager or assistant. Your Human Resources specialist will assist you.

PERSONNEL POLICIES AND PROCEDURES

DISTRIBUTION:		SUBJECT: PROBLEM-SOLVING PROCEDURE	
EFFECTIVE DATE:	PAGE 2 OF 2	FILE UNDER SECTION	
REVISION DATE:	APPROVED BY:		

Division Manager

If a satisfactory answer to your problem cannot be reached at plant level, an appointment will be made with the division manager to appeal your plant manager's decision if you desire to do so. Your plant Human Resources specialist will also help arrange this meeting.

Vice President and President

If your problem is not solved at the fourth step, you will be given a final opportunity to discuss your problem with the vice president and/or the president. They are keenly interested in the welfare and problems of every associate. The decision made at this step shall be final.

You may be certain that every effort will be made to secure all the facts related to your problem.

PERSONNEL POLICIES AND PROCEDURES

DISTRIBUTION:		SUBJECT: SUGGESTIONS AND COMPLAINTS	
EFFECTIVE DATE:	PAGE 1 OF 1	FILE UNDER SECTION	
REVISION DATE:	APPROVED BY:		

GENERAL:

A clear and open channel for the expression of employee suggestions and complaints is a fundamental principle of sound employee relations. Therefore, each employee should be encouraged to talk with his/her supervisor about any problem, complaint, or suggestion that might arise concerning his/her work.

PROCEDURE:

A. The employee talks about his/her problem or suggestion to his/her immediate supervisor, and the supervisor is given the first opportunity to act on the suggestion or to settle any complaint.

B. It should then be made clear to the employee that if he/she is not fully satisfied with his/her supervisor's decision, or if there is any uncertainty in his/her mind, he/she is at liberty to take his/her problem to the department head.

If the complaint is beyond the scope of the immediate supervisor's jurisdiction, he/she should suggest that the employee discuss it with the next higher level of management who is in a position to answer the question.

When an employee's complaint moves beyond the immediate supervisor, it is suggested that the complaint be reduced to writing to establish the facts of the case and prevent the facts from being changed. (This tends to keep the story straight.) This will assure those to whom the case is appealed that they are considering the same problem that was presented to the immediate supervisor. When requested, the Industrial Relations Department will help the employee prepare his/her written complaint.

Although it is important to preserve the immediate supervisor's authority and dignity, to uphold his/her decision, and to back him/her up, it is vital that nothing be done by higher management to undermine the employee's confidence in the company's desire to be fair and act in good faith.

Should the immediate supervisor make an error and his/her decision have to be reversed, the higher supervisor should review the facts with him/her, explain the situation and the reason why a different decision is necessary, and then encourage him/her to make the reversal—thus preserving his prestige.

C. If the employee's complaint or suggestion is still not settled to the employee's satisfaction, the employee may take his/her complaint or suggestion to the company officer in charge of his/her group and/or department for a hearing.

Speedy handling of complaints and suggestions is a vital part of any procedure. When a complaint or suggestion is presented, quick attention and quick action in getting the right answer, followed by prompt communication with the employee, will greatly enhance the success of the system.

One word of caution: Do not give an employee advice on any elections or choice of benefits due him/her. If your advice should prove unreliable or result in any loss to the employee, the company could be held liable.

PERSONNEL POLICIES AND PROCEDURES

DISTRIBUTION:		SUBJECT: SUGGESTION PROGRAM	
EFFECTIVE DATE:	PAGE 1 OF 2	FILE UNDER SECTION	
REVISION DATE:	APPROVED BY:		

POLICY:

The "Suggestion Program" is established to supply all employees with an opportunity to express their own creative and original ideas on methods and procedures that ultimately will:

- Improve efficiency
- Improve attitudes and working conditions
- Improve the company's competitive position

It is further the desire of management to encourage ongoing effort in creative thinking and originality by the establishment of a flexible recognition program.

PROCEDURE:

The procedure for administration of the "Suggestion Program" is:

1. Suggestion Boxes will be placed and maintained at key travel areas at each operation.

    A. Standard suggestion forms will be readily available for use (but not required).

    B. Boxes will remain locked at all times, with one designated person holding the key.

2. All employees will be notified of the revitalized effort on the suggestion program by means of:

    A. A personal letter stressing the importance of the program and encouraging employee utilization; a detailed listing of the "characteristics of a good suggestion"; and a brief summary of the structure of the review and consideration process, including basic rules.

    B. Posters and timely reminders such as flyers and information distributed with payroll checks, verbal encouragement, etc.

3. Suggestions will be collected each month and submitted to a review committee once a month. The committee will assign the suggestion to the appropriate department manager for consideration and "functional" review. A report will be presented to the committee by the department manager as to the potential of the suggestion. The committee will then appraise the value of the suggestion, recommend an award, and send its recommendation to the President for his approval.

    A. All suggestions will be acknowledged with a letter of gratitude and a token of appreciation for participation in the program (baseball caps, decals, gloves, etc.).

    B. Suggestions will be reviewed and considered on the basis of a four-level system as follows:

    Level 1: Suggestions that clearly are not conducive or acceptable to the process, procedure, or direction of the operation.

    Acknowledgment: A letter of gratitude and an award of a baseball cap, decals, gloves, etc.

    Level 2: Suggestions that appear to have merit but need further development for implementation.

    Acknowledgment: A letter of gratitude and an award of a baseball cap, decals, gloves, etc., along with an explanation that further consideration will be given if the idea is returned in a more fully developed manner.

    Level 3: Suggestions that appear to have true merit, with their possibilities fully developed, that can be easily implemented, and that will result in "probable improvement to the company's competitive position"—but through nonmeasurable means (e.g., improved personnel policy resulting in better employee attitude).

DISTRIBUTION:		SUBJECT: SUGGESTION PROGRAM	
EFFECTIVE DATE:	PAGE 2 OF 2	FILE UNDER SECTION	
REVISION DATE:	APPROVED BY:		

Acknowledgment: A letter of gratitude that emphasizes the understanding and need of improvements in systems that cannot be readily measured in terms of dollars but are critically important all the same. Award of $25 up to $260.

Level 4: Suggestions that are extraordinarily well developed with immediate implementation possibilities that should result in a measurable annual savings of $10,000 or more.

Acknowledgment: A letter of gratitude along with a presentation of an award of $600 at the time of implementation. Further, present a follow-up award of 10 percent of the actual first full year's savings after the suggestion has been implemented and utilized for twelve months.

To further encourage participation in the Suggestion Program, a random drawing will be conducted each time twenty-five suggestions have been received, with the winner being awarded $50.

NOTE: All suggestions must be of a legitimate nature and must at least present some supportive reasoning as to what, who, when, where, and how the suggested activity may be beneficial to the company and its employees.

Simplistic statements will not be considered as suggestions. Examples:

1) Burn more coal.
2) Hire more people.
3) Fire the Boss.
4) Make more money.

Characteristics of a Good Suggestion

A good suggestion, one that is meaningful and useful, should accomplish one or more of the following:

- Reduce cost.
- Improve company product.
- Reduce the chance of accidents.
- Prevent/reduce waste of time and materials.
- Eliminate bottlenecks in production. Improve coordination between units.
- Speed up delivery.
- Speed up production.
- Allow the use of less costly materials without loss of product quality.
- Cut energy/fuel consumption.
- Prevent/reduce environmental pollution.
- Simplify/eliminate paperwork.
- Make productive use of slack or downtime.
- Improve health conditions.
- Create feeling of teamwork.
- Improve communications.
- Streamline procedures.

Please avoid suggestions that:
- Do not result in net benefit to the company and its employees.
- Are vague and unspecified.
- Repeat ideas already suggested.
- Involve enforcing policies that already exist.

PERSONNEL POLICIES AND PROCEDURES

DISTRIBUTION:		SUBJECT: EMPLOYEE SUGGESTION PROGRAM	
EFFECTIVE DATE:	PAGE 1 OF 3		FILE UNDER SECTION
REVISION DATE:	APPROVED BY:		

PURPOSE:

To define the policy and responsibilities associated with the employee suggestion program.

GENERAL:

Pursuant to the policy of the corporation to provide employees "the opportunity to express their views and ideas on how the company might improve its products, services, and operations," a formal employee suggestion program has been established to provide recognition for employee suggestions of value to (Company Name).

POLICY:

1. General
   1.1 All employees of the company may submit suggestions.
   1.2 All salaried, nonexempt, and hourly-rated employees are eligible for cash awards, as are similar employees of the customer services, controller's, and office administration departments, and the engineering and manufacturing facilities.
   1.3 While most suggestions are eligible for cash awards, the employee suggestion program rules list subjects that are not eligible.
   1.4 To be eligible for a cash award, a suggestion must be submitted on the applicable suggestion form and be signed by all who contribute to it. The suggestion must contain specific details as to the situation to be improved and the specific solution that, when implemented, will result in savings or improvement to the company.

2. Cash Awards
   2.1 An eligible suggestion will be determined to have tangible value (measurable savings as defined in the employee suggestion program manual) or intangible value (cannot be measured in precise monetary terms).
   2.2 For tangible-value suggestions, the award will be 20 percent of the measurable net savings during the first twelve-month period following implementation, with a minimum of $50 and a maximum of $100,000.
   2.3 For intangible-value suggestions, the award will normally range from $50 to $150, with a maximum of $2,500.
   2.4 When the net award is estimated to be $2,500 or less, the full amount of the award will be paid when the suggestion is implemented. When an award is estimated to be greater than $2,500, it will be paid in two installments. The initial payment will be made at the time of implementation and will be the greater of $2,500 or 50 percent of the estimated total award. The remainder of the award will be paid after a calculation of the measurable net savings during the first twelve-month period following implementation of the suggestion. (If this calculation reveals that the initial payment was too high, the suggester will not be asked to reimburse the company.)
   2.5 When an employee receives multiple awards for the same suggestion, the total of such awards is not to exceed the maximum amount allowable.

407

DISTRIBUTION:		SUBJECT: EMPLOYEE SUGGESTION PROGRAM	
EFFECTIVE DATE:	PAGE 2 OF 3	FILE UNDER SECTION	
REVISION DATE:	APPROVED BY:		

2.6 Cash awards for suggestions submitted by employees of an engineering and manufacturing facility will be paid by the location(s) that implement the suggestion.

2.7 Cash awards for product-related suggestions submitted by marketing or customer services employees will be paid upon implementation by the marketing or customer services organization involved (even though the engineering and manufacturing facility with design cognizance may benefit from the suggestion).

3. Approval Authority

   3.1 The adoption of an employee suggestion by a suggestion program committee represents a commitment by the company to disburse funds for:

   ... Actual payment of the suggestion award to the employee

   ... Expenses necessary to implement the suggestion

   3.2 The committee may not adopt a suggestion if either of these commitments exceeds the limits in the chart of approval authority. In such cases, the appropriate approvals must be acquired prior to adoption of the suggestion.

   3.3 The corporate chart of approval authority authorizes the following approval authorities for the payment of employee suggestion awards and/or necessary to implement a suggestion:

Corporate Unit President	$100,000
Corporate Unit Vice President	$ 50,000
Facility General Manager/Plant/Corporate Suggestion Committee	$ 20,000
Manager—Central Clearing House	$ 500

RESPONSIBILITIES:

1. Overall

   1.1 The employee suggestion program is the responsibility of local and group management. It is the responsibility of local and group management at all facilities to ensure the integrity of the program by monitoring the processing of suggestions and reviewing the accuracy of program statistics.

   1.2 Each employee suggestion program corporate unit (one that has a corporate unit identifier number) will have an administration staff, directed by an administrator/manager.

   1.3 In addition to the administrator, an employee suggestion program staff typically will be composed of full/part-time evaluator(s), financial analyst(s), and clerical personnel.

   1.4 The focal point of the program is the administrator, whose responsibilities include receiving and acknowledging receipt of suggestions, screening suggestions for duplication and subject eligibility, forwarding the suggestions for evaluation, monitoring and communicating to employees the status of their suggestions, scheduling and conducting suggestion program committee meetings, coordination of award payments and presentations, maintaining records and submitting reports, and promoting and publicizing the program.

   1.5 Critical to the success of the program is the evaluator, whose responsibilities include assuring thorough, objective, and timely evaluations of all suggestions (either personally or by investigators selected on the basis of their individual expertise); presenting recommendations to the suggestion program committee as to the adoption/nonadoption of a suggestion, as well as to the amount of the cash award; and assisting employees in rewriting their suggestions to meet the suggestion eligibility requirements.

PERSONNEL POLICIES AND PROCEDURES

DISTRIBUTION:		SUBJECT: EMPLOYEE SUGGESTION PROGRAM	
EFFECTIVE DATE:	PAGE 3 OF 3		FILE UNDER SECTION
REVISION DATE:	APPROVED BY:		

1.6 A suggestion program committee will be established in each corporate unit and will consist of at least four exempt/professional members selected by senior management from engineering, manufacturing, finance, and the product assurance and support activity in an engineering and manufacturing facility, with additional members at local option. It is the finance member's responsibility to analyze and approve the reasonableness and appropriateness of estimated cost savings.

1.7 It is the committee's responsibility to review the evaluation of a suggestion and determine whether or not it will be adopted; and, if it is adopted, to approve or to secure the approval authorities for payment of the suggestion award and/or expenses necessary to implement the suggestion.

1.8 Expenses involved in the investigation of a suggestion will be charged to the investigating party.

2. Administration/Evaluation Process

    2.1 Coordination of suggestions from engineering and manufacturing facilities, customer services, and headquarters/corporate offices employees, as well as liaison between these organizations, will be the responsibility of the central clearing house (CCH).

    2.2 The CCH will prepare and distribute monthly/quarterly management reports of employee suggestion program activity, relying upon data supplied from each of the operating units.

    2.3 The CCH staff will evaluate all nonproduct suggestions received, utilizing administrative unit evaluators as required.

    2.4 The CCH staff will forward suggestions requiring product evaluation to the engineering and manufacturing facility with design cognizance.

    2.5 Corporate human resources will be responsible for the expense and personnel budgets of the CCH.

3. Engineering and Manufacturing Facilities

    3.1 Product-related suggestions that involve any aspect of life-cycle product cost will be evaluated by the facility having design cognizance for the product. The product assurance and support activity will calculate potential field savings on product-related suggestions.

    3.2 Should a marketing or customer services operating unit request review of an engineering and manufacturing suggestion program committee's decision, such review will be conducted by corporate human resources with appropriate corporate representation (e.g., corporate engineering).

    3.3 Each engineering and manufacturing facility, in addition to evaluating suggestions from its own employees, will evaluate suggestions forwarded from other facilities through the CCH.

    3.4 The plant general manager will be responsible for the expense and personnel budgets of the employee suggestion program in each facility.

4. Evaluation Period

    A decision as to the adoption or nonadoption of a suggestion should be reached within ninety calendar days from the date the suggestion is date-stamped by the suggestion program administrator.

PERSONNEL POLICIES AND PROCEDURES

DISTRIBUTION:		SUBJECT: ROUNDTABLE MEETINGS	
EFFECTIVE DATE:	PAGE 1 OF 1	FILE UNDER SECTION	
REVISION DATE:	APPROVED BY:		

PURPOSE:

The purpose of this policy is to allow associates the opportunity to meet periodically with company representatives to ask questions or discuss concerns they may have regarding the company.

POLICY:

It is the policy of this company to keep the channels of communications open. In keeping with our commitment for better communication, associates are encouraged to meet in a group setting to discuss issues that affect them and the company.

PROCEDURES:

A. Group meetings will be held bimonthly or as determined by plant management.

B. Associates from all areas of the facility will attend.

C. Associates will be selected on a random and rotating basis. The objective of the program is to eventually include all associates.

D. Meetings will be conducted by representatives of management at each facility.

E. Associates will be allowed to ask any questions and make any comments they wish regarding the company. No one will be allowed to make negative personal comments about individuals during the meetings. Matters that are critical of individuals may be discussed following the meeting.

F. Copies of the minutes will be shared with the appropriate management staff and associates.

PERSONNEL POLICIES AND PROCEDURES

DISTRIBUTION:		SUBJECT: 24-HOUR HOTLINE	
EFFECTIVE DATE:	PAGE 1 OF 2	FILE UNDER SECTION	
REVISION DATE:	APPROVED BY:		

PURPOSE:

The purpose of this policy is to establish a telephone-based communication system that will enable the company to receive and respond to associates' questions, suggestions, concerns, and complaints.

POLICY:

As part of our communication system, the company will maintain a Hotline Program that will provide our associates with the opportunity to call and voice their questions, suggestions, concerns, or complaints and have them considered and addressed by the company.

PROCEDURE:

The Hotline system will consist of a telephone answering/recording device maintained on a dedicated phone extension in the Administration Office.

The Hotline extension number will be published by the company on Controlled Communication Centers and in the associate handbook. Associates are invited to call the Hotline whenever they have a question or a concern, or whenever they want to provide feedback to the company.

Detailed below is the description of how the Hotline Program will operate:

A. The Associate Relations Section will maintain responsibility for the Hotline Program. This includes receiving the calls, transcribing them, making sure that inquiries are considered/addressed, and, when appropriate, preparing answers that will be posted on plant Communications Centers.

B. When an associate calls the Hotline, the telephone device will answer the call, and a prerecorded message from a representative of Associate Relations will explain the Hotline Program and will invite the caller to leave his/her question/inquiry on the recorder.

   The prerecorded message will also notify each caller that if he/she would like a personal response to his/her inquiry, he/she should leave his/her name, address, and phone number, along with his/her work location and message.

C. The Associate Relations Section will monitor the Hotline regularly, and when a Hotline message is received, will transcribe the call and erase the caller's message. If the caller does not provide identification, no attempt will be made to identify the voice of the person making the call.

D. A copy of the transcribed message will be forwarded to the Associate Relations manager or his/her designee.

E. The Associate Relations Section will review the associate's inquiry, research the situation, and work to resolve and/or answer the question with appropriate departmental/plant management.

F. After the situation has been addressed and the answer has been formulated, the matter will be discussed and reviewed with departmental/plant management.

PERSONNEL POLICIES AND PROCEDURES

DISTRIBUTION:		SUBJECT: 24-HOUR HOTLINE	
EFFECTIVE DATE:	PAGE 2 OF 2	FILE UNDER SECTION	
REVISION DATE:	APPROVED BY:		

G. If a Hotline caller chooses to leave his/her name along with his/her inquiry and requests a personal discussion, the Associate Relations manager or his/her designee will meet the associate and discuss the problem.

H. The Associate Relations Section will maintain a historical file of all Hotline inquiries and answers.

POLICY FORMAT:

A. All Hotline inquiries that are received will be considered thoroughly investigated and, as appropriate, addressed by the company.

B. There will be no reprisals against an associate because of his/her use of the Hotline.

PERSONNEL POLICIES AND PROCEDURES

DISTRIBUTION:		SUBJECT: KAIZEN SUGGESTION PROGRAM	
EFFECTIVE DATE:	PAGE 1 OF 1	FILE UNDER SECTION	
REVISION DATE:	APPROVED BY:		

PURPOSE:

The purpose of this policy is to define the procedure for administration of the company Kaizen Suggestion Program.

POLICY:

The company encourages all associates to submit suggestions that will improve the workplace. Hourly and salaried nonexempt associates may receive cash awards for suggestions for improvement in the following areas:

- Safety
- Material savings
- Quality
- Productivity
- Work environment

Suggestions concerning wages, benefits, or other conditions of employment are not appropriate and will be rejected without consideration.

Associates whose suggestions are approved by the immediate supervisor/coordinator will receive a five-dollar award. In cases where two associates submit one suggestion, each will receive two dollars and fifty cents. If more than two associates submit one suggestion, each will receive a two-dollar award.

Some approved suggestions may not be implemented because of cost or other considerations. Associates whose suggestions have been implemented for more than ninety days are eligible for the Section Manager's Award. These awards are given to associates whose suggestions provide the greatest contribution to safety, material savings, quality, productivity, or work environment. Recipients will receive twenty-five dollars. In cases where two associates submit one suggestion, each will receive twelve dollars and fifty cents. If more than two associates submit a single suggestion, each will receive ten dollars.

Associates whose suggestions have received the Section Manager's Award will be considered for the President's Award. These awards are given to associates whose suggestions, after being evaluated by the president of the company, are determined to have provided the greatest contribution to safety, material savings, quality, productivity, or work environment. Recipients will receive one hundred dollars. In cases where two associates submit one suggestion, each will receive fifty dollars. If more than two associates submit a single suggestion each will receive thirty-five dollars.

PROCEDURE:

Kaizen suggestion forms will be made available at all locations.

Associates should return completed suggestion forms to their immediate coordinator/supervisor for approval.

PERSONNEL POLICIES AND PROCEDURES

DISTRIBUTION:		SUBJECT: EMPLOYEE COUNSELING POLICY FOR SALARIED EMPLOYEES	
EFFECTIVE DATE:	PAGE 1 OF 1	FILE UNDER SECTION	
REVISION DATE:	APPROVED BY:		

POLICY STATEMENT:

Management wants all employees to be fully informed on policies and procedures affecting them and wants to give them every opportunity to express their opinions, to discuss their complaints and misunderstandings, and to seek information on matters affecting their jobs and particular interests.

Managers, to the best of their ability, are required to inform, listen, and counsel employees on all matters affecting them; and management recognizes the right of the employee to appeal in these matters without fear of retribution or prejudice.

In administering this policy, all levels of management should realize that employees do not always feel free to express their true concern, in which case the Personnel Manager, or the comparable management representative assigned to the Human Resources function, might be in a better position to assist.

All barriers affecting upward communication should be removed; otherwise, problems will become severe and morale can be adversely affected.

PERSONNEL POLICIES AND PROCEDURES

DISTRIBUTION:		SUBJECT: SOUNDING BOARD	
EFFECTIVE DATE:	PAGE 1 OF 1	FILE UNDER SECTION	
REVISION DATE:	APPROVED BY:		

PURPOSE:

To provide associates with a system to confidentially communicate their problems and concerns to corporate management in writing without being bound by a chain of command or other restrictions at the plant or facility level.

POLICY:

The Associate Handbook and notices on Controlled Communication Centers at all company facilities will publicize the Sounding Board as an effective means of problem resolution and communication of concerns. Preposted Sounding Board letter forms will be made available to all associates.

The Corporate Associate Relations Section will investigate each Sounding Board letter and will work with facility or section management to provide an appropriate, accurate, and timely response to the associate who initiated the Sounding Board letter.

PROCEDURE:

A. The Associate will complete and mail a Sounding Board letter form that details the associate's problem or concern and explains the situation.

B. Sounding Board letters will be received by the Associate Relations Section, where they will be logged and passed to the Associate Relations manager.

C. An investigation of the problem/concern will be conducted by the Associate Relations manager, and a response will be drafted with the input of the appropriate plant/section managers. The response will be sent within fourteen (14) days of the date the letter was received.

D. The identity of the associate who sent the Sounding Board letter will be kept confidential by the Associate Relations manager unless the nature of the complaint makes it necessary to identify the associate in order to come to a satisfactory resolution of the problem.

E. Sounding Board records will be maintained for a minimum of one (1) year, and periodic reports on Sounding Board activity will be made by the Associate Relations Section to the General Manager.

SECTION 12

Employment Expenses and Reimbursement

The following checklist can be used to help you determine the various policy items that should be incorporated in your policy manual. Sample policy statements covering many of the items in your checklist appear in this section. They can be used to guide your policy statements.

Our Policy Manual Should Cover:

Relocation

		Yes	No
1.	Management relocation	Yes___	No___
2.	Nonmanagement relocation	Yes___	No___
3.	New hire relocation	Yes___	No___
4.	Premove expenses	Yes___	No___
5.	Sale of old residence	Yes___	No___
	A. Company purchase	Yes___	No___
	B. Company assistance—real estate firm	Yes___	No___
	C. Closing costs	Yes___	No___
6.	Purchase of new residence	Yes___	No___
	A. Bridge loan	Yes___	No___
	B. Mortgage differential	Yes___	No___
	C. Closing costs	Yes___	No___
	D. Miscellaneous allowance	Yes___	No___
7.	House-hunting trips	Yes___	No___
8.	Temporary living expenses	Yes___	No___
9.	Household moving expenses	Yes___	No___
10.	Use of personal automobile	Yes___	No___
11.	Explanation of tax liability	Yes___	No___

12. "Gross-up" procedure   Yes_____   No_____

13. Authorization required   Yes_____   No_____

14. Expense reports   Yes_____   No_____

15. Receipts required   Yes_____   No_____

Business Trips

1. Travel advance   Yes_____   No_____

2. Travel authorization   Yes_____   No_____

3. Rental automobile   Yes_____   No_____

4. Personal automobile   Yes_____   No_____

5. Spouse/family travel   Yes_____   No_____

6. Meal allowance   Yes_____   No_____

7. Air travel   Yes_____   No_____

8. Nonallowable expenses   Yes_____   No_____

9. Travel expense report   Yes_____   No_____

10. Receipts required   Yes_____   No_____

Other Expense Subjects

1. Payment of employment expenses   Yes_____   No_____

2. Temporary assignment expenses   Yes_____   No_____

3. Automobile usage   Yes_____   No_____

4. Customer entertaining   Yes_____   No_____

5. Meal reimbursement   Yes_____   No_____

6. Membership in clubs and civic organizations   Yes_____   No_____

7. Participation in trade and professional associations   Yes_____   No_____

RELOCATION

In many industries, upward mobility may involve accepting periodic transfers to new company locations for the purpose of gaining experience, learning new skills, or simply taking the next step up the ladder. Relocations are often met with some resistance by employees, especially those with families and working spouses, so employers have tried to make moving somewhat more attractive by offering relocating employees a number of forms of financial assistance. These are usually covered under the heading of ''moving expense'' or ''relocation expenses'' in the company policy manual.

While most of these policies are aimed at employees who are transferred at the company's request, some apply to newly hired employees as well. Often a company must recruit a high-level executive from a distant location or fill highly skilled jobs in an area where the needed skills are lacking. In such cases, newly hired individuals would be reimbursed for moving expenses associated with the accepting of employment. Another possible benefit that can be included is reimbursement of travel and living expenses for prospective employees who come to be interviewed for employment, to observe the company's operations, and to evaluate the area in which they would have to live if they accepted a job with the firm.

Reimbursement for relocation expenses is usually associated with large companies where transfers are frequent and company facilities are located in different states or even different countries. But when home mortgage rates and housing costs reached an all-time high, many medium-sized and smaller firms had to establish policies in this area. While twenty or thirty years ago it was unthinkable for an employee to turn down a promotion that necessitated relocating, today's employees may regard such offers with well-founded suspicion. When it means uprooting the whole family, selling a home (perhaps at a loss) and buying another in a far more expensive location, and frequently forcing a spouse with a career commitment to leave his or her job and look for a new one as well, even advancement-oriented employees cannot really be blamed for hesitating. While a liberal policy on moving expenses cannot be expected to change these attitudes, it can be the deciding factor as far as the economic decision is concerned. No employee is going to jump at a promotion for which he or she will pay dearly in a financial, as well as a personal, sense.

Listed below are several points that should be included in your relocation policy:

- Eligibility
- Moving expenses
- Travel expenses
- Interim living expenses
- Miscellaneous expense
- Rental assistance
- Selection of a mover
- Documentation
- Claims for loss or damage
- Storage
- Housing loans
- Tax implementations
- International relocations
- Paperwork
- Responsibility for approval and implementation
- Termination of employment

Here are some additional issues that you may wish to discuss in your policy:

1. *The current and anticipated economic conditions affecting housing.* Mortgage interest rates, which have been variable during the past few years, will obviously have an effect on your policy. Many employers now offer what is called a ''Mortgage Interest Differential Allowance'' (MIDA), which helps relocated employees cope with high interest rates on their new mortgage. Recessions and inflation can also make it more difficult for individuals to sell their homes, and the cost of housing in some areas of the country has increased astronomically.

2. *Your company's plan for expansion.* If your firm is planning to open a number of new facilities over the next few years, you should consider this when developing your relocation policy.

3. *Working spouses.* With the two-career family fast becoming the norm, an increasing number of employers have had to address the problem of how to make relocation look more attractive to the employee's

spouse as well. Some companies have had to arrange job interviews for the spouse or to set him or her up in a comparable position at the same facility. Others offer career counseling for the spouse at the new location in order to help him or her obtain a suitable job.

Should a substantial number of present employees be required to relocate or should your organization make a local move, we would suggest that an employee attitude and opinion survey be undertaken. It would be very helpful to you to know your employees' opinions, attitudes, and suggestions before the actual move is required. A professionally conducted survey by an outside consultant has the advantage of assuring participants anonymity and allowing for freedom of response. Of course, the survey will also give the company the benefit of objective, quantifiable information upon which to base its decisions and plans.

Conducting a survey can provide management with important information about its employees' concerns and wishes. It gives a more objective picture of doubts and apprehensions about the move. Having this knowledge puts management in a better position to make plans and allocate resources regarding the people, the physical aspects of the move, and the relocation process itself.

Although there may be surprises, survey results enable a company to act more securely, knowing that it is not just guessing what its employees are thinking.

Relocation policies tend to be quite long, usually with good reason. There are so many different expenses associated with looking for and purchasing a new home, and with selling an existing one, that it is wise to be as thorough as possible in detailing what the company will or will not cover.

The following pages contain policies covering:

Relocation for Transferred Employees
Relocation Service
Payment of Employment Expenses
Fee Payment for Employment Procurement
Automobile Usage
Customer Entertainment Expenses
Meal Reimbursement
Club and Civic Organizations Memberships
Trade and Professional Associations
Request for Paid Relocation

PERSONNEL POLICIES AND PROCEDURES

DISTRIBUTION:		SUBJECT: RELOCATION POLICY FOR COMPANY TRANSFERRED EMPLOYEES	
EFFECTIVE DATE:	PAGE 1 OF 4	FILE UNDER SECTION	
REVISION DATE:	APPROVED BY:		

PURPOSE:

It is the policy of (Company Name) to provide a service to the employee at the time of a company-required transfer that will enable the employee to relocate himself/herself and his/her family as conveniently and economically as possible.

RESPONSIBILITY:

♦ Employee—Responsible for completing the form entitled "Request for Company-Paid Relocation" and, if approved, following policy as described herein.

♦ Executive Committee Member—Responsible for first approval of the form entitled "Request for Company-Paid Relocation" and for approving all expenses charged to his/her relocation account.

♦ Vice President—Human Resources—Responsible for administration of the Relocation Policy.

♦ President—Responsible as final approving authority for the form entitled "Request for Company-Paid Relocation" and for approving any expenses that are not covered by policy or that are deviations from the policy.

ELIGIBILITY:

A. All salaried (exempt) employees who are transferred at the request of (Company Name) are eligible to apply for assistance as prescribed by this policy.

B. Employees who transfer at their own request are NOT eligible for benefits under this policy.

C. The new job site has to be at least fifty miles from the previous location.

D. This policy does not apply to New Hires who relocate to the job location.

E. No expenses will be paid under this policy if the employee concerned terminates his/her employment, even though said expenses may have been incurred prior to the termination date.

F. From the effective date of the personnel action, as reflected on the Change of Status Form, up to a period of one year is considered to be the maximum time benefits will be available under this policy to the individual concerned.

BENEFITS:

A. A miscellaneous expense allowance as follows:
   1. Selling home and purchasing home at new location—one month's salary.
   2. When an employee is not a homeowner—one-half month's salary.
   3. Selling home and renting at new location—one-half month's salary.

PERSONNEL POLICIES AND PROCEDURES

DISTRIBUTION:		SUBJECT: RELOCATION POLICY FOR COMPANY TRANSFERRED EMPLOYEES	
EFFECTIVE DATE:	PAGE 2 OF 4		FILE UNDER SECTION
REVISION DATE:	APPROVED BY:		

B. Selling home:
   1. Real estate commission not to exceed 5 percent (not available if employee sells home without the services of a real estate firm).
   2. Up to 1 percent of selling price of home to cover legal, transfer, etc., expenses.

C. Purchasing home:
   1. Loan discount points up to a maximum of 3 percent.
   2. Up to 1 percent of purchase price of home to cover closing costs, etc.

D. Interim living expenses:
   1. If married, living expenses including room and board for the employee at the new location while dependents are at the old location—maximum of thirty days or $1,000, whichever occurs first.
   2. If single, living expenses for a maximum of fifteen days or $500, whichever occurs first.

E. Premoving expenses: The employee will be reimbursed for the following travel expenses incurred in connection with the transfer:
   1. Trip from home to report to new location.
   2. Travel to the new location incidental to finding new housing.
   3. Two trips to the new location for employee's spouse to select new housing (maximum of eight calendar days).
   4. Trips home to visit family if they are still residing at the old location. This will be a maximum of one trip each two-week period, for a total of three trips.

F. Household goods:
   1. All reasonable and customary expenses incurred for the packing and relocation of household goods.
   2. Costs for temporary storage of household goods for a period not to exceed thirty calendar days.

G. Travel:
   1. Twenty-two cents per mile compensation for driving personal automobile to new location (maximum of two automobiles).
   2. Meal and lodging while en route with family to new location.
   3. Up to a maximum of fourteen days' temporary lodging/meals for family after arriving at new location while waiting to move into new residence.
   4. Airline transportation costs for employee and immediate family if no personal automobile is involved.

H. Expenses not covered:
   1. Losses above the insured amount for household goods to be relocated.
   2. Shipping household plants, trees, etc.
   3. Shipping firewood, etc.

DISTRIBUTION:		SUBJECT: RELOCATION POLICY FOR COMPANY TRANSFERRED EMPLOYEES	
EFFECTIVE DATE:	PAGE 3 OF 4	FILE UNDER SECTION	
REVISION DATE:	APPROVED BY:		

4. Tuning or servicing pianos/organs, etc.

5. Disassembling or assembling playground equipment.

6. Baby sitters.

7. Dry cleaning.

8. House cleaning.

9. Rug cleaning.

10. Hanging of draperies, rods, etc.

11. Maid service.

12. Boats, trailers, etc.

13. Shipping pets/domestic animals.

14. Loading or transporting vehicles by common carrier or driving service.

15. Tips/gratuities to movers.

16. All other extraordinary services.

(NOTE: The expenses not covered list does not include all categories. The miscellaneous expense allowance is designed to cover such expenses.)

I. Federal and State Income Tax: Any amount received by an employee, either directly or indirectly, from the company as a payment or reimbursement for expenses of moving from one residence to another must be included in the employee's gross income and reported on Form W-2, Wage and Tax Statement.

The employee will be permitted to deduct expenses to the extent to which they qualify as deductible moving expenses on Form 1040, Individual Income Tax Return.

The nondeductible moving expenses, as defined in the U.S. Income Tax Regulations, reimbursed by the company will be considered taxable income to the employee. To help defray the resulting tax liability, the company will:

1. Include in the employee's Form W-2 (wages subject to withholding section) all moving expenses, both deductible and nondeductible, plus an additional 25 percent of all nondeductible moving expenses.

2. A like amount of 25 percent of all nondeductible moving expenses will also be added to the employee's Form W-2 taxes withheld section. This amount is paid by the company to the U.S. government as additional withholding tax on behalf of the employee.

If, when the employee completes the final income tax calculation for the year in which reimbursement is made, the federal and state income tax on the moving expense is greater than the amount of gross-up calculated under the above formula, the employee may apply through the Human Resources Department for additional tax reimbursement. Employee calculations will be checked against the individual's actual tax return by an employee in (Company Name) Tax Department, and any necessary additional tax gross-up will be authorized by the Tax Department.

A Moving Expense Summary Form will be issued by Accounting to each employee who has incurred moving expenses during the year up to October 31. All expenses incurred after this date will appear in a summary

DISTRIBUTION:		SUBJECT: RELOCATION POLICY FOR COMPANY TRANSFERRED EMPLOYEES
EFFECTIVE DATE:	PAGE 4 OF 4	FILE UNDER SECTION
REVISION DATE:	APPROVED BY:	

prepared in the following year. This form will contain both the deductible and nondeductible amount of moving expenses and the employee withholding tax, which will be included in the employee's W-2, Wage and Tax Statement.

MISCELLANEOUS:

A. A "Request for Company-Paid Relocation" form must be submitted and approved by all concerned before any expenses may be incurred.

B. A "Travel Expense Report" form is to be used to reflect expenses.

C. Bridge loans or company-guaranteed loans are not covered by this policy. Financial matters with lending institutions or real estate firms are the sole responsibility of the employee concerned.

PERSONNEL POLICIES AND PROCEDURES

DISTRIBUTION:		SUBJECT: RELOCATION	
EFFECTIVE DATE:	PAGE 1 OF 5	FILE UNDER SECTION	
REVISION DATE:	APPROVED BY:		

PURPOSE:

The purpose of this policy is to describe the nature and extent of the Corporation's Relocation Assistance Program. This policy will also outline the conditions and procedures that govern the payment or reimbursement of expenses.

POLICY:

The company relocation program is designed to assist newly hired and transferred associates in most situations encountered in the relocation and moving process. The eligibility requirements are as follows:

A. Newly hired exempt salaried associates whose initial assignment requires a permanent change in residence.

B. To qualify for reimbursement, the distance between the associate's new principal work location and the former residence must be at least fifty (50) miles further than the former residence was from the previous work location.

C. New hires must complete the movement of household goods within a reasonable time period [up to twelve (12) months from the effective date of hire] to be eligible for any reimbursement under this program.

DUTIES AND RESPONSIBILITIES:

A. Associate responsibilities are outlined in the "Move" brochure.

B. The location's Human Resources Department will advise the associate concerning policies and procedures and assist in completion of the necessary forms. The following forms must be completed and approved by the corporate relocation coordinator before any expenses are incurred:
   - Relocation Expense Request and Authorization
   - Movement of Household Goods Authorization

C. The Corporate General Affairs Department is responsible for the overall effective and equitable administration of the Corporate Relocation program.

D. The Corporate Finance Department is responsible for the maintenance of records for tax purposes and will furnish each relocated associate with a Relocation Expense statement at year-end. The Corporate Finance Department will administer the "tax gross-up allowance" and the allocation of charges to the appropriate control centers.

ASSISTANCE PROVIDED:

A. Pre-Move House-hunting Trip
   1. The associate and one other person upon approval will be reimbursed for the reasonable and documented travel and living expenses for one round trip, not to exceed five (5) days, to obtain a residence at the new location. If the associate requires additional time and a second trip appears advisable, that trip shall require the approval of the Corporate General Affairs Department.

424

PERSONNEL POLICIES AND PROCEDURES

2. If the associate's personal car is used, reimbursement will be at the established corporate mileage rate.

3. Reasonable cost of child care, if required.

B. Travel to New Location

1. The associate and his/her immediate family will be reimbursed for reasonable and documented travel and living expenses while en route to the new location. Any in transit vacation or personal stopovers are at the associate's expense.

2. Whenever possible, the associate should use his/her personal automobile when traveling to the new location. Mileage will be reimbursed at the established, standard corporate rate based on the most commonly traveled direct route.

3. If the associate's immediate family does not travel to the new location by automobile, reimbursement will be made for the cost of their transportation by either coach-class air or first-class rail accommodations.

C. Temporary Living

When the associate and/or his family arrive at the new location, receipted reasonable meals and lodging will be reimbursed as required for a period of sixty (60) days while awaiting occupancy of the new residence. It is understood that the temporary living provision is applicable when the associate has started in his/her new job or, with the company's approval, has arrived early and is waiting to start work.

1. Expenses not eligible for reimbursement are as follows:

    ◆ Above reasonable and customary telephone charges.

    ◆ Normal meal expenses incurred by the associate that would have occurred if the family were relocated; e.g., lunches during the week.

2. Family Visitations

    If the associate's family does not accompany him/her to the new location when employment commences, the associate may be reimbursed for periodic travel (transportation only) to the former location. Reimbursement will be limited to two weekend trips per thirty- (30-) day period.

D. Shipment and Movement of Household Goods

In order to obtain assistance in the movement of his/her household goods, the relocating associate must complete and submit a "Movement of Household Goods Authorization" form for approval.

The company will arrange and directly pay for the following services relative to the movement of an associate's household goods:

1. Packing, shipping, delivery, and unpacking of household goods and personal effects.

    Household goods and personal effects shall be defined so as to include clothing; furniture; household furnishings; luggage; appliances; canned goods and nonperishable food items; books; properly registered firearms; motorcycles; mopeds and scooters; and canoes under fourteen (14) feet long.

2. Reasonable expenses for commercial towing of a mobile home that is not installed on a permanent foundation and is the associate's principal residence.

3. Disconnection and reconnection of household appliances to existing facilities. This does not include television antennas or lighting fixtures.

4. Temporary storage-in-transit of household goods, if required, for a period up to sixty (60) days.

5. Transit insurance. Insurance coverage for home furnishings during shipment. However, it is highly recommended

DISTRIBUTION:		SUBJECT: RELOCATION	
EFFECTIVE DATE:	PAGE 3 OF 5	FILE UNDER SECTION	
REVISION DATE:	APPROVED BY:		

that goods of extraordinary value, such as fine art and antique furnishings, be appraised at the associate's expense. In the unlikely event of loss or damage, the appraisal will be helpful in filing a claim.

6. Shipment/transit of a secondary automobile, not to exceed the equivalent of the current corporate mileage allowance times the total mileage when taking the most direct route to the new location.

Items not reimbursable under this section.

- Boarding or shipment of nonhousehold pets/animals.
- Shipment or storage of boats over fourteen (14) feet; recreational vehicles; plants; shrubs; lumber; steel; heavy machinery; explosives; flammable, hazardous, or contaminating materials; firewood; inoperable automobiles; perishables; small structures such as playhouses or doghouses; and other such items not considered as usual household furnishings.
- Shipment or storage of aircraft; currency; securities, notes, deeds, and other valuable papers; stamp and coin collections; gold; silver; furs; and jewelry.

E. Moving Oneself

This program is designed for those persons who have a minimum amount of household goods to relocate and, because of cost savings, prefer to move themselves utilizing a U-Haul type of service. Under this program, the company will reimburse the associate at a rate of 125 percent actual and approved charges.

When selecting this option, the associate agrees to:

1. Contract with a truck or trailer rental agency (not a moving van company) for the sole purpose of moving his/her household goods; and

2. Assume responsibility for packing, loading, and unloading. Costs reimbursable by the company are as follows:

- Truck or trailer rental charges, insurance premiums (cargo, physical damage, and medical), packing, rental of pads and hand dollies. Deposits will not be reimbursed.
- Automobile towing charges up to the equivalent of the current mileage allowance rate for the most direct route to the new location.
- Reasonable and actual fees charged by the truck rental agency for packing, loading, and unloading services, where available.

F. Disposition of Former Residence

The company provides the following regarding disposition of a former residence:

1. Reimbursement of documented fees for canceling the current mortgage loan on the associate's primary residence. (Reimbursement maximum shall not exceed 1 percent of the loan balance.)

2. Reimbursement of documented fees for canceling of a lease to a maximum of two (2) months' rent at the former location. Security deposits will not be reimbursed.

G. Purchase/Rental of New Residence

The company will reimburse the following expenses in connection with locating a new home/apartment.

1. Approved travel and lodging

2. Finder's fees/rental
   For associates choosing to rent at the new location, a finder's fee for the assistance of a real estate agent or rental service will be reimbursed to a maximum of one (1) month's rent at the new location. A security deposit is different from a finder's fee.

3. Renter's differential

PERSONNEL POLICIES AND PROCEDURES

DISTRIBUTION:		SUBJECT: RELOCATION	
EFFECTIVE DATE:	PAGE 4 OF 5	FILE UNDER SECTION	
REVISION DATE:	APPROVED BY:		

The associate will be reimbursed to a maximum of $150 per month for one (1) year if the rental/lease cost at his/her destination is higher than that at his/her old location, provided the residences are of comparable size and neighborhood. The amount is based on the original documented rental/lease cost at destination less documented rental/lease cost at origin.

4. Purchase of new residence

The associate will be reimbursed for the following reasonable and documented expenses incurred in the acquisition of the new home, which are customarily borne by the buyer and required by the lender in accordance with local practice.

- Attorney services to a maximum of $500
- Title fees, including title search, judgment search, abstracting, title insurance premium, and legal opinion on title
- Recording fees
- Mortgage origination fee (up to 1½ percent), credit report, appraisal, inspection, and property survey

Expenses not reimbursable

- Loan discount fees
- Points
- Taxes
- Homeowner insurance
- Assumption fees

H. Miscellaneous Allowance

There are numerous hidden costs associated with moving, and it is impossible to predict each cost in advance. Therefore, the company will provide a single lump-sum payment for these miscellaneous items. The special allowance for miscellaneous items is a one-time payment of $1,000.00, payable upon submission of a signed rental or purchase agreement at the new location.

TAXES:

Whenever an associate is being relocated, certain expenses paid by the company on the associate's behalf are considered as income to the associate. To determine what expenses are considered as income, the federal government has established certain rules and regulations. (In some instances, state and local governments may have similar rules and regulations.) Those paid expenses that are established as income under these rules and regulations are subject to payroll taxes and will be reported on the associate's W-2 as income.

To lessen the increased tax liability to the associate resulting from the increased income due to payment of these expenses, the Corporation will pay to the government on behalf of the associate the estimated tax associated with this additional income. This tax calculation will be made in accordance with the tax law in effect at year-end.

Because tax laws are complex and change frequently, it is recommended that each relocating associate seek the advice of a tax consultant for more information on moving and how it can affect his/her taxes.

Examples of expenses paid by the company and considered income to the associate are as follows:

- Pre-move house hunting trip
- Temporary living expenses
- Reimbursement of expenses for purchase of a home
- Reimbursement of expenses for sale of a home
- Payment of miscellaneous allowance

427

DISTRIBUTION:		SUBJECT: RELOCATION	
EFFECTIVE DATE:	PAGE 5 OF 5		FILE UNDER SECTION
REVISION DATE:	APPROVED BY:		

RECEIPTS:

Government regulations require most relocation expenses to be documented before they are allowed as personal tax deductions or Corporate Business Expenses. As a result, company policy requires receipts wherever possible. This will speed processing of expense reports and could save the associate and the company money in taxes. While associates should try to get receipts for everything, there are some expenses for which receipts are mandatory. These include:

* Any cost related to the sale of the associate's former residence
* Any costs related to the culmination of lease or forfeiture of deposits on the associate's residence
* Charges for travel by public transportation
* Meals over $25
* Lodging costs for the associate and his/her family
* Any costs related to the purchase or rental of a new residence
* All truck or trailer rental costs and related applicable expenses when moving oneself

SPECIAL CIRCUMSTANCES AND EXCEPTIONS TO THE POLICY:

The company's Relocation Program is designed to assist associates in most situations encountered in the move process. While unlikely, situations may arise that require special consideration. If this occurs, the associate should describe the circumstances in writing to his/her new location manager. If the request appears to have merit, the request will be submitted to the corporate vice president of the General Affairs Department for further consideration. The associate will be notified as soon as possible of the company's evaluation of the matter and should not make any related commitments until approval has been either granted or denied.

PERSONNEL POLICIES AND PROCEDURES

DISTRIBUTION:		SUBJECT: RELOCATION POLICY SUPPLEMENT	
EFFECTIVE DATE:	PAGE 1 OF 2	FILE UNDER SECTION	
REVISION DATE:	APPROVED BY:		

PURPOSE:

The purpose of this policy is to describe the nature and extent of the corporation's Relocation Assistance Program. This policy also outlines the conditions and procedures that govern the payment or reimbursement of expenses.

POLICY:

The Company provides designated associates with the following programs to assist in the disposition of their former residence:*

A. Disposition of Former Residence

1. Market Assistance—This is provided through a third-party relocation service company that is recognized nationally for its expertise in home sales. The third-party consultant will work with the associate to generate a fair market sales price on his/her residence, including two independent appraisals; develop a marketing strategy; recommend repairs or improvements; recommend a qualified broker; monitor market and sales activity; and, when an offer is made, assist in the closing of the sale.

2. Home-finding Assistance—The third-party relocation consultant will conduct a needs analysis with the associate to use as a guideline in identifying communities/neighborhoods; gather financial data to establish a price range; prequalify the associate for a mortgage; and assign a broker at the new location.

B. Selling Expenses Reimbursed

1. Realtor's commissions that are customary in the area up to a maximum of seven (7) percent of the sale price of the house. In lieu of a real estate broker's commission, an associate who sells a principal residence without the assistance of a broker will receive three and one half (3-1/2) percent of the sale price.

2. Attorney's fees not to exceed $500.

3. Reasonable documented costs of internal revenue stamps, transfer taxes, recording fees, termite inspection fees, and other closing expenses that are customarily borne by the seller in accordance with local practice.

4. Approved travel and living expenses for associate and spouse for up to two (2) days for closing if required.

5. Reimbursement of documented fees for canceling the current mortgage loan on the associate's primary residence. [Reimbursement maximum shall not exceed one (1) percent of the loan balance.]

Note: Discount points borne by the seller are not reimbursable.

C. Protecting Your Investment

This provision is provided if the associate sells his/her home below the original purchase price under the following conditions:

1. The company will reimburse up to ten (10) percent of the purchase price of the former home on sales below

---

* "Former residence" shall mean a single-family or two-family residence that is used by the associate as his/her principal residence and is owned by the associate and his/her spouse, with associated property customarily considered part of the realty, but exclusive of any land in excess of a normal lot for the neighborhood in which the residence is located. The term "home" shall include a condominium but shall not include a cooperative apartment or a residence any part of which is used for nonresidential purposes. The home shall include all personal property normally sold with a house in accordance with local custom.

PERSONNEL POLICIES AND PROCEDURES

DISTRIBUTION:		SUBJECT: RELOCATION POLICY SUPPLEMENT	
EFFECTIVE DATE:	PAGE 2 OF 2	FILE UNDER SECTION	
REVISION DATE:	APPROVED BY:		

investment value. Investment value is defined as the contract price of the former home. The maximum reimbursement is $15,000. Mobile homes that are installed on a permanent foundation are also included in this program.

2. The home sale must be completed within a reasonable amount of time, normally up to twelve (12) months from the effective date of transfer/hire.

3. When an associate accepts an offer, proof of two independent appraisals must be submitted to the Associate Relations Department.

D. Miscellaneous Allowance

There are numerous hidden costs associated with moving, and it is impossible to predict each cost in advance. Therefore, the company will provide a single lump-sum payment for these miscellaneous items. The special allowance for miscellaneous items is a one-time payment of $3,000.00, payable upon submission of a signed rental or purchase agreement at the new location.

PERSONNEL POLICIES AND PROCEDURES

DISTRIBUTION:		SUBJECT: RELOCATION SERVICE	
EFFECTIVE DATE:	PAGE 1 OF 2	FILE UNDER SECTION	
REVISION DATE:	APPROVED BY:		

POLICY STATEMENT:

(Company Name) will provide a Relocation Service involving the sale of a transferred employee's home when said employee is unable, after concentrated effort, to dispose of his/her family dwelling.

ELIGIBILITY:

This service applies only to Salaried (Exempt) employees who are at a salary level of $30,000 per annum and over.

FINAL APPROVING AUTHORITY:

No relocation service will be granted without the final approval of the President.

GUIDELINES:

1. The company has an agreement with the Equitable Relocation Service whereby that firm will purchase the home of (Company Name) employees.

2. Under this arrangement, Equitable Relocation Service requests two appraisals to determine the fair market value. The relocation firm will then offer to purchase the home from the employee, and the employee has thirty days to accept the offer. If the offer is accepted, the firm then takes title to the home and responsibility for its maintenance and resale. The employee will receive a sufficient amount of money to cover the down payment requirement on the new home and will receive the entire equity at the time he/she closes on his/her new home or moves from his/her former home, whichever comes first. During the thirty-day offer period, if the employee receives an offer on his/her own at a higher price than that offered by the relocation firm, the employee may "assign" the sale. In either of these situations, the company assumes the fees for the relocation service.

3. PROCEDURE

   It is important to advise the transferee that the following provision should be stated in any listing agreement executed with a Realtor:

   "We hereby reserve the right to sell our home to Equitable Relocation Service at any time during the term of this listing agreement, and in such event, this agreement is canceled with no obligation for commission or continuance of listing thereafter."

   An employee who wishes to use the relocation service should telephone the director of Human Resources, who will make the necessary arrangements. Once the company authorizes Equitable to proceed, all future contacts and arrangements will be handled directly between Equitable and the employee.

PERSONNEL POLICIES AND PROCEDURES

DISTRIBUTION:		SUBJECT: RELOCATION SERVICE	
EFFECTIVE DATE:	PAGE 2 OF 2	FILE UNDER SECTION	
REVISION DATE:	APPROVED BY:		

In accordance with the Equitable contract, the following company representatives are designated to authorize a request for an offer to purchase:

- Director of Human Resources
- Vice President—Finance

4. EXPENSE ALLOWANCES

If an employee elects to accept the offer from the relocation service, he/she will NOT be eligible for real estate commission on the sale of a house or loan discount points.

PERSONNEL POLICIES AND PROCEDURES

DISTRIBUTION:		SUBJECT: PAYMENT OF EMPLOYMENT EXPENSES	
EFFECTIVE DATE:	PAGE 1 OF 3	FILE UNDER SECTION	
REVISION DATE:	APPROVED BY:		

SCOPE:

This procedure defines the expenses that will be reimbursed and the conditions applying to both employees and prospective applicants/new hires to fill exempt-level positions related to interviews and preliminary trips.

GENERAL:

Applicants are required to submit all expenses on an actual and reasonable expenditure basis supported by applicable receipts. The guidelines for reasonable expenditures are set out in the relocation assistance program.

INTERVIEW TRIPS:

1. Prospective applicants who are requested by a Human Resources Department to travel outside the areas in which they reside to keep employment interview appointments are reimbursed for transportation, meals, and lodging.

2. The cognizant employment function only authorizes such payment.

3. If the applicant uses a personal automobile in lieu of public transportation, reimbursement for mileage incurred is made in accordance with the current domestic rate, plus tolls.

4. If air transportation is used, the applicant is reimbursed for the cost of coach/economy air fare.

5. At the discretion of the cognizant employment department, and with advance written approval, a spouse may be authorized to accompany the interviewee to the interview site and be reimbursed for related expenses. When a spouse accompanies the interviewee, one subsequent preliminary trip is forfeited.

6. All interviewee expenses are charged to account, within the respective organizational budget.

PRELIMINARY TRIP:

Employees and prospective applicants/new hires and their spouses may, at management's discretion, be authorized to take preliminary trips to review available accommodations, educational facilities, and other family requisites and are reimbursed for transportation, meals, and lodging.

1. Two preliminary trips in total may be authorized. Submitted expenses for both trips may not exceed eight days. Expenses related to travel time are in addition.

2. Employees may be authorized to take a preliminary trip prior to accepting or rejecting the new position.

   Viable outside applicants may be authorized to take a preliminary trip, prior to accepting or rejecting the new position, after a written offer of employment has been made and it is recognized that a preliminary trip is essential to assist the candidate in making the employment decision.

DISTRIBUTION:		SUBJECT: PAYMENT OF EMPLOYMENT EXPENSES	
EFFECTIVE DATE:	PAGE 2 OF 3	FILE UNDER SECTION	
REVISION DATE:	APPROVED BY:		

3. The host location Human Resources Director, or his/her designee, authorizes such trips and the payment of the expenses.

4. If a personal car is used in lieu of public transportation, reimbursed for mileage incurred is made in accordance with the current domestic rate, plus tolls.

5. The cost of renting a midsize car while visiting the new location, if a personal car is not used, is reimbursed.

6. If air transportation is used, the cost of coach/economy air fare is reimbursed.

7. The cost of child care during the absence of parents to $35 per day is reimbursable.

8. All expenses that occur are to be billed to account within the respective organizational budget.

PROCEDURES:

Interviews or preliminary trips at major locations

Responsibility	*Action*

Human Resources/Employment Manager	1. Schedules the preliminary trip or interview with the parties at interest
	   ◆ If requested (for prospective new hires), arranges for an air travel ticket to be picked up at point of departure.
	2. Provides copy of the Reimbursement of Applicant Expense Form to applicants upon arrival, requesting provision of expense information on the form during the visit or immediately following trip completion.
	   ◆ Employees complete travel expense reimbursement form.
	3. Reviews the expense report, enters the account distribution, and submits the report to accounts payable.

Interviews or preliminary trips at field branch office

Responsibility	*Action*
Requesting Field Management	1. Requests approval of the cognizant Human Resources Department Representative to invite selected applicant(s) for local interview.
Cognizant Human Resources Representative	2. Schedules the interviews or preliminary trip with the parties at interest. If requested, arranges for an air travel ticket (for prospective new hires) to be picked up at point of departure.

PERSONNEL POLICIES AND PROCEDURES

DISTRIBUTION:		SUBJECT: PAYMENT OF EMPLOYMENT EXPENSES	
EFFECTIVE DATE:	PAGE 3 OF 3		FILE UNDER SECTION
REVISION DATE:	APPROVED BY:		

Interviewing Manager/Director

3. Gives a copy of the Reimbursement of Applicant Expense to each new hire upon arrival, requesting completion of expense information on the form during the visit or immediately following trip completion.

  ◆ Employees complete a travel expense reimbursement form.

4. Reviews the expense report, approves it if appropriate, and submits it to the cognizant Human Resources Representative.

Cognizant Human Resources Representative

5. Reviews the expense report, enters the account distribution, and submits the report to accounts payable.

PERSONNEL POLICIES AND PROCEDURES

DISTRIBUTION:		SUBJECT: FEE PAYMENT FOR EMPLOYMENT PROCUREMENT: TRAINEE AND SALESPERSON	
EFFECTIVE DATE:	PAGE 1 OF 1	FILE UNDER SECTION	
REVISION DATE:	APPROVED BY:		

POLICY STATEMENT:

Employment agency fees for procurement of (Company Name) Sales Trainees and Salespersons will be borne by the Company.

GUIDELINES:

Use of Agencies

1. Personnel responsible for the recruiting of Sales Trainees and Salespersons (i.e., Manpower Development Manager, Regional Manager, District Manager, Human Resources Manager) will minimize the use of employment agencies. Agencies should be used as a last resort and only after all other sources of recruiting have been exhausted.

2. Agencies must guarantee the new employee for ninety days. That is, should an agency-procured employee leave the Company's employ within three months from the date of employment, the agency must agree to furnish a suitable, fully qualified replacement.

LIMITATION OF FEES:

Agency fees in excess of 15 percent of the candidate's yearly base salary will not be paid unless approved in advance by the Director of Human Resources.

Method of Payment

1. Invoices will be approved by the Regional Manager concerned and forwarded to the Human Resources Department for payment. (This expense is charged to Employment Procurement Account.)

2. In no event may costs be charged to the Employee Procurement Account without the prior knowledge and approval of the Director of Human Resources. These include costs incurred in employment advertisements, interview expenses, employment agency fees, etc.

PERSONNEL POLICIES AND PROCEDURES

DISTRIBUTION:		SUBJECT: AUTOMOBILE USAGE	
EFFECTIVE DATE:	PAGE 1 OF 1	FILE UNDER SECTION	
REVISION DATE:	APPROVED BY:		

POLICY:

It is the policy of (Company Name) to own and maintain automobiles for use by employees while on company business. Also, an employee may be required to use his/her own personal automobile for company business, if necessary, in accordance with the following guidelines.

PROCEDURE:

A. Company automobiles are assigned to those departments that have demonstrated a continuing need for them. Also, additional automobiles are maintained in a pool for use by employees as needed.

B. Employees who are required to travel in the course of their regular, daily work may be assigned company automobiles for their use while on company business. All other employees who have only an occasional need for an automobile in travel for the company may draw from the motor pool. Employees may use their personal automobile for company business only with the prior approval of their supervisor/manager.

C. Company automobiles are not to be used for an employee's personal use without the prior approval of their supervisor/manager. Nonbusiness use should be limited to special situations and for short periods of time.

D. Any cost of fuel or other expenses directly related to company automobiles paid for by the employee will be fully reimbursed by the company. Employees who use their own automobiles for company business shall receive a mileage allowance reimbursement of 25¢ per mile to cover the applicable expenses. The only expenses that may be in addition to this allowance are costs of parking and tolls. Claims for reimbursement must be approved by the supervisor/manager before being submitted to Accounts Payable for payment. Employees who use their own personal automobile for company business are required to have insurance coverage to adequately cover damage to the vehicle, other property damage, and injuries sustained by individuals as a result on the accident. It is the responsibility of the particular supervisor/manager to verify insurance coverage before allowing a personal automobile to be used for company business.

E. Every employee who operates a vehicle on company business shall be required to possess a valid driver's license. The particular supervisory manager shall be responsible for checking the driver's license of each employee assigned to travel on company business. Any fines incurred while on company business shall be paid by the employee.

F. Any employee using a company automobile is responsible for its proper maintenance. Any malfunctions or maintenance requirements must be reported to the supervisor of the motor pool. Permanently assigned automobiles should be returned to the pool for scheduled maintenance.

G. A report of any accident, regardless of extent or damage, must be made if a company automobile or personal automobile used on company business is involved. Such report must be made to the supervisor of the motor pool within forty-eight hours of the accident. Employees should always cooperate fully with the authorities in case of an accident. However, employees should not make any voluntary statements other than in reply to questions of investigating officers.

PERSONNEL POLICIES AND PROCEDURES

DISTRIBUTION:		SUBJECT: PROCEDURES FOR BUSINESS TRAVEL AND ENTERTAINMENT EXPENSE REPORTING
EFFECTIVE DATE:	PAGE 1 OF 5	FILE UNDER SECTION
REVISION DATE:	APPROVED BY:	

Employees are reimbursed for reasonable and necessary expenses incurred in carrying out preauthorized travel and other business-related assignments. At no time shall an officer, manager, or other company employee deviate from this policy. Any report submitted that is not in compliance with this policy or is improperly completed will be returned to the approving manager. A Travel Expense Report must be completed for all travel. Expense reports must be forwarded to Accounts Payable within two weeks of the return from the trip.

1. All travel expense reports must include the employee's name, employee #, the date, location and purpose of trip, and account coding. Persons other than employees must complete the report with a current address and note whether they are temporary or interviewees. Original receipts (a copy is acceptable) should be attached to the expense report for reimbursement. Documentation of motel charges, auto rental costs, and airfare must also be included, even if billed directly to the company. The name of the motel, auto rental agency, etc., should be included along with the dollar amount of the charge.

2. Travel advances may be issued one week prior to the trip. These may be cash advances from petty cash or a check from Accounts Payable. A request for a check received in Accounts Payable by noon on Wednesday will be processed that week and will be available the following Monday.

3. A company credit card may be available for travel purposes. A Funds Request marked "Credit Card" must be completed showing the estimated expenses to be charged to the credit card. For use of the company credit card, see your Petty Cash Custodian or contact the Accounting Department. Do not sign the back of the credit card. Once an individual signs the card, that card cannot be used as a company credit card. The company credit card is not to be used for cash advances from banks or motels. Upon returning from your trip, return the card within two days along with a copy of the charge receipts.

4. Complete and correct expense reports received prior to noon on Wednesday will be processed in that week's Accounts Payable check run and will be distributed via intercompany mail the following Monday. Expense reports for mileage, tolls, and gas only that are under $25.00 may be reimbursed from petty cash. All other expense reports must be sent to Accounts Payable for processing.

5. Expense reports must be completed in INK, signed, and approved. All receipts must be attached. If the expense report indicates moneys due to the company, you must have a check, traveler's checks, a money order, or a copy of a payroll deduction form attached. Do not send cash through the mail.

Travel Information Required

The employee should complete the Travel Expense Report with his/her employee number, name, plant location, department, date, and account code information.

Check what type of vehicle was used—i.e., personal or company car. The dates and location of travel should be noted. Personal automobile mileage is reimbursed at the rate of $.31 per mile for business-related use. Write in the miles traveled for each day. If you claim both mileage and gasoline receipts for the same day, explain under Remarks. Only mileage in excess of your normal mileage to and from work may be claimed.

Receipts are required for reimbursement of gasoline for company cars and rental cars.

All airfare, car rental, taxi fare, parking, and toll charges must be supported by receipts for reimbursement. Reimbursement for toll charges between plants need not be supported by receipt.

PERSONNEL POLICIES AND PROCEDURES

DISTRIBUTION:		SUBJECT: PROCEDURES FOR BUSINESS TRAVEL AND ENTERTAINMENT EXPENSE REPORTING
EFFECTIVE DATE:	PAGE 2 OF 5	FILE UNDER SECTION
REVISION DATE:	APPROVED BY:	

All motel charges must be supported by the necessary receipts. If the charges are directly billed to the Company, please note the name of the motel and obtain the amount of charges to be included on your expense report. Charges on these bills for excess telephone calls, movies, meals, etc., will be deducted from the amount due the employee or added to the amount due the company.

Employees traveling together must submit separate expense reports. If motel rooms and rental cars are shared, one person should include all shared charges, and this should be noted in the Remarks section.

On overnight trips for employees with only one family car, where the trip would leave the employee's family without access to any transportation, the company will make the following exceptions:

1. If available, a company car should be used for the trip. Only actual gasoline purchases made by the employee will be reimbursed.

2. If a company vehicle is not available and the trip is less than 150 miles one way, the employee's spouse can drive the employee to the destination or airport and return home, then return to pick up the employee after the Company business is completed. The employee would be reimbursed for mileage for all four trips. However, this must be noted in the Remarks section of the expense report.

3. If a company car is not available, a rental car may be obtained by notifying the Travel Clerk in the office.

Mileage

Personal automobile mileage is reimbursed at the rate of $.31 per mile for business-related use. Write in the miles traveled. If you claim both mileage and gasoline receipts for the same day, explain under Remarks. Travel between plant locations is based upon the standard mileage chart below. Any deviation from this mileage must be fully explained and is subject to approval by Accounting.

Only mileage in excess of your normal mileage to and from work may be claimed. If you have excess miles, please explain in the Remarks section. Otherwise, the excess miles will not be reimbursed.

Gasoline

Reimbursement of gasoline purchases for Company vehicles or rental cars will be made if a copy of the receipt is attached. Rental cars must be returned with a full tank of gas; excess charges for gasoline purchased from rental car companies may not be reimbursed. Gasoline purchases for personal vehicles are not reimbursed.

Parking/Tolls

Parking fees and tolls for nonplant travel for which you have receipts are reimbursed. Receipts for tolls between plants are not necessary. Enter the correct toll amount on your expense report.

Auto Rental

The Company uses both Avis and National Car Rental for travel. These reservations must be made by the Travel Clerk, unless there is a substantiated emergency. Avis will bill the Company directly in most cases, as will National Car Rental. Include these charges on the appropriate line of your expense report and deduct as Less Charges to Company. Make sure you fill the rental car with gasoline before returning. The Company may deduct the excess gasoline charges from the Rental Car Company from your reimbursement.

DISTRIBUTION:		SUBJECT: PROCEDURES FOR BUSINESS TRAVEL AND ENTERTAINMENT EXPENSE REPORTING
EFFECTIVE DATE:	PAGE 3 OF 5	FILE UNDER SECTION
REVISION DATE:	APPROVED BY:	

Do not accept the full collision insurance offered by car rental agencies. These charges are not reimbursable. The Company's insurance will cover any rental vehicle as long as the driver possesses a valid driver's license.

Air Fare

Travel arrangements involving air transportation for all employees must be made through the Travel Clerk, unless there is a substantiated emergency. All air fare should be charged to the Company but must appear on your expense report. Please include this under Air Fare and attach a copy of your Airline Receipt as backup.

Local Transportation

Expenses for traveling by cab, limo, or bus are reimbursable by the Company. Please use discretion when selecting your form of local travel. Whenever possible, use the most economical. Obtain a receipt and attach it to your expense report. If a receipt is not available for bus/subway transportation, you may be reimbursed for reasonable charges.

Lodging

Motel reservations should be made through the Travel Clerk. It is the employee's responsibility to pay for lodging expenses and request reimbursement through the completed expense report. Please make sure you obtain a copy of the receipt, to be attached with your expense report. The room charges must be listed under Lodging. The Company will not reimburse for in-room movies or room service charges.

Meals

A per diem allowance for meals is paid for any overnight travel or trips over 125 miles one way. Breakfast per diem is allowed for travel beginning before 7:00 A.M., and dinner per diem is allowed for travel if you cannot reasonably be expected to return prior to 7:00 P.M. Tips are included in the per diem rates.

The per diem allowance is as follows:

	Standard Rate	High Per Diem Rate
Breakfast	$ 4.00	$ 6.00
Lunch	$ 8.00	$10.00
Dinner	$16.00	$20.00
Total per Day	$28.00	$36.00

Meals provided or furnished by others are not to be included in per diem. This includes those meals included in the cost of seminars, those provided by vendors or customers, and those paid for by other employees. Because of tax law changes, most of the cost of meals is not deductible by the Company as a business expense.

Phone & Fax

Reasonable charges for personal phone calls are reimbursable on overnight trips. All business-related calls are reimbursable, but the person called and the business connection must be indicated. Management should review these expenses and disallow any excessive charges.

Business-related fax charges and telegrams are reimbursable with receipt.

Cellular phone charges for Company business calls are reimbursable within the Company guidelines. Following is the policy for Company and personal cellular phones:

PERSONNEL POLICIES AND PROCEDURES

DISTRIBUTION:		SUBJECT: PROCEDURES FOR BUSINESS TRAVEL AND ENTERTAINMENT EXPENSE REPORTING
EFFECTIVE DATE:	PAGE 4 OF 5	FILE UNDER SECTION
REVISION DATE:	APPROVED BY:	

Cellular Telephones

◆ Company Cellular Phone:

— These cellular phones are for business calls. Employees should reimburse the Company for all personal calls. On a monthly basis, contact Accounts Payable for a copy of the phone bill, review all calls, mark all personal calls, and submit a check made payable to the Accounting Department.

— When traveling outside your local coverage area, try to use the regular telephone service for nonemergency calls. Roaming charges and premium rates for air time are very costly. You might want to look into subscribing to more than one carrier service to avoid roaming charges.

◆ Personal Cellular Phone:

— Cellular business calls will be reimbursed with proper approval. The employee should supply a copy of his/her detailed cellular bill, highlight each business call, total the cost, attach this to an expense report form, and submit it to your manager for approval. Management should review each line item and determine if these costs should be reimbursed. When reviewing these items, check the date and day of the week, the time of the call, roaming charges, and the length of the call. Management should offer suggestions on ways to reduce cellular business calls.

Other

Reasonable laundry expenses will be reimbursed on trips over seven days. Receipts are necessary if charges exceed $5.00. Excess laundry charges, such as those charged by motels, will not be fully reimbursed.

An employee may be reimbursed one time for safety shoes required by the company. Safety glasses are provided for all employees and therefore are not reimbursable. Employees should be informed of the necessity of these items before leaving for the trip.

Tips for meals are included in the per diem rates. The Company does not reimburse for tips at hotels for bellhops or parking, at airports for luggage assistance, etc., unless preapproved for physical conditions.

Occasional purchases of office supplies, etc., may be put under this category with an explanation under Remarks as to the reason for the purchase and the account number to be charged.

The expense report form should not be used for the purchase of passports and/or visas.

Entertainment Expenses

Entertainment expenses for business purposes that involve company employees are charged as internal entertainment expenses. Only authorized persons may claim entertainment expenses.

Entertainment involving nonemployees is reimbursable if it is determined to have a business purpose and is held in the best interest of the Company. Only authorized persons may claim external entertainment expenses.

The Entertainment portion of the expense report must be completed, listing the names of all persons and the business purpose. All entertainment expenses must be approved by the Treasurer. Use discretion when entertaining, since because of new tax laws, much of this cost cannot be deducted as a business expense.

Nonreimbursable Expenses

The following items are not reimbursable.

◆ Personal items such as clothing, toiletries, eyeglasses/sunglasses, barber, movies, etc.
◆ Purchased luggage, briefcases, etc.

PERSONNEL POLICIES AND PROCEDURES

DISTRIBUTION:		SUBJECT: PROCEDURES FOR BUSINESS TRAVEL AND ENTERTAINMENT EXPENSE REPORTING	
EFFECTIVE DATE:	PAGE 5 OF 5	FILE UNDER SECTION	
REVISION DATE:	APPROVED BY:		

- ◆ Child care fees
- ◆ Liquor and tobacco (except approved entertainment/gifts)
- ◆ The cost of circuitous side trips or excursions
- ◆ Personalized Christmas cards
- ◆ Travel and accident insurance
- ◆ Full collision insurance offered by car rental agencies
- ◆ Gifts
- ◆ Speeding tickets
- ◆ Parking tickets or towing charges for unauthorized parking
- ◆ Locksmith charges
- ◆ Kennel fees for pets
- ◆ All expenses associated with family members who accompany you on business trips. This includes hotel cost, meals, and additional charges for cab or limo services.

PERSONNEL POLICIES AND PROCEDURES

DISTRIBUTION:		SUBJECT: EXPENSE REPORTING	
EFFECTIVE DATE:	PAGE 1 OF 1	FILE UNDER SECTION	
REVISION DATE:	APPROVED BY:		

PURPOSE:

The purpose of this policy is to provide guidelines for reimbursing associates for reasonable and necessary expenses incurred while carrying out preauthorized travel and other business-related assignments.

POLICY:

Each manager should ensure that his/her subordinates who travel on company business understand proper procedures for requesting reimbursement for covered expenses and how to correctly complete a Travel Expense Report.

A copy of the "Procedures for Business Travel and Entertainment Expense Reporting" should be provided to each manager for his/her information and for the purpose of communicating the relevant procedures to subordinates.

Questions concerning reimbursibility of specific expenses or proper procedures for expense reporting should be directed to the Accounting Section of Business Planning and Control Department.

PERSONNEL POLICIES AND PROCEDURES

DISTRIBUTION:		SUBJECT: CUSTOMER ENTERTAINMENT EXPENSES	
EFFECTIVE DATE:	PAGE 1 OF 1		FILE UNDER SECTION
REVISION DATE:	APPROVED BY:		

POLICY:

It is the policy of (Company Name) to reimburse employees for expenses incurred in business entertainment in accordance with the following guidelines.

PROCEDURE:

A. Usually entertainment of business associates will be conducted by management personnel. On occasions where circumstances justify business entertainment by nonmanagement employees, prior approval of the employee's department head must be obtained.

B. Entertainment expenses will be reimbursed only for business meals or in cases where entertainment is directly related to, or associated with, the company's business. Since it is difficult to establish precise guidelines concerning business and personal entertainment, management must rely on the judgment and good faith of its employees in this area. Expenses for entertainment of a personal nature are not deductible by the company and are not eligible for reimbursement.

C. Requests for reimbursement of entertainment expenses must be approved by the appropriate department head and submitted to accounting on an expense voucher. Such vouchers should contain a detailed itemization of expenses; the date, place, and business reason for the entertainment; and the names of those present including relationships to the company. Vouchers must include receipts for expenditures of $25.00 or more.

D. Entertainment expenses should be reasonable and will not be reimbursed if they are extravagant or lavish. An unusual or large expenditure for entertainment must be approved prior to the event by management.

E. Reimbursement of entertainment of company employees must have the approval of management in advance.

PERSONNEL POLICIES AND PROCEDURES

DISTRIBUTION:		SUBJECT: MEAL REIMBURSEMENT	
EFFECTIVE DATE:	PAGE 1 OF 1	FILE UNDER SECTION	
REVISION DATE:	APPROVED BY:		

POLICY:

It is the policy of (Company Name) to reimburse employees for the cost of meals under the following guidelines.

PROCEDURE:

A. Nonexempt employees shall receive a meal allowance of $0.00 when required to work a minimum of four hours of unscheduled overtime.

B. Employees who are required to travel overnight on company business shall be reimbursed for actual expenses of meals to a maximum of $00.00 per day.

C. Upon approval by the Human Resources Department, eligible employees may be permitted to sign for meals purchased in the company cafeteria or be reimbursed for actual expenses incurred with a maximum of ——— per day.

D. Cafeteria meal slips for eligible expenses shall be submitted with an expense voucher with approval by the department head to the accounting department for processing.

PERSONNEL POLICIES AND PROCEDURES

DISTRIBUTION:		SUBJECT: MEMBERSHIP IN CLUBS AND CIVIC ORGANIZATIONS
EFFECTIVE DATE:	PAGE 1 OF 1	FILE UNDER SECTION
REVISION DATE:	APPROVED BY:	

POLICY:

It is the policy of (Company Name) to reimburse employees under certain guidelines for membership in social clubs and civic organizations as outlined below.

PROCEDURE:

A. All employees are encouraged to seek membership in worthwhile clubs and organizations regardless of whether they are eligible for reimbursement of expenses under this policy.

B. When an employee is proposed for membership in a social club or civic organization, he/she may request reimbursement of expenses by submitting a written request approved by the employee's department head to the Human Resources Manager.

C. The decision whether to reimburse an employee for membership expenses will be based on the following considerations:

1. The nature and purpose of the club or organization.

2. The benefit to the company from the employee's membership.

3. The extent to which the company is already represented in the club or organization.

4. The level of responsibility and length of service of the employee requesting reimbursement.

5. The cost to the company.

D. Except in unusual cases, only executive and supervisory personnel will be reimbursed for membership expenses.

E. Reimbursable expenses shall include charges for dues and initiation fees. If initiation fees are paid by the company, the member employee shall execute a reimbursement agreement with the company providing for repayment to the company of any amount of initiation fee that may be refunded upon termination of the employee's membership in the organization or employment with the company.

F. Employees reimbursed for membership expenses are encouraged to use their clubs for business entertainment and must keep detailed records of their use of such organizations. The employee shall substantiate all expenses incurred, the date and business reason for use of the facilities, and the names of the persons entertained and their business relationship with the company. If any membership reimbursement is disallowed as a deduction by the Internal Revenue Service, such reimbursement may be terminated.

PERSONNEL POLICIES AND PROCEDURES

DISTRIBUTION:		SUBJECT: PARTICIPATION IN TRADE AND PROFESSIONAL ASSOCIATIONS	
EFFECTIVE DATE:	PAGE 1 OF 1	FILE UNDER SECTION	
REVISION DATE:	APPROVED BY:		

POLICY:

It is the policy of (Company Name) to encourage employees to participate in trade and professional associations.

PROCEDURE:

A. Employees are encouraged to apply for membership and take an active interest in trade and professional associations, when eligible.

B. The company will reimburse employees for membership fees or dues for trade and professional associations, subject to the prior approval or recommendation of management. Each approved membership is subject to annual review by management.

C. The company, subject to the prior approval of management, will reimburse employees for registration fees and reasonable expenses to attend meetings and conferences of trade and professional associations.

D. Employees are encouraged to submit articles, present papers, or give talks to trade and professional associations and their publications. However, prior approval must be obtained from management if any subject involves company confidential information or trade secrets and/or if such communication might be construed as representing the company's position on any subject.

E. Employees who are invited to seek or serve in any official position of a trade or professional association must obtain management approval before accepting. The company may, upon management approval, reimburse employees for reasonable expenses incurred in attending to their duties and compensation for working time lost. Any absence from work duties requires management approval.

Section 13

Safety and Health

The following checklist can be used to help you determine the various policy items that should be incorporated in your policy manual. Sample policy statements covering many of the items in the checklist appear in this section. They can be used to guide your policy statements.

Policy Manual Checklist

Our Policy Manual Should Cover:

Health and Safety Checklist

1. Is there a dispensary or first aid station?	Yes_____	No_____
A. Company-operated	Yes_____	No_____
B. Outside source	Yes_____	No_____
C. Nurse in attendance	Yes_____	No_____
D. Physician in attendance	Yes_____	No_____
E. Ambulance service available in case of emergency	Yes_____	No_____
F. Accurate records made of employee contacts:	Yes_____	No_____
(1) Health	Yes_____	No_____
(2) Accident	Yes_____	No_____
(3) General	Yes_____	No_____
G. Request employees to use dispensary when necessary? (A properly equipped first aid station with a trained nurse or physician in attendance often prevents loss of production time by preventing a slight cut or scratch from becoming infected. Arrangements can often be made for ambulance service in case of emergency.)	Yes_____	No_____
2. Are there arrangements for medical services?	Yes_____	No_____
A. Entrance physical examination. (Often uncovers handicaps unknown to new employees that can be medically corrected.)	Yes_____	No_____
B. Periodic physical examination for all workers. (Often prevents long absence by locating trouble and enabling prompt treatment. Also makes known any contagious development.)	Yes_____	No_____
C. Medical examination for employees returning to work from:	Yes_____	No_____
(1) Brief absence (determines if employee is able to work).	Yes_____	No_____
(2) Long or repeated illness (may locate cause of repeated illness).	Yes_____	No_____
D. Vaccination and inoculation services (to prevent spread of contagious diseases).	Yes_____	No_____
E. Distribution of vitamin preparations. (Used as a builder to prevent illness and disease.)	Yes_____	No_____

   F. Distribution of salt tablets (to build chemical needs of body lost
      through perspiration).   Yes_____ No_____

   G. Visiting nurse services. (May locate and correct causes of
      sickness and thereby prevent absenteeism from this cause.)   Yes_____ No_____

3. Is there a safety and accident prevention program?   Yes_____ No_____
   A. Safety engineer   Yes_____ No_____
   B. Committee   Yes_____ No_____
   C. A specific written program   Yes_____ No_____
   D. Are records kept of all accidents?   Yes_____ No_____
      (1) Analyzed to determine causes?   Yes_____ No_____
      (2) Analyzed by department and shift?   Yes_____ No_____
      (3) Is the cause analyzed to determine methods to prevent
          recurrences?   Yes_____ No_____
      (4) Is a report made to top management showing: Yes_____ No_____
          a. Accidents and causes?   Yes_____ No_____
          b. Progress in accident prevention program? (Facts must be
             compiled and causes analyzed by department and shift
             before corrective measures can be attempted.)   Yes_____ No_____
   E. Is a periodic check made on all safety devices? (This may detect
      faulty equipment before an accident occurs.)   Yes_____ No_____

4. Are safety rules and practices explained to new employees as they
   apply to each particular job?   Yes_____ No_____

5. Does company make use of first aid training?   Yes_____ No_____
   A. Have any employees taken courses in first aid?   Yes_____ No_____
   B. Is first aid practice provided for in the establishment? Yes_____ No_____

6. Is the health and safety program designed to make all employees
   "good health and safety" conscious?   Yes_____ No_____

7. Do we insist that (when indicated) workers must not wear bracelets,
   rings, and other jewelry around machines?   Yes_____ No_____

8. Do we require workers to wear (when indicated) safe wearing
   apparel and hair covering?   Yes_____ No_____

9. Does the company investigate the possibility of: Yes_____ No_____
   A. Fatigue due to too long working periods?   Yes_____ No_____
   B. Fatigue due to inadequate food?   Yes_____ No_____
   C. Need for accommodation of some employees?   Yes_____ No_____
   D. Excessive physical effort?   Yes_____ No_____
   E. Undue exposure? (Continuous fatigue may eventually result in
      illness. This means a loss of productive time. Reengineering of
      jobs may reduce fatigue.)   Yes_____ No_____

10. Do we have adequate facilities for comfort? (Consideration should
    be given to these factors to help safety and health program.) Yes_____ No_____
    A. Sanitary facility   Yes_____ No_____
    B. Matron service   Yes_____ No_____
    C. Good housekeeping   Yes_____ No_____

11. Guidelines for access to medical records   Yes_____ No_____

A. By employees   Yes_____ No_____
B. By other interested parties   Yes_____ No_____

Security

1. Guard force   Yes_____ No_____
    A. Employees of company   Yes_____ No_____
    B. Contract services   Yes_____ No_____
    C. Provided by lessee   Yes_____ No_____

2. Emergency procedures   Yes_____ No_____
    A. Medical   Yes_____ No_____
    B. Fire   Yes_____ No_____
    C. Weather   Yes_____ No_____
    D. Work stoppage   Yes_____ No_____

3. Fire drills—frequency?   Yes_____ No_____

4. Security incident report   Yes_____ No_____

5. Entrance/exit procedure for employees   Yes_____ No_____

6. Entrance/exit procedure for visitors   Yes_____ No_____

7. Investigative policy   Yes_____ No_____

Alcohol/Drug Abuse

1. Possession of drugs/alcohol on company property   Yes_____ No_____

2. Requirements of duties   Yes_____ No_____

3. Definitions—drugs, etc.   Yes_____ No_____

4. Training for management   Yes_____ No_____

5. Referral to employee assistance program   Yes_____ No_____

6. Disciplinary procedures   Yes_____ No_____

7. Searches and investigations   Yes_____ No_____

8. Drug testing   Yes_____ No_____
    A. Pre-employment   Yes_____ No_____
    B. Promotion/transfer   Yes_____ No_____
    C. Company physicals   Yes_____ No_____
    D. Investigative   Yes_____ No_____
    E. Random testing   Yes_____ No_____
    F. Chain of custody requirements   Yes_____ No_____

9. Procedure if drug tests are positive   Yes_____ No_____

10. Exams/testing after first tests   Yes_____ No_____

11. Prescription medication   Yes_____ No_____

12. Employee education program   Yes_____ No_____

AIDS

1. Company philosophy   Yes_____ No_____

2. Group insurance coverages   Yes_____ No_____

3. Legal responsibilities of company   Yes_____ No_____

4. Accommodation measures for affected employees   Yes_____ No_____

5. Education of employees   Yes_____ No_____

6. Confidentiality of information   Yes_____ No_____

7. Refusal of nonaffected employee to work with AIDS-affected
   employee   Yes_____ No_____

8. Company and community resources for treatment and counseling Yes_____ No_____

9. Requirement for medical certification of AIDS-affected employee   Yes_____ No_____

Employee Assistance Program (EAP)

1. Purpose of EAP   Yes_____ No_____

2. Who provides services (company vs. outside agency)   Yes_____ No_____

3. Guidelines for availability   Yes_____ No_____
   A. What problems are covered   Yes_____ No_____
   B. How to receive help—who to contact   Yes_____ No_____
   C. Who covered—employee, family, etc.   Yes_____ No_____
   D. Cost to employee/family   Yes_____ No_____
   E. Coordination with group health plan   Yes_____ No_____

4. Responsibilities of employee   Yes_____ No_____

5. Responsibilities of immediate supervisor   Yes_____ No_____

6. Responsibilities of EAP coordinator   Yes_____ No_____

7. Confidentiality of information   Yes_____ No_____

8. Coordination with disciplinary policies   Yes_____ No_____

9. Effect upon other company policies/procedures   Yes_____ No_____

10. Education of manager/supervisors   Yes_____ No_____

11. Education of employees/families   Yes_____ No_____

OSHA—Hazard Communication Standard

1. Notices to employees—where, etc.	Yes_____ No_____
2. Inventory of all chemicals	Yes_____ No_____
3. Identification of hazardous substances	Yes_____ No_____
4. Material Safety Data Sheets (MSDS)	Yes_____ No_____
A. Availability to employees	Yes_____ No_____
B. Availability to others	Yes_____ No_____
5. Labeling requirements	Yes_____ No_____
6. Training requirements	Yes_____ No_____
7. Hazardous substance spill cleanup procedures	Yes_____ No_____
8. Coverage of contractors (subcontractors)	Yes_____ No_____
9. Record retention requirements	Yes_____ No_____

How to Maintain a Drug-Free Workplace

Most organizations realize that there are no neat or easy solutions to the problems associated with employee substance abuse. Alcohol and drug abuse usually mask deeper problems with family, marriage, finances, or some other area.

Substance abuse in the workplace is now recognized as a monumental problem that has reached crisis proportions. Chemical dependency is not limited to high-powered, intense, competitive industries, nor is it confined to big cities or special groups. Every profession, every occupation, every level in the labor-management hierarchy, and every region of the country is affected or has the potential to be affected.

The statistics are not encouraging. It is believed that between 10 percent and 23 percent of all U.S. workers use dangerous drugs on the job. Upwards of 73 percent of drug abusers hold full-time jobs. Additionally, drug users have ten times greater absenteeism, four times greater accident rates, 30 percent lower productivity, five times greater workers' compensation experiences, and three times higher health-care costs. Additionally, 50 percent of accidents reported by companies are alcohol- or drug-related.

Management teams are divided into two groups in their approach to substance abuse problems. One approach is passive—dealing with problems as they arise rather than confronting the issue and planning preventive and corrective measures. Under this approach, management may even appear to accept employees' drug problems, and the resulting drop in productivity, as one of the costs of running a company in today's world. This approach is really a holding action that appears to buy management time to study the problem instead of jumping in with quick solutions, such as a blanket firing policy, that could do more harm than good.

On the other hand, a more active approach can be beneficial if it includes a policy that clearly states that the company will not tolerate drug use, not only because drug abuse poses moral and legal dangers to our society as a whole, but because it endangers employees' health and the company's well-being. It is prudent for management to devise a plan to deal with the problem and take the initiative.

Listed below are ten essential steps that will aid you in developing a plan of action for effective intervention and treatment:

1. *Early intervention.* Intervention needs to occur at the earliest possible point. The problem seldom

improves when left alone. Protection of a substance abuser usually supports chronic use and leads to a drop in employee morale and productivity.

2. *Involve the employee's family.* Denial, projection, and avoidance of treatment are basic to the substance abuse process. Success is very dependent on the involvement of all members of the employee's support system.

3. *Be certain.* It is essential that you be certain that there is a problem involving substance abuse. The employee will often admit the problem when faced with specific evidence of behavioral and performance deficits.

4. *Be firm.* When it has been established that there is a substance abuse problem, it is essential that there be very specific and definite expectations for treatment. Follow up on every detail of the agreement. It is what you inspect that will determine success—not what you expect.

5. *Treatment takes at least one year.* The substance abuser's prognosis depends very much upon extended treatment. Total abstinence during and after treatment is essential.

6. *Treatment should include the family.* Substance abuse is a family system's problem. If treatment is to be successful, the entire family must change.

7. *In-patient and out-patient treatment work.* Success rates are determined more by the quality of the treatment program than by where or how it is provided. Use the most cost-effective form.

8. *The employee should share in the cost of the treatment.* There is less resistance to treatment when costs are shared.

9. *Confidentiality is important.* While others may know that there is a problem, discussion should be restricted to management and the employee. The employee's family should be involved only with the employee's permission.

10. *Be optimistic.* Positive expectations are important and should be maintained. Good employees are worth investing in. However, remember that addiction is powerful and that toughness and active follow-up are the foundations of success.

The formation of a written policy is also a very important step. Several points to be considered and addressed in a policy would include the following:

1. *Prohibitions must be specific.* The policy should state the behaviors that will cause discharge, such as possession of illegal drugs, proven use of illegal drugs, sale of illegal drugs, etc.

2. *Disciplinary steps must be specific.* The policy should state the procedures for confronting, warning, disciplining, referring, and counseling employees who have been found to be drug-impaired.

3. *Firing procedures must be clear.* The policy should state whether discharged employees will be eligible for future employment and the conditions employees must meet for rehire, including how seniority is affected by termination.

4. *Drug testing must be fair to all employees.* The policy should state the methods and procedures that will be used to prove that employees are free from drug impairment, as well as secondary procedures to verify positive results.

5. *Exceptions to the rule must be stated clearly.* For example, those employees who take medical prescriptions may be asked to submit proof that they are under a qualified medical doctor's care, etc.

6. *The policy must be widely publicized.* Every employee must be aware of the policy. This means that management must disseminate the policy frequently and explain the related program to all new hires. Confidentiality of results is equally as important.

AIDS

The Center for Disease Control estimates that one in 250 persons in the United States is infected with HIV, and that by the year 2000, an estimated 40 million people worldwide will be infected with HIV.

The estimated average annual cost to treat a person with AIDS is $17,000, and with new drug treatments, the life expectancy is increasing. American businesses, faced with this problem, must act in a way that will enable them to meet the challenges of the AIDS epidemic.

Of Fortune 500 companies, about 20 percent have a formal policy and/or practice for dealing with AIDS in the workplace. The percentage is probably half that if small firms, where the majority of Americans are employed, are included.*

In a recent survey, only 39 percent of the businesses questioned had begun to map any strategy for dealing with AIDS. Alarmingly, only 18 percent had formalized their strategies as policy statements.

Why should businesses wait until an employee develops AIDS or until other circumstances force the company to develop an AIDS policy? To encourage you and to make the effort less difficult, we would offer the following comments, in addition to a sample policy statement and actual policies:

1. Determine your company's philosophy toward and strategy for dealing with AIDS by using a team of key personnel.
2. Understand the legal responsibilities of the company and its employees.
3. Make sure that health insurance provides broad but cost-effective coverage for all catastrophic illnesses.
4. Develop a written AIDS policy—consider AIDS as a handicap, and assure confidentiality and reasonable accommodation.
5. Prepare an educational program for all employees, especially managers and supervisors.

The following policies are found in this section:

Safety—General
Safety Program
Safety Rules and Procedures
Safety Protection
Access to Medical Records
Medical Information Request/Authorization Form
Emergencies
Fire Prevention
Security
Alcohol/Drug Abuse
AIDS in the Workplace
Employee Assistance Program

* *Los Angeles Times*, November 11, 1991.

PERSONNEL POLICIES AND PROCEDURES

DISTRIBUTION:		SUBJECT: SAFETY—GENERAL	
EFFECTIVE DATE:	PAGE 1 OF 3	FILE UNDER SECTION	
REVISION DATE:	APPROVED BY:		

SUPERVISOR'S RESPONSIBILITY:

1. Employee safety on the job is the primary responsibility of every foreman and supervisor. The Safety Department acts only as a coordinator. Employee safety cannot succeed without the supervisor's utmost sincerity and effort. The company has gone to great expense to provide safe working conditions throughout the plant. It is the supervisor's duty to see that there is complete safety in his/her area at all times.

2. Both the employee and his/her environment are contributing factors in over 60 percent of all accidents. The supervisor must, therefore, be constantly on the alert for incidents of human error and mechanical failure. He/she must take the initiative to make corrections where he/she has authority to do so. And, lacking direct authority, he/she must report any condition or employee practice that is likely to cause an accident.

3. The supervisor must be convinced that accidents are caused; they don't just happen. An act of negligence, disregard for established rules or procedures, being in a hurry, improperly guarded machinery, lack of or improper maintenance, can all cause an accident.

4. The supervisor must also be convinced that an accident does not affect the employee alone. Accidents cost money and have a direct impact on company profitability. Accidents affect production and directly reflect on the efficiency of the department.

SUPERVISOR'S ACTION:

To make the program effective, every member of management shall ensure that:

1. Work that is hazardous or located in a hazardous area is not assigned until all steps have been taken to provide for the safety of the employee.

2. All employees have received proper job instruction and are familiar with pertinent safety and health rules and regulations.

3. Work areas are frequently examined to ascertain that the work environment is safe and that employees are working in a safe manner.

4. All safety and health deficiencies are corrected immediately and not repeated.

5. Accidents are investigated and corrective action is initiated where necessary.

Like the supervisor, every employee has a specific role in our loss-prevention efforts. Each employee is expected to participate actively in the Safety Program and observe all established precautionary measures.

REPORTING INJURIES:

Injuries, no matter how minor, are to be reported to the Medical Department immediately. If circumstances permit, the employee shall be given a First Aid pass. In no case shall the injured be moved before examination by the Medical or Safety Department if the injury is serious. It is equally important that all spectators be kept away from the scene of an

455

DISTRIBUTION:		SUBJECT: SAFETY—GENERAL	
EFFECTIVE DATE:	PAGE 2 OF 3	FILE UNDER SECTION	
REVISION DATE:	APPROVED BY:		

accident. A supervisor should not permit employees to leave their work areas to go to the scene of an accident. Doctor's notes, etc., brought in by the employee should be forwarded directly to the Safety Department.

Failure to report injuries or illnesses may result in a delay or denial of workers' compensation benefits.

CORRECTING DEFICIENCIES:

The department supervisor or foreman is responsible for correcting or causing to be corrected any hazard that is found as a result of his/her department inspections or investigation of an accident, or is brought to his/her attention by an employee. All corrective action must be followed up to ensure completion.

Where necessary, assistance should be requested from the Safety Department.

ACCIDENT INVESTIGATION:

Upon receipt of an investigation form, it shall be completed as soon as possible and returned to the Safety Department. Instructions on the form should be followed explicitly.

WORKERS' COMPENSATION:

Employees who sustain an occupational injury or illness will be compensated in accordance with the state workers' compensation act. In order to receive such benefits, the appropriate notification and medical reports must be provided by the employee.

Any lost time as a result of work-related injury that also qualifies as a medical leave of absence will be charged against an eligible employee's annual FMLA entitlement.

PHYSICAL EXAMINATION:

Physical examinations are required of all employees:

A. Upon employment or re-employment.

B. Upon return to work after a leave of absence for an illness of longer than three (3) calendar days in duration.

C. Upon return to work after an absence from the plant of six (6) months' duration or longer.

D. As required by OSHA: blood work, air sample tests, dental checks, urine samples, hearing tests, physicals, etc.

PERSONAL PROTECTIVE EQUIPMENT:

Where necessary, by reason of hazard, the company will provide the necessary personal protective equipment to ensure the well-being of the employee. These items include:

DISTRIBUTION:		SUBJECT: SAFETY—GENERAL	
EFFECTIVE DATE:	PAGE 3 OF 3	FILE UNDER SECTION	
REVISION DATE:	APPROVED BY:		

A. Safety glasses

B. Gloves

C. Aprons

D. Safety shoes

E. Respiratory equipment

Supervision must review operation and provide or request to be provided (by Safety Department) the necessary protection. Items such as clothing, gloves, aprons, protective creams, etc., must be supplied and issued by the department head.

PERSONNEL POLICIES AND PROCEDURES

DISTRIBUTION:		SUBJECT: SAFETY PROGRAM	
EFFECTIVE DATE:	PAGE 1 OF 3		FILE UNDER SECTION
REVISION DATE:	APPROVED BY:		

RESPONSIBILITY:

The Employee Relations Manager shall coordinate Division safety activities, establishing procedures for promoting safe working conditions, conducting safety meetings, reviewing accidents, and recommending measures to reduce accidents and health hazards; he/she shall work with the workers' compensation carrier and with local, state, and federal agencies to assure that safety and health standards fully meet applicable requirements.

Line management, including the Plant Manager, the Manufacturing Manager, and all foremen and supervisors, shall be responsible for incorporating safety and good housekeeping into the day-to-day activities of their departments, including taking corrective and preventive action on problems within their departments.

The Safety and Housekeeping Committee shall meet on a monthly basis. Consisting of hourly and salaried employees representing all departments and shifts, the Committee shall bring to management's attention for corrective action any safety and housekeeping problems noted during the preceding month. The Committee shall review progress on solving problems previously brought up, recommending solutions wherever possible. Promotion of interest and cooperation on safety and housekeeping matters shall be a prime concern of the Committee.

SAFETY RULES:

Employees and supervisors have cooperated in the establishment of Division safety rules. Each foreman and supervisor is responsible for seeing that the rules are observed within his/her own department, and for taking corrective or disciplinary action as required to assure that work is carried out within these rules.

EMPLOYMENT:

The Human Resources Department shall screen applicants for employment so as to ensure that they are placed in jobs to which their physical capacities are suited. Questionable cases shall be referred to outside medical authorities for evaluation.

ORIENTATION:

Foremen and supervisors shall double-check the hiring/placement decision, noting any physical problems with applicants and new employees, and recommending corrective action as required. They shall also be responsible for ensuring that the new employee knows all safety, health, and housekeeping rules to which his/her job is subject.

TRAINING AND EDUCATION:

The Human Resources Department shall coordinate the use of meetings, films, discussion groups, communications, and other activities to train selected groups and educate all employees for awareness of safety and housekeeping problems. Line management shall recommend specific areas where such training and education may be required.

ACCIDENTS:

The foreman or supervisor shall report each industrial accident or health problem requiring outside treatment to the Human Resources Department on the Supervisor's Accident Investigation Report. The foremen and the Human Resources

PERSONNEL POLICIES AND PROCEDURES

DISTRIBUTION:		SUBJECT: SAFETY PROGRAM	
EFFECTIVE DATE:	PAGE 2 OF 3	FILE UNDER SECTION	
REVISION DATE:	APPROVED BY:		

Department, together with members of management as required, shall investigate reported accidents, taking corrective action as necessary to prevent recurrence.

INSPECTIONS:

Together with a representative of the workers' compensation carrier, with personnel of local, state, and federal agencies, or with other Division personnel, the Employee Relations Manager, Plant Manager, Manufacturing Manager, and foremen shall inspect the facility regularly for safety and housekeeping problems. Such problems as may be found shall be evaluated and corrective action taken as required.

ENGINEERING:

Plant, manufacturing, industrial, and product engineering activities shall be carried out so as to eliminate hazards involving defective equipment and inadequate facilities on both a preventive and a remedial basis.

FACILITIES:

The company shall maintain facilities for first aid, fire extinguishers, emergency exits, walkways, parking lots, control panels, air temperature and cleanliness, lavatories, lighting, and other environmental factors that fully meet the requirements applicable to the Division.

DEFICIENCIES:

Such deficiencies as may be found in Division safety and housekeeping procedures by insurance personnel or representatives of local, state, and federal agencies shall be evaluated and corrected as required.

SAFETY RULES FOR ALL DEPARTMENTS:

These safety rules have been established by the Division Safety Housekeeping Committee and approved by Division management for the protection of each employee. All employees are requested to cooperate in observing these rules, and to help in making the Division a safe and orderly place to work.

1. Never operate any machine or equipment unless you are specifically authorized to do so by your supervisor.

2. Do not operate defective equipment. Do not use broken hand tools. Report defective or hazardous equipment to your supervisor.

3. Obtain full instructions from your supervisor before operating a machine with which you are not familiar.

4. Never start on any hazardous job without being completely familiar with the safety techniques that apply to it. Check with your supervisor if in doubt.

459

PERSONNEL POLICIES AND PROCEDURES

DISTRIBUTION:		SUBJECT: SAFETY PROGRAM	
EFFECTIVE DATE:	PAGE 3 OF 3	FILE UNDER SECTION	
REVISION DATE:	APPROVED BY:		

5. Make sure that all safety attachments are in place and properly adjusted before operating any machine.

6. Do not operate any machine or equipment at unsafe speeds. Shut off equipment that is not in use.

7. Wear all protective garments and equipment necessary to be safe on the job. Wear proper shoes; sandals or other open-toed or thin-soled shoes should not be worn.

8. Do not wear loose, flowing clothing or long hair while operating moving machinery.

9. Never repair or adjust any machine or equipment unless you are specifically authorized to do so by your supervisor.

10. Never oil, clean, repair, or adjust any machine while it is in motion.

11. Never repair or adjust any electrically driven machine without opening and properly tagging the main switch.

12. Put tools and equipment away when they are not in use.

13. Do not lift items that are too bulky or too heavy to be handled by one person. Ask for assistance.

14. Keep all aisles, stairways, and exits clear of skids, boxes, air hoses, equipment, and spillage.

15. Do not place equipment and materials so as to block emergency exit routes, fire boxes, sprinkler shutoffs, machine or electrical control panels, or fire extinguishers.

16. Stack all materials neatly and make sure piles are stable.

17. Keep your work area, machinery, and all company facilities that you use clean and neat.

18. Do not participate in horseplay or tease or otherwise distract fellow workers. Do not run on company premises—always walk.

19. Power-truck operators must safeguard other workers at all times; workers must show courtesy to power-truck operators.

20. Never take chances. If you're unsure, ask your supervisor. Let good common sense be your guide.

PERSONNEL POLICIES AND PROCEDURES

DISTRIBUTION:		SUBJECT: SAFETY AND OPERATING RULES AND REGULATIONS	
EFFECTIVE DATE:	PAGE 1 OF 1	FILE UNDER SECTION	
REVISION DATE:	APPROVED BY:		

POLICY:

Providing safe working conditions and maintaining continuity of employment are of continual concern. In this regard, it is important that adequate policies and procedures be developed and adhered to in order to ensure safe, efficient operating conditions, thereby safeguarding employees and facilities.

The company will not knowingly permit unsafe conditions to exist, nor will it permit employees to indulge in unsafe acts. Violations of company rules and regulations will result in disciplinary action.

The company believes that the safety of employees and physical property can best be ensured by a meaningful program.

A. Employee—Since the employee on the job is frequently more aware of unsafe conditions than anyone else, employees are encouraged to make recommendations, suggestions, and criticisms of unsafe conditions to their immediate supervisor so that they may be corrected.

B. Supervisors—Supervisors are responsible for the working conditions within their department and the plant generally. A supervisor should remain alert at all times to dangerous and unsafe conditions, so that he/she may recommend corrective action, discipline employees who habitually create or indulge in unsafe practices, assess new or changed situations for inherent dangers, and follow up on employee suggestions for corrective action so that unsafe conditions are not instituted or permitted to exist.

COMMITTEE MEETINGS:

Safety—It is company policy to establish an effective Safety and Health Committee, made up of six to ten management and warehouse employees.

It is recommended that plant employees be appointed to the Safety Committee for a six-month term, thereby allowing other employees a chance to participate.

Plant inspections are to be made weekly by designated Committee members and the findings reported in writing to the entire Committee and the President.

In order to be effective, regular monthly meetings are scheduled to include, but are not limited to, the following agenda:

1. Review minutes from last meeting.

2. Determine those areas that continue to present a safety hazard.

3. Review building inspection reports and, where unfavorable, unsafe, or potentially unsafe conditions exist, determine action to be taken in order to eliminate such conditions.

4. Review those work-related injuries and illnesses and workers' compensation cases that have arisen since the last meeting; determine actions required in order to reduce the possibility of further injuries.

5. Review OSHA violations and/or citations (if any) to assure prompt compliance. It is the responsibility of the Committee Secretary to prepare minutes of each meeting.

It is the responsibility of the Safety Committee to develop procedures covering the Safety Programs, to distribute the inspection procedure and checklist, to provide supervisory guidance procedures for analyzing and investigating accidents, to review the fire drill schedule and procedure, and to establish and monitor progress as the Committee deems appropriate.

PERSONNEL POLICIES AND PROCEDURES

DISTRIBUTION:		SUBJECT: SAFETY/PROTECTION	
EFFECTIVE DATE:	PAGE 1 OF 1	FILE UNDER SECTION	
REVISION DATE:	APPROVED BY:		

EYE PROTECTION:

Supervisors may obtain eye protection (safety glasses, goggles, etc.) for their employees from First Aid.

If the eye protection is lost or destroyed due to the employee's negligence, the employee will be responsible for the cost of a replacement pair.

PRESCRIPTION SAFETY GLASSES:

Employees working in potential eye-hazard areas who need prescription glasses may submit a request through their supervisor to First Aid for prescription safety glasses. The prescription safety glasses can be obtained through a company-approved source. The company will assume the cost of the glasses.

If the prescription safety glasses are lost or destroyed due to the employee's negligence within one year of the date of issue, the employee will be responsible for the cost of a replacement pair.

EAR PROTECTION:

Employees working in areas where the noise level is 80 decibels or more may obtain ear protection through their supervisor from First Aid.

Personnel in 80-decibel-or-more areas are given a yearly hearing test.

FOOT PROTECTION:

All employees should wear substantial shoes to protect their feet and toes.

The company allots $10 per year, per person, for safety shoes for those employees who work in areas where safety shoes are recommended. The safety shoes must meet federal standards and can be purchased through several local suppliers.

HAIR/HEAD PROTECTION:

Employees with long hair (down to the shoulders) should tie their hair back or wear hair nets or caps when working on drill presses, vertical milling machines, or equipment with rotating spindies or other moving machinery.

Riders of tow trucks should wear a hard hat when operating the vehicle.

GENERAL:

Loose clothing must not be worn near moving machinery.

Neckties must be securely clipped to the shirt.

Employees working in areas where chemicals, solvents, other irritants, or caustic acids are used (e.g., tumbling room) will be supplied with rubber face shields, boots, aprons, etc.

Rings and jewelry must not be worn when working on machinery.

Work gloves (leather-palmed) must be worn by anyone handling raw material coils.

PERSONNEL POLICIES AND PROCEDURES

DISTRIBUTION:		SUBJECT: ACCESS TO MEDICAL RECORDS	
EFFECTIVE DATE:	PAGE 1 OF 1	FILE UNDER SECTION	
REVISION DATE:	APPROVED BY:		

POLICY:

This policy describes procedures for providing employees with access to: (1) records maintained by the company on exposure to toxic substances and harmful physical agents, and (2) personal medical records. These procedures have been adopted to comply with Occupational Safety and Health Administration (OSHA) standards and state law.

The policy and procedures described herein are intended to: (1) safeguard exposure and medical records; (2) maintain confidentiality; and (3) provide access within fifteen (15) days from the date such records are officially requested.

IMMEDIATE SUPERVISOR:

When employees request access to their exposure and/or medical records, a copy of the Information Request and Authorization Form must be completed. Supervisors are to follow the procedures outlined in the steps below:

1. Provide the requesting employee with a copy of the Information Request and Authorization Form for completion and return it to the employee's immediate supervisor.

2. Check to be certain that the completed form is accurate, complete, and legible.

3. Sign and date the form in the spaces provided.

4. Immediately send the form, via company mail, to the Health Services Unit.

5. Upon receipt of the requesting employee's medical records, sign and date the accompanying Medical Records Receipt Form. Do not open the envelope within which the requesting employee's medical records are contained.

6. Obtain the requesting employee's signature on the Medical Records Receipt Form and the date of receipt.

7. Give the envelope containing the medical records to the requesting employee.

8. Send the Medical Records Receipt Form to the Health Services Unit by company mail.

PERSONNEL POLICIES AND PROCEDURES

DISTRIBUTION:		SUBJECT: EMERGENCIES	
EFFECTIVE DATE:	PAGE 1 OF 1	FILE UNDER SECTION	
REVISION DATE:	APPROVED BY:		

EMERGENCY NUMBER: (Fire, Police, Ambulance) _____

Medical—To summon an ambulance in the event of a medical emergency, dial _____.

Advise administration. Have an employee posted at the service elevator to wait for the ambulance service and to direct them to the proper department quickly. A member of the department should accompany the person being treated.

Fire—Each department of the company has an acting Fire Warden. At Branch A there are two fire wardens on each floor. Each building has an exit procedure to be followed in case of a fire. These procedures are rehearsed in periodic drills; however, you should make a point of contacting your Fire Warden and asking him/her to tell you about the procedure and show you the location of emergency exits and fire extinguishers. In this way, you will not be completely unprepared if there is an emergency when the Fire Warden is out of the building.

In the event of a fire, leave the building by means of the stairways and proceed down to the street. At Branch B, do not stop on the plaza level. Fire Department regulations require that this area be cleared to facilitate their operations.

ELEVATORS SHOULD NEVER BE USED IN FIRE OR STORM EMERGENCY:

Weather—In the event of snow, heavy rains, or other unusual weather conditions creating hazardous travel during working hours, the Executive Vice President in charge of Administration will decide if and when the office will be closed early to permit personnel to leave. Such announcements will also include the closing hours of the switchboard, the mailroom, and the telex room. If such weather conditions occur at night or on weekends, you must use your own judgment. We do, however, expect all employees to make every reasonable effort to report to work.

PERSONNEL POLICIES AND PROCEDURES

DISTRIBUTION:		SUBJECT: SAFETY HABITS/FIRE PREVENTION	
EFFECTIVE DATE:	PAGE 1 OF 1	FILE UNDER SECTION	
REVISION DATE:	APPROVED BY:		

The company expects each employee to do everything possible to safeguard the plant from damage by fire.

Each employee can help prevent such a disaster by keeping his/her work area clean and free of rubbish, and by observing all rules regarding fire prevention.

Combustible and Flammable Materials

Flammable materials such as paper, cardboard, oily rags, etc., must never be placed near steam pipes or radiators. All oily waste and other materials of no value must be placed in the metal receptacles provided.

Care must be exercised in the handling of flammable materials, especially flammable liquids. Extreme caution should be taken to see that such materials are not spilled or splashed, particularly on clothing. Flammable liquids must be kept only in properly labeled safety containers provided for that purpose.

Fire Exits and Drills

Supervisors should instruct each new employee of the location of the two exits nearest his/her working place.

In case of fire, WALK to your assigned exit. Do not shout or say anything that might lead to panic among fellow employees. A building can be emptied quickly if everybody keeps calm.

Fire drills are held a minimum of once a year to ensure the prompt and safe exit of employees from all buildings in case of an actual fire. Prompt obedience to supervisors' and fire captains' instructions is required during these drills.

PERSONNEL POLICIES AND PROCEDURES

DISTRIBUTION:		SUBJECT: OSHA—HAZARD COMMUNICATION STANDARD	
EFFECTIVE DATE:	PAGE 1 OF 3	FILE UNDER SECTION	
REVISION DATE:	APPROVED BY:		

POLICY:

It is the policy of (Company Name) to fully comply with the Hazard Communication Standard (better known as the Right to Know Law) as enacted by the Occupational Safety and Health Administration.

PROCEDURES:

A. It is the responsibility of the company Safety Supervisor (or designee) to post notices throughout the company facilities informing employees of the times and locations the written hazard communication program and Material Safety Data Sheets (MSDSs) are available for inspection. This information is to be posted on all company bulletin boards.

B. It is the responsibility of the Safety Supervisor, assisted by the company's Purchasing Agent, to compile an inventory of all chemicals used at the facility. It should then be determined which chemicals are regulated by (1) determining if they appear on any of the base lists and (2) if not, requesting the chemical supplier to indicate whether or not the chemical as been determined to be hazardous.

(Company Name) will identify and consider the available scientific evidence concerning the physical and health hazards of all substances in the facility. If the substances are combustible liquids, compressed gases, explosive, flammable, organic peroxides, oxidizers, pyrophoric, unstable, or water-reactive as defined in the federal standard, they are regulated as hazardous chemicals. The company will also follow the guidelines in the standards' appendices, to determine if the substances present a health hazard because of any "statistically significant evidence" that acute or chronic health effects may occur in employees exposed to the substances.

C. (Company Name) has requested and obtained Material Safety Data Sheets (MSDSs) for all regulated chemicals in the facility. The Safety Supervisor is responsible for reviewing incoming MSDSs to assure that they are complete. If a MSDS is not received or is incomplete, he/she should send a written request for a complete MSDS to the supplier and retain a copy of the request to document the company's attempts to obtain the MSDS.

Copies of MSDSs are retained in the work area where each hazardous substance is present. A master file of all MSDSs is available in the Safety Supervisor's office. Employees are allowed to view and read MSDSs at any time. To obtain copies of MSDSs, employees should submit a written request to the Safety Supervisor. Request forms are available in the Safety office. The company will provide the requested MSDS within three working days. If the requested MSDS is not immediately available, the company will provide it within fifteen days of the request. If the company fails to provide the requested MSDS within this timeframe, the employee may request to be temporarily transferred from the area in which contact with the particular substance exists. Copies of MSDSs are also kept in the Maintenance Department for use in emergency situations. The Employee Safety Training Manual describes this system in greater detail. Upon written request, MSDSs will be provided to an employee's authorized designated representative. The designated representative must have written authorization from the employee. (Editor's Note: An employee's collective bargaining agent does not need written authorization from the employee to obtain an MSDS.)

D. All containers of regulated chemicals at (Company Name) will be labeled to identify their contents and to alert

466

employees to hazards. Labels on containers brought into or shipped out of the facility are to be checked by the Safety Supervisor to assure that they include:

1. The name of all hazardous substances—i.e., trade name, common name, part number that exactly references the appropriate MSDS.

2. The name and address of the chemical manufacturer, importer, or other responsible party.

3. Appropriate hazard warnings (i.e., words, symbols, pictures) that convey the hazard of the contained chemical.

E. (Company Name) shall provide training to its employees about the hazard communication standard and about safety measures for working with hazardous substances. Training is to be given during normal working hours, with pay.

Employees also shall receive training when they are first hired or assigned to work in an area where they may be exposed to hazardous substances. Training will be done annually thereafter. If new hazards are introduced into the workplace, additional training and information will be required. The Safety Supervisor also shall publish an Employee Safety Manual for each employee that includes:

1. An explanation of the hazard communication standard.

2. Instructions in various aspects of the standard, including:

    a. Hazardous substance identification.
    b. MSDS preparation and availability.
    c. Labeling requirements.
    d. Training requirements.

3. Employee rights, including protection from discrimination and disciplinary action.

4. An explanation of the information that MSDSs contain, including a sample MSDS.

5. An explanation in nontechnical terms of the MSDSs for the specific substances used, handled, or stored by employees in each work area.

6. An explanation of the health effects of hazardous substances.

7. An explanation of how and why to use protective clothing and equipment.

8. A description of the equipment and procedures used by the company to monitor work areas and to detect the release of hazardous substances.

9. Instruction in the way employees can detect the release of hazardous substances.

The training manual is to be used by all employees and explained verbally to all employees by the Safety Supervisor. Training should include verbal instruction and demonstrations concerning the hazards and the correct fitting and use of protective equipment.

Records shall be kept by the Safety Supervisor of the training each employee receives. The records should include a description of the training, dates given, attendance records, and name of the instructor. These records shall be maintained for three years after each employee has ceased to be an employee of the company.

F. Hazardous substance spill cleanup shall be conducted under the supervision of the Safety Supervisor. Necessary instructions and protective equipment will be provided employees involved in these tasks. Training for these tasks should include a brief review of the hazards of the substances involved and, especially, the protective equipment and other measures necessary for the safe performance of the task.

PERSONNEL POLICIES AND PROCEDURES

DISTRIBUTION:		SUBJECT: OSHA—HAZARD COMMUNICATION STANDARD	
EFFECTIVE DATE:	PAGE 3 OF 3	FILE UNDER SECTION	
REVISION DATE:	APPROVED BY:		

G. Employees of contractors operating in the company's facilities will be given necessary protective equipment. It is company policy to require that such equipment be worn by employees of contractors when working in the facility. If these employees are performing work that involves specific substances, they will be informed of the hazards and safety precautions before entering areas that contain hazardous substances and will be allowed to see MSDSs, if they wish.

H. All MSDSs obtained, compiled or prepared by (Company Name) are maintained for a period of thirty years.

I. It is the responsibility of the Safety Supervisor to assure the company's compliance with the Federal Hazard Communication Standard, as well as any state/local regulations that may apply. Any question should be addressed to the Safety Supervisor.

[*Editor's Note:* Additional state right to know regulations and community right to know standards—including regulations under the Superfund Amendment and Reauthorization Act of 1988 (Title III)—will also apply to your company. Before adopting this policy for your company, you should examine all state, county, etc., regulations involving hazardous substances. These regulations may impose more stringent guidelines than those mentioned above. Also, please note that Safety Supervisor in this policy may be exchanged for the individual in your company responsible for safety.]

PERSONNEL POLICIES AND PROCEDURES

DISTRIBUTION:		SUBJECT: PERSONNEL FILE ACCESS	
EFFECTIVE DATE:	PAGE 1 OF 3	FILE UNDER SECTION	
REVISION DATE:	APPROVED BY:		

PURPOSE:

The purpose of this policy is to define procedures to allow associates access to their personnel and medical files.

POLICY:

Upon the written request of an associate, personnel files or medical files containing records relating solely to that associate will be made available to the individual, with the following exceptions: investigative files, files dealing with potential or actual litigation and claims, and personnel planning documents (other than performance appraisals).

This access will be given to the associate in the presence of a Human Resources representative at a time convenient to the associate and facility management without disruption of normal business operations. The associate will be permitted to make notes concerning any such information; however, no photocopies will be allowed.

A. Personnel Records:

Personnel files containing records relating solely to that associate will be made available to the associate in the presence of a representative of the Human Resources Section. The associate will be permitted to make notes concerning any information.

B. Medical and Industrial Records:

Medical and industrial hygiene records should be kept separate from associate personnel files. The records should be retained for the duration of employment plus thirty (30) years. This includes records of occupational injury and all types of treatment and testing by the company. Medical records to which an associate may be given access include reports of physical examinations and laboratory tests made by physicians acting for the company. Physicians' statements concerning leaves of absence or work restrictions may also be reviewed by the associate, as well as records of associate exposure to workplace conditions.

Associates interested in obtaining information must fill out a "Request for Access to Associate Medical Records" form and turn it in to the Human Resources Department.

"Associate Medical Records" does not include:

1. Records concerning health insurance claims,
2. Records created solely in preparation for litigation, which are privileged from discovery under applicable rules of procedure or evidence, or
3. Records concerning voluntary associate assistance programs (alcohol, drug abuse, or personal counseling programs).

Unless provided for by state law, access to associate personnel files is limited to the individual only.

ACCESS BY INDIVIDUALS OTHER THAN THE ASSOCIATE:

Access to such information is to be limited to those persons having a legitimate need thereof in the performance of their job responsibilities. Such persons are to be given access only to those associate records that are necessary or relevant to the proper discharge of their job responsibilities. While in some situations a given individual may need to have access to several different types of associate records, Human Resources representatives should take precautions to protect associate records from unauthorized release, transfer, access, or use.

PERSONNEL POLICIES AND PROCEDURES

DISTRIBUTION:		SUBJECT: PERSONNEL FILE ACCESS	
EFFECTIVE DATE:	PAGE 2 OF 3	FILE UNDER SECTION	
REVISION DATE:	APPROVED BY:		

Personal information or any information other than that described above is not to be disclosed to individuals outside the company without the associate's written authorization, with the exception of information required to be disclosed by law or legal process.

Requests from agencies of government for disclosure of information concerning individual associates not otherwise required by law to be disclosed must have the approval of the general manager. Such requests will be considered only when made in writing by an authorized agency official, describing the information required and the reason for which the information is sought.

Terminated associates are not permitted access to their personnel files.

CONSENT TO RELEASE RECORDS:

(Name of Company) (hereinafter "Employer"), acting by and through its agents, is hereby authorized to release _____

_____

(specify records)

records in its possession relating to _____

(associate to print name)

(hereinafter "Associate"). All records released pursuant to this consent shall be released only to the Associate. Associate hereby releases Employer from all claims that may arise against Employer as a result of releasing any such records to Associate. Associate agrees to indemnify and hold Employer harmless against any damage or claim that may arise as a result or releasing Associate's records, including payment of Employer's attorney's fees.

Associate Signature: _____ Date: _____

Associate Date of Birth: _____ Associate Social Security Number: _____

Witness Signature: _____

REQUEST FOR ACCESS TO ASSOCIATE PERSONNEL/MEDICAL RECORDS:

Associates Section to complete:

I, _____ , hereby request the opportunity to examine records

(Associate Name)

regarding my employment as _____

470

PERSONNEL POLICIES AND PROCEDURES

DISTRIBUTION:		SUBJECT: PERSONNEL FILE ACCESS	
EFFECTIVE DATE:	PAGE 3 OF 3	FILE UNDER SECTION	
REVISION DATE:	APPROVED BY:		

at (Name of Company). Further, I give my permission for this information to be used for the following purposes: _____ _____ but do not give permission for any other use or redisclosure.

_____   _____
Associate Signature   Date

_____   _____
Medical Department   Date

_____   _____
Human Resources Representative   Date

MEDICAL WAIVER AND CONSENT:

I, _____, having filed a claim
      (Print Your Full Name)

for workers' compensation benefits, do hereby waive any physician-patient, psychiatrist-patient privilege I may have and hereby authorize any physician, psychiatrist, chiropractor, podiatrist, hospital, or health care provider to furnish to (Name of Company) or (Name of Physician) any information or written material reasonably related to my work-related injury or my past relevant medical history.

The authorization includes, but is not restricted to, a right to review and obtain copies of all records, x-rays, x-ray reports, medical charts, prescriptions, diagnoses, opinions, and courses of treatment.

This authorization shall remain valid for 180 days following its execution. A photocopy of the authorization may be accepted in lieu of the original.

Signed at _____, this _____ day of _____, 19 _____.

SIGN YOUR FULL NAME _____

DATE OF BIRTH _____

SOCIAL SECURITY NUMBER _____

Pursuant to KRS 343.020(4), any physician, psychiatrist, chiropractor, podiatrist, hospital, or health care provider shall, within a reasonable time, provide the requesting party with any information or written material reasonably related to the injury for which the associate claims compensation.

PERSONNEL POLICIES AND PROCEDURES

DISTRIBUTION:		SUBJECT: SECURITY	
EFFECTIVE DATE:	PAGE 1 OF 1	FILE UNDER SECTION	
REVISION DATE:	APPROVED BY:		

Security problems and violations cannot be handled in a constructive manner unless company management knows about them. Our security policy therefore places a strong emphasis on reporting security-related incidents so that the proper action can be taken.

SECURITY INCIDENT REPORTS:

Written reports should be prepared by department heads (or appropriate personnel) and submitted to the Human Resources Manager immediately after a security-related incident has occurred or been discovered. The report should cover any and all information relating to the who, what, when, where, why, and how aspects of the incident. If time is a critical factor, the report should first be made over the telephone and later confirmed in writing.

The following types of incidents must be reported:

- Criminal acts on company property, including gambling, possession or use of narcotics, and money lending at unreasonable rates of interest.
- Bomb threats via telephone, mail, etc., or actual bomb incidents.
- Theft or misappropriation of company assets.
- Loss, theft, or suspected theft of proprietary information. Also, any inadvertent or unauthorized disclosure of proprietary data.
- Damage to company property or an employee's personal property while on company premises involving actual or suspected mischief, vandalism, or criminal negligence.
- Natural or man-made disasters.
- Attempts by persons to misrepresent themselves as employees or agents.
- Actual or suspected espionage or subversive activity.
- Any riot, civil disorder, or insurrection.
- Any illegal action proposed by a purchasing agent, contractor representative, or employee thereof.

PERSONNEL POLICIES AND PROCEDURES

DISTRIBUTION:		SUBJECT: ENTRANCE/EXIT PROCEDURE FOR EMPLOYEES AND VISITORS	
EFFECTIVE DATE:	PAGE 1 OF 2	FILE UNDER SECTION	
REVISION DATE:	APPROVED BY:		

POLICY STATEMENT:

This policy is established in order to specify proper procedures to be followed by all employees and visitors when entering or leaving the manufacturing and office facilities that make up (Company Name and Location).

DEFINITION OF TERMS:

1. Normal Business Hours—That period of time from 7:30 A.M. until 6:00 P.M., Monday through Friday of each work-week.

2. Main Entrance—The entrance to the building in which the Human Resources and Purchasing Departments are located.

3. Research/Administration Building Entrance—The entrance to the building in which the Scientific Affairs, Marketing, Accounting, and Research/Product Development Departments are located.

EMPLOYEE ENTRANCE/EXIT:

1. During Normal Business Hours—Employees may enter or leave the facilities through all doors not identified as "Security Doors." During emergencies such as fire drills, "Security Doors" may be utilized.

2. Other than Normal Business Hours—Employees may enter or leave the facilities only through the main entrance. A Security Officer will be on duty at the main entrance from 6:00 P.M. until 12:00 midnight, Monday through Friday, to "sign in" and "sign out" all employees who have permission to be on the premises.

3. Saturdays, Sundays, and Holidays—Employees may enter or leave the facilities only through the main entrance. A Security Officer will be on duty at the main entrance from 7:00 A.M. until 6:00 P.M. to "sign in" or "sign out" all employees who have permission to be on the premises.

4. No Admission Hours—Employees may not be on the premises without prior approval by the appropriate Management Committee Member and Director of Human Resources at the following times:

   Monday through Friday: 12:00 midnight until 7:00 A.M.

   Saturdays, Sundays, or Holidays: 6:00 P.M. until 7:00 A.M.

5. Hourly and Salaried (Nonexempt) employees who have business reasons to be on the premises during the weekday hours of 6:00 P.M. to 12:00 midnight and Saturdays, Sundays, and holidays from 7:00 A.M. to 6:00 P.M. must have prior approval in the form of an Overtime Authorization executed by the appropriate Management Committee Member. Salaried (Exempt) employees need only reflect their hours on their Employee Weekly Record cards, which are submitted to Payroll each Friday.

PERSONNEL POLICIES AND PROCEDURES

DISTRIBUTION:		SUBJECT: ENTRANCE/EXIT PROCEDURE FOR EMPLOYEES AND VISITORS
EFFECTIVE DATE:	PAGE 2 OF 2	FILE UNDER SECTION
REVISION DATE:	APPROVED BY:	

6. Visitors

   A. Visitors may enter or leave the facilities during normal working hours by either the main entrance or the Research/Administration Building entrance.

   B. In no event is it permissible for visitors to enter or be in the facilities during other than normal working hours without prior approval of the Director of Human Resources.

   C. All visitors must report to the receptionist on duty during normal working hours at either of the two entrances and register by signing their name in the "Guest Book" provided. Visitors will be required to wear a (Company Name) identification badge at all times while they are in any of the facilities.

   D. If a visitor wishes to call upon personnel in different locations, the hosting (Company Name) supervisor is responsible for notifying the employees concerned and escorting the visitor to the next person. Under no circumstances may visitors be allowed to wander through the facilities unaccompanied.

7. Workers (Outside)

   A. All persons not employed directly by (Company Name), such as contractors, etc., will be required to wear company identification badges while working in and around the facilities.

   B. Outside workers may not work after normal working hours without special written permission forwarded through the Management Committee member concerned. This written permission must be presented to the Director of Human Resources no later than 4:00 P.M. on the day the work is to be performed.

   C. Except at those times when equipment is being loaded or unloaded, workers' vehicles may not be parked near the plant buildings.

8. Security Log

   All persons who enter or leave the facilities during other than normal working hours must "sign in" and "sign out" in the security log located at the main entrance.

9. Miscellaneous

   A. As a condition of continued employment, all employees may be asked to submit to a personal check by authorized personnel. This may include, but is not limited to, an examination of briefcases, lunch boxes or bags, pocketbooks, boxes, and any other such containers. This check may be conducted at any time or place while the employee concerned is on company premises.

   B. A Security Officer will be on duty at the main entrance during other than normal working hours (as specified earlier). It will be the Security Officer's responsibility to check each employee or visitor in and out to ensure that plant security is maintained.

   C. It will be the responsibility of each Management Committee Member to arrange reporting relationships in his/her division so that any visitor entering his/her area without a company identification badge is reported to him/her immediately.

   D. It will be the responsibility of each supervisor concerned to ensure that all visitors entering his/her work area obtain and wear company identification badges.

   E. It will be the responsibility of each employee to report to his/her immediate supervisor any visitor who is observed at any location in the facilities without an escort or who is not wearing the company identification badge.

PERSONNEL POLICIES AND PROCEDURES

DISTRIBUTION:		SUBJECT: INVESTIGATIVE POLICY	
EFFECTIVE DATE:	PAGE 1 OF 1	FILE UNDER SECTION	
REVISION DATE:	APPROVED BY:		

The company has a policy of maintaining a safe and healthy work environment for all of its employees. Use or possession of illegal and unauthorized drugs, alcoholic beverages, firearms, and weapons is not permitted on company property.

To enforce this policy, the company reserves the right to conduct searches or inspections (including medical exams) of employees' persons, personal effects, or lockers for the purpose of determining if any employees are using or in possession of any such illegal or unauthorized items. Such searches may be made from time to time by authorized company representatives without prior warning.

The refusal by any company employee to submit to a search, inspection, or examination of his/her personal property may result in discipline up to and including discharge.

Any company employee found to be using or in the possession of any such illegal or unauthorized items will be immediately discharged.

PERSONNEL POLICIES AND PROCEDURES

DISTRIBUTION:		SUBJECT: ALCOHOL/DRUG ABUSE	
EFFECTIVE DATE:	PAGE 1 OF 4	FILE UNDER SECTION	
REVISION DATE:	APPROVED BY:		

STATEMENT:

(Company Name) provides a safe and productive work environment for all employees. It is the policy of the company that employees shall not be involved with the unlawful use, possession, sale, or transfer of drugs or narcotics in any manner that may impair their ability to perform assigned duties or otherwise adversely affect the company's business. Further, employees shall not possess alcoholic beverages in the workplace or consume alcoholic beverages in association with the workplace or during working time. The specific purpose of this procedure is to outline the methods for maintaining a work environment free from the effects of alcohol/drug abuse or other substances that adversely affect the mind or body.

If we are to continue to fulfill our responsibility to provide reliable and safe service to our customers and a safe working environment for our employees, employees must be physically and mentally fit to perform their duties in a safe and efficient manner.

IMPLEMENTATION:

1. Introduction
    A. Employees are expected to report for work and remain at work in condition to perform assigned duties free from the effects of alcohol and drugs.
        (1) Alcohol/illegal drug use and its physiological effects represent a threat to the well-being and security of employees and could cause extensive damage to the company's reputation, liability exposure, and community standing.
        (2) Any involvement with alcohol/drugs that adversely affects the workplace or the work environment will not be tolerated.
        (3) Off-the-job illegal drug activity or alcohol abuse that could have an adverse effect on an employee's job performance or that could jeopardize the safety of other employees, the public, company equipment, or the company's relations with the public will not be tolerated.
        (4) The company considers alcoholism and other drug addictions to be treatable illnesses. Absences directly or indirectly caused by the use of alcohol/drugs, for the specific purpose of company-approved treatment, will be excused. Such absences may qualify for FMLA leave for eligible employees.
    B. Illegal drugs are those drugs defined as illegal under federal, state, or local laws, including, but not limited to:
        ◆ Marijuana
        ◆ Heroin
        ◆ Hashish
        ◆ Cocaine
        ◆ Hallucinogens
        ◆ Depressants and stimulants not prescribed for current personal treatment by an accredited physician
        Illegal use of drugs includes significant deviations from prescribed dosages.
    C. Training is provided to assist management in recognizing potential symptoms of alcohol/drug abuse that may lead to or be causing a performance problem.

2. Use of the Employee Assistance Program
    A. (Company Name) provides the services of professionally trained counselors to assist employees in the treatment of alcohol or substance abuse problems. Our counseling resources may be contacted by any employee to discuss

DISTRIBUTION:		SUBJECT: ALCOHOL/DRUG ABUSE	
EFFECTIVE DATE:	PAGE 2 OF 4		FILE UNDER SECTION
REVISION DATE:	APPROVED BY:		

such problems. Based on a confidential consultation, you may be referred to another resource within our community for additional assistance if necessary. There is no charge for the services of the Employee Assistance Program. However, the cost of any treatment received from services outside the program that are not covered by company insurance or other benefits are the employee's responsibility.

B. Employees experiencing problems with alcohol or other drugs are urged to voluntarily seek assistance through the Employee Assistance Program to resolve such problems before they become serious enough to require management referral or disciplinary action.

C. Employees whose job performance deteriorates may be referred by management to the Employee Assistance Program for diagnosis of the performance problem(s).

D. Participation in the Employee Assistance Program for an alcohol/drug problem, in itself, will in no way jeopardize an employee's job. In fact, successful treatment will be viewed positively. However, participation will not:

(1) Prevent normal disciplinary action for a violation(s) that may have already occurred; or

(2) Relieve an employee of the responsibility to perform assigned duties in a safe and efficient manner.

3. Consequences of Alcohol/Drug Abuse

A. Drug Abuse

The use, sale, or personal possession (for example, on the person or in a tool box, desk, or vehicle) of illegal drugs while on the job, including rest periods and meal periods, or on company property is a dischargeable offense and may result in criminal prosecution. Any illegal drugs found will be turned over to the appropriate law enforcement agency.

Employees taking prescription or nonprescription drugs must report this use to supervision when the use of such drugs may affect the employee's ability to perform assigned duties. This reporting requirement is intended to protect the safety of the employee, coworkers, property, and the public. Employees failing to follow this instruction may be subject to disciplinary action.

B. Alcohol Abuse

The use or personal possession (for example, on the person or in a desk, tool box, or locker) of alcohol during work time of on company property is a dischargeable offense.

(1) For all employees, alcohol consumption is prohibited during the workday, including rest periods and meal periods. Notwithstanding this, there may be occasions, removed from the usual work setting, at which it is permissible to consume alcohol in moderation, with management approval. Employees who consume alcohol under such circumstances shall not report back to work during that workday.

(2) The possession of alcohol in a company or personal vehicle on or off of company property is prohibited by this procedure.

(3) Personal possession of alcohol or illegal drugs in company vehicles is expressly prohibited.

C. Where there is no evidence of consumption of alcohol during regular work time, including breaks and meal periods, the following will apply:

(1) For the purpose of this policy, an employee will be considered under the influence when, in the judgment of the supervisor, the employee's ability to perform his or her job safely and effectively is affected by the use of alcohol.

(2) Any employee, in any job, who is perceived to be under the influence of alcohol will be immediately removed from service and evaluated by medical personnel, if reasonably available. Management will take further appropriate action (i.e., referral to Employee Assistance Program and/or disciplinary action) based on the medical information, past history, and other relevant factors, such as performance, record of disciplinary actions, etc.

477

PERSONNEL POLICIES AND PROCEDURES

DISTRIBUTION:		SUBJECT: ALCOHOL/DRUG ABUSE	
EFFECTIVE DATE:	PAGE 3 OF 4	FILE UNDER SECTION	
REVISION DATE:	APPROVED BY:		

(3) An employee who is not perceived to be under the influence of alcohol, but who displays evidence of alcohol consumption, such as the smell of alcohol on the breath, will be immediately removed from service. Management will take appropriate action based on past history and other relevant factors, such as performance, record of disciplinary actions, etc.

D. Off-the-job selling, distributing, or manufacturing of illegal drugs by a (Company Name) employee is a dischargeable offense. Likewise, illegal selling, distributing, or manufacturing of alcohol is a dischargeable offense. Decisions regarding discharge shall be made by management after consultation with the Human Resources Manager.

4. Special Action

A. In order to protect the best interests of employees, the public, and (Company Name), the company will take whatever measures are necessary to find out if alcohol or illegal drugs are located on or being used on company property. These measures will not be taken unreasonably, but when the company believes them to be completely justified and necessary. The measures that may be used will include but not be limited to the following:

(1) Searches of people, and of personal property located on company premises, may be conducted by security officers or by management. Searches of the person and of noncompany property (where reason to suspect exists) will not be conducted if an individual refuses to submit to a search. Upon refusal to submit to such searches, the purpose of the requested search and the potential implications of refusal will be carefully explained to the employee. Further refusal to submit will result in immediate removal from service and may result in termination for insubordination.

(2) Federal, state, and/or local authorities may be called upon to assist in an investigation.

B. The decision to use the measures described above, or other similar measures, must be approved by a senior management official.

Physical searches of employees and property searches may be conducted with location management approval without approval of a senior management official in situations where time is critical to the success of the search.

C. As a supplement to other means of detecting drug and alcohol use, urine and blood testing will be conducted.

(1) Drug tests will be conducted as a routine part of the pre-employment physical examination for all regular full-time and regular part-time job applicants. Applicant must satisfactorily pass both the examination and the drug screen prior to reporting to work. Offers of employment may be made contingent upon satisfactorily meeting these requirements. If the drug screening procedures indicate the presence of drugs or controlled substances, the applicant will not be considered further for employment until a confirming test is performed.

(2) Drug tests will be conducted as a routine part of promotion/transfer for all employees being considered for positions for which a company-mandated physical is required and/or that may directly affect public safety or employee safety. If the drug screening indicates the presence of drugs, other than prescription drugs, the employee will not be considered further for the position until a confirming test is performed.

(3) Drug tests will be conducted as a routine part of company-mandated physicals for certain positions considered sensitive from a health and safety standpoint. Positive results on a drug screening will be cause for referral to the Employee Assistance Program and/or consideration for disciplinary action.

(4) Drug and/or alcohol tests may be conducted at the option of management as a part of the investigation involving an accident (vehicular or personal) or ''near accident'' in which safety precautions were violated and/or unusually careless acts were performed.

(5) Drug and/or alcohol tests will be conducted when an employee's supervisor has cause to believe that the employee is ''unfit for duty.''

DISTRIBUTION:		SUBJECT: ALCOHOL/DRUG ABUSE	
EFFECTIVE DATE:	PAGE 4 OF 4	FILE UNDER SECTION	
REVISION DATE:	APPROVED BY:		

(6) Drug tests will be conducted when there is reason to suspect use or possession of illegal drugs.

(7) When there is a change in group behavior, a high rate of accidents or injuries, reliable information about drug involvement, and/or reason to suspect the use of illegal drugs within a work group, there may be cause for testing all employees in the work group after approval of senior management.

D. In cases where a drug screen indicates illegal drug use, the following steps will be taken:

(1) In the case of a first-time positive result on a drug screen, but where no evidence exists of use on the job, the following steps will be taken:

   a. The employee will be suspended without pay.

   b. The employee must visit the staff of the company-approved Employee Assistance Program at least once to learn what drug counseling resources are available. The employee will be required to seek treatment for drug abuse from a recognized professional and/or institution. Refusal to do so will be viewed as insubordination, and the employee will be subject to discharge. The employee will be required to co-operate with Employee Assistance Program staff in carrying out its responsibility to coordinate the treatment process.

   c. The employee must have a negative test result in a screen administered by the company within a period of six weeks from the date of suspension. In the event the employee fails to do so within this six-week period, the employee will be discharged. If, after negative results within such six-week period, an employee is unable to return to work for good reason (e.g., participation in a treatment program not yet completed), the time at which such employee shall return to work may be extended beyond the end of the six-week period.

   d. Employees who have been suspended following a positive drug screen and who have subsequently had a negative test result will be subject to random screening for an indefinite period of time. Supervisors shall have the responsibility to require follow-up random screening.

(2) Employees in positions where a physical is required and/or that may affect public or employee safety who have a first-time positive drug screen and a negative follow-up screen within six weeks will be allowed to return to their positions only upon providing to the Employee Assistance Program certified documentation from a recognized professional that would give a reasonable degree of confidence that the individual would be capable of performing his/her assigned job duties without impairment. Until certification acceptable to the Employee Assistance Program is provided, the company may, but shall have no obligation to, provide a work assignment.

(3) Employees who have been suspended for a positive drug screen and allowed to return to work, in accordance with this procedure, will be discharged for a positive test result on a subsequent drug screen.

5. When urinalysis and/or blood tests are requested or necessary, samples will be taken under the supervision of an appropriate health care professional. Your supervisor can advise you of the medical facility providing these services for you.

President/CEO

PERSONNEL POLICIES AND PROCEDURES

DISTRIBUTION:		SUBJECT: SUBSTANCE ABUSE	
EFFECTIVE DATE:	PAGE 1 OF 1	FILE UNDER SECTION	
REVISION DATE:	APPROVED BY:		

POLICY STATEMENT:

If we are to continue to fulfill our responsibility to provide reliable and safe service to our customers and a safe working environment for our employees, employees of (company name) must be physically and mentally fit to perform their duties in a safe and efficient manner. Therefore, no employee shall work or report to work while under the influence of alcohol, illegal drugs, or drugs that would affect his/her ability to perform the job in a safe and efficient manner. No employee shall consume, display, or have in his/her possession on (Company Name) property, including in the workplace or in company vehicles, alcoholic beverages or illegal drugs at any time during the workday, including during lunch, breaks, and on-call hours. To do so could jeopardize the safety of other employees, the public, company equipment, and the company's relations with the public, and is a prime cause for disciplinary action, up to and including dismissal. The exception to this rule is when consumption of alcoholic beverages is authorized by the President at company functions, such as Open Houses or other business activities.

PROCEDURES:

Should employees be required to take any kind of prescription or nonprescription medication that may potentially affect their job performance, they are required to report this to their supervisor, who will determine if it is necessary to temporarily place them on another assignment to ensure their safety and the safety of our employees and the public.

To protect the best interests of employees and the public, management at (Company Name) will take whatever measures are necessary to determine if alcohol or illegal drugs are located on or are being used on company property. These measures will not be taken unreasonably, but when the company believes them to be completely justified and necessary. Measures that may be used will include but not be limited to searches of people and of personal property located on company premises, which may be conducted by law enforcement authorities or by management, as well as drug and/or alcohol tests to be conducted when there is reasonable suspicion of substance abuse. When urinalysis and/or blood tests are requested or necessary, samples will be taken under the supervision of an appropriate health-care professional. The above-mentioned searches and drug tests will not be conducted if an individual refuses to submit; however, refusal to submit will result in immediate removal from service and may result in termination.

Employees experiencing problems with alcohol or other drugs are urged to voluntarily seek assistance to resolve such problems before they become serious enough to require management referral or disciplinary action. A portion of the cost of treatment may be covered by our company insurance program, and employees may have to assume responsibilities for the cost of a portion of the treatment. Successful treatment will be viewed positively. However, participation in a treatment program will not prevent normal disciplinary action for a violation that may have already occurred, nor will it relieve an employee of the responsibility to perform assigned duties in a safe and efficient manner.

While supervisors are not expected to be diagnosticians, nor is it acceptable to assume that an employee is impaired, supervisors are expected to identify performance or behavioral problems and to begin investigative or corrective action, as appropriate, based on behaviors demonstrated by employees and observed by supervisory personnel.

PERSONNEL POLICIES AND PROCEDURES

DISTRIBUTION:		SUBJECT: DRUG AND ALCOHOL ABUSE	
EFFECTIVE DATE:	PAGE 1 OF 2	FILE UNDER SECTION	
REVISION DATE:	APPROVED BY:		

BACKGROUND:

(Name of Hospital) will strive to maintain a drug-free environment.

POLICY:

* An employee found to be in possession of or utilizing illegal drugs, other controlled substances, or alcohol on work time or on hospital property will be subject to disciplinary action up to and including dismissal.
* The presence of illegal drugs, unauthorized controlled substances, or alcohol in any body fluid while the employee is on work time is prohibited and will result in disciplinary action up to and including termination.

PROCEDURE:

If an employee is suspected of being under the influence of alcohol, illegal drugs, and/or other controlled substances, the supervisor will notify the administrator responsible for that area or the administrator on-call, if after normal working hours. The employee will immediately be requested to submit to body fluid testing. If use is confirmed as a result of the test, the employee will be subject to action as stated above. If circumstances make the determination of the appropriate action difficult at that time, the employee should be suspended *after* body fluid tests have been conducted so that all facts pertaining to the incident can be evaluated.

If the employee is suspected of selling or furnishing such substances, the supervisor will notify the administrator responsible for the area, and a full investigation will be conducted.

Employees on-call for their departments are subject to this policy and procedure should they be called to work after hours.

IMPLEMENTATION:

1. Body Fluid Testing

Where there is a reasonable cause to suspect the use of illegal drugs or unauthorized controlled substances or alcohol abuse by an employee, or where the nature of the work assignment will involve substantial safety, security, or economic risk, the hospital may require the employee to take a medical examination and/or a body fluid test. Employees who refuse to be tested will be subject to disciplinary action, up to and including termination. Employees who test positive will be subject to disciplinary action up to and including termination.

Body fluid tests (urinalysis in cases of nonalcohol incidents or blood alcohol content in cases of alcohol-related incidents) will be referred to the Outpatient Department (or the Emergency Department if the Outpatient Department is closed).

2. Employee Assistance Program (EAP)

   A. In certain instances employees who have substance abuse problems will be required to participate in the Employee Assistance Program (EAP). However, participation in the EAP in no way exempts such employees from the usual disciplinary process.

   B. Refusal of an employee to participate in the EAP and adhere to the program established for rehabilitation will be cause for disciplinary action up to and including termination.

DISTRIBUTION:		SUBJECT: DRUG AND ALCOHOL ABUSE	
EFFECTIVE DATE:	PAGE 2 OF 2	FILE UNDER SECTION	
REVISION DATE:	APPROVED BY:		

C. Self-referral and participation in the EAP will be held confidential *except* as provided under laws of mandatory disclosure and hospital policy regarding safety.

3. Search

Search procedures such as inspections of employee personal property or lockers will be conducted as appropriate. All employees will also be expected, as a condition of employment, to cooperate with special drug/alcohol searches of personal property where there is reason to believe that an employee may be in possession of illicit drugs or alcohol. Failure of an employee to cooperate with searches will be cause for disciplinary action up to and including termination. Searches of hospital premises and property may be conducted at any time.

DEFINITIONS:

- *Reasonable Cause* means:
    A. That the employee has been involved in a workplace accident or an incident resulting in personal injury or damage to property, or workplace circumstances that could have resulted in personal injury or damage to property, and a supervisory employee has a reasonable suspicion that the employee's acts or omissions contributed to the occurrence or severity of the accident, incident, or circumstance; or
    B. Behavior, appearance, and/or bodily odor of an employee causes a supervisory employee to have reasonable suspicion that the employee is currently under the influence or impaired by alcohol, drugs, or a controlled substance, based upon specific personal observations of the supervisor concerning the behavior, speech, or body odors of the employee; or
    C. The return to work of an employee following participation in a rehabilitation program such as EAP; and/or
    D. Other circumstances that would indicate that the employee is reporting to work in other than a sober and reliable state, free from the influence of alcohol or drugs. Such circumstances may include, but shall not be limited to, excessive tardiness, absenteeism, or reduction in job productivity.

- *Controlled Substance*
Means any substance listed in the Controlled Substance Act of 1970 as amended. This Act includes the regulations covering drugs subject to abuse and divides narcotic and other drugs into five schedules according to the legitimacy of medical use and potential for abuse.

- *Illegal Drugs*
Means any mind-altering substance, including any active substance and including, but not limited to, controlled substances used without regard to standard medical practices and/or contrary to the directions provided by a physician.

- *Hospital Property*
Means all real or personal property owned, leased, or otherwise under the control of (Name of Hospital) or a related company. Includes, but is not limited to, building, plant facilities and offices, parking lots, automobiles, desks, cabinets, lockers, closets, etc.

PERSONNEL POLICIES AND PROCEDURES

DISTRIBUTION:		SUBJECT: ALCOHOL AND DRUG ABUSE	
EFFECTIVE DATE:	PAGE 1 OF 2	FILE UNDER SECTION	
REVISION DATE:	APPROVED BY:		

PURPOSE:

The company prohibits the use, transfer, distribution, manufacture, or possession of alcohol, controlled substances, unauthorized drugs, intoxicants, drug paraphernalia, or any combination thereof on any company premises or work sites, including company vehicles and private vehicles parked on company premises or work sites.

Use or possession of prescription drugs consistent with a physician's directions is not considered a violation of this policy.

Employees who fail to conform to these rules will be subject to removal from the facility and appropriate disciplinary action up to and including termination of employment. This policy applies to all employees.

SELF-IDENTIFICATION:

Employees who volunteer information concerning their chemical dependency problems may receive the support and aid of the company for rehabilitation. However, any support or aid offered to an employee is a discretionary management decision and will be based partly on the employee's circumstances, the manner in which the company obtained the information, and the seriousness and frequency of other company violations.

The decision to request a diagnosis and accept treatment for a chemical dependency is the personal responsibility of the individual. An individual's refusal to accept referral for diagnosis or to follow prescribed treatment will be considered insubordination and a violation of this policy.

FITNESS FOR DUTY:

As a condition of employment, employees must report to their jobs in a condition that will allow them to be mentally and physically alert.

When a manager has reason to believe that an employee's fitness for duty is impaired because the employee is under the influence of alcohol, drugs, or other controlled substances, the employee's fitness should be witnessed by another supervisor (if possible). If he/she concurs that the employee's fitness for duty is impaired, the company will administer appropriate disciplinary action, including discharge.

TESTING:

All alcohol and drug testing procedures will conform to all local, state, and federal regulations.

No testing procedures will be implemented that will not meet the company's professional and certifiable standards.

All laboratories, hospitals, and their professional staffs must meet the standards of the National Institute on Drug Abuse. The company will require, but not limit, alcohol and drug testing for:

* Accidents,
* Annual physicals (as permitted by law),
* Specific incidents,
* Fitness for duty,
* Pre-employment (where permitted by law), and
* Probable cause (unusual behavior).

Employees testing positive for alcohol and/or drugs may be required to enroll in at least one of the following:

DISTRIBUTION:		SUBJECT: ALCOHOL AND DRUG ABUSE	
EFFECTIVE DATE:	PAGE 2 OF 2	FILE UNDER SECTION	
REVISION DATE:	APPROVED BY:		

- ◆ Employee Assistance Program,
- ◆ Education and/or training program, or
- ◆ Rehabilitation program.

The selection of an appropriate program and/or appropriate disciplinary action for the employee violating the alcohol and drug abuse policy is completely a discretionary decision of management, and the company reserves the right to take disciplinary action up to and including discharge.

If an employee is required to enroll in a rehabilitation, education, or assistance program, continued employment is conditional upon the following requirements:

1. The employee must present written certification that he/she has successfully completed the appropriate rehabilitation program.

2. The employee must satisfactorily complete an alcohol and drug test.

CONFIDENTIALITY:

The company will maintain the highest standards of confidentiality for all records and information concerning alcohol and drug dependencies. No employee is authorized without the express consent of the President to release, communicate, or leave unsecured information on alcohol or drug abuse problems. Any employee violating this policy will be subject to disciplinary action including possible termination of employment. Nonemployees, contractors, vendors, and agencies that disclose unauthorized information will be subject to legal recourse.

Nothing in this statement of policy is to be interpreted as constituting a waiver of management's responsibility to maintain discipline, or the right to take disciplinary measures in the case of poor performance or misconduct.

PERSONNEL POLICIES AND PROCEDURES

DISTRIBUTION:		SUBJECT: SUBSTANCE ABUSE	
EFFECTIVE DATE:	PAGE 1 OF 4	FILE UNDER SECTION	
REVISION DATE:	APPROVED BY:		

PURPOSE:

To establish a policy for the administration and implementation of the Substance Abuse Program, which includes the testing and discipline related to substance abuse.

POLICY:

Company policy related to substance abuse has been stated in the ''Employee Handbook'' and administered by the company for several years. In addition to that, substance abuse is included in the ''Personal Rules of Conduct,'' which has been used as a measurement of employee behavior for several years. The Employee Handbook states the policy on drug abuse as follows:

It is the company's policy to make every effort to provide its employees with a safe, clean, and wholesome place to work. The sale, purchase, use, or possession of drugs by any employee while on company premises is obviously inconsistent with that policy. Consequently, we want all employees to know that the sale, purchase, use, or possession of illegal drugs by employees on company premises or while on company business is prohibited. The services of any employee who engages in such conduct will be subject to termination.

In the Personal Rules of Conduct, the policy is stated as follows:

Included among the more serious offenses considered for immediate discharge are the following: using, possessing, or being under the influence of intoxicants or/and narcotics.

This policy shall continue to be an active part of the company's position in conjunction with this Standard Practice.

GENERAL:

The company has a strong commitment to its employees and its customers to provide a safe, healthy, and secure work environment. The critical nature of the work performed by our company and its employees at all levels can involve life-threatening equipment and processes if failure occurred. Equipment that is certifiably safe and properly designed is constructed with materials and workmanship of the highest standard. For those reasons, the company expects its employees to maintain a high level of productivity, efficiency, and moral standards.

The presence of drugs and other mind-altering substances in the workplace and the influence of these substances on employees during performance of these critical activities is inconsistent with company policies and objectives. Therefore, the company expects all its employees to perform their duties in a safe and productive manner.

Our drug testing procedure will include 100 percent testing of all employees to assure the certifiability of a drug-free workplace. Activities in violation of these policies will not be tolerated at our company and will be cause for immediate suspension, subject to termination.

In the best interest of the objectives stated, the company will take whatever measures are necessary to determine that our goals are met. Measures, in addition to testing, that may be used will include searches of people and personal property located within the fenced area on company premises. The searches will be for just cause and will be conducted by law enforcement authorities or by company security. The above-mentioned searches will not be conducted if an individual refuses to submit. However, refusal to submit to these searches may result in immediate suspension, subject to termination.

The company intends to implement immediately a drug testing program in accordance with procedures outlined in this Standard Practice. This drug testing program will include 100 percent of the employees at the company. No one will be exempt. Refusal on the part of employees to submit to drug testing will be reason for immediate suspension, subject to termination. The drug testing program will be conducted by a certified, federally approved laboratory hired and paid for

DISTRIBUTION:		SUBJECT: SUBSTANCE ABUSE	
EFFECTIVE DATE:	PAGE 2 OF 4	FILE UNDER SECTION	
REVISION DATE:	APPROVED BY:		

by the company. These tests will be conducted on whatever levels are necessary to assure that the presence or abuse of drugs is accurately determined. When drug testing indicates "positive," this laboratory will be authorized to use the latest technology to assure the accuracy of its tests. The company will accept that data as being accurate and will move to disciplinary action based on those test results.

In addition to testing for illegal drugs, the company is aware that there are mind-altering drugs sometimes prescribed by physicians for the purpose of pain relief or for other medical reasons. It is every employee's responsibility to report to the company nurse or the Personnel Department the use of these prescription drugs. The company will accept the employee's private physician's statement that it is safe to work while taking a prescribed medication. If changes to those prescriptions occur, it is the obligation of the employee again to indicate to the Personnel Department or the company nurse those changes.

In the past, the excessive use of alcohol has been a matter for immediate termination. We would expect that policy to remain in effect. Although a legal intoxicant, alcohol will not be permitted on company property. The use of or being under the influence of alcohol while on duty at the company will be cause for immediate suspension, subject to termination.

All of the requirements of this substance abuse policy will be enforced with the attitude that it is best for all our employees, for our customers, and for the company to adhere strictly to these rules. We expect your sincere cooperation in this matter.

Nothing contained in this policy is to be interpreted as constituting a waiver of the Employer's rights to take disciplinary measures for just cause or the Union and its members' rights to avail themselves of provisions in the collective bargaining agreement, including the grievance and arbitration procedures for violations of any provision of this policy.

PROCEDURE:

1. Personnel will be selected for drug tests under the following conditions:

    1.1 All new applicants for jobs prior to hiring.

    1.2 A return of an employee after an absence exceeding thirty calendar days.

    1.3 After a serious accident involving one or more employees.

    1.4 When an employee appears to be unstable or unfit for duty.

    The following may constitute reasonable cause to believe that an employee is under the influence of drugs and therefore unfit for duty.

    1.4.1 Incoherent, slurred speech.
    1.4.2 Staggering gait, disorientation, or loss of balance.
    1.4.3 Red and watery eyes, if not explained by environmental causes.
    1.4.4 Paranoid or bizarre behavior.
    1.4.5 Unexplained drowsiness.

    1.5 At any time an employee's Social Security number is drawn in a lottery as conducted under the following rules:

PERSONNEL POLICIES AND PROCEDURES

1.5.1 A committee of employees will be designated as the Drug Monitoring Committee and will work with the Personnel Department and the company nurse in the matters of drug testing. The Committee will be present at all lottery drawings, while the sample is sealed by the plant nurse, and during the review of the results from the Laboratory. All employees will have sufficient privacy while giving a sample.

1.5.2 The Drug Monitoring Committee will consist of one bargaining unit employee, selected by the Union local president; one nonexempt employee, elected by his/her peer employees; and one member of management, appointed by the President of the Company.

1.5.3 Every employee of our company will have his/her Social Security number entered on a lottery pill. The pills will be divided into equal lots and deposited in two lottery drums. One time every other week four pills will be drawn from each drum. These Social Security numbers will be translated to names and those names handed to the Personnel Director or the company nurse for notification that drug testing will be conducted on that same day.

1.5.4 The pills will be returned to the opposite drum. The pills drawn from lottery drum #1 will be placed in lottery drum #2, and the pills drawn from lottery drum #2 will be placed in drum #1. If an employee is absent on the day of testing, his/her pill will be returned to the drum it was drawn from, and another pill will be drawn. All new employees coming to work at our company will be divided equally, and half their Social Security numbers will be placed in drum #1 and half in #2.

1.6 By this method, all employees can be assured of a fair and equitable selection of names to be tested.

2. The Personnel Director will supervise the sample taking.

   2.1 Only certified government-approved drug testing laboratories will be employed for this purpose.

3. Duplicate samples will be taken with tamper-proof seals. One will be sent to the laboratory and the second retained in a sealed container by the company in the secured freezer.

   3.1 If the first sample tests positive, the second sample will be sent to another NIDA laboratory for testing. The employee may choose this laboratory at the Company's expense. If the laboratory results conflict, both samples will be retested.

   3.2 If the first sample tests negative, the second sample will be destroyed. The Drug Testing Committee and the plant nurse will assure the chain of custody.

   3.3 Employees who are determined to be positive in terms of being beyond the legal guidelines established by the Government shall be suspended, pending discharge. If an employee loses wages and/or benefits and ultimately prevails, he/she will be reinstated and made whole regarding wages and benefits.

4. The company has a rehabilitation program included in the company medical plan. An employee turning himself/herself in to a rehabilitation program prior to the date of notification that he/she will be the subject for drug tests may do so without disciplinary action. Company policy will continue to be that the company recommends that those who are addicted to drug use or have a significant problem turn themselves in for treatment and rehabilitation.

   4.1 All employees, including those on layoff, will have a thirty-day grace period from the date of this notice to submit to a company-paid, voluntary rehabilitation program.

5. The Company agrees to hold the Union harmless from any litigation arising out of the Company's activities in carrying out the drug testing program.

PERSONNEL POLICIES AND PROCEDURES

DISTRIBUTION:		SUBJECT: SUBSTANCE ABUSE	
EFFECTIVE DATE:	PAGE 4 OF 4	FILE UNDER SECTION	
REVISION DATE:	APPROVED BY:		

6. All subcontractors performing work on the company's property must conform with all sections of this policy. This includes being tested at the company or being tested by their company immediately prior to site work at the company. Long-term contractors will be subject to retest.

METHODOLOGY:

	Stage 1 (Screening)	Screening Cutoff	Stage 2 (Confirmation)	Confirmation Cutoff
Amphetamines	EMIT	1.00 μg/ml	GC/MS	0.50 μg/ml
Barbiturates	EMIT	0.30 μg/ml	GC/MS	0.20 μg/ml
Benzodiazepines	EMIT	300.00 μg/ml	GC/MS	250.50 μg/ml
Benzoylecgonine	EMIT	0.30 μg/ml	GC/MS	0.15 μg/ml
Cannabinoids	EMIT	100.00 μg/ml	GC/MS	15.00 μg/ml
Opiates	EMIT	0.30 μg/ml	GC/MS	0.30 μg/ml
Phencyclidine	EMIT	25.00 μg/ml	GC/MS	25.00 μg/ml
Methadone	EMIT	0.30 μg/ml	GC/MS	0.25 μg/ml
Propoxyphene	EMIT	0.30 μg/ml	GC/MS	0.30 μg/ml
Methaqualone	EMIT	300.00 μg/ml	GC/MS	250.00 μg/ml

EMPLOYEE AUTHORIZATION—SUBSTANCE SCREENING:

By my signature below, I voluntarily and knowingly agree to the following:

a. I consent to take any physical or medical examinations, including blood and urine or other tests for alcohol and drugs, requested by the Company in connection with the processing of my application for employment, and further agree to take any such physical or medical examinations requested by the Company during my employment if I am offered and accept a job. I understand that such an examination is needed in order to determine my competence to perform the job or work for which I was hired, or to identify any physical or mental condition bearing on my job performance. I understand that refusal to submit to any physical or medical examination ordered by the Company is grounds for rejection for employment or for disciplinary action up to and including immediate discharge. I further understand that any information obtained through such exams may be retained by the Company and is exclusively the Company's property. I also understand that the examinations will be performed by medical personnel, clinics, or laboratories qualified to do the necessary work and that costs for such examinations will be borne by the Company.

b. I consent to submit and cooperate in any questioning or any searches of my assigned vehicle, locker or storage area, or bags or other belongings on or in the Company's property that the Company in its discretion may request, and I understand that the refusal to submit or cooperate in these procedures is grounds for disciplinary action up to and including immediate discharge.

c. I acknowledge I have read, understand, and will abide by the above notice. I further acknowledge that a copy has been furnished to me, and another copy is made a part of my personnel file.

_____   _____

Employee's Signature   Date

PERSONNEL POLICIES AND PROCEDURES

DISTRIBUTION:		SUBJECT: SAMPLE SUBSTANCE ABUSE POLICY/CONSENT FORM	
EFFECTIVE DATE:	PAGE 1 OF 1	FILE UNDER SECTION	
REVISION DATE:	APPROVED BY:		

If we are to continue to fulfill our responsibility to provide reliability and safe service to our customers and a safe working environment for our employees, employees of XYZ Services, Inc., must be physically and mentally fit to perform their duties in a safe and efficient manner. Therefore, no employee shall work or report to work while under the influence of alcohol, illegal drugs, or drugs that affect the ability to perform the job in a safe and efficient manner. No employee shall consume, display, or have in his/her possession alcoholic beverages or illegal drugs while on company property. To do so could jeopardize the safety of other employees, the public, and the company's relations with the public, and is a prime cause for disciplinary action, up to and including dismissal.

Should an employee be required to take any kind of prescription or nonprescription medication that may potentially affect job performance, the employee is required to report this to his/her supervisor. The supervisor will determine if it is necessary to temporarily place the employee on another assignment to ensure his/her safety and the safety of other employees and the public.

Intoxication at work is grounds for disciplinary action, including immediate discharge. As used in this policy, intoxication means both being under the influence of drugs or alcohol and physical evidence that indicates that drugs or alcohol have been consumed. If any employee is suspected of being intoxicated at work, he/she will be suspended pending investigation. During this investigation, the company may discuss the employee's intoxication with his/her coworkers and supervisors.

The company reserves the right to test applicants and to randomly test employees for the presence of drugs or alcohol, and a refusal to take such a test is grounds for refusal to hire or immediate discharge. The company is not obligated to test any employee. An employee must make arrangements for any testing not requested by the company. Results of any drug test may be shared with an employee's supervisors or others in management who have a legitimate interest in the suspected violation. When urinalysis and/or blood tests are requested or necessary, samples will be taken under the supervision of an appropriate health-care professional.

To protect the best interests of employees and the public, management at XYZ Services, Inc., will take whatever measures are necessary to determine if alcohol or illegal drugs are located on or are being used on company property. Measures that may be used will include, but will not be limited to, searches of people and of personal property located on company premises. Searches may be conducted by law enforcement authorities or by management. The above-mentioned searches and drug tests will not be conducted if an individual refuses to submit; however, refusal to submit will result in immediate suspension and may result in termination.

Employees experiencing problems with alcohol or other drugs are urged to voluntarily seek assistance to resolve such problems before they become serious enough to require management referral or disciplinary action. Successful treatment may be viewed positively, but it will not prevent normal disciplinary action for a violation that may have already occurred or relieve an employee of the responsibility to perform assigned duties in a safe and efficient manner.

As a condition of employment, each of the company's employees, including management, must acknowledge by signature that he/she has received and understands this policy.

I certify that I have read and fully understand the company's drug policy, which is set forth above, and I agree to be bound thereby.

_____   _____
Date   Employee

NOTE: The above sample is provided as a guide; counsel should be consulted before final policy development and implementation.

PERSONNEL POLICIES AND PROCEDURES

DISTRIBUTION:		SUBJECT: AIDS	
EFFECTIVE DATE:	PAGE 1 OF 1	FILE UNDER SECTION	
REVISION DATE:	APPROVED BY:		

POLICY STATEMENT:

After consultation with medical experts, and in view of the gravity of the issue, as well as its potential impact on our staff, the company asks for your serious attention and cooperation regarding this issue.

Our policy is to be both compassionate and in line with current medical and legal counsel. Simply stated, AIDS and Pre-AIDS employees are fully entitled to the ethical considerations and legal rights awarded anyone with any other illness. This includes protection of the individual's privacy, confidentiality, and civil liberties. This disease should be treated like any other medical problem with attendant absence and disability.

Medical evidence available indicates that AIDS is not communicated by normal activity within an office or manufacturing environment. There is no evidence that other employees are exposed to an increased risk because of the presence of AIDS or Pre-AIDS employees.

If the occasion arises, please manage this issue in a manner consistent with this policy. Any questions may be addressed to _____.

PERSONNEL POLICIES AND PROCEDURES

DISTRIBUTION:		SUBJECT: AIDS AND AIDS-RELATED CONDITIONS IN THE WORKPLACE	
EFFECTIVE DATE:	PAGE 1 OF 1	FILE UNDER SECTION	
REVISION DATE:	APPROVED BY:		

(Company Name) recognizes that Acquired Immune Deficiency Syndrome (AIDS), its related conditions such as AIDS-Related Complex (ARC), and persons with seropositive test results pose significant and delicate issues for employees in the workplace. Because we are committed to maintaining a healthy and safe work environment, we have established the following guidelines for handling employee issues that arise when an employee is affected by this fatal disease.

A. The company is committed to maintaining a safe and healthy work environment for all employees.

B. Consistent with this commitment, the company will treat AIDS the same as other life-threatening illnesses, in terms of all our employee policies and benefits. Employees who are affected by AIDS or any other life-threatening illness will be treated with compassion and understanding, and will be given support to the full extent possible in dealing with their personal crisis.

C. Based on the overwhelming preponderance of available medical and scientific opinion, there is no evidence that the AIDS virus is casually transmitted in ordinary social or occupational settings or conditions. Therefore, subject to changes in available medical information, it is the policy of the company to allow employees with AIDS or any of its related conditions to continue to work as long as they are medically able to perform and do not pose a danger to their own health and safety or the health and safety of others. Concomitantly, coworkers have no basis upon which to refuse to work or withhold their services for fear of contracting AIDS by working with an AIDS-affected person. Employees who engage in such refusals or withholding of services or who harass or otherwise discriminate against an AIDS-affected employee will be subject to discipline.

D. Recognizing the need for employees to be able to be accurately informed about AIDS, the company will provide information regarding the facts about this disease, how it is transmitted and not transmitted, and how best to contain it from spreading to all employees.

E. Employees affected by AIDS or any of its related conditions or concerned about AIDS are encouraged to contact their Human Resources Representative to discuss their concerns and to obtain additional information.

F. The company will treat all medical information obtained from employees with AIDS or any of its related conditions confidentially as required by law.

The company reserves the right to change this policy or make appropriate revisions, additions, amendments, or corrections.

PERSONNEL POLICIES AND PROCEDURES

DISTRIBUTION:		SUBJECT: AIDS AND OTHER ILLNESSES	
EFFECTIVE DATE:	PAGE 1 OF 2	FILE UNDER SECTION	
REVISION DATE:	APPROVED BY:		

POLICY:

We recognize that employees with a potentially life-threatening and/or infectious illness, including but not limited to cancer, heart disease, and AIDS, may wish to continue to engage in as many of their normal pursuits as their condition allows, including their employment. (Current medical opinion indicates that AIDS is not transmitted through casual contact between individuals. The U.S. Centers for Disease Control recommend against removing AIDS-affected workers from their jobs or routinely screening employees to determine whether they have been exposed.) As long as these employees are able to meet acceptable performance standards, and medical evidence indicates that their conditions are not a threat to themselves or others, managers should be sensitive to the employees' conditions and ensure that they are treated consistently with other employees. At the same time, we have an obligation to provide a safe work environment for all employees. Reasonable precautions should be taken to ensure that an employee's medical condition does not present a health and/or safety threat to other employees.

The company believes that the best method of combating public fears with respect to an illness is to educate the workers as to the means and risk of transmission of such illnesses and accordingly will implement educational and informational programs. Efforts will also be made to provide individual counseling and referral services for infected or ill employees and for coworkers to assist them in dealing with these issues and to minimize the workplace impact of these illnesses.

PROCEDURE:

When dealing with situations involving employees with an illness, managers should:

A. Remember that an employee's health condition is personal and confidential, and take reasonable precautions to protect the confidentiality of information regarding an employee's health condition.

B. Contact the Medical Department or your Human Resources Representative if you believe that you or other employees need information about a specific illness or if you need further guidance in managing a situation that involves an employee with an illness.

C. Contact the Medical Department or your Human Resources Representative if you have any concern about the possible contagious nature of an employee's illness.

D. Contact the Medical Department or your Human Resources Representative if a statement should be obtained from the employee's attending physician that the employee is able to perform his/her job duties or that his/her continued presence at work will pose no threat to the employee, coworkers, or customers. Accordingly, we reserve the right to request an examination by a medical doctor appointed by the company.

E. If warranted, make reasonable accommodation for employees with an illness consistent with the business needs.

F. Be sensitive and responsive to the employee's and coworkers' concerns and emphasize the education programs available through the Medical Department or your Human Resources Representative.

PERSONNEL POLICIES AND PROCEDURES

G. Recognize and deal with situations arising from unwarranted fear on the part of employees concerning a coworker's actual or perceived illness by promoting adequate education and counseling. Job transfers or reassignments in these situations are not considered to be acceptable solutions.

H. Encourage concerned employees to contact the Medical Department or the Human Resources Representative for information on company or community resources for medical treatment and counseling services.

These guidelines are subject to change as more information on illnesses and methods of illness transmission becomes available.

PERSONNEL POLICIES AND PROCEDURES

DISTRIBUTION:		SUBJECT: AIDS: EDUCATION GUIDELINES	
EFFECTIVE DATE:	PAGE 1 OF 2	FILE UNDER SECTION	
REVISION DATE:	APPROVED BY:		

Education is the primary strategic tool for the control of AIDS in the workplace. The key to resolving the potential issues on this subject is communication to educate management and employees. Because of the rapid expansion of medical knowledge on AIDS and the impact of new laws and developing legal opinion on AIDS employment issues, procedures should be implemented to monitor these changes and ensure that the education programs are kept up to date.

A. MANAGEMENT EDUCATION

The Medical Department, in conjunction with the Human Resources Department, will prepare presentations and provide brochures on guidelines for training all management and supervision on how to handle life-threatening illnesses. Training material should include:

1. Historical background of AIDS
2. Transmission
3. Medical issues
4. Legal issues
5. Liability
6. Economic threats
7. Confidential precautions to protect employee's health condition

All training material should be screened by a professional medical authority to assure accuracy.

B. HEALTH CARE EMPLOYEES/EMERGENCY RESPONSE EMPLOYEES

Guidelines should be prepared for company nurses, emergency brigade members, and first aiders. Guidelines should include recommendations for managing parenteral and mucous membrane exposures to blood or other body fluids, precautions to be taken with needles and sharp instruments, appropriate use of equipment to minimize the need for mouth-to-mouth resuscitation, sterilization and disinfecting procedures, housekeeping procedures, and appropriate use of gloves and other protective garments. Guidelines should be on file in the departments where employees have been assigned health care duties.

C. FOOD SERVICE WORKERS

With respect to food service workers, all evidence from epidemiological and laboratory studies indicates that blood-borne and sexually transmitted infections such as AIDS are not transmitted in connection with the preparation or serving of food or beverages.

Guidelines should be prepared that state that food service workers should follow established standards and practices of good personal hygiene and food sanitation. Food service workers should not prepare or serve food when they have lesions or weeping dermatitis, and they should take care to avoid injury to their hands when preparing food. If such injury should occur, food contaminated with blood must be discarded.

Food service workers known to be infected with the AIDS virus need not be restricted from work unless they show evidence of another infection, condition, or illness for which there should be such a restriction.

494

PERSONNEL POLICIES AND PROCEDURES

DISTRIBUTION:		SUBJECT: AIDS: EDUCATION GUIDELINES	
EFFECTIVE DATE:	PAGE 2 OF 2	FILE UNDER SECTION	
REVISION DATE:	APPROVED BY:		

D. GENERAL EMPLOYEE EDUCATION

Employee guidelines should be prepared to emphasize that AIDS is not spread by the kind of nonsexual, person-to-person contact that occurs among workers in the office or factory settings. Workers known to be infected with the AIDS virus should not be restricted from work, nor should they be restricted from using telephones, office equipment, toilets, showers, eating facilities, and water fountains. In case of accidents in the workplace, employees and management should be trained that when equipment is contaminated with blood or other body fluids, whether known to be infected or not, a procedure is in place to clean it with soap and water, detergent, or a disinfectant.

The Medical Department or departments having functional medical responsibility should have health education materials available for both heterosexual and homosexual employees.

A listing of resource sources should be disseminated to employees seeking further information.

E. AIDS VICTIM EDUCATION

Risk reduction education should be provided to an employee known to have AIDS. The Medical Department should have procedures that guarantee confidentiality to provide the ability to collect epidemiological data. An education program should also allow counseling by the Medical Department to reduce risk to uninfected employees. All employees tested for LAV/ARV antibodies and found to be positive should be counseled and educated on transmission.

PERSONNEL POLICIES AND PROCEDURES

DISTRIBUTION:		SUBJECT: AIDS: LEGAL CONCERNS	
EFFECTIVE DATE:	PAGE 1 OF 2	FILE UNDER SECTION	
REVISION DATE:	APPROVED BY:		

The AIDS crisis presents a significant number of legal issues with no current, definitive answers. However, existing federal and state laws protect AIDS victims and establish parameters for dealing with AIDS victims and coworkers.

Prospective legal restrictions include: (1) federal and state discrimination laws, (2) occupational safety and health laws (for example, OSHA), (3) state workers' compensation statutes, (4) the National Labor Relations Act (NLRA), (5) privacy and confidentiality laws, (6) wrongful discharge laws and court decisions, and (7) defamation laws. Compounding the impact of these restrictions is the fact that some of them may require conflicting action on the part of the employer.

A. ANTIDISCRIMINATION LAWS

The antidiscrimination laws have the biggest potential impact on the company's handling of employees with AIDS. AIDS is a disability specifically protected by the Americans with Disabilities Act and most state antidiscrimination laws. The laws would protect those with AIDS, as well as those perceived as having AIDS or associating with another person who has AIDS, who are otherwise capable of doing the job, from discharge, rejection for hire, and other adverse employment actions. The ADA also requires reasonable accommodation for AIDS victims, such as minor restructuring of the job and time rescheduling.

B. RIGHT OF PRIVACY VS. RIGHT TO KNOW

The Americans with Disabilities Act prohibits the company from notifying managers and coworkers of an employee's AIDS condition. On the other hand, OSHA may require the company to notify managers and coworkers of AIDS to protect their health and provide a safe work environment. The OSHA impact is less likely, given the guidelines published by the Centers for Disease Control regarding the AIDS virus. The guidelines provide that AIDS is not transmittable through the type of casual contact found in the workplace. The company should be able to rely on these guidelines to avoid OSHA or tort liability for failure to notify coworkers of a fellow employee's AIDS condition.

C. COWORKER REFUSAL TO WORK

An employee who refuses to work with an AIDS victim is arguably acting on behalf of fellow employees as to a group safety issue. Any adverse action against that employee might be viewed as interfering with the employee's right to engage in concerted activity and a violation of the NLRA. Disciplining a group of employees for refusing to work with an AIDS victim might also be viewed as an NLRA violation. Nevertheless, refusal to work with or cooperate with an employee who has AIDS would constitute harassment under ADA and, unless corrected by the company, could subject the company to injunctive relief and punitive damages of up to $300,000.

D. LEGAL PARAMETERS

Realizing that the identification of an AIDS employee may create an initial employee relations crisis, the probable application of the above laws suggests the following parameters:

1. AIDS should be treated in all respects like any other life-threatening illness such as cancer and heart disease. Confidentiality of medical information should be respected and the company medical benefits applied.

2. The AIDS victim should not be terminated or placed on unpaid leave of absence. The resulting economic loss to the employee could force a lawsuit, result in bad publicity, and expose the company to legal liability.

3. The company should implement management guidelines on AIDS to promote consistency of approach and to respond to the uncertainty and questions among the workforce raised by this highly publicized disease.

4. An AIDS case will present medical problems and may present employee relations and legal problems; therefore,

DISTRIBUTION:		SUBJECT: AIDS: LEGAL CONCERNS	
EFFECTIVE DATE:	PAGE 2 OF 2	FILE UNDER SECTION	
REVISION DATE:	APPROVED BY:		

a response to an AIDS case should involve a coordinated effort among the cognizant medical and human resources departments.

5. When an employee with AIDS is otherwise capable of working, a confirming company medical opinion should be considered, necessary work restrictions identified, and the circumstances analyzed on a case-by-case basis, and the employee should be allowed to work with reasonable accommodations as warranted.

6. Routine screening of applicants is not recommended, since the company would not be able to reject the applicant based on the AIDS condition, and it could not test solely for AIDS, but would also have to test for other diseases.

In summary, AIDS has raised many legal questions, but few answers. Current laws, however, provide some guidance in the proper course of action to deal with AIDS in the workplace.

PERSONNEL POLICIES AND PROCEDURES

DISTRIBUTION:		SUBJECT: AIDS	
EFFECTIVE DATE:	PAGE 1 OF 1	FILE UNDER SECTION	
REVISION DATE:	APPROVED BY:		

The unfortunate spread of AIDS has caused us to adopt a policy regarding the employment of those who have this disease. According to the best medical evidence available, casual office contact with employees who have AIDS, or who have been exposed to the AIDS-related virus, will not result in the transmission of AIDS.

Accordingly, our policy will be to employ persons who have AIDS as long as they perform their jobs to our standards. Exceptions may be necessary, but our goal will be to employ persons with AIDS while at the same time preserving the safety and morale of all employees.

If you have any questions about this policy, please contact _____. If you wish to review medical information upon which the policy is based, we will be glad to make it available.

PERSONNEL POLICIES AND PROCEDURES

DISTRIBUTION:		SUBJECT: AIDS	
EFFECTIVE DATE:	PAGE 1 OF 1	FILE UNDER SECTION	
REVISION DATE:	APPROVED BY:		

PROCEDURE REGARDING THE TREATMENT OF AN EMPLOYEE WITH AIDS:

An employee with AIDS should be treated like any other ill employee; and

1. If fit to work, provided with work in accordance with normal procedures and appropriate accomodation if necessary. Usually, no special precautions in the workplace are indicated.

2. If unable to work, treated in the same manner with the same consideration as any other ill employee.

Managers should consult with the Human Resources Department concerning any exceptions and for assistance in managing any employee.

PERSONNEL POLICIES AND PROCEDURES

DISTRIBUTION:		SUBJECT: AIDS	
EFFECTIVE DATE:	PAGE 1 OF 1	FILE UNDER SECTION	
REVISION DATE:	APPROVED BY:		

POLICY:

It is our policy to allow employees with AIDS who are medically fit to work to continue employment by providing reasonable work accommodation for them while accommodating the need for everyone else's safety.

PROCEDURES:

The physical and emotional health and well-being of all employees must be protected, and reasonable accommodation for the employee with AIDS who is medically fit to work must be provided. To meet these goals, these guidelines are to be followed:

1. The manager who learns that an employee has AIDS is to notify the Human Relations Department.

2. The employee with AIDS, when requested by the company, must obtain a written medical certification of the illness and that the employee is medically fit to work and any work restrictions required. The company has the right to require an examination of the employee and the employee's medical records by a physician of its choice in order to obtain a second medical opinion. If the two opinions do not agree, the matter will be referred to the Human Relations Department.

3. The company will assess the need for job modification or transfer for the employee to accommodate any work restrictions and to minimize the employee's exposure to further infections.

4. If a healthy employee refuses to work with an employee with AIDS who has been medically approved as fit to work, the employee will be counseled by the Human Relations Department to alleviate the employee's concerns, but will be informed that further refusal to work with or otherwise cooperate with the employee with AIDS will subject the employee to disciplinary action, including possible termination.

5. To ensure that all employees have accurate medical information regarding AIDS, and to reduce unnecessary fear, managers will distribute brochures on AIDS to all employees.

PERSONNEL POLICIES AND PROCEDURES

DISTRIBUTION:		SUBJECT: AIDS	
EFFECTIVE DATE:	PAGE 1 OF 2	FILE UNDER SECTION	
REVISION DATE:	APPROVED BY:		

The facility's primary obligation is to protect the health and welfare of its patients and employees. These guidelines shall apply to patients, employees, and applicants who have or are suspected of having infection with HIV (including AIDS, AIDS-Related Complex [ARC], and asymptomatic carriers of AIDS).

PATIENT CARE:

A. Patients known or suspected of having infection with HIV shall be placed on appropriate precautions pursuant to Nursing and Infection Control policies and procedures as determined by the patient's physician. These policies and procedures shall be based on standards of practice for infection control including, among others, those recommended by the Centers for Disease Control.

B. The Infection Control Committee is responsible for addressing facility policies and procedures for patients with HIV infection.

C. Confidential information regarding medical tests, test results, medical findings, or diagnosis shall be maintained in the same confidential manner as all other medical information. Only persons having a need to know should be informed of the exact nature of the diagnosis. Pursuant to Infection Control policies and procedures, persons at risk will be informed and educated regarding recent medical information about Acquired Immunodeficiency Syndrome, and instructed to follow appropriate blood/body fluid precautions.

FACILITY PERSONNEL:

A. Reasonable efforts shall be made either to permit facility personnel diagnosed as having HIV infection to continue to perform their assigned duties (unless they are unable to perform the essential functions of the position or would pose a significant danger to the health, welfare, or safety of themselves, facility patients, or other employees) or to offer them a position that they are able to perform and that would not pose a significant danger to the health, welfare, or safety of themselves and/or others. In determining the significance of the danger posed, the facility shall consult public health officials, as well as appropriate guidelines that may be promulgated by public health authorities regarding the state of medical knowledge concerning:

  ◆ The nature of the risk (how the disease is transmitted),

  ◆ The duration of the risk (how long the carrier is infectious),

  ◆ The severity of the risk (what is the potential harm to third parties), and

  ◆ The probabilities that the disease will be transmitted and will cause varying degrees of harm.

Such decisions will also be based on considerations of the reasonable accommodations that can be provided to eliminate any substantial risk. These determinations will be made on an individualized, case-by-case basis.

B. Confirmed cases of HIV infection in facility personnel should be reported immediately to Infection Control so that it can immediately respond to the health and educational needs of patients and employees. This information shall be maintained by Infection Control in a confidential manner and shall be disclosed only to persons having a need to know and only to the extent required to protect the health, welfare, and safety of patients and employees.

C. Employees who believe they have been exposed to the body fluids of an individual with HIV infection shall immediately report the matter to Infection Control so that Infection Control may evaluate the need for appropriate testing

DISTRIBUTION:		SUBJECT: AIDS	
EFFECTIVE DATE:	PAGE 2 OF 2	FILE UNDER SECTION	
REVISION DATE:	APPROVED BY:		

and treatment. If an individual is suspected of having AIDS and refuses to consent to appropriate testing, Infection Control and the exposed employee's physician shall make determinations regarding appropriate testing and treatment for the employee based on the individual's current available medical information. Follow-up testing may be indicated and performed according to Infection Control policies and procedures.

D. Facility personnel who refuse to work with other facility personnel or patients either suffering or suspected of suffering from HIV infection should be referred to Infection Control by their supervisor or department head. Infection Control shall provide these individuals with the latest information concerning HIV infection, its transmission, and adequate safeguards against transmission, as necessary. Facility personnel who have a reasonable basis for refusal (such as pregnancy or undergoing chemotherapy) may be offered a temporary or permanent transfer if such is available.

E. Facility personnel suffering from HIV infection shall be eligible for employee benefits (such as disability and Workers' Compensation) in the same manner as any other employee who may be entitled to such benefits.

APPLICANTS FOR EMPLOYMENT:

A. Persons offered employment shall complete a health screening questionnaire that shall include a question as to whether or not he/she suffers from or is susceptible to any immunity disorder.

B. Persons diagnosed with immunity problems may be considered for employment the same as any other applicant, based on their experience, qualifications, abilities to perform the job, and other appropriate factors. Persons diagnosed with immunity problems may be required to obtain medical clearance from their physicians. Employee Health or Infection Control will provide instructions and education as necessary. The same policy guidelines regarding assigned duties as stated in Section II (A) shall apply.

EMPLOYEES OR APPLICANTS WITH OTHER DISABLING OR INFECTIOUS DISEASES:

A. Applicants for employment with confirmed or suspected disabling infectious diseases other than AIDS shall be considered for employment as described in Section III.

B. The policy guidelines contained herein regarding continuing employment, assigned duties, eligibility for benefits, and employee education shall apply to facility employees either confirmed or suspected of having a disabling or infectious disease other than AIDS.

ADVISORY COMMITTEE ON INFECTIOUS DISEASE:

An ad hoc advisory committee shall be established from time to time to advise the facility's administration on medical matters pertaining to employees or applicants offered employment with infectious, disabling, or contagious diseases (including HIV infection). Each such ad hoc advisory committee shall include at least one representative from the Infection Control Committee together with other appropriate professionals. The committee shall consider all available medical information regarding the employee's or applicant's condition and shall provide advice to the facility administration regarding such matters as the individual's ability to perform or to continue to perform the job, the significant risks of infection to others, or unnecessary significant risk to the individual. The committee shall consult with facility legal counsel as necessary, provide findings and recommendations to the appropriate administrative officers, and otherwise maintain the information it receives and its findings and recommendations in a confidential manner.

PERSONNEL POLICIES AND PROCEDURES

DISTRIBUTION:		SUBJECT: EMPLOYEE ASSISTANCE PROGRAM	
EFFECTIVE DATE:	PAGE 1 OF 2	FILE UNDER SECTION	
REVISION DATE:	APPROVED BY:		

It is the intent of the company to provide meaningful assistance for employees with personal problems that may affect job performance. We want to provide assistance in ways that will allow and cause employees to exercise personal initiative in pursuit of problem control and solutions. It is our desire to provide for complete confidentiality regarding the circumstance, up to the point where confidentiality itself may reduce the probability of providing effective assistance. In other words, it is our intention to include, in any form of communications, only those who are in a position to assist in providing meaningful help for the employee. It must be recognized that problems affecting work performance will often require help from supervision.

We believe that the personal lives of employees are their own affair. However, when an employee's personal problems seriously affect job performance, sound business practice and an obligation rooted in personal concern for employees require that the problems be resolved. The basic purpose of this program is to offer employees assistance in such a way as to restore individual productivity and enable employees to lead meaningful lives. In so doing, the company will retain valued employees.

HELP AGENCIES:

(Company Name) has contracted with _____ to run the day-to-day business of the EAP. Employees are given cards with the number they can call twenty-four hours a day.

_____ has the responsibility for keeping updated files on various help agencies. Recognizing that different agencies may approach problems in significantly different manners, they endeavor to maintain files that will provide information on more than one source of help.

These files shall include, but will not be limited to, agencies that are able to help with problems relating to the following:

1. Alcohol
2. Chemical dependence (drug addiction)
3. Mental/emotional/psychological problems
4. Personal stress arising from conditions within the home, such as divorce, physical abuse, etc.

AVAILABILITY AND USE OF EMPLOYEE ASSISTANCE PROGRAM (EAP):

+ Any employee with a serious problem should be encouraged to ask for assistance. Supervisors are responsible for communicating the availability of this program to members of their own departments. It is desired that participation be on a voluntary basis.

+ No employee shall have his or her job security jeopardized solely because of his or her need for diagnosis, treatment, or help.

+ Employees may ask for Employee Assistance through their own supervisor, the Open Door, the Director of Human Resources, or by directly calling _____ .

+ The company representative receiving a request for Employee Assistance shall keep the matter in the strictest confidence and discuss it only with persons whose help and/or understanding is needed.

+ Absences needed for drug or alcohol treatment may qualify for FMLA leave for eligible employees.

PERSONNEL POLICIES AND PROCEDURES

DISTRIBUTION:		SUBJECT: EMPLOYEE ASSISTANCE PROGRAM	
EFFECTIVE DATE:	PAGE 2 OF 2	FILE UNDER SECTION	
REVISION DATE:	APPROVED BY:		

KEY RESPONSIBILITY OF THE EMPLOYEE USING THE EAP:

♦ To recognize that the responsibility of employees using the EAP is to themselves, their family, and their jobs, not to the program itself.

♦ To recognize that the EAP in itself provides assistance, and that participation in the program cannot automatically ensure job security.

♦ To recognize that the company is working with, and in the interest of, the employee in a special way to provide meaningful assistance that will ultimately result in the employee's again becoming a productive and successful employee.

♦ To work cooperatively with the supervisor and/or other sources to cause efforts at problem resolution to be successful and permanent.

KEY RESPONSIBILITIES OF THE IMMEDIATE SUPERVISOR:

♦ To observe deteriorating and/or unsatisfactory job performance and take remedial action.

♦ To discuss job performance with the employee, establish common expectations regarding job performance, and reach agreement that performance must be improved to a satisfactory level. During this step, when appropriate, explain the EAP to the employee and refer to the Director of Human Resources with appropriate communications. Document carefully for personnel file.

♦ To work with troubled employees on a concerned but no-nonsense basis, confronting them with the facts of their performance. Present the EAP to them as an alternative to discharge when appropriate.

♦ To take suitable corrective action to restore employee productivity and maintain performance standards in the department. Employees who do not bring their job performance up to a satisfactory level after a reasonable period of time shall be terminated.

♦ To document all activity related to performance on the job, actions taken, and employee responses. Communicate appropriately with the Director of Human Resources.

KEY RESPONSIBILITIES OF THE DIRECTOR OF HUMAN RESOURCES FUNCTIONING AS EAP COORDINATOR:

♦ To act as a liaison with troubled employees and community resources.

♦ To work with troubled employees, supervisors, outside resources, and family members to enhance the probability of benefit to the employee from using the EAP.

♦ To ensure the confidentiality of employees using the EAP. To document activity related to the EPA.

PERSONNEL POLICIES AND PROCEDURES

DISTRIBUTION:		SUBJECT: EMPLOYEE ASSISTANCE PROGRAM	
EFFECTIVE DATE:	PAGE 1 OF 3	FILE UNDER SECTION	
REVISION DATE:	APPROVED BY:		

POLICY:

(Company Name) considers alcoholism and other chemical dependencies, emotional disturbances, and many personal stresses as health problems that can be successfully treated. Employees who have these problems that adversely affect job performance will receive equal consideration with employees who have other illness. Such health problems may qualify for related benefits that are available under the company's group insurance program.

The company will become concerned only when job performance, attendance, or job responsibilities are affected by behavioral/medical problems, and intends that such problems be diagnosed and treated at the earliest possible stage. Since management and supervision normally do not have the professional qualifications to diagnose and treat such illnesses, this Employee Assistance Program (EAP) has been established.

EAP has been developed to supplement existing Benefit Programs and assure maximum effort in assisting the "problem employee." This program has four objectives:

1. To retain valued employees.
2. To restore performance through early identification of personal behavior problems.
3. To motivate employees to seek help.
4. To refer employees to the appropriate assistance resources.

Technical support for EAP will be provided by the _____, which will assist in developing employee and supervisor training programs, assist in locating appropriate community resources in other states to which company personnel may be referred for diagnosis and treatment, and function as the community resource for area referrals.

PROCEDURES:

The Employee Relations Department will be responsible for implementation of this Program, and a member of the Employee Relations staff will be assigned the role of Director of Employee Assistance. The Director will perform the services outlined in the following procedures and will be available at all times for advice, guidance, or assistance on any part of the Program. It will further be the Director's responsibility to provide and promote confidentiality and privacy in the handling of cases, train management and supervisory personnel in the proper way to deal with such situations, provide employee educational programs, and help remove some of the moral stigma often associated with behavioral/medical problems.

A. PROBLEM IDENTIFICATION

The possibility that a behavioral/medical problem exists arises when an employee's performance has deteriorated; normal supervisory corrective interviews have been conducted; the employee has been given a reasonable period of time to improve; and job performance has not improved significantly. This will differ from other job performance problems in that this "problem employee" will have been a person of proven capability or a person with high potential and in either case would be expected to be capable of reversing a trend of deteriorating job performance but has been unable to do so for no apparent reason.

B. PRECONTACT PROCEDURES

1. Document the occurrences and nature of performance deficiencies of the "problem employee," which may include absenteeism, poor quality of work, missed deadlines, loss of credibility, unsatisfactory evaluations, problems with other employees, errors in judgment, and poor decisions.

2. Review the facts with the Director of EAP. He/she will assist in planning the contact interview with the employee.

PERSONNEL POLICIES AND PROCEDURES

DISTRIBUTION:		SUBJECT: EMPLOYEE ASSISTANCE PROGRAM	
EFFECTIVE DATE:	PAGE 2 OF 3	FILE UNDER SECTION	
REVISION DATE:	APPROVED BY:		

Experience has indicated that such assistance is very important to the effectiveness of the interviews that will follow. It will not be a normal performance interview because the supervisor knows that something is wrong or the individual would have been able to bring his/her performance up to standard before this point in time.

C. CONTACT PROCEDURES

1. Talk to the employee and review the performance record and the employee's failure to meet the agreed-upon plan and objectives. Offer the help of EAP.

2. If the employee accepts the offer of help, call the Director of EAP and arrange a meeting with the employee. If the employee says nothing or is noncommittal or refuses the offer of help, there is nothing further to do at this time except to note in the records that the employee did not accept the offer of help. Record the date of this interview with a brief summary of the content and the agreed-upon plan and objectives for performance improvement.

3. After a short but reasonable period of time, if there is no significant improvement in job performance, conduct a second interview. Tell the person that his/her work has still not improved and that it would be to his/her advantage to meet with the Director of EAP to get help on whatever it is that is adversely affecting job performance. Emphasize to the employee that he/she has been given two chances already and that the job could be in jeopardy if something is not done. If the individual agrees, schedule the appointment at that moment. If the individual refuses, note this in your record and contact the Director of EAP to review the case.

4. If no substantial performance improvement follows from these steps, initiate a final interview. Tell the employee that he or she must make a choice: either see the Director of EAP to try to get help on whatever it is that has caused the continuing performance decline so that performance can be brought back to standard, or face the consequences now in terms of job action up to and including termination. If the employee accepts the offer of help, telephone the Director of EAP immediately and schedule an appointment. If for any reason the individual refuses the offer of help here, proceed with the agreed-upon job action to be taken.

5. In any individual case, the number of interviews with the employee may vary with the circumstances. However, it is essential that the employee not be allowed to avoid the "either/or" interview—that is, the one where the individual is offered the firm choice of either accepting help or receiving appropriate job action up to and including termination.

6. In some instances, a leave of absence for treatment may be necessary.

7. After an employee completes the prescribed treatment and returns to work, the manager should resume the normal job-monitoring procedure and advise the Director of EAP if any difficulty should arise.

8. If an employee who accepts treatment fails to respond or after completing treatment resumes unsatisfactory job performance, he or she will be subject to termination or whatever administrative action is appropriate.

D. THE ROLE OF THE SUPERVISOR

1. The supervisor has one of the most effective tools—that is, the desire that employees have to hold their jobs. The role of the supervisor is to identify the "problem employee" through poor job performance, attendance, or job responsibility, and to use that poor performance to motivate the employee to seek help through EAP. In addition, the supervisor should encourage self-referrals to the program.

2. The key to successful motivation of an employee to seek help lies in the fair and constructive use of the supervisor's authority. Employees must be made to understand that unless their problem is corrected and their performance brought up to standard, they will be subject to termination for unsatisfactory job performance. They will also need assurance that participation in EAP will not jeopardize their job or promotional opportunities.

3. The purpose of EAP is to motivate employees to accept treatment by offering referral to qualified professionals. The supervisor can motivate employees to accept help through EAP. Supervisors cannot solve the problem alone.

DISTRIBUTION:		SUBJECT: EMPLOYEE ASSISTANCE PROGRAM
EFFECTIVE DATE:	PAGE 3 OF 3	FILE UNDER SECTION
REVISION DATE:	APPROVED BY:	

What the Manager or Supervisor SHOULD NOT DO:

a. DO NOT try to diagnose the problem.

b. DO NOT raise any questions with the employee that might reveal the nature, severity, or prognosis of a disability or any underlying health condition.

c. DO NOT discuss drinking or other drug use unless it occurs on the job or the employee reports to work in an impaired condition.

d. DO NOT moralize. Restrict comments to job performance.

e. DO NOT be misled by sympathy-evoking tactics.

f. DO NOT cover up. A misguided "kindness" can lead to a serious delay in real help reaching the employee.

g. DO NOT discuss the employee's problem with anyone except the Director of EAP or immediate superiors.

E. EFFECT ON JOB SECURITY

Referral to the Employee Assistance Program for diagnosis and treatment will not jeopardize an employee's job security or promotional opportunities, but it will be the responsibility of the employee to comply with the referral and to cooperate with the prescribed treatment and administrative procedures. An employee's refusal to accept diagnosis or treatment, or failure to respond to treatment, will be handled in the same manner as for other illnesses when job performance continues to be adversely affected.

F. EFFECT ON COMPANY RULES

This policy and any subsequent Employee Assistance Program will not in any way change any company or project rules relating to employee conduct, and any behavior that heretofore subjected an employee to reprimand or discharge will continue to receive the same degree of disciplinary action.

Section 14

Miscellaneous Policies and Procedures

The following checklist can be used to help you determine the various policy items that should be incorporated in your policy manual. Sample policy statements covering many of the items in the checklist appear in this section. They can be used to guide your policy statements.

Policy Manual Checklist

Our Policy Manual Should Cover:

Business Ethics

1. Compliance with laws and regulations   Yes_____ No_____

2. Dealing with customers, suppliers, etc.   Yes_____ No_____
   A. Contract negotiations   Yes_____ No_____
   B. Product quality   Yes_____ No_____
   C. Information from competitors   Yes_____ No_____
   D. Costs/timecard and reporting   Yes_____ No_____
   E. Hiring restrictions   Yes_____ No_____

3. Company resources   Yes_____ No_____
   A. Political contributions   Yes_____ No_____
   B. Business gifts   Yes_____ No_____
   C. U.S. government regulations   Yes_____ No_____
   D. Relations with foreign officials   Yes_____ No_____
   E. Financial responsibility   Yes_____ No_____

4. Conflict of interest   Yes_____ No_____

5. Insider trading   Yes_____ No_____

6. Acceptance of business gifts, etc.   Yes_____ No_____

7. Restricted company information   Yes_____ No_____

8. Classified information   Yes_____ No_____

9. Reporting violations   Yes_____ No_____

10. Discipline procedures   Yes_____ No_____

Personal Computers and Software

1. Access to PCs and authorization to use   Yes_____ No_____

2. Control of data (programs, files, etc.)   Yes_____ No_____

3. Record of PC use   Yes_____ No_____

4. Security of files (backup, etc.)   Yes_____ No_____

5. Loan of PCs to employees   Yes_____ No_____

6. Safeguarding equipment/software   Yes_____ No_____

7. Training on PC use   Yes_____ No_____

8. Access to company files/records   Yes_____ No_____

Other Miscellaneous Policies/Procedures

1. Loan of company equipment/supplies to employees   Yes_____ No_____

2. Smoking policy   Yes_____ No_____
   A. No-smoking areas   Yes_____ No_____
   B. Designated smoking areas   Yes_____ No_____

3. Company bulletin boards and contents   Yes_____ No_____

4. Telephone usage by employees   Yes_____ No_____

5. E-mail   Yes_____ No_____

6. Other employment   Yes_____ No_____

7. Company keys   Yes_____ No_____

8. Expressions of sympathy by company   Yes_____ No_____

9. Contract personnel and services   Yes_____ No_____

10. Press releases   Yes_____ No_____

11. Personnel records   Yes_____ No_____
    A. Requirements to update   Yes_____ No_____
    B. What they should/should not contain   Yes_____ No_____
    C. Providing access to employees   Yes_____ No_____
    D. What information is to be provided to employee   Yes_____ No_____

12. Requests for employee information   Yes_____ No_____
    A. Written requests   Yes_____ No_____
    B. Telephone requests   Yes_____ No_____
    C. Requests from government agencies—federal, state, county,
       unemployment, etc.   Yes_____ No_____

D. Requests from tax units	Yes_____	No_____
E. Requests from courts and law enforcement agencies	Yes_____	No_____
F. Subpoena	Yes_____	No_____
G. Employee release	Yes_____	No_____
13. Company confidential information	Yes_____	No_____
14. Employee agreements	Yes_____	No_____
A. Not to compete	Yes_____	No_____
B. Inventions, patents, etc.	Yes_____	No_____
15. Company property escrow account	Yes_____	No_____
16. Guidelines on solicitation and distribution	Yes_____	No_____

Should You Let Employees See Their Personnel File?

If one of your employees came to see you and asked to see his or her personnel file, what would you do? There is currently no federal law covering access to personnel files. However, many states, such as Michigan, Massachusetts, and Maryland, have regulations giving employees the right to see their own personnel files. Usually there are certain requirements concerning access to personnel files, such as, the employee must make the request in writing, and the file may not be removed from the premises. However, in Michigan, for instance, an employee is allowed to copy anything in his or her personnel file. While not all states have enacted file access legislation, it is expected that this will come in time.

Many employers are reluctant to allow an employee to review his or her own personnel file. In contrast, some employers will open the file to just about anybody who wants to look at it. It is recommended that employees have access to their personnel files, as the personnel file should be defensible and each employee should be able to know what is in his or her file. If there is something detrimental in the file, then the employee should know about it, and the detrimental information should be correct. If the information is incorrect, the error should be corrected so the file reflects only the true circumstances.

Therefore, in looking to the future, we would recommend that employers begin to establish policies about an employee's right to review and even copy his or her personnel file. We also want to ensure that an employee's right to privacy concerning what is contained in his or her file is protected. We recommend that the following procedures be established:

1. The personnel file should contain only items that have been seen by the employee or that the employee knows about.
2. Each item that is placed in the personnel file should be true and accurate.
3. If employees wish to review their personnel file, they should be allowed to do so provided they review it in your office and, if you wish, they make their request in writing.
4. Depending on your particular state law, you may be required to allow the employee to make and take copies of the items in his or her personnel file.
5. No person other than the employee, his or her supervisor, and other concerned members of management or someone with a definite need to know may look at an individual's personnel file.
6. Medical information, psychological testing results, and anything that is not job-related should be kept in a separate confidential, locked file with limited access.

The contents of personnel files should basically be limited to the application form, tax form, insurance applications, discussions concerning questionable job performance, formalized performance appraisal reviews, employment history, disciplinary measures, commendations, absenteeism records, attendance at training sessions and seminars, special achievements, authorization for payroll deductions, exit interview forms, and separation of employment forms. We suggest that you check your state law to see what the requirements are for an employee's access to his or her personnel files. Barring any state restrictions, the foregoing procedures should provide a sound system of personnel file accessibility and review.

The following miscellaneous policies are found in this section:

Access to Employee's Personal Information
Confidential Information
Request for Employee Information
Employee Agreements
Ethical Conduct in Business
Entrance/Exit Procedures for Employees and Visitors
Investigative Policy
Loan of Company Equipment/Supplies to Employees
Smoking
Bulletin Boards
Telephone Usage
E-mail
Holding Other Jobs
Company Keys
Expressions of Sympathy
Contract Personnel and Services
Press Releases
Workplace Violence
Company Property Escrow Account
Guidelines for Solicitation and Distribution

PERSONNEL POLICIES AND PROCEDURES

DISTRIBUTION:		SUBJECT: ACCESS TO EMPLOYEE'S PERSONAL INFORMATION	
EFFECTIVE DATE:	PAGE 1 OF 2		FILE UNDER SECTION
REVISION DATE:	APPROVED BY:		

OBJECTIVE:

This policy is established to protect and safeguard the privacy of employees' personal information to the fullest extent possible, consistent with business and legal practices.

DEFINITIONS:

1. Employee—Any person currently employed, laid off with re-employment rights, or on leave of absence. The term does not include applicants for employment, designated agents, or any other persons.

2. Personnel File—Any record maintained within (Company Name) that has been used or may be used to affect an employee's qualifications for employment, promotion, transfer, additional compensation, or disciplinary action.

3. Records Representative—For plant locations, the records center manager or designee. For marketing field locations, the Human Resources Director or designee at operations office, or the branch manager or designee at branch offices.

POLICY:

It is the policy of (Company Name) that:

1. (Company Name) collects, maintains, and uses employee personal information in such a manner as to ensure its accuracy and relevancy, preserve the confidentiality of the information, satisfy business needs, and conform to applicable legal requirements.

2. To preserve privacy, only those who have a legitimate "need to know" may have access to employee information. The disclosure of such data is governed by company policy.

3. Upon completion of a personnel file information request, sent to the designated records representative, an employee may review his or her personnel file. Within ten (10) days of the request, a mutually convenient time during normal business hours is scheduled. Any records indicated in item 4 may be reviewed; if they are not maintained by the records representative, they will be obtained by the representative from the maintaining department for the scheduled review. The review is conducted in the presence of the records representative without disruption of normal business operations. Such reviews are permitted at reasonable intervals, but generally not more frequently than twice a year. Employees who believe that the file information is incorrect may, after review, recommend correction, deletion, or modification to the cognizant Human Resources representative. Appropriate corrective action will be taken when justified, or the employee may submit a statement for attachment to the disputed record. Although file documents are not to be removed from the place of inspection, or reproduced unless prescribed by law, employees may take notes on the contents of their file.

4. Personnel files should be reviewed to ensure that only pertinent and necessary data is kept. Personnel files for each employee are retained in accordance with the established records retention schedule. The personnel file should contain only documentation that pertains to and is officially used to record or affect qualification for employment, promotion, compensation increase, termination, or disciplinary action, such as:

PERSONNEL POLICIES AND PROCEDURES

DISTRIBUTION:		SUBJECT: ACCESS TO EMPLOYEE'S PERSONAL INFORMATION	
EFFECTIVE DATE:	PAGE 2 OF 2		FILE UNDER SECTION
REVISION DATE:	APPROVED BY:		

    A. Employment applications, résumés, employment offer letters, acceptance letters, etc.

    B. Wages or salary information.

    C. Documentation of compensation changes, hire date, job titles, seniority, birth date, authorization for pay deductions and withholdings, etc.

    D. Commendations, disciplinary warnings, etc.

    E. Layoffs, leaves of absence, attendance records, etc.

    F. Fringe benefit information.

    G. Retirement records.

    H. Performance evaluations.

    I. Educational information from colleges, technical schools, company courses, etc.

5. Certain information should not be included in an employee's personnel file, such as:

    A. Medical records/information.

    B. Security information.

    C. Company personnel planning data, salary increase forecasts, replacement charts, etc.

    D. Civil, criminal, grievance, administrative agency, and other such proceedings.

    E. Letters of reference.

    F. Information that would disclose personal information about another individual.

    G. Materials available to the employee under the Fair Credit Reporting Act.

6. If required by federal or state law, applicants and employees are advised, prior to the preparation of an investigative report by an outside agency, that such a report on them may be prepared.

7. Employees are advised of the company's practices regarding privacy and information disclosure through orientation programs, employee handbooks, and company publications.

PERSONNEL POLICIES AND PROCEDURES

DISTRIBUTION:		SUBJECT: CONFIDENTIAL INFORMATION	
EFFECTIVE DATE:	PAGE 1 OF 1	FILE UNDER SECTION	
REVISION DATE:	APPROVED BY:		

POLICY STATEMENT:

Confidential information regarding the company of the customers we serve should in no way be divulged; divulging confidential information will result in immediate discipline.

PROCEDURE:

Information regarded as personal and confidential, including payroll, financial statements, and other information, should be handled carefully. Managers should instruct their staff coming in contact with this information as to what is personal and confidential and should require that staff write ''PERSONAL AND CONFIDENTIAL'' on such materials on the outside of any envelopes and correspondence. Additionally, employees should be instructed by management that upon receipt of materials marked Personal and Confidential, these materials should be left sealed, to be opened by the individual to whom they are addressed.

PERSONNEL POLICIES AND PROCEDURES

DISTRIBUTION:		SUBJECT: REQUESTS FOR EMPLOYEE INFORMATION	
EFFECTIVE DATE:	PAGE 1 OF 2	FILE UNDER SECTION	
REVISION DATE:	APPROVED BY:		

OBJECTIVE:

This policy is established to prevent disclosure of personnel, medical, or payroll information to unauthorized persons.

POLICY:

It is the policy of (Company Name) that:

1. Requests for information and/or records concerning employees are referred to the appropriate Human Resources Manager or designee except as provided in paragraphs 4(B) and 4(C) below.

2. Except as provided in paragraphs 4(B), 4(C), and 5 below, Non-Human-Resources employees do not furnish information concerning employees to external sources without prior approval of the appropriate Human Resources Manager.

3. Human Resources employees do not furnish any employee information unless the identity of the requester is clearly defined. Written requests must be on the letterhead of the organization requesting the information. Telephone requests may be handled on a "callback" basis. Information given by telephone is limited to confirming that the inquirer has the correct dates of employment and most recent occupation description. If requested, this information alone can be confirmed in writing.

4. Requests for employee information from organizations that have the legal right and authority to obtain this information are handled as follows:

    A. Requests from government agencies and federal, state, county, and local courts and law enforcement agencies are directed to the Human Resources Department, and the requester's legal right to the requested information is reviewed with the Human Resources Manager and the law department prior to release.

    B. Requests from federal, state, county, and municipal tax units concerning employees' earnings are referred to the payroll department, and information is furnished to the requester.

    C. Requests from the Bureau of Unemployment Compensation and Welfare usually result from a claim filed by employees. Information that expedites the settling of the claim is to be furnished. Earnings information is supplied by the payroll activity, except in those states serviced by the (Company Name) unemployment compensation counselor.

5. All other requests for information contained in personnel records are not honored unless:

    A. Clear written permission to release specific information is obtained from the employee. (The employee's written authorization is to be reviewed by the law department prior to the release of any information, unless the written authorization is to release special information for credit references, loans, mortgages, credit card applications, etc.)

    or

    B. A subpoena or other request having the force of legal compulsion is served to (Company Name). The employee receiving the document contacts Human Resources immediately.

PERSONNEL POLICIES AND PROCEDURES

DISTRIBUTION:		SUBJECT: REQUESTS FOR EMPLOYEE INFORMATION	
EFFECTIVE DATE:	PAGE 2 OF 2	FILE UNDER SECTION	
REVISION DATE:	APPROVED BY:		

The Human Resources representative, upon receipt of the document, contacts the appropriate law or industrial relations department as indicated below, and forwards the subpoena or other document bearing the force of law, with any relevant information on file, as follows:

(1) To the industrial relations department for subpoenas dealing with equal employment, labor relations, or occupational safety and health administration matters.

(2) To the law department for all other subpoenas.

NOTE: When the above-mentioned documents are referred to the law department, the Human Resources representative telephones the employee and confirms, with a memorandum like that shown in exhibit A, that (Company Name) is compelled to supply the requested items.

6. An employee served with a subpoena addressed to (Company Name) for the purpose of furnishing employee information or records does not furnish such information or records without prior approval of the law or industrial relations department, as appropriate, nor will the employee appear in court or at a hearing without counsel unless prior approval of the law department is obtained.

EXHIBIT A

TO: (Employee's Name)

FROM: (Human Resources Representative)

COPY: (Attorney in law department who is handling the matter. Show both the name of the carbonee and the law department's name so that the employee knows why the attorney is receiving a carbon copy.)

SUBJECT: Subpoenaing of Personnel Files
John Q. Employee

As I advised you by telephone on (the date), we have received a subpoena for certain documents from your personnel file. A copy of this subpoena is attached.

Prior to the actual court hearing, it is a fairly common practice in this county that if no objections are raised by any party, the employer will send copies of the relevant documents to the attorney who had the subpoena issued and thereby satisfy its obligation under the subpoena. This practice may be observed in this situation unless you or your attorney advises us on or before (the date on which the documents would be mailed) not to do so.

If you have any questions on this matter, please feel free to contact either me or Attorney (Name), who is coordinating this for the law department.

PERSONNEL POLICIES AND PROCEDURES

DISTRIBUTION:		SUBJECT: EMPLOYEE AGREEMENTS	
EFFECTIVE DATE:	PAGE 1 OF 1	FILE UNDER SECTION	
REVISION DATE:	APPROVED BY:		

OBJECTIVE:

This policy is established to provide for the protection of confidential information and inventions of the (Company Name) group.

POLICY:

It is the policy of (Company Name) that:

1. Each employee hired, or rehired, is required to sign an employee confidential information and invention agreement, as a condition of employment. The agreement must be properly executed before the employee starts to work.

2. The term employee, as used here, refers to all persons directly employed by the company. It excludes all contract personnel performing in-house services and all outside consultants under contract.

PERSONNEL POLICIES AND PROCEDURES

DISTRIBUTION:		SUBJECT: LOAN OF COMPANY EQUIPMENT AND SUPPLIES TO EMPLOYEES
EFFECTIVE DATE:	PAGE 1 OF 1	FILE UNDER SECTION
REVISION DATE:	APPROVED BY:	

POLICY STATEMENT:

Items of equipment and supplies that are the property of (Company Name) may be loaned to company employees for their personal use outside the plant. Such loans will be made by the company according to the guidelines noted herein.

RESPONSIBILITY:

Employee—It is the responsibility of each employee wishing to borrow an item of company property to complete a Loan Authorization Form and secure the necessary approval signatures. In addition, the employee is responsible for the condition of the tools, equipment, or supplies upon their return to the company.

Department Head—The lending of company property shall be at the discretion of the department head who has custody of and/or is responsible for the property.

GUIDELINES:

1. A Loan Authorization Form will be used to authorize and record the loan of tools, equipment, and supplies. Such forms will be made available through the Human Resources Department.

2. After completing the Loan Authorization Form, the employee must present it to the department head who has custody of and/or is responsible for the property for his/her approval. It is the responsibility of the Department Head to determine whether the person seeking the loan of an item has the technical knowledge and skill to operate or use the item without risk of damage or personal injury.

3. Whether or not approval is granted, the original copy of the Loan Authorization Form should be forwarded to the Human Resources Department, with a copy retained by the employee and by the issuing department.

4. For property not returned by the due date, the issuing department should inform the Human Resources Department and follow-up procedures will be initiated.

5. Certain items of company property (such as vehicles) will not be available to employees on a loan basis. Those items that may be loaned will be determined by the appropriate department head.

6. If office equipment is loaned on a long-term basis, a copy of the Loan Authorization Form must be sent to the manager, office services.

PERSONNEL POLICIES AND PROCEDURES

DISTRIBUTION:		SUBJECT: SMOKING	
EFFECTIVE DATE:	PAGE 1 OF 2	FILE UNDER SECTION	
REVISION DATE:	APPROVED BY:		

The company places an emphasis on wellness and staying fit. Our aggressive nonsmoking policies and health education program are designed to promote good health among our employees, improve productivity, and reduce health-care claims. We firmly believe that prevention, in the first place, is far superior to incurring illness and its associated costs.

The smoking policy of the company is based on the following reasons:

1. There is indisputable evidence that smoking is detrimental to good health, and we can no longer fail to act on this significant health risk;

2. The company feels a responsibility to be a leader in the community in practicing healthy lifestyle behaviors;

3. Smoking-related illness and death is the number one health problem in the United States today;

4. The prevention of heart disease, cancer, emphysema, and stroke is promoted by the elimination of cigarette smoking;

5. Although smokers do have a right to smoke, the nonsmoking majority have a right to breathe comfortably and safely, since sidestream smoke is a health hazard to nonsmokers;

6. Smokers can be expected to have 25 to 35 percent more health-care claims, and

7. Smoking is responsible for many business-related fires.

   To help achieve our wellness goal, a three-part program has been developed as follows:

1. Current employees who smoke should be assured that their jobs are not in jeopardy because they are smokers. We are not making "quitting smoking" a condition of continued employment. Also, company policy will not allow negative consequences on an employee's performance evaluation because he/she is a smoker. However, normal disciplinary procedure will be used for employees who disregard established nonsmoking areas.

2. We will encourage our current people who are smokers to stop smoking. This encouragement will be in the form of educational information about the health risk of smoking and financial incentives for becoming a nonsmoker. Anyone who stops smoking is eligible for a $100 incentive bonus by contacting his/her supervisor or manager (this bonus must be returned if smoking is reinitiated).

3. Smoking areas in company facilities and buildings will be more restricted in the future. Due to this policy and fire insurance requirements, smoking will be permitted only in designated areas (see company handbook).

PERSONNEL POLICIES AND PROCEDURES

DISTRIBUTION:		SUBJECT: SMOKING	
EFFECTIVE DATE:	PAGE 2 OF 2	FILE UNDER SECTION	
REVISION DATE:	APPROVED BY:		

NONSMOKING AWARD:

Effective _____,19 _____, _____ an employee
of (Name of Company), ceased smoking and thereby qualifies for the $100.00 smoking cessation award.

In accepting this award, (Name of Employee) acknowledges that should he/she begin smoking cigarettes, cigars, or pipes, the full $100.00 must be refunded to the company.

_____

Employee

_____

Manager

_____

Corporate Officer

_____

Date

PERSONNEL POLICIES AND PROCEDURES

DISTRIBUTION:		SUBJECT: SMOKING	
EFFECTIVE DATE:	PAGE 1 OF 1	FILE UNDER SECTION	
REVISION DATE:	APPROVED BY:		

ADMINISTRATIVE GUIDELINES:

The option to smoke or not to smoke is an individual's right and choice. The location at which a person can smoke at our facility is restricted to designated areas.

Smoking is prohibited in common public areas such as hallways, conference rooms, meeting and class rooms, open work areas or work stations, and other public, common areas.

Smoking is permitted in areas where it doesn't affect nonsmokers, such as designated sections of cafeterias, individual offices if designated by the occupant, and other such designated areas.

Smokers are urged and encouraged to stop smoking. Employees who are interested in cessation programs should be encouraged to participate in medical and health programs sponsored by the company or community organizations.

The policy will be communicated to all employees and to contractors, vendors, and visitors as may be deemed necessary and appropriate.

Any state or local statutes on smoking will supersede the company policy when the statutes are more stringent.

Areas identified as no smoking as part of a safety and fire protection program remain applicable.

PERSONNEL POLICIES AND PROCEDURES

DISTRIBUTION:		SUBJECT: SMOKING	
EFFECTIVE DATE:	PAGE 1 OF 1	FILE UNDER SECTION	
REVISION DATE:	APPROVED BY:		

POLICY STATEMENT:

Although smoking is not prohibited at (Company Name) facilities, we require that employees restrict smoking to designated areas and within break and meal periods.

PROCEDURE:

Safe smoking habits must be observed at all times. Receptacles are provided where smoking is permitted and must be used. Supervisors and managers are responsible for monitoring employees' smoking to ensure that it is done within designated areas, within break or meal periods, and in compliance with safety standards.

Restricted Areas:

- New Manufacturing Building (basement and all floors)
- Printing Building (basement and first floor)
- General Office Building:
  Maintenance and Sanitation (basement)
  Control Laboratory (third floor)
- Research/Administration Building
  Research Laboratories (fourth and fifth floors)
- Antibiotics Plant
- Animal House Building
- Warehouse
- All restrooms

In all other areas, the "no smoking" rule is in effect with the following exceptions:

- Employee Cafeteria (except for food preparation areas)
- Smoking Canteens
- Main Office Reception Room
- Conference Rooms
- Private Offices (outside "no smoking" areas referred to above)
- Outside of buildings

MISCELLANEOUS:

1. If there is a doubt as to whether smoking is permitted in a given area, assume that it is a "no smoking" area until you ask the Director of Human Resources and get a specific answer.

2. All managers and supervisors are responsible for reporting "no smoking" violations and enforcing the "no smoking" rule.

3. In locations where smoking is permitted, ashtrays and fireproof containers will be provided and must be used to discard ashes, etc.

   Watch for fire hazards. Report fires by activating the fire alarm box in your area or by telephoning the switchboard operator.

PERSONNEL POLICIES AND PROCEDURES

DISTRIBUTION:		SUBJECT: BULLETIN BOARDS	
EFFECTIVE DATE:	PAGE 1 OF 2	FILE UNDER SECTION	
REVISION DATE:	APPROVED BY:		

POLICY STATEMENT:

In order to supplement other existing forms of employee communications, bulletin boards are installed throughout the (Company Name) facility for the convenience of all employees. This policy is established in order to specify authorized bulletin boards, and to define proper access thereto.

AUTHORIZED LOCATIONS:

Authorized bulletin boards are installed at the following locations:

1. Employee cafeteria

2. Outside maintenance storeroom

3. Across from maintenance department—beside men's dressing room

4. Powder department—next to elevator

5. Printing department—snack area

6. Packaging department—between restrooms

7. Packaging department—next to clerk's office

8. Liquid department—beside elevator

9. Tablet department—beside men's room

10. Suppository department—inside door

11. Capsule department—inside door

12. First aid—around corner in hallway

13. Marketing department

14. Medical department—hall outside of entrance

15. Veterinary department

16. Accounting department—opposite elevator

17. Research—hall opposite conference room

18. Library—next to card file

DISTRIBUTION:		SUBJECT: BULLETIN BOARDS	
EFFECTIVE DATE:	PAGE 2 OF 2	FILE UNDER SECTION	
REVISION DATE:	APPROVED BY:		

19. Warehouse—between offices and warehouse

20. Blow molding department—inside office

21. APB—main entrance

Boards at locations other than the above are unauthorized and therefore prohibited.

CONTENTS OF BOARDS:

Authorized information appearing on company bulletin boards falls into three general categories:

1. Required notices in conformance with state and federal regulations (e.g., Equal Employment Opportunity, OSHA, Minimum Wages, etc.).

2. Communications setting forth information necessary for safety or proper departmental procedures (e.g., fire exit routes, safety and health regulations, operational procedures).

3. Notices concerning information of general interest to employees (e.g., job announcements, activities, awards, etc.).

All notices may be posted only on authorized bulletin boards, and must have prior approval of the respective department head in whose work area the board is located and the Human Resources Department.

PERSONNEL POLICIES AND PROCEDURES

DISTRIBUTION:		SUBJECT: COMPANY KEYS	
EFFECTIVE DATE:	PAGE 1 OF 1	FILE UNDER SECTION	
REVISION DATE:	APPROVED BY:		

POLICY STATEMENT:

The company utilizes a controlled key system for buildings and vehicles. Duplicate copies of all company vehicle keys are maintained in the home office. If employees require duplicates, they must advise their supervisor.

PROCEDURE:

If an employee requires a key for a building, a requisition form must be filled out stating what key is desired and the reasons why. This form should be approved by proper management personnel and forwarded to the President's Administrative Assistant.

If the request is approved, the key will be assigned and the employee will be required to sign the form for the designated key. The signed requisition form will be kept on file until the key is returned. At that point, the key form will be destroyed.

PERSONNEL POLICIES AND PROCEDURES

DISTRIBUTION:		SUBJECT: VISITATION	
EFFECTIVE DATE:	PAGE 1 OF 1	FILE UNDER SECTION	
REVISION DATE:	APPROVED BY:		

PURPOSE:

The purpose of this policy is to allow for limited visitation by immediate family members of associates while avoiding interruptions of work and ensuring efficiency and safety.

POLICY:

1. Immediate family members may visit active associates only during lunch and supper breaks in the cafeteria.

2. All visitors must enter through the main entrance of plants rather than through the associate entrance.

3. Visiting family members must sign in with the receptionist or guard and receive a visitor's badge. This badge must be displayed at all times.

4. The presence of unauthorized visitors on company property should be reported to a member of plant management. If any associate notices someone on company property whom he/she believes to be an unauthorized visitor, he/she should notify his/her supervisor/coordinator immediately.

5. No one except active associates assigned to work during the shift may enter production areas.

6. Guidelines for visitation must be posted at each location.

PERSONNEL POLICIES AND PROCEDURES

DISTRIBUTION:		SUBJECT: EXPRESSIONS OF SYMPATHY	
EFFECTIVE DATE:	PAGE 1 OF 1	FILE UNDER SECTION	
REVISION DATE:	APPROVED BY:		

OBJECTIVE:

This policy covers expressions of sympathy for the death of an employee or a member of the employee's immediate family.

DEFINITIONS:

Employee's immediate family is defined for the purpose of this policy as the employee's spouse, parents, children, and mother- or father-in-law.

POLICY:

It is the policy of (Company Name) that:

1. The manager of employee services or the managerial authority of the involved branch or administrative location for the field operations, after notification by the employee's supervisor, is responsible for providing an expression of sympathy on behalf of the company for the funeral of a deceased employee or a deceased member of the employee's immediate family.

   NOTE: The invoice being paid must indicate the name of the deceased and the relationship to the employee.

2. Expressions of sympathy other than those referred to above require the approval of the Director of Human Resources administration and support programs or, for field operations, the cognizant Director of Human Resources operations.

PERSONNEL POLICIES AND PROCEDURES

DISTRIBUTION:		SUBJECT: FLOWERS	
EFFECTIVE DATE:	PAGE 1 OF 1	FILE UNDER SECTION	
REVISION DATE:	APPROVED BY:		

PURPOSE:

The intent of this policy is to define the procedure of sending flowers to associates.

POLICY:

It is the policy of (Name of Company) to send flowers to an associate who is admitted to a hospital for an anticipated stay of three days or more or who gives birth, or for a death in the associate's immediate family as defined below. Flowers will also be sent to the appropriate family member upon the death of an associate.

An associate's immediate family is defined as full or step-members, as follows:

- Mother/father (and in-law)
- Wife/husband
- Daughter/son (and in-law)
- Sister/brother (and in-law)
- Half-brother/sister
- Grandchildren
- Grandparent
- Great-grandparent

PROCEDURE:

When a situation occurs that requires the sending of flowers as outlined in this policy, the associate's direct supervisor is responsible for obtaining all of the relevant information concerning the situation (name, location where the flowers should be sent, etc.) and then contacting the person responsible for ordering flowers at that location. It is the responsibility of the Human Resources Section to ensure that the flowers have been sent on behalf of the company.

PERSONNEL POLICIES AND PROCEDURES

DISTRIBUTION:		SUBJECT: CONTRACT PERSONNEL AND SERVICES	
EFFECTIVE DATE:	PAGE 1 OF 2	FILE UNDER SECTION	
REVISION DATE:	APPROVED BY:		

OBJECTIVE:

This policy is established to provide for obtaining contract personnel and services as required to meet specific (Company Name) objectives.

DEFINITIONS:

1. Contract personnel—applies to contract personnel involved in one of the following areas:
   a. Clerical/typing
   b. Cafeteria help
   c. Security guards

2. Service personnel—applies to service personnel visiting (Company Name) on an "on-call," occasional, or irregular basis to perform maintenance or preventive maintenance on their own equipment. The following service personnel are covered:
   a. Copy machine service
   b. Telephone installation and service

3. Outside service personnel—applies to service personnel working outside the building proper. The following outside service personnel are covered:
   a. Outside maintenance (includes snow removal personnel)
   b. Service of equipment—equipment that is sent out of the building

4. Outside consultants and other professional services

POLICY:

It is the policy of (Company Name) that:

1. All contract personnel and service persons are obtained after appropriate evaluation of the need and approval of the expenditure to be incurred.

2. Contract personnel are required to sign a confidential information and invention agreement—contract services. The agreement must be properly executed before such personnel may start to work on behalf of (Company Name).

3. Any contract for obtaining personnel or services shall include, as a provision therein, that all persons furnished or providing services under the contract are required to execute a confidential information and invention agreement—contract services.

DISTRIBUTION:		SUBJECT: CONTRACT PERSONNEL AND SERVICES	
EFFECTIVE DATE:	PAGE 2 OF 2	FILE UNDER SECTION	
REVISION DATE:	APPROVED BY:		

4. Each person classified as "service personnel" is required to sign a confidential information agreement (visitor's agreement).

5. Personnel classified as "outside service personnel" are not required to sign a confidential information and invention agreement or a confidential information agreement (visitor's agreement).

PERSONNEL POLICIES AND PROCEDURES

DISTRIBUTION:		SUBJECT: PRESS RELEASES	
EFFECTIVE DATE:	PAGE 1 OF 1	FILE UNDER SECTION	
REVISION DATE:	APPROVED BY:		

POLICY STATEMENT:

Employees are not authorized to release information regarding (Company Name) to representatives of print or broadcast media.

PROCEDURE:

Should an employee or manager be approached by the press for information about or related to (Company Name), all such requests for information must be forwarded to the President.

PERSONNEL POLICIES AND PROCEDURES

DISTRIBUTION:		SUBJECT: MEDIA RELATIONS	
EFFECTIVE DATE:	PAGE 1 OF 1	FILE UNDER SECTION	
REVISION DATE:	APPROVED BY:		

PURPOSE:

The purpose of this policy is to describe the company's position with respect to dealing with representatives of the media. For the purpose of this policy, the term "media" shall refer to representatives of newspapers, magazines, television, and radio.

POLICY:

1. Requests Initiated by Media Representative

    A. Any associate of the company who is contacted by a representative of the media with a request for an interview with a company spokesperson, a visit to a company facility, or permission to come on company property and photograph or videotape company facilities or operations should refer the individual making the request to the facility General Manager.

    B. All requests from a media representative must be submitted in advance in writing to the facility General Manager. Any request that fails to meet this requirement will be denied.

    C. Approval of a request from a media representative requires the concurrence of both the facility General Manager and the Senior Vice President.

    D. While on company property, media representatives must be accompanied by a Management Associate designated by the facility General Manager.

2. Company Press Releases

    A. Requests by the General Manager of any company location for a press release to be issued to the media should be directed through Corporate General Affairs. Proposed releases are to be submitted to the General Affairs Department for editing, approval, and release. If the local facility would prefer, the Corporate General Affairs Department will prepare the press release and distribute it to the media.

PERSONNEL POLICIES AND PROCEDURES

DISTRIBUTION:		SUBJECT: EMERGENCY PLANT CLOSING	
EFFECTIVE DATE:	PAGE 1 OF 1	FILE UNDER SECTION	
REVISION DATE:	APPROVED BY:		

PURPOSE:

The purpose of this policy is to define the company's intention concerning work for associates during severe weather conditions and/or other conditions beyond the control of the company that may affect plant operation.

POLICY:

It is the intention of the company to provide work for associates even under severe conditions.

Severe Weather Conditions:

1. A decision to close manufacturing functions will be based on the severity of weather conditions throughout the area. Decisions will be communicated to all associates at the earliest possible time.

2. A committee composed of at least one person from manufacturing, Human Resources, and one general manager will meet and decide if weather conditions are severe enough to cause associates to be late for work. In such a case, if an ''inclement weather day'' is declared, associates who are less than one hour late will not be considered tardy.

3. Associates who leave early or fail to report to work because of conditions beyond company control will not be paid, and it will affect their attendance record.

4. Closure decisions based upon other conditions beyond the control of the company—for example, ice storms, fires, floods, earthquakes, power failures, and road blocking—will be dealt with based on likelihood of the company to effectively operate the plant.

5. Announcements regarding the operation of company facilities will be made through designated radio and/or television stations. Identification of these stations will be posted at each facility, and associates are responsible for monitoring these sources of information.

PERSONNEL POLICIES AND PROCEDURES

DISTRIBUTION:		SUBJECT: ASSOCIATE RECOGNITION PROGRAM	
EFFECTIVE DATE:	PAGE 1 OF 2		FILE UNDER SECTION
REVISION DATE:	APPROVED BY:		

PURPOSE:

(Name of Company) recognizes outstanding performance with an Associate Recognition Program for each location.

POLICY:

One person per month from each major workgroup at each facility will be recognized as an outstanding associate.

Associates will be selected at the beginning of each calendar month based on performance for the preceding month.

To be recognized, an associate must have demonstrated above-average quality and productivity, have an overall good attendance record, including perfect attendance for the month, and be cooperative and helpful to other members of the workgroup.

Each month the facility general manager will invite the outstanding associates to a luncheon/dinner and discussion to be held in their honor. Also, a letter of appreciation will be sent by the general manager to the home of each associate selected and a reserved parking space will be provided in the associate parking lot.

PROCEDURE:

A. The outstanding associates will be announced at the first plant meeting of the calendar month. This recognition will be for outstanding performance during the preceding calendar month.

B. The general manager will decide on the appropriate grouping of associates for this recognition. Very small groups should be combined to standardize the size of the groups as much as possible.

C. The names of all the outstanding associates in each facility will be posted on the Personal Communication Center.

D. An associate recognized as an outstanding associate is not eligible for consideration again during the same calendar year.

E. A letter of recognition (see page 3) will be sent to each outstanding associate's home and a copy of the letter will be placed in the associate's personnel file. It is the general manager's responsibility for seeing that the letter is sent.

F. Human Resources specialists and/or coordinators/supervisors will be responsible for explaining to each outstanding associate the benefits to which he/she is entitled.

G. The Human Resources Section at each location is responsible for maintaining a record of those who were selected as outstanding associates.

(Date)

Dear (Name of Employee)

Congratulations on being recognized as an ''Outstanding Associate'' for the month of ———.

534

PERSONNEL POLICIES AND PROCEDURES

DISTRIBUTION:		SUBJECT: ASSOCIATE RECOGNITION PROGRAM	
EFFECTIVE DATE:	PAGE 2 OF 2	FILE UNDER SECTION	
REVISION DATE:	APPROVED BY:		

We feel that this is recognition that you richly deserve due to your excellent job performance, sense of responsibility, and spirit of cooperation. I want you and your family to know how important you are to our plant's success and how very much we value your contributions.

It is our philosophy that people are our most valued resource. We will always try to recognize outstanding associates, and we feel that it is appropriate that you are being recognized in this manner.

Thank you for being an outstanding team member!!!

Sincerely,

PERSONNEL POLICIES AND PROCEDURES

DISTRIBUTION:		SUBJECT: CONTROLLED COMMUNICATION CENTERS	
EFFECTIVE DATE:	PAGE 1 OF 4	FILE UNDER SECTION	
REVISION DATE:	APPROVED BY:		

PURPOSE:

The purpose of the policy is to describe the administrative procedures that will be utilized by the company in the area of the Controlled Communication Centers (bulletin boards). This policy will also detail the requirements/restrictions on the use of Controlled Communication Centers in our facilities. The types of Controlled Communication Centers will be:

A. Controlled Communication Centers

B. Personal Communication Centers

C. Classified Communication Centers

POLICY:

The company believes that an effective internal communications program is essential if we are to be a successful company. In order to establish credibility within our workforce and develop "associate spirit," we must implement an ongoing strategy of communicating openly and honestly with our associates.

Our plant Controlled Communication Centers system is one of the most important methods we use to disseminate information to associates. These Controlled Communication Centers are used as daily communication tools to provide our associates with important information about our company, its programs, and its people.

(Name of Company) will maintain large Controlled Communication Centers at the main entrances to plants and other areas designated by the Human Resources Section. Each Controlled Communication Center will be glass-enclosed and secured by a lock.

PROCEDURE:

A. The General Affairs Department will be responsible for maintaining lists of all postings that are required at every facility, copies of the required notices, and dates for notices and removal of those notices. This list includes, but is not limited to, those notices required by law, changes of company policy or practices on a corporate level, and items of special interest to associates. This list will be provided to the plant Human Resources Section.

B. The plant Human Resources Section will be responsible for maintaining the plant's Controlled Communication Centers.

C. Sections wishing to post a notice on the plant's Communication Centers should submit the material to the Human Resources Section.

D. The Human Resources manager or his/her designee will review all material submitted for posting to ensure that it meets the company guidelines.

PERSONNEL POLICIES AND PROCEDURES

DISTRIBUTION:		SUBJECT: CONTROLLED COMMUNICATION CENTERS	
EFFECTIVE DATE:	PAGE 2 OF 4	FILE UNDER SECTION	
REVISION DATE:	APPROVED BY:		

E. If the notice meets all posting guidelines, the Human Resources Section will prepare the material for posting. The notice will include a posting date and the date on which it should be removed from the board, and will be initiated by the Human Resources manager or his/her designee to indicate his/her approval.

F. The Human Resources Section will post the notice. It will also be the Human Resources Section's responsibility to remove the notice on the appropriate date.

No other associate/section may post/remove notices on/from the Controlled Communication Centers.

G. Controlled Communication Centers' notices will remain posted for a minimum period of three days, with the exception of job postings. However, the period for which a notice is posted must include at least one day in two consecutive workweeks.

CONTROLLED COMMUNICATION CENTERS:

The following guidelines will apply to the posting of material:

A. No materials/notices will be permitted on any plant walls, doors, etc., unless specifically approved by the local Human Resources representative or his/her designee. This does not apply to meeting room schedules, which are posted on the doors of meeting rooms. In addition, this guideline is not meant to restrict the company from posting job-related information.

B. No materials/notices will be permitted on the external glass of any Controlled Communication Center.

C. Materials/notices advertising sale of personal items or services will not be permitted on the plant Controlled Communication Center. These types of postings, however, may qualify for posting on the Classified Communication Centers.

D. Materials/notices advertising non-company-sponsored activities/meetings will not be permitted without the approval of the Human Resources Section.

E. Materials/notices advertising services or items for sale involving individuals not employed by the company will not be permitted, nor will for-profit items advertised by company associates.

HISTORICAL FILE:

The Human Resources Section at each location will maintain a chronological file for one year of all material notices that are posted on the plant's Controlled Communication Center.

DISTRIBUTION:		SUBJECT: CONTROLLED COMMUNICATION CENTERS	
EFFECTIVE DATE:	PAGE 3 OF 4	FILE UNDER SECTION	
REVISION DATE:	APPROVED BY:		

PERSONAL COMMUNICATION CENTERS:

In addition to the plant Controlled Communication Centers each location will provide a Personal Controlled Communication Center. The purpose of this board is to provide a method of communicating information of interest to the associates at each facility.

A. GUIDELINES.

The following types of information may be posted on the Personal Communication Centers:

1. Items of local interest concerning associates or their immediate family
2. Newspaper articles containing birth and wedding announcements of associates
3. Thank-you notes from associates
4. Notices that recognize associates for accomplishments or achievements
5. Notices of company activities

B. PROCEDURE:

1. All materials/notices that are posted on the Personal Communication Centers must be approved in advance by the local Human Resources representative or his/her designee.
2. The Human Resources Section will post/remove all notices on/from the Personal Communication Centers.
3. Notices for the Personal Communication Centers will normally be posted for two weeks.

CLASSIFIED COMMUNICATION CENTERS:

In order to provide associates with a method of buying/selling/trading their own personal items, the company will provide and maintain Classified Communication Centers in each location. These boards will be glass-enclosed and will be controlled or maintained by the plant Human Resources Section.

Company associates may submit items for posting to the Human Resources Section in accordance with the following procedures/rules:

A. Any associate wishing to have an item posted on the Classified Communication Center should present a written description of the item(s) that he/she wishes to buy/sell/trade to the Human Resources Section. The information provided should include an outside telephone number where interested parties can contact the associate. The description submitted should also be signed and dated by the associate. A photo of the item for sale may also be submitted.

B. All notices received for posting will be edited by the Human Resources Section and will be typed or written on a 3″ × 5″ index card. The date the notice was posted and the date on which it should be removed from the board will also be included.

C. The local Human Resources representative must review all Classified Communication Center advertisements. He/she will initial the posting to indicate approval for posting.

PERSONNEL POLICIES AND PROCEDURES

DISTRIBUTION:		SUBJECT: CONTROLLED COMMUNICATION CENTERS	
EFFECTIVE DATE:	PAGE 4 OF 4		FILE UNDER SECTION
REVISION DATE:	APPROVED BY:		

D. Requests for Classified Communication Centers postings will be subject to available space on the board.

- Classified Communication Centers advertisements will remain posted on the board for a period not to exceed two weeks.
- Once an item posted on a Classified Communication Center has been sold, the associate who had the item for sale should contact a Human Resources representative so that the advertisement can be removed.
- All transactions resulting from Classified Communication Centers advertisements should take place during the associate's nonwork time.
- No materials/notices will be permitted on the external glass of Classified Communication Centers.
- Materials/notices advertising non-company-sponsored activities/meetings will not be permitted.
- Materials/notices advertising services or items for sale involving individuals not employed by (Name of Company) will not be permitted, nor will for-profit items advertised by company associates.

PERSONNEL POLICIES AND PROCEDURES

DISTRIBUTION:		SUBJECT: BUSINESS ETHICS	
EFFECTIVE DATE:	PAGE 1 OF 1	FILE UNDER SECTION	
REVISION DATE:	APPROVED BY:		

POLICY STATEMENT:

(Company Name) will maintain high standards of business ethics. In today's business climate, anything less would be dangerous for the company and its employees. Even minor or ambiguous instances of misconduct can today prove ruinous for a company that depends for its success on public confidence and customer trust. (Company Name) has an enormous stake in serving governments—national and local—around the world and in being accepted as a close business partner by the world's most eminent corporations. To protect this vital investment, every company unit and employee must maintain very exacting standards of ethical conduct.

Management is expected to make the company's ethical policy an integral part of doing business. It is the job of all company managers to see that every employee understands and observes our ethical policy, both in letter and in spirit, at all times. Please give this objective your highest management priority.

The company's ethics policy will be governed by a corporate Ethics Committee, which will report regularly to the Audit Committee of the Board of Directors. Front-line responsibility rests with general management throughout the company.

PERSONNEL POLICIES AND PROCEDURES

DISTRIBUTION:		SUBJECT: ETHICAL CONDUCT IN BUSINESS	
EFFECTIVE DATE:	PAGE 1 OF 3	FILE UNDER SECTION	
REVISION DATE:	APPROVED BY:		

POLICY:

The commitment of (Company Name) to conduct its business lawfully and ethically is fundamental to our very existence as a corporation. It is critically important that all employees meet the highest standards of legal and ethical conduct. Nothing less will do.

Each of us has an obligation to behave at all times with honesty and propriety—because such behavior is morally and legally right, and because (Company Name) depends for its business success on its reputation for integrity and on the trust and confidence of everyone with whom we deal.

At (Company Name), the commitment to ethical behavior is not a matter of vague principles and generalized rhetoric. We have a strict code of conduct. The rules are set forth within these procedures. You should be certain that you read, understand, and adhere to these rules and that you keep this policy for future reference.

PROCEDURE:

A. Comply with all laws and regulations.

As a (Company Name) employee, you must scrupulously comply with all laws and government regulations applicable in your nation, state, and other governing jurisdiction. For any interpretation or clarification of legal or regulatory requirements, consult the corporate legal department.

B. Deal honestly with customers, suppliers, and consultants.

1. Contract Negotiations—In negotiating contracts, be accurate and complete in all representations. The submission to a United States government customer of a proposal quotation or other document or statement that is false, incomplete, or misleading can result in civil and criminal liability for the corporation and the involved employees who condone such a practice. In negotiating contracts with the federal government, we have an affirmative duty to disclose current, accurate, and complete cost in pricing data where such data is required under appropriate regulation.

2. Product Quality—(Company Name) is committed to developing, manufacturing, and delivering quality products that meet all contractual obligations and quality standards.

3. Competitive Analysis—In conducting market analysis, do not accept or use information proprietary to our competitors. Supervisors must ensure that competitor proprietary information is not obtained or used in any fashion.

4. Charging of Cost/Timecard Reporting—Employees who file timecards must be particularly careful to do so in a complete, accurate, and timely manner. Government-sector employees must be particularly careful to ensure that hours worked and cost are applied to the account for which they were in fact incurred.

5. Hiring of Federal Employees—Complex rules govern the recruitment and employment of U.S. government employees in private industry. Prior clearance to discuss possible employment with, make offers to, or hire any current or former government employee must be obtained from the human resources department.

C. Use company resources properly.

1. Making Political Contributions—Do not contribute or donate company funds, products, services, or other resources for any political cause, party, or candidate without the advance written approval of the legal department.

2. Providing Business Courtesies to Customers or Suppliers—Our success in the marketplace results from providing

PERSONNEL POLICIES AND PROCEDURES

DISTRIBUTION:		SUBJECT: ETHICAL CONDUCT IN BUSINESS	
EFFECTIVE DATE:	PAGE 2 OF 3	FILE UNDER SECTION	
REVISION DATE:	APPROVED BY:		

superior products and services at competitive prices. Our company does not seek to gain improper advantage by offering business courtesies such as entertainment, meals, transportation, or lodging. Employees should never offer any type of business courtesy to a customer for the purpose of obtaining favorable treatment or advantage. Do not provide any customer or supplier with gifts or promotional items of more than a nominal value. As a gift, as noted below, you may pay for reasonable refreshments and/or entertainment expenses for customers and suppliers that are incurred only occasionally, are not requested or solicited by the recipient, and are not intended to or likely to affect the recipient's business decision with respect to the company.

3. U.S. Government Customers—You may not provide or pay for any meal, refreshment, entertainment, travel, or lodging expenses without the advance written approval of the legal department. Company employees doing business with all government bodies are expected to know and respect all such restrictions.

4. Dealing with Foreign Officials—Do not promise, offer, or make any payments in money, products, or services to any foreign official in exchange for or in order to induce favorable business treatment or to affect any government decision. Minor payments to clerical personnel to expedite performance of their duties in foreign companies can be made only with the express approval of the legal department.

5. Accurate Books and Accounts—All company payments and other transactions must be properly authorized by management and be accurately and completely recorded on the corporation's books and records in accordance with generally accepted accounting principles and established corporate accounting policies. Do not make false, incomplete, or misleading entries. No undisclosed or unrecorded corporate funds shall be established for any purpose, nor should any company funds be placed in any personal or noncorporate account. All corporate assets must be properly protected and asset records regularly compared with actual assets, with proper action taken to reconcile any differences.

D. Do not abuse your position of trust at the company.

The company expects you to devote your full working time and efforts to the corporation's interests and to avoid any activity that may distract from or conflict with the corporation's interests. In particular:

1. Conflict of Interest—You may not have any employment, consulting, or other business relationship with a competitor, customer, or supplier of our company, or invest in any competitor, customer, or supplier of the company (except for moderate holdings of publicly traded securities) unless you have the advance written permission of the legal department. Outside employment may also constitute a conflict of interest if it places an employee in the position of appearing to represent the company, involves providing goods or services substantially similar to those of the company, or lessens the efficiency, alertness, or productivity normally expected of employees on their jobs. All outside employment must be approved in advance by the employee's immediate supervisor and the Human Resources Department.

2. Insider Trading—Do not trade in the securities of the company or any other company, or buy or sell any property or assets, on the basis of nonpublic information you have acquired through your employment at (Company Name), whether such information comes from the company or from another company with which we have a confidential relationship.

3. Acceptance of Business Courtesies—Never accept anything of value from someone doing business with the company when the gratuity is offered or appears to be offered in exchange for any type of favorable treatment or advantage. To avoid even the appearance of impropriety, we do not accept any gifts or promotional items of more than a nominal value. You may accept meals, drinks, or entertainment only if such courtesies are unsolicited, infrequently provided, and reasonable in amount. Such courtesies must also be directly connected with business discussions. Do not accept reimbursement for lodging or travel expenses, or free lodging or travel without the written approval of the legal department.

DISTRIBUTION:		SUBJECT: ETHICAL CONDUCT IN BUSINESS	
EFFECTIVE DATE:	PAGE 3 OF 3	FILE UNDER SECTION
REVISION DATE:	APPROVED BY:	

4. Company Restricted Information—Do not disclose to any outside party, except as specifically authorized by management, pursuant to established policies and procedures, any nonpublic business, financial, personnel, or technological information, plans, or data that you have acquired during your employment at (Company Name). Upon termination of employment, you may not copy, take, or retain any documents containing restricted information. This prohibition against disclosing company-restricted information extends indefinitely beyond your period of employment. Your agreement to protect the confidentiality of such information in perpetuity is considered an important condition of your employment.

5. Government Classified Proprietary Information—We have special obligations to comply with laws and regulations that protect classified information. Employees with valid security clearances who have access to classified information must ensure that such information is handled in accordance with pertinent federal procedures. These restrictions apply to any type of information, whether in written or electronic form.

E. Violations and discipline.

Strict adherence to this policy is vital. Supervisors are responsible for ensuring that employees adhere to provisions of the policy. For clarification or guidance on any point, please consult your supervisor, your human resources representative, or the legal department.

Employees are expected to report any suspected violation of the policy or other irregularities to their supervisor or the legal department. No adverse action or retribution of any kind will be taken against any employee because he or she reports a suspected violation of this policy or other irregularities. Such reports shall be treated confidentially to the maximum extent consistent with fair and rigorous enforcement of this policy.

Violations of the policy may result in disciplines ranging from warnings and reprimand to discharge or even the filing of a criminal or civil complaint. Employees will be informed of the charges against them and will be given the opportunity to explain their actions before any disciplinary action is imposed.

PERSONNEL POLICIES AND PROCEDURES

DISTRIBUTION:		SUBJECT: BUSINESS GIFTS OR GRATUITIES	
EFFECTIVE DATE:	PAGE 1 OF 1	FILE UNDER SECTION	
REVISION DATE:	APPROVED BY:		

POLICY STATEMENT:

(Company Name) believes that the practice of accepting gifts or gratuities is not only unnecessary and undesirable but also contrary to the best interest of employees and the division alike. The integrity of any business relationship can always be questioned, regardless of the degree of personal relationship, if gifts or gratuities are made, received, or exchanged by parties to the relationship.

GENERAL:

Employees of (Company Name) may not accept gifts or gratuities, except for advertising ''gimmicks'' of nominal value, that result from a business contact with any supplier or with any person or company. Any gift or gratuity that is received, whether at the office, a plant location, or an employee's home, must be returned to the sender, collect. Any violation of this policy will subject the employee concerned to disciplinary action. This policy applies equally to all employees—from top management to the newest temporary employee—and refers to product samples or any other items, regardless of how insignificant.

PERSONNEL POLICIES AND PROCEDURES

DISTRIBUTION:		SUBJECT: CONFLICTS OF INTEREST	
EFFECTIVE DATE:	PAGE 1 OF 1	FILE UNDER SECTION	
REVISION DATE:	APPROVED BY:		

Exactly what constitutes a conflict of interest or an unethical business practice is both a moral and a legal question. The company recognizes and respects the individual employee's right to engage in activities outside of his or her employment that are private in nature and do not in any way conflict with or reflect poorly on the company. Management reserves the right, however, to determine when an employee's activities represent a conflict with the company's interests and to take whatever action is necessary to resolve the situation—including terminating the employee.

It is not possible in a general policy statement of this sort to define all the various circumstances and relationships that would be considered "unethical." The list below suggests some of the types of activity that would reflect in a negative way on the employee's personal integrity or that would limit his or her ability to discharge job duties and responsibilities in an ethical manner:

1. Simultaneous employment by another firm, particularly if the other firm is a competitor or supplier.

2. Carrying on company business with a firm in which the employee, or a close relative of the employee, has a substantial ownership or interest.

3. Holding a substantial interest in, or participating in the management of, a firm to which the company makes sales or from which it makes purchases.

4. Borrowing money from customers or firms, other than recognized loan institutions, from which our company buys services, materials, equipment, or supplies.

5. Accepting substantial gifts or excessive entertainment from an outside organization or agency.

6. Speculating or dealing in materials, equipment, supplies, services, or property purchased by the company.

7. Participating in civic or professional organization activities in a manner whereby confidential company information is divulged.

8. Misusing privileged information or revealing confidential data to outsiders.

9. Using one's position in the company or knowledge of its affairs for outside personal gain.

10. Engaging in practices or procedures that violate antitrust laws or other laws regulating the conduct of company business.

REMEMBER: Employment by the company carries with it a responsibility to be constantly aware of the importance of ethical conduct. Employees must refrain from taking part in, or exerting influence in, any transaction in which their own interests may conflict with the best interests of the corporation.

PERSONNEL POLICIES AND PROCEDURES

DISTRIBUTION:		SUBJECT: ETHICAL CONDUCT	
EFFECTIVE DATE:	PAGE 1 OF 1	FILE UNDER SECTION	
REVISION DATE:	APPROVED BY:		

POLICY STATEMENT:

Employment by (Company Name) carries with it a responsibility to be constantly aware of the importance of ethical conduct. Employees must never accept gifts, gratuities, or rewards from our customers for any service that they perform in their job. Employees must refrain from taking part in, or exerting influence in, any transaction in which their own interests may conflict with the best interest of the company. Employees are not permitted to approach or negotiate with customers we serve under any circumstance that would in any way result in personal gain, exclusive of the company's compensation plan, for the employee.

PROCEDURE:

Behavior reflecting conflict of interest will result in immediate suspension leading to dismissal.

PERSONNEL POLICIES AND PROCEDURES

DISTRIBUTION:		SUBJECT: PERSONAL COMPUTERS AND SOFTWARE	
EFFECTIVE DATE:	PAGE 1 OF 2	FILE UNDER SECTION	
REVISION DATE:	APPROVED BY:		

POLICY:

It is the policy of (Company Name) to provide employees with personal computers (PCs), or access to them, when a need for such equipment has been established and control can be assured. The company also will provide certain third-party software for such computers as the need arises. Such software is purchased for company use only and is not to be duplicated unless provided for in the license agreement.

PROCEDURE:

A. When a PC is assigned to a department, the supervisor is responsible for delegating responsibility for its use and control to an employee or group of employees who will be using it. Each employee authorized to use a PC shall be given specific responsibility for maintaining and preserving the information he/she uses.

B. Employees may use a PC and its software only after they have been authorized by the responsible supervisor, and then only after they have received instruction on the rules and procedures for its use. Employees may not use programs, files, or other data from outside their assigned area of responsibility without the prior approval of the supervisor. Any unauthorized use of a PC or software will subject the employee to disciplinary action.

C. A written log of user time shall be maintained for each PC, including files created, changes made, backup files, and the project for which the PC/software was used. Authorized PC users are responsible for the use, storage, and security of their files and the maintenance of backup or duplicate disks of essential files.

D. Portable units (laptops, etc.) may be assigned to specific employees for their use on business calls, on trips, and at home. Advance approval for assignment and use must be obtained from the department head. Assignment will be based upon departmental priorities and availability.

E. Employees assigned PCs are responsible for the security of their equipment and software. This includes safeguarding it from loss or damage and ensuring that it is used only by authorized personnel. You may not copy, disclose, or transfer any software provided by the company without written permission.

F. Special training in PC applications and operations will be provided authorized users by the company. Each supervisor is responsible for arranging such training and will determine if it is best handled internally or externally.

G. The company maintains official files on a central mainframe computer operated by the Data Processing Department. These files are the sole source of official company information, and therefore their accuracy and integrity must be safeguarded. Authorized PC users who require access to these files must receive prior approval from the department head and must receive special access codes from the Data Processing Manager. Such codes will limit access to the specific files needed and are subject to strict confidentiality. No changes are to be made to the company's official files without written permission from the Data Processing Manager. Similarly, no unauthorized software may be downloaded or installed on any computer without the written permission of the Data Processing Manager. You may not intentionally write, produce, generate, copy, propagate, or attempt to introduce any computer code designed to

DISTRIBUTION:		SUBJECT: PERSONAL COMPUTERS AND SOFTWARE	
EFFECTIVE DATE:	PAGE 2 OF 2	FILE UNDER SECTION	
REVISION DATE:	APPROVED BY:		

self-replicate, damage, or otherwise hinder the performance of any computer's memory, file system, or software. Such software is often called a virus, worm, Trojan Horse, or some similar name.

H. All software purchased by the company is to be properly maintained as per the license agreement from each vendor. No company employee is authorized to make additional copies of the software for any use whatsoever in violation of the individual license agreements. Employees who violate this procedure are subject to disciplinary action as determined by the Human Resources Manager.

I. Computers are for company use only. No employee is to use company time and resources for personal gain. Any personal use of the computer requires written permission from the Data Processing Manager. Likewise computers are not to be used for playing games on company time.

ELECTRONIC MAIL POLICY:

Every (Company Name) employee is responsible for seeing that the electronic mail (E-mail) system is used properly and in accordance with this policy. Any questions about this policy should be directed either to the Human Resources Department or to the company's E-Mail Administrator.

1. The E-mail system of (Company Name) is part of the business equipment and technology platform and should be used for company purposes only. Personal business should not be conducted by means of the E-mail system.

2. Employees should disclose information or messages from the E-mail system only to authorized employees.

3. Employees do not have a personal privacy right in any matter created, received or sent from the (Company Name) E-mail system. Employees should not enter personal matter into the E-mail system. The company, in its discretion, reserves the right to monitor and to access any matter created, received or sent from the E-mail system.

4. No messages or information should be entered into the (Company Name) E-mail system without a good business reason for doing so. Copies of E-mail messages should be sent only for good business reasons.

5. Even if you have a password for the E-mail system, it is impossible to assure the confidentiality of any message created, received or sent from the (Company Name) E-mail system. Any password you use must be known to the company as your account may need to be accessed in your absence by the company.

6. The provisions of (Company Name)'s no solicitation–no distribution policy (see Employee Handbook) apply fully to the E-mail system.

7. No E-mail messages should be created or sent which may constitute intimidating, hostile or offensive material on the basis of sex, race, color, religion, national origin, sexual orientation, or disability. (Company Name)'s policy against sexual or other harassment applies fully to the E-mail system, and any violation of that policy is grounds for discipline up to and including discharge.

8. (Company Name) expressly reserves the right to access, retrieve, read, and delete any communication that is created, received or sent in the E-mail system to assure compliance with this and other Company policy.

9. Any employee who becomes aware of misuse of the E-mail system should promptly contact either the Human Resources Department or the E-Mail system administrator.

PERSONNEL POLICIES AND PROCEDURES

DISTRIBUTION:		SUBJECT: TELEPHONE USAGE	
EFFECTIVE DATE:	PAGE 1 OF 1	FILE UNDER SECTION	
REVISION DATE:	APPROVED BY:		

POLICY STATEMENT:

The telephone is an important public relations tool for the company. Our only contact with many of our customers and suppliers is through the telephone. A "busy signal" causes frustration and fails to promote our image of prompt and efficient service. Telephones should always be attempted to be answered on or before the third ring in a prompt and courteous manner, and the use of company telephones for personal business is not permitted.

PROCEDURE:

Personal calls to employees must be limited to those of an emergency nature. Employees will be notified immediately of any emergency calls for them. Managers should monitor the telephone usage to ensure employees are complying with this policy.

Any problems with the telephone system should be directed either to the switchboard operator or to supervisory or management personnel.

PERSONNEL POLICIES AND PROCEDURES

DISTRIBUTION:		SUBJECT: PHONE AND E-MAIL	
EFFECTIVE DATE:	PAGE 1 OF 1	FILE UNDER SECTION	
REVISION DATE:	APPROVED BY:		

COMMENTARY:

E-mail and phone mail provide many advantages to the Corporation, including:

1. reducing telephone tag

2. speeding up decision making

3. shortening the communication cycle

These are factors that improve productivity and provide the ability to communicate with other employees at virtually any time and at any location.

The disadvantage is that employees assume that their messages are private, but privacy is not guaranteed. E-mail and phone mail files are like other company files and can be used in the discovery process linked to litigation. Additionally, because E-mail and phone mail allow users to respond immediately, many do so without a second thought. The potential risk is increased due to the ability to respond so quickly that a person may later regret what was written or said.

PURPOSE:

To ensure that the use of electronic and telephonic communication systems and business equipment is consistent with (Name of Company)'s business interests.

SCOPE:

All electronic and telephonic communication systems and all communication and information transmitted by, received from, or stored in these systems are the property of (Name of Company), and these systems are to be used for job-related communications only.

POLICY:

E-mail or phone mail shall not be used to transmit vulgar, profane, insulting, or offensive messages such as racial or sexual slurs. Prohibited uses of E-mail and phone mail include, but are not limited to, soliciting outside business ventures, advertising for personal enterprises, or soliciting for non-company-related purposes. This policy does not prohibit personal messages of a social nature that do not contain otherwise prohibited content.

Employees are not permitted to use passwords, access a file, or retrieve any stored communication unless authorized to do so, or unless they have received prior clearance from an authorized company representative. All passwords are the property of the company.

Authorized representatives of (Name of Company), from time to time, may monitor the use of such equipment. Such monitoring may include accessing recorded messages and printing and reading data files by company employees who are authorized to do so by management.

Employees who violate this policy are subject to disciplinary action up to and including termination.

PERSONNEL POLICIES AND PROCEDURES

DISTRIBUTION:		SUBJECT: ELECTRONIC MAIL	
EFFECTIVE DATE:	PAGE 1 OF 1	FILE UNDER SECTION	
REVISION DATE:	APPROVED BY:		

PURPOSE:

To ensure that the electronic mail (E-mail) system is used properly and in accordance with company policy.

POLICY:

1. The E-mail system of (Name of Company) is part of the business equipment and technology platform and should be used for company purposes only. Personal business should not be conducted by means of the E-mail system.

2. Employees should disclose information or messages from the E-mail system only to authorized employees.

3. Employees do not have a personal privacy right in any matter created, received, or sent from the company E-mail system. Employees should not enter personal matter into the E-mail system. The company, in its discretion, reserves the right to monitor and to access any matter created, received, or sent from the E-mail system.

4. No messages or information should be entered into the company E-mail system without a good reason for doing so. Copies of E-mail messages should be sent only for good business reasons.

5. Even if a password is used for the E-mail system, it is impossible to ensure the confidentiality of any message created, received, or sent from the company E-mail system. Any password must be known by the company.

6. The provisions of the company's No Solicitation/No Distribution policy apply fully to the E-mail system.

7. No E-mail messages should be created or sent that may constitute intimidating, hostile, or offensive material on the basis of sex, race, color, religion, national origin, sexual orientation, or disability. The company's policy against sexual or other harassment applies fully to the E-mail system, and any violation of that policy is grounds for discipline up to and including discharge.

8. The company expressly reserves the right to access, retrieve, read, and delete any communication that is created, received, or sent in the E-mail system to ensure compliance with this and other company policy.

9. Any employee who becomes aware of misuse of the E-mail system should promptly contact either the Human Resources Department or the E-mail system administrator.

PERSONNEL POLICIES AND PROCEDURES

DISTRIBUTION:		SUBJECT: CORE WORK SCHEDULE	
EFFECTIVE DATE:	PAGE 1 OF 2	FILE UNDER SECTION	
REVISION DATE:	APPROVED BY:		

Core schedules of six hours plus lunch will be established at all locations. To meet a family care need, an employee may elect a nonstandard schedule that includes the core hours. This schedule then becomes the employee's regular work schedule, equal to the length of the former schedule.

There may be circumstances, such as production lines, where the nature of the work will not permit a flexible schedule. In such cases, managers will accommodate desired schedules where practical.

INTENT:

This policy provides an option for employees when they require nonstandard start/stop times to accommodate their family care needs. Typically the need is for an extended period of time, but, in unusual circumstances, schedules can be changed for a few weeks. Managers are expected to make every effort to accommodate employees.

Actual core schedules for various groups of employees will be established by each business. In all cases, the core hours will be six work hours plus a lunch period, and employees will be able to work their other two hours (in whole or in part) either before or after the core schedule.

APPLICABLE SITUATIONS INCLUDE BUT ARE NOT LIMITED TO:

- Employee has child care arrangements that conflict with standard company hours, such as center opening or closing time or caregiver availability.
- Employee has a parent or spouse who requires ongoing, routine care and supervision.
- Employee has school-age children who require before- or after-school care.
- Employee has an ill or injured family member.
- Employee has a newborn or newly adopted child.
- Employee has a temporary family care need caused by school vacations or child custody visitations.

QUESTIONS AND ANSWERS:

- *How often can I change my schedule?*

There is no arbitrary limit to how often schedules can be changed. It is expected that employees will not frequently change schedules because that could be disruptive to the business. A new schedule is expected to be the employee's regular schedule.

- *Can I have a flexible work schedule so that I can get to my aerobics class?*

No. Not under this policy. This policy specifies that the only reasons for adjusted work schedules are family care needs. An aerobics class, though recognized as promoting better health for the employee, is not considered a family care need.

- *I already have a flexible work schedule so that I can attend class, but I don't work the core hours you talked about. What happens to my arrangements?*

This policy specifically covers only employees with family care needs. A manager continues to have the authority to handle special employee situations on an exception basis. Therefore, your manager can continue to approve your special schedule.

- *Does this apply to all shifts?*

This applies to all shifts where management has determined that the nature of the work permits adjustments to the start and end of the shift.

DISTRIBUTION:		SUBJECT: CORE WORK SCHEDULE	
EFFECTIVE DATE:	PAGE 2 OF 2	FILE UNDER SECTION	
REVISION DATE:	APPROVED BY:		

◆ *What can I do if my manager says I cannot have a flexible work schedule because he/she doesn't believe in them?*

Managers are expected to accommodate employees' needs for an alternative schedule except where the nature of the work prohibits it. Employees have three options if they feel their managers are making arbitrary or unreasonable decisions:

—Appeal to the manager's manager
—Seek assistance from the Work and Family Coordinator
—Seek assistance from their HR representative

PERSONNEL POLICIES AND PROCEDURES

DISTRIBUTION:		SUBJECT: TEMPORARY PART-TIME SCHEDULE
EFFECTIVE DATE:	PAGE 1 OF 3	FILE UNDER SECTION
REVISION DATE:	APPROVED BY:	

To accommodate family care needs, a temporary, part-time work schedule may be established to assist an employee in making the transition back to full-time work.

Such arrangements may be for 20 or more hours per week and may last up to one year. There may be circumstances, such as extensive customer contact, where the nature of the work will not permit a part-time schedule. Managers will accommodate part-time schedules where practical.

INTENT:

This policy provides an option for employees when their needs are best met by working reduced schedules and devoting increased time to their families. A part-time schedule is intended to provide a transition period of up to one year, after which the employee returns to full-time. Employees must work at least twenty (20) hours per week, but may elect to work up to thirty-two (32) hours. Managers are expected to make every effort to accommodate an employee's request for a part-time schedule, including changing the employee's work assignment if practical.

Benefits of part-time employees will be continued, with some being proportional to the hours the employees elect to work. It is also expected that part-time employees will be considered "1/2 heads" for purposes of head count measurements. Final details are being worked out and will be communicated prior to implementation. Temporary part-time employees should be considered along with full-time employees for all appropriate personnel actions, including upgrades, promotions, salary increases, and layoffs.

Family is primarily intended to be parent, spouse, and child, but other significant relatives who require the employee to provide care may be reasons for managers to approve part-time schedules.

APPLICABLE SITUATIONS INCLUDE BUT ARE NOT LIMITED TO:

- Employee has an ill or injured family member.
- Employee has adopted a child.
- Employee wishes to provide routine care for an infant.
- Employee has a terminally ill family member.
- Employee has to provide temporary, routine care for an aging parent or spouse.

QUESTIONS AND ANSWERS:

- *Can I work three (3) days per week?*

Temporary part-time schedules can be structured any way that meets the needs of both the business and the employee as long as the schedule is for twenty (20) hours or more per week. Three eight- (8-) hour days per week would be acceptable. Other examples could be four (4) hours per day or a combination of half and full days.

- *I am nursing my baby and would like to work from 10:00 A.M. to 2:00 P.M. every day until he's about a year old. Is that a legitimate reason?*

Yes. Nursing an infant is a family care reason, and a 10:00 A.M. to 2:00 P.M. schedule meets that twenty- (20-) hour-per-week minimum.

- *Can part-time arrangements ever be for more than one year?*

Managers have the authority to approve part-time arrangements for longer than one year on a rare exception basis.

PERSONNEL POLICIES AND PROCEDURES

DISTRIBUTION:		SUBJECT: TEMPORARY PART-TIME SCHEDULE	
EFFECTIVE DATE:	PAGE 2 OF 3	FILE UNDER SECTION	
REVISION DATE:	APPROVED BY:		

- *I already work part-time so that I can get my Master's Degree. Does this new policy affect me?*
No. This temporary part-time policy covers only temporary part-time schedules for family care needs. Any special arrangements, made for other reasons, are handled as individual exceptions between employees and their managers.

- *My grandmother will be living with me for three (3) months until she can get a space in a residential home. She needs someone with her, and my wife can cover three days a week. I'd like to work a part-time schedule and work those three days and be home the other two days. Does this qualify?*
Yes. In situations where a manager can accommodate a part-time schedule, a grandmother living in an employee's home who requires care would be considered a legitimate reason to have a temporary part-time schedule.

MANAGERIAL GUIDELINES:

While details regarding the temporary part-time schedules for family care reasons have yet to be clarified, the following is a brief look at how an employee's pay may be affected.

1. Personal Illness

   No change in eligibility. Each half-day taken is counted as a half-day. If the employee is scheduled to work more than four hours but less than eight and only works up to four hours, the remainder would be paid and charged as a half-day personal illness.

2. Personal Business

   No change in eligibility. Same as personal illness, but managers may want to suggest personal business be done during non-scheduled work time whenever possible.

3. Jury Duty Pay and Death in Family

   Paid if absence occurs on day scheduled to work for number of hours scheduled to work.

4. Overtime

   Time worked up to eight (8) hours per day paid at straight-time rate. Any time worked beyond eight (8) hours paid in accordance with normal overtime policy. All Saturday and Sunday hours will be eligible for overtime premium in accordance with normal overtime policy, unless employee's regular schedule includes Saturday and/or Sunday.

5. Vacation Pay

   No change in eligibility (based on years of service). Paid at rate on December 31 of previous year or current rate, whichever is higher. Day of vacation is counted as day taken, whether or not work schedule is eight (8) hours.

   Additional guidelines on how vacation pay and holiday pay are specifically affected will be forthcoming.

BENEFITS SUMMARY:

1. SAME AS FULL-TIME—No change in coverage or contributions.

PERSONNEL POLICIES AND PROCEDURES

DISTRIBUTION:		SUBJECT: TEMPORARY PART-TIME SCHEDULE	
EFFECTIVE DATE:	PAGE 3 OF 3	FILE UNDER SECTION	
REVISION DATE:	APPROVED BY:		

- Comprehensive Medical Benefits (No change in coverage, but contributions for the medical plan will be reduced according to the part-time salary.)
- Dependent Life Insurance
- Dental Assistance Plan
- Personal Accident Insurance
- Dependent Personal Accident Insurance
- Flexible Spending—Health Care and Dependent Care
- Emergency Aid Plan
- Product Purchase Plan
- Life Insurance (a)
- Additional Life Insurance (a)
- Savings Bond Program
- Personal Excess Liability Plan
  (a) Benefits based on highest annual pay in last five years

2. SAME AS FULL-TIME, Except Contribution and Company Share Based on Earnings

- Savings and Security Plan
- Pension Plan

3. LIMITED ELIGIBILITY

- Tuition Refund
- Individual Development Program

(Employees will be eligible IF the course(s) would otherwise have been approved for payment AND if the course is NOT offered during the employee's regularly scheduled full-time shift. For example, a first-shift employee who is now temporarily working only until 1:00 cannot take an afternoon class and be reimbursed, but could take an evening course and be reimbursed.)

4. CHANGE IN BENEFITS POSSIBLE, Based on Last Week's Paid Salary

- Exempt Layoff Benefit
- Income Extension Aid
- Long-Term and Short-Term Disability

PERSONNEL POLICIES AND PROCEDURES

DISTRIBUTION:		SUBJECT: FLEXIBLE TIME OFF FROM WORK	
EFFECTIVE DATE:	PAGE 1 OF 2	FILE UNDER SECTION	
REVISION DATE:	APPROVED BY:		

PURPOSE:

Our organization recognizes that employees may need to take a break from their daily routine in order to renew and refresh themselves, take care of pressing personal business needs, or take sick leave for their own health-related reasons or those of a family member. Because we understand that reasons for time off may fluctuate from year to year, our organization provides approved flexible time off from work as a benefit to employees.

SCOPE:

This policy applies to all regular employees. It includes procedures for determining the circumstances under which employees may take flexible time off, and guidelines for eligibility requirements, accrual schedules, obtaining approvals, and policy limitations.

POLICY AND PROCEDURE:

1. *Eligibility*

    1.1 All regular full-time and part-time employees (on a pro-rata basis) are eligible for paid flexible time off.

    1.2 Accrued flexible time off may be taken by eligible employees for reasons including, but not limited to:

    (1) vacation time to give employees an opportunity to renew and refresh themselves;

    (2) personal and/or floating holiday paid time off; and

    (3) health-related reasons of the employee or for members of his or her family, such as a seriously ill child, parent, or spouse.

    1.3 Employees are not eligible to use paid flexible time off until the completion of nine months of continuous service with the organization.

    1.4 Temporary employees are not eligible for paid flexible time off.

    1.5 If a temporary employee becomes a regular employee without a break in service, his or her eligibility for flexible time off is computed from the initial start date as a temporary employee.

2. Accrual Period

    2.1 Regular full-time and regular part-time employees accrue flexible time off from January of the year before the flexible time off period through December of the flexible time off period.

    2.2 The flexible time off period, which is that period of time in which an employee may take accrued flexible time off, is January 1 through December 31.

    2.3 Employees must be employed for the entire month for accrual purposes (e.g., if hired on February 25, an employee would not earn flexible time off for that month).

    2.4 This paid time may be used at any time during the year; however, with the exception of time off for sick leave, direct supervisors should be given at least one week's notice.

    2.5 Employees do not have to wait for their actual anniversary dates to be eligible for extended flexible time off (e.g., if an employee will have completed two years of service by December 31, he or she may take the entitled flexible time off any time during that anniversary year.)

557

PERSONNEL POLICIES AND PROCEDURES

DISTRIBUTION:		SUBJECT: FLEXIBLE TIME OFF FROM WORK	
EFFECTIVE DATE:	PAGE 2 OF 2	FILE UNDER SECTION	
REVISION DATE:	APPROVED BY:		

3. Accrual Schedule

   3.1 The amount of time accrued each month for all employees is based on length of service as follows:

     (a) Less than 2 years of service: 1 day per month $\times$ 12 = 12 days.
     (b) 2 years but less than 5 years: 1-¼ days per month $\times$ 12 = 15 days.
     (c) 5 years but less than 10 years: 1-⅔ days per month $\times$ 12 = 20 days.
     (d) 10 years or more: 2-½ days per month $\times$ 12 = 30 days.

4. Unused Flexible Time Off

   4.1 No payments will be made for unused days.

   4.2 Flexible time off must be used during the calendar year of the current flexible time off period, since unused days will not be carried over past the calendar year for which time off was accrued. Exceptions to this rule require prior approval of the Personnel Department and the President.

   4.3 If an exception is approved, all flexible time off carried over must be taken in the first quarter of the year following its accrual.

5. Scheduling of Flexible Time Off

   5.1 Employees should schedule their flexible time off with their direct supervisor's approval.

   5.2 In case of a conflict of flexible time off among employees, the direct supervisor will assign flexible time off periods according to the operating needs of the organization.

   5.3 It is the responsibility of each direct supervisor to maintain a record of all flexible time off for each employee.

6. Advance for Flexible Time Off

   6.1 On an exceptional basis, employees may request a salary advance on their flexible time off.

   6.2 Requests for flexible time off advances must have prior written approval of the employee's direct supervisor and the Personnel Department.

   6.3 Each flexible time off advance request will be limited to one standard pay period.

7. Holidays and Weather Closings During Flexible Time Off

   7.1 If a recognized organization holiday, which an employee would normally observe, occurs during flexible time off, the extra day will not be counted as a flexible time off day.

   7.2 If the organization grants time off because of bad weather conditions or other unusual circumstances during the flexible time off, an additional day off is not allowed.

8. Termination

   8.1 Employees who have at least nine months of active service will be paid for any unused current year's flexible time off accruals upon termination of employment.

   8.2 Unless otherwise determined by state or local laws, accrued flexible time off for employees with less than nine months of service is forfeited without payment upon termination.

9. Death Benefits

   9.1 Payment for the current year's accrued and unused flexible time off is made to the estate of a deceased employee.

PERSONNEL POLICIES AND PROCEDURES

DISTRIBUTION:		SUBJECT: UNIONIZATION OF HOSPITAL EMPLOYEES	
EFFECTIVE DATE:	PAGE 1 OF 1	FILE UNDER SECTION	
REVISION DATE:	APPROVED BY:		

SAMPLE STATEMENT OF POLICY CONCERNING UNIONIZATION OF HOSPITAL EMPLOYEES

_____ Hospital believes in, has practiced, and will continue to be guided by fair employee relations policies. It has expressed this belief in a Pledge to Employees and a Code for Employee Relations, a copy of which is attached. This policy and Code have been carried out through policies and regulations issued in an employee handbook and various memoranda and applied by supervisors fairly and equitably throughout the hospital.

This hospital meets its obligations to employees by providing adequate pay, appropriate benefits and good working conditions; observing all laws applicable to employment; and recognizing their rights as individuals. Because of these, we believe that unions are not necessary to protect the best interests of our employees or those of our patients. There is no need for third parties and third-party tactics to intervene between our employees and the management of the hospital.

We believe that adherence to these principles is the best policy for our employees and that their interests are best served by our direct voluntary action on their behalf and by their direct personal communication through their supervisor with the hospital. We believe there is no need for a union at _____ Hospital in order to obtain these ends. We believe, further, that the disadvantages to employees arising from unions are: expense of union dues and assessments; the obligation to take part in affairs not connected with the hospital; the control by outsiders of employee relationships with the hospital; and, because a union contract must be written for the group, the limitation of management's freedom to recognize the individual abilities and needs of each employee.

The primary obligation of _____ Hospital is to make continuously available to the community it serves, the best possible care of the sick and injured. This is a continuing round-the-clock obligation to which all other obligations are secondary.

Unionization of hospital employees has the further and critical disadvantage of interfering with this obligation to the community and to the individual patient. Unionization and the application of union techniques can have an adverse effect upon the availability, continuity, and cost of patient care because of conditions created by the union, such as boycotts, jurisdiction disputes, slowdowns, and restrictions on the work performed.

We, therefore, believe that the interests of _____ Hospital employees, the patients we treat, and the hospital itself are all best served if our employees deal directly with us rather than through an outside labor union. As a good corporate citizen we will comply with the applicable laws and regulations in respect to labor unions and will act in good faith with any union certified as the bargaining representative of our employees. We hope, however, that the majority of our employees are of the same conviction as we, that it is better to continue to discuss with their hospital directly any concern they may have.

We believe further that we should make our views known to all employees and should discuss frankly the disadvantages to all concerned if a union is allowed to intervene in hospital affairs. We pledge ourselves to do all we can to further the interests of our employees and to assure fair pay and working conditions for all employees at _____ Hospital.

DISTRIBUTION:		SUBJECT: GUIDELINES FOR SOLICITATION AND DISTRIBUTION	
EFFECTIVE DATE:	PAGE 1 OF 1	FILE UNDER SECTION	
REVISION DATE:	APPROVED BY:		

PURPOSE:

The purpose of this policy is to define the company's position with respect to solicitation and distribution of literature or other materials on company property and/or company work time.

POLICY:

In order to prevent disruptions in the operations of the company, and in order to protect employees from harassment and interference with their work, for the following rules regarding solicitation and distribution of literature or other materials on company property/time must be observed.

A. Associates

    1. During working time, no associate shall solicit or distribute literature or other materials to another associate for any purpose. Working time refers to that portion of any working day in which the associate is supposed to be performing actual job duties. It does not include such times as lunch, break time, or time before or after a shift. No associate who is on ''working time'' shall solicit or distribute literature or other materials to another associate. No associate who is on ''nonworking time'' shall solicit or distribute literature or other materials to an associate who is on working time.

    2. No associate shall distribute literature or other materials to another associate for any purpose in working areas of the company.

    3. No associate shall solicit or distribute literature or other materials to any visitors at any time for any purpose.

    4. Violation of these rules will be cause for appropriate discipline.

B. Nonassociates

Persons who are not employed by the company shall not distribute literature or other materials or solicit associates or visitors at any time for any purpose on company grounds or inside the company's plants or offices.

PERSONNEL POLICIES AND PROCEDURES

DISTRIBUTION:		SUBJECT: WORKPLACE VIOLENCE	
EFFECTIVE DATE:	PAGE 1 OF 1	FILE UNDER SECTION	
REVISION DATE:	APPROVED BY:		

POLICY:

Workplace violence will not be tolerated. Any employee who commits an act of violence at work against a person or property will face disciplinary action up to and including discharge. Where appropriate, the matter will be referred to legal authorities for prosecution.

Workplace violence is violence against employers and employees that takes place in the workplace, is committed by persons who either have an employment-related connection with the company or are outsiders, and involves: (1) physical acts against persons or employer property, or (2) verbal threats, or vicious statements that are meant to harm or cause a hostile environment, or (3) written threats, vicious cartoons or notes, and other written conduct of intense distortion that is meant to threaten or create a hostile environment, or (4) visual acts that are threatening or intended to convey injury or hostility.

PROCEDURE:

Workplace violence can and must be prevented! To achieve that goal requires the combined efforts of all employees. Anything less than total commitment to the elimination of workplace violence is not enough—we intend to see that it is stopped, and all employees must do their part to see that it is. These are the five keys to prevention that employees are expected to observe:

1. Understand what violence is
2. Understand themselves, including their attitudes, motivations, and decision-making styles, so that they will not resort to violence
3. Follow prescribed security measures
4. Use designated security devices
5. Report any persons who may or have committed a violent act

All employees are entitled to perform their work, regardless of location, whether on the employer's premises or elsewhere, free from violence.

All employees are expected to report any act of violence or a threat of violence. Employees should bring their concern directly to the attention of line management or the Human Resources Manager. All such reports shall be fully investigated. Any employee who takes any reprisal, regardless of the magnitude of the reprisal, against a person who reports any act of violence or a suspicion of violence shall be subject to immediate discipline, up to and including discharge.

PERSONNEL POLICIES AND PROCEDURES

DISTRIBUTION:		SUBJECT: COMPANY PROPERTY ESCROW ACCOUNT	
EFFECTIVE DATE:	PAGE 1 OF 1	FILE UNDER SECTION	
REVISION DATE:	APPROVED BY:		

COMMENTARY:

Many employers incur losses when an employee is terminated (resignation, discharge) and fails to return company property, such as uniforms, tools, et al.

Many states have laws regarding termination pay and prohibit deductions that are not required by law unless specifically authorized in writing by the employee. In such cases, pre- or post-employment blanket deduction employee authorizations ordinarily do not suffice for termination deductions because the required written authorization typically must be specific as to the purpose and the amount to be deducted. Also, federal and state wage laws prohibit deductions that would bring the terminated employee's pay below the minimum wage.

Finally, some resigning or discharged employees may be disinclined to sign such authorizations.

To address this problem, an employer may elect to have a policy whereby a nominal sum would be deducted from each paycheck during the employee's first (e.g.) twelve months of employment until a total of (e.g.) $200 is reached. Larger (but still nominal) sums could be deducted during the first three months of employment. This sum would be held in the employee's name in escrow in an interest-bearing account, reimbursable with interest upon termination of employment.

The policy should stipulate that upon termination, applicable amounts would be deducted from the accumulated sum for any unreturned company property. This not only would preclude the employer's loss (up to the accumulated sum), but would provide an incentive for terminated employees to return company property in their possession.

A signed payroll deduction authorization is essential. A signed acknowledgment and receipt describing the specific property assigned to the employee is also essential.

The policy may be reworded in any manner to accommodate the employer's specific circumstances.

The policy is permissible in all states, with the following exceptions:

EXCEPTIONS:

—Indiana: Not permissible
—Kansas: Not permissible
—North Carolina: Not needed
—South Carolina: Not needed, but handbook policy should spell out what deductions from final pay will be made
                   upon termination of employment
—South Dakota: Not needed

PURPOSE:

To prevent losses when an employee is terminated (resignation, discharge) and fails to return company property, such as uniforms, tools, et al.

POLICY:

During the first _____ months of employment, the company will deduct $ _____ from an employee's paycheck to be placed in an interest-bearing escrow account under the employee's name. The employee must sign a payroll deduction authorization for this purpose.

Upon termination of employment, the company will deduct from the employee's account an appropriate amount to cover any unreturned company property. The balance of the account, including interest, will then be fully reimbursed to the employee.

Index of Sample Policies

About the Author

Joseph W. R. Lawson II is Chairman of the Board and Chief Executive Officer of SESCO Management Consultants.

Lawson has authored the following publications for management: *How to Develop an Employee Handbook, Second Edition; How to Meet the Challenge of the Union Organizer; How to Reduce Absenteeism, Cure Tardiness, and Build Employee Morale; Management's Complete Guide to Employee Benefits; How to Comply With the Equal Opportunity Act;* and *Management's Guide to the Americans with Disabilities Act.* He received his B.A. degree from King College in Bristol, Tennessee, and his M.S. degree in Industrial Relations from the University of North Carolina. Since 1961, Lawson has represented clients in business and industry as an employee and labor relations consultant to management. He specializes in employee and labor relations, human resources management systems, and employer-labor negotiations and arbitration. He is a member of the Commericial Panel of the American Arbitration Association. Lawson serves as a professional speaker and instructor for human resources management seminars and union-free employee relations workshops for clients and trade associations.

About SESCO Management Consultants

SESCO Management Consultants is a professional consulting firm specializing in human resources management consulting and labor relations. The firm was founded in 1945 by J. W. Lawson, Sr., following his early career with the U.S. Department of Labor. For more than fifty years, Dr. Lawson has brought together a staff of professional employee relations and labor relations specialists from business and industry. The firm provides a broad variety of consulting services and publishes a monthly newsletter, the *SESCO Report.*

The SESCO staff represents clients who are engaged in heavy and light manufacturing, retail and wholesale services, mining, transportation, banking, savings and loan, electronics, automobile dealerships, the health care industry, and several national and state trade/business associations.

CPSIA information can be obtained at www.ICGtesting.com
Printed in the USA
LVOW020104281212

313478LV00003BA/34/A